Implementing Application Frameworks

Object-Oriented Frameworks at Work

Mohamed E. Fayad

Douglas C. Schmidt

Ralph E. Johnson

Wiley Computer Publishing

John Wiley & Sons, Inc.

NEW YORK · CHICHESTER · WEINHEIM · BRISBANE · SINGAPORE · TORONTO

Publisher: Robert Ipsen
Editor: Marjorie Spencer
Assistant Editor: Margaret Hendrey
Managing Editor: Marnie Wielage
Text Design & Composition: North Market Street Graphics

Library of Congress Cataloging-in-Publication Data:
Implementing application frameworks : object-oriented frameworks at
   work / editors: Mohamed Fayad, Douglas Schmidt, Ralph Johnson.
       p.   cm.
    "Wiley Computer Publishing."
    Includes bibliographical references and index.
    ISBN 0-471-25201-8
    1. Object-oriented programming (Computer science)   2. Computer
software—Reusability.   I. Fayad, Mohamed, 1950–   . II. Schmidt,
Douglas C.   III. Johnson, Ralph.
    QA76.64.I527   1999
    005.1'17—dc21
                                                      99-26925
                                                      CIP

*To the memory of my mom and dad,
to my lovely wife Raefa, to my beautiful
daughters Rodina and Rawan, and to my
handsome son Ahmad.*

—Mohamed E. Fayad

*To Sonja, for helping me appreciate what's
important in life.*

—Douglas C. Schmidt

*To the creators of Simula and Smalltalk,
who were the first to see the vision.*

—Ralph E. Johnson

Contents

Preface

This book is for anyone who wants to implement large-scale software reuse through object-oriented (OO) application frameworks. Its purpose is to help the reader understand one of the hottest technologies related to software reuse—*frameworks*—and provide guidelines for making decisions about this technology. Decision makers such as presidents and vice presidents, as well as software project managers and project leaders, will benefit from the experience and lessons in this book. It illustrates the development and use of frameworks technology in several domains, such as business, artificial intelligence, agents, tools, environments, and system applications. In 28 chapters and 4 sidebars, we describe diverse application frameworks and discuss our real-world experience.

Implementing Application Frameworks follows three central themes:

- How to build and adapt OO application frameworks through examples
- How to overcome problems with application frameworks
- What we can learn from our experience with domain-specific application frameworks

Outstanding Features

This book provides valuable insight into successful OO application framework examples. All the material has been derived from actual experience and is presented in a practical, easy-to-understand manner. We explain in detail both the philosophy behind the frameworks and how to apply the frameworks to different domains. After reading this book, you will:

- Understand, through extensive examples, how to build OO application frameworks.
- Be prepared to utilize frameworks.

- Understand diverse application framework architectures.

- Be ready to face problems with frameworks, by learning from our experience.

- Be familiar with the design of more than 20 application-oriented frameworks.

- Be ready to explore new areas of application-oriented framework technology.

Who Should Read This Book

This volume draws on the experience and collective wisdom of its numerous contributors to explore problems and present insights into the design, development, and deployment of specific application and enterprise frameworks. It will prove invaluable to software vendors in building frameworks that are both robust and flexible, to managers in identifying the most appropriate frameworks for the specific enterprise they are engaged in, and to application developers in effectively exploiting frameworks to construct complete applications quickly and efficiently.

This volume is intended for a broad community of computer and software professionals involved in the management and development of software projects, including company executives, project managers, engineering staff, technologists, software managers, object-oriented business owners, presidents, and CEOs. Software engineers, system engineers, system analysts, software developers, software process groups, contract administrators, customers, technologists, software methodologists, and enterprise program developers will greatly benefit from this book.

Supplemental Materials

Supplemental materials can be found in the contributors' URLs included in the authors index at the end of this book. Updates, news, question and answer sessions, and comments to the authors can be found at www.cse.unl.edu/~fayad and the companion Web site at www.wiley.com/compbooks/frameworks.

The companion Web site includes the following:

- Extended preface

- Extended acknowledgments that acknowledge the work of the contributors and reviewers of this book

- Brief table of contents

- Detailed table of contents

- Chapter abstracts

- Complete chapter references

- Miscellaneous listings of theme issues, special interest groups, conferences, and so on

- Extended authors index

- Annotated references
- Question-and-answer session
- FAQ: Application and enterprise frameworks

CD-ROM Contents

The CD-ROM that accompanies this book contains several complete or partial application frameworks that are mostly described in this book. The CD-ROM contains several items, such as complete application frameworks, demos, framework code, sample models, manuals, documentation, presentations, design patterns, freeware and shareware, and more. Appendix C, "About the CD-ROM," provides more information about the CD-ROM contents.

Acknowledgments

This book would not exist without the help of many great people. I am grateful to all the contributing authors for their submissions and their patience, and to all the reviewers for valuable and useful reviews of all the submissions to this book. I would like to take this opportunity to say that I am honored to work with the two editors of this book, Douglas Schmidt and Ralph Johnson, and with all the authors and reviewers. This has been a terrific and enjoyable project because of their tremendous help and extensive patience. Thanks to both of you for believing in me.

I, along with all of the authors who contributed to this volume, wish to thank all of those who have had a part in the production of this book. First and foremost, we owe our families a huge debt of gratitude for being so patient while we put their world in a whirl by injecting this writing activity into their already full lives. We also thank the various reviewers and editors who have helped in so many ways to coordinate this book. We thank our associates who offered their advice and wisdom in defining the content of the book. We also owe a special thanks to those who worked on the various projects covered in the case studies and examples.

A special thanks to my wife Raefa, my lovely daughters Rodina and Rawan, and my son Ahmad for their great patience and understanding. Special thanks to my friend Mauri Laitinen for his encouragement and long discussions about the topics and the issues in this book. Thanks to all my students—in particular Amr Yassin, Jinkun Hu, David Naney, Sanjeev Sagen, and Adam Altman; to my friends Jun Gu, Marshall Cline, W.T. Tsai, Solomon Gabraiel, and Yasser alSafadi, for their encouragement during this project; and to the staff of *Communications of ACM*—Diana Crawford, Tom Lambert, and Robert Fox—for their support. I am very grateful to the editors at John Wiley & Sons. Thanks to Marjorie Spencer for her belief and support of the book, and to Margaret Hendrey for her patience and sharing of help for putting this text together, and to Marnie Wielage for overseeing the production of such a gigantic project.

Contributor Acknowledgments

Thank you to all the contributors for their tremendous effort and patience in making this volume a reality. Thanks also to all the contributors who participated in the review process for their valuable comments and excellent reviews. This volume provides a unique source of information and a wide spectrum of knowledge intended to aid software vendors, managers, developers, and users in their journey toward managing, developing, adapting, and utilizing application and enterprise frameworks. It is an appropriate book for a variety of graduate courses in advanced software engineering and framework technology. It was a great honor to work with all of those who contributed. This volume was made possible only by the enormous efforts of the contributors—sincere thanks to all of them is in order (see the companion Web site at www.wiley.com/compbooks/frameworks).

Reviewer Acknowledgments

Special thanks to all the reviewers for their useful reviews, helpful critiques, and pertinent insights that resulted in a clearer presentation and more integrated book than anything I could have produced alone. This manuscript is one of a three-volume set and has been thoroughly reviewed by more than 500 reviewers. Their comments and reviews were invaluable contributions to the making of this book. I have been honored to work with all of them and their valuable comments have led to improvements in the content and presentation of this book. Thank you all. (See the companion Web site at www.wiley.com/compbooks/frameworks.)

Mohamed E. Fayad

Special Acknowledgments

The authors of Chapter 3 (Martine Devos and Michel Tilman) would like to thank their team members: Rudy Breedenraedt, Hilde Deleu, Jan Geysen, Els Goossens, Wouter Roose, Fred Spiessens, Du Thanh-Son, Danny Ureel, and Leen Van Riel. They would also like to thank the Programming Technology Lab at the Vrije Universiteit Brussel for their many good ideas, and the pioneer users at Argo who helped to make this framework happen. Finally, they would like to thank Ralph E. Johnson for his many helpful comments during the review process.

The authors of Chapter 7 (Davide Brugali and Katia Sycara) acknowledge that the work presented here has been supported by the project Tecnologie di elaborazione distribuita nei servizi multimediali per l'azienda virtuale e il commercio elettronico, in collaboration with CSELT, Turin, Italy; by DARPA grant F33615-93-1-1330; by ONR grant N00014-96-1-1222; and by NSF grant IRI-9508191.

The authors of Chapter 8 (Pierre Marcenac and Remy Courdier) would like to express their gratitude to the Institut de Recherche En Mathématiques et Informatique

Appliquées (IREMIA) for providing them with a simulating intellectual environment, as well as financial support for this project. They are also grateful to S. Calderoni for reading and commenting on earlier drafts of this chapter. Finally, they tip their hats to J.C. Soulié, for Java programming, and S. Giroux, for Smalltalk advice, in acknowledgment of services rendered during experimentation with the first version of the platform.

The author of Sidebar 4 (Zakaria Maamar) thanks Professors B. Moulin, G. Babin, and Y. Bédard of Laval University for their contributions to this research.

The author of Chapter 12 (Raman Kannan) acknowledges that this chapter is a report on an ongoing project (since 1994) at Asset Enterprise Technologies Corporation, New Jersey. The author also would like to thank William Sweeney, Byron Nicas, Vadim Dosychev, Mitch Haviv, Angelo Susi, Dan Marcellus, Nachum Greenspan, Robert Sachs, Virendra Agarwal, Joel Rosner, Peter Delucia, Karen Minasia, Florian Miciu, Henry Ming, Paul Kennery, John Sabini, Marge Kaelis, Kris Stala, Kathy Delligatti, Joseph Costantini, and the many contributors to the ACE Mailing List. The author is grateful to his family, Concurrent Engineering Research Center, West Virginia University, Jorge Diaz, and Larry Dworkin of Monmouth University for their encouragement and support.

The authors of Chapter 15 (Jurg Gutknecht and Michael Franz) would like to thank Niklaus Wirth. They acknowledge the work of Hannes Marais, whose Gadgets framework and toolkit have led the way. They also gratefully acknowledge the contributions of Emil Zeller, Ralph Sommerer, Patrick Saladin, Joerg Derungs, and Thomas Kistler in the areas of compound and distributed documents, descriptive object composition, and compiler construction, respectively. Their sincere thanks also go to Pieter Muller, implementor of the native PC Oberon kernel.

The authors of Chapter 16 (Wade Holst and Duane Szafron) would like to thank Karel Driesen for several discussions during the research involved in this chapter. Jan Vitek and the ECOOP Program Committee also provided helpful information. This research was supported in part by NSERC research grant OGP8191.

The authors of Chapter 19 (Görel Hedin and Jørgen Lindskov Knudsen) would like to thank Patrik Persson and Anders Ive for commenting on the readability of this chapter.

The author of Chapter 20 (Vinny Cahill) would like to thank Brendan Tangney, Neville Harris, Paul Taylor, and Alan Judge for their contributions to the work described in this chapter.

Introduction

Frameworks are generally targeted for a particular application domain, such as user interfaces, business data processing systems, telecommunications, or multimedia collaborative work environments. A framework is more than a class hierarchy. It is a semicomplete application containing dynamic and static components that can be customized to produce user-specific applications [Fayad 1999]. Due to the generic nature of framework components, mature frameworks can be reused as the basis for many other applications. This book is comprised of 27 chapters and 4 sidebars; it describes several sizes of application frameworks in multiple and different domains, and discusses experiences related to OO application frameworks.

This book helps organizations apply framework technology effectively by citing examples from the real world. This book combines the actual experiences and lessons learned from developing and/or adapting different application frameworks. This book is intended to provide valuable, real-world insight into successful OO application framework examples. All the material has been derived from actual experiences, successes, and failures, and is presented in a practical, easy-to-understand manner. This book provides different framework architectures and explains in detail the philosophy behind the frameworks and how to apply it to several domains. This is information that students can apply today. This book covers the following domains: business application frameworks, artificial intelligence applications and agent-oriented application frameworks, specialized tool application frameworks, language-specific frameworks, and system application frameworks. It also covers experiences and lessons learned in working with application frameworks.

1.1 Application Framework Classifications

The application frameworks in this book map well to the application framework classifications in [Fayad 1999; Fayad-Schmidt 1997]. Application frameworks are classified based on their scope. Most of the application frameworks in this book are *system infrastructure frameworks*—such as all the system application frameworks introduced in Part Five. A few application frameworks are *enterprise application frameworks*—such as the IBM San Francisco Project discussed in Sidebar 3. Also, application frameworks in this book can be classified by the techniques used to extend them, which range along a continuum from *whitebox frameworks* to *blackbox frameworks* [Fayad 1999].

1.2 Organization of This Book

This book is organized into six major parts: Part One, "Business Frameworks"; Part Two, "Artificial Intelligence and Agent Application Frameworks"; Part Three, "Specialized Tool Frameworks"; Part Four, "Language-Specific Frameworks"; Part Five, "System Application Frameworks"; and Part Six, "Experiences in Application Frameworks."

Part One has two chapters (Chapters 2 and 3) and three sidebars (Sidebars 1, 2, and 3). This part introduces framework technology in the business domain, such as sales promotions, the Argo administration framework, and the IBM San Francisco project. The sales promotion application framework (Chapter 2) is used to build an application for product managers. The Argo administration framework (Chapter 3) is developed to support Argo administration, where Argo is a semi-government organization managing several hundred public schools. It uses this framework to develop its applications, which share a common business model and require database, electronic document, workflow, and Internet functionality. This part also introduces the IBM SanFrancisco project (Sidebar 3), which delivers business process components written in Java that provide an object-oriented design and default business logic for mainline business applications. Part One also discusses the notion of rule patterns as generic rule-based solutions for realizing business policies (Sidebar One) and promotes the realization of workflow management systems (WFMSs) in framework technology (Sidebar Two).

Part Two contains five chapters (Chapters 4 through 8) and one sidebar (Sidebar 4). This part discusses artificial intelligence application frameworks, such as speech recognition (Chapter 4) and neural networks (Chapter 5), and agent-oriented application frameworks, such as intelligent and mobile agents (Chapter 6), RETSINA (Chapter 7), and agent-oriented platforms in Java (Chapter 8). Sidebar 4 discusses the notion of software agents in frameworks.

Part Three has 4 chapters (Chapters 9 through 12). This part discusses specialized tool frameworks, such as the CSP++ framework for executable specifications (Chapter 9); applying inheritance beyond class-based languages (Chapter 10); Luthier frameworks for a flexible support for the construction of tools for object-oriented framework analysis and visualization (Chapter 11); and scalable architecture for reliable and high-volume datafeed handlers (Chapter 12).

Part Four contains 7 chapters (Chapters 13 through 19). This part discusses issues related to programming languages and defines the impact of programming language constructs on component and application framework development, such as the integration of the constraint programming (CP) paradigm with the object-oriented (OO) paradigm (Chapter 13); a generative methodology for the design and rapid prototyping of component-based systems for supporting real-time distributed domain and hardware-software codesign (Chapter 18); and the relationship between framework design and language constructs (Chapter 19). This part also describes language-specific application frameworks, such as a framework for capturing the application-important relationships between objects, as well as a mechanism for using these relationships when implementing the changing nature of the objects (Chapter 14); Oberon with Gadgets (Chapter 15), an inheritance management and method dispatch framework (Chapter 16), and a framework for building efficient and powerful constraint-satisfaction programming environments (Chapter 17).

Part Five has six chapters (Chapters 20 through 25). This part describes several system application frameworks, such as Tigger (Chapter 20), Déjà vu (Chapter 21), Graphics Recognition (Chapter 22), Cryptographic Protocols (Chapter 23), and Component User Interface (Chapter 25).

Part Six contains three chapters (Chapters 26, 27, and 28). This part discusses experiences and lessons learned in the application framework arena. Chapter 26 shows how framework development can be aided by using common design patterns with a file reader framework. Chapter 27 presents some experience gained in the evolution of a framework architecture through its application in a number of projects over a period of years. Chapter 28 describes a scalable strategy for model-based development as implemented at a major financial services institution.

1.3 Summary

This book contains real samples of business application frameworks (Part One), artificial intelligence application frameworks and agent-oriented application frameworks (Part Two), specialized tool frameworks (Part Three), language-specific application frameworks (Part Four), and system application frameworks (Part Five). This shows that application frameworks are becoming mainstream and that developers at all levels are increasingly adopting framework technologies and succeeding with them. These application framework samples are just the beginning of the spread of framework technology in key domains. In addition, these application framework samples show the way for learning about effective, efficient approaches for building, implementing, and utilizing application frameworks, and they introduce lessons learned through experience for avoiding adaptation traps and pitfalls. We encourage you to get involved with others working on frameworks by attending conferences, participating in online mailing lists and newsgroups, and contributing your insights and experience.

1.4 References

[Fayad 1999] Fayad, M.E., D. Schmidt, and R. Johnson. *Building Application Frameworks: Object-Oriented Foundations of Framework Design*. New York: John Wiley & Sons, 1999.
[Fayad-Schmidt 1997] Fayad, M.E. and D. Schmidt. Object-oriented application frameworks. *Communications of the ACM* 40(10), October 1997.

PART One

Business Frameworks

Object-oriented (OO) frameworks are considered an important step forward in developing software applications efficiently. Success of frameworks has, however, predominantly been limited to structured domains. This part introduces framework technology in the business domain. Part One consists of Chapters 2 and 3 and Sidebars 1, 2, and 3.

Chapter 2, "Domain Framework for Sales Promotions," describes a method for developing OO domain frameworks for semistructured domains. The complexity of such domains requires the use of more elaborate analysis and design techniques than those normally used in OO analysis and design. In the method described in this chapter, the knowledge of domain experts forms the basis for developing the framework. The OO framework is constructed on the design level using a CASE tool. Using the design model, the framework can be customized and extended to develop a variety of applications for the domain. The approach is illustrated by developing a framework for the sales-promotions domain and using this framework to build an application for product managers. The chapter concludes that the approach described is beneficial for building and using OO frameworks for semistructured domains.

Analogous to design patterns in object-oriented systems development, Sidebar 1, *Business Policies and Rule Patterns,* introduces the notion of rule patterns as generic, rule-based solutions for realizing business policies. The advantages of rule patterns are their predefined, reusable, and dynamically customizable nature, allowing the designer to reuse existing experience for building rule-based applications. For this, a framework of rule patterns extracting business policies from an object-oriented modeling method is provided. The approach of rule patterns has been evaluated by applying the framework for the realization of different interaction policies.

Chapter 3, "A Reflective and Repository-Based Framework," describes a framework developed to support the Argo administration. Argo is a semigovernment organization managing several hundred public schools. It uses this framework to develop its applications, which share a common business model, and requires database, electronic document, workflow, and Internet functionality. The framework is based on a repository in two ways. First, it consists of a set of tools for managing a repository of documents, data, and processes, including their history and status. These tools enable users to select applications, enter and view data, query the repository, access the thesaurus, and manage electronic documents, workflow processes, and task assignments. More important, the framework behavior is driven by the repository. The repository captures formal and informal knowledge of the business model. None of the business model is hardcoded. The tools consult the repository at runtime. End users can change the behavior of the system by using high-level tools to change the business model. Thus, this chapter separates descriptions of an organization's business logic from the application functionality. The framework helps develop applications iteratively and interactively. It enables the application developer to build increasingly complete specifications of applications that can be executed at once. The resulting system is easy to adapt to changes in the business. Argo can develop new applications through modeling and configuration, rather than through coding.

Sidebar 2, *Workflow Management Frameworks*, discusses how object-oriented technology, and in particular the idea of frameworks, promotes the realization of workflow management systems (WFMSs). The idea of capturing and controlling business processes by means of computer technology is relatively old, the first systems dating back to the 1970s. However, mainly due to immature technology, it took more than 15 years until business process automation spread beyond research communities and conquered the market as WFMSs. Nowadays, not least due to recent developments in object-oriented technology, WFMSs are able to keep their promise of raising the productivity and competitive edge of an organization

Sidebar 3, *IBM SanFrancisco Business Components,* discusses the IBM SanFrancisco Project. IBM SanFrancisco delivers Business Process Components written in Java that provide an object-oriented design and default business logic for mainline business applications. The Business Process Components use Common Business Objects (objects that are used in more than one application domain) and are built on the Foundation, which provides a Java server infrastructure for managed, distributed objects. The Business Process Components and Common Business Objects are designed as frameworks so that they can be easily modified and extended. The first two releases have provided Business Process Components in the domains of Business Financials, Order Management, and Warehouse Management. Additional information is available at the IBM SanFrancisco web site at www.software.ibm.com/ad/sanfrancisco/.

CHAPTER 2

Domain Framework for Sales Promotions

Like other business areas, marketing has seen a true information revolution. Effective and efficient use of heterogeneous data has become crucial, especially in highly competitive markets. In this quest for information, the time factor is important: Knowledge is most valuable when it is acquired before the competition gets it. The companies that can design the best marketing campaigns in the shortest period of time are the winners in the marketplace.

Computer systems currently available to companies offer a variety of data retrieval and optimization procedures (such as production planning and supermarket shelf space allocation). Although these systems are often adaptable in parameters, they are mostly static representations of problems that do not fit the dynamic nature of the marketing domain. As new types of data become available in increasing amounts and the human factor in decision making becomes more central, attention seems to be shifting to building adaptable systems that fit the mental models of decision makers.

A product manager is one important marketing decision maker who is responsible for development, pricing, distribution, advertising, and sales promotion of one or more products. Product managers make semistructured decisions, mostly under heavy time pressure. To perform successfully, these managers need well-designed software applications, based on their mental models, to support their decision making.

Mental models of product managers consist of building blocks that are typical marketing concepts—brands, prices, advertisements, sales, market share—or typical marketing actors—customers, competitors, producers, retailers. In this mental counterpart of the real world, the product manager replays, simulates, and forecasts things that happen in order to be able to respond to the opportunities and threats that occur.

In order to facilitate the development of software applications for product managers, we developed a domain framework of the mental models of product managers. The framework focuses on sales promotion decision making, which is a prominent task of product managers. Sales promotions are marketing events aimed at having a direct impact on the buying behavior of consumers. Examples of sales promotions are price-offs, premiums, cash refunds, samplings, and coupons. As the effects of mass media are diminishing, sales promotions are becoming an increasingly important tool for product managers to increase sales [Blattberg-Neslin 1990].

Once constructed, the general domain framework can be reused to build a variety of specific applications for the domain. In a multinational corporation a sales promotion domain framework can serve as the basis for the development of applications for sales promotion decision making in different countries, for different divisions, adapted to the needs of individual managers, and for the various tasks that have to be performed within the domain. The development of such a framework is possible and beneficial because despite circumstantial differences (for example, individual differences in the product they manage, their decision-making style), product managers tend to have similar tasks and share a comparable mental model.

Early reports on object-oriented (OO) frameworks have mainly described system-level frameworks (such as file-access or networking aids) and user interface application frameworks. Recently, research into domain frameworks has emerged, primarily focusing on more-structured and well-studied domains such as accounting or logistics. The framework developed in the present study concerns a semistructured domain. In this domain, as Table 2.1 shows, creativity and experience as well as hard data are important.

Table 2.1   Importance Ratings* of Factors of Sales Promotion Decision Making

FACTORS	AVERAGE
Creativity	6.0
Experience	5.8
Hard data	5.6
Judgment	5.3
Soft data	5.0
Discussions	4.9
Intuition	4.9
Heuristics	4.7
Experiments	4.0
Models	3.0
Theory	3.0

*Ratings obtained from 20 respondents in interviews that we report on later in this chapter (scale: 1–7).

It is the objective of this chapter to describe and illustrate a method to develop frameworks for semistructured domains such as sales promotions. The method has three features that we argue are essential in building such frameworks successfully:

The development method should start with an analysis of the thinking processes of the domain expert—the mental models underlying his or her actions. In this chapter we show the use of think-aloud protocols, which subsequently are analyzed by means of content analysis.

The development method should employ an OO analysis and design methodology in combination with the use of patterns. OO modeling enhances the correspondence between the system and the problem domain. Encapsulation hides the internal details of the framework and inheritance facilitates extension and reuse of the framework. The advantages of OO modeling are further enhanced by using analysis patterns, which are documented solutions to common modeling problems.

The framework should be modeled in a computer-aided software engineering (CASE) environment capable of translating the model into different programming languages. In this way, the framework can be used in many different projects, regardless of specific platform or language needs. Furthermore, using, adapting, and extending the model can be done at the design level (in the CASE environment), preventing important semantic modeling information from being lost [Fayad-Laitinen 1998].

The following section describes this development method in more detail and illustrates it by discussing the development of the sales promotion framework. In *Section 2.2,* a possible application (re)using the framework is shown. In *Section 2.3,* we evaluate our approach, and in *Section 2.4,* we suggest possible extensions.

2.1 Framework Development

Figure 2.1 depicts the development method of the framework and the specific application. Steps 1 to 3, which concern a general approach to the building of the framework, are explained in the next section. In later sections, steps are illustrated for the sales promotion domain. *Section 2.2* shows the use of the framework for the development of a specific client application.

2.1.1 The Framework Development Method Step by Step

The framework development method consists of three major steps:

- Solving sample problems
- Analyzing protocol contents
- Creating the object-oriented framework using CASE tool

These steps are discussed in detail in the following sections.

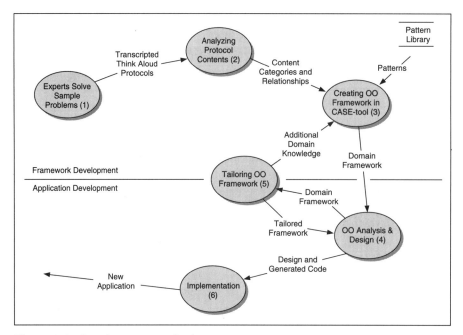

Figure 2.1 Development method.

Step 1: Experts Solve Sample Problems

Developing software to support decision making in semistructured domains without involving domain experts easily leads to incomplete, poorly constructed, and unused software. It has been widely recognized that it is essential to have domain experts involved in OO modeling of software [Rumbaugh 1991; Yourdon 1994]. Framework development also requires input from domain experts, but differs from application development in that end users do not directly benefit from the results. Hence, they are not likely to be available for extensive training and modeling sessions. Also, it is generally agreed that conceptual modeling of a framework is harder and more abstract than modeling an actual application and therefore requires good modeling skills. Conceptual modeling is probably the most difficult and expensive activity performed in the process of framework development.

We propose an indirect yet thorough way to utilize domain expertise for framework development. In this approach, think-aloud protocols of domain experts are used to construct a domain framework. A set of sample problems that can, more or less, be considered representative for the domain are collected or constructed and presented to a group of domain experts. The solutions the experts produce are recorded on tape and transcribed so they can be used for further analysis. The output of this first step is the transcribed think-aloud protocols.

Step 2: Analyzing Protocol Contents

The methodological framework of content analysis is used for the analysis of the protocol data. Content analysis is an accepted research technique in the social sciences and is concerned with the analysis of the content of communications. A central idea in content analysis is that the many words of a text can be classified into fewer content categories that are presumed to have similar meaning. On the basis of this categorization, the researcher tries to draw valid inferences from the text. For an introduction to this field see [Krippendorff 1980; Weber 1985].

The purpose of the analysis is to find out how domain experts conceptualize (make mental representations of) their domain. In order to achieve this, the protocols generated previously are coded by applying two coding procedures. The first procedure is meant to *discover content categories*. Coders are given instructions to look for nouns related to the domain. The coding units (in other words, the pieces into which the text is subdivided) in this procedure are *word* (such as, "budget") or *word sense* (for example, "the money that is available for the promotion") [Weber 1985], the latter being the part of a sentence that refers to a single entity but is expressed with more than one word.

The coders then classify the units in categories according to equal semantic meaning. For example, "our budget," "the available $300,000," "the money we can spend," can be attributed the same semantic meaning (budget) and put into one category. Each category receives a name that adequately covers the semantics of the units it contains.

We can now rank the categories based on the frequency with which they occur. If several different cases were solved by various experts, the ranked (cumulative) frequency gives us clear insight into the relative importance of the concepts as used by the experts.

The second procedure is performed to find relationships among the content categories. Themes are used as coding units [Weber 1985]. A theme is a unit of text that has no more than the following elements: (1) the perceiver, (2) the agent of action, (3) the action, and (4) the target of action. For example, "I want consumers to pay attention to my product" is divided as follows:

> "I [the perceiver] (want) consumers [agent of action] to pay attention to [action] my product [target of action]."

A relationship consists of two or more themes ("If I want consumers to pay attention to my product *Theme 1*, I could promote by giving an introduction discount *Theme 2*"). All relationships should be coded from all collected transcripts.

Step 3: Creating the Object-Oriented Framework Using a CASE Tool

The Unified Modeling Language (UML) [Booch-Rumbaugh 1997] can be used to model the framework. The OO paradigm holds the promise of being highly suitable for constructing applications for semistructured domains such as marketing, since such domains cannot be modeled in a single proper way and are, moreover, inherently dynamic. These factors impose strong demands on the adaptability of software. The promise of OO to deliver adaptable software systems matches these demands [Gibson-Senn 1989; Korson-McGregor 1990]. Reuse of OO components should enable quick delivery of new system functionality, though adaptability must be explicitly engineered into the system. Frameworks and patterns provide a vehicle to achieve adaptability and reuse [Fayad-Cline 1996]. A framework can be used to build applications by creating new subclasses [Johnson-Foote 1988]. Software developers often lack the domain expertise that is encapsulated in the framework. The knowledge incorporated in a domain framework exceeds that of other reusable components. Unlike other reusable components, OO frameworks incorporate object interaction and define default behavior [Taligent 1997].

Most OO analysis methods suggest that analysts should mark all the nouns they find in domain-related texts as candidate classes. In semistructured domains, this easily leads to unmanageable numbers of classes.

In our method, this problem is tackled by the initial reduction of the set of nouns by putting them into content categories (Step 2, first procedure), and by a further reduction of the initial number of classes by mapping only the top 20 or 30 content categories to object classes. This mapping is the first step in the actual construction of the framework. The exact number of categories included in the initial object model can be decided by the developer while taking into consideration factors like the estimated size of the framework and the distribution of the frequencies over the categories. The classes selected in this way make up the initial object model, which, thus constructed, forms the basis for the rest of the modeling process.

The modeling process proceeds by refining this initial framework using the relationships that were found in the protocols (Step 2, second procedure). Within relationships, verbs relate one word or word sense to another, implying the way classes are related to one another. The text of a relationship is mapped to the OO model by (1) checking whether the classes the relationship refers to are correctly represented in the initial object model and (2) modeling relevant verbs either as relationships between objects or as behavior.

It is hard to delimit the inferences that can and cannot be made by the modeler. There are two important criteria that can be set to judge modeling choices [Krippendorff 1980]. First, the modeler should aim at as little impairment of the original text as possible. Second, inferences based on few relationships yield a lower degree of certainty than those often encountered, indicating more stable relationships. The modeler should administer the modeling choices that are made, for instance, by storing them in tables or by administering them directly in the CASE tool, thus relating source text references to classes, attributes, relationships, or behavior.

2.1.2 Using the Development Method for the Sales Promotion Domain

This section shows how to apply the framework development method in the sales promotion domain.

Step 1: Experts Solve Sample Problems

We devised two sample problems representative of the domain of sales promotions. Each interviewee (10 product managers and 10 sales promotion authorities) had to solve a problem on the design of a sales promotion plan for the introduction of a new salad dressing (see Exhibit 2.1) and another one in which a sales promotion plan had to be devised for a troubled fashion magazine (not displayed here). The respondents were asked to think aloud so their solutions could be recorded and transcribed.

EXHIBIT 2.1
PRESTO-DRESS SAMPLE PROBLEM

Presto-Dress is a new salad dressing. The producer has developed a new package concept using a transparent plastic box with a handy spout that allows the user to dose the salad dressing very accurately. The market for salad dressing has two submarkets: the regular dressings market and the special dressings market. Goals are "making Presto-Dress a flourishing brand in the special dressings market, in terms of market share and profit,'" and "to promote brand-switching from Creamy-Dress (a product in the special dressings market that the producer wants to eliminate) to Presto-Dress."

   The assignment: Design a sales promotion plan for the introduction of Presto-Dress. The budget is $300,000.

Step 2: Analyzing Protocols Contents

The purpose of the interviews and the analysis of the protocols was to find out how sales promotion managers conceptualize (make mental representations of) their domain.

   Exhibit 2.2 displays a small piece of protocol transcript collected in Step 1. The 20 transcripts were coded by business school students enrolled in a course on sales promotion decision making. Each interview was coded by two students to assess coding reliability.

   The first coding procedure was meant to discover the important concepts in the sales promotion domain. The instructions were to look for nouns, either related to products or to sales promotions, in order to simplify the coding process and reduce the number of categories beforehand, eliminating irrelevancies. Table 2.2 shows the top 30 content categories, indicating the number of units in each category. Brand, product, and promotion name appeared so frequently that counting them would have distracted the coders (labeled N/A in Table 2.2).

   Categories with a high frequency for one problem and a zero frequency for the other mark problem-specific concepts. For example, the concept of Package is relevant only for

---

EXHIBIT 2.2
PART OF A DOMAIN EXPERT PROTOCOL

Well, I think, you could . . ., I would wonder whether I want a promotion the first year at any rate? I mean, since it is a new product. It is new. The package is great. I'm going to campaign, I could imagine to . . ., well, because what I really want is to drive consumers to make trial purchases. Well, if I'm going to campaign, I'd probably promote by giving an introduction discount; so no added value promotions. That would distract attention from the product since added value is already in the product. I mean, suppose I would give a CD that would, . . ., no . . ., I want to focus on my product and drive people to buy the product. If I want consumers to pay attention to my product, I could promote by giving an introduction discount. Or I would do a refund promotion. In other words: Give the consumer cash money back immediately, or . . ., I could promote by refunding the entire product price if people send in the bar code of the product.

Table 2.2 Ranked Average Number of Occurrences of Categories in Protocols (Number of Protocols = 20)

RANK	CATEGORY	PRESTO-DRESS	MARIE-FRANCE	AVERAGE	RANK	CATEGORY	PRESTO-DRESS	MARIE-FRANCE	AVERAGE
1	Brand	N/A	N/A	N/A	16	Market	24	12	18
2	Product	N/A	N/A	N/A	17	Shape of Package	27	0	14
3	Promotion Name	N/A	N/A	N/A	18	Promotion Strategy	27	0	14
4	Promotion Budget	68	86	77	19	Character	0	17	9
5	Sales	3	102	53	20	Proposition	16	0	8
6	Promotion Costs	40	52	46	21	Producer	11	2	7
7	Promotion Goal	61	29	45	22	Distribution	11	0	6
8	Consumer	19	56	38	23	Added Value	10	0	5
9	Advertiser	0	71	36	24	Reach	5	5	5
10	Price	30	29	30	25	Promotion Communication	10	0	5
11	Package	58	0	29	26	Awareness	7	2	5
12	Trial	44	4	24	27	Promotion Prospect	0	9	5
13	Ad	24	20	22	28	Product Content	4	4	4
14	Market Share	35	3	19	29	Profit	8	0	4
15	Target Market	3	34	19	30	Promotion Location	0	8	4

the salad dressing problem, and the concept of Advertiser is relevant only for the troubled fashion magazine (see Table 2.3). These categories are deliberately included in further analysis, since they indicate important problem-related concepts. When we design the framework, such concepts point at *hinges* of the framework (in other words, places where adaptability has to be engineered into the framework explicitly) [Fayad-Cline 1996].

With the second coding procedure we intend to *find relationships among the content categories*. Table 2.3 shows relationships and their references to content categories that were extracted from the protocol fragment displayed in Exhibit 2.2.

Step 3: Creating the Object-Oriented Framework in a CASE Tool

Marketing decision making is strongly oriented toward certain common concepts and actors with characteristics and behavior. A strong mapping between the real world and potential software objects exists. As is noted in the marketing literature [Wierenga-Van Bruggen 1997], managers are not willing to accept systems based on models that are at

Table 2.3 Sample Relationships

REFERENCE	RELATIONSHIPS	CONTENT CATEGORIES
ns1-1	Do I want a promotion the first year, since I'm dealing with a new product here?	Promotion, Date, Product
ns1-2	I'm going to do a promotion, since I want consumers to make trial purchases.	Promotion, Consumer, Trial Purchase
ns1-3	If I'm going to campaign, I'd probably promote by giving an introduction-discount.	Promotion, Product Introduction, Introduction Discount
ns1-4	No added-value promotions because the added value is already in the product.	Added-Value Promotion, Product Added Value, Product
ns1-5	If I want consumers to pay attention to my product I could promote by giving an introduction discount.	Consumer, Attention, Product, Promotion, Introduction Discount
ns1-6	If I want consumers to pay attention to my product I could do a refund promotion.	Consumer, Attention, Product, Refund Promotion
ns1-7	If I want consumers to pay attention to my product I could promote by giving an immediate refund.	Consumer, Attention, Product, Refund
ns1-8	I could promote by refunding the entire product price if people send in the bar-code of the product.	Refund, Product Price, Bar Code

variance with their own mental model. Object orientation makes it possible to build systems that closely match reality as perceived by its users. Also, product managers act in a dynamic environment where products and actors quickly appear, disappear, and change position. The promise of OO to deliver adaptable software systems matches this dynamic nature of the domain.

We started building the sales promotions framework by mapping the top 30 content categories (see Table 2.2) to object classes. This initial object model forms the basis for the rest of the modeling process.

We subsequently refined the framework with the use of the relationship that we found in the protocols of the sales promotion decision makers (Step 2, Table 2.3). Figure 2.3, for example, displays an inheritance relation between Purchase and Trial. This link was created during modeling when we came across the statement, "I'm going to do a promotion since I want consumers to make trial purchases." (see Table 2.3 [ref. ns1-2]). In the initial model (top 30 classes), only the class Trial was modeled. By analyzing the relationships, we found that a trial purchase is a specialized version of a regular purchase; hence, we created Purchase and made Trial a specialization of this class.

The sales promotion domain framework model is too complex to remain comprehensible while being displayed in one diagram. The model is decomposed into six smaller units (see Figure 2.2)—so-called packages—that can contain all kinds of modeling elements [Booch-Rumbaugh 1997]. In partitioning the model, we strove for high cohesion based on grouping classes addressing similar domain aspects and loose coupling between distinct classes. Arrows between the packages indicate visibility relationships: If a client object in the Product package wants to make use of a server object in the Consumer package, then a visibility relationship must exist between the client and server classes [Fowler 1997]. The Consumer and Product packages have mutual visibility. The framework is too extensive to be described here entirely. To illustrate both the generic as well as the domain-specific classes of the framework, we highlight the contents of the Consumer, Promotion, and QuantityHistory package in this section.

Figure 2.3 displays an explosion of the Consumer package. Consumer is one of the central concepts of the framework and captures data on individual consumers and their purchase histories. The interview results indicated that sales promotion managers have a high interest in data on the level of the individual. Sales promotions and direct-marketing activities (telemarketing, direct mailing) have increasingly been linked and merged. Producers can buy individual data available either from scanners in stores (linked to con-

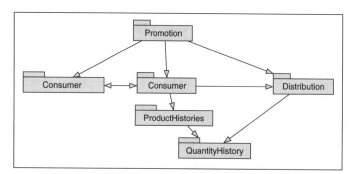

Figure 2.2 The packages and their dependencies.

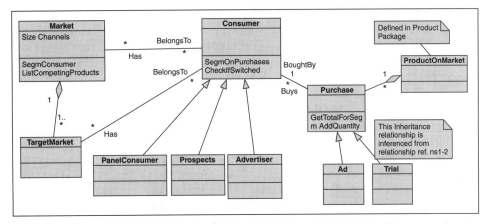

Figure 2.3 The Consumer package. The frequencies of the corresponding categories are displayed in the top-left corner of the class.

sumer data by electronic cards) or from consumer panels (samples of consumers whose purchases, media consumption, preferences, and so on, are recorded over a longer period of time). This individual data can be represented by the Purchase class. The subclasses Ad and Advertiser illustrate how a simple extension to the framework enables the manager to store data on a special consumer: an Advertiser that buys an Ad in a Magazine.

An example of framework behavior that was modeled in the Consumer package pertains to the activity of segmenting. Many relationships extracted from the protocols addressed this prominent marketing strategy, which concerns the finding groups of more or less homogeneous consumers according to some prespecified characteristic(s). Figure 2.4 zooms in on this behavior in the Consumer package, by showing how the manager interacts with the system when he or she wants to segment consumers, based on their Purchases.

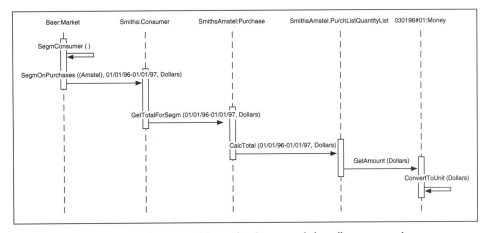

Figure 2.4 A sequence diagram of how the framework handles segmenting consumers. Note: Interaction with files and GUI components are not shown in order to simplify this figure.

Suppose a product manager of Amstel Beer wants to gain insight into how consumers are grouped over categories based on how much Amstel they purchased in the year 1996 (for example, divide them into three segments: heavy, medium, and light users).

First, the manager is presented a list of attributes by which consumers can be segmented (method: SegmConsumer). In this example, the manager chooses the variable Purchases, also indicating the period and currency he or she wants to consider. This request generates a message that is sent to each consumer of Amstel (in the diagram the message is sent to consumer Smiths, invoking the method SegmOnPurchases, passing the arguments 01/01/96–01/01/97, Dollars). Each consumer object now retrieves its total purchases of Amstel in that year (message to Purchase objects, invoking the method GetTotalForSegm, arg 01/01/96–01/01/97, Dollars). If necessary, the currency is converted to Dollars (message to Money objects, invoking the method ConvertToUnit, arg Dollars). The CalcTotal message illustrates how polymorphism is used, since the message can be sent to any consumer characteristic for which a history is kept (for example, TotalExpenditures, NrOfVisitsToStore).

Figure 2.5 shows an explosion of the Promotion package and displays the sales promotion types the managers commented on in the interviews. The promotion types were grouped based on similarity in characteristics and behavior, as extracted from the protocols. Promotions based on price discounts, for example, were put in one group, since they all share a mechanism that influences the product price. The other sales promotion types influence the added value of the product. A (virtual) pricing method (Pricing) was defined on the level of the abstract class (Price) and was overridden at the subclass level: Discount directly lowers the price, Coupon discounts the price when a coupon is handed over, ProductPlus promotions give an extra quantity of the product for the same price, and Refund gives a discount on the sale directly or after send-

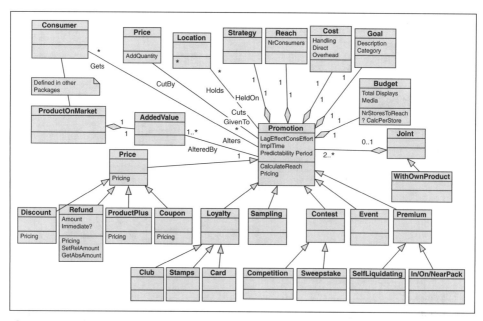

Figure 2.5   The promotion package.

ing in a proof of purchase. The Pricing method is another example of how polymorphism is used in the framework.

A special type of promotion often used by our interviewees was the joint promotion. A joint promotion can be any type of promotion and is a coordinated effort among several different producers. The solutions managers proposed to the Presto-Dress sample problem (see Exhibit 2.1) often had a joint character: giving away samples of the salad dressing when consumers buy lettuce, or gluing coupons on packages of other products of the producer's product range (WithOwnProduct).

The managers choose a promotion type based on the goal of the promotion and, among other things, the available time and the budget. In specifying their promotion they set attributes such as the period in which the promotion will be executed, the distributors with whom they will operate, the trade conditions, the displays they will provide to the stores that adopt the promotion, media expenditures, and many others, not displayed in Figure 2.5 for reasons of clarity.

The Quantity History package shown in Figure 2.6 includes classes that allow the storage of a variety of data over time. The interview data showed that product managers depend heavily on real-world data such as product sales, consumer purchases, market share, and awareness. Variations in product and market require different units of measurement. For example, a bottle of spring water has a price in U.S. dollars and a volume in gallons in the United States, whereas in the Netherlands guilders and liters would be used. These diverse measurements are not present in the programming systems currently available. Anticipating that many analysts have to deal with this problem, Fowler proposed Quantity patterns: analysis patterns describing solutions to this problem based on his experience in modeling hospital systems [Fowler 1997]. As suggested in these patterns, a general Quantity class is introduced, containing a number and a unit of measurement. Specific quantity types we needed for the framework were subclassed. The Money class, for instance, contains Amount and (a currency) Unit. Typical needs of the Money type, such as displaying the quantity using a fixed-point notation, are implemented in the Money class itself. We elicited the subclasses of Quantity from the protocol data: Share (for example, market share), BooleanFactor (for example, a consumer is aware or not aware of a product), and different units for mea-

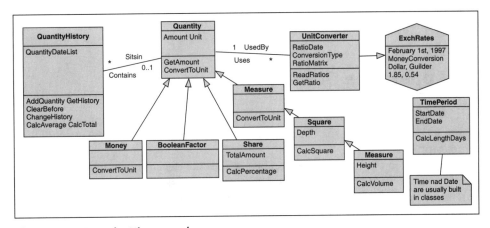

Figure 2.6 Quantity History package.

suring sizes and contents. Product managers look at data from different countries and view quantities on different aggregation levels. This requires conversion of quantities to other units. As suggested by Fowler, a UnitConverter class is designed to perform such conversions. Figure 2.6 shows a sample object, ExchangeRates, that performs such unit conversions for Money objects.

The manager is not only interested in current information, but tends to base many of his or her decisions on historical developments—that is, product sales in the last six months. A system built for the sales promotion domain must be able to store a variety of quantities over a period of time. The QuantityHistory class was designed based on Fowler's Historic Mapping patterns. This class can contain any number of objects from the quantity hierarchy and the dates at which the quantities are valid. The class contains methods like CalcAverage, a method that calculates the average over the Quantities within a specified time period. Many classes in the framework—for example, Purchase and Awareness—are descendants of QuantityHistory and thus are able to store histories data.

The framework was modeled in MetaEdit, a CASE tool that supports UML, which allows methodology engineering and methodology adaptation, and generates source code in different programming languages such as C++, Smalltalk, and Delphi. In case source code cannot be generated for the programming environment the system is built in, custom instructions can be programmed in the CASE tool in order to do so [Smolander 1991]. We discovered that using the CASE tool (in combination with UML) had a number of advantages. First, UML support gave us a combination of well-known diagramming techniques. Useful in handling the complexity of design, for instance, the package construct serves as an entry point to lower-level diagrams. Second, the meta-level adaptability permits extra documentation fields (such as extra comments, references to protocol relationships) to be added to UML concepts. This domain information is crucial to enable future users (developers) to understand the framework. Third, source code generation facilitates adaptation of the framework on the design level whenever a new application is being created. The class operations are implemented in a pseudocode. CASE tools exist that allow source code (or a generic formal language) to be entered directly into the CASE environment. However, including this level of detail into a framework can easily distract the designers from the domain issues and may destroy the advantage of working at a higher level of abstraction. Delivering the framework as programming code would cause a loss of much semantic information.

2.2 Application Development

This section will briefly describe Steps 4 through 6 of the development method (see Figure 2.1) by describing the Sales Promotion Intelligence Data EngineeR (SPIDER) sample application.

The sales promotion framework can be used for the development of a whole range of applications. Software can be designed for different tasks that need to be performed in relation to sales promotions, such as an application for calculating the profitability of sales promotions or time scheduling of different promotional events through the year. The framework can also be used to build sales promotion software for different industries like banking, automobiles, or fast food. The sample application we developed is SPIDER, a system that can store and retrieve sales promotion events for managers who need to design sales promotion plans for products in fast-moving consumer-good markets. The remainder of this section elaborates on this system.

Product managers can gather a lot of experiential data on their sales promotion activities. Most managers manage multiple brands, each of which has multiple variants (different sizes, flavors, packages). Each product has its own promotional agenda that often comprises multiple promotional events a year, executed in different markets, in different regions, and for different customers. Promotional events are considered great learning opportunities by managers. One problem with the available promotion data is that the information is scattered over various sources throughout the organization: databases, market research reports, videotapes, documentation maps, and the manager's mind. In markets where competition is fierce, decisions have to be made fast and information has to be available instantly. A product manager is generally unable to recollect all relevant experiences that can be used for decisions.

For SPIDER, we needed both a technique to represent the domain and its knowledge and a reasoning mechanism for using that knowledge in the proper way. The sales promotion framework was used for the representation of the domain. This provided the developers, for instance, with the semantics for storing data, organizing it on the basis of the domain knowledge. Promotion Package objects (see Figure 2.5) are used to store data on the promotion itself (for example, Type, Budget, Media), Consumer Package objects (see Figure 2.3) store data on consumers who participate in the promotion (such as Name, Address, AmountPurchased), Distribution objects store data on the retailers that adopt the promotion (for example, Allowance, NrOfStores), and so on.

SPIDER is based on the problem-solving technique known as case-based reasoning. Put simply, case-based reasoning is the computerized equivalent of what we refer to as reasoning on the basis of analogy when it is performed by humans. New problems are solved by using previously designed solutions to similar problems. A case-based reasoning system can serve as a central repository in which experiences can be collected. Algorithms are available for retrieval of the right cases at the right time. Certain case-based reasoning systems have functionality for adapting cases to the new problem situations, which is useful since problems are seldom identical. [Aamodt-Plaza 1994; Schank 1982] provide a good introduction into the field of case-based reasoning.

The domain framework is used by SPIDER, by having its data stored in, and retrieved from, the framework's objects. Objects once defined (as specific consumers, products, and retailers) can remain stored in the system, making entry of new cases an easy job. Most data can be reused: A new sales promotion occurs in an already defined market, was held by a known competitor, and so on.

Figure 2.7 shows the basic architecture of SPIDER and its use of the sales promotion domain framework.

The system is implemented in KAPPA-PC, a hybrid environment combining multiple representation paradigms, including objects, rules, and procedures. The CASE tool we used (MetaEdit) could not generate code for this environment, but provides the possibility to customize code generation. We used this possibility and put in custom-made instructions that are used by the CASE tool to generate KAPPA-PC code.

We performed a UML-use scenario analysis [Booch-Rumbaugh 1997] for finding out the scope and required functionality of SPIDER. The use scenarios comprise the basic

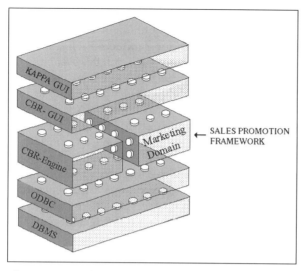

Figure 2.7   Architecture of SPIDER.

functional elements of the system (Exhibit 2.3 shows a textual example of such a scenario). The scenarios were input for the rest of the modeling process: drawing class diagrams and interaction diagrams (see Figure 2.1, Step 4). After this stage, an assessment is made of how the framework can be tailored for the specific application (Step 5). Then, modeling trajectory source code was generated and final implementation issues were addressed (Step 6).

2.3 Lessons Learned

We learned a number lessons in applying the framework development method.

As opposed to our initial expectations, new candidate classes were still found after analyzing a substantial number of expert protocols (see Figure 2.8). We think this will be the case in many semistructured domains, since there is not an objective, fixed set of

EXHIBIT 2.3
AN EXAMPLE USE SCENARIO FOR BUILDING SPIDER

The user selects *Improve brand image* and *Increase loyalty* as values for the *Goals* attribute: The attribute *Goals* is a multivalued text attribute with different options to choose from. As soon as the user clicks the mouse over such an attribute, a list becomes visible, displaying the options from which the user can choose. This attribute allows the selection of multiple items from the list (such as *Improve brand image* and *Increase loyalty*). In case multiple items are selected, the user can express the wish to enter weights for the different items. If the user does so, each item will be displayed along with a slider, ranging from 0–100, with which he or she can set the weights.

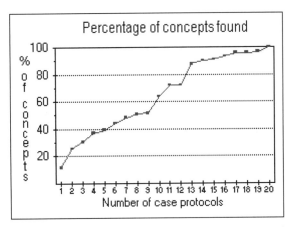

Figure 2.8 The percentage of concepts found against the number of protocols.

elements that play a role. Structured domains, on the other hand, have such a set, making modeling more easy. Ninety-five percent of the candidate objects were found after analyzing 17 protocols. Though such an analysis is a considerable effort, it eliminates the need for expensive domain experts to undergo OO training and modeling sessions. In our approach, each expert spends only about one hour.

In refining the model, we find the recent developments of analysis patterns very useful. We feel that future developments in this area can be of benefit to all OO developers. The CASE tool and methodology (UML) we use provide enough power and flexibility for modeling frameworks. Frameworks for semistructured domains, such as sales promotion, require the use of abstraction techniques like bottom-up design and information hiding, which are supported by CASE tools. We found that creating sequence diagrams is very useful in validating the classes designed.

Reuse is an important theme when building software for domains such as marketing. Although no two product managers have the exact same job, the vast majority of what such a manager does is the same across companies, products, markets, and countries. A sales promotion domain framework can serve as the basis for the development of applications for sales promotion decision making in different companies, markets, and countries, adapted to the needs of specific products, of individual managers, and for the various tasks that have to be performed within the domain. This type of structure probably exists for many such domains, making the development of a domain framework, as we have shown in this chapter, very beneficial.

2.4 Summary

In this chapter we have presented a methodology for developing domain frameworks in semistructured domains, such as marketing. The procedure starts from protocols of experts solving sample problems, after which content analysis is used to derive concepts and relationships between concepts from these texts. In building the OO model, content analysis provides a vehicle for finding classes and relationships that is much more powerful than those specified by many of the guidelines given in OO literature. Once developed, such a framework can be used for building different applications within the task domain of the user. The illustration of the framework development method presented in this paper concerns decision making about sales promotions.

The work described here can be extended in several directions. For example, the number of sample problems (in this case, two) and the number of experts (20) can be increased. Also, this methodology can be applied to other decision domains with a semistructured character, for example, investment decisions, management development, personnel selection, and legal problem solving.

This chapter has shown that the development of a domain framework, combining methods from behavioral sciences such as content analysis with OO modeling, can make a major contribution to the development of software applications for supporting decision makers in semistructured domains.

2.5 References

[Aamodt-Plaza 1994] Aamodt, A., and E. Plaza. Case-based reasoning: Foundational issues, methodological variations, and system approaches. *AICOM* 7(1), January 1994.

[Blattberg-Neslin 1990] Blattberg, R.C., and S.A. Neslin. *Sales Promotion: Concepts, Methods, and Strategies.* Englewood Cliffs, NJ: Prentice Hall, 1990.

[Booch-Rumbaugh 1997] Booch, G., and J. Rumbaugh. Unified Modeling Language: Metamodel Description Version 1.0. Rational Software Corporation, www.rational .com/uml/.

[Fayad-Cline 1996] Fayad, M., and M.P. Cline. Aspects of software adaptability. *Communications of the ACM,* Theme Issue on Software Patterns, Douglas Schmidt, Mohamed Fayad, and Ralph Johnson, editors, 39(10), October 1996:58—59.

[Fayad-Laitinen 1998] Fayad, M.E., and M. Laitinen. *Transition to Object-Oriented Software Development.* New York: John Wiley & Sons, 1998.

[Fowler 1997] Fowler, M. *Analysis Patterns: Reusable Object Models.* Reading, MA: Addison-Wesley, 1997.

[Gibson-Senn 1989] Gibson, V.R., and J.A. Senn. System structure and software maintenance performance. *Communications of the ACM* 32(3), March 1989:347–358.

[Johnson-Foote 1988] Johnson, R.E., and B. Foote. Designing reusable classes. *Journal of Object-Oriented Programming* 2(1), January–February 1988.

[Korson-McGregor 1990] Korson, T.D., and J.D. McGregor. Understanding object-orientation: A unifying paradigm. *Communications of the ACM* 33(9), September 1990: 40–60.

[Krippendorff 1980] Krippendorff, K. *Content Analysis: An Introduction to Its Methodology.* Thousand Oaks, CA: Sage Publications, 1980.

[Rumbaugh 1991] Rumbaugh, J., M. Blaha, W. Premerlani, F. Eddy, and W. Lorensen. *Object-Oriented Modeling and Design.* Englewood Cliffs, NJ: Prentice Hall, 1991.

[Schank 1982] Schank, R. *Dynamic Memory: A Theory of Learning in Computers and People.* New York: Cambridge University Press, 1982.

[Smolander 1991] Smolander, Kari, Kalle Lyytinen, Veli-Pekka Tahvanainen, and Pentti Marttiin. MetaEdit—A flexible graphical environment for methodology modeling. *Advanced Information Systems Engineering, Third International Conference CAiSE 1991:*

Proceedings, pp. 168–193, R. Andersen, J.A. Bubenko, Jr., A. Solvberg, editors. Berlin: Springer-Verlag, 1991.

[Taligent 1997] Taligent, I. *Building Object-Oriented Frameworks.* Taligent, www.taligent .com, 1997.

[Weber 1985] Weber, R.P. *Basic Content Analysis.* Beverly Hills, CA: Sage Publications, 1985.

[Wierenga-Van Bruggen 1997] Wierenga, B., and G.H. Van Bruggen. The integration of marketing problem solving modes and marketing management support systems. *Journal of Marketing,* July 1997, pp. 21–37.

[Yourdon 1994] Yourdon, E. *Object-Oriented Systems Design: An Integrated Approach.* Englewood Cliffs, NJ: Prentice Hall, 1994.

SIDEBAR 1
BUSINESS POLICIES AND RULE PATTERNS

SB1.1 Characteristics of Rule Patterns

Application development has to cope with frequently changing requirements that are to a large extent due to changes in the business environment [Loucopoulos 1991]. These facets of business environments are often referred to as *business policies*. They may be based on ethics, law, culture, and organizational commitments by either prescribing a certain action or by constraining the set of possible actions [Odell 1994].

Two main problems arise in the context of implementing business policies. First, business policies are often blurred with code for implementing the basic, rather stable functionality of an application. This makes it difficult to cope with their dynamic nature. The problem can be resolved by factoring out business policies from single applications and representing them in terms of *Event/Condition/Action rules (ECA rules)*. These rules allow the designer to monitor situations represented by events, together with conditions, and execute the corresponding actions when the events occur and the conditions are true. ECA rules may be stored as first-class objects in active object-oriented database systems [Kappel-Retschitzegger 1998]. The second problem concerns reusability. Application designers have to decide on the implementation of a particular business policy over and over again for each application domain since appropriate abstraction mechanisms are not available. This problem can be captured by introducing *rule patterns,* which describe business policies in an abstract way [Kappel 1996].

When looking at rules implementing specific business policies, one can find components that are applicable to a number of application domains as well as components specific to a single application domain. Let us consider two business policies from a warehouse application and a bank application. The former states that every time goods are removed from the stock, the remaining number of goods is checked. If it has fallen below a given limit, new goods have to be ordered. The latter states that every time money is withdrawn from an account, the balance is checked and—if overdrawn—the bank charges are increased. A common formulation of these two policies in terms of a generic rule pattern would express that as soon as a certain property's value is changed and falls below a defined threshold, some reaction has to be undertaken.

The value, the threshold, and the reaction would be the parameters of the rule pattern constituting its application-specific components. Next to parameterization, composition makes rule patterns even more general and versatile than they could be otherwise. A composed rule pattern consists of several component rule patterns working together to realize some specific kind of business policy.

SB1.2 A Framework of Rule Patterns

Assuming an object-oriented design in the first place, one way to systematically identify an application's business policies is to extract them out of the three basic perspectives of an object-oriented modeling method representing the application. The three perspectives are the object view, the dynamic view, and the interaction view [Fowler 1997]. Business policies that are identified in this way comprise different kinds of static and dynamic constraints, real-time constraints, and interaction policies, to mention just a few. By transforming these business policies into rule patterns, a framework of rule patterns is established. Adapting the framework notion [Johnson 1997], we do not represent the *whole* application skeleton in the framework but rather an essential part of it, namely, the context-dependent and time-dependent organizational knowledge of an application domain typically captured by business policies. By factoring them out into a reusable framework of rule patterns, knowledge independence is reached [Ceri-Fraternali 1997]. The power of knowledge independence is that, on the one hand, business policies are automatically shared by, and therefore also imposed on, all applications, and, on the other hand, evolution of knowledge is much more feasible and controllable.

A design environment for both extending our pattern framework and using it as a basis for rule-based application development is operational. To evaluate our approach, we realized different *interaction policies* between objects, such as *synchronous, asynchronous,* and *future synchronous* by means of rule patterns [Kappel 1996]. These rule patterns are called *interaction rule patterns*. They enhance sequential message passing in such a way that interactions in a concurrent object-oriented environment based on multiple threads of control are specifiable. Instead of having to accept messages implicitly, or unconditionally, any object accepts messages explicitly, depending on its actual state. By now, we support 11 interaction patterns, differing in how the sender of a message synchronizes with the receiver. They are basically classified according to the two dimensions, *start of interaction* and *end of interaction*. Concerning the start of an interaction, both the acceptability of the receiver and what has to be done if the receiver is not immediately ready to satisfy the request must be specified. Basically, the sender can either be blocked until the receiver is in the right state for accepting the request (synchronous begin) or proceed irrespective of the receiver's state (asynchronous begin). Considering the end of an interaction, it must be specified whether the sender is blocked until the receiver has finished execution (synchronous end) or not (asynchronous end). Concerning the latter, the sender may wait for the result of the receiver at some future point in time (future synchronous end).

At this time we do not claim completeness of our framework of rule patterns. The proper design of rule-based applications, however, is one of the most pressing research issues in this area [Ceri-Fraternali 1997]. As a consequence, our objective is to support application designers by a framework of high-level rule patterns rather than letting them alone with low-level objects and rules.

SB1.3 References

[Ceri-Fraternali 1997] Ceri, S., and P. Fraternali. *Designing Database Applications with Objects and Rules: The IDEA Methodology.* Reading, MA: Addison-Wesley, 1997.

[Fowler 1997] Fowler, M. *UML Distilled: Applying the Standard Object Modeling Language.* Reading, MA: Addison-Wesley, 1997.

[Johnson 1997] Johnson, R.E. Frameworks = (components + patterns). *Communications of the ACM,* Theme Issue on Object-Oriented Application Frameworks, Mohamed E. Fayad and Douglas Schmidt, editors, 40(10), October 1997.

[Kappel 1996] Kappel, G., S. Rausch-Schott, W. Retschitzegger, and M. Sakkinen. From

Continues

SIDEBAR 1
BUSINESS POLICIES AND RULE PATTERNS *(Continued)*

rules to rule patterns. *Proceedings of the 8th International Conference on Advanced Information Systems Engineering (CAiSE 1996),* pp. 99–115, P. Constantopoulos, J. Mylopoulos, and Y. Vassiliou, editors, Heraklion, Crete, Springer LNCS 1080, 1996.

[Kappel-Retschitzegger 1998] Kappel, G., and W. Retschitzegger. The TriGS active object-oriented database system—An overview. Accepted for publication at the *ACM SIGMOD Record,* September 1998.

[Loucopoulos 1991] Loucopoulos, P., C. Theodoulidis, and D. Pantazis. Business rules modeling: Conceptual modeling and object-oriented specifications. *Proceedings of the IFIP WG8.1 Working Conference on the Object-Oriented Approach in Information Systems,* F. Van Assche, et al. editors, Quebec City, Canada, North-Holland, 1991.

[Odell 1994] Odell, J.J. Specifying requirements using rules. *Journal of Object-Oriented Programming (JOOP)* 6(2), 1994.

CHAPTER 3

A Reflective and Repository-Based Framework

3.1 Context

Argo is a semigovernment organization that manages the public schools (nondenominational) within the Flemish community in Belgium. It consists of a central administration and a few hundred semi-autonomous local sites (boards and schools).

The project started in early 1994. At the start, Argo was going through an external audit, which made it likely that there would be major changes of procedures, organizational structure, accountability rules, and delegations of responsibility. Future requests for changes were a given at the start of the project.

So Argo needed a framework to build applications that would be sufficiently flexible to cope with changing and emerging needs and opportunities, both functional and technological, imposed or desired. It wanted an environment that not only would survive the expected reorganization and decentralization but would stimulate users to envision better ways of working.

We started with three pilot applications to provide input for initial framework requirements and design:

A documentation center that provided flexible search and retrieval of data and documents such as legislative texts and parliamentary decrees concerning education. Many documents have a complex structure of interrelationships, such as appendixes, references to subsequent changes and juridical decrees based on multiple laws.

A system to support the central board's decision procedures from initial draft version to the final text, and then to monitor the implementation of the decisions by the administration or the local boards and schools. These decisions include motions that have been passed or tabled, contracts with teachers, and changes to curricula and budget reports. The path through the administration is not clear-cut and it changes depending on the parties involved or the subject of the decision. The procedures are not always limited to a strict hierarchical structure; some involve temporary workgroups or external committees.

An application to import, index, store, and route large volumes of documents sent in by the local boards. Examples include attendance records, decisions, meeting notes, and any large addenda.

Halfway through the project the pending reorganization was effectively carried out. Although the nature and extent of it were largely unknown at the onset, we were able to adapt the existing applications through reconfiguration without additional coding.

Since then, several new end-user applications have been delivered. We are now in the process of extending the framework, most notably to give schools and local boards access to the central data and information through the Internet. We are converting large existing relational database applications, we added web functionality and an Internet discussion system.

These applications, together with new technological possibilities, are our major sources of requirements for the evolving framework. Within this process we further refined and redesigned many framework components. The persistency component, for instance, has been completely reimplemented. In addition, we created some applications to support the development process, such as a bug reporting system with follow-up, training-session management, and framework documentation management.

Not only do we build end-user applications with data, document, workflow, and Internet functionality, but we also use the same framework to develop the tools that we use to build and manage these applications. In this way users can use their interface, known from their business objects, to adapt applications.

End users at Argo are gradually taking over the management of applications and configuration from the development team. Key users teach and write parts of the documentation. User groups organize workshops to discuss how to put the technology to better use. This process was initially driven by small teams of highly motivated pioneer users and has gradually started to embrace the end-user community at large. Given the high degree of computer-illiteracy within Argo at the start of the project, we believe this to be a significant achievement on behalf of the end users.

3.1.1 Project Requirements

There are four major project requirements that are described in this section: functionality, support for change, integrated environment, and configuration and administration tools.

Functionality

The technology has to support applications containing a mixture of database (school database, patrimonies, personnel, budget, inventory), electronic documents (educational documentation, research papers, articles, laws and decrees), workflow management (task assignments and follow-up, decision routing, process management), and has to give local sites access to the central repository of data and documents.

Database

Users have to be able to enter, modify, remove, query, list, browse, report, print, import, and export data. They need tools to set up appropriate views and to store queries for later reuse.

Electronic Document Management

Users need to create, index, search, edit, annotate, print, export, and process documents. These can be either electronic (such as files or email) or scanned paper documents. Structured information, thesaurus keywords, and full-text indexing are used for indexing and searching. Optical character recognition enables users to extract text from scanned documents. Users need tools to manage document versions. They must be able to choose the most appropriate alternative representations of the same document, depending on the environment or the job at hand. A document created and adapted with a word processor must be frozen once it has passed the decision process and can be presented in Portable Document Format (PDF) files to schools.

Workflow Management

Users must be able to plan and handle incoming tasks, keep track of outgoing task assignments, and manage workflow processes, which can be more or less well defined or completely ad hoc. Argo wants workflow functionality to suggest opportunities to its users, guiding rather than restricting them.

Alternative Access Modes

In addition to the applications running in client-server mode at the central site, Argo needs alternative ways of accessing its applications, data, documents, and processes in the central repository, such as the following:

- Using an offline version of the system so that employees can occasionally take work home for specific tasks, such as preparing a proposal for the central board

- Using the system online by means of a direct dial-up connection, such as a modem or ISDN for board members and employees working in remote locations

- Using email and web browsers to access the repository through the Internet for schools and teachers

Infrastructure

The applications must be able to operate in a Windows-Novell environment. The database is an Oracle server. Internet mail is used for external communication; cc:Mail for internal communication. The framework must be developed in VisualWorks/Smalltalk.

Support for Change

To cater to changing needs, the system should forgo hardcoding as much as possible: The technology should support iterative and incremental development through the use of prototypes. Moreover, it must act as a catalyst for a learning process when introducing this new technology, thus effectively complementing a business process reengineering project at Argo.

Integrated Environment

The applications must be integrated in one environment. All applications must use a common business model. This model supplies the cohesion expected in a large administration, providing formal procedures and policies (such as hierarchy, responsibilities, indexing vocabulary of documentation, and global validation- and authorization rules), but giving ample scope and freedom to adapt the technology to the most appropriate local or personal working practices. For some legal activities, all departments have to abide by strict rules requiring a prescribed number of signatures, while less formal processes are in use for more everyday tasks.

Configuration and Administration Tools

There must be tools to define the object model, constraints, and behavior; to configure and manage applications, views, and stored queries; to define and manage workflow processes; to set up access control; to manage the database; and to configure caching and backup of documents.

 At the end of the project, Argo's users need to be able to apply these tools. Hence, the deliveries do not include just end-user applications, but also the necessary tools to empower users to model and configure applications.

3.2 Using the Framework

We give a short overview of a documentation center application, a decision procedure application, and an incoming mail registration application. We will illustrate how the user applies the various tools to build and configure applications.

3.2.1 Examples

This section provides a brief overview of two different applications: document center applications and workflow process applications.

Documentation Center

The documentation center applications let users manage and search authors, publishers, and several types of books, periodicals, editions, and other kinds of documentation, including the framework documentation. Librarians use one application to import, index, and administrate the documents. Regular end users use a simpler application to search for the documents they want to consult.

 Some documentation exists only on paper. In this case we maintain references to the physical location. Most documentation is made accessible online, in original format or as scanned documents. Part of the documentation is made available on the Internet, in an alternative representation, such as PDF.

For indexing and querying we rely extensively on thesaurus and full-text indexing. Librarians manage distribution lists to notify users automatically about new documentation. They also keep track of loans. In addition to the standard printing facilities, librarians print documentation in ISBD-specific format.

The object model is complex. To reduce complexity and make the application more dynamic, we use some explicitly typed objects and associations. For instance, several types of documents share the same attributes and associations, but require different query and forms screens. We use the Type Object pattern for increased flexibility. Similarly, we model several types of associations by one attributed association. The attribute dynamically types the association, representing, for instance, "replaces" and "is an addendum to" associations between documentation.

Workflow Processes

Argo does not use workflow as a means to single-mindedly automate existing processes. Too many exceptions occur in the office to prescribe the flow in most cases. Although some processes follow a strict plan, in general, users need the freedom to deviate from this plan. And in some cases there is no fixed plan.

The central board decision procedure formally describes the process for submitting a dossier for approval by the central board, starting from a department's manager. The preparation phase prior to this process depends on each department's culture, which in some cases is very team-oriented and in other cases is inspired by a hierarchical structure. The general manager has the right to advise on the dossier, but he or she is not part of the actual process flow. To keep the general manager informed of upcoming dossiers, notifications are sent when the process enters a particular phase. When decisions result in a concrete action plan, management needs to check when and if the goals are actually met, by monitoring the state of specific data, documents, and processes.

A typical ad hoc process is the mail registration application for handling incoming (paper) mail. The users register these documents in the system, setting properties such as date, reference of sender, subject, summary, and keywords using Argo's thesaurus. They indicate if the information is confidential. The actual (paper or electronic) documents may be stored in the system using native Windows documents, such as HTML, PDF, and scanned TIFF. The documents are routed to the persons who have the authority to assign tasks and set priorities and deadlines. Depending on the nature of the documents, they are routed through the organization for further handling. The actual process flows depend on the contents of the documents. The recipients of the tasks are notified by email. They change the status of a task when they complete it or delegate it to someone else. The employees responsible for the dossiers keep track of the status of the tasks and report to superiors if needed.

3.2.2 Building Applications

Starting from the model in the repository at a certain moment, we build applications by going through a set of steps. These steps can be performed in any order, even interactively. The development process unfolds incrementally. We can try out and correct ideas dynamically, together with our users.

An end-user application usually starts by extending an existing model. Developing an application consists of the following:

- Extending (and possibly refactoring) the object model
- Setting up application environments and defining window layouts
- Extending or refining authorization rules
- Defining action rules
- Defining workflow process templates

This process is illustrated in Figure 3.1. Solid arrows denote the products of the tools; other arrows denote dependencies of the tools.

Extending the Object Model

With the object model editor, as shown in Figure 3.2, we define the object model: object and association types and basic constraints, such as uniqueness of value and totality of associations.

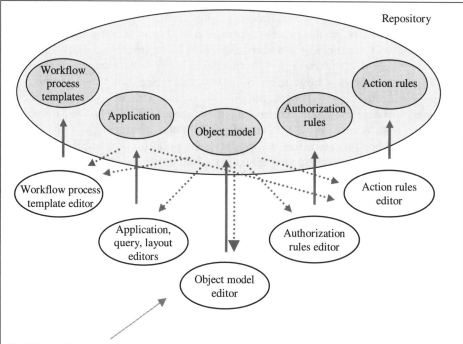

Building applications starts with an object model. All configuration tools depend on the object model.
Application environments depend on the object model only. Within these environments, stored queries and layouts customize screens.
Action rules and workflow process templates depend on object model and application environments. Authorization rules only depend on the object model.

Figure 3.1   Building applications.

Object behavior and user-defined constraints may be added now or later on, for example, to ensure correct initialization. Object behavior and constraints are common to all applications.

The object model editor defines the supertypes and subtypes of a new object type. It also defines the properties of a type, which can be either attributes, containing, for example, strings or dates, or references to associated objects.

When we have defined the model, we generate the necessary database structures. We select the mapping strategies for representing objects in the database. These strategies may be mixed, and even changed later on, to optimize the database mapping and to ease integration of existing databases.

Setting Up the Application Environment

This step starts with defining a filter on the shared business model: objects and properties to be accessed, created, and queried within the context of an application. Once this basic environment has been stored in the repository and access privileges have

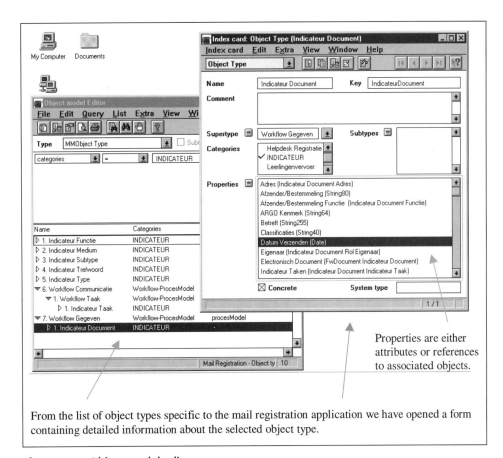

From the list of object types specific to the mail registration application we have opened a form containing detailed information about the selected object type.

Figure 3.2   Object model editor.

been set, users get a default application that is available for immediate use. Users can log on, choose this environment, enter data, query the repository, and list or print results. They can keep track of task assignments, manage electronic documents, and access the thesaurus. Functionality can be added or removed. The environment can be further refined for individual or shared use through views, queries, and subenvironments.

In the following example, we define the environment for the mail registration ("Indicateur") application (see Figure 3.3). We select the object types to be used in the application environment. For each object type we indicate accessible properties and how they are used and created.

Using the Default Application

Having defined the application environment, users have access to a fully functional default application by logging on in the main application window. What users perceive as an application is essentially determined by the objects they can manage and the functionality of the tools we provide, filtered by the application environment. Thus, we always present users with a similar set of tools, but these tools adapt themselves to the specifications of the application.

The main window tool (here on the default mail registration application) presents users with the query editor and an overview list. It also provides access to other functionalities, such as additional query and list windows, forms, document management, the thesaurus browser, workflow processes, in-/out-baskets, preference settings, and online help (see Figure 3.4).

Queries can be saved for individual or shared reuse within the application. Each query can have its own list layout. This list layout is selected automatically when the query is executed.

Users create, view, edit, print, export, and browse objects through the form tools. Each form is generated on the fly, according to a default strategy, subject to the authorization rules. The form generator selects appropriate editors for the individual properties and the object type at hand. In Figure 3.5 we opened a form on the two elements selected in the overview list.

Defining Window Layouts

Layout editors enable users to define new forms and overview lists and change old ones. The form layout editor presents the available editors for each type of property. For instance, the default association editors may be replaced with embedded list views and forms, enabling reuse of existing layouts. In the layout editor list, hierarchical relationships can be used to define threaded list views. Furthermore, association chains can be followed when defining the list of properties to be displayed, allowing users to denormalize views. Layouts can be defined as the default layout for a particular object type within a given application. In that case they will be selected automatically in overview lists and forms for the corresponding object type (see Figure 3.6).

Object types and properties with a check mark are accessible in the application.

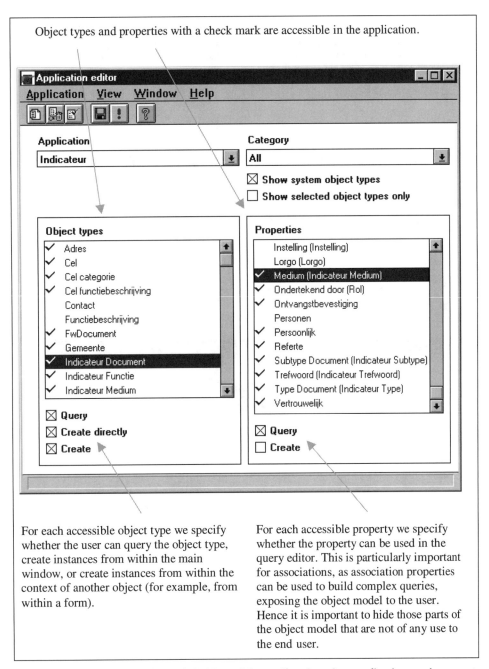

For each accessible object type we specify whether the user can query the object type, create instances from within the main window, or create instances from within the context of another object (for example, from within a form).

For each accessible property we specify whether the property can be used in the query editor. This is particularly important for associations, as association properties can be used to build complex queries, exposing the object model to the user. Hence it is important to hide those parts of the object model that are not of any use to the end user.

Figure 3.3 Application editor—definition of the mail registration application environment.

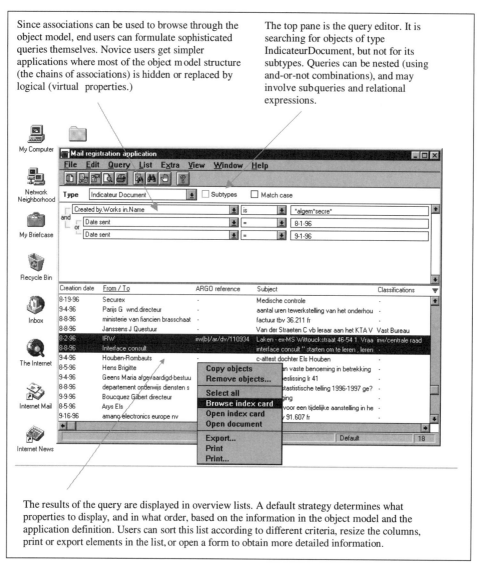

Since associations can be used to browse through the object model, end users can formulate sophisticated queries themselves. Novice users get simpler applications where most of the object model structure (the chains of associations) is hidden or replaced by logical (virtual properties.)

The top pane is the query editor. It is searching for objects of type IndicateurDocument, but not for its subtypes. Queries can be nested (using and-or-not combinations), and may involve subqueries and relational expressions.

The results of the query are displayed in overview lists. A default strategy determines what properties to display, and in what order, based on the information in the object model and the application definition. Users can sort this list according to different criteria, resize the columns, print or export elements in the list, or open a form to obtain more detailed information.

Figure 3.4   Default mail registration application.

Extending or Refining Authorization Rules

Access control is based on a set of authorization rules. These are not tied to any specific business model and can be used to set up both very fine- and course-grained access. Authorization rules can be context- and content-sensitive. Some rules apply to everyone; other rules apply to groups of people whose members are determined at runtime. This way, authorization rules support cohesion, while giving considerable flexibility in supporting different team cultures.

This is a form that views an IndicateurDocument. The form contains property editors to view and edit the accessible properties. Some are simple text input fields; others represent associations of this object with related objects.

Here we opened a form on the associated address. This form is generated dynamically, based on the object model and the application definition.

Association editors (often identified by a chain-like icon in front) enable users to browse through the object relationships. This traversal may be bidirectional, depending on the application environment definition.

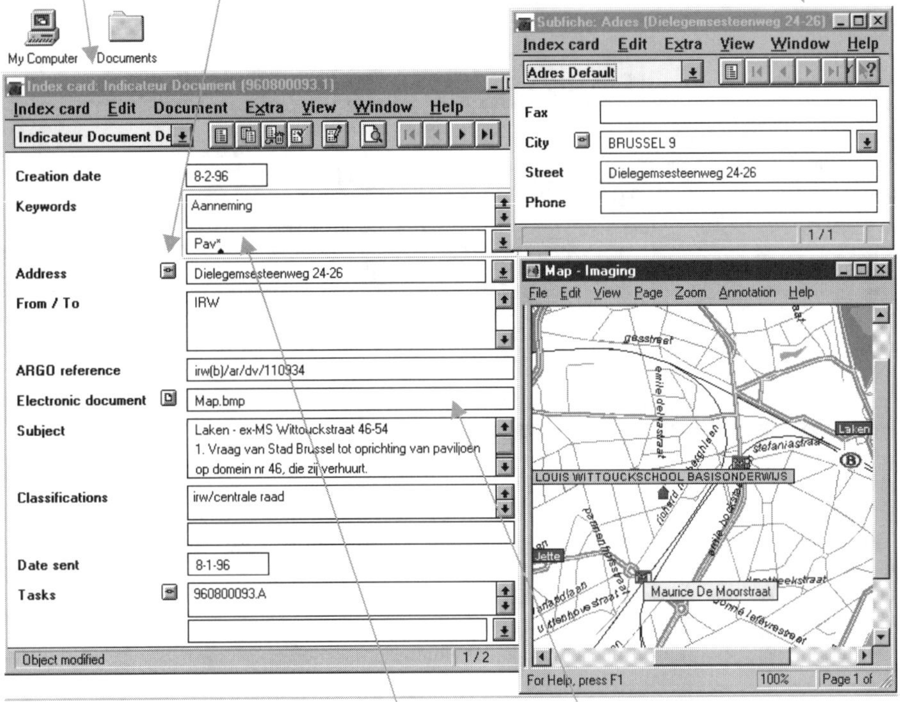

Associations with existing objects can be established by entering a search pattern and selecting the element from the resulting list. In case of thesaurus keywords the query may include synonyms, too. In order to thesaurus-enable an application, we only need to define an association between an object type and thesaurus descriptors.

Document-enabling an application is only a matter of defining an association between a particular object type and electronic documents. When a user opens a form on an instance of this object type, a special editor provides by default the functionality to attach, export, version, view, edit, and print electronic documents. In this example we imported a bitmap file and opened a Windows application to view the document.

Figure 3.5 Forms and document viewer.

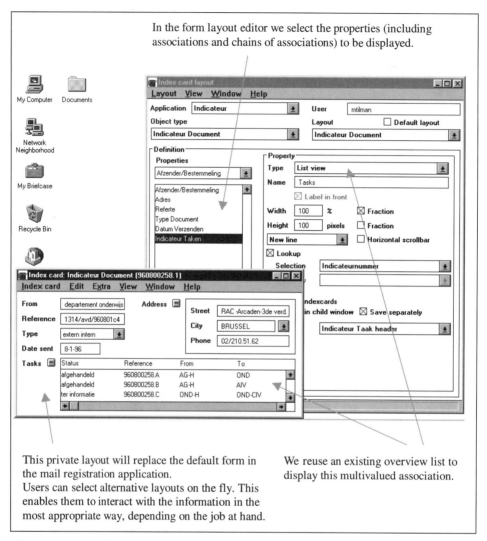

Figure 3.6   Form layout editor.

Authorization rules contain four parts. The *agent* (whom we are granting or denying access) and *object* (what objects the rule is about) conditions are defined using the query editor component. The *aspect* specifies to what aspects (properties) the rule applies and *rights* denotes the privileges (read and export), as shown in Figure 3.7.

Defining Action Rules

These rules capture business-semantics, set defaults, perform extra validation, impose constraints, and add functionality. Action rules can cover an entire organization or particular functions, or they can be limited to a specific application environment. Hence,

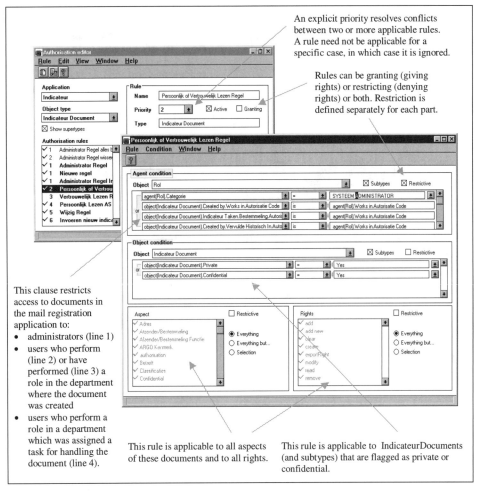

Figure 3.7 Authorization editor.

action rules give extensive support to autonomous teams while preserving overall consistency. Action rules come in two flavors: high-level template rules for defining workflow processes and script rules for handling more specific cases, as shown in Figure 3.8.

Defining Workflow Process Templates

Workflow process templates, as shown in Figure 3.9, specify default scenarios that the user typically follows in the context of a business process. Users can (usually) deviate from these scenarios and snap back into the predefined flow later on. Processes can be configured incrementally, for example, between departments first and within each department later on. Depending on team culture, these individual subprocesses are more or less strictly defined. In addition, there are automated tasks and dedicated private or shared in-/out-baskets to manage incoming and outgoing work.

This script rule initializes IndicateurDocuments in the mail registration application. It is triggered immediately whenever an object of this type is created, whether by means of forms or in the scripting language.

Events can be system events (create, update, delete) to impose constraints, time events (to set up automated tasks easily), application events (such as login or application switch events), and GUI events. The latter are triggered by application- and object-specific menu options, and add context-sensitive functionality.

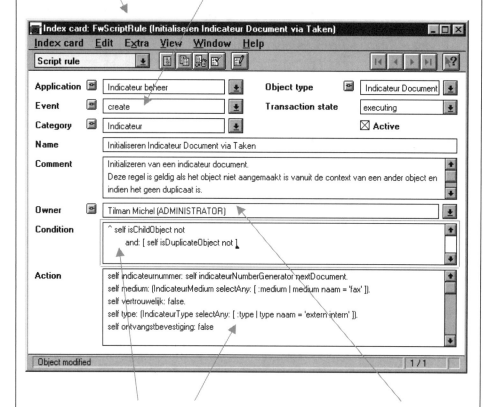

Rules consist of a condition and action part. Conditions specify if the rule is applicable to the object. An event may trigger several rules. The action parts of rules with valid conditions are executed. The scripting language in condition and action parts extends the Smalltalk language with a dynamic accessor protocol, automatic translation of Smalltalk-like select methods into query expressions, and implicit access control when accessing or updating an object property.

Access privileges are validated for the login user, unless we define a rule owner. In the latter case we check the owner's privileges when accessing or updating objects.

Figure 3.8 Script rules editor.

Action rules enable us to implement business rules and to offer extra functionality, depending on the job at hand. High-level rules capture many recurrent themes in script rules. We define high-level rules by means of extended forms.

Workflow process templates can be defined either graphically or by means of high-level rules. The graphical editor translates process diagrams into high-level rules.

In this example we are defining a rule to create a new task in the process flow and to assign default values for the task properties.

This new task's modification date is set to the creation date (relative expression).

This expression specifies to include the documents enclosed in the preceding task (relative expression) and to add the document with reference number 961100045.1 (object reference constant expression).

Attribute constant expression (primitive data, e.g., a date or string).

Object reference constant expression (repository object).

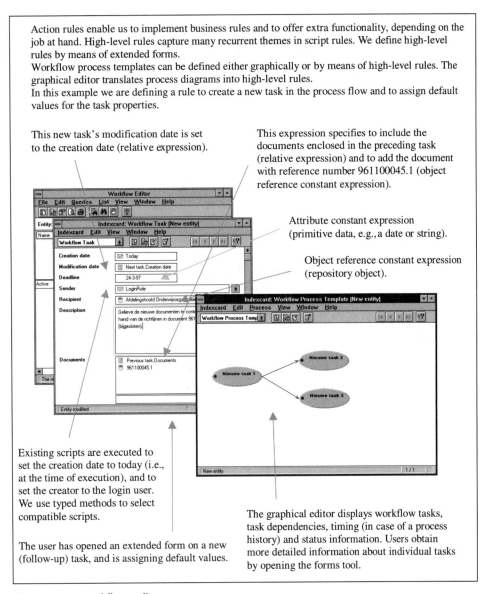

Existing scripts are executed to set the creation date to today (i.e., at the time of execution), and to set the creator to the login user. We use typed methods to select compatible scripts.

The user has opened an extended form on a new (follow-up) task, and is assigning default values.

The graphical editor displays workflow tasks, task dependencies, timing (in case of a process history) and status information. Users obtain more detailed information about individual tasks by opening the forms tool.

Figure 3.9   Workflow editor.

3.3 Our Framework Approach

We aim to combine the high-level modeling power of CASE tools with the open-ended nature of object-oriented frameworks. Our approach is based on the following observations:

Users tend to describe their requirements in terms of how they currently work. It is difficult for them to picture how new technology can or will influence their future working practices. Hence, they need to try out new software, to learn from it, and to correct it. This requires extensive prototyping. Too often, however, prototypes are used to validate the design, rather than help users and developers capture and explore the real requirements. Prototypes can be expensive, as they usually have to be thrown away. This is particularly true when developing many applications, each one requiring several iterations to get the requirements right.

A business model is particular to each organization at a particular point in time [Stowell-West 1994]. However, functional requirements, such as data-entry, querying, reporting, and document management, are generic.

Extensions or enhancements to functionality can often be made into reusable assets, independent of the actual business model, and vice versa. This can be done by using hooks and hot spots [Fayad 1999, Chapters 9, 15, and 16].

3.3.1 Architecture

The core of the architecture is a three-level repository that is consulted dynamically by two sets of tools, which are discussed in the following sections.

Business Objects Repository and End-User Tools

The framework uses the first repository to capture knowledge of a particular business model, including documents, data, state of processes, organization structure, and the roles each person can play (see Figure 3.10).

We provide the user with tools to access this repository. These tools enable the user to select applications; to enter and view data; to query the repository; to display, print, and export the results of a query; to access the thesaurus; and to manage electronic documents, workflow processes, and task assignments.

This way, we deliver the functionality demanded by the end user: applications for database, document management, and workflow and access to all these over the Internet.

Configuration Tools and Meta-Information

We want end users to be able to tailor, configure, and manage their applications. Therefore, we provide a second set of high-level tools. These tools define and manage the specifications of end-user applications, such as the structure and behavior of documents, data, processes, organization, and roles; private and shared views on data; predefined queries for later reuse; authorization and business rules; and additional end-user functionality.

We store this meta-information in a second (meta-)repository (see Figure 3.11).

We do not generate code for the end-user applications. Both sets of tools consult the meta-repository at runtime. Changes made to the meta-information, such as object structure and views, are immediately available to clients.

Example. We use the meta-information to dynamically generate query screens and forms. This process is based on the object model. Because we store the meta-information about the objects in the repository, the screens in the end-user tools

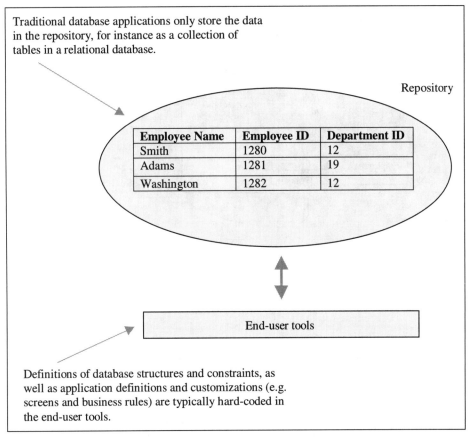

Traditional database applications only store the data in the repository, for instance as a collection of tables in a relational database.

Repository

Employee Name	Employee ID	Department ID
Smith	1280	12
Adams	1281	19
Washington	1282	12

End-user tools

Definitions of database structures and constraints, as well as application definitions and customizations (e.g. screens and business rules) are typically hard-coded in the end-user tools.

Figure 3.10   Repository–Business objects.

will adapt to changes in the object model, for example, the addition or removal of properties.

All tools are fully operational and provide, out of the box, both end-user functionality and the means to configure and fine-tune applications. They only need the meta-information to get the system up and running.

Secondary Goals

To make these tools easily accessible to users, we give them the same interface and functionality as the regular end-user applications. The ideal situation would be to have one single set of tools, thus enhancing reuse and ease of maintenance.

Support of a bootstrapping process became an important secondary design goal: Administration and configuration tools are gradually expressed in terms of the framework itself. We replace most hardwired administration and configuration tools with configured applications. This leads to a small but powerful kernel of generic and orthogonal tools.

The meta-model used to describe the object model is expressed in terms of itself and is stored in the repository. This is a third-level repository, a meta-metarepository. This

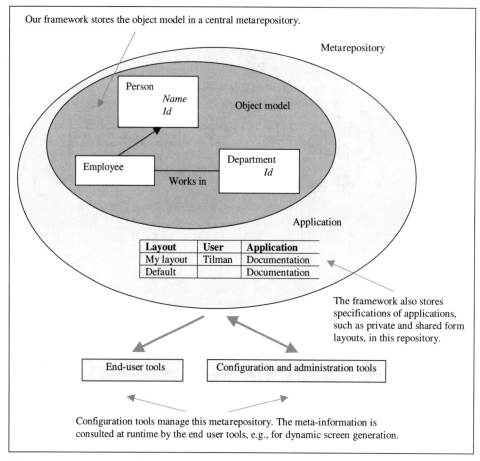

Our framework stores the object model in a central metarepository.

Metarepository

Person
Name
Id

Object model

Employee

Department
Id

Works in

Application

Layout	User	Application
My layout	Tilman	Documentation
Default		Documentation

The framework also stores specifications of applications, such as private and shared form layouts, in this repository.

End-user tools

Configuration and administration tools

Configuration tools manage this metarepository. The meta-information is consulted at runtime by the end user tools, e.g., for dynamic screen generation.

Figure 3.11   Meta-repository.

started as an experiment to push the limit of flexibility, but proved to be useful. It enables us to extend the semantics of an object model.

> **Example.** In the first version of the framework the semantics of cascaded deletes were hardwired. Now we define and store rules in the repository that overwrite built-in default behavior. More intelligent delete rules can now be adapted to cope with particular needs in an application.

In practice, the three repositories are one and the same, managed with the same tools, as shown in Figure 3.12.

3.4 Framework Components

In this section we look in more detail at some key elements stored in the repository: object model, meta-model, system objects, application environments, electronic docu-

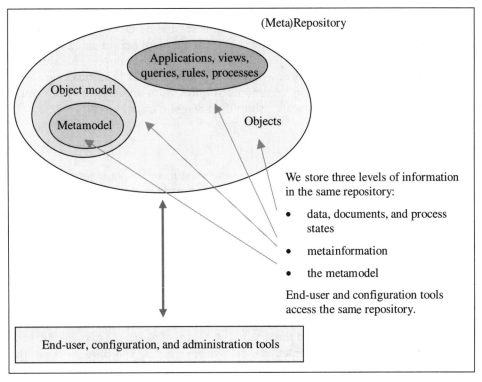

Figure 3.12 Repository.

ments, in-/out-baskets, workflow process templates, authorization rules, action rules, and background processing rules.

We borrow some terminology from the GOF design pattern system [Gamma 1995].

3.4.1 Example: The Mail Registration Application

The mail registration application is used to register information about incoming documents and dossiers, to assign tasks for handling them, and to keep track of their status.

When users receive a document they create an instance of the IndicateurDocument object type and set the appropriate attribute and association properties, including thesaurus keywords. Some properties, such as the identity of the employee who works with the document and the creation and modification date, are given default values. The actual document may be stored in the system as an electronic document linked to the IndicateurDocument object.

Handling mail requires several types of objects: IndicateurDocument, ElectronicDocument, Employee, OrganizationalUnit (department), and ThesaurusDescriptor (taxonomy of keywords and synonyms). We do not write code to represent these objects but model them in the repository. Nor do we code the relationships between these objects. Association types like "IndicateurDocument created by Employee" and "Employee member of OrganizationalUnit" are stored in the repository along with their cardinality constraints, such as "every IndicateurDocument is created by exactly one Employee" and constraints on attributes, such as "the name of the Employee is mandatory."

We reuse objects from existing applications—for example, Employee, ThesaurusDescriptor (managed within the documentation application), and ElectronicDocument. The IndicateurDocument inherits common attributes from an abstract type (WorkflowDocument). Figure 3.13 presents a simplified diagram of an object model.

3.4.2 Repository

Hot spots should be easy to change. The framework stores hot-spot objects in the central repository so that they can be changed without any programming. They can be changed by end users, configurators, or administrators, rather than by developers.

Object Model

The repository contains three kinds of objects. The first kind are end-user objects, which are the objects that make up the business model. These are the objects that the end user talks about. The second kind are system objects, which are objects that the developers or configurators talk about, but that are not part of the business model. For example, authorization rules and the internal structure of electronic documents, such as versions and various representations, are system objects. The third kind are the objects that describe the business model and system objects (object model).

The object model describes the elements stored in the repository: object structures, associations, and constraints. The meta-model describes the structure of the object model. It is expressed in terms of itself and is stored in the repository, too.

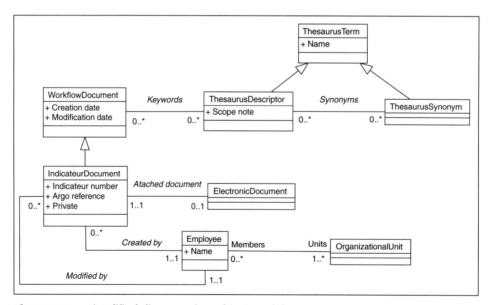

Figure 3.13   Simplified diagram of an object model.

End-User Objects

End-user objects model organization structure, processes, tasks, data, and relationships. The tools make no a priori assumptions about these end-user objects. This enables us to construct different business models. In fact, several models of the organization can be made to coexist, which is useful for simulating future scenarios.

An IndicateurDocument keeps track of its creator and the organizational units its creator works in. There are different kinds of organizational units, for example, departments and temporary project teams. Instead of modeling these different kinds of units through different object types, we use the Type Object pattern to classify the units dynamically. This enables us to replace the organization model without having to change the object model. A mere change of repository population suffices.

Meta-Model

Each object has a specific type. An object type has a name and defines a set of properties. Each property has a name and a type, and also has other attributes such as whether it is mandatory and unique and represents a symmetric relationship.

If an object is of a particular type, then it is allowed to have properties that the type specifies. The values of a property of an object of type T must match the type of the property specified in T. Attribute property values have primitive types, such as dates, strings, or numbers, and enumerated values over these types. Association properties reference other objects.

Object types can have subtypes. The property type may be overridden in subtypes. This is particularly useful for specializing abstract associations between two abstract types. Figure 3.14 shows a simplified diagram of the meta-model.

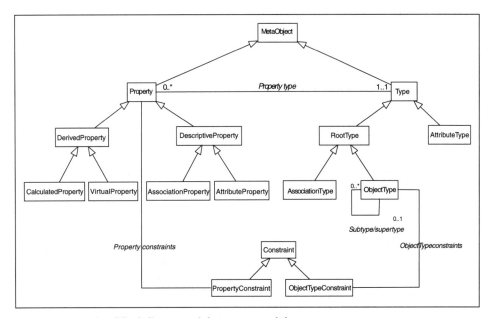

Figure 3.14 Simplified diagram of the meta-model.

The instance diagram shows, as in Figure 3.15, a small portion of the meta-model population, part of the mail registration object model.

Our model supports *N*-ary and attributed associations. We use an example of attributed associations in the documentation center application. A document may be related to other documents. For example, it may be an addendum to or a modification of other documents. We model this relationship as a symmetric association. The nature of the relationship is represented by means of an attribute of the association. The attribute takes its values from an enumeration set.

Individual properties can be constrained to take values in a subset of the type value set. Object and interproperty constraints describe conditions to be satisfied prior to committing changes to (groups of) objects. These constraints are specified by means of script expressions (Smalltalk code). Property types and constraints may be overridden in subtypes.

As an abstraction mechanism to hide details of the object model or to denormalize the user's perception of the object model (for example, when using the query editor or defining layouts in the forms tools) we use derived properties. These are read-only

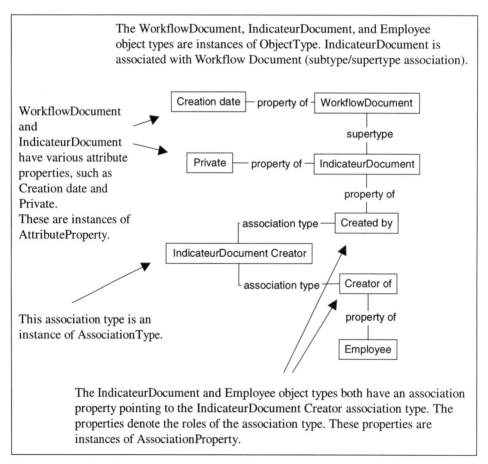

Figure 3.15 Simplified instance diagram of the meta-model.

properties representing values or aggregates of properties. They are defined by means of query expressions (virtual properties) or script expressions (calculated properties). Derived properties can be used as regular properties in most cases (calculated properties cannot be used in queries).

Our framework treats objects that make up the object model in the same way as objects managed by end-user applications. Thus we can reuse the forms tool to edit the object model. Authorization and action rules apply to this object model editor application. For instance, we can define action rules that are triggered whenever the model changes—for example, to update database tables and columns, or to invalidate layouts. And expressing the meta-model in terms of itself enables us to go one step further: The definition of our kernel meta-model can be extended to specify new types of constraints; the semantics can then be implemented by means of action rules.

System Objects

The end-user and configuration tools require several types of *system objects*.

We use many of these system objects to specify end-user applications, such as application environments, stored queries, action rules, and object behavior. These types of objects are often associated with meta-level objects, such as object types and properties.

Several types of system objects, such as action rules and stored queries, contain parts that would require complex models and need not be queried or updated separately. These parts are modeled as encoded objects that provide an interface to encode (decode) Smalltalk objects into (from) a string representation when updating or accessing the object.

> **Example.** The Indicateur example shows how initialization rules can set the default values of new IndicateurDocuments (for instance, IndicateurDocument is not confidential and the CreationDate is today). The CreationDate rule is defined in the supertype WorkflowDocument and inherited by all its subtypes.

All these rules are stored in the repository. Rules have an association with object types. Condition and action scripts of script rules are modeled as strings containing the (Smalltalk) source code. The compiled versions of these scripts are modeled as encoded objects, associated with the rules. When a script rule is changed, another script rule is triggered that validates the script's expressions and generates the compiled code. Figure 3.16 shows the simplified rule object model.

Other system objects represent special business objects, such as login users, electronic documents, and thesaurus keywords, that need some dedicated framework components. These objects are usually presented to the end user through special tools, such as the query editor and viewers for scanned documents. But since system objects are explicitly modeled and stored in the repository, for administration purposes such as querying and reporting we don't need additional tools. The generic end-user tools can be used instead to set up management applications.

Object Representation

By default, repository objects are represented at runtime by instances of a Smalltalk class (FwEntity). These instances keep track of the identification (object and type references) of the repository objects they represent. In addition, the class provides an interface for accessing and updating the properties. Instances typically contain partial

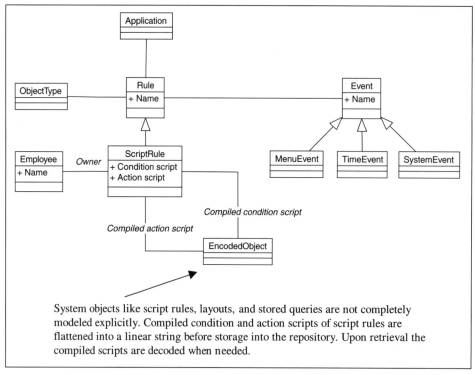

System objects like script rules, layouts, and stored queries are not completely modeled explicitly. Compiled condition and action scripts of script rules are flattened into a linear string before storage into the repository. Upon retrieval the compiled scripts are decoded when needed.

Figure 3.16   Simplified rule object model.

information; in other words, we load only those properties from the database we actually need. Accessor methods are created on the fly when using the scripting language, and object behavior is loaded when needed.

This approach usually suffices for end-user objects. In the case of system and meta-model objects, the framework components often require extra behavior or state. We provide the means to add subclasses to FwEntity and to link these classes to specific types of repository objects.

Application Environments

Application environments restrict the view on the repository by specifying what objects can be accessed, queried, and created. Environments can be structured hierarchically: Nested environments further specialize the view on the shared object model. Action rules, views, and queries are inherited.

For every object type, layouts can be configured for use in list, print, export, and forms tools. These views are either private or shared among all users of the environment. Default views can be defined. Individual views take precedence over shared ones. Views may be reused in other views.

In a similar way, queries may be saved for private or shared reuse. Defaults can be specified. Queries can be reused in other queries. List views can be coupled to specific queries.

Action rules can be defined within the context of the environment, such as to set appropriate defaults, to trigger a cascaded delete, or to add specific functionality—for instance, a batch update of a list of objects.

The use of nested environments typically leads to the following strategy: definition of an abstract application with reusable assets, followed by dedicated subapplications, such as full management and retrieval applications, and even simplified applications with many predefined queries and layouts for novice users.

Electronic Documents

Electronic documents represent unstructured information and require dedicated tools for creating, viewing, editing, and printing. Making electronic documents available in end-user applications is straightforward: We only need to associate documents with the relevant object types in the application. Thus, electronic documents are not perceived as stand-alone objects by the end user; rather, they are enclosed in objects having more domain-specific meaning.

The apparently simple document structure hides a more complex object model that contains the necessary information for the various tools, such as versions, different representations, storage information, and instructions to delete or copy documents.

Versions

Documents are perceived by the end user as logical documents, which have a name and can exist in one or more versions. One version is the preferred one. We do not maintain a version tree, as it would needlessly complicate use of the tools, nor are new versions created automatically by default. If necessary, we define rules to override this default behavior.

Document versions come in two flavors:

Basic documents. Correspond to physical documents, which have a well-defined format and type.

Complex documents. Containing different representations (basic documents) for the same logical document version.

Basic documents are stored on physical media in one or more copies, which are managed by the document-caching process manager.

Representations

Representations enable users to use different views on the same logical document, for example, to create a text representation of a scanned document, which can subsequently be stored in a full-text indexing database. Other examples are alternative representations using a more widely available format, such as PDF for Internet, or a TIFF representation of a frozen Word document that may only be annotated.

One of these representations is the master document. Invalidating the master invalidates the other (slave) representations as well.

Document-Caching Process Manager

A document can exist in one or more copies on several caches and the optical storage medium. A background process (implemented by means of background processing rules) keeps track of the status of these copies to make sure that the up-to-date copy is stored and retrieved.

Instructions to cache or delete documents are not necessarily carried out immediately. Instead, they are listed as instructions to be executed by the background process. This condition takes into account the model and contents of the objects in which the document is enclosed (the document owner). This enables us to set up very flexible caching strategies.

Whether an electronic document is persistent is ultimately derived from the repository information: An electronic document must be owned by a repository object. Hence, in case of failure, our recovery strategy makes the document base consistent by starting from the information in the database.

In- and out-baskets

In- and out-baskets maintain lists of incoming and outgoing work. What appears in a basket is defined by means of a query expression, hence it is not restricted to task objects only. Each user has a generic in-basket containing tasks sent to him or her. In addition, dedicated baskets may be set up, for example, to follow up particular dossiers.

The in-/out-baskets tool uses a special application environment that reuses several system objects from other environments, such as layouts.

Workflow

Workflow processes represent cause-connected activities to be performed in a (not necessarily unique) particular order to achieve a specific goal, such as the central board decision process, ad hoc processes to register and handle incoming documents, or the process to create and distribute new norms and regulations toward the school.

Activities are modeled by means of task types. Tasks may involve several participants, for example, the person who issued the task assignment and the recipient of the task.

Predefined process templates provide options to guide the user through default process scenarios. Processes can also be triggered automatically by specific events, for instance, at the start of each day.

Tasks

A task specifies the interaction between participants necessary to perform a specific activity. Participants can be any object, since object types are independent of the actual rule engine, process editor or in-/out-basket model.

Some workflow tools, such as the graphical process editor, assume the existence of a minimal set of common properties defined for all task objects:

- The status property defines the various relevant states for a task with regard to commitment of the participants involved in the task.

- The previous task/next task association maintains task dependencies.

- Timing information includes date sent, reminder date, and deadline.

Other properties can be added as needed in the various subtypes of the Task object type. These properties can be viewed or edited using regular list views and forms, or they can be listed in the graphical process history overview.

Processes

Processes represent the running history of an ad hoc or predefined workflow process (or a combination of both)—in other words, the tasks performed so far. Tasks are always associated with exactly one process. A process will automatically be created when the user activates a process template from scratch. Within the context of a process, subprocesses may be started by activating process templates.

Process Templates

A process template defines default scenarios for a workflow process, by listing the default tasks (more precisely, types and default values) to be performed, and, at each step, the options to move from one task to another. These default scenarios are modeled by means of a collection of action rules.

Whether users may deviate from this default process is ultimately determined by the authorization mechanism. Instead of relying on programmed exceptions, the process template definition gives users the means to let nondefault processes snap back into the default flow if some rule condition is satisfied. Alternatively, users can synchronize explicitly with one or more key steps in the template by activating a rule specifically configured for these purposes.

The mixture of ad hoc or predefined processes and tasks or subprocesses allows us to define process templates incrementally. For instance, a process template may be initially defined at the level of individual departments and refined later within each individual department. These subprocesses may be more or less strict, depending on each department's working practices.

Implementing Other Process Models

Other workflow process models can be implemented, too. We illustrate two existing approaches here:

Workflow processes based on intelligent work objects [Karbe 1990] can be modeled using script rules. The work object contains the necessary data and state information. A script rule describing the routing algorithm is activated whenever the user opens a form on the work object.

Process models based on speech acts [Flores 1993] can be modeled using high-level rules. Conversation objects contain the necessary data and state information. The condition expression refers to a matrix describing permissible state transitions. Default acts on conversations, such as promise, decline, or counteroffer, can be configured by means of action rules.

Authorization Rules

The authorization mechanism makes no a priori assumptions about a particular model. It allows simple user/user group access controls, as well as more sophisticated, fine-grained context- and content-sensitive access privileges. It relies on a knowledge base of authorization rules. Each rule explicitly either grants or denies rights to users for certain aspects (mostly properties) of objects, or tells us nothing at all (in other words, the rule may be irrelevant or undecided). Thus, the authorization mechanism revolves around a strategy to find the most appropriate rule that conclusively answers the question, "Does this user have these rights for these aspects of this object," with yes or no. The main idea is to capture the default cases in rules with a large scope and to add rules catering to exceptions in a piecemeal fashion. The actual solution depends on the problem domain (for example, do we restrict access in the default cases and explicitly grant access in the exceptions, or vice versa?), but often reflects global policies within the organization regarding access control and privacy of information.

For example:

- All users may read all documents (default case for all users, aspects, and types of documents, granting).

- No user, except administrators, may update documents (default case, denying in the former case, granting in the latter case).

- The colleagues of an employee may update a document he or she created (specific case, granting).

- In the mail registration application we use documents that may be flagged as private. Only members of the same department as the document creator or employees higher up in the hierarchy have access to private documents (specific case, denying).

Because rules may conflict, it is necessary to provide conflict-resolution strategies.

Definitions

Each authorization rule consists of the following four-tuple:

- The agent set (Ag), which specifies the users to whom access is granted or denied.

- The object set (O), which specifies the subjects of the rule.

- The object aspects (As), for example, a selection of properties.

- The rights (R), such as read, write, add, remove, and export.

These sets (called *dynamic sets*) can be dynamic, based on a condition that specifies the elements belonging to the set. Conditions make use of query expressions defined with the end-user query editor or, in some cases, Smalltalk expressions. In addition, static sets can be defined by explicit enumeration. In practice, agent and object sets are usually dynamic; the aspects and rights, static. Dynamic sets can refer to context variables, such as the login user.

Each of the sets can be made *restrictive* (denoted as [S], S a dynamic set). A rule is restrictive if at least one of its sets is restrictive. A rule can also be *granting*. Rules can be both granting and restrictive. Using these rules, we explicitly grant or deny access control.

Rule Semantics

The following example illustrates the semantics of authorization rules.

Applying a rule {Ag, [O], [As], R} to an agent-object-aspect-right tuple {ag, o, as, r} will answer true, false, or undecided according to the following strategy:

- True if (ag $\in$ Ag) and (o $\in$ O) and (as $\in$ As) and (r $\in$ R) and (the rule is granting).

- False if (ag $\in$ Ag) and (o $\notin$ O) and (as $\notin$ As) and (r $\in$ R) and (the type of o is a subtype of the type of the object set O, that is, the rule must be *relevant*).

- Undecided otherwise.

If we substitute Ag = {Department heads}, O = {Proposals}, As = {Visa property}, and R = {Edit}, then this rule translates into: "Department heads may only edit the visa property of proposals." This rule is not relevant for objects of types other than proposals.

Combining Rules

Rules can be inherited according to the object set type hierarchy. Rules defined for a particular object type have precedence over inherited rules. Rules defined within the same object type are explicitly prioritized to resolve conflicts.

As rule evaluation may be undecided for a particular tuple {ag, o, as, r}, at least one default rule is needed that answers true or false for all tuples. This can be a rule defined at the common supertype of all object types.

Using Authorization Rules

Authorization rules can capture complex requirements succinctly.

> **Example.** "A user has access to all documents created within a workflow process if at least one of these documents has been created by a member of his or her organizational unit or a unit further down in the hierarchy." This rule can be defined in the configuration tool without any scripting. Rules like these will typically use context variables—for instance, to refer to the login user.

Rules can be applied to all elements in the repository, including system objects such as document annotations, applications, and even authorization rules.

The authorization mechanism is very expressive, but managing the rule base may become less evident if number and complexity of the rules grow too large. Two techniques can be applied to simplify maintenance of access control:

- Reification of hidden elements in the rule definitions.

  > **Example.** To specify the applications a user has access to, a simple end-user application has been configured. This application maintains explicit associations between users and environments. Several authorization rules have been reduced to one meta-rule checking this information. Note that this rule applies to the application itself.

  > Similar techniques can be used to manage, for example, large numbers of users.

- Modeling additional, simpler authorization rule types to be managed through end-user tools. Transformation methods are needed to convert these rules into system-level rules.

Thus, we can configure specific authorization applications, targeted toward a particular use, with a minimal effort.

Optimizing Performance

By default, authorization rules are executed locally. In some cases, this generates considerable overhead when many objects are retrieved from the repository, only to find out that the user has no access. And even if the user has access to a particular object, the authorization rules may require additional associated objects to be downloaded in order to verify the access privileges. To optimize performance, rules are combined with database queries if appropriate.

Design

The authorization mechanism presents one aspect of the framework [Xerox 1996]. At first sight, its functionality should be woven together with the object store's to ensure consistency. However this behavior is not always required or even wanted. Performance issues take precedence in some cases. The Facade pattern provides a clean mechanism to have different framework components access the object store in different ways—for instance, with or without access control. Ideally, however, this requires context-sensitive access control for objects [Richardson 1992], whereby only trusted components may access the object store directly.

Action Rules

Objects obey constraints defined in the model and exhibit behavior that is used across all applications. End-user applications sharing these objects may, however, require additional, often context- and contents-sensitive functionality and semantics (business rules) [Graham 1994]. Action rules capture these requirements. While action rules allow semantics to be different across applications or workflow processes, they do not violate the global constraints defined in the model.

The main elements of action rules are events, conditions, actions, and rule scope. The type of event determines whether the rules implement some business rule or provide some additional functionality to the user. Following are some examples:

- When creating documents we set the creation date and creator. When committing a modified document, we update modification date and remember the last author. Documents in the mail registration application need extra initialization to generate a unique id based on the context: Is the document the start of a new workflow process or is it created within the scope of an existing process?

- When removing objects, we delete attached electronic documents (if any) by default.

- We add extra functionality to perform operations not directly provided by the generic tools (such as a particular report) or to support repetitive work. In the context of workflow processes, we often need to synchronize the state of different related objects and guarantee the overall consistency; instead of complicating the tasks of both users and configurators, we provide extra functionality to perform the necessary operations in a controlled way. All these rules are typically triggered by menu events corresponding to menus that appear only in the relevant context (application environment and object type).

- Several tasks must be performed automatically, often at regular times. Rules can be triggered by time events generated by the clock.

Events

Action rules are triggered by events. These may be generated by the system or by explicit user actions.

Rules triggered by system events generally affect the semantics and include creating, duplicating, saving, deleting, or modifying an object. The transaction state specifies when the event is actually generated. For instance, rules triggered by changes of individual property values will typically be executed at once, whereas rules triggered by more global object updates are usually delayed until precommit time.

User action events correspond either to extra menu options providing additional functionality or to generic events, such as switching applications and selecting an object or layout.

A single event can trigger several rules, which enables us to add behavior in a modular way. All enabled rules (rules for which the condition is satisfied) will be activated.

Activating Rules

Action rules have access to context variables, such as the login user or the interface component that triggered the rule. To activate a rule we apply it to a particular object (the receiver) in a given context. If the condition is satisfied, the action will be executed.

A rule is scoped: It can be applied only to objects of a given type (including subtypes). The scope can be further limited to a particular application or workflow process.

Types of Rules

We provide essentially two types of rules: script rules and high-level rules.

Script rules. Script rule condition and action expressions require our scripting language (basically Smalltalk with dynamic object accessor methods, implicit access control, and high-level query access to the repository); hence, they are not targeted toward the average end user. The rule scripting language has access to several context variables and can reuse object behavior (the latter uses the same scripting language, but has no access to the context variables, making it context-independent).

High-level rules. To allow end users to add their own rules, we provide high-level rule types. High-level rules explicitly model common script practices in the repository, such as:

- Initializing objects to default values ("constants" or "results of query expressions").

- Updating an object at commit time or when a property has been modified ("update expressions").

- Creating a follow-up task in a workflow process, based on certain conditions, and updating the state of the current task ("stepwise structuring").

Results of query expressions. Conditions are specified by means of query expressions. These can be created by the query editor. The action part uses one or more *update expressions* to specify new values for object properties. The first expression refers to the receiver. Executing the expression updates the receiver. Additional expressions specify type and initial values for new objects to be created when the rule is activated. Following are some examples:

- Rules with one expression are typically used to set default values for a newly created or duplicated object, or to update an object's properties as the result of a user action. The latter is often used in batch procedures to update a series of objects.

■ Rules with two expressions are used to support definition of workflow processes. Given a task (the receiver), a rule can be defined to create a follow-up task and update the current task state. We define a workflow process consisting of a set of tasks by describing for each task the options (and conditions) to start other tasks. Each option then corresponds to a rule.

High-level rules can model recursive processes, such as to implement an approval procedure that mirrors the hierarchy.

Update expressions. Update expressions can be edited by means of extended forms. No scripting is needed. These expressions behave similarly to regular objects, in other words, they have a type and properties, but the latter accept expressions in addition to values. The following expressions can be used:

■ Constant expressions, such as a date value (attribute property) or a reference to another object (association property).

■ Query expressions.

■ Property expressions (chains of associations ending in an attribute or association property).

■ Scripts (using typed methods).

For multivalued properties, individual elements may be flagged for addition or removal. The approval rule (in pseudolanguage) in Figure 3.17 illustrates the idea.

The example shown in Figure 3.17 can be read as: "When the user has approved a request (condition) and has selected the "forward" menu item (event), the current task will be flagged as finished (current task expression). A new request for approval will be sent to the finances manager. The documents enclosed in the current task will be attached and the date will be set to today's date (new task expression)."

Stepwise structuring. Operations on objects such as saving, deleting, or locking often require that the same operation be performed on related objects (cascaded saves, deletes, and locks). A variant of the high-level rules can be used to model

```
event
        select "forward" menu item

condition
        currentTask.approved = true

current task expression (type ApprovalTask)
        currentTask status: finished

new task expression (type ApprovalTask)
        newTask recipient: (Manager selectAny: [ :mgr | mgr division = 'Finances' ])   (query)
        newTask documents: currentTask documents                                        (relative)
        newTask approved: false                                                         (constant)
        newTask dateSent: self dateToday                                                (message)
```

Figure 3.17   High-level rule example.

these practices. Extended forms can be used equally well to edit these new types of rules. This incremental process of formalizing practices in the repository is an example of stepwise structuring [Hägglund 1989].

Authorization

When executing rules, it may be necessary to override the current user's privileges. Hence, each rule can be given an owner, whose privileges will be used instead. In addition, the user must have the necessary privileges to execute the rule.

Background Processing Rules

Background processing rules specify activities to be performed automatically on elements in the repository. Typical uses are process managers handling requests to migrate document copies to a particular storage medium or to convert notification requests generated by the system into email messages, and automated tasks within the context of a particular application or workflow process.

Background processing rules used to be dedicated objects and framework components. Now they are implemented by means of action rules triggered by time events. Time events enable us to set up elaborate scheduling strategies, including recurrent events.

The action rule manager automatically schedules any background rules defined in a specific application whenever the user selects the application. Whether the background rules run within the context of an end-user application on his or her client or on a dedicated client PC is solely a matter of configuration. Thus, we can easily set up appropriate applications on separate clients in order to achieve the right degree of load balancing.

3.5 Bootstrapping Process

The bootstrapping process is driven by our observations that most configuration tools essentially manage specific types of objects in the repository, to which we need to add some extra functionality, validation, consistency rules, and specific caching. Often, an alternative plug-in property editor is all that is required to access these objects easily through end-user tools.

3.5.1 Examples

To bootstrap the system, we initially developed a hardwired object model editor. About one year into the project we were able to configure end-user tools for accessing the object model. Now we are enhancing this application to support the functionality offered by the new persistency component.

While access to in- and out-baskets is still managed through a dedicated application, baskets are defined through regular forms. We applied a bit of whitebox reuse to make the query editor fit in the property editors scheme, and we modeled the basket definition explicitly. Its properties include a query expression specifying the basket's contents.

Most of our latest tools are configured applications or are developed with configuration in mind. Examples of the former are the object behavior and action rules applications. The graphical workflow on the other hand is designed as an alternative property editor for use in forms.

3.5.2 Reflection

We are increasingly using existing tools to build new (typically configuration) tools. Reflection [Foote-Yoder 1996] is a useful technique to support this kind of approach. Many people still view reflection as rather obscure and difficult. Yet, given our framework approach, we consider this idea of bootstrapping as a very natural thing to do: The system already contains so many tools to build applications that we would take a step back by not trying to reuse this functionality. The locality of change that can be achieved with reflection is also a very important asset. In fact, reflection makes our design both cleaner and simpler.

3.6 Framework Evolution

We started the framework initially building three applications. At this moment we have built and maintain many more. We tuned, adapted, and extended our framework and business model, based on what we learned from the needs and shortcomings of our applications and from feedback from configurators and end users.

Since the business objects, object model, scripts, and application specifications are all stored in the same repository, we use the repository as a sort of centralized knowledge base. Some recurring business practices or functional requirements may be less evident at the start, but may come to surface later on—for example, in the form of similar custom scripts. When we identify these patterns, we try to make them more explicit either in the repository or in the tools.

For example, the form layout editor initially provided the means to include Smalltalk scripts describing how to represent associated objects on the screen. After a few years, these scripts have been replaced by parameterized strings. The parameters refer to properties or property chains of the associated objects and may include conditional expressions. These expressions capture the existing scripting patterns more explicitly. They are also much simpler and more robust than the original scripts.

When developing applications with the framework we identify the following:

Working practices specific to the organization. We create reusable assets in the repository, refactor the object model, or develop more specific end-user and configuration applications using the existing tools.

Practices that transcend applications. We change the framework functionality and refactor the framework [Foote-Opdyke 1995].

Functionality specific to a particular application. Depending on its nature, we change the functionality of the repository, the framework, or both. For instance, some applications require a simple procedure to automatically generate standard reply letters based on repository information. In this case, we store extra behavior in the repository. If a new external tool is required, we usually add a component to the framework.

Technological needs and opportunities. We use subframeworks for components that are strongly coupled to technology, such as the persistency layer and the document storage. These subframeworks can easily be replaced.

Additional functionality. To support new types of applications, such as Internet applications.

This way, the framework explicitly supports evolution and reuse at different levels [Tilman-Devos 1996].

3.7 Summary

The main goal of the framework design was a small kernel of generic components acting dynamically upon the repository. Hardcoding was to be avoided as much as possible. Initially, we focused on achieving this goal for end-user applications. We developed hardwired administration and configuration tools to help us bootstrap the system. As the framework evolved and the tools became more flexible, we reused components of end-user tools in some of our administration tools. In a third phase, we started to replace some of the hardwired tools with applications configured in the system.

The framework configuration functionality will be enhanced, in order to further increase the expressiveness of the tools and to allow end users to adapt the tools to their own needs even better, thus obviating the need for developers to a larger degree.

Some additional components are being developed, most notably to make the repository Internet-aware. The main component will act both as a client of the repository and as a generic Internet application server. This will empower Argo to develop Internet applications through modeling and configuration, too.

At first sight, one might wonder whether this approach does not make the design more complex or affect performance negatively. We do not believe that the design is more complex. In fact, the framework goals help us focus more clearly on the responsibilities of the various components, in particular with regard to reuse and evolution. As is often the case, reifying implicit responsibilities actually makes the design simpler. And the bootstrapping principle is an additional asset in validating the design.

Although we initially encountered some performance problems, these were not essentially related to the approach as such, but to the use of a persistency component that was not really suited for our purposes. We must be aware, however, that the flexibility of the system allows end users to build equally good and bad queries. Proper training is of primary importance, as is the need to hide more complex elements of the tools from novice users.

After three years, we are convinced that the approach is a valid one. End-user applications can be developed iteratively and incrementally, even interactively. We do not code (apart from some custom scripting) and we do not generate end-user applications. Neither do we use or need throwaway prototypes. Instead, we build increasingly complete specifications of end-user applications. These specifications are available for immediate execution. Thus, we help close the gap between specification, development, and use of the applications. This way we can afford to stimulate the users to think and rethink their processes and redesign them.

3.8 References

[Flores 1993] Flores, Fernando, Michael Graves, Brad Hartfield, and Terry Winograd. Computer systems and the design of organizational interaction. In *Readings in Groupware and Computer-Supported Cooperative Work*. Morgan Kaufmann, 1993.

[Foote-Opdyke 1995] Foote, Brian, and William F. Opdyke. Lifecycle and refactoring patterns that support evolution and reuse. *Pattern Languages of Program Design*. James O. Coplien and Douglas C. Schmidt, editors. Reading, MA: Addison-Wesley, 1995.

[Foote-Yoder 1996] Foote, Brian, and Joseph Yoder. Evolution, architecture, and meta-morphosis. *Pattern Languages of Program Design—2*. John M. Vlissides, James O. Coplien, and Norman L. Kerth, editors. Reading, MA: Addison-Wesley, 1996.

[Gamma 1995] Gamma, Erich, Richard Helm, Ralph Johnson, and John Vlissides. *Design Patterns: Elements of Reusable Object-Oriented Software*. Reading, MA: Addison-Wesley, 1995.

[Graham 1994] Graham, Ian. *Object Oriented Methods*. Reading, MA: Addison-Wesley, 1994.

[Hägglund 1989] Hägglund, S. Iterative design and adaptive maintenance of knowledge-based office systems. *Proceedings of the IFIP WG 8.4 Working Conference on Office Information Systems: The Design Process*, North-Holland, 1988.

[Karbe 1990] Karbe, B., N. Ramsperger, and P. Weiss. Support for cooperative work by electronic circulation folders. *Proceedings of the ACM OIS 1990 Conference*, Cambridge, Massachusetts, 1990.

[Richardson 1992] Richardson, J., P. Schwarz, and L.-F. Cabrera. CACL: Efficient fine-grained protection for objects. *Proceedings of the ACM OOPSLA 1992 Conference*, Vancouver, British Columbia, Canada, October 1992.

[Stowell-West 1994] Stowell, Frank, and Duane West. *Client-Led Design: A Systemic Approach to Information System Definition*. New York: McGraw-Hill, 1994.

[Tilman-Devos, 1996] Tilman, Michel, and Martine Devos. Object-orientation and evolutionary software engineering. *OOPSLA 1996 Workshop on Object-Oriented Software Evolution and Reengineering*, San Jose, California, October 1996.

[Xerox 1996] Xerox Parc. Aspect-oriented programming project. *ACM Workshop on Strategic Directions in Computing Research, Working Group Object-Oriented Programming*, MIT, June 14–15, 1996.

SB2.1 Requirements of WFMSs

Workflow Management Framework Systems (WFMSs) support the design, execution, and monitoring of long-lasting business processes that typically involve multiple activities and multiple collaborating resources in a distributed and heterogeneous environment. To achieve this goal, various requirements have to be considered [Kappel 1997]. First, WFMSs demand *reusability* in the sense that existing specifications of business processes can be reused within a certain domain as well as for similar application domains. Second, since business processes are subject to frequent changes, it must be possible to easily *adapt* their functional and organizational aspects on the fly—without having to stop and restart running workflows. Third, the architecture of a WFMS has to be *open* in that legacy applications performing an activity of the business process can be incorporated. Fourth, in order to control the execution of a business process, WFMSs have to coordinate multiple, possibly *heterogeneous,* resources, which are usually *distributed* over the company's network or belong to several participating companies. Finally, *reliability* is crucial since, on the one hand, WFMSs have to be tolerant with respect to failures due to distribution, and, on the other hand, they have to ensure the consistency of data processed by the workflows. Whereas heterogeneity, distribution, and reliability are mainly covered by means of middleware and database technologies [Alonso 1997], reusability, adaptability, and openness can be met by applying object-oriented framework concepts, as illustrated in the following.

SB2.2 Mapping WFMS Requirements to Framework Characteristics

Following the idea of frameworks, the generic domain-independent building blocks of a WFMS, such as activities, resources executing and controlling activities, and worklists, should be preimplemented as *abstract* and *concrete* classes. This would enhance reusability and adaptability for different application domains, either through *blackbox reuse* by means of composition or through *whitebox reuse* by means of inheritance and specialization. Concerning the latter, *template* methods and *hook* methods can be used to separate the stable parts of a WFMS from the hot spots of the system [Pree 1996]. These hot spots denote both those parts of the system that have to be adapted to the specifics of a particular organization employing the WFMS and the volatile, frequently changing elements of the WFMS. Another advantage of encapsulating the implementation details of hot spots and providing well-defined and stable interfaces is that those parts of the implementation that are affected by changes in the workflow specification can be more easily localized [Fayad-Schmidt 1997].

By reusing the single, generic building blocks of a WFMS, not only source code but also the architectural design of a WFMS gets reused [Pree 1996]. Due to *inversion of control*, the main control flow is predefined within the WFMS and controlled by means of events signaled by resources participating in the business process. Existing resources can

Continues

SIDEBAR 2
WORKFLOW MANAGEMENT FRAMEWORKS *(Continued)*

be incorporated into the business process by simply registering them within the framework, thus enhancing the *openness* of the system. These resources are then called back by the WFMS according to the inherent event-dispatching mechanism.

SB2.3 An Example for Implementing WFMSs as Domain-Specific Frameworks

Some systems that are implemented on the basis of object-oriented framework technology already exist, for example, FlowMark, InConcert, Workflo, and TriGS$_{flow}$ [Alonso 1997; Kappel 1999]. TriGS$_{flow}$ implements the basic building blocks of a WFMS in terms of a generic object-oriented workflow model in the sense that business processes for different kinds of application domains, such as an application for scholarship or reordering of goods, are modeled by simply inheriting, customizing, and instantiating the corresponding predefined classes. A specialty of TriGS$_{flow}$ is that the framework is built on the basis of both object-oriented constructs and Event/Condition/Action (ECA) rules. ECA rules are used mainly to encapsulate the business policies necessary to coordinate the various activities and resources. Thus, ECA rules represent some major hot spots of a business process. ECA rules can be seen as the glue between the basic building blocks of the generic object-oriented workflow model by providing selection policies for resources and ordering policies for activities, to mention just a few. Consequently, the realization of the volatile elements of the TriGS$_{flow}$ framework is split into hook methods of the generic object-oriented workflow model and ECA rules of the active model. The advantage of using ECA rules is that organizational knowledge can be represented explicitly, which in turn enhances reusability and adaptability. In addition, since ECA rules in TriGS$_{flow}$ are first-class objects, business policies may be adapted and extended on the fly. Furthermore, they provide some kind of inversion of control, since, analogous to hook methods, their action is called back, once having been registered by means of appropriate event and condition specifications monitoring the execution of the business process.

Most recently, the standardization efforts in terms of a generic workflow reference model by the Workflow Management Coalition [WMC 1998] and by the Object Management Group (OMG) [Schulze 1998] may serve as a good basis for implementing a WFMS as a domain-specific framework. In addition, component technology may foster the independent development of WFMS components being interoperable within a standardized WFMS framework [Johnson 1997, Schmidt 1998].

SB2.4 References

[Alonso 1997] Alonso, G., D. Agrawal, A. El Abbadi, and C. Mohan. Functionality and limitations of current workflow management systems. *IEEE-Expert* 12(5), September/October 1997.

[Fayad-Schmidt 1997] Fayad, M.E., and D.C. Schmidt. Object-oriented application frameworks. *Communications of the ACM* 40(10), October 1997.

[Johnson 1997] Johnson, R.E. Frameworks = (components + patterns). *Communications of the ACM,* Theme Issue on Object-Oriented Application Frameworks, Mohamed E. Fayad and Douglas Schmidt, editors, 40(10), October 1997.

[Kappel 1997] Kappel, G., S. Rausch-Schott, and W. Retschitzegger. Hypermedia document and workflow management based on active object-oriented databases. *Proceedings of the 30th Hawaiian International Conference on System Sciences (HICSS 1997)*, IEEE, Maui, HI, January 1997.

[Kappel 1999] Kappel, G., S. Rausch-Schott, and W. Retschitzegger. A framework for workflow management systems based on objects, rules and roles. Accepted for publication in *ACM Computing Surveys Symposium,* Mohamed E. Fayad, editor, March 1999.

[Pree 1996] Pree, W. *Framework Patterns.* New York: SIGS Management Briefings, 1996.

[WMC 1998] Workflow Management Coalition, www.aiai.ed.ac.uk/project/wfmc/, last accessed June 1998.

[Schmidt 1998] Schmidt, R., U. Assmann, P. Biegler, R. Kramer, P.C. Lockemann, and C. Rolker. The interrelatedness of component-oriented systems and workflow-management—What they can do for each other. *OMG-DARPA Workshop on Compositional Software Architectures,* Monterey, CA, www.objs.com/workshops/ws9801/papers/paper043.html, January 6–8, 1998.

[Schulze 1998] Schulze, W., C. Bussler, and K. Meyer-Wegener. Standardising on workflow-management—The OMG workflow management facility. *SIGGROUP Bulletin* 19(1):24–30.

SIDEBAR 3
IBM SANFRANCISCO BUSINESS COMPONENTS

IBM SanFrancisco delivers Business Process Components written in Java that provide an object-oriented design and default business logic for mainline business applications. The Business Process Components use Common Business Objects (objects that are used in more than one application domain) and are built on the Foundation, which provides a Java server infrastructure for managed, distributed objects [Bohrer 1997; 1998]. The Business Process Components and Common Business Objects are designed as frameworks so that they can be easily modified and extended. The first two releases have provided Business Process Components in the domains of Business Financials, Order Management, and Warehouse Management [IBM 1997, 1998]. Additional information is available at IBM SanFrancisco's web site: www.software.ibm.com/ad/sanfrancisco/.

SB3.1 Layered Architecture

IBM SanFrancisco includes three layers of reusable software for use by application developers. The top layer consists of the Business Process Components for key day-to-day business activities. These are called the *Core Business Processes,* and each provides business objects and default business logic for a particular application area [Bohrer 1997]. The second layer, called the *Common Business Objects,* provides implementation for commonly used business objects that can be used as the basis for consistency and interoperability between applications. The lowest layer, called the *Foundation,* provides the infrastructure and services that are required to build applications using distributed, managed objects on multiple platforms. Application developers can choose to use SanFrancisco at any of the three layers. For example, they could choose to build directly on the Foundation and develop their own frameworks and business objects. Or they could choose to use the Core Business Processes and make the extensions needed to complete their application.

The Core Business Processes that are delivered are not intended to be finished applications. Developers will use them as the base for their application and complete it by making changes such as adding additional attributes, changing default business rules, and overriding default methods with their specific logic. A major part of the remaining work will be in the area of the user interface. SanFrancisco does provide a Java graphical user interface (GUI) framework that can be used to complete the user interface. However, developers do not need to use this and are free to use other tools to develop their GUI if they wish.

SB3.2 Design Principles

Several key design principles have been followed in building the Core Business Processes and Common Business Objects. First, the application software provided by IBM SanFrancisco is designed to be modified. This means that we have identified extension points, where we expect the code to be modified, and have designed the code so that changes can be easily made at these points. A second principle used in the development of SanFrancisco was to identify and use design patterns whenever possible. This approach improves the quality of the solution because proven design concepts are being reused and because the consequences of those design decisions are well understood. It is also easier for developers to understand the system because they can learn a handful of patterns, rather than having to understand a multitude of unique designs.

In addition, IBM SanFrancisco has concentrated on providing an infrastructure that helps developers build applications that are portable and flexible. In part, this is achieved by the SanFrancisco programming model, which provides operations necessary for distributed business objects, without requiring developers to have a detailed understanding of the underlying services. This approach insulates business objects from changes in specific technologies, provides separation of programming and administrative roles, and masks platform-specific function. Applications can be moved to other platforms that support SanFrancisco and may use any of the available persistent storage options without having to change the application code.

SB3.3 Content Overview

The IBM SanFrancisco project has three major components:

- Core business processes
- Common business objects
- Foundation

These components are covered in more detail in the following sections.

SB3.3.1 Core Business Processes

The Core Business Processes are the top layer of the SanFrancisco architecture. They provide an object design and default business logic for an application domain. They are designed as frameworks with extension points to allow for easy extension of function and overriding of the default behavior. Core Business Processes in the domains of Business Financials, Order Management, and Warehouse Management have been delivered. We are working with our partners to identify additional domains that should be addressed. Figure SB3.1 shows the IBM SanFrancisco Project Content Overview.

The Business Financial domain includes the areas of Accounts Payable, Accounts Receivable, and General Ledger. Some of the functions provided are definition of the general ledger (account structure), support for interactions with banks, multicurrency and multiple period journaling, and creation of invoices (in conjunction with other related financial transactions). The Order Management domain includes both Sales and Purchase Orders. Examples of the function provided include creation and management of orders, pricing and discounts, and sales order invoicing. The Warehouse Management domain includes receiving and shipping of materials. Examples of the function provided are costing, picking, receiving, manual stock transactions, and quality control.

Continues

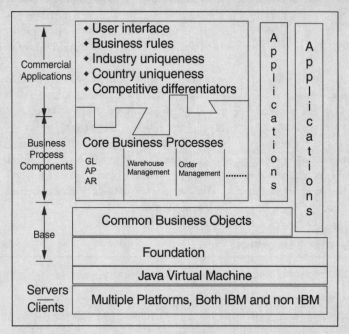

Figure SB3.1 IBM SanFrancisco Project Content Overview.

SB3.3.2 Common Business Objects

The Common Business Objects (CBOs) implement basic objects and rules that are needed for many applications. They fall into three general types: business objects commonly used in multiple application domains, business object interfaces that provide interoperability between applications, and objects that implement frequently used design patterns for business applications.

The first type of CBO is the objects that are used in more than one vertical application domain. SanFrancisco provides these objects to promote consistency across applications. Examples of these business objects include Address, Business Partner, Calendar, and Currency.

The second type of CBO enables application interoperability by providing interfaces to the Core Business Processes. These CBOs allow independently developed SanFrancisco applications to work together and allows SanFrancisco applications to interoperate with legacy applications. An example is the interface to post an entry to the General Ledger. The interface could be called from either a SanFrancisco–based application or a legacy application.

The last type of CBO supports design patterns that have been found to be useful in many different application domains. Examples of these are Keyables (used to create composite keys and to manipulate objects across different composite keys) and Classification Types (used to represent user-defined types).

SB3.3.3 Foundation

The lowest layer of the SanFrancisco architecture is called the Foundation. It provides the infrastructure that is used to build the Common Business Objects and the Core Business Processes. The Foundation includes two sets of interfaces that are visible to application developers. The first set is the base classes that provide a consistent programming model for use by application developers. Examples include Entity (independent, shareable objects), Dependent (objects that must be owned by an Entity), and Command (a group of operations on one or more objects).

The same interfaces are used by application developers regardless of the platform on which the application will eventually execute. This means that developers can write their applications once, deploy them on many different platforms, and use different persistence mechanisms, without changing the application code.

The second set of interfaces used by application developers is the application utilities. These provide services that will be needed by most applications built using the SanFrancisco. Examples include Security Administration, Persistent Store Configuration, Server Configuration, and Schema Mapping.

SB3.4 Summary

IBM SanFrancisco has worked with many software companies to develop a functionally rich set of infrastructure and default application functions that can be used to develop distributed object applications [Bohrer 1997]. The Foundation, Business Process Components, and Common Business Objects are written in Java, so they, and applications built using them, will be able to run on many different platforms. The object design and default business logic that are provided allow applications to be built by extending existing code, rather than having to build them from scratch. Underlying technology is masked from application developers so that choices such as object location and type of persistent storage can be made without requiring changes to the application code.

The second release of SanFrancisco is now available. It includes updates to the General Ledger component, new Order and Warehouse Management components, and beta versions of Accounts Payable and Accounts Receivable components. Over 400 companies have licensed the SanFrancisco code, and over 4000 downloads of the evaluation code have taken place. For additional information on SanFrancisco products, evaluation code, and more, visit the web site: www.ibm.com/java/sanfrancisco.

SB3.5 References

[Bohrer 1997] Bohrer, K. Middleware isolates business logic. *Object Magazine,* November 1997.

[Bohrer 1998] Bohrer, K., V. Johnson, A. Nilsson, and B. Rubin. Business process components for distributed object applications. *Communications of the ACM* 41(6), June 1998.

[IBM 1997] *IBM Systems Journal,* Technical Forum 36(3), 1997.

[IBM 1998] *IBM Systems Journal,* Theme Issue 37(2), 1998

PART Two

Artificial Intelligence and Agent Application Frameworks

Part Two is devoted to artificial intelligence application frameworks, such as speech recognition and neural networks, and agent application frameworks. Agents appear in a wide range of applications. Agent-based systems have been developed in response to the following requirements (see Chapter 6):

■ Personalized and customized user interfaces that are proactive in assisting the user

■ Adaptive, fault-tolerant distributed systems that solve complex problems

■ Open systems where components come and go and new components are continually added

■ Migration and load balancing across platforms, throughout a network

■ New metaphors, such as negotiation, for solving distributed, multidisciplinary problems

Agents are the next significant software abstraction, especially for distributed systems. They will soon be as ubiquitous as graphical user interfaces.

Part Two consists of Chapters 4 through 8 and Sidebar 4.

Chapter 4, "Speech Recognition Framework," illustrates the effectiveness of object-oriented frameworks in creating flexible architectures that encapsulate the complexities inherent in any application domain. The principal contribution of this chapter is the design and development of an application framework for a specific problem domain: speech recognition. Developers who may not fully comprehend the complexities of the speech recognition applications domain can benefit from the derived abstractions and rapidly incorporate speech technology into applications. This chapter also describes the benefits of the object-oriented paradigm rich with design patterns that provide a natural way to model complex concepts and capture system relationships effectively, along with achieving a high level of software reuse. While adhering to the classical definition of framework design, the novel contribution of this chapter is the evolution of a powerful, resilient architecture for speech applications as a result of iterative design over several framework applications.

Chapter 5, "Neural Network Components," describes the design and implementation aspects of framework architecture for decision support systems that rely on artificial neural network technology. Besides keeping the design open for supporting various neural network models, a smooth integration of neural network technology into a decision support system forms another important design goal. Many conventional implementations of such decision support systems suffer from a lack of flexibility; that is, they are built for a particular application domain and rely on one specific algorithm for the intelligent engine. In general, for different application domains, large portions of the decision support system have to be reimplemented from scratch. The principal contributions of this chapter are (1) the description of flexible and reusable components for core aspects of neural network implementations, (2) the integration of different neural network models in a decision support system, and (3) the presentation of a decision support system architecture that can be easily adapted to handle different domain problems.

Chapter 6, "A Framework for Agent Systems," summarizes research and experience in designing and developing an application framework for intelligent and mobile agents. This chapter also presents agents and agent-based systems as a new and important area for application frameworks. The application framework described in this chapter captures and clarifies the key aspects of agent-based systems. It provides a reusable and industrial-strength agent architecture, design patterns, and components for agent application development. The framework is documented with patterns to facilitate understanding and to expedite future extension and modification; this is necessary because agents are a new and evolving paradigm. Individual agents developed with the framework can cooperate and form agent societies. Java has been utilized as the implementation language because of its support for platform independence, concurrency, and mobility.

Chapter 7, "A Model for Reusable Agent Systems," shows the effectiveness of agent technology concepts. It may be better exploited if the development process is guided by a consolidated reuse methodology and shows how agent technology can enhance the flexibility and adaptability of object-oriented systems and simplify the development of reusable application frameworks for the distributed systems domain. The main contribution of this chapter is the description of the RETSINA agent model and the RETSINA application framework for the development of interoperable heterogeneous agents. The framework has been evaluated through the development of a variety of applications in the information-gathering domain.

Chapter 8, "Experimentation with an Agent-Oriented Platform in Java," invites the reader to share the experience and lessons learned from designing and implementing a Java agent-oriented development environment for simulation applications. The framework is a generic software tool, allowing the user to experiment with complex systems models, such as those found in natural phenomena in geophysics or artificial societies in economics. The family of related applications is then the simulation, which is used to adequately capture any behavior likely to be observed, to exhibit unknown parameters, and to emphasize complex processes that are brought into action by such poorly understood mechanisms. The use of a centralized program, which aims at considering a complex system as a unique entity, fails in this framework, because intrinsic application complexity describes nonlinear and nonpredicted worlds. The principal contribution is to investigate the use of the agent paradigm to thwart the previous issues. The agent paradigm allows the representation of the real world in independent and autonomous components called *agents,* where system behavior emerges from local interactions between such agents. As agents can extend the object paradigm, the architecture design was tackled with object-modeling technique (OMT). The principal innovation is the implementation following three abstraction levels: a microlevel, describing atomic and determinist behaviors in simple (reactive) agents; a medium-level, arranging intermediate structures; and a macrolevel, describing the whole system where emerging behavior will be observed and analyzed.

Sidebar 4, *Software Agents in Frameworks,* describes frameworks whose components are software agents. A software agent-oriented framework offers services to users and to other frameworks. Such a framework is an environment based on a supervisor agent and one or several teams of software agents that cooperate in order to achieve the services offered by the framework.

Speech Recognition Framework

Speech recognition–based computing is already a reality [Benet 1995; Lai-Vergo 1997]. The domain in which speech recognition may be applicable can vary from highly interactive user interfaces for creating text from speech, to telephony applications, which may have no graphical user interface. Systems that support the synergistic use of speech and direct manipulation using keyboard or mouse hold the appeal of improved usability by providing a more natural interface to the computer. The medical, legal, and journalism industries have been using speech recognition to create their documents in order to eliminate transcription time and improve productivity.

Speech recognition may be used in one of two ways in an application. The first is aimed at text entry or document creation applications such as dictation for electronic mail or word processing, and is referred to as *dictation*. The second is targeted for transaction processing and data entry systems and is referred to as *command and control* or *navigation*. Advances in technology are making significant progress toward the goal of any individual being able to speak naturally to a computer on any topic and be understood accurately.

However, we are not there yet. Even continuous speech recognition with a high degree of accuracy requires the user to speak clearly, enunciate each syllable properly, and have one's thoughts in order before starting. Factors inhibiting the pervasive use of speech technology today include the lack of availability of general-purpose, high-accuracy continuous speech recognition; lack of systems that support the synergistic use of speech input with other forms of input; and the challenges associated with designing speech user interfaces for increased user productivity despite speech recognition inaccuracies.

After an initial assessment of a problem domain shows it to be suitable for the application of speech recognition, a true understanding of the advantages and limitations of speech can be obtained only by prototyping the system. The emergence of the object-oriented paradigm resulting in the evolution of object-oriented frameworks provides an important enabling technology for rapid prototyping, together with achieving a high degree of reuse. Different levels of reuse such as reuse-in-the-small, reuse-in-the-medium, and reuse-in-the-large have been identified [Lajoie-Keller 1994]. Most object-oriented systems exhibit reuse-in-the-small by the usage of inheritance and object composition. Reuse-in-the-medium is exemplified by framework applications that contain object class interactions, or micro-architectures [Gamma 1995]. Reuse-in-the-large refers to the highest form of reuse, whereby application objects that are independent systems are reused, and the system that reuses the framework may not have been developed based on frameworks or even in the same language. With the design of the speech framework, we strive to achieve all three forms of reuse for speech applications.

In this chapter, we first define basic speech recognition technology concepts. We then describe the design of a framework, which enables the rapid development of speech applications using ViaVoice, IBM's speech recognition technology [IBM 1997]. We illustrate the encapsulation of speech complexities within the framework using a sample framework application. While we describe the technical underpinnings of such a system, we do not focus on design criteria and trade-offs related to speech user interface design. This chapter is intended to present a bridge between object-oriented design groups and user interface groups by demonstrating a complex, but real, solution to a real-world interface development problem.

4.1 Speech Concepts

At a simplistic level, if we think about the difference between two speech applications, it boils down to what specific words or phrases you say to the application and how the application interprets what you say. What one can say to the application so as to be understood is determined by what it is listening for, or its active *vocabulary*. Vocabulary defines the set of words or phrases that can be translated by a speech engine and is one of the resources that the engine uses to process spoken input. Speech grammars are an extension of the single words or simple phrases supported by vocabularies. They are a structured collection of words and phrases bound together by rules that define the set of speech streams that can be recognized by the speech engine at a given point in time. The speech recognition engine matches the acoustics from the speech input to words in the vocabularies; therefore, only words in the vocabulary are capable of being recognized. Constraining the size of the active vocabulary leads to higher recognition accuracy; therefore, applications typically change the active vocabulary depending on context.

Words in a vocabulary are recognized based entirely on their pronunciations or how they sound. Pronunciations are the possible phonetic representations of a word. Words can have multiple pronunciations; for example, *the* will have at least two pronunciations, "thee" and "thuh." Punctuation symbols are often associated with several different verbal representations; for example, the symbol "." may have the pronunciations "period," "point," "dot," and so on [IBM 1997].

Word-usage models are another resource used by the speech engine to provide statistical information on word sequences. They assist the speech engine in decoding speech by biasing the output toward high-probability word sequences. Within a particular application domain such as radiology, perplexity is a measurement of the number of equally likely word choices given a sequence of words [Markowitz 1995; Schmandt 1994]. Together, vocabularies and word-usage models are used in the selection of the best match for a word or phrase by the speech recognition engine. We refer to the results returned by the speech recognition engine in navigational mode as *recognized commands* (or, interchangeably, as *recognized words*) and *phrases,* and to the results returned by the speech recognition engine in dictation mode as *recognized text*. In the context of a graphical user interface (GUI) application, the active vocabulary and recognized commands may be different for each window *and* may vary within a window, depending on the state of the application.

4.2 Speech Application Complexities

Several factors contribute to the complexity in developing speech recognition applications:

The recognition technology in itself is inherently asynchronous and requires adhering to a well-defined handshaking protocol. Adhering to the rules that govern engine communication relative to the engine state is a complex task.

Speech programming interfaces typically reflect technology-level functionality such that a series of calls may be necessary to accomplish a single application-level task. An example is the initiation of dictation mode. Starting dictation, depending on the state of the speech engine, might involve up to seven application program interface (API) calls.

The asynchronous nature makes it possible for the user to initiate an action "during" an application-level task. The application must either disallow or defer any action until all previous speech engine processing has been completed.

The aim for a high degree of accuracy requires the application to constantly monitor the size of the active vocabulary. The application must define vocabularies and recognize the active vocabulary.

The uncertainty associated with recognition forces the application to deal with recognition errors. The application must detect any recognition errors and the causes of them.

The speech recognition engine communicates with applications at a process level and carries no notion of GUI windows or window-specific vocabularies. The application must, therefore, build its own infrastructure to direct and dispatch messages at the window level.

Recognized text returned by the speech engine is unformatted. Each word and punctuation mark is returned as a token and the application must assume responsibility for all aspects of formatting such as capitalizing, justification, insertion of new lines and paragraphs, and the placement of spaces between words.

Recognized text is returned to the application with associated audio information. This audio information is necessary for playback and the correction of recognition errors. The application must maintain an accurate association between the text and the associated audio, even in the face of text editing using the keyboard and mouse.

4.3 Speech Framework Architecture

The speech framework is a semicomplete application where the responsibilities of a system are partitioned among its fixed and variable components. The fixed component or the reusable design for a speech application is expressed as a set of collaborating object classes that abstract speech interface concepts and encapsulate engine-level complexity. The commonalities in the application domain include establishing a recognition session, defining and enabling a pool of vocabularies, ensuring a legal engine state for each call, and directing recognized word messages and engine status messages to different windows in the application. Explicit hot-spot [Pree 1994] identification is necessary to provide the variations such as the active window, the active vocabulary in a specific active window, the recognized words received by the active window based on the active vocabulary, and the action that an active window must take based on the recognized word.

Each major speech component modeled by an abstract class in the framework is realized in the application by the creation of a concrete derived instance of the abstract class. Due to the object-oriented features of inheritance and dynamic binding, the concrete instances encapsulate large parts of functionality and control flow in the application, provided by the abstract classes [Johnson-Foote 1988]. Application-specific logic must be performed by the concrete realizations of the abstract classes. The partitioning of the framework into distinct classes that support kernel functionality and interactive interface functionality allows for a flexible system architecture where different aspects may be allowed to vary independently.

Figure 4.1 shows a high-level view of the layered framework architecture adopted in order to embody this theory with maximum flexibility and reuse. The speech recognition engine and speech application are separate processes. The first layer, the core framework, encapsulates the speech engine functionality in abstract terms, independent of any specific GUI class library. A GUI speech recognition application usually involves the use of a GUI class library; therefore, the second layer extends the core framework for different GUI environments in order to provide tightly integrated seamless speech recognition functionality. Each GUI speech application is an instance of customizing the GUI extension to the core framework.

Figure 4.2 focuses on the flow of recognition events between the speech engine and the core framework classes. The SpeechClient class provides the command-and-control or navigational functionality and the SpeechText class provides the dictation functionality. SpeechClient is responsible for enabling vocabularies and receiving window-level recognition events; the SpeechText for edit control–level recognition events; the VocabularyManager class for vocabulary definition functions, and the SpeechObserver class for observing speech engine status changes. Prior to invoking any speech functionality, a recognition session must be established, and vocabularies

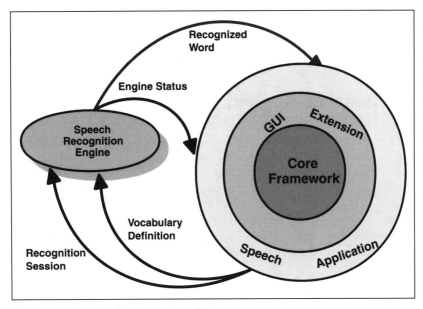

Figure 4.1   Layered framework architecture.

must be defined and enabled. The user may then begin speaking words from any of the active vocabularies. The speech engine processes the audio stream and directs recognized commands and phrases to the SpeechClient class, and recognized text to the SpeechText class. Speech engine status is maintained within the framework and broadcast to registered SpeechObservers.

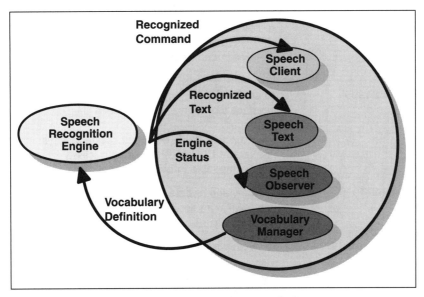

Figure 4.2   Recognition events and core framework classes.

Thus, the abstract classes in the core framework provide the flexible system composition where their collaborations provide the infrastructure to abstract, direct, dispatch, and receive speech engine events at a level that is meaningful to the application. The concrete instances of these abstract classes must be implemented by the application.

4.4 Design Patterns Applied

We describe some aspects of the framework design by identifying concrete realizations of design patterns that describe successful solutions to known software engineering problems and facilitate the direct reuse of design and code. We have used patterns to guide the creation of abstractions in the design phase, necessary to accommodate future changes and yet maintain architectural integrity. These abstractions help decouple the major components of the system so that each may vary independently, thereby making the framework more resilient. Table 4.1 summarizes the design patterns used in the framework together with the requirements that they satisfy.

4.4.1 Façade/Singleton

We defined a Façade object, the SpeechManager class, used internally by the framework to provide a unified, abstract interface to a set of interfaces supported by the

Table 4.1   Design Patterns Employed in Speech Framework

DESIGN PATTERN USED	WHY?
Façade [Gamma 1995]	To provide an abstract interface to a set of interfaces supported by the speech subsystem. To abstract speech concepts to facilitate the use of a different speech recognition technology.
Singleton [Gamma 1995]	To create exactly one instance of the speech subsystem interface class per application since the recognition system operates at the process level.
Adapter [Gamma 1995]	To enable the use of existing GUI classes whose interface did not match the speech class interface. To create a reusable class that cooperates with unrelated GUI classes that don't necessarily have compatible interfaces.
Observer [Gamma 1995]	To notify and update all speech-enabled GUI windows in an application when speech engine changes occur.
Active Object [Schmidt 1995]	To decouple method invocation from method execution in the application when a particular word is recognized.
Asynchronous Completion Token [Schmidt 1996]	To provide state information associated with the completion of asynchronous engine tasks.

speech subsystem. The Façade class is not exposed in the framework's public interface. However, the core abstract classes, such as SpeechText, SpeechClient, VocabularyManager, and SpeechObserver, communicate with the speech subsystem by sending requests to the Façade object, which in turn forwards the requests to the appropriate subsystem objects. The Façade class internally consists of various classes that assume responsibility for distinct functional areas of the speech subsystem. The Façade also implements the Singleton pattern, where it guarantees a single instance of the speech subsystem for each client process. Figure 4.3 shows the set of subsystem interfaces that have been encapsulated by the Façade class in the core framework. We

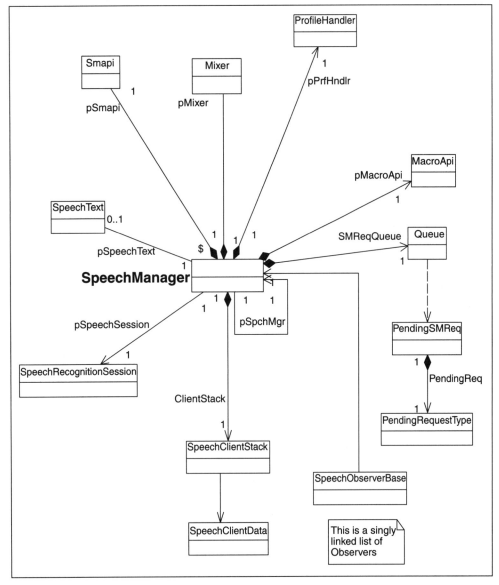

Figure 4.3 The Façade class: SpeechManager.

use the Unified Modeling Language (UML) [Rumbaugh 1991] notation, as generated by the tool Rational Rose, to represent the class diagrams (see Figure 4.8).

The use of the Façade and Singleton were straightforward applications of the patterns, given the context of the problem they addressed in the framework. However, they address some of the recognition technology issues we faced by abstracting speech concepts so as to hide differences in philosophy adopted by potentially different speech recognition technology providers. For example, IBM's speech technology requires the engine to be in a halted state when a vocabulary is enabled. The mechanics of halting the speech engine, enabling the vocabulary, and then restarting the speech engine were encapsulated by the Façade object in the Smapi class. Another example of encapsulating IBM speech technology–specific behavior is in the collaboration of the Smapi, Queue, and PendingSMRequest classes, which handle the asynchronous engine behavior.

4.4.2 Adapter

We used the class Adapter pattern to create a reusable speech class that cooperates with other existing and unrelated graphical user interface classes that do not have a speech interface. One way of implementing a speech-enabled GUI window class is to create a new class that inherits from the abstract SpeechClient class *and* a specific GUI window class. Similarly, a speech-enabled edit control class may be implemented by creating a new class that inherits from the abstract SpeechText class *and* a GUI edit control class.

The use of this pattern has been critical to the design and evolution of the framework and has been responsible for the level of reuse achieved. It enabled us to encapsulate the speech-aware behavior in abstract framework classes such that existing GUI classes did not have to be modified in order to exhibit speech-aware behavior. In addition, the Adapter pattern also addresses a key development environment issue of supporting speech functionality in a non-C++ environment because the abstract speech components do not contain GUI components and yet they provide speech-aware behavior [Srinivasan-Vergo 1998].

We also used the object Adapter pattern internally in order to ensure that the core framework classes remain independent of any specific GUI class library. Figure 4.4 shows a subset of the extensions to the core framework for one particular GUI class library, the IBM VisualAge class library; the class naming convention uses the prefix "I" for the GUI framework extension classes. For example, the class ISpeechClient refers to the VisualAge framework extension class, which provides the core SpeechClient class functionality. The application makes its request to the ISpeechClient class. The style and argument classes of ISpeechClient match the style and argument classes supported by the GUI class library. The SpeechClient class maintains class library independence, as illustrated by the following class declarations and the implementation of the method, setClientVocabState( ).

```
class ISpeechClient{
public:
    ...
    void setClientAndVocabState(const IText &vocabState="");
    ...
```

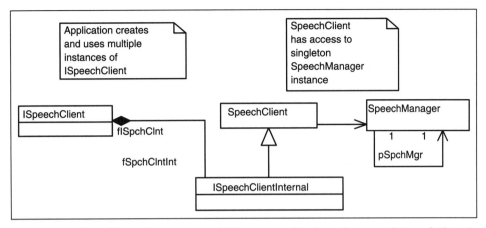

Figure 4.4 The object adapter: ISpeechClientInternal is the adapter and SpeechClient is the adaptee.

```
private:
    ISpeechClientInternal *fSpchClntInt;
};


class ISpeechClientInternal:public SpeechClient{
public:
    ...
};


class SpeechClient{
public:
    ...
    void SetSpeechClientData(const char *szVocabState, SpeechClient
                        *pSpchClient=NULL);
    ...
};
```

We observe that the signature of ISpeechClient::setClientVocabState( ) is consistent with the VisualAge class library (use of IText in the argument), while SpeechClient::Set-SpeechClientData( ) is not, and can remain independent of any particular GUI class library.

```
void ISpeechClient::setClientAndVocabState(const IText &vocabState)
{
    try {
        fSpchClntInt->SetSpeechClientData((const char*)vocabState,
                                fSpchClntInt);
    }
    catch(Exception const &e){
        ISpeechError ise(e);
        ITHROW(ise);
    }
}
```

The implementation of ISpeechClient::setClientVocabState( ) also shows the conversion of core framework classes into VisualAge-specific classes where the Exception class has been converted to an instance of ISpeechError, so as to be consistent with VisualAge's error handling mechanism.

4.4.3 Observer

We used the Observer pattern to implement the notification mechanism in order to observe speech engine changes and reflect them in the user interface as appropriate. Having partitioned the system into a collection of cooperating classes such as Speech-Clients and SpeechTexts, these objects needed to maintain consistency with the state of the speech engine. The Observer pattern implements the publish-subscribe mechanism where each instance of the SpeechObserver class registers itself to be notified of engine status changes through a broadcast mechanism implemented within the framework. The introduction of this class addresses some of the application-level issues by simplifying the accurate maintenance of speech engine state in the application.

4.5 A GUI Framework Extension

The class diagram in Figure 4.5 shows the core framework extension for the VisualAge GUI class library. The collaborations of the IVocabularyManager, ISpeechSession, ISpeechClient, ISpeechText, and ISpeechObserver classes provide the necessary speech

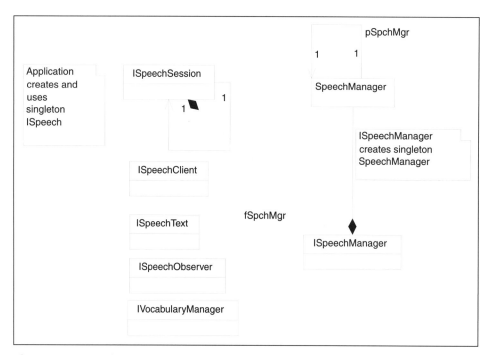

Figure 4.5   Speech framework public classes.

abstractions in the framework extension. The ISpeechSession class provides the ability to establish a recognition session with the engine. An application creates a speech-enabled GUI window using multiple inheritance by deriving from the ISpeechClient class and a GUI window class such as IFrameWindow (the class Adapter pattern). This provides speech functionality and speech engine addressability at a GUI window level such that recognized words may be directed to a particular GUI window by the framework. Similarly, an application creates a speech-enabled text widget using multiple inheritance by deriving from the ISpeechText class and a GUI text widget class such as IRichEditControl. This provides speech functionality and speech engine addressability at a text widget level. Concrete ISpeechObserver classes provide a publish-subscribe protocol necessary to maintain a consistent speech recognition engine state across all windows in the application. The IVocabularyManager class supports the dynamic definition and manipulation of vocabularies. The collaboration of these classes is internally supported by the singleton ISpeechManager, which encapsulates the core singleton class, the SpeechManager.

Figure 4.6 shows the realization of one of the primary hot spots in the system, the processing of recognized words by the active ISpeechClient. DictationSpeechClient is a concrete class derived from the abstract ISpeechClient class. The speech engine invokes the pure virtual method, recognizedWord( ), when it recognizes a word; this gives DictationSpeechClient the ability to process the recognized word in an application-specific manner. This works as designed only if the application obeys the accompanying contract [Helm 1990], which states that before a user speaks into the microphone (which causes the recognizedWord( ) method to be invoked), the application must specify the active ISpeechClient and its corresponding vocabularies.

Let us examine how an application might implement the basic variable aspects identified. Consider a GUI application that contains several windows, each of which is a multiply derived instance of ISpeechClient and IFrameWindow. The framework user must, at all times, keep track of the currently active ISpeechClient and ensure that the correct one is designated as being active. Likewise, enabling the appropriate vocabulary based on the active ISpeechClient is the framework user's responsibility. One way to do this is to designate the foreground window as the active ISpeechClient. The application must track change in the foreground window and designate the appropriate derived ISpeechClient as active. This means that the application must process the notification messages sent by the IFrameWindow class when the foreground window

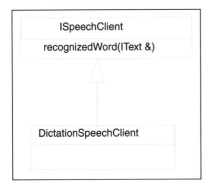

Figure 4.6 Hot spot: What is recognized?

changes and update the active ISpeechClient and vocabulary. Only then will the implementation of the hot spot in Figure 4.6 ensure delivery of the recognized words to the correct window by calling the active ISpeechClient's recognizedWord( ) method.

4.6 A Speech Framework Application

Consider the implementation of a speech application using the VisualAge speech framework. We describe a sample application that consists of a single GUI window containing a rich edit control field, a microphone button, an audio indicator, and a few other GUI controls, as shown in Figure 4.7. The user may issue speech commands to the window and dictate text into the rich edit field. We step through the concrete classes that must be implemented by the application to achieve this functionality.

The window in Figure 4.7 is a concrete instance of ISpeechClient implemented in the ISpeechFrame class. The leftmost button on the toolbar is a concrete instance of ISpeechObserver implemented in the MicObserver class. The audio indicator to the left of the Exit button is a concrete instance of ISpeechObserver implemented in the AudioObserver class. The text area below the toolbar is an instance of ISpeechRichEdit,

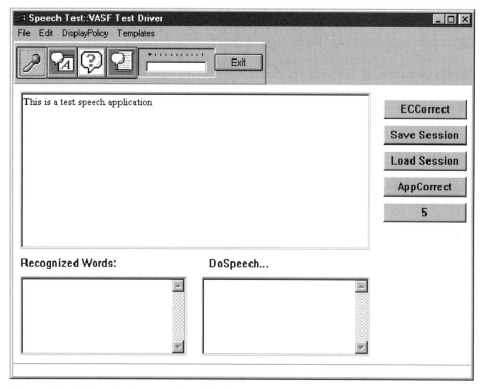

Figure 4.7   A Speech framework application.

a concrete framework class. The application uses the class Adapter pattern to implement the ISpeechFrame class. This class contains an instance of the MicObserver class, the AudioObserver class, and the ISpeechRichEdit in addition to other nonspeech GUI classes.

```
class ISpeechFrame:public IFrameWindow, public ISpeechClient{
public:
    ...
protected:
    // overridden methods from ISpeechClient
    ...
    void recognizedWord(const ISpeechCommandWord &commandWord);
    ...
private:
    ...
    IspeechRichEdit *iSpchRichEdit;
    MicObserver     *iMicButton;
    AudioObserver *iAudioObs;
    ...
};

class ISpeechRichEdit:public ISpeechText, public IRichEditControl{
    ...
};

class MicObserver:public ISpeechObserver, public IToolBarButton{
public:
    ...
    virtual void update();
    ...
};
```

The main module of the application instantiates the following classes and invokes the methods shown in order to create the main window, define vocabularies, and set the active vocabulary.

```
try {
    //establish a recognition session with speech engine
    ISpeechSession *sess;
    sess = new SpeechSession(getenv("SF_UID"),
                             getenv("SF_EID"),appName,
                             sessionData,10000,
                             "startus", "En_US", "text");
    // Create the main window
    ISpeechFrame aFrame("Speech Text");

    // define vocabularies
    IVocabularyManager VocMgr;
    IText pWords[MAX_WORDS];
    // define the main command vocabulary
    pWords[0] = "Begin Dictation";
    pWords[1] = "Exit";
```

```
    IText vocab("MainCommandVocab");
    VocMgr.defineVocab(vocab, pWords, 2);

    // define the main command state
    IText VocabNames[1];
    VocabNames[0] = "MainCommandVocab";
    IText vocstate("CommandState");
    VocMgr.defineVocabState(vocstate, VocabNames, 1 );

    //set active ISpeechClient and active vocabulary
    aFrame.setClientAndVocabState("CommandState");
}
catch(IException &e){
    ...
}
```

The constructor of ISpeechFrame contains the necessary method calls to register the rich edit class and the observer classes, so they may receive the appropriate notifications from the framework.

```
ISpeechFrame::ISpeechFrame(const IText &appName):IFrameWindow(...)
{
    ...
    iSpchRichEdit->setSpeechText();
    iMicButton->attach();
    iAudioObs->attach();
    ...
}
```

Executing this code will display the speech-enabled window shown in Figure 4.7. The user may now speak any of the words from the active vocabulary. In our example, "Begin Dictation" and "Exit" are the only two words that are defined in the active vocabulary. When either of these commands is spoken, the framework invokes the recognizedWord() method in the ISpeechFrame class. This method must implement application-specific action for each of the possible speech commands that may be returned by the speech recognition engine, as shown in the following:

```
void ISpeechFrame::recognizedWord(const ISpeechCommandWord &commandWord)
{
    if (commandWord.spelling() == "Begin Dictation")
        {
            ...
            BeginDictation("DictationState");
        }
    else if (commandWord.spelling() == "Exit")
        ...
}
```

In response to the "Begin Dictation" speech command, the ISpeechFrame class invokes the BeginDictation method, which changes the state of the speech engine from command mode to dictation mode. At this time, the user may begin speaking sentences from the dictation vocabulary, such as "This is a test speech application . . ." The recognized text returned by the speech engine automatically flows into the rich edit control, as shown in Figure 4.7, because of the behavior built into the ISpeechRichEdit class. The ISpeechRichEdit class also maintains synchronization between the audio data and the text in order to support other functionality such as playback, error correction, and so forth.

When other relevant speech events occur, the framework notifies the registered speech observers by invoking the update( ) method where application-specific behavior must be implemented. For example, the MicObserver changes the bitmap on the button based on the state of the microphone. Similarly, the AudioObserver adjusts the indicator based on the audio level.

```
void MicObserver::update()
{
    // get status of the microphone and display bitmap
    if (ISpeechSession::instance().isMicOn()) {
        setBitmap(micOnBmp);
    }
    else
        setBitmap(micOffBmp);
}


void AudioObserver::update()
{
    int level = 10 * ISpeechSession::instance().micAudioLevel();
    moveArmToTick(level);
}
```

The recognizedWord( ) and update( ) methods are examples of hot-spot implementations enabling the application to customize the framework using the Adapter and Observer patterns.

4.7 Summary

We have described the design of a framework for speech recognition applications using IBM's speech recognition technology. A layered approach has been adopted in the framework to maximize flexibility and reuse. The core framework abstracts speech concepts in distinct classes and the GUI extensions to the core framework provide seamless speech functionality in the GUI class library. The design patterns embodied in the framework help create the abstractions necessary to accommodate changes and yet maintain architectural integrity, thereby making the framework more resilient. This framework successfully encapsulates speech recognition complexities and provides a simplified interface enabling the rapid development of speech applications.

4.8 UML Notation

Unified modeling language (UML) is a standard modeling language for software—a language for visualizing, specifying, constructing, and documenting the artifacts of a software-intensive system [Jacobson 1999]. Figure 4.8 shows the UML graphical notation.

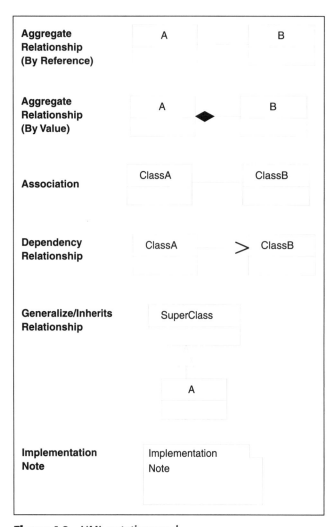

Figure 4.8   UML notation used.

4.9 References

[Benet 1995] Benet, B. Dictation system for Windows: Dragon, IBM, Kurzweil. *Seybold Report on Desktop Publishing,* 9(10), June 10, 1995:12–19.

[Gamma 1995] Gamma, E., R. Helm, R. Johnson, and J. Vlissides. *Design Patterns: Elements of Reuseable Object Oriented Software.* Reading, MA: Addison-Wesley, 1995.

[Helm 1990] Helm, R., I.M. Holland, and D. Gangopadhyay. Contracts: Specifying behavioral compositions in object oriented systems. *Proceedings of OOPSLA 1990,* Ottawa, ON, October 1990.

[IBM 1997] IBM Corporation, ViaVoice Dictation. *ViaVoice Developers Toolkit.* 1997.

[Jacobson 1999] Jacobson, I., G. Booch, and J. Rumbaugh. The Unified Software Development Process. Reading, MA: Addison-Wesley, 1999.

[Johnson-Foote 1988] Johnson, R.E., and B. Foote. Designing reusable classes. *Journal of Object-Oriented Programming* 1(2), June/July 1988:22–35.

[Lai-Vergo 1997) Lai, J., and J. Vergo. MedSpeak: Report creation with continuous speech recognition. *Proceedings of CHI 1997,* Atlanta, GA, March 1997.

[Lajoie-Keller 1994] Lajoie, R., and R. Keller. Design and reuse in object-oriented frameworks: Patterns, contracts and motifs in concert. *Proceedings of the 62nd Congress of the Association Canadienne Francaise pour l'Avancement des Sciences,* Montreal, QC, May 1994.

[Markowitz 1995] Markowitz, J. Talking to machines. *Byte,* December, 1995, pp. 97–104.

[Pree 1994] Pree, W. *Design Patterns for Object-Oriented Software Development.* Reading, MA: Addison-Wesley, 1994.

[Rumbaugh 1991] Rumbaugh, J. *Object-Oriented Modeling and Design.* Englewood Cliffs, NJ: Prentice Hall International, 1991.

[Schmandt 1994] Schmandt, C. *Voice Communication with Computers.* New York: Van Nostrand Reinhold, 1994.

[Schmidt 1995] Schmidt, D.C., and G. Lavender. Active object—An object behavioral pattern for concurrent programming. *Proceedings of the Second Pattern Languages of Programs Conference,* Monticello, IL, September 6–8, 1995, and as a chapter in *Pattern Languages of Program Design.* James Coplien and Douglas Schmidt, editors. Reading, MA: Addison-Wesley, 1995.

[Schmidt 1996] Schmidt, D., T. Harrison, and I. Pyarali. ACT—An object behavioral pattern for efficient asynchronous event handling. *Proceedings of the 3rd Annual Pattern Languages of Programming,* Monticello, IL, September 4–6, 1996.

[Srinivasan-Vergo 1998] Srinivasan, S., and J. Vergo. Object oriented reuse: Experience in developing a framework for speech recognition applications. *Proceedings of ICSE-20,* Kyoto, Japan, April 1998.

[Vlissides 1996] Vlissides, John M., James O. Coplien, and Norman L. Kerth, eds. *Pattern Languages of Program Design 2.* Reading, MA: Addison-Wesley, 1996.

Neural Network Components

5.1 An Overview of the Domain Area

One characteristic of computer-based decision support systems is that they deal with complex, unstructured real-world tasks. Let's take a look at a sample application of a decision support system in the realm of a mail order reseller. Customers order goods usually via telephone or by sending an order form. The information associated with an order, such as the value of ordered goods, the customer's home address, and the customer's age are useful for customer classification. For example, the marketing department needs such a classification to optimize the selection of customers who receive information brochures regularly. In order to implement a computer-based decision support system for the classification task, the mail order reseller provides a large amount of customer data from recent years that describe customer behavior.

The construction of decision support systems requires the integration of several methods from knowledge engineering and artificial intelligence (AI) research areas. An adequate decision support system should

- Have sufficient knowledge about the problem domain
- Be able to learn
- Have logical, deductive, and inductive reasoning capabilities
- Be able to apply known solutions to analogous new ones
- Be able to draw conclusions

Expert systems represent a well-known example of this kind of system. In order to overcome several problems of expert systems, such as difficulties in building up a large, consistent knowledge base, so-called hybrid systems were proposed [Leão-Rocha 1990]. They try to integrate various single AI technologies—in particular, expert systems, artificial neural networks, fuzzy logic, genetic algorithms, and case-based reasoning.

Artificial neural networks support knowledge acquisition and representation. Fuzzy logic [Kosko 1992] is useful to model imprecise linguistic variables, such as predicates and quantifiers (expressions like "high," "short," and so forth). Genetic algorithms excel in the ability to do deductive learning [Lawrence 1991]. Case-based reasoning remembers previous problems and applies this knowledge to solve or evaluate new problems.

5.1.1 Why Build a Framework for Decision Support Systems?

One difficulty in implementing hybrid systems is the smooth integration of the various single AI technologies. A hybrid system should also be flexible enough to solve problems in several application domains. [Medsker-Bailey 1992] discuss the former aspect, whereas this chapter focuses on the latter aspect—constructing a flexible hybrid system. We assume that the reader is familiar with the most basic concepts of artificial neural networks and expert systems.

In artificial neural networks (ANNs) software development, it is common to redevelop models from scratch each time a different application must be accomplished. There are tools that try to avoid this and help with the main ANN development aspects, offering some predefined building blocks. Unfortunately, in general, these tools are commercialized software and their structure is not open for analysis. Furthermore, ANN software developers usually:

- Think about only one neural model to solve a specific application problem.

- Come up with too-specific implementations for a particular problem.

- Concentrate on ANN performance and not on the construction of different ANN models and their reusability in different problem domains.

Thus, object-oriented (OO) design and implementation have hardly been applied so far in this domain area. Our intention is to build a flexible OO architecture in order to solve the following problems related to the implementation of decision support systems:

- The architecture should be sufficiently flexible/extensible to deal with various neural models.

- Flexible ANN architectures that can change their structure and behavior at run-time allow experiments to gain better results.

- It should be easy to have different neural network models distributed over a network. In this way, a suitable solution to a decision problem can be found more quickly.

- In the long term, the OO architecture could form the basis for building up hierarchies of ANNs working together, cooperating, and acting as intelligent agents in a distributed environment.

We chose Java as the implementation language. Neural networks form a good test bed for Java performance evaluation, in particular when just-in-time (JIT) compilation is applied. The first comparisons with the conventional C implementations revealed that there are no significant performance losses, if the virtual machine and JIT compiler are reasonably well implemented.

5.2 Characteristics and Problems of a Conventional Architecture

Hycones (short for Hybrid Connectionist Expert System; [Leão-Reátegui 1993a]) is a sample hybrid system that is especially designed for classification decision problems. The core technology is artificial neural networks based on the Combinatorial Neural Model (CNM) [Machado-Rocha 1989, 1990]. The experiments with this model proved that it is powerful for classification problems, having good results ranging from medical diagnosis to credit analysis [daRosa 1995; Leão-Reátegui 1993b; Reátegui-Campbell 1994]. This section begins with a discussion of the principal features of Hycones. Based on this overview, the problems regarding its flexibility are outlined. These problems were encountered when Hycones was applied to different domains.

5.2.1 Hycones as Generator of Decision Support Systems

The fact that Hycones is a generator system already indicates that the design of a generic architecture constitutes an important goal right from the beginning. Unfortunately, the conventional design and implementation did not provide the required flexibility, as will be outlined in *Section 5.2.2.*

The first step in using Hycones is to specify the input nodes and output nodes of the ANNs that are generated. In the case of a customer classification system, the input nodes correspond to the information on the order form. Hycones offers different data types (string values, fuzzy value ranges) to specify the input neurons. The output neurons, called *hypotheses,* correspond to the desired decision support. In the case of the customer classification system, the customer categories become the output neurons.

Based on the information already described, Hycones generates the CNM topology depending on some additional parameters (various thresholds, and so on). Figure 5.1 schematically illustrates this feature of Hycones. Each combination of input neurons contributes to the overall decision.

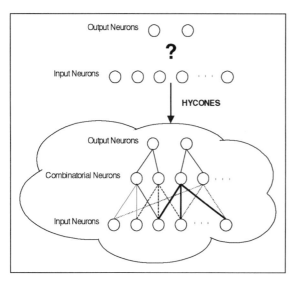

Figure 5.1   Hycones as ANN generator.

Learning

We differentiate inductive and deductive learning mechanisms:

Inductive learning is performed through the training of the generated ANN based on available data using a punishment and reward algorithm and an incremental learning algorithm [Machado-Rocha 1989]. Inductive learning allows automatic knowledge acquisition and incremental learning.

Deductive learning can be implemented through genetic algorithms. This might imply further modifications in the topology of the ANN, creating or restoring connections between neurons. Deductive learning is not implemented in the current version of Hycones.

Inference

Once the generated ANN is trained, Hycones pursues the following strategy to come up with a decision for one specific case (for example, a customer). The ANN evaluates the case and calculates a confidence value for each hypothesis. The inference mechanism finds the winning hypothesis and returns the corresponding result.

Expert Rules

Additional expert knowledge can be modeled in expert rules [Leão-Rocha 1990]. For example, rules describing typical attributes of customers belonging to a particular category could be specified for the mail order decision support system. Such rules imply modifications of the weights in the ANN. Figure 5.2 exemplifies this Hycones property.

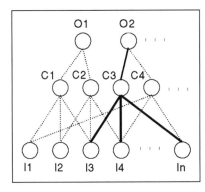

Figure 5.2 Incorporating expert rules into the ANN topology.

The expert rule, I3 & I4 & In => O2, corresponds to the strengthened connections among the input nodes I3, I4, and In; the combinatorial node C3; and the output node O2 of an ANN.

5.2.2 Adaptation Problems

Despite the intention of Hycones to be a reusable generator of decision support systems, the Hycones implementation had to be changed fundamentally for each application domain in recent years. In other words, the Hycones system had to be implemented almost from scratch for each new application domain. What are the reasons for this unsatisfying situation?

Limits of Hardware and Software Resources

The first Hycones version was implemented in Common Lisp Object System (CLOS). CLOS simplified the implementation of core parts of Hycones, but the execution time turned out to be insufficient for the domain problems at hand.

In subsequent versions of Hycones, parts of the system were even implemented on different platforms to overcome performance problems and memory limits. For example, the ANN training algorithm is implemented in C on a Unix workstation. C was chosen to gain execution speed. Other parts of Hycones, such as an interactive tool for domain modeling by means of specifying expert rules, are implemented on PCs and use Borland Delphi for building the GUI.

Complex Conceptual Modeling

This issue is also related to performance problems: Hycones manages the complex ANN topology by storing the information about all the connections and their corresponding weights in main memory. (Hycones provides no parallelization of ANN training and testing.) Due to memory limits, only parts of the ANN structure can be kept there, and the rest is stored in a database. Roughly speaking, database records represent the connections and weights of one ANN topology. All this forms quite a complex conceptual model, involving overhead when swapping ANN weights between memory and database. The way in which the information about the generated ANN is stored in database tables has had to be changed several times to be optimal for the database system in use. These changes are not only tedious, but also error-prone.

The fact that Hycones also became a hybrid system with regard to its implementation implies complex data shifting between different computing platforms. The parameters comprising the specification for the ANN generation are entered on PCs, but the ANN training and testing are done on Unix workstations. Finally, if the user prefers to work with the decision support system on PCs, the generated and trained ANN has to be transferred back from the Unix platform to the PC environment.

Neural Network Models

Hycones supports only one ANN model, the Combinatorial Neural Model, but it should be possible to choose from a set of ANN models the one that is best suited for the decision support problem at hand.

Conversion of Data

Companies that want to apply Hycones must provide data for ANN training and testing. Of course, various different ways of dealing with this data have to be considered. For example, some companies provide data in ASCII format, others as relational database tables, and still others as object databases. The data read from these sources must be converted to valid data for the ANN input. This conversion is done based on the domain knowledge, which also changes from application to application. Though this seems to be only a minor issue and a small part of the overall Hycones system, experience has proven that a significant part of the adaptation work deals with the conversion of training and test data.

In order to overcome these problems, Hycones is completely redesigned based on framework construction principles. The problems of the conventional Hycones implementation form a good starting point for identifying the required hot spots [Fayad 1999, Chapters 9, 15, and 16]). *Section 5.3* presents the hot-spot-driven redesign and implementation of Hycones.

5.3 Design of a Neural Network Framework Architecture

We use the term Java-ANN-Business-Components, Java-ABC for short, because the resulting set of frameworks is implemented in Java. The hot spots of Java-ABC can be summarized as follows:

- ANN training: Java-ABC should support several ANN models (as already pointed out, Hycones is restricted to one specific model, the Combinatorial Neural Model).

- The ANN internal structure and behavior change from model to model, but some significant aspects can be kept flexible in order to facilitate any ANN model implementation.

- Data conversion: Java-ABC should provide flexible mechanisms for converting data from various sources.

Modeling the core entities of the ANN—neurons and synapses—as objects solves the complex conceptual modeling of Hycones. Instead of storing the generated ANN in database tables, the topologies are saved as objects via Java's serialization mechanism. The object-oriented model also forms the basis for the parallelization and distribution of ANN learning and testing. These aspects are not related to frameworks, however, and we will not discuss them in this chapter. Finally, Java being a portable language and system solves the problem of splitting the original system into subsystems implemented in various programming paradigms on different platforms. Java-ABC runs on all major computing platforms.

5.3.1 Object-Oriented Modeling of the Core Entities of Neural Networks

The neurons and synapses of ANNs mimic their biological counterparts and form the basic building blocks of ANNs. Java-ABC provides two classes, Neuron and Synapse, whose objects correspond to these entities. Both classes offer properties that are common to different neural network models. The idea is that these classes provide basic behavior independent of the specific neural network model. Subclasses add the specific properties according to the particular model.

An object of class Neuron has the activation as its internal state and provides methods to calculate its activation and to manage a collection of Synapse objects. A Synapse object represents a direct connection between two neurons (here distinguished by the names Receptor and Source). The receptor neuron manages a list of incoming synapses (represented by the straight arrows on Figure 5.3) and computes its activation from these synapses. A Synapse object has exactly one Neuron object connected to it, which is the source of the incoming sign. The dashed arrows on Figure 5.3 represent the computational flow (set of incoming signs from all source neurons). The incoming sign

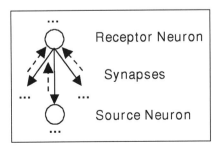

Figure 5.3 Relationship between Neuron and Synapse objects.

from one source neuron is processed by the synapse and forwarded to the receptor neuron on its outgoing side.

As the synapse knows its source neurons, different neuron network topologies can be built, such as multilayer feedforward or recurrent networks. The process of creating the neural network architecture is controlled by a method called generateNet( ) and belongs to the class NetImplementation, which is explained in *Section 5.3.2*. Each neural network model is responsible for its topological construction. Different neural models use the Neuron and Synapse classes as the basic building blocks for the neural network structure and behavior construction. Example 5.1 shows some aspects of the Neuron and Synapse classes to make clear how these classes are implemented. The core explanations for them will be provided in subsequent sections.

Example 5.1   Neuron and Synapse Classes

```
public class Neuron extends Object implements Serializable {
    float currentActivation; // stores the resulting activation
computation
    Vector incomingSynapses; // vector of input Synapse objects
    ComputationStrategy compStrategy; /* strategy for processing input
values (see explanation in the text) */
    Neuron () {incomingSynapses = new Vector();}
    Neuron (ComputationStrategy cs) {
        incomingSynapses = new Vector();
        compStrategy = cs;
    }
    void compute() {
        Synapse s;
        for (int i=0; i<incomingSynapses.size; i++) {
            s = incomingSynapses.elementAt(i);
            s.compute(); // calculates next synapse current flow
        }
        // takes incomingSynapses's currentFlow and applies its own
calculation strategy
        currentActivation = compStrategy.compute(incomingSynapses);
    }
    void generateSynapses(Vector sourceNeurons, ComputationStrategy
synapsesCompStrategy) {
        Synapse s;
        for (int i=0; i<sourceNeurons.size; i++) {
            s= new Synapse(sourceNeurons.elementAt(i),
synapsesCompStrategy);
            incomingSynapses.addElement(s);
        }
    }
    float getCurrentActivation() {return (currentActivation);}
    ...// other methods are implemented
}
```

Example 5.1 *(Continued)*

```
public class Synapse extends Object implements Serializable {
   Neuron sourceNeuron; // the neuron that the synapse receives
computation
   ComputationStrategy  compStrategy; /* strategy for processing input
values (see explanation in the text) */
   float weight;         // synaptic weight
   float currentFlow;        // stores the result of synapses
computation
   Synapse(Neuron addtlSourceNeuron, ComputationStrategy  cs) {
       weight = (float)1.0;
       sourceNeuron = addtlSourceNeuron;
       compStrategy = cs;
   }
   void compute() {
       sourceNeuron.compute();
       currentFlow =
compStrategy.compute(sourceNeuron.getCurrentActivation(),weight);
/* calculate currentFlow using the incoming activation from the
sourceNeuron and the synaptical weight */
   }
   void setWeight(float calcWeight) {weight = calcWeight;}
   float getWeight() {return (weight);}
   float getCurrentFlow() {return (currentFlow);}
}
```

Using Neuron and Synapse Classes to Create Neural Network Topologies

In the case of implementing a multilayer feedforward neural network, the neurons for all necessary neuron layers are created initially. Later, the necessary synapses to connect the neurons at different layers are created and correctly connected to the neuron layers. A list of synapses (called incomingSynapses) controls each instance of Synapse that connects an output neuron to a hidden neuron. The class Neuron (see Example 5.1) implements this list. When creating instances of the class Synapse (see Example 5.1), it is informed in its constructor to which hidden neuron it must be connected. The reference to the hidden neuron is stored in the instance variable sourceNeuron. This process is repeated for all network layers. The method generateSynapses(Vector sourceNeurons, ComputationStrategy, synapsesCompStrategy) in class Neuron is responsible for the generation of Synapse instances and their appropriate connection to source neurons.

The software architecture explained here was successfully used to implement different neural network models involving different neural network architectures. Besides the CNM model, the Backpropagation [Rumelhart-McClelland 1986] network was implemented as another feedforward network. The Self-Organizing Feature-Mapping (SOM) [Kohonen 1982] was implemented representing lattice structures with a two-dimensional array of neurons. Finally, the Hopfield Network [Hopfield 1982] was implemented as a recurrent network architecture example.

The implementation of recurrent computation in the proposed architecture implies synchronization of the computational flow. It is necessary to select the next neuron to do the computation in a learning step. The typical solution is to choose the neuron randomly [Haykin 1994].

A class called NetImplementation is tightly associated with class Neuron (this class is explained in *Section 5.3.2*). Roughly speaking, a NetImplementation object harnesses the ANN in order to make decisions. The NetImplementation object represents the inference engine (that is, the neural network model) of the running Java-ABC system. Its abstract interface reflects the needs of the decision-making process. For example, a method, getWinner( ), computes which output neuron has the maximum activation. Due to the design of NetManager and Neuron, Java-ABC supports different inference engines. How to switch between different ANN models is discussed in the next section.

5.3.2 Support of Different Neural Network Models through the Separation Pattern

Java-ABC should be flexible regarding its underlying ANN model. The choice of the most appropriate ANN model depends on the particular decision problem at hand, and usually it is necessary to try some different ANN models to see which one performs better. Thus, the design should allow the trial of different ANN models.

Java-ABC should be able to manage various ANN models, trying the solution for a specific problem in a distributed way. Several neural models can then run at the same time. To handle this idea, the class NetManager was created. The NetManager class is responsible for controlling, at runtime, a set of instances of different neural models, or even a set of instances of the same neural model but with different configurations.

As the learning of a neural model can take days, it could be interesting to change the underlying ANN model at runtime. It is necessary to allow the user to add new ANN models at runtime in order to start different learning trials during the learning or testing process of other neural models, without stopping the processes already started. It is also desirable to allow modifications to the ANN that is already learning. This means the possibility of adding or deleting neurons and synapses on the ANN structure and changing its behavior by changing learning strategies and tuning learning parameters. To have these kinds of simulation characteristics, it is necessary to have quite a flexible architecture design. This design was obtained through the hot-spot-driven design methodology [Pree 1995]. The use of hot-spot cards to identify the flexibility points on the design matured the object model. From the hot-spot cards, the appropriate patterns were chosen as explained subsequently.

To permit the addition of new neural models at runtime, it is necessary to abstractly couple the NetManager with the class NetImplementation, that is, to rely on the Separation pattern. The NetManager has a list of instances of the NetImplementation class that are responsible for different ANN implementations. A specific ANN model is defined by subclassing NetImplementation and overriding the corresponding hook

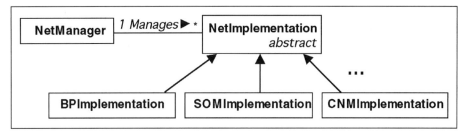

Figure 5.4   ANN models as subclasses of NetImplementation.

methods such as getWinner( ) and compute( ). Figure 5.4 exemplifies how three commonly used ANN models can be incorporated in Java-ABC: BPImplementation (Back-propagation), SOMImplementation, and CNMImplementation.

Neural Network Behavior

Specific ANN models also imply the need for specific behavior of the classes Neuron and Synapse. A simple solution would be to create subclasses of Neuron and Synapse, but this solution would generate a nested hierarchy, because for each neural model, similar subclasses of Neuron and Synapse would be created. For example, in the case of CNM, the subclasses would have the names CNMNeuron and CNMSynapse. CNM-Neuron would factor out commonalities of the CNM-specific classes CNMInputNeuron, CNMCombinatorialNeuron, and CNMHypothesisNeuron. For Backpropagation the same would be required.

To avoid this, the Bridge pattern was used [Gamma 1995]. This pattern is equivalent to the Separation Metapattern [Pree 1997], and thus has the ability to change neural network behavior at runtime. Figure 5.5 shows the application of this pattern to the class Neuron. Its application is analogous to the class Synapse. Neuron is an abstract class having the three most common neuron types as its subclasses: InputNeuron, HiddenNeuron, and OutputNeuron. These three classes are the most common in the ANN implementations. The names refer to the layers they belong to. The ANN layers are built using those classes. Each layer can be of any size. There can be any number of hidden layers, and the NetImplementation class controls its generation. Finally, any neural model is based on these Neuron classes.

The necessary behavior of each neural model is added to these classes by composition through the associated interface ComputationStrategy (see Figure 5.5). The dif-

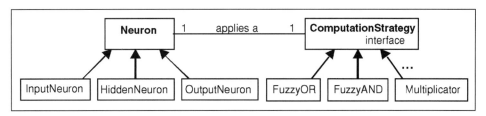

Figure 5.5   Design of flexible behavior based on the Bridge pattern.

ferent behaviors are implemented through the ComputationStrategy interface. The instances of the classes that implement this interface can be used by different neural model implementations through the classes Neuron and Synapse. The classes Neuron and Synapse have a relationship with this interface through the instance variable compStrategy.

The ComputationStrategy also implements the pattern Flyweight [Gamma 1995]. The framework has only one instance of each class that implements it. Each instance is shared by a large number of Neuron and Synapse instances. This keeps the memory footprint significantly smaller and improves the behavior reusability.

An important design issue is that a developer who uses Java-ABC does not have to worry about which specific subclasses of Synapse and Neuron are associated with a particular ANN model. In order to resolve this, the Factory pattern [Gamma 1995] was applied. A concrete class that implements NetImplementation, such as CNMImplementation, already takes care of the correct instantiation of Neuron and Synapse subclasses.

CNM Adaptation of Java-ABC

A sample adaptation of Java-ABC exemplifies the necessary steps to adjust the framework components to a specific neural network model. For this reason, it is necessary to discuss the inner workings (see Figure 5.6):

1. The CNMImplementation object is responsible for the creation of OutputNeuron objects (called Hypothesis neurons in the CNM definition [Machado 1990]), with the FuzzyOR behavior and for the creation of InputNeurons, whose behavior is explained in *Section 5.3.3*.

2. An OutputNeuron instance then creates Synapse objects, which automatically create HiddenNeuron instances (called *combinatorial neurons* in the CNM defini-

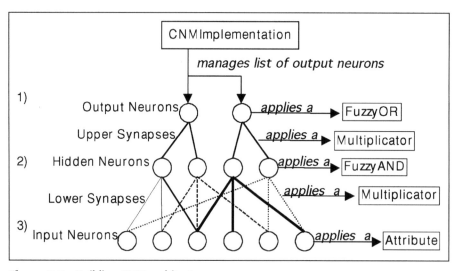

Figure 5.6 Building CNM architecture.

tion [Machado-Rocha 1990]), with the FuzzyAND behavior. As the CNM model has only one hidden layer, the neurons of the hidden layer are then directly connected to the input layer.

3. The connections between the HiddenNeuron instances and the InputNeuron instances are established in an analogous way. The Synapse instances of a CNM model have behavior similar to the Backpropagation model using the same Multiplicator computation strategy, which simply does the multiplication of the input activation with the synaptic weight and returns the result.

For the neural network generation process, the classes that implement NetImplementation (in this case, the CNMImplementation) rely on problem-specific domain knowledge, the representation of which is discussed in *Section 5.3.3*. The basic idea behind the CNM inference machine is that numerous combinations (the small networks that form the CNM hidden layer) all test a certain case for which a decision is necessary. Adding the activation from all combinations amounts to the OutputNeuron activation. The OutputNeuron with the maximum accumulated activation is the winner (FuzzyOR). The CNM object also provides an explanation by calculating those input neurons that most strongly influenced the decision. [Machado-Rocha 1989, 1990] discuss the CNM-specific algorithm.

Adding Behavior to a Multilayer Feedforward Architecture

The computation of a case, either learning or testing, is done in the following way: The object NetImplementation knows the instances of output neurons that are implemented in the structure already created. The result value of a case computation is implemented by the output neurons' compute( ) method and can be retrieved by the getCurrentFlow( ) method (see Example 5.1). The NetImplementation object requests computation from the output neurons by calling the compute( ) methods of all existent output neurons. When the output neuron is requested to do its computation, it first requires its list of incoming synapses to do the same. The synapses also have a source neuron, which is requested to do its own computation (see Example 5.1).

The source neuron is a hidden neuron in the architecture and its compute( ) method implementation also requests the computation of the connected synapses. In this way, the request of computation flows from the output neurons to the input neurons. The input neuron instance's behavior is simply to take the activation from outside to be able to start the ANN data processing. This activation comes from the class Attribute, explained in *Section 5.3.3*. In short, the instances of the Attribute class prepare the activation values from the data read in the data sources. These prepared data (activation) are transferred to the input neuron instances on demand.

When the computation flow goes back from the input neurons to the output neurons, each synapse and neuron object is then able to do the necessary calculation it is supposed to do and return it to the object that requested it (other neurons and synapses). The instances of the classes that implement ComputationStrategy do this calculus. Finally, the compute( ) method of each output neuron gets the computational results of all connected synapses and does its appropriate computation. Then the resulting values can be consulted through the output neurons' getCurrentFlow( )

method. The NetImplementation object is able to evaluate these values and to make a decision.

The computational flow explained here is a parallel process internal to the neural network architecture. Instances of Synapse and Neuron in the same layer can be completely independent processes. Depending on the neural model, synchronization must be implemented in order get the correct results and to have optimal performance. The parallel implementation strategy of the computational flow is specific to each model and is not explained here.

To complete the appropriate behavior of the implemented neural networks, it is necessary to have them related to the knowledge representation of the problem domain. *Section 5.3.3* explains how the domain model influences and interacts with the neural network architecture.

5.3.3 Domain Representation and Data Conversion

As the principal application domain of Java-ABC is classification problems, the chosen object-oriented design of this system aspect reflects common properties of classification problems. On the one hand, so-called evidences form the input data. Experts use evidences to analyze the problem in order to come up with decisions. Evidences in the case of the customer classification problem would be the age of a customer, his or her home address, and so on. One or more Attribute objects describe the value of each Evidence object. For example, in the case of the home address, several strings form the address evidence. The age of a customer might be defined as a fuzzy set [daRosa 1997; Kosko 1992] of values: child, youth, adult, and senior (see Figure 5.7).

On the other hand, the hypotheses (classification categories) constitute a further core entity of classification problems. In Java-ABC, an instance of class Domain represents the problem by managing the corresponding Evidence and Hypothesis objects. Class Domain again applies the Singleton pattern. Even based on classification problems and focused on neural networks learning algorithms, the design presented here can also be extended to support general domain representation for symbolic learning strategies. [Blurock 1998] works intensively on the domain representation for machine learning algorithms. Although they are completely independent works, both lead to

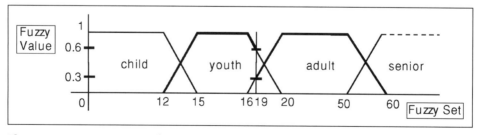

Figure 5.7   Fuzzy set example.

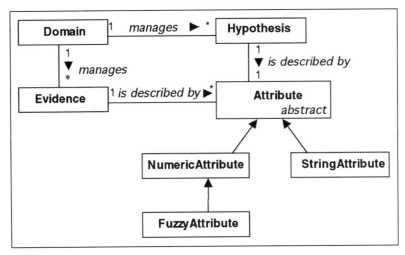

Figure 5.8   Domain representation.

quite similar designs. Figure 5.8 shows the relationship among the classes involved in representing a particular domain.

The training and testing of an ANN are the principal features of Java-ABC. For both tasks, data must be provided. For example, for training an ANN to classify customers, data might come from an ASCII file. One line of that file represents one customer—in other words, the customer's evidences and the correct classification. After training the ANN, customer data should be tested. To do this, Java-ABC gets the evidences of a customer as input data and must classify the customer. The data source might, in this case, be a relational database management system. It should be clear from this scenario that Java-ABC has to provide a flexible data conversion subsystem. We are also considering the integration of Apple's Enterprise Object Framework for converting data in relational databases into Java Classes/Objects. Data conversion must be flexible at runtime, as the user may wish to change the data source anytime during learning or testing. Thus, the Separation pattern is the appropriate construction principle underlying this framework.

Two abstract classes constitute the framework for processing problem-specific data: class Fetcher and class EvidenceFetcher. Class Fetcher is abstractly coupled with the class Domain (see Figure 5.9). A Fetcher object is responsible for the preparation/ searching operations associated with a data source. If the data source is a plain ASCII file, the specific fetcher opens and closes the file. This includes some basic error handling.

Class Evidence and class Hypothesis are abstractly coupled with class Evidence- Fetcher (see Figure 5.10). Specific subclasses of EvidenceFetcher know how to access the data for the particular evidence. For example, an EvidenceFetcher for reading data from an ASCII file stores the position (from column, to column) of the evidence data within one line of the ASCII file. An EvidenceFetcher for reading data from a relational database would know how to access the data by means of SQL statements. Figure 5.10

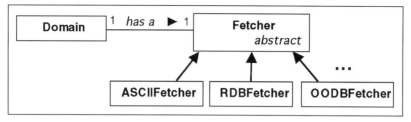

Figure 5.9   Dealing with different data sources.

shows the design of these classes, picking out only class Evidence. The class Hypothesis has an analogous relationship with the class EvidenceFetcher.

Note that the Attribute objects prepare the data from external sources so that they can be directly fed to the input neurons of the ANN (see Figure 5.6). This works in the following way: Each Evidence instance fetches its value from the data source, and this value is applied automatically to all attributes of the evidence. Each attribute applies the conversion function that is inherent to the specific Attribute class. For example, the StringAttribute conversion function receives the string from the database and compares it to a given string modeled by the expert, returning 1 or 0 based on whether the strings match. This numeric value is stored by the attribute object and will be applied in the ANN input by request. The ANN input nodes have a direct relationship with the attributes of the evidence (see Figure 5.6). When the learning or testing is performed, each input node requests from its relative attribute the values previously fetched and converted. The attribute simply returns the converted value.

Visual/interactive tools support the definition of the specific instances of Evidence-Fetcher and Fetcher subclasses. For example, in the case of fetching from ASCII files, the end user of Java-ABC, who does the domain modeling, simply specifies the file name for the ASCIIFetcher object and, for the ASCIIEvidenceFetcher objects, specifies the column positions in a dialog box.

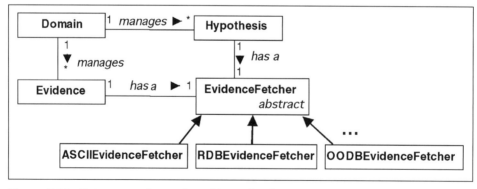

Figure 5.10   Data conversion at the evidence level.

5.4 Summary

This chapter illustrates how the uncompromising application of framework technology leads to decision support systems with appropriate flexibility. The chosen case study corroborates that a sound object-oriented design of neural network components delivers the expected benefits that a conventional solution could not provide. The current design and implementation of Java-ABC is a generic decision-making system based on neural networks. An ambitious goal would be to enhance the framework further, so that other decision support problems, such as forecasting, can be supported. Also ambitious would be to allow the implementation of other learning mechanisms, that do not rely only on neural networks, such as machine learning algorithms.

This framework developed in the Java-ABC project is the basis for the new Hycones implementation that is planned to be a new product for decision support. The framework design gives flexibility and reliability to the system. Its goals are being expanded from a classificatory system with only one learning algorithm to the possibility of implementing many different learning algorithms, such as clustering. Furthermore, some experiments of the technology as a data mining tool have been carried out. The design also allows the framework to easily add other implementation facilities such as parallelization and distribution.

Currently, most excellent frameworks are products of a more or less chaotic development process, often carried out in the realm of research-like settings. In the realm of designing and implementing Java-ABC we found that hot-spot analysis is particularly helpful for coming up with a suitable framework architecture more quickly. An explicit capturing of flexibility requirements can indeed contribute to a more systematic framework development process.

5.5 References

[Blurock 1998] Blurock, Edward S. ANALYSIS++: Object-oriented framework for multi-strategy machine learning methods. *OOPSLA 1998*, www.risc.uni-linz.ac.at/people.

[daRosa 1995] da Rosa, S.I.V., B.F. Leão, and N. Hoppen. Hybrid model for classification expert system. *Proceedings of the XXI Latin American Conference on Computer Science*. Canela, Brazil, 1995.

[daRosa 1997] da Rosa, S.I.V., F.G. Beckenkamp, and N. Hoppen. The application of fuzzy logic to model semantic variables in a hybrid model for classification expert systems. *Proceedings of the Second International ICSC Symposium on Fuzzy Logic and Applications (ISFL 1997)*. Zurich, Switzerland, 1997.

[Fayad 1999] Fayad, M.E., D. Schmidt, and R. Johnson. *Building Application Frameworks: Object-Oriented Foundations of Framework Design,* New York: John Wiley & Sons, 1999.

[Gamma 1995] Gamma, E., R. Helm, R. Johnson, and J. Vlissides. 1995. *Design Patterns: Elements of Reusable Object-Oriented Software*. Reading, MA: Addison-Wesley, 1995.

[Haykin 1994] Haykin, S. *Neural Networks: A Comprehensive Foundation*. Upper Saddle River, NJ: Prentice Hall, 1994.

[Hopfield 1982] Hopfield, J.J. Neural networks and physical systems with emergent collective computational abilities. *Proceedings of the National Academy of Sciences of the U.S.A.* 79: 2554–2558, 1982.

[Kohonen 1982] Kohonen, T. Self-organized formation of topologically correct feature maps. *Biological Cybernetics* 43: 59–69, 1982.

[Kosko 1992] Kosko, B. *Neural Networks and Fuzzy Systems.* Englewood Cliffs, NJ: Prentice Hall, 1992.

[Lawrence 1991] Lawrence, D. *The Handbook of Genetic Algorithms.* New York: Van Nostrand Reinhold, 1991.

[Leão-Reátegui 1993a] Leão, B.F., and E. Reátegui. Hycones: A hybrid connectionist expert system. *Proceedings of the Seventeenth Annual Symposium on Computer Applications in Medical Care—SCAMC.* Los Alamitos, CA: IEEE Computer Society, 1993.

[Leão-Reátegui 1993b] Leão, B.F., and E. Reátegui. A hybrid connectionist expert system to solve classificational problems. *Proceedings of Computers in Cardiology*, London: IEEE Computer Society, 1993.

[Leão-Rocha 1990] Leão, B.F., and A.F. Rocha. Proposed Methodology for Knowledge Acquisition: A Study on Congenital Heart Disease Diagnosis. *Methods of Information in Medicine* 29(1), January 1990:30–40.

[Machado-Rocha 1989] Machado, R.J., and A.F. Rocha. *Handling Knowledge in High Order Neural Networks: The Combinatorial Neural Model.* Technical report CCR076. Rio de Janeiro: IBM Rio Scientific Center, 1989.

[Machado-Rocha 1990] Machado, R.J., and A.F. Rocha. The combinatorial neural network: A connectionist model for knowledge based systems. In *Uncertainty in Knowledge Bases,* B. Bouchon-Meunier, R. R. Yager, and L.A. Zadeh, editors. Springer-Verlag, 1990.

[Medsker-Bailey 1992] Medsker, L.R., and D.L. Bailey. Models and guidelines for integrating expert systems and neural networks. In *Hybrid Architectures for Intelligent Systems*, A. Kandel and G. Langholz, editors. CRC Press, 1992.

[Pree 1995] Pree, W. *Design Patterns for Object-Oriented Software Development.* Reading, MA: Addison-Wesley/ACM Press, 1995.

[Pree 1997] Pree, W. *Komponentenbasierte Softwareentwicklung mit Frameworks.* Heidelberg, Germany: dpunkt, 1997 (German translation of: Pree, W. *Framework Patterns.* New York: SIGS Books, 1997).

[Reátegui-Campbell 1994] Reátegui, E., and J. Campbell. A classification system for credit card transactions. *Advances in Case-Based Reasoning. Second European Workshop EWCBR-94.* Chantilly, France, November 1994. J.P. Haton, M. Keane, M. Manago, editors. Springer-Verlag, 1994.

[Rumelhart-McClelland 1986] Rumelhart, D.E., and J.L. McClelland. *Parallel Distributed Processing: Explorations in the Microstructure of Cognition*, vol. 1. Cambridge, MA: MIT Press, 1986.

A Framework
for Agent Systems

Agents appear in a wide range of applications, including personalized user interfaces, electronic commerce, enterprise integration, manufacturing, and business process support [Bradshaw 1997; BTRL 1997; Jennings 1996; Nwana 1998; Tenenbaum 1992]. However, agent development to date has primarily been homegrown [Bradshaw 1997] and done from scratch, independently, by each development team. This has led to the following problems [Bradshaw 1997]:

Lack of an agreed definition. Agents built by different teams have different capabilities.

Duplication of effort. There has been little reuse of agent architectures, designs, or components. Agent systems to date have primarily been point solutions [Nwana 1997, 1998] rather than general techniques.

Inability to satisfy industrial-strength requirements. Agents must integrate with existing software and computer infrastructure. They must also address security and scaling concerns.

Incompatibility. Standardization efforts have begun [Dickinson 1997], but they are still in process.

This chapter describes the product of several years of research, development, and implementation in agent systems that have been carried out at RMIT [Kendall 1997a, 1997b, 1997c]. The effort has concentrated on producing methodology, tools, and techniques for developing robust and maintainable agent systems. The approach has centered on extending techniques from object-oriented software engineering, especially design and analysis patterns, to agent-based systems. The framework discussed here presents the results in agent design and implementation. It is known as JAFIMA, for Java Framework for Intelligent and Mobile Agents.

JAFIMA is an application or horizontal framework [Rogers 1997]. An agent is a general-purpose software module, and this framework captures expertise that is applicable to many diverse client domains. Agents are a new abstraction, and the framework is still evolving. This means that it will be significantly modified and used in many unforeseen ways; as such, this chapter provides documentation regarding the framework's design via patterns [Johnson 1992]. Additionally, due to these challenges, this framework is architecture-driven rather than data-driven [Rogers 1997], and clients must customize the classes and behavior for their problem domain.

The framework is the result of a research and academic activity, rather than a commercial endeavor. It has been utilized on research projects on agent-based systems, in network management and agent-based intrusion detection and prevention. A fairly substantial amount of effort is required by the user. Other agent frameworks are commercial [Bradshaw 1991; Ingrand 1992; Nwana 1998; Walsh 1998]; however, the framework discussed here is distinct from them in the following ways:

This framework is more comprehensive, with the exception of KAoS [Bradshaw 1997], and addresses all aspects of agency. Whereas this is not necessary for every application, an agent architecture and design should be flexible enough to address the various kinds of agents found today, such as weak, strong, collaborative, and mobile agents [Nwana 1997].

This framework is the only agent framework that has been designed and documented with patterns. This facilitates future extension and documents the design's motivation.

In contrast to other agent frameworks, this framework emphasizes integration issues. The view is that agent-based solutions must easily integrate to other system software.

The RMIT agent framework addresses these four issues, which have plagued agent-based systems to date. It accomplishes this by capturing and documenting the following, which represent the contributions of the work:

- JAFIMA provides a detailed definition of an agent that is flexible enough to encompass simple and sophisticated agents and agent societies.

- This chapter presents the primary design issues, invariants, and abstractions of agent-based systems that were uncovered during the analysis and design of JAFIMA. As a result, recurring design patterns are uncovered and brought together.

- JAFIMA comprises a layered architecture, subframeworks for each layer, design patterns, and Java code. Thus, during an implementation of an agent-based system, a software developer can use, extend, or customize the framework with respect to a specific application. This reuses the associated architecture, design, and code.

This chapter has the following outline. *Section 6.1* presents the application area of agent systems. *Section 6.2* describes the underlying architecture for the framework. *Section 6.3* through *Section 6.6* describe the design of the subframeworks found internal to the individual layers. The subframework detailed in *Section 6.7* deals with infrastructure for integrating the layers. In *Section 6.2* through *Section 6.7*, each subframework is documented in terms of its key abstractions and design patterns. For brevity, well-known patterns are not described in detail. *Section 6.8* illustrates how the framework can be employed in a sample application via Java code; it also provides a set of interaction diagrams. *Section 6.9* compares JAFIMA to other agent frameworks.

6.1 Agent-Based Systems

Agent definitions, agent applications, and agent behaviors are discussed in the following sections.

6.1.1 Definitions and Applications

A weak agent is autonomous, social, reactive, and proactive, and a strong agent, in addition to these features, is knowledge-based and can adapt or learn [Wooldridge 1995]. An agent can migrate, and a multiagent system is open because agents can enter and depart the system at any point. It is the combination of autonomous, social, reactive, and proactive behavior that distinguishes an agent from objects, actors [Agha 1986], and robots. Agents are the next significant software abstraction, especially for distributed systems. The following two examples illustrate the kinds of problems that agents will address [Wooldridge 1995].

> **The air traffic control systems in the country of ABC suddenly fail, due to weather.** Fortunately, agent-based air traffic control systems in neighboring countries negotiate between themselves to deal with affected flights, and the potentially disastrous situation passes without incident.

> **Upon logging into your computer, you are presented with a list of newsgroup items, sorted into order of importance by your agent-based personal digital assistant (PDA).** The assistant draws your attention to one article about new work in your area. After discussion with other PDAs, yours obtains a technical report for you from an FTP site. When a paper you have submitted to an important conference is accepted, your PDA makes travel arrangements for you.

Although these applications might seem farfetched, two agent-based systems in existence today are major steps toward making them reality. The OASIS (Optimal Aircraft Sequencing with Intelligent Scheduling) system [AAII 1998] built by the Australian Artificial Intelligence Institute is a prototype agent-based system for air traffic control. It has been commercialized to the HORIZON system and demonstrated at the airport in Sydney, Australia. The RADAR personal agent [BTRL] proactively seeks documents that it believes a user will find to be of interest from databases and libraries worldwide. RADAR operates while a user is authoring a paper, using keywords entered in the document and its acquired model of the user's preferences.

6.1.2 Model of Agent Behavior

The RMIT agent framework is based on the following model of agent behavior [Ingrand 1992; Kendall 1997a, 1997b, 1997c]. Strong agents use knowledge-based techniques to select a capability that could achieve their stated goal(s). A plan from the capabilities library is instantiated when a triggering event occurs, and an instantiated plan is an intention. An intention executes in its own thread, and an agent may have several intentions executing concurrently. Agents negotiate with each other in conversations or protocols [Barbuceanu-Fox 1995] and agent societies may have centralized or decentralized management. Strong agent collaboration across disciplines often requires the use of ontologies [Tenenbaum 1992] to exchange cross-disciplinary semantics.

These aspects of agent behavior are summarized in Figure 6.1. Agents have sensors that update their model of the outside world or environment. Agents review their models and those of themselves to select a capability or plan to address the present situation. In a strong or knowledge-based agent, this selection requires artificial intelligence; in a weak agent, it is a direct response to a stimulus. Once invoked, each plan executes in its own thread, and several of these may execute concurrently. Agents negotiate with each other; agent collaboration across disciplines may require that semantics can be translated or exchanged.

In an air traffic control application, each agent would have plans for managing a runway or for bringing a plane in safely. There would be many plans, addressing weather conditions and emergency situations, and other possibilities. The agents' models of the outside world would reflect the status of the planes and the runways,

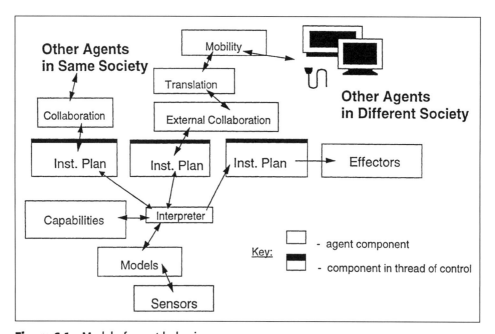

Figure 6.1 Model of agent behavior.

and sensors would be used to update the models with respect to plane positions and speeds, and weather conditions. The agents would select a plan on the basis of the present situation. They would negotiate with each other for landing times, and their effectors would provide landing instructions and send messages directly to plane navigation systems.

Three sample capabilities that have been selected and instantiated into plans are shown in Figure 6.1. One involves an effector that impacts objects in the outside world; the other two feature collaboration with other agents. One case of collaboration involves another agent within the original society; the other involves an agent in a different society on another computer platform. Because the agents are in different societies that are separated physically, one of them must become mobile and migrate, either virtually or in reality, in order for them to collaborate. This illustrates the openness of agent societies; mobile agents can come and go as needed.

6.2 The Layered Agent Architectural Pattern

The Layered Agent Architectural pattern addresses both simple and sophisticated agents and is discussed in the following section.

6.2.1 Intent

How can agent behavior be best organized and structured into software? What software architecture best supports the behavior of agents? The Layered Agent Architectural pattern [Kendall 1997a] supports all aspects of agent behavior but is flexible enough to address simple and sophisticated agent systems.

6.2.2 Motivation

An agent system is complex; it also spans several levels of abstraction. There are many dependencies between neighboring levels. All of the interactions feature two-way information flow. The software architecture must encompass autonomous, social, reactive, and proactive behavior. Agents also interact with their environment, through sensors and effectors. These sense changes in external objects and send messages back to them to effect changes. The architecture must be flexible enough to address agent mobility, translations between agent ontologies, virtual and actual migration, and different approaches to collaboration.

6.2.3 Solution

Agents should be decomposed into layers [Brooks 1986; Buschmann 1996] because (1) higher-level behavior depends on lower-level capabilities, (2) levels only depend on their neighbors, and (3) there is two-way information flow between neighboring levels. The layers can be identified from the model of the agent's real world. Figure 6.2 structures Figure 6.1 into seven layers as follows:

Sensory. The agent gathers sensory input from its environment.

Beliefs. The agent models itself and its environment.

Reasoning. The agent determines what to do next, based on its goals, plans, capabilities, and models. The plans may generically specify requests for services or responses to requests.

Action. The agent's intentions (instantiated plans from the reasoning layer) are carried out. Pending actions for the agent are queued, and these are derived from incoming requests.

Collaboration. The agent determines how to collaborate with another agent. This includes accepting or rejecting an incoming request for services.

Translation. The agent formulates a message for another agent, translating it into another language or semantics (ontology), if necessary.

Mobility. When collaborating agents are in different locations, this layer is required for messaging.

In Figure 6.2, top-down information flow is shown on the left side, while bottom-up is on the right. In bottom-up transactions (following the arrows in the figure along the right side), an agent's beliefs are based on sensory input. When presented with a problem, an agent reasons about its beliefs to determine what to do. When the agent decides on an action, it can carry it out directly if it is within its capabilities, but an action that involves other agents requires the Collaboration layer. Within this layer, the agent decides how to negotiate with another agent. Once the approach to col-

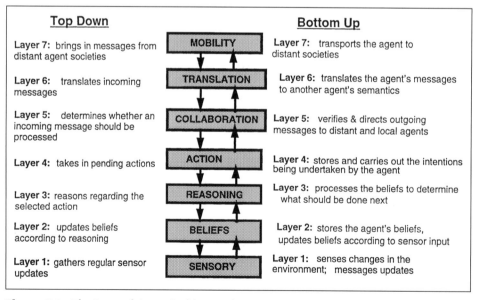

Figure 6.2 The Layered Agent Architectural pattern.

laboration is determined, the actual message is formulated at the Translation layer if the collaborating agents have different semantics. Messages to distant societies are delivered by the Mobility layer; the Mobility layer may also accomplish actual migration.

Top-down (following the arrows on the left side of the figure), distant messages arrive at Mobility. An incoming message is translated into the agent's semantics. The Collaboration layer stores contacts and conversations, and determines whether the agent should process a message. If the message should be processed, it is passed to the Action layer. When the action is dequeued for processing, it is passed to the Reasoning layer. Depending on the type of request, processing may continue to the Beliefs and Sensory layers. Once a plan is instantiated as an intention and placed in the Action layer, it does not require the services of any lower layers. An intention calls on higher layers when it needs to involve other agents in its tasks.

6.2.4 Variations

The Layered Agent Architectural pattern addresses simple and sophisticated agents. A weak agent has a simple Reasoning layer (see *Section 6.3.3*), while a strong agent can have advanced expertise. Collaboration may be centralized or decentralized (see *Section 6.5*).

All agents do not have the seven layers shown in Figure 6.2. A Translation layer is needed only for multidisciplinary agent societies, which are presently rare. A static agent isn't mobile, so layer 7 is not needed. Many agent societies have one Collaboration layer for agents to share. Mobility and Collaboration layers may be combined if an agent society is dispersed over several platforms and no agents are actually located together. This is often the case for a personal agent that travels the Internet; it is alone on its platform, and it only collaborates with agents on other platforms. If an agent's beliefs about the environment or external objects do not change, the Sensory layer is not needed.

Further, aspects of the Layered Agent pattern may be conceptual rather than architectural if, due to performance issues, direct connections between nonadjacent layers are required. For example, Reasoning and Collaboration may be directly linked if the agent's dominant activity is to service fairly simple requests from other agents and no multithreading is required.

6.3 Sensory, Beliefs, and Reasoning Layers

Section 6.3 through *Section 6.6* summarize key aspects of each of the layers. Key abstractions are discussed first. Design problems and solutions are then provided as recurring design patterns. Additional details are provided in *Section 6.7* and *Section 6.8*, which address integration and a sample application. A sequence of interaction diagrams (Figures 6.23 through 6.28) appears in *Section 6.8.3*; these figures are also noted in the relevant text in *Section 6.3* through *Section 6.6*.

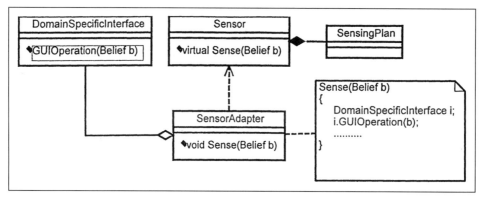

Figure 6.3   Use of the Adapter pattern in the Sensory layer.

6.3.1 Sensory Layer

The Sensory layer of an agent is responsible for sensing the environment and updating the beliefs; the key abstraction of the subframework is a Sensor that needs to cooperate with domain-specific interface classes. The design of the Sensory layer uses the Adapter pattern [Gamma 1995], shown in Figure 6.3. The subframework supplies the abstract Sensor's interface (the method Sense()), while the application developer or user of the framework provides the domain-specific Sensor Adapter. The Sensory layer has a list of external objects that need to be sensed; these are stored in the Sensing Plan. The Sensing Plan may be just a collection of the sensors and their relevant messages, or it may suggest alternatives and address data or sensory fusion. For additional details, refer to the interaction diagram in Figure 6.23.

6.3.2 Beliefs Layer

The Beliefs layer has a Beliefs Repository that stores several beliefs. These beliefs can be primitive or composite. The composite beliefs are composed of several primitive beliefs. Thus, when any of the primitive beliefs changes, the associated composite beliefs have to be notified. This design uses two patterns: Composite and Observer [Gamma 1995]. Also Figure 6.4 shows that the Reasoning layer is also an observer of the beliefs. When a belief changes, an interpret cycle in the Reasoning layer is needed, as discussed in the next section. For additional details, refer to the interaction diagrams in Figures 6.24 and 6.25.

6.3.3 Reasoning Layer

The Reasoning layer determines what the agent should do next. For strong and weak agents, Reasoning interprets beliefs and requests to determine an appropriate reaction. In a strong agent, the Reasoning layer encompasses mentalistic notions to emulate

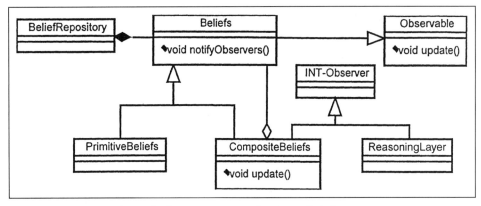

Figure 6.4   Composite and Observer patterns for the Beliefs layer.

human intelligence, whereas in a weak agent it matches an action to a stimulus. Reasoning defines objects for the grammar used to define stimuli, conditions, goals, and actions, and these are abstracted as Expressions and Plans.

The Interpreter and Strategy patterns [Gamma 1995] are employed as shown in Figure 6.5. An agent's plans are represented in expressions and interpreted using the Interpreter pattern. In Figure 6.5, RegularExpression is a general clause, LogicalExpression involves a logical operator, and BeliefExpression is a terminating symbol. In Reasoning, the Strategy pattern is employed, so each plan is an object.

The Reasoning layer in this framework is relevant for weak agents and for strong agents with about 10 capabilities or plans. We believe that this is appropriate for the distributed nature of agent-based systems; in a truly distributed system, no single agent should have more than 10 plans. If more sophisticated reasoning, such as goal-based backward chaining [Ingrand 1992; Nwana 1998] or scheduling and resource allocation [Nwana 1998] is required, a more advanced Reasoning layer needs to be utilized.

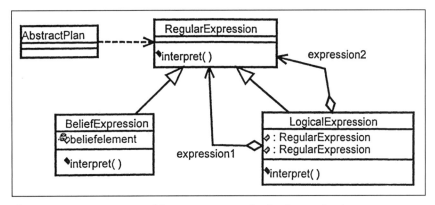

Figure 6.5   Interpreter and Strategy patterns in the Reasoning layer.

6.4 The Action Layer Subframework

An overview of the Action layer subframework and its key abstractions are discussed in *Section 6.4.1* through *Section 6.4.7*.

6.4.1 Overview and Key Abstractions

The Action layer is responsible for carrying out the plan selected by the Reasoning layer. A plan is instantiated in a separate thread called an Intention. There will be many different kinds of plans, and they will be application-specific. However, the framework divides them into two categories: Collaboration Intentions that utilize an interface to the Collaboration layer known as Collaborators, and Reaction Intentions that use an environment-specific interface known as the Effectors. An agent may have many options for what to do next; there is a need to provide a Scheduler and a Prioritizer for scheduling and prioritizing actions.

The Action layer subframework consists of the following patterns:

Command. Used to make a plan into a command [Gamma 1995].

Abstract Factory. Creates a plan object based on a given class library [Gamma 1995].

Factory Method. Creates intention thread objects dynamically [Gamma 1995].

Decorator. Implements the Prioritizer [Gamma 1995].

Future [Kafura 1998], with Observer [Gamma 1995]. Accomplishes asynchronous method invocation by an intention thread.

Active Object. Schedules actions that affect the environment and also forwards messages (or requests) from the Collaboration layer to Reasoning [Lavender 1995].

6.4.2 Command Pattern

In this section, the Command pattern is explained.

Motivation

Plans are central to the Action layer; they must be queued and logged, and they must be able to be undone. A plan specifies primitive actions that are to be taken, where a primitive action is an operation that can be executed directly by the effectors or collaborators. Each intention has a plan to execute. Plans are known only at the runtime; this framework can't explicitly implement plans. There is a need to define a structure for plans that provides high-level operations based on primitive ones.

Solution

The Command pattern [Gamma 1995] encapsulates a request as an object, and it is employed in the Action layer, as shown in Figure 6.6. Each ConcretePlan is a command object that implements the ActionPlan interface that declares the high-level operation

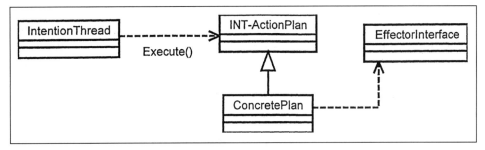

Figure 6.6 Use of the Command pattern in the Action layer.

Execute( ). The receiver of this message is a ConcretePlan object that is instantiated at runtime based on the configuration information provided by the user. Each Concrete Plan will use primitive methods of EffectorInterface in their Execute method.

6.4.3 Abstract Factory

In this section, the Abstract Factory pattern is explained.

Motivation

A plan is instantiated for every new intention. Plans will be highly variable and application specific. The framework is concerned with providing an abstract interface that each concrete plan can implement; it is not concerned with implementation. Each application developer will provide a collection of plan classes where each separate class implements the ActionPlan interface. Therefore, there is a need for a creational framework for instantiating plans that reveals their command interfaces but not their implementations.

Solution

The Abstract Factory pattern [Gamma 1995] is used to solve the problem. In Figure 6.7, the PlanFactory is the abstract factory; it declares the interface to instantiate the

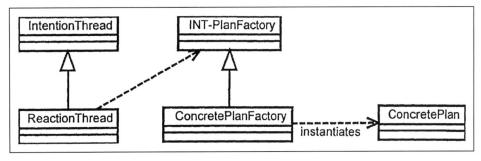

Figure 6.7 The Abstract Factory instantiates concrete plans.

ConcretePlans. The ConcretePlanFactory provides the required implementation. This plan object is then used by the IntentionThread. The user of the framework (the application developer) can determine how the Concrete Plan Factory instantiates the plans.

6.4.4 Factory Method Pattern

The Factory Method pattern is employed to delegate the responsibility of instantiating intention objects to the respective subclasses. Thus, depending on the ActionPlan type, ReactionIntention or CollaborationIntention subclasses will be instantiated.

6.4.5 Decorator Pattern

In this section, the Decorator pattern is explained.

Motivation

In an agent-based system the intention threads may share some resources, such as effectors. Thus, there is a need to prioritize the intentions. There will be several different kinds or levels of prioritization. Further, once an agent intends (or begins to execute) a plan, it can't be stopped. Thus, priority handling should be done before the execution of the action plan.

The IntentionThread is executed by calling its run( ) method, which implements Java's Runnable interface. A ConcretePlan is executed in this run( ) method, as discussed in *Section 6.4.2* and *Section 6.4.3*.

Solution

Priority handling is done by instances of the ConcretePrioritizer class (see Figure 6.8), and the Decorator pattern is employed to attach additional responsibilities to an intention object dynamically. This is a flexible alternative to subclassing for extending functionality [Gamma 1995].

Each ConcretePrioritizer class can provide different priority-handling strategies. The ConcretePrioritizer calls its superclass's run method, and it adds the priority-handling functionality before or after this function call. Priority handling can be changed at runtime with the dynamic class loading provided in Java so that different ConcretePrioritizers can be loaded and instantiated.

6.4.6 The Future and Observer Patterns

In this section, the Future and Observer patterns are explained.

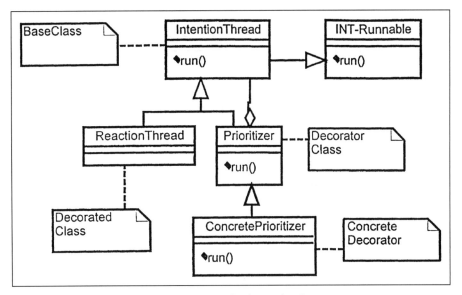

Figure 6.8 Use of the Decorator pattern in the Action layer.

Intent

The Future object provides a placeholder for a result that is expected in the future [Kendall 1997a].

Motivation

In Java, actions running in threads can not return results directly, because Runnable .run() has a void return type. However, in an agent two separate threads, one of the intention and another of a concurrent server, have to be able to communicate asynchronously when a result is returned from the server thread. There is a need to identify a mechanism for supporting asynchronous communication at the completion of a thread, and this mechanism must simulate returning a value.

Solution

In the Future pattern [Kafura 1998] (see Figure 6.9), an instance of Future is used as a placeholder for a future value. The Client will execute an asynchronous operation, DoOperation(), which instantiates a Future object and returns its reference. The Client will message the Future object's read(), which will block thread execution if the Future is not in its updated state. Later on, the concurrently executing CoexistingServer updates the state of the Future object.

The Observer pattern [Gamma 1995] is also used, so that each Future object is an Observable or a Subject for the corresponding Observer Clients that register themselves with the related Futures. When a Future is updated by the CoexistingServer, it notifies these observers. This notification will execute the update method of the Client, and the blocked (or suspended) Client thread is resumed in this method.

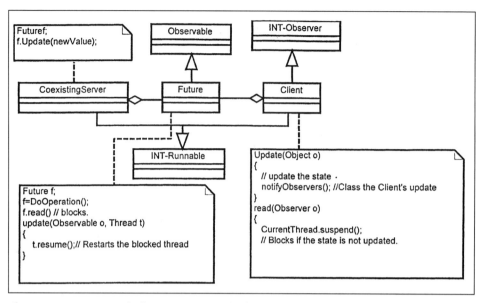

Figure 6.9   Future and Observer patterns in the Action layer.

6.4.7 Active Object Pattern

In this section, the Active Object pattern is explained.

Intent

The Active Object pattern decouples method execution from method invocation in order to simplify synchronized access to a shared resource [Lavender 1995].

Motivation

Agent intentions act concurrently in different threads of control. However, an object in the environment may need to be affected or impacted by the agent in a sequential manner. For example, an external object may not be multithreaded. Therefore, intentions may invoke the methods to affect the environment concurrently, but the execution of these methods may actually need to be done sequentially. Thus, a mechanism for queuing and dispatching is required to convert from concurrent to sequential flow.

Effectors will be application specific; there will be many different kinds of effectors, and this framework can provide only an interface for them.

Solution

The Active Object pattern [Lavender 1995] fulfills the design requirements. It encapsulates a method call into a method object and places it in a queue. It then dequeues and dispatches the method object on a priority basis. This dispatching is done in a separate thread, hence the name *Active Object*.

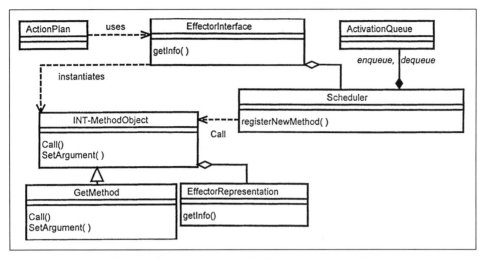

Figure 6.10   Use of the Active Object pattern in the Action layer subframework.

The Active Object pattern is comprised of a client interface, scheduler, queue, method object, and a resource representation. The client uses the interface to pass in messages that it wants to be received by the resource representation. Messages are encapsulated into method objects, prioritized by the scheduler, and placed in a queue. The scheduler then is responsible for dequeuing or dispatching the method objects to the resource representation, according to their priority.

The classes involved in this utilization of the pattern are shown in Figure 6.10. The EffectorInterface forms the client interface, and an ActionPlan uses or sends messages to this interface when it needs to affect the environment. The interface declares several methods; however, all of these methods are stubs. The actual functionality is provided in the EffectorRepresentation.

Scheduler and ActivationQueue classes provide enqueuing and dispatching behavior. The MethodObject declares a Call( ) method, which encapsulates a method call to EffectorRepresentation. Also, each MethodObject has sufficient state information for the method execution.

The stub methods in the EffectorInterface instantiate a MethodObject and enqueue it into the ActivationQueue using the Scheduler. The dispatcher thread of the Scheduler dequeues the MethodObject and executes the Call( ) method. The Call( ) method, in turn, messages the EffectorRepresentation. The interaction diagram shown later in this Chapter (see Figure 6.26). provides further detail regarding this utilization of the Active Object pattern.

6.5 Collaboration Layer Subframework

The Collaboration layer is responsible for carrying out negotiations and the exchange of services between agents. It determines how to collaborate, and it addresses different coordination protocols. The collaboration layer handles sending, accepting, and rejecting requests, along with replying.

Section 6.5.1 discusses a centralized design; the decentralized approach follows in *Section 6.5.2. Sections 6.5.3 to 6.5.5* discuss specific instances of the decentralized approach.

6.5.1 Centralized Collaboration: The Mediator Pattern

Centralized collaboration is the responsibility of a Mediator or Facilitator [Gamma 1995]. In a given agent society, each agent may not have knowledge of every other agent. Proliferating interconnections and dependencies increase complexity, complicate maintenance, and reduce reusability. With a Mediator, agents do not have to have direct knowledge of one another for collaboration.

6.5.2 Decentralized Collaboration

In decentralized collaboration, agents deal directly with one another. They must retain knowledge of each other's capabilities, and they must communicate via structured messages that are known agent protocols. The agents must also maintain the state of each conversation or negotiation to avoid endless loops. Decentralized collaboration is more complicated than centralized collaboration, and the subframework is still under development; this section describes the present state of the design. Key abstractions are discussed in this section, along with recurring design patterns.

During decentralized collaboration, the role of an individual agent changes; it can be a client or a server. For example, when agent A passes a request to agent B, agent A is a client and agent B is a server. But if the information provided by A is not sufficient, B makes a counterrequest for extra information, making B the client and A the server. Each negotiation session needs to be uniquely identifiable. An agent always sends a message in the protocol of the receiving agent, and messages are converted before being sent. Because the Collaboration layer communicates with more than one agent concurrently, this layer is multithreaded. The many activities of the Collaboration layer are managed by the CollaborationInterface, including message delivery and reception, which are addressed by Connectors and Acceptors, respectively.

The Collaboration layer subframework consists of the following patterns.

Synchronized Singleton. Used to manage the collaboration threads so there is a centralized point of access.

Decorator. Changes the behavior of the thread dynamically so that it can either send or receive messages [Gamma 1995].

Active Object. Used to schedule the requests forwarded by the Action layer to the Collaboration layer [Lavender 1995].

Future. Used in combination with Observer for asynchronous method invocation [Kafura 1998].

Strategy. Used to convert a message into the corresponding language of the destination agent [Gamma 1995].

6.5.3 Synchronized Singleton Pattern

In this section, the Synchronized Singleton pattern is explained.

Motivation

There is a group of threads in the Collaboration layer, and a single access point is necessary for a thread to be able to process a message. Moreover, the state of each thread should be maintained. All these tasks should be done by a single object; moreover, another object of this type should not be able to be instantiated.

Solution

The Synchronized Singleton pattern, a variation on the Singleton pattern [Gamma 1995], is used in this framework to solve this problem.

In sequential programming this can be achieved by making a ThreadPool object a Singleton. But in concurrent programming the Singleton pattern does not work, because if multiple threads executing simultaneously try to instantiate the Singleton, two objects of the same type are created. Double-Checked Locking [Schmidt 1996] can be used to solve this problem. However, in Java, this can be achieved by wrapping the constructor of the Singleton [Gamma 1995] in a synchronized method. This is shown in Figure 6.11.

6.5.4 Decorator Pattern

In this section, the Decorator pattern is explained (also see *Section 6.4.5*).

Motivation

There is a need to provide specialized kinds of threads for sending and receiving messages, such as connectors and acceptors. However, there is only a limited number of threads overall, and you don't want to run the risk of not being able to provide the desired behavior.

The Collaboration layer needs a thread every time it sends or receives a message. This can be done with dedicated thread objects, such as acceptor and connector threads. The other way to achieve the required behavior is to reuse the primitive thread

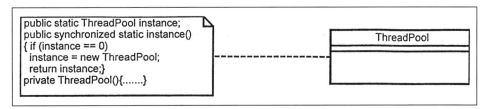

Figure 6.11   The Synchronized Singleton pattern.

class by delegation, and this approach is more efficient. But this means that there is a possibility that all sending (or receiving) threads will be busy when one is needed. In this case, there could be an idle acceptor (or connector) thread, but it couldn't be used because it couldn't perform the desired behavior. This would decrease the performance of the agent. The Strategy pattern [Gamma 1995] can be used, but behavior should be added dynamically rather than through specialization.

Solution

Use of the Decorator pattern is shown in the Figure 6.12. As in *Section 6.4.5,* the Decorator pattern is used to attach additional responsibilities to an object dynamically.

The abstract Command class is refined by two concrete command classes: AcceptorCommand and ConnectorCommand. There is also a decorator subclass, CommandDecorator. AcceptorCommand processes a message received by the agent in its execute( ) method. Similarly, ConnectorCommand sends a message to other agents in its execute( ) method. As shown in Figure 6.12, a CommandDecorator contains instances of the superclass; this can be used to place a connector or an acceptor inside it.

The execute( ) method of CommandDecorator wraps the execute method of the Command class. This means that the CommandDecorator object's execute( ) method calls the execute( ) method of whatever Command object is contained in it.

ConcCommandDecorator is a concrete subclass of CommandDecorator. The user of the framework can add new behavior to the thread, such as an authentication algorithm, by defining a new concrete decorator. CollabThread instantiates a ConcCommandDecorator and passes a Command object (for example, an AcceptorCommand object or a ConnectorCommand object as per the requirement).

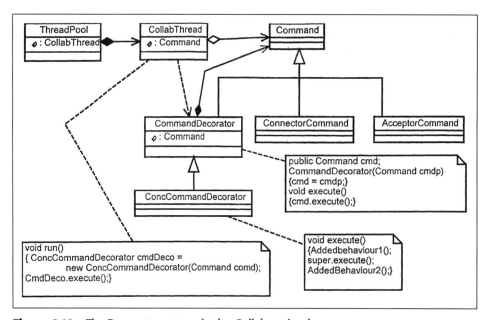

Figure 6.12   The Decorator pattern in the Collaboration layer.

Interaction diagrams for sending and receiving collaboration messages are provided later in this chapter (see Figure 6.28).

6.5.5 The Collaboration Interface

The many activities of the Collaboration layer are managed by the CollaborationInterface. This involves receiving, queuing, dispatching, and forwarding messages, in addition to ascertaining whether an incoming message is part of a conversation that the agent has already been involved in. Agents need to be able to send and receive messages in multiple agent dialects or protocols, such as KQML, COOL [Barbuceanu-Fox 1995], and ACL.

6.5.6 Active Object with Future

In this section, the Active Object with future pattern is explained (also see *Sections 6.4.6* and *6.4.7*).

Motivation

There may be many intention threads in the Action layer forwarding messages to the Collaboration layer concurrently. However, the CollaborationInterface may need to receive the messages from the Action layer in a sequential manner. Therefore, the CollaborationInterface's method to forward the messages may be called or invoked concurrently, but the execution of those methods may actually need to be done sequentially. Thus, a mechanism of queuing and dispatching is required to convert from concurrent to sequential flow.

Also, an outgoing message can be a request to start a new conversation, or a reply to a conversation that has already been started with another agent. In either situation, the intention thread will need to wait for the reply or acknowledgment from the other agent. Because the required time to wait is variable, the intention thread needs a placeholder for an incoming message.

Solution

The Active Object pattern can be used to address the synchronization and concurrency issues. The Future pattern is added in this context to solve the problem caused by the need to wait for a reply or an acknowledgment. For the CollaborationInterface, the interface of Active Object has been modified to return a Future object for each intention thread when a method is invoked and a return is expected. The FutureMesg acts as a placeholder for the message the intention thread is expecting.

As shown in Figure 6.13, the CollabInterface provides the required interface for the intention threads of the Action layer. The invocation of a CollabInterface object method by the intention thread triggers a corresponding method in the CollabScheduler. This method triggers the construction of a Message object and also a FutureMesg object. The Message object is enqueued on the ActivVector by the CollabScheduler and the FutureMesg object is returned to the intention thread in the Action layer. There is an

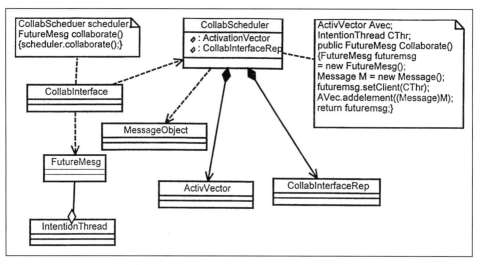

Figure 6.13 Design of the Collaboration interface.

observer-observable relationship between the FutureMesg object and the intention thread.

When the FutureMesg gets updated, it notifies the corresponding intention thread that it needs to take the message. The CollabScheduler creates and contains the CollabInterfaceRep and the ActivVector; this is done at configuration time. When the CollabInterfaceRep is available, the CollabScheduler removes a Message object from the queue and dispatches it to the CollabInterfaceRep. CollabInterfaceRep is the actual object to which the intention threads have directed their messages. The use of the Active Object pattern with Future is shown in Figure 6.13.

The Collaboration Interface Representation

The behavior of the CollabInterfaceRep is as follows:

1. Check the sessionID, to determine if it is a new session or an existing session.

2. Delegate the message to NewReqHandler or ReplyAckHandler, accordingly.

3. Obtain the destination agent's ID from the information repository.

4. Compose a new sessionID if it is a new session.

5. Compose the message in the correct protocol.

6. Forward this message to a MessageHolder.

When a message arrives or is ready to be sent, the ThreadPool may not have an idle thread for message handling. In this situation, there is a chance that the other agent's connection or the message to be sent is lost. Therefore, it is necessary to hold the message in a separate thread until an idle CollabThread is available. A MessageHolder is used for this purpose.

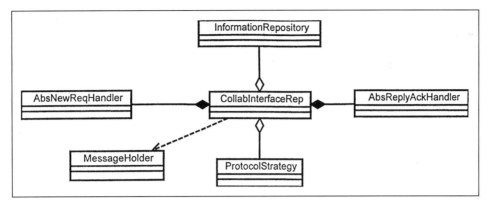

Figure 6.14 Design of the Collaboration interface representation.

The CollabInterfaceRep of the active object in Figure 6.13 has to carry out several activities before forwarding the message to MessageHolder. These include passing the message to NewReqHandler or ReplyAckHandler (concrete classes of AbsNew-ReqHandler and AbsReplyAckHandler in Figure 6.14). The NewReqHandler determines which agent can service the request, and it also creates a sessionID. If the message already has a sessionID, ReplyAckHandler uses the decomposer to obtain the destination agent's ID. After NewReqHandler or ReplyAckHandler performs its tasks, CollabInterfaceRep uses the InformationRepository to find the protocol of the other agent and then converts the message appropriately. The CollabInterfaceRep creates a MessageHolder and forwards the futureID, sessionID, and message to the Message-Holder. The objects involved in these steps are depicted in Figure 6.14.

Additional objects are required to accept a message from a peer agent, forward a message to the Action layer, and actually send a message to another agent. These are shown in Figure 6.15.

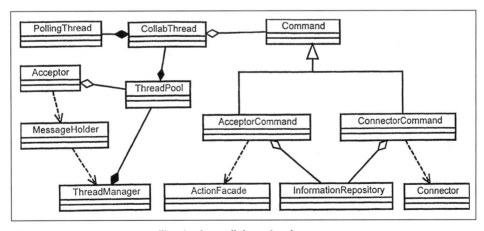

Figure 6.15 Message Handling in the Collaboration layer.

The Acceptor object consists of a listening port which is in an infinite loop waiting for the request for connection. Whenever there is a request for connection from the peer agent, the Acceptor object forwards the request to the MessageHolder object and waits for the next available connection. The MessageHolder object, which runs in its own thread of control, requests a thread from the ThreadManager to handle the request from the peer agent.

When an AcceptorCommand receives a message from another agent, it checks for the sessionID. If one is present, the SIdFuture hashtable is checked so the message can be placed in the corresponding Future. If there is no sessionID, the Acceptor inserts one, and then forwards it to the Action layer.

When the CollaborationInterface forwards a message to a ConnectorCommand object, it inserts a new sessionID into the SIdFuture hashtable before sending the message to the destination agent. The ConnectorCommand object uses the Information-Repository to find the public port of the destination agent in order to send the message to the other agent.

Some interaction diagrams later in this chapter (see Figures 6.27 and 6.28) provide additional information about the behavior of the Collaboration layer.

6.6 The Mobility Layer Subframework

An overview of the Mobility layer sub-framework and its key abstractions are discussed in *Sections 6.6.1* to *6.6.5*.

6.6.1 Overview and Key Abstractions

The Mobility layer is shared by several agents and agent societies. It supports virtual migration by providing location transparency between collaborating agents that may be on different platforms. It supports actual migration by providing a framework for cloning an agent in another environment. If agent A has to migrate physically from society 1 to society 2, then a clone of agent A is generated in society 2, and the cloned agent has sensors and effectors that are compatible with the new environment.

Figure 6.16 shows the architecture of the centralized Mobility layer. This design is based on the Broker pattern [Buschmann 1996]. The Mobility layer consists of a shared region and a region that belongs to an individual agent. It is made up of the following key abstractions:

The Client Proxy. Marshals the service request messages. It also acts as a class loader and as a proxy server to the lower layers, providing location transparency for virtual migration.

The Remote Configurator. Supports actual migration by cloning an agent dynamically at runtime in a way that may be specific to a given destination.

The Broker. The central object for agent mobility. Each agent, Client Proxy, and Remote Configurator object is registered by the Broker. The Broker also provides the bus through which interagent transactions are done.

The Information Repository. Stores information about the registered objects.

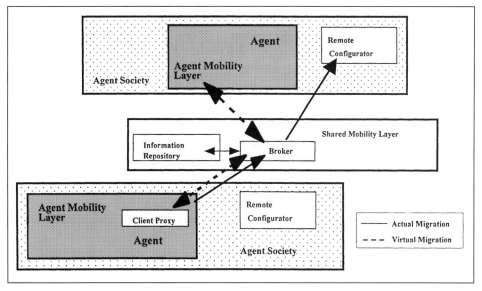

Figure 6.16   Architecture of the Mobility layer.

The design of the Mobility layer is based on the following design patterns:

The Factory Method pattern. Allows virtual and actual migration handlers to be instantiated as needed at runtime [Gamma 1995].

The Active Object pattern. Addresses access to shared resources, such as the InformationRepository [Lavender 1995].

The Visitor pattern. Used for remote configuration [Gamma 1995].

The Proxy pattern. Employed for aspects of virtual migration [Gamma 1995].

6.6.2 Factory Method Pattern

An agent can request a service from another society (virtual migration), or it can migrate physically. The type of the request is known only at runtime, and the behaviors required for each type are very different. Thus, there is a need to dynamically create the handler object according to the incoming request. The framework also should be extensible so new services can be added, and this requires an abstract class Handler that can be specialized.

Figure 6.17 shows the design of the Broker in which the abstract class Handler declares the factory method MakeHandler in its interface and uses this factory method in the Create method (also see *Section 6.4.4*). The concrete definition of this factory method is given by the subclasses VirtualMigration and ActualMigration. The HandlerCreator selects the appropriate subclass according to the client request and instantiates it. It then calls Create( ) on this object, which then composes itself and creates the object by using MakeHandler( ).

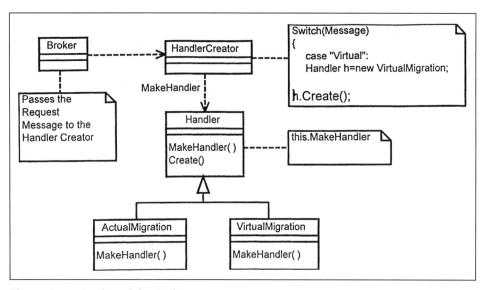

Figure 6.17 Design of the Broker.

6.6.3 Active Object Pattern

In this section, Active Object pattern is explained (also see *Section 6.4.7* and *Section 6.5.5*).

Motivation

VirtualMigration and ActualMigration are in their own thread of control; thus, more than one thread can access an InformationRepository concurrently. (An Information Repository may be a ServiceRepository or a SocietyRepository.) There is a need to provide synchronized access to these shared objects. One way to do this is by associating mutual exclusion locks, but this means that any class that inherits from ServiceRepository inherits the associated synchronization mechanism.

Solution

As discussed in *Section 6.4.7* and *Section 6.5.5*, the Active Object pattern solves this problem. The VirtualMigration and ActualMigration objects are clients of the interface of Information Repository, such as a Service Repository. The interface wraps up the method call into a MethodObject. The ServiceRepository has a Scheduler object that places the MethodObject in the ActivationQueue. Each MethodObject encapsulates the interface to the shared resource, which in this case is the representation of the ServiceRepository. The dispatcher thread of the Scheduler dequeues the MethodObject and executes its command method. This design is very similar to the designs in *Section 6.4.7* and *Section 6.5.5*.

6.6.4 Visitor Pattern

In this section, the Visitor pattern is explained.

Motivation

For actual migration, an agent has to be cloned in the destination society. Some aspects of its configuration might be specific to the destination, such as effectors, sensors, and collaboration protocols.

The RemoteConfigurator needs configuration details for cloning, such as the plan library and the beliefs. However, the configuration details and their format depend on the requirements of a given society's RemoteConfigurator. In such a case the agent's configuration must be adapted to the destination society. Thus, each agent potentially has to support various kinds of operations for configuration.

Each agent from this framework has a similar object structure. Thus, there is a need to represent the functions and behavior for configuration separately from the agent structure; otherwise each agent has to support many distinct and unrelated operations in its object structure.

Solution

The Visitor pattern [Gamma 1995] lets you define a new operation without changing the class of the elements on which it operates. As discussed in [Gamma 1995], the client passes the Visitor object to the object structure by calling its public interface method.

In an agent-based system, the Visitor class and the object structure that is to be visited (or operated on) will be in physically different societies. Figure 6.18 shows that the ClientProxy in the agent's Mobility layer downloads the Visitor class and instantiates it. Once the Visitor is instantiated, its Visit() method is called, and a reference to the ClientProxy is passed. In Figure 6.18, only one method Visit(Agent) is shown.

The RemoteConfigurator in the destination society downloads a visitor when the migrating agent requests permission and assistance to migrate. The RemoteConfigurator in the destination society may have many visitors, or just one; it determines which visitor to send. Such a concrete visitor could be an instance of the StandardVisitor class, as shown in Figure 6.18.

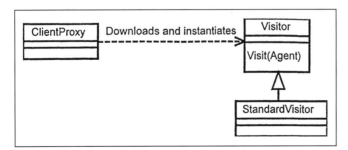

Figure 6.18   The Visitor pattern in the Mobility layer.

6.6.5 Proxy Pattern

The ClientProxy acts as a proxy server when an agent is performing virtual migration. This provides location transparency of the server and creates an effect similar to migration. Thus the client proxy acts as a local representative for an agent that actually resides remotely in another society.

ClientProxy is a proxy class, and it defines the methods that allow the agent to perform intersociety collaborations across platforms. In the centralized mobility architecture, the ClientProxy provides virtual migration services by using a Connector to connect to the Broker, and then requesting the Broker for virtual migration or location transparency. This is accomplished by the VirtualMigration Handler, and it is transparent to the client.

6.7 Subframework for Agent Configuration and Integration

An overview of the agent configuration and integration subframework and its key abstractions are discussed in *Sections 6.7.1 to 6.7.3*.

6.7.1 Context and Overview

The process of creating and configuring an agent consists of creating the various layers and then integrating them. The design uses the Agent Builder and Layer Linker patterns.

6.7.2 Agent Builder Pattern

In this section, the agent builder pattern is explained.

Intent

To separate the construction of the complex object structure of the agent from its representation so that the same construction process can create different representations.

Motivation

Each agent has fundamentally the same structure. The creation process of the agent should be isolated so that the same process can be used to generate different object structures.

Solution

The AgentCreator collects the user configuration details and passes the information to the Creator object. According to the Builder pattern [Gamma 1995], Creator is a direc-

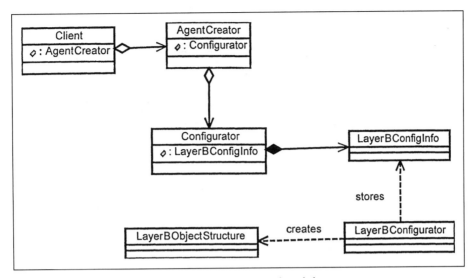

Figure 6.19 Agent Builder creates the structure of each layer.

tor object (see Figure 6.19). It stores the process used to create an agent. The AgentCreator instantiates the Creator with seven Configurator objects, and the Configurator objects are the builder objects that actually create the object structure of each individual layer based on the configuration information. The Configurator declares a virtual method Configure( ). The concrete definition of this method is provided by the layer-specific subclasses.

6.7.3 Layer Linker Pattern

In this section, the Layer Linker pattern is explained.

Intent

To integrate the various individual layers found in the agent.

Motivation

It is necessary to provide an interface to each layer but also to decouple the layers as much as possible.

Solution

Each Configurator creates a Façade object and other objects which form the structure stipulated by the application developer. The use of the Façade pattern [Gamma 1995] (see Figure 6.20) both provides a simple interface and decouples the layers. The Façade object implements the unified interface for the layer, promoting layer independence and portability.

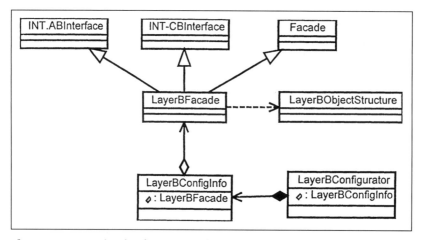

Figure 6.20   Design for the Layer Linker pattern.

For example, layers A and C are both adjacent to layer B. Then, as shown in the figure, INT-CBInterface declares the interface from layer C to layer B, and, correspondingly, INT-ABInterface declares the interface from layer A to layer B. The Configurator registers them in the configuration repository object LayerBConfigInfo. These repositories are used to get the Façade object reference during the integration phase executed by the Creator object's integrate( ). This is explained further in *Section 6.8*.

6.8 Using the Framework

Application programming interface (API), sample applications, and sample interaction diagrams are discussed in the following sections.

6.8.1 Application Programmers Interface (API)

Figure 6.21 depicts an AgentAPI module, which is a group of classes provided to help the application developer create agents. There are several classes in this module, including one for each layer: SensoryAPI, BeliefsAPI, ReasoningAPI, ActionsAPI, and CollaborationAPI. There are also classes for creating effectors. Details of each class in the AgentAPI are provided in this section, along with details of how they can be employed in a sample application. All these classes are final classes that cannot be further extended. They are directly instantiated by the application developer.

Class SensoryAPI has the following methods:

```
SetSensor(String sensorname);
```

sensorname is the name of the implementation or subclass of class Sensor that is an interface to the environment.

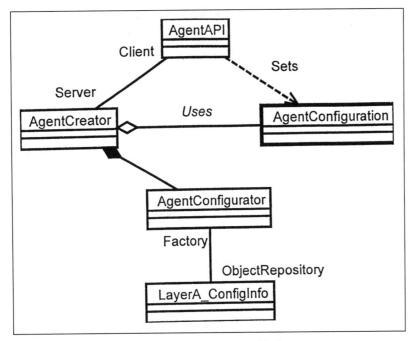

Figure 6.21 Design for agent configuration with the AgentAPI.

```
SetEnvBeliefs(String Beliefs, Sensor givensensor);
```

This method identifies which beliefs are to be sensed. The sensing can be done by asynchronous events or by polling, depending on the sensor object.

Class *BeliefsAPI* has the following methods:

```
Register(FILE Beliefsfile, char delimiter);
```

Beliefsfile should have the following structure. Each line in the file should contain two fields. The first field should contain the BeliefId, and the second field should contain the corresponding Belief.

Class ReasoningAPI has the following methods:

```
WriteRule(FILE ReasoningFile, char delimiter);
```

ReasoningFile should have the following structure. Each line in the file should contain two fields. The first field should contain the rule, and the second field should contain the corresponding action. The delimiter provided should be used to separate the two columns.

The syntax of the rule is identified as follows:

```
SetParser(Parser someparser);
```

The parser must follow infix notation. This parser is used to parse the rules.

Class ActionsAPI has the following methods:

```
RegisterPlans(FILE Planfile, char delimiter);
```

Each line in the file Planfile should contain two fields. The first field should contain the planID and the second field should contain the name of the Plans class which is a subclass or implementation of ActionPlan. The delimiter should be used to separate the two columns.

```
setEffector(String effectorname)
```

effectorname is the name of the implementation or subclass of EffectorInterface. It implements method stubs, an example is shown in Figure 6.11. Plans should use the methods provided in the effector.

Class CollaborationAPI has the following methods:

```
SetAgentId(String AgentId);
SetPort(int PORTNO);
SetLanguage(String Languagename);
```

Languagename is an implementation or subclass of ProtocolStrategy if the language is a simple message-passing language; it will be an implementation or subclass of AbsStateDepStrategy if the language is a state-dependent or conversational strategy. It is assumed that all agents in a society converse in a single language.

```
SetPeerAgents(FILE Collabfile, char delimiter);
```

Collabfile should have a first field that provides the agent id and a second field that provides the portno. The remaining fields are for the services provided by that particular agent.

```
SetConversationCapacity(int NoOfConversations);
```

This sets the number of conversations that can be handled by the agent simultaneously.

Class Agent has the following methods:

```
main(String[]args)
```

This is the main function that should configure the agent using the preceding API.

```
Start()
```

This starts the agent's main thread; therefore, with this command, the agent becomes active in a society. The user should extend the Agent class and define its main function.

6.8.2 Sample Application

This section presents a network management agent as an example use of the framework; it also provides additional classes that are necessary for the agent to interact with or affect its environment. This network management agent (NMA) has a network management server (NMS) and mail server as its coexisting objects in the environment. The NMS performs information management for that host, and this server can be specific to a particular host operating system. The mail server performs the event reporting via mail. The management information is represented as managed objects in the NMS, and the NMA has beliefs that model this information. The NMA senses or obtains this information by requesting it from the server by issuing a get command or message; in addition, it affects the environment by sending set commands to the server. This situation is depicted in Figure 6.22.

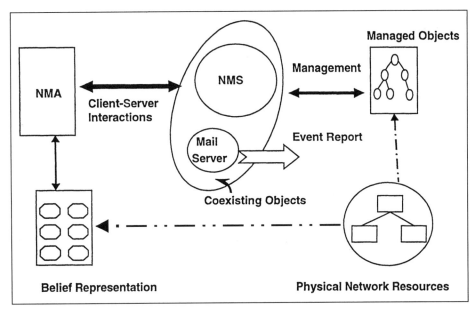

Figure 6.22 The network management application.

The NMA does not work alone; it provides information to a human system administrator. There are also other agents that are subordinate to it. These provide more specialized expertise and services, such as network intrusion detection and prevention, and fault diagnosis and maintenance.

Each NMA instance should be a separate process, as each agent is separate entity. In this example, NMA is implemented by the NMAAgent class. The main() function is detailed following:

```
public class NMAAgent extends Agent{
public static void main(String[] args)
{
```

In the main function, any number of command line arguments that can be used to configure and create an agent can be passed. In this example, main expects one command line argument, which is the agent's unique identification number. This is used for collaborating and negotiating with other agents. The piece of code from the main() function shown following uses the API defined in *Section 6.8.1.*

```
SensoryAPI NMASensor; // For sensory layer
      ActionsAPI NMAActions; // For action layer
      ReasoningAPI NMAReasoner; // For reasoner layer
      BeliefsAPI  NMABeliefs; // For beliefs layer
      CollaborationAPI NMACollab; // For Collaboration layer.
      //error handling is not shown here.
      // Set the sensor class.
      NMASensor.SetSensor("java.lang-----.NMSSensor");
```

```
// The next line  sets the belief with beliefId of NMA1100
// which should be sensed by the NMSSensor.
    NMASensor.SetEnvBeliefs("NMA1100");
    // The NMABeliefsFile.x files stores the beliefs.
    NMABeliefs.Register("NMABeliefsFile.x",'|');
```

The NMABeliefsFile.x has the following line:

```
NMA1100 | NMA1100.class
```

Here NMA1100.class is the class which implements this belief.

In this example, the NMSSensor is an adapter. It looks into its sensing plan and finds the NMA1100 belief. This belief is part of the representation in the NMA (see Figure 6.22) that represents a physical resource of the NMS. Thus, the sensor adapts the NMA1100 belief to the interface of its actual managed object. In other words, the NMASensor will actually poll the particular object by sending a get request to the NMS.

```
Continuing with the main function,
// The next line sets the rules for interpretation.
NMAReasoner.WriteRule("NMAReasonerFile.x", '|');
```

The NMAReasonerFile.x has the following rule, which equates NMA1100 to some integer value and also checks another belief NMA89 that may represent some alarm. If this rule equates to TRUE, then a intention is executed with an action plan identified by ACTION1100.

```
((NMA1100 == 100) AND (NMA89==TRUE)) | ACTION1100
```

Each rule in the Reasoning layer is represented by an object that is the observer of the beliefs object (see *Section 6.3.3*). When the belief NMA1100 changes its state, it notifies the object representing the preceding rule. If the rule interprets itself as being TRUE, then an action plan ACTION1100 is triggered. The ReasoningrAPI will parse the preceding line and create a rule object from it.

```
// The next line sets the Action plans.
NMAActions.RegisterPlans("NMAActionPlans.x",'|');
The NMAActionPlans.x file has following line,
ACTION1100 | java.lang.------.NMAMailAdmin.class
```

Thus NMAMailAdmin.class has the functionality to carry out ACTION1100. For carrying out the plan, this class uses an object from the EffectorInterface class. The next line sets the Effector Interface. Plans use this to affect the environment.

```
NMAActions.SetEffector("java.lang.---.NMSEffectorIF);
```

The following sets an ID for the agent in the society; other agents use this to collaborate.

```
NMACollab.SetAgentId(args[0]);
```

The next lines of code perform the following functions:

- Set a port number where the agent waits for the incoming messages.
- Identify the agent dialect.
- Identify an information repository for collaboration.
- Set the maximum number of conversations that the agent can have.

```
NMACollab.SetPort(10006);//some port number
NMACollab.SetLanguage("KQML");
NMACollab.SetPeerAgentsFile("NMACollabAgentsFile.x",'|');
NMACollab.SetConversationCapacity(25);
```

The last step is to call the start method of this agent. This method internally starts the NMSensor thread, which is executed eternally. Once the agent is activated, it can be stopped or suspended via collaboration messages:

```
this.Start(); // Start this agent's sensor's thread.
} // End of main().
} // End of NMAAgent.
```

The action plan class that is utilized to determine what the agent actually does is a user-supplied class that should implement the ActionPlan interface supplied by the framework. There are two methods that this interface declares, SetEffector(Object e) and Execute. The user has to typecast the Object instance passed in the SetEffector method to its desired interface. Here in our example the effector interface is MailServerIF. The Execute method should implement the functionality using this effector.

During configuration (see *Section 6.7*), the framework calls the SetEffector method of the plan object and passes the effector interface class instance—that is, NMSEffectorIF—to it. The NMAMailAdmin class is shown following.

```
public class NMAMailAdmin implements ActionPlan
{
        private MailAddress adminAddress; // mail address
        private MailServerIF Eff; // Effector Interface
        public SetEffector(Object e)// this method will be called by
        {Eff= (MailServerIF)e;} // configurator in framework

        public Execute()// this executes this plan of sending a mail.
        {Eff.sendMail(adminAddress);}
}
```

The NMSEffectorIF may implement more than one interface. This is a wrapper class that can be used by different categories of plans. In this example, the NMSEffectorIF class implements the MailServerIF interface's sendMail method. Referring to *Section 6.4.7*, this class is the method interface in the Active Object pattern. Thus, it has only the stub methods that instantiate and register the method objects in the scheduler. This is shown following. In the code, the C_MethodObject has access to C-compliant primitive methods. These primitive methods form the EffectorRepresentation discussed in *Section 6.4.7.*

```
public class NMSEffectorIF implements MailServerIF
{
      private Scheduler sch;
      public sendMail(MailServer o)
      {sch.Register(new C_MethodObject("sendMail",(MailServer)o));}
      public any_other_method(Type Arg)
      {sch.Register(new C_MethodObject("any_other_method",
(Type) Arg);}
}
```

6.8.3 Sample Interaction Diagrams

Figures 6.23 through 6.28 are interaction diagrams. Together they depict the sequence of events that occurs bottom up in the framework. Figure 6.23 shows how a Sensor object utilizes a Sensing Plan and a Sensor Adapter to get domain-specific data regarding changing beliefs. For the NMA, this would obtain information about network traffic and faults and suspected intrusions, for example.

Figures 6.24 and 6.25 focus on the Beliefs layer. Once the sensor has obtained a new value for a belief, this change needs to be propagated through the Beliefs layer, via the

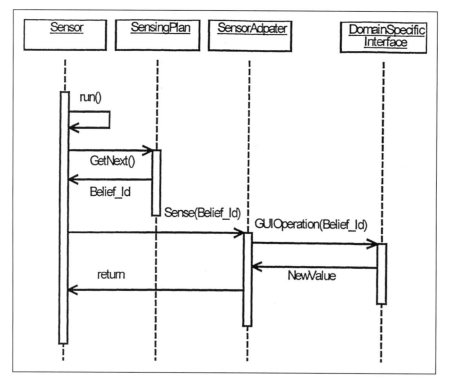

Figure 6.23 Updating Beliefs with Sensors.

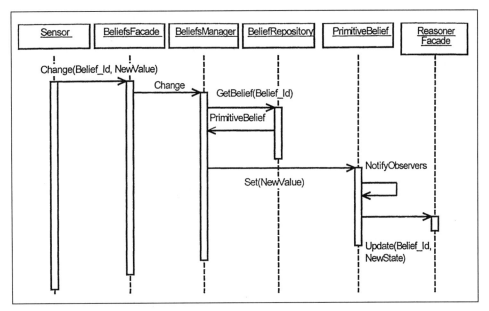

Figure 6.24 Updating a PrimitiveBelief.

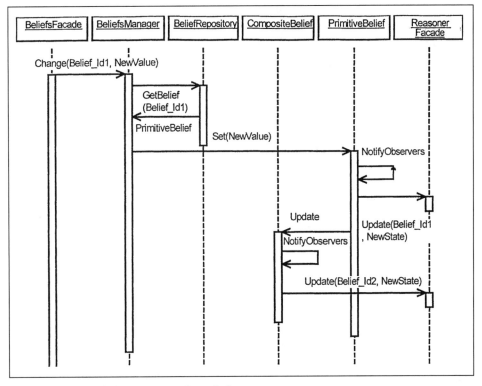

Figure 6.25 Updating a CompositeBelief.

BeliefsFaçade, the BeliefsManager, and the BeliefRepository, to the actual PrimitiveBelief. Figure 6.24 is for the case when the belief or fact appears only once in the belief database. Figure 6.25 considers what happens when the belief also appears in composite beliefs.

In either case, through the Observer pattern (*see Section 6.3.3*), the Reasoning layer is notified of the change via its Reasoning Façade, signifying that an interpret cycle is needed. The interpret cycle determines whether any plan should be triggered on the basis of the change in beliefs.

For example, in the NMA application, a Sensor might note a fault, such as a lost connection. This connection might appear in only one belief, if it is a leaf, or it might appear in many beliefs, if it is a key link. The agent has plans for dealing with faults, including rerouting. So, when one or more beliefs change, it runs an interpret cycle to decide what to do.

Figure 6.26 depicts what happens when an instantiated plan (an intention) needs to deal with an effector. As the effector may operate sequentially, the Active Object

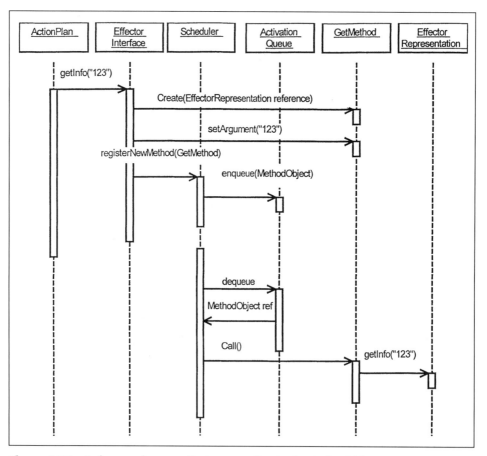

Figure 6.26 A plan employs an effector according to the Active Object pattern.

pattern is used (see *Section 6.4.7*). (The sequence is the same in all the cases throughout this chapter wherever the Active Object pattern has been used.) As in any use of the Active Object pattern, five objects are used: an interface, representation, scheduler, queue, and a method object. In Figure 6.26, the method object is named *Get-Method*.

In the application, Figure 6.26 is valid when the NMA needs to impact or affect a sequential object in the environment. One example is an interface to a human system administrator; time sequences of events must be preserved and presented. This is also true for an audit trace for network management.

Figures 6.27 and 6.28 deal with collaboration between agents; Figure 6.27 is for an outgoing message, while Figure 6.28 is for an incoming one. The NMA agent requests information from its subordinates; this may involve asking them for detailed information about local faults that the NMA agent can assimilate into an overall picture of the network's status. The subordinates then reply with the requested information. Alternatively, the subordinates may note something and bring it to the attention of the NMA. The objects that appear in Figures 6.27 and 6.28 are discussed in detail in *Section 6.5.2*.

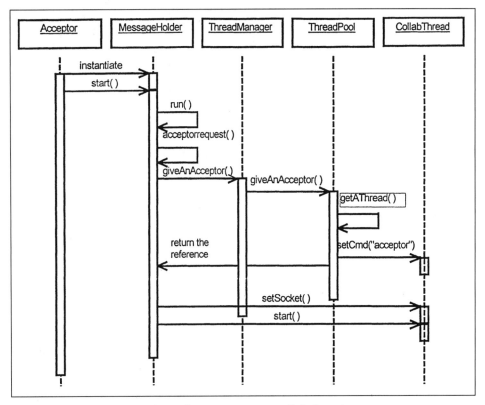

Figure 6.27   Assigning an incoming message to a collabThread.

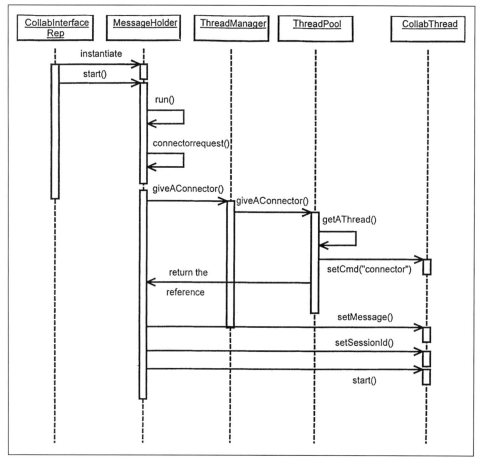

Figure 6.28   Placing an outgoing message in a MesgHolder and passing it on to another agent.

6.9 Summary of the Framework

This summary highlights the contributions of this chapter and compares the agent system framework with other existing agent-based frameworks. In this section, future work is also explained.

6.9.1 Contributions

The framework described in this chapter is ambitious. However, it represents a considerable contribution to agent system understanding and design, and it provides a platform for further development of agent-based systems. Further, this framework demonstrates that agents can be designed and implemented using design and architectural patterns.

The framework has been utilized to develop agent-based systems for network management and for detecting network intrusion. It has also been used for an application in enterprise integration that utilizes mobile agents.

All of these simple applications could have been developed without agents. However, these have been built to illustrate the enabling technology. They represent a starting point; agent technology is still in its infancy. Agents represent a new paradigm, and although significant applications have been recognized, they have not yet been developed.

6.9.2 Comparison to Other Agent Frameworks

In comparison to other frameworks for agent-based systems, this is the only agent framework that utilizes patterns for design and documentation. This facilitates future extensions and modifications, which are bound to occur.

Further, with the exception of KAoS [Bradshaw 1997], JAFIMA is more comprehensive, addressing more aspects of agency. Concordia [Walsh 1998] emphasizes mobility, but does not address reasoning; ZEUS [Nwana 1998] and dMARS [Ingrand 1992] concentrate on reasoning and collaboration, but they do not cover mobility. In KAoS [Bradshaw 1997], agents have intelligent behavior and aspects of mobility are being incorporated. KAoS is a commercial system, and only limited information about its design is available. Therefore, a more detailed comparison is not possible between JAFIMA and KAoS.

ZEUS and dMARS feature advanced agent reasoning and resource allocation. The reasoning is goal based and accomplishes backward chaining rather than the simple forward chaining in this framework. This is important for some strong agent applications, such as those that involve knowledge-based planning, and this type of Reasoning layer could be added to the RMIT framework for these kinds of applications.

Although ZEUS and dMARS emphasize reasoning and strong agents, both require that additional agents be generated for most purposes of sensing and affecting the environment. In dMARS an agent that deals with the environment is called a Foreign Agent, and in ZEUS it is a Database Proxy Agent. In an agent-based application that requires substantial integration, it is anticipated that this approach will prove to be cumbersome and complex; it could also lead to bottlenecks.

In addition, to support the sophisticated reasoning backward chaining, the belief data structures in ZEUS and dMARS are *structures*, rather than objects. This means that inheritance and data encapsulation cannot be used. It also makes it difficult to place domain objects in an agent's internal model of its environment; they must be written in and out of the belief data structures, complicating the design and the implementation.

The framework presented here is highly modular. This has resulted in some additional complexity and in a multitude of objects. However, it is believed to be superior to a more monolithic approach which would be more difficult to change. As agents are new and not yet mature, change is inevitable.

6.9.3 Future Work

The RMIT framework is still under development, as follows:

Standardization. Agent proxies and effectors should be supplied with the framework so that it meets standards.

Beliefs layer. An object-oriented database could be used to represent the beliefs.

Collaboration layer. Agent collaboration is an active area of research, especially with respect to conflict management and opportunistic, rather than prescriptive, cooperation.

Translation layer. No work has yet been done on the Translation layer.

Mobility layer. Agent mobility requires further investigation, especially CORBA compatibility for virtual migration. Security is crucial for actual migration.

6.10 References

[Agha 1986] Agha, G. *A Model of Concurrent Computation in Distributed Systems.* Cambridge, MA: MIT Press, 1986.

[AAII 1998] Australian Artificial Intelligence Institute. *OASIS: Optimal Aircraft Sequencing with Intelligent Scheduling.* AAII, 1998, www.aaii.com.au/proj/oasis

[Barbuceanu-Fox 1995] Barbuceanu, M., and M.S. Fox. COOL: A language for describing coordination in multi-agent systems. *First International Conference on Multi-Agent Systems (ICMAS '95),* San Francisco, CA, June 1995.

[Bradshaw 1997] Bradshaw, J.M., S. Dutfield, P. Benoit, and J.D. Woolley. KAoS: Toward an industrial-strength open distributed agent architecture. *Software Agents,* J.M. Bradshaw, editor. Cambridge, MA: AAAI/MIT Press, 1997.

[BTRL 1997] British Telecom Research Laboratories. *Intelligent Agent Research: The RADAR Personal Agent.* BTRL, 1997, www.labs.bt.com/projects/agents/research/personal4.htm

[Brooks 1986] Brooks, R.A. A robust layered control system for mobile robot. *IEEE Journal of Robotics and Automation,* 2(1), 1986.

[Buschmann 1996] Buschmann, F., R. Meunier, H. Rohnert, P. Sommerlad, and M. Stal. *Pattern-Oriented Software Architecture: A System of Patterns.* New York: John Wiley & Sons, 1996.

[Dickinson 1997] Dickinson, I. *Agent Standards.* Agent Technology Group, http://drogo.cselt.stet.it/fipa, 1997.

[Gamma 1995] Gamma, E.R., R. Helm, R. Johnson, and J. Vlissides. *Design Patterns: Elements of Reusable Object-Oriented Software.* Reading, MA: Addison-Wesley, 1995.

[Ingrand 1992] Ingrand, F.F., M.P. Georgeff, and A.S. Rao, An architecture for real time reasoning and control. *IEEE Expert,* 7(6), 1992.

[Jennings 1996] Jennings, N.R., P. Faratin, M. Johnson, P. O'Brien, and M. Wiegand. Using intelligent agents to manage business processes. *First International Conference on the Practical Application of Intelligent Agents and Multiagent Technology,* London, 1996.

[Johnson 1992] Johnson, R.E., Documenting frameworks with patterns. OOPSLA 1992. Vancouver, British Columbia, Canada, October 1992, *ACM SIGPLAN Notices* 27(10). Reading, MA: ACM Press, 1992.

[Kafura 1998] Kafura, D.G. *A Polymorphic Future and First Class Function type for Concurrent Object Oriented Programming.* www.cs.utexas.edu/users/lavender/papers /future.ps.

[Kendall 1997a] Kendall, E.A., C.V. Pathak, P.V. Murali Krishna, and C.B. Suresh. The Layered Agent Pattern Language. *Pattern Languages of Programming Conference* (PloP 1997). Monticello, IL, September 1997.

[Kendall 1997b] Kendall, E.A., M.T. Malkoun, and C.H. Jiang. Multiagent system design based on object oriented patterns. *Report on Object Oriented Analysis and Design,* in conjunction with the *Journal of Object-Oriented Programming,* June 1997.

[Kendall 1997c] Kendall, E.A., M.T. Malkoun, and C.H. Jiang. The application of object-oriented analysis to agent based systems. *Report on Object Oriented Analysis and Design,* in conjunction with *Journal of Object-Oriented Programming,* February 1997.

[Lavender 1995] Lavender, R.G., and D.C. Schmidt. Active Object: An object behavioral pattern for concurrent programming. *Pattern Languages of Programming Conference* (PloP 1995). Monticello, IL, 1995.

[Nwana 1997] Nwana, H.S., and D.T. Ndumu. An introduction to agent technology. *Software Agents and Soft Computing,* H.S. Nwana and N. Azarmi, editors. Lecture Notes in Artificial Intelligence 1198. New York: Springer, 1997.

[Nwana 1998] Nwana, H.S., Ndumu, D.T., and Lee, L.C. ZEUS: An advanced tool kit for engineering distributed multi-agent systems. *Practical Applications in Agent and Multi-Agent Systems,* March 1998: 377–391.

[Rogers 1997] Rogers, G.F. *Framework-Based Software Development in C++.* Prentice Hall Series on Programming Tools and Methodologies. Upper Saddle River, NJ: Prentice Hall, 1997.

[Schmidt 1996] Schmidt, D.C., and Tim Harrison. Double-checked locking—An object behavioral pattern for initializing and accessing thread-safe objects efficiently. *Pattern Languages of Programming Conference* (PloP 1996). Monticello, IL, 1996.

[Tenenbaum 1992] Tenenbaum, J.M., J.C. Weber, and T.R. Gruber. Enterprise integration: Lessons from SHADE and PACT. *Enterprise Integration Modeling Proceedings of the First International Conference,* C.J. Petrie, editor. Cambridge, MA: MIT Press, 1992.

[Walsh 1998] Walsh, T., Paciorek, N., and Wong, D. Security and reliability in Concordia. Hawaii International Conference on Systems Science (HICSS-31). HI, January 1998.

[Wooldridge 1995] Wooldridge, M.J., and N.R. Jennings. Agent theories, architectures and languages. *ECAI-94 Workshop on Agent Theories, Architectures, and Languages.* Amsterdam, 1995.

A Model for
Reusable Agent Systems

Due to advances in networking technology, increasingly heterogeneous distributed computing resources are becoming available on the Internet. This proliferation has introduced new requirements in the design of distributed systems.

Scalability. The critical scaling issue is not the size of the applications to be developed or the number of applications that can be interconnected, but rather the flexibility of the distributed system to the introduction of new components or new interconnections.

Interoperability. The distributed system should be able to interoperate with applications that were unknown or nonexistent prior to the creation of the system.

Adaptability. A distributed system continually evolves: It should be able to rapidly adapt to new environmental conditions and requirements.

Effective use of the Internet by end users and application designers calls for technology that allows distributed resources to be flexibly combined, and their activities coordinated. Object-oriented (OO) technology has proved to be an extremely powerful software development technique which promotes modularity, composability, and reusability of complex systems. Unfortunately, it has turned out to be excessively brittle with respect to the specific requirements of distributed systems [Guerraoui 1996], especially for the development of reusable application frameworks. This is due to the fact that in OO programming the interactions between two components are specified and implemented as operations on one of the two: The more likely the interactions are to be changed in future applications, the less reusable is the component that expresses the joint behavior [Mili 1995]. There is a need for a computational model that increases the adaptability of the reusable components of a framework in terms of the interactions with other components.

The goal of this chapter is to show how agent technology can enhance the flexibility and adaptability of object-oriented systems and simplify the development of reusable application frameworks for the distributed systems domain.

The main contribution of this chapter is the definition of the reusable task structure-based intelligent network agents (RETSINA) [Sycara 1996], an agent-based application framework that builds on the corresponding RETSINA agent model and has been conceived for the distributed system domain.

The chapter is organized as follows. *Section 7.1* reviews some extensions to the traditional object models. *Section 7.2* presents the RETSINA agent model. *Section 7.3* defines three types of relationships between agents that are used to build complex multiagent organizations. *Section 7.4* presents the RETSINA application framework and emphasizes its flexibility with respect to the relationships between its components. *Section 7.5* describes how a framework is transformed into a specific application and discusses the effectiveness of agent-based application frameworks as a reuse technique. *Section 7.6* reports on some related works. Finally, *Section 7.7* draws some conclusions.

7.1 From Objects to Agents

Several attempts to extend the traditional object model have been proposed in the literature, with the goal of enhancing its flexibility in the development of distributed applications.

Interaction protocols. A formalism for describing object interactions, which can be processed automatically by a compiler. The formalism is mainly intended to validate the correctness of an application [Bokowski 1996].

Contracts. An implementation mechanism for encapsulating object interaction behaviors. Only a limited form of abstraction of contracts is possible [Holland 1992].

Actors. An extension of object-style data abstraction to concurrent open systems: Actors have an identity that can be communicated to other actors at runtime. This means that relationships between actors can be created and destroyed dynamically and that actors can freely enter or exit a system. Actors have been shown to offer better support for modeling fine-grained concurrency in low-level processing (such as computer vision) than for large-grained concurrency in large-scale distributed systems.

The distributed object model underlying Object Management Group (OMG) Common Object Request Broker Architecture (CORBA). Enhances the traditional object model by hiding the location and implementation language of distributed objects from their clients. In so doing, CORBA provides interoperability between heterogeneous and distributed applications. However, in this model each object has a distinct immutable identity, interface, and implementation [Vinoski 1997].

Software agents. Integrated systems that incorporate major capabilities drawn from several research areas: artificial intelligence, databases, programming languages, and theory of computing. Usually, software agents are conceived as one-off systems built to investigate a single application. A new trend in distributed artificial intelligence (DAI) considers software agents as software units of design that may be customized and composed with other similar units to build complex systems. (For a survey, see [Riecken 1994].)

7.2 The RETSINA Agent Model

In the following, the RETSINA agent model is presented as an extension of the traditional object model. In particular, the RETSINA agent model is described in terms of *agent state*, *agent behavior*, *agent interface*, and *agent identity*.

7.2.1 Agent State

Agents, like objects, have an internal state that reflects their knowledge. However, this knowledge may be partially specified or based on default assumptions [Conrad 1997]. During its life span, an agent may extend or refine its knowledge by performing inferences on its past and present states or by acquiring information from the outside environment.

The RETSINA agent model does not make any assumption with respect to how the agent's knowledge is represented (for example, assertions, productions, and so forth) or to the kind of knowledge the agent possesses (complete world knowledge, default assumptions, and so forth). In contrast, the RETSINA model does assume uniform access to knowledge, so that all of the agents in the system can share their knowledge and interoperate. Uniform access to knowledge is achieved by assuming that the agents in the system share the same semantics for common knowledge domains and, as will be explained later on in this chapter, the same communication language. Shared semantics are represented by domain ontologies [Falasconi 1996]. Like a conceptual schema, an ontology provides a logical description of special-purpose concepts common to a specific knowledge domain and allows different agents to interoperate independently of internal representation structures.

7.2.2 Agent Behavior

Agents have a behavior that is determined by the set of admissible operations on their internal state. As in the RISC model the internal operations of a RETSINA agent are represented by first-class objects, called *actions*. In contrast to traditional objects, whose behavior is specified in a procedural way inside a method definition, the behavior of a RETSINA agent may be specified inside actions in a declarative way (by rules, constraints, goals, and so forth) as well.

The explicit representation of actions allows agents to reason about their own behavior (reflection) and to schedule the use of their resources by serializing actions or grouping them for concurrent execution. Actions can be composed with each other to form higher-level behavioral aggregates, such as tasks, plans, and so forth.

Like active objects [Minoura 1993], RETSINA agents encapsulate and manage one or more independent threads of control. They can act on behalf of another agent (human or software), providing services on demand; they can react to external or internal events (such as a clock); or they can perform background activities such as monitoring their own activity or the external environment.

7.2.3 Agent Interface

The RETSINA agents have a message-based interface, which is defined in terms of the set of messages that the agent can interpret. The RETSINA agents adopt the declarative approach to communication, which is based on the Speech Act theory [Searle 1969]. A declarative communication language, such as KQML [Genesereth 1994], is a messaging protocol, where a message is an expression composed of (1) a communication primitive, called a *performative*, that corresponds to a specific linguistic action (for example, query, answer, assert, or define); and (2) its content. The content of a message is a sequence of declarative statements, an expression built using a knowledge representation language, such as KIF [Genesereth 1994], and formed from words defined in an ontology. The use of a declarative communication language allows agents implemented using different programming languages to interoperate. The messages received by an agent are internally represented by first-class objects called *objectives*. We use the word *objective* to indicate a potentially complex specification of a desired outcome and its associated multiple-attribute utility characteristics. Because objectives can be created and destroyed dynamically, the agent's behavior in response to a specific message can change during the agent's lifetime.

Whenever the agent receives a message, a new objective object is created and inserted into a private list. The objective list may have different behaviors (queue, stack, and so forth), allowing different dispatching policies for the incoming messages. In the simplest case, an objective is satisfied by the execution of a specific *action*. In the general case, an objective may be satisfied by the execution of a high-level task, which has to be reduced by a planner and finally results in the execution of a sequence of actions (plan).

7.2.4 Agent Identity

An agent's identity is that property of the agent which distinguishes it from all other agents in the same system. An agent's identity is represented by an identifier, such that no two distinct agents in the system are allowed to have the same identifier. The identity of a RETSINA agent is expressed in terms of a symbolic name. Because real systems may consist of a large number of agents, it may be not feasible to assign a unique name to each agent. A common approach is to group agents into *domains* (as for the Internet) and assign unique names to agents belonging to the same domain. The symbolic name of an agent can be associated to several addresses, one for each transport mechanism that the agent can use (email, TCP/IP, HTTP, and so forth). An agent refers to other agents using their symbolic names and leaves the resolution of these names of transport addresses to specialized agent name servers (ANSs) [Finin 1995].

The use of symbolic names allows agents to move from one location to another without changing their identity. Whenever an agent enters the system or migrates, it notifies the ANS of its new location. The RETSINA model gives each agent the responsibility of querying the ANS for the current location of other agents. This means that agents may hold dangling identifiers of other agents. The identity of an agent can be communicated to other agents.

7.3 Agent Relationships

One of the basic problems facing designers of open, multiagent systems for the Internet is the connection problem—finding what information is available from whom (and at what cost). There are two special types of information used in this process, preferences and capabilities. In multiagent systems, a *preference* is knowledge about what types of information have utility for a requester. A *capability* is knowledge about what types of services can be requested from a provider. Agents that deal with information about preferences or capabilities and are neither the requester nor the provider (from the standpoint of the transaction under consideration) are called *middle agents* [Sycara 1997]. Middle agents enhance the flexibility of a multiagent system by reducing visibility dependencies between service providers and customers.

The following sections consider three specific types of middle agents: *MatchMaker*, *Broker*, and *Ontology Agent*. They are used to help agents establish three kinds of relationships among each other, namely *use*, *composition*, and *specialization*, which closely resemble the three basic relationships between objects: use, inclusion, and inheritance [Booch 1991].

7.3.1 The Use Relationship

An agent can use the services provided by other agents if it knows their names and their capabilities. In an open distributed system (such as the Internet), agents are free to appear and disappear. Any agent that enters the system and intends to let other agents use its services must clearly declare this intention by making a long-term commitment to taking on a well-defined class of future requests. This declaration is called an *advertisement* and contains a specification of the agent's capability with respect to the type of request it can accept. Since it is obviously not feasible for an agent to broadcast its identity and capabilities, a specific agent in the organization takes on the role of *MatchMaker*. The MatchMaker is an agent that knows the name of many agents and their corresponding capabilities. The MatchMaker has a well-known name; that is, all agents have a predefined, static procedure to contact it. When an agent needs the collaboration of another agent with a specific capability, it queries the MatchMaker for the names of all the available agents in the system that provide that capability. The requester agent has the responsibility to contact the prospective collaborators and negotiate with them for the use of their capabilities.

7.3.2 The Composition Relationship

For reasons of privacy, some agents may want to keep their identity secret while providing a service to other agents in the system. Some agents may want to filter the access to their services through other agents. As in Object Orientation, the simplest solution is to hide those agents by encapsulating their identity inside specialized agents called *Broker* agents. The Broker is an agent that knows the names of some provider agents and their corresponding capabilities, and advertises its own capabilities as a function of the capabilities of those provider agents. From the requester's point of view, the Broker assumes the role of provider. From a provider's point of view, the Broker accepts advertisements and acts as a MatchMaker. The Broker mainly differs from the MatchMaker in that neither the requester nor the provider ever directly knows the identity of the other in a transaction.

Because a Broker stands at a filtering and control point in the information flow of an organization, one natural service that is provided is load balancing—the Broker can choose providers not just to satisfy service requests, but also to optimize usage of the provider. Load balancing is feasible under the assumption that providers cannot advertise with more than one Broker.

7.3.3 The Specialization Relationship

It is likely (and desirable) that in the future a large number of agents will populate the Internet. It is also likely that similar capabilities will be provided by different agents. It is obviously desirable, in order to enhance interoperability, that agents with similar capabilities be related to each other. Capability descriptions can differ in the name they have been assigned, which may be synonyms (for example, *BuyStocks* and *Purchase-Stocks*). They can differ in expressing different concepts, which may derive from a common ancestor concept (for example, *Magazine* and *Newspaper*). These kinds of mismatches can be solved by specific agents, called *Ontology Agents*. An Ontology Agent essentially plays the role of an ontological library manager and distributor [Falasconi 1996]. Ontology Agents manage multiple and evolving classifications of terms and concepts, and allow other agents (such as MatchMakers and Brokers) to classify agents' capabilities in specialization and generalization hierarchies. When a requester asks a MatchMaker for the name of a specific service provider which is not available in the system or is not known to the MatchMaker, it may be answered with the name of an agent that provides a more general capability.

7.3.4 Agent Organizations

Middle agents can be used by a multiagent system to form several organizational structures:

Uncoordinated teams. Agents use a basic shared behavior to ask a middle agent about who might be able to provide a requested service. If the middle agent returns more than one service provider, the requester can choose from among them and contact the provider. Such organizations are characterized by low overheads, but with potentially unbalanced loads.

Economic markets. Agents use price, reliability, and other utility characteristics in choosing another agent. Middle agents can supply to each agent the appropriate updated pricing information as new agents enter and exit the system or alter their advertisements. Agents can dynamically adjust their organization as often as necessary, the only limitation being transaction costs. Such organizations potentially provide efficient load balancing and the ability to effectively provide truly expensive services (expensive in terms of the resources required).

Federations. Agents give up individual autonomy in choosing who they will do business with to a locally centralized facilitator that brokers requests. Centralization of message traffic potentially allows greater load balancing and the provision of automatic translation and mediation services [Wiederhold 1992].

Bureaucratic functional units. Traditional manager-employee groups of a single multisource information agent (manager) and several simple information agents (employees). Being organized into functional units—that is, related information sources—such organizations concentrate on providing higher reliability (by using multiple underlying sources), simple information integration (from partially overlapping information), and load balancing.

7.4 The RETSINA Framework

This section presents the RETSINA application framework. It builds on the agent model defined in *Section 7.2* and is the result of a generalization process from a set of applications that we have developed for distributed information gathering. Following the classification defined in [Brugali 1997], the RETSINA framework consists of elemental, basic design and domain-dependent components.

Elemental components determine the language in which the agent architecture is written. In the early stages of the framework's life span [Brugali 1997], they are conceived as whitebox components. As the framework evolves, concrete implementations are provided, examples being communication modules that are to be specialized to embed specific protocols, knowledge representation modules, and reasoning modules.

Basic design components are agent architectures that integrate elemental components of the framework. They differ from each other according to their internal structure.

The other components are domain dependent and consist of concrete implementations of agents with specific functionalities.

7.4.1 Elemental Components

The elemental components of the RETSINA framework are classified as functional modules and synchronization modules. *Functional modules* are active objects that concurrently perform specific activities. The Communicator, the Planner, the Scheduler, the ExecutionMonitor, and the Coordinator are the functional modules that belong to the framework. *Synchronization modules* are blocking objects that offer the wait primitive to suspend any calling process until a specified condition is verified. The ObjectiveQueue, the TaskQueue, and the Schedule Queue are used to synchronize the functional modules of the framework. In addition, the framework provides the Belief-

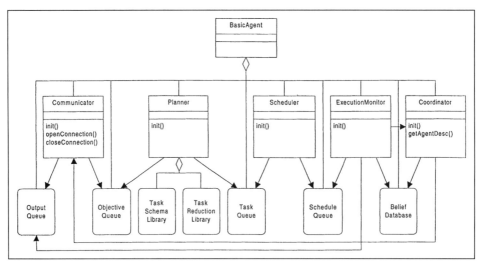

Figure 7.1   The RETSINA basic agent architecture.

Database module, which is a blocking object used to store the agent's knowledge. The elemental components of the framework are integrated in the RETSINA basic agent architecture, as depicted in Figure 7.1, and are described as follows.

The Communicator module periodically monitors a specific input port for messages coming from other agents. Messages can contain service requests, which are translated into first-class objects called *objectives* and inserted into the ObjectiveQueue. The Communicator encapsulates a parser, which is specific to the communication language used by the agent. The parser is a hot spot [Pree 1994] of the Communicator and has been designed following the Strategy and Interpreter patterns [Gamma 1995]. Currently, we have implemented a subclass of the Communicator which encapsulates a parser for KQML messages. Furthermore, the Communicator periodically monitors the OutputQueue for messages that have to be sent to other agents.

The Planner module retrieves objectives from the ObjectiveQueue and produces plans that enable the agent to satisfy the objectives. A *plan* consists of a sequence of interrelated actions that are to be executed concurrently or in a specific order. In our current implementation, the agent planning process is based on a hierarchical task network (HTN) planning formalism [Tsuneto 1996]. Each objective is associated with a high-level task (*task schema*), which has to be reduced into subtasks using specific *task-reduction schemas*. Task-reduction schemas relate a task with a set of subtasks and actions and describe the information-flow relationships between them. That is, a reduction may specify that the result of one subtask (such as the action of retrieving the name of an agent) be provided as an input to another subtask (such as sending a KQML message). Each agent has a library of task schemas and task-reduction schemas. They characterize the kind of services provided by the agent and define its behavior in response to service requests. Simple actions are the final result of a task reduction (for a complete description of our task network representation, see [Sycara 1996]). The reduction of a task into actions is independent of their execution. This means that several tasks can be reduced concurrently before their corresponding objectives have been satisfied. The actions instantiated by the planner but not yet executed are called *active actions* and are inserted into the PlanQueue.

The Scheduler module schedules the execution of the active actions that are present in the PlanQueue. It has to decide when to allocate the agent's resources to a specific action or group of concurrent actions. Although scheduling can be very sophisticated, in our current implementation we use a simple earliest-deadline-first schedule execution heuristic. The Scheduler has been implemented following the Strategy pattern [Gamma 1995]. The sequence of the actions that have been scheduled for execution are stored inside the ScheduleQueue.

The ExecutionMonitor module prepares, monitors, and completes the execution of an action. It assigns a thread of execution to each action retrieved from the Schedule-Queue and monitors their execution with respect to resource usage and completion progress. For example, the action may have a completion deadline which, if not met, results in the action being interrupted. Another example of monitoring strategy is illustrated when a certain external information source is temporarily out of service. The agent that needs data from this information source shouldn't just wait passively until the service is back; instead, the agent might want to try another information source or switch its attention to other tasks for a certain period of time before returning to the original task. The execution of an action may consist of control operations on software or hardware devices that affect the external environment, or in communicative acts to other agents. In the latter case, a message is generated and inserted into the Out-putQueue.

The BeliefDatabase contains facts, constraints, and other knowledge reflecting the agent's current model of the environment. It also contains assertions, such as the names, addresses, and service description of the agent's collaborators. The Knowledge base is dynamically updated at runtime, based on the occurrence of environmental events and interactions with other agents.

The Coordinator module manages the interactions with the other agents in the organization. In particular, it is responsible for updating the BeliefDatabase with information concerning the agent's collaborators. For example, when the execution of an action requires an external service, the Coordinator first queries the BeliefDatabase for the name of a collaborator that can provide that service. If such a collaborator is unknown, the Collaborator queries the MatchMaker for a list of prospective collaborators, chooses one specific collaborator, and updates the BeliefDatabase with the corresponding identity information.

7.4.2 Basic Design Components

Concrete implementations of the basic agent architecture may include additional modules with specific capabilities and specific resources. They can be classified in four broad categories: task agents, interface agents, information agents, and middle agents.

> **Task agents.** Support decision making by formulating problem-solving plans and carrying out these plans through querying and exchanging information with other software agents. Task agents have knowledge of the task domain, and of how to collaborate with other task agents or information agents that can help to perform various parts of the task. They are implemented by specializing all the

elemental components that belong to the basic agent architecture. Usually, the Planner and the Scheduler are highly sophisticated.

Interface agents. Manage a graphical interface in order to interact with the user that is receiving user specifications and delivering results. They acquire, model, and utilize user preferences to guide system coordination in support of the user's tasks. Because they do not perform complex planning and scheduling activities, the Planner and the Scheduler modules have very simple capabilities. On the contrary, they have a sophisticated Coordinator module, because it is responsible for identifying the collaborators (task agents) that are able to satisfy the user requests.

Information agents. Tightly coupled to information sources so as to find information in response to queries and actively monitor them for specified conditions; they do not perform complex planning and scheduling activities and do not need to establish complex interactions with other agents. Therefore, the Planner, Scheduler, and Coordinator modules have very simple capabilities. On the contrary, they have a sophisticated BeliefDatabase module, which is responsible for managing and updating the information coming from the external information sources.

Middle agents. A specific kind of information agent; they manage information regarding other agents. In addition, they provide the advertise and unadvertise services. In particular, the Broker agent has capabilities similar to those of task agents, because it acts as a service provider.

7.4.3 Domain-Specific Components

A variety of applications have already been designed and implemented using the RETSINA framework. Examples are WARREN, for financial portfolio management; PLEIADES, for personal productivity and organizational integration; and THALES, for satellite visibility forecasting. These applications consist of organizations of software agents, some of which have been reused across different applications in the same application domain and are now part of the framework component library. Usually, they manage specific resources and provide specific functionalities (for example, an asset allocation critic that uses a model from finance theory to offer suggestions regarding a portfolio's allocation of assets).

Reusing these agents requires that their specific capabilities be customized. RETSINA agents support the so-called *graybox* customization: For each specific agent implemented when the framework is used, the developer has to specify the agent's knowledge and reasoning capabilities. As indicated by the agent model, a RETSINA agent's knowledge and reasoning capabilities are defined in a declarative way, in terms of assertions, rules, constraints, and task descriptions, which are implemented as data and stored in the agent's knowledge base and Task Schema library.

7.5 Framework Reuse

This section presents a set of guidelines for the development of multiagent applications using the RETSINA framework, with an example in the domain of financial portfolio management [Decker 1996]. Portfolio management (PM) is the task of providing an investment portfolio over time, using the information resources already available over the Internet. The goal, as stated in modern portfolio theory [Markowitz 1991], is to provide the best possible rate of return for a specified level of risk or, conversely, to achieve a specified rate of return with the lowest possible risk. In current practice, portfolio management is carried out by investment houses that employ teams of specialists in order to find, filter, and evaluate relevant information. A multiagent system approach is natural for portfolio management, in that it provides a natural mapping of multiple types of expertise into a set of interconnected agents. Agents, like objects, provide mechanisms for abstraction and modularity, which allow the designer to organize software systems as an aggregation of software units.

Developing a multiagent application is a process, which is closely related to well-known object-oriented praxis. Based on our experience, we have identified a set of guidelines, which in some steps resemble well-consolidated OO methods (such as object modeling technique (OMT) [Booch, 1991]), but that also exploit the characteristic elements of the agent model:

Find the key abstractions in the problem space. In the PM example, the key abstractions are the sources of information, the experts of the investment house, and the user.

Assign a role and a responsibility to each abstraction. In the PM example, each expert has a specific responsibility (for example, evaluating relevant information) and plays an intermediary role between the user and the sources of information.

Model each abstraction as an agent, choosing the appropriate architecture. In the PM example (see Figure 7.2), we have identified the following agents. Portfolio Manager is an interface agent that interacts graphically and textually with the user to acquire information about the user's profile and goals. The Analyst Tracking agent is a task agent that elaborates information about what human analysts are thinking about a company. The Fundamental Analysis agent is a task agent that calculates a stock's fundamental value by taking into consideration information such as a company's finances, forecasts of sales, earnings, and expansion plans. The Technical Analysis agent is a task agent that uses complex stochastic models to try to predict the near future in the stock market. The Market Tracker agent and the Economic Indicator agent are information agents that monitor stock-reporting Internet sources. The Historical Market agent is an information agent that manages a local repository.

Identify the knowledge and capabilities that each agent needs in order to fulfill its assigned responsibility, and the tasks it must be able to carry out to exploit its role. Build the domain-specific and agent-specific TaskSchema library and TaskReduction library (possibly by reusing those which already exist). For example, in order to evaluate relevant information the agent needs storage capabilities so as to gather information; it also must be able to execute tasks such as comparing the acquired information and distinguishing between relevant and irrelevant information by means of metrics, which are part of its knowledge.

For each agent, define the services it provides to other agents and the communication protocol to query those services. For example, the Market Tracker agent recognizes the request message with content "current price of IBM stock." The agent will interpret the message and will instantiate a goal to find and provide the information requested.

For each agent, identify the external resources and functionalities that the agent needs in order to fulfill its tasks and that may be provided by other agents in the system. The same functionality may be provided by different agents and the same agent may provide several functionalities. For example, in PM the Analyst Tracking agent needs information that can be provided by the Historical Market agent.

Identify the type of organization that the agents belong to (as defined in *Section 7.3.4*). Choose the appropriate middle agents. The PM problem is best modeled by a bureaucratic functional units organization, where the manager of the investment house is represented by a task agent that delegates some tasks to teams of specialists.

Figure 7.2 shows the snapshot of a possible pattern of relationships between the agents in the organization. In particular, The Economic Indicator agent is advertising its capabilities; the Analyst Tracking agent is querying the MatchMaker for the identity of a Fundamental Analysis agent; the Portfolio Manager is requesting services to the Analyst Tracking agent and to the Technical Analysis agent.

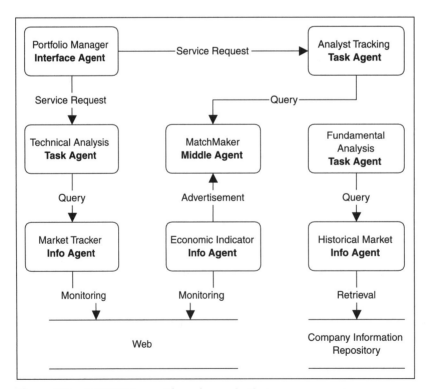

Figure 7.2 A RETSINA agent-based organization.

7.5.1 Comparison with other Reuse Techniques

As a reuse technique, agent-oriented (AO) application frameworks closely resemble both component off-the-shelf (COTS) development [Boehm 1995] and OO application frameworks [Fayad-Schmid 1997].

Component-based development consists of building new applications by assembling previously existing blackbox software components. The developer designs the architecture of the application and writes the main function that defines the control flow and information flow between the components. Integrating components requires a considerable effort because their design and implementation is fixed and cannot be customized.

On the contrary, OO application frameworks support the so-called *inversion of control:* The framework provides the application architecture and the main control flow, which defines how the user-provided components are executed. The developer builds a new application by customizing the variable aspects of the framework; usually, a framework supports both whitebox and blackbox customization. Whitebox customization of a framework requires a deep understanding of the framework implementation.

Both component development and OO application frameworks require the developer to code a considerable part of each new application. AO application frameworks mainly differ from them in that they are intended to promote graybox customization. Ideally, a new application is built by selecting concrete implementations of agents with a specific functionality and integrating them to form a multi-agent organization.

Different from COTS development, agent integration does not require the developer to write a high-level function that coordinates the agent activities. Instead, the developer creates relationships between the agents and determines the information and control flow between them by customizing the variable aspects of each single agent. In particular, for each agent the developer specifies (1) the knowledge and capabilities (data, rules, and constraints) that the agent needs in order to fulfill the assigned responsibility, (2) the interagent communication protocol (that is, how the agent may be used by other agents), and (3) the external dependencies between an agent's functionality and resources (TaskSchema).

We call this approach to software integration *reinversion of control* [Brugali-Sycara 1999] so as to emphasize its differences with the more common approach of OO application frameworks. The behavior of the whole application is determined by the behavior of each single agent and the agents' mutual interactions. Interoperability between agents is guaranteed by the common infrastructure and architecture provided by the framework used to implement them.

AO application frameworks also differ from *horizontal frameworks* such as CORBA [Vinoski 1997] in their approach to system integration. CORBA provides a set of middleware services for object distribution and interoperability. Specific applications are built on top of the CORBA infrastructure and have to be designed from scratch. On the contrary, AO application frameworks are semidefined applications that solve most of the difficult problems in a specific application domain.

7.6 Related Work

Researchers have applied multiagent technology in several application domains: electronic markets [Merz 1996], telecommunications [Magedanz 1996], and concurrent engineering [Petrie 1996]. In the following, we describe some of the more interesting systems and frameworks that have been developed for creating multiagent applications.

Coracle. A framework developed at Brown University that supports distributed computing and multiagent coordination. The framework consists of components organized in three abstraction levels. At the base level, the components provide functionalities for agent communication. At the next level, the components embed common control protocols (such as client-server, pipelines, and so forth). At the highest level, the components embed different coordination protocols (such as contract net) [Lejter-Dean 1996].

DESIRE. A modeling methodology developed by the Artificial Intelligence Group at Vrije University, Amsterdam. In DESIRE, multiagent systems are modeled and specified as compositional systems, and agents as interacting complex components [DESIRE 1997].

JAFMAS. A framework developed by Deepika Chauhan and Bert Baker at the Department of Electrical and Computer Engineering and Computer Science, University of Cincinnati. It provides guidelines for the development of multiagent systems along with a set of classes for agent deployment in Java. It supports multicast and directed communication, KQML or other speech-act performatives, and coordination protocols among a collection of intelligent agents forming the multiagent system [Chauhan 1997].

IBM Aglets Workbench. A visual environment for building network-based applications that use mobile agents to search for and transfer information. IBM Aglets are mobile Java programs which may travel and execute in specialized nodes in the network [IBM Aglets 1996].

JATLite. Currently being developed by the Computer Science Department at Stanford University. It provides a set of Java packages that facilitates agent framework development using the Java language. JATLite provides basic communication tools and templates for developing agents that exchange KQML messages through TCP/IP [Petrie 1996].

InteRRaP. A layered agent architecture developed at the German Artificial Intelligence Research Institute (DFKI). It is meant for designing complex dynamic agent societies for manufacturing scheduling applications and for robotics. It consists of an agent knowledge base and its associated control unit on top of a perception-action component [InteRRaP 1994].

dMARS. An agent-oriented development and implementation environment designed for building distributed, time-critical systems. It is being developed by the Australian Artificial Intelligence Institute (AAII). It is intended to help with system design and maintenance [dMars 1996].

7.7 Summary

A number of researchers are reexamining OO's basic potential, that the object paradigm can give the programmer tremendous flexibility [Guerraoui 1996]. In some application domains (such as open distributed systems) the object model has turned out to be too brittle.

Several researchers are exploiting ideas from other disciplines in order to enhance the flexibility and usability of the object model in the development of complex systems. Agent technology is an attempt to accommodate basic OO concepts (such as abstraction and modularity) and advanced artificial intelligence techniques (such as reasoning and learning). The aim is to provide the programmer with a basic unit of design (the agent) that enhances software modularity, maintainability, and reuse. Through the development of RETSINA, we are pursuing this idea further, by raising the level of reuse from single agent components to entire architectures (multiagent systems) and up to the development of application frameworks.

7.8 References

[Agha 1992] Agha, G., I. Mason, S. Smith, and C. Talcott. Towards a theory of actor computation. *Proceedings of the Third International Conference on Concurrency Theory (CONCURR 1992)*. Lecture Notes in Computer Science (LNCS) Vol. 630, Stony Brook, NY, August 1992, pp. 565–579. Springer-Verlag, 1992.

[Boehm 1995] Boehm, C. Reuse emphasized at next process workshop. *Software Engineering Notes*, 20(5), November 1995.

[Bokowski 1996] Bokowski, B. Interaction protocols for composing concurrent objects. *Proceedings of ECOOP 1996, Workshop on Composability Issues*. Linz, Austria, July 1996. Heidelberg, Germany: dpunkt, 1996.

[Booch 1991] Booch, G. *Object Oriented Design with Applications*. Redwood City, CA, Benjamin/Cummings, 1991.

[Brugali 1997] Brugali, D., G. Menga, and A. Aarsten. The framework life span. *Communications of the ACM*, Theme Issue on Object-Oriented Application Frameworks, Mohamed E. Fayad and Douglas Schmidt, editors, 40(10), October 1997.

[Brugali-Sycara 1999] Brugali, D., and K. Sycara. Towards agent oriented application frameworks. *ACM Computing Surveys*, Symposium on Application Frameworks, March 1999.

[Chauhan 1997] Chauhan, D. JAFMAS: A Java-based agent framework for multiagent systems development and implementation. Ph.D. thesis, University of Cincinnati, www.ececs.uc.edu/~abaker/JAFMAS/, 1997.

[Conrad 1997] Conrad, S., G. Saake, and C. Tuerker. Towards an agent-oriented framework for specification of information systems. *Proceedings of the International Conference on Autonomous Agents (Agents 1997)*. Marina del Rey, CA, February 5–8, 1997.

[Decker 1996] Decker, K. Sycara, and D. Zeng. Designing a multi-agent portfolio management system. *Proceedings of the AAAI-96 Workshop on Internet-Based Information Systems*. Portland, August 4–9, 1996.

[DESIRE 1997] DESIRE 1997. Artificial Intelligence Group, www.cs.vu.nl/vakgroepen/ai/projects/desire/. Vrjje University, Amsterdam, 1997.

[DMars 1996] DMars 1996. Australian Artificial Intelligence Institute, www.aaii.oz.au/proj/dMARS-prod-brief.html, 1996.

[Falasconi 1996] Falasconi, S., G. Lanzola, and M. Stefanelli. Using ontologies in multi-agent systems. *Tenth Knowledge Acquisition for Knowledge-Based Systems Workshop (KAW 1996).* Banff, Canada, November 9–14, 1996.

[Fayad-Schmidt 1997] Fayad, M., and D. Schmidt. Object-oriented application frameworks. *Communications of the ACM,* 40(10), October 1997.

[Finin 1994] Finin, T., R. Fritzson, D. McKay, and R. McEntire. KQML as an agent communication language. *Proceedings of the Third International Conference on Information and Knowledge Management (CIKM 1994).* Gaitherburg, MD, November 29–December 2, 1994, Reading, MA: ACM Press, 1994.

[Gamma 1995] Gamma, E., R. Helm, R. Johnson, and J. Vlissides. *Design Patterns: Elements of Reusable Object Oriented Software.* Reading, MA: Addison-Wesley, 1995.

[Genesereth 1994] Genesereth, M., and S. Ketchpel. Software Agents. *Communications of the ACM,* 37(7), July 1994.

[Guerraoui 1996] Guerraoui, R. Strategic research directions in object oriented programming. *ACM Computing Survey,* 28(4), December 1996.

[Holland 1992] Holland, I. Specifying reusable components using contracts. *Proceedings of ECOOP 1992.* Utrecht, The Netherlands, June 1992, Proceedings: Lecture Notes in Computer Science (LNCS), Vol. 165, Springer-Verlag, 1992.

[IBM Aglets 1996] IBM Aglets: Programming mobile agents in Java. White paper, IBM Tokyo Research Laboratory, www.ibm.co.jp/trl/aglets/whitepaper.html, 1996.

[Lejter-Dean 1996] Lejter, M., and T. Dean. A framework for the development of multi-agent architectures. *IEEE Expert,* Special Issue on Intelligent Systems and their Applications, 11(6), December 1996: 47–59.

[Magedanz 1996] Magedanz, T., K. Rothermel, and S. Krause. Intelligent agents: An emerging technology for next generation telecommunications? *Proceedings of INFO-COM 1996.* San Francisco, CA, March 24–28, 1996.

[Markowitz 1991] Markowitz, H. *Portfolio Selection: Efficient Diversification of Investments,* 2d ed. Cambridge, MA: B. Blackwell, 1991.

[Merz 1996] Merz, M., and W. Lamersdorf. Agents, services, and electronic markets: How do they integrate? *Proceedings of the IFIP/IEEE International Conference on Distributed Platforms.* Dresden, Germany, February 27–March 1, 1996.

[Mili 1995] Mili, H., F. Mili, and A. Mili. Reusing software: Issues and research directions. *IEEE Transactions on Software Engineering.* 21(6), June 1995.

[Minoura 1993] Minoura, T., S. Pargaonkar, and K. Rehfuss. Structural active object systems for simulation. *Proceedings of OOPSLA 1993.* Washington, DC, October 1993.

[Petrie 1996] Petrie, C. Agent-based engineering, the web, and intelligence. *IEEE Expert,* Special Issue on Intelligent Systems and their Applications, 11(6), December 1996: 24–29.

[Pree 1994] Pree, W. *Design Patterns for Object-Oriented Software Development.* Reading, MA: Addison-Wesley, 1994.

[Riecken 1994] Riecken, D. Intelligent agents. *Communications of the ACM,* (37)7, July 1994.

[Searle 1969] Searle, J. *Speech Acts*. Cambridge, England: Cambridge University Press, 1994.

[Sycara 1996] Sycara, K., A. Pannu, M. Williamson, and D. Zeng. Distributed intelligent agents. *IEEE Expert,* Special Issue on Intelligent Systems and their Applications, 11(6), December 1996.

[Sycara 1997] Sycara, K., K. Decker, and M. Williamson. Middle-agents for the internet. *Proceedings of the International Joint Conference on Artificial Intelligence (IJCAI 1997).* Nagoya, Japan, August 23–29, 1997.

[Tsuneto 1996] Tsuneto, R., K. Erol, J. Hendler, and D. Nau. Commitment strategies in hierarchical task network planning. *Proceedings of the Thirteenth National Conference on Artificial Intelligence (AAAI 1997).* Providence, RI, August 1–3, 1997.

[Vinoski 1997] Vinoski, S. CORBA: Integrating diverse applications within distributed heterogeneous environments. *Proceedings of IEEE Communications Magazine,* 14(2), February 1997.

[Wiederhold 1992] Wiederhold, G., P. Wegner, and S. Cefi. Toward megaprogramming. *Communications of the ACM,* 33(11), 1992: 89–99.

CHAPTER 8

Experimentation with an Agent-Oriented Platform in JAVA

The flapping of a single butterfly's wings today produces a tiny change in the state of the atmosphere. Over a period of time, what the atmosphere actually does diverges from what it would have done. So, in a month's time, a tornado that would have devastated the Indonesian coast doesn't happen. Or maybe one that wasn't going to happen, does.
—I. Stewart [Stewart 1989]

8.1 Modeling Complex Systems for Simulation Purposes

This chapter begins by showing that simulation plays an important role for understanding complex systems and framework specifications.

8.1.1 Simulation as a Solution to Understanding Complex Systems

Complex systems arise in the social, biological, physical, and behavioral sciences, in phenomena from urban traffic networks to price movements on financial markets. The frightening complexity of natural systems emphasizes simulation applications as the best actual solution to understanding and predicting their underlying phenomena. Simulation is an appropriate methodology whenever a phenomenon is not directly accessible, either because it no longer exists, or because its structure or behavior is so complex that the user cannot know what is going on [Conte-Gilbert 1995]. It may help to reformulate the system behavior model in more specific and empirically relevant terms. The boom of computer science in systems modeling during the past 20 years has greatly increased the understanding of complex systems through the use of virtual simulation. This technology is proposed by both researchers and industrial engineers, constituting a real research–industry transfer. From accumulated experience, simulation is now considered to be ahead of theoretical approaches, and is becoming a promising tool in this framework.

Our framework relates to the SWARM system [Minar 1996], one of the best-known simulation platforms with agents. In SWARM the agent's behavior is defined by the emergent phenomena of the agents inside its swarm. However, a swarm does not explicitly dispose of any organizational structure, no further information being needed when the phenomenon appears; this causes the difference with our approach.

To make the best use of simulation, the first step is to aggregate data, knowledge, and hypotheses to build a model of the physical world. A *model* is defined as an abstraction of the real system, governed by laws and structured concepts. This model is generally expressed by mathematical relationships between variables, such as differential equations. Simulation consists of making a system abstraction (a model) evolve over time in order to try to understand the system's working and behavior and to analyze the properties of the theoretical models. Simulations run on computers provide tests to validate the theoretical model, or they may simply allow the experimenter to observe and record the target system's behavior. Results can then be processed and exploited with the help of statistical techniques to verify the given hypotheses.

8.1.2 Framework Specifications and Challenges

Our "customers" are industrial engineers and researchers who want to explore and understand the field of potential actions in a specific domain by simulation. In the domain to be investigated, the question is not what has happened, or even what might have happened, but rather what the sufficient conditions are for a given result to be obtained.

This chapter discusses the design and implementation of a development environment (sometimes called a *tool* or *platform*) that is intended to model and simulate complex systems. For instance, this kind of tool is meant for researchers who need to simulate complex physical models, without having to implement the whole application on their own. In terms of software engineering issues, this objective requires generic applicability and reusability as first objectives of the platform design, which justifies the use of object-oriented design methodology such as object modeling technique (OMT) [Rumbaugh 1991]. Indeed, our purpose is to produce a complete toolkit as a virtual laboratory for designing a large scope of dynamic systems and studying the informational structure of complex systems, and to provide generic interfaces to set and control the simulation.

The project is then dictated by the facts that (1) there are no appropriate tools (especially in simulation), (2) reducing complexity to model complex systems requires appropriate structures, and (3) intrinsic mechanisms of global behavior emergence are complex and not clearly identified. As the system complexity can not be globally expressed, the challenge is to find a computational model able to represent and distribute complexity in individual elements, represent the system's dynamics as local interactions between agents, and provide mechanisms so that simulation results emerge by interpreting such local interactions.

The following section presents the design of a platform conforming to such specifications.

8.2 Matching the Agent Paradigm with Framework Challenges

This section gives an overview of different views, and levels of abstraction and matches the agent paradigm with framework challenges.

8.2.1 A Global View of the Platform Analysis

Figure 8.1 gives a general view of the platform analysis, which is briefly exposed here before being detailed in the following sections.

Horizontally, the platform is described following three software engineering layers:

Language layer. Describes Java as an object-oriented language, which has been chosen to implement the platform. The reasons for this choice are twofold. The first concerns the clarity and cleanness of the language, according to the object-oriented philosophy and mechanisms (all-is-object, static and dynamic inheritance, dynamic overloading, polymorphism, and so forth), as well as its utilities, such as threads, which are useful for agent implementation. The second is Java's safety catch when using applets—that is, small, subordinate or embeddable applications to be run and used within the context of a larger application, such as a web browser [Neimeyer-Peck 1996].

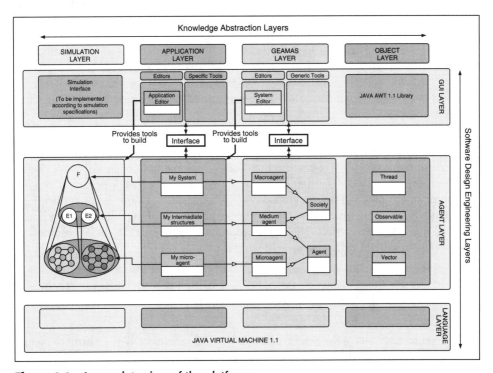

Figure 8.1   A complete view of the platform.

Agent layer. Adds the agents' capabilities to Java—that is, independence, autonomy, and evolution features.

GUI layer. Hides the complexity of languages and agents to the user by introducing interfaces needed to build applications and derive simulations with the platform. The GUI layer helps in integrating the platform as a toolkit and a virtual laboratory for complex systems simulation purposes. This chapter does not go further into this layer for reasons of space.

The platform is also vertically based on four knowledge abstraction layers:

Object layer. This is the language layer. It is composed of each Java class being used or derived to implement the subabstraction layers. Figure 8.1 illustrates some of these classes—for instance, Thread, to allow parallel tasking; Observable, to allow the use of demon functions; or Vector, to dynamically manage a list of values.

Generic Architecture for Multiagent Simulation (GEAMAS) layer. This layer implements a computational model of agents to match the specifications required by complex systems simulation. The GEAMAS layer constitutes the heart of the system. It includes a specific architecture (composed of a macroagent, medium agents, and microagents), the description of an agent and a society model, and self-organization mechanisms required by complex systems simulations. Figure 8.2 illustrates such a layer, which is described in the following sections. In Figure 8.2, a double arrow means that the two objects that participate in the relationship mutually need to be known to each other. A simple arrow from A to B means that A objects need to know about B objects to act, but that B objects do not require the opposite; therefore, the connection of the relationship from B to A is not to be implemented (it is represented between square brackets in Figure 8.2). Finally, if any object needs to be mutually known, the relationship is dropped (that is the case between the Structure and Agent classes, information being assumed to transit between Agent and Society).

Application layer. This layer can be seen as the result of the GEAMAS layer applied on a specific domain. An application is then understood as a real-world translation in terms of agents following the model implemented in the GEAMAS layer. Building an application then consists of describing the real world by deriving some or all classes of the previous layer by using GUIs. Examples of applications might be the description of a volcano in geophysics or of the evolution of a financial market in economics. The Application layer is a set of classes, whose definition is provided by the system editor.

Simulation layer. This is the instance level of the application. It defines the set of instances of the previous classes. The instantiation of such classes is graphically set with the help of the application editor, which proposes some fill-in-the-blanks windows to set each parameter value.

The next section details the design of the GEAMAS layer, which gives birth to agents as the basic units to model real-world components in our platform.

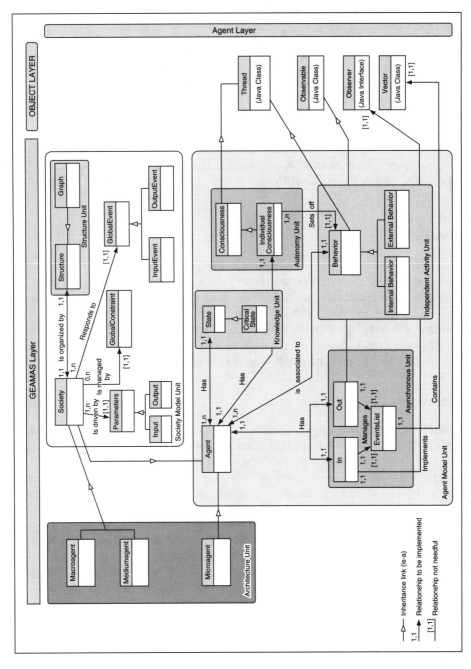

Figure 8.2 Object-oriented design of the GEAMAS layer.

177

8.2.2 The GEAMAS Layer: Macro, Micro, and Medium

The architecture is based on three abstraction levels. Each successive level represents a higher level of abstraction. Each abstraction level describes a degree of knowledge complexity and applies a model of agents, through the expression of knowledge, behavior, and evolution capabilities. Each level is independent, executing processes asynchronously and representing a higher level of abstraction than the one below it. Furthermore, the architecture implements the *recursion* property to greatly reduce the design of the system, by applying the same agent-model to coarse-grain and fine-grain components. To move up and down levels, two fundamental mechanisms are introduced: Decomposition and Recomposition. *Decomposition* allows the transfer of information to lower levels, until *Recomposition* allows the transfer of information back to higher levels.

Macrolevel

The macrolevel describes a *coarse-grain agent* as a related element in which global solutions will be observed. It builds on the underlying agents' organization in a society. In multiagent systems, such an organization has no reason to be if it is unable to represent interaction facilities between agents. The society is therefore organized as a network of acquaintances, managing agents in the system to match global specifications. The role of the whole system is expressed through an external behavior, and driven by an input/output interface with the external world (software or human).

Microlevel

The microlevel corresponds to *fine-grain agents*. It describes the microlevel as reactive agents. Each reactive agent is described by interactions, microbehaviors, and evolution capabilities. At runtime, agents interact in a concurrent way with their surroundings. The microlevel masks the complexity of the whole system, which is encapsulated in agents describing low-level and basic actions. Such reactive agents are often called *cells* in some related areas (biology or medicine, for instance), or *microagents*, in a more general way. A microagent is reactive, as it generates behavior without explicit representation of the domain or global task constraints; microagents just interact with their surroundings and evolve over time by updating their internal state. They get close to each other and form a compact group. They act in response to events that are too fine-grained to be understood (or explained) by a macroagent. Interactions between microagents are thus provided by signals which do not bear semantics, their meaning depending on the interpretative ability of the receiver.

Medium Level

However, as we have seen before, a complex system should integrate the nonpredictable dimension: The critical state of the system leads to catastrophes. Our assumptions are then to consider the critical state as assigned to particular states of microagents, and the avalanche to a *spatiotemporal aggregation*, in some particular context and environment, and under specific conditions, of microagents taking part in the phenomenon. The result of this aggregation is then an emergent structure created by self-organization in the multiagent system.

Therefore, the main issue is to look for a computational model that can represent and characterize self-organization from local interactions between agents. Considering a two-level architecture in the system makes the catastrophe-modeling task difficult for two reasons. On one hand, as a microlevel is described by fine-grain agents, the organization of new structures cannot be processed at such a microscopic level; it does not have enough knowledge to do so. Beyond this microscopic dimension, emergent structures can arise only in one macroscopic level, disposing of missing knowledge. On the other hand, it is often impossible for a macrolevel to characterize and correctly identify the whole set of emergent structures. As the complex system is nonpredictable and badly understood, trying to explain emergence mechanisms at the global level of the system fails. As a matter of fact, a significant number of microagents could intervene in the whole emergence process, making the system too complex to be analyzed at a macrolevel.

It is then elegant to introduce an intermediate-grain level between the macrolevel and the microlevel, embedded as suborganizations. Such an intermediate level is called the *medium level,* and the suborganizations, *medium agents.* The medium level is designed before the simulation begins by giving suborganizations structure and behavior. This point of view enforces the necessity of finding the most efficient abstraction when designing this level, which is totally dependent of the context tackled [Marcenac-Calderoni 1997]. However, medium agents are not dynamically predefined in the system, because they spontaneously appear during the simulation as the result of self-organization. When self-organization arises (meaning that the system's critical state is reached), a new medium agent will be created within the system to model the catastrophe.

This approach seems handy, because it allows consideration of the catastrophe as an entire entity able to compute its own properties. Moreover, it is at the right place to distribute new computed values after the critical point is reached in order to constrain the affected part of the system. Medium agents' properties are computed and set when the organization is built. Such properties are then reintroduced in underlying lower-level agents as constraints to apply in their own structures, a mechanism called *back-propagation.* In this way, a medium agent plays its causal role for the rest of the simulation, by constraining a part of the system.

8.2.3 A Detailed View of the Society Model

The macrolevel manages agents in the system in order to match global specifications of the application; it is inscribed in a model called the *society model.* The society model describes the role, the interface, and the whole organization of the system: The system's role is expressed through behaviors (global events and global constraints); the interface with the external world (software or human) describes input and output parameters for simulation needs; and the organization is managed through a structure of interrelated agents.

Society Knowledge

Input parameters govern the whole system and describe all agents' states. In a sense, input parameters restrict the system extent by constraining agents' states. Output parameters express the role of the system. Such parameters are used to measure the simulation results of the system outputs. They express the external behavior of the system to be observed by the user that constitutes the system's goal. They are managed by a graphical user interface (GUI) described by the GUI editors of the Application layer.

Society Structure

The structure of the society describes how agents are organized, and is then responsible for the collective of agents representing interagent connections (as interaction possibilities between agents). This organization is defined as the description of agents' dynamic relationships used to structure interactions within the system. The structure is then organized as a *network of acquaintances*, forming a competence network, wherein agents correspond to nodes, and interaction possibilities (acquaintances relationships) correspond to edges. The choice of a network as a data structure to organize agents is justified by its flexibility and its general nature of adaptability to several situations [Marcenac 1996]. In addition, it allows the description of some real-world topologic representations, where the geometry can be implicitly represented. Indeed, the number of acquaintances of each agent determines the topology, and constitutes a very interesting feature, showing how a real world could be designed as a three-dimensional network. This parameter is called the agents' *connectivity*. As connections determine the ability of an agent to communicate, a part of the communication protocol is then defined by setting this parameter. This number of connections describes the influence an agent can have on another, and defines a spatial and geometric disposition of the agents.

In addition, some more information has been added in the diagram in Figure 8.3.

First, edges can be strengthened to take the signal intensity between two agents into account. This feature allows a certain priority of messages among agents to be expressed by the application designer. Indeed, the intensity of a signal emitted by an agent decreases as a function of the distance between agents, and agents' behavior is

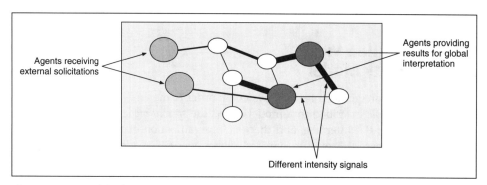

Figure 8.3   Model of agents' organization in the society.

strongly dictated by their relative position in the topological structure. In our model, agents evolve in a world whose structure is defined by the agents' communication network, and an agent can interact solely with its immediate neighborhood. Agents' behavior and state are therefore influenced by the actions of their neighbors. When an agent acts or changes state, some of its neighbors may react more or less strongly according to the signal intensity.

Second, some agents are shown as able to receive external solicitations. This kind of agent will be considered first when an external event has to be performed by the system. In descriptive real worlds, such as physics, for instance, such agents generally model the system's side. Finally, along the same idea, some agents are shown as able to provide results, modeling, for instance, the opposite side of the system. This information allows the system to compute simulation results or adapt its behavior (see Figure 8.3).

Society Behavior

The behavioral part of the society describes what the system has been designed for. It includes the following:

> **Global events description.** This describes events being performed by the system. Each external event is first interpreted by the society that controls the event. As the system's behavior is nonlinear, this event cannot be performed at the global level. The external event is therefore decomposed on underlying agents able to receive external solicitations, according to the general decomposition mechanisms described following.

> **Global constraints definition.** This defines parameters that could constrain the whole structure by applying specific behaviors. They are composed of general strategies and laws according to the domain tackled. For instance in a financial market, there can be a law prohibiting certain types of trades when the Dow Jones Industrial Average has declined more than 50 points from its previous close (this rule was instituted by the New York Stock Exchange shortly after Monday, October 19, 1987, to prevent the kind of panic seen on that Black Monday).

> **Acquaintance establishment.** When simulation begins, each agent looks for acquaintances in the organization according to the network topology, so agents might communicate with neighbor ones.

General Mechanisms

What is not shown in Figure 8.2 is a set of global mechanisms that assures general tasks at the society level. Two kinds of mechanisms are identified: first, a set of decomposition mechanisms that allows a global input event to be distributed over the network in order to be performed by lower-level agents; second, the part of the self-organization mechanisms needed to create, manage, and preserve consistency of medium agents during phenomena emergence.

Decomposition Mechanisms

The *Decomposition* process is defined to propagate a message to underlying agents. Decomposition allows information to be transferred in lower levels of the architecture.

When receiving a Decomposition message, the agent gets information given by its society. Two kinds of information can be addressed by such a message. First, a Decomposition message could specify that an external event is to be performed by lower-level agents. For instance, the external perturbation has to be distributed between all concerned sublevel agents, such as between the society and the microagents. This type of message helps microagents to be ready to perform the event. The event is thus divided up, and subevents are transferred to the microagents that are best able to process them. Conversely, there may be laws or knowledge on a macrolevel that must be observed by microagents—for instance, knowledge that constrains microagents' movements. A society is the right place to express such knowledge; it may constrain part of the state and behavior of its subordinate microagents, by acting on either the world structure or on individual microagents.

A process is also defined to find the *handling* underlying agents that can perform an event, according to agents defined as able to receive external solicitations in the organization. It defines a kind of process that is responsible for localizing the necessary agents to perform a kind of event and that remains coherent with the current goal of the society.

Finally, a *filtering function* receives an external event in input and provides discretized subevents in output. Such a function is application-relative, as the method of transforming an event in such tiny simulated events cannot be generic in any case. For instance, in a geophysical application, such as modeling volcanic eruptions, external perturbations are caused by specific behaviors; for instance, to simulate external fluid feeding, such as from the earth's core, magma volumes are injected within the system. When drained, the society modeling the edifice has to distribute the external injection to microagents modeling magma lenses. The event is divided in order to model the fluid flow: If a volume of magma V is transferred to a lens during the simulation, the input volume is discretized in multiples n of V, and an amount of magma nV is injected into each microagent. From a programming point of view, nV values represent time units required to recompute the internal pressure between two messages. Indeed, microagents modify their state rapidly, in order to maintain the correct pressure value and be ready for the arrival of new disturbances. At the injection of the next nV, the microagent is then ready to process the new computation.

Global Self-Organization Mechanisms

When self-organization is required to represent emergent phenomena, a global mechanism is used to create a medium agent, aggregating some microagents or adding them to an existing suborganization. If a suborganization already exists, the underlying medium agent managing the suborganization is advised, and the new microagent is integrated within the existing structure. Note that if the two microagents are members of two different suborganizations, they can be integrated on both suborganizations, to take different emergent phenomena into account. If no medium agent already exists, the global creation mechanism creates a new medium agent responsible for the emergent structure. This agent will then be populated step by step. Finally, note that such an encapsulated microagent can leave the structure at any time, if its state evolves again. If only one agent remains in the structure, the suborganization is deleted.

Beyond this mechanism, backpropagation involves a medium agent to act as a feedback on each member of its structure. At the design phase of the application, the designer gives the void structure of a medium agent defining properties that are independent of the microagents' properties. During the simulation, when the medium agent is entirely populated, the global mechanism computes appropriate values for the new agent's state. Setting new properties in a medium agent becomes easy at this point, mainly because the global creation mechanism can pick up information from lower levels. This set of new properties defines a kind of constraint or restriction governing the new structure. This constraint acts as a global law for all underlying microagents belonging to the structure, and backpropagation is the way to inform such microagents. Therefore, when the emergent structure backpropagates a constraint, it forces the behavior of underlying agents by applying some of its properties to them. This view is very close to reality: For instance, during an eruption each magma lens releases energy and moves into the system. The remaining energy is then low, and the microagents should be properly reinitialized so that the whole system behavior might be modified accordingly.

8.2.4 A Detailed View of the Agent Model

The agent model is the most important part of the platform, as it defines the agent as the only unit to be handled when modeling. It describes the agent's knowledge, role, independence and autonomy capabilities, and local mechanisms for self-organization purposes. Knowledge is given by states; role is expressed though internal and external behaviors; asynchronous part is ensured by two mailboxes (In and Out); and autonomy is managed by a kind of metacontrol of the agent's behavior, named *consciousness*.

Agent's Knowledge

The agent's state is represented with a *state vector,* from which each coordinate describes an internal property. A subset of these internal properties, called *state parameters*, is limited by *thresholds* giving the agent's critical state. A specific behavior is then associated with each threshold. Thresholds and state parameters are set during the designing phase of the application. The agent's stability is defined as a satisfaction state with regard to its role. An agent is then stable when state parameter values do not reach the thresholds.

Agent's Behavior

The agent's behavior represents what the agent is able to do during its life. In our model, the agent's behavior can be internal or external. *Internal behaviors* allow agents to work without external solicitations. They describe a life cycle of the agent and perform actions continually by updating the state vector. Internal behaviors ensure the independent part of the agent. For this reason, the agent's behavior should be implemented as a Thread (in the Java sense, that is, as a parallel process). *External behaviors* are provided by the agent when receiving external solicitations (such as events). For instance, one of the scenarios for such an external behavior might be: (1) update the state vector, (2) compute the rest of the constraints to propagate in the neighborhood,

(3) choose agents to which to propagate the event, and (4) propagate the event in the chosen agents.

Agent's Asynchronous Part

The asynchronous part of the agent is derived from the use of two mailboxes, In and Out. The *In* class stores input messages that should be performed by the agent, ordered by intensity. The *Out* class stores each message to be propagated in the agent's neighborhood after being locally performed. The mechanism used to set the appropriate behavior in a neighbor agent is not given by a traditional message, but is based on the observer mechanism in Java. Each In mailbox observes the agent's acquaintances' Out mailboxes. When an object B wants to propagate an event to its neighborhood, it leaves the message in the Out box. The Out box is observed by the In boxes of all acquaintances (agent A for instance), which automatically catch the message. This mechanism is similar to those of demon functions used in knowledge representation systems in the 1980s. Figure 8.4 illustrates such a mechanism.

Agent's Autonomous Part

The autonomous part of the agent is managed by a kind of metacontrol that controls the agent's behavior and determines which action to invoke. This mechanism allows maintaining room for decision making, because the agent's behavior is dynamically self-adapted during the simulation. This characteristic then authorizes an agent to reproduce adequate behaviors—that is, behaviors that are the best adapted to the environment and to the current situation. Such a mechanism is called *Consciousness*. As it constitutes the overcontrol of the agent, this process should itself be independent in order to be able to stop the agent's current behavior if some conditions change. This is why Consciousness inherits from Thread.

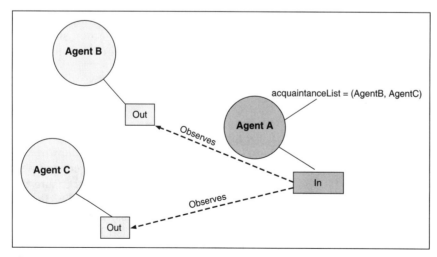

Figure 8.4 Observers and asynchronous message passing.

Recomposition

Recomposition is the bottom-up mechanism that is at the root of emergent behaviors of the system. It transfers information on the agent's stability from microlevel to macrolevel. The values of state parameters evolve during the simulation, based on multiple local interactions between microagents. When one threshold is reached, the agent is assumed to be unstable, and information is then transferred to the agent's society with a Recomposition message. Therefore, a Recomposition message is provided by microagents to alert the society that something unusual is happening. Shifting from the microlevel up to the upper level, the society collects data on microbehaviors, combines them to determine macrobehavior, and then adapts itself to the situation. Recomposition then requires that the society have some abilities to interpret information at low levels. A higher-level behavior then emerges from such an ability. In such cases, the dynamic of low-level agents governs emerging behaviors.

Local Self-Organization Mechanisms

Agents interact according to the organizational structure described at the macrolevel. If some agents are looking for cooperation to act together in a common purpose, others, on the contrary, will get clash. In this way, some groups of agents will be self-organized through interactions, forming new organizational structures. Self-organization then requires the following mechanisms:

A global mechanism to create and manage the new structure within the system. This mechanism was previously presented in the society model.

A local detection mechanism, distributed over microagents, to detect and identify an effective cooperation between interacting agents, leading to an emergent phenomenon. At the time an interaction occurs, an agent A alerts an agent B to look for its intentions. Then, a local observer mechanism compares agent A's intentions with those of agent B. As the similarity is detected, cooperation is established, and the agents can be considered to have organized for a common purpose. From this self-organization, an organizational structure emerges locally that has never been described in the system before. This structure is semantically based on the similarity between agents.

A mechanism in charge of ending the self-organization process when the emergent phenomenon stops. This mechanism, usually called an *observer*, acts as an end-detection mechanism by examining the neighborhood to look for potential agents that are not stable enough to propagate the phenomenon again. The end-detection mechanism computes the number of microagents remaining unstable. Thus, when the counter registers nil, the end of propagation is detected. In traditional multiagent systems, the programmed observer is generally implemented as a global loop inserted over the multiagent system or as a part of the society, to inspect the stability of underlying agents forming the structure. In our architecture, the programmed observer is distributed and locally defined, to remain close to the agent paradigm.

The next section describes some elements of the implementation, as well as hints to better design applications with the platform.

8.3 Java Implementation and Application Generation

The following section outlines the Java classes that have been implemented according to the design steps presented in *Section 8.2* and shows how to develop applications with the platform.

8.3.1 Java and Agents

To translate the design into implementation accurately, some simple rules have been followed by programmers. Each inheritance link has been implemented using the Java inheritance keyword extends, and multiinheritance has been avoided. As a consequence, the concept of Interface in Java has been reserved for defining parsers between each layer in the platform rather than for solving multiinheritance issues. An exception has been made for the observer mechanism, which requires the use of intrinsic interfaces. Each relationship size has been implemented by holding each size arrow and looking at its connections (see Figure 8.5):

Case 1,1. A parameter is added in the needed class.

Case 1,n. A container is created (Vector or List) and a parameter is added to refer to the container created.

Figure 8.6 gives a complete illustration of the Java class hierarchies defined to implement the whole platform according to the design.

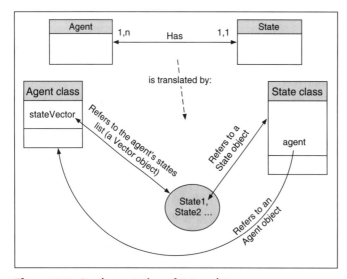

Figure 8.5 Implementation of 1,1 and 1,n.

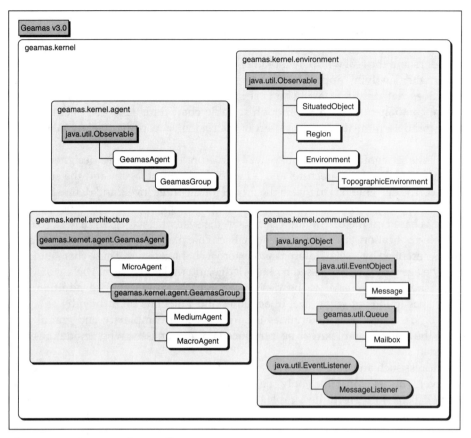

Figure 8.6   GEAMAS classes diagram.

8.3.2 Developing Applications with the Platform

After collecting a number of observations of the real world, empirical pattern rules are constructed which constitute the starting point of the real-world theory to be modeled. This description of the field to be investigated is called the *application*. Simulations are then derived from the application, and can be considered as application instances. To describe an application, the user must adapt an abstracted model of the real world to the three-level architecture. This foundation is inherent to the problem to be solved, namely modeling and reducing complexity. Modeling then consists of describing all levels in the architecture by applying the agent model and the society model at each appropriate level. After modeling, simulations are instanced from the application so built, and the real-world theory is tested against observation. If results are not satisfying, the theory can then be easily refined by deriving a new simulation from the application and repeating the experiment.

This section offers some hints in order to give the user the means to design an application in the best way. When using object-oriented analysis methods such as Coad and Yourdon's [Coad-Yourdon 1991] or OMT [Rumbaugh 1991], the first step is to understand the real world by looking at "business objects," which is particularly difficult when evolving applications in an unfamiliar environment. Designing with agents does not defy the law: The first step is to look at the real world to find software components that have enough suitable characteristics to be agents in the system and determine the logical aspect of the system, according to external specifications.

Then, the designing task is quite well structured, because the designer drives through a three-level architecture, and a model for both the agent and the society is provided. The designer has to match the model for the three levels and define the right level of complexity at each level. To find the adequate separation, the methodology we propose is based on the distribution of *roles* in the system. Each agent plays a role for the whole application, and bears semantics. Each role played by the agent in the application is described by a set of internal and external characteristics. These characteristics define the agent model, expressed by knowledge, internal and external behaviors, and consciousness, which have to be designed for each agent type. In addition, the designer has to look at what level of activities and functions performed by an agent should be described. This determines the right level of complexity and granularity. Finding the limit of complexity to be introduced is the main issue when modeling complex systems.

To address such an issue, three steps should be taken. First of all, begin to build the microlevel. This level inscribes only the agent model (no lower level, so no society to describe). Behaviors are quite simple, and can easily be split up into tiny pieces. Because a microagent can not be decomposed again, it describes the most tiny grain. The right level of granularity is reached when the agent cannot be described in any further detail, following the triad *knowledge–behavior–consciousness.* At this step, the stability of a reactive agent also has to be determined. Because the stability is given by some parameter thresholds, such an agent is stable when the values of associated parameters do not reach the thresholds. These values will then be computed according to messages handled by the microagent during the simulation. The computation depends on the complexity of the network described in the organization, and the neighboring agents' states.

The second step is to design the macrolevel. As the microlevel matches the agent model, a macroagent matches the society model. So the designer must define the input and output parameters of the system and the agents' organization (connectivity and intensity), as well as global events and constraints to be considered. Finally, the last step is to design the medium level. Two remarks could help the designer at this step: On one hand, a medium agent should apply both the agent and society models to respect the recursion property; on the other hand, a medium agent will be dynamically created by self-organization mechanisms. The medium level is then designed before the simulation begins by giving suborganizations structure and behavior according to agent and society models. However, medium agents are not dynamically predefined in the system because they spontaneously appear during the simulation as the result of self-organization.

8.4 A Real Example: Agricultural Biomass Management

Agricultural biomass management is becoming an important stake today, driven by environmental and pollution considerations. The objective of this application is a better understanding and management of stockbreeding operation effluents on Reunion Island, in the Indian Ocean, by using and comparing several simulation approaches. The system to carry out must, a priori, be centered on the simulation of matter flow, information flow, and financial flow. This will be achieved on the basis of the system structure (physical, technical, and geographical), of actor behavior, and of decisional choice. The model must make analyses possible. These analyses should point out relevant issues to the question of what would occur if one gathered a certain subset of stockbreeders around a certain composting platform, and those stockbreeders adopted a certain rule of management.

8.4.1 Agents and Situated Objects

Figure 8.7 represents the model structure on the basis of interactions between two Exploitation agents. In terms of agent classes, we thus distinguish Conveying agents (carriers) and Exploitation agents (made up of breeding and culture agents). Exploitation agents are equipped with an internal function of coordination and external communication. The internal function is determined by the *role*, an important notion of the application. The role describes either an offer or a demand.

These agents operate in an environment described as a whole of located objects. The distinction takes place on the basis of capacity to act: Whereas the agents are dynamic entities and have the capacity to act on other agents and their environment, the objects located are static entities that impose constraints on agents' actions, and can be modi-

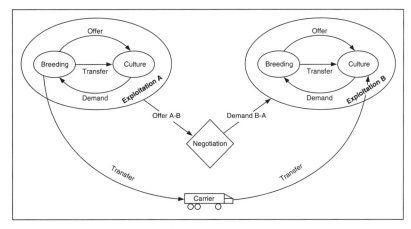

Figure 8.7 Illustration of Exploitation agents.

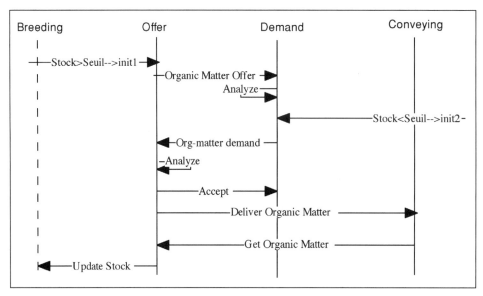

Figure 8.8   Negotiation between Exploitation agents.

fied only by them. The main identified objects located describe parcels, livestock buildings, and transportation communication channels (the roadway system). The application is then implemented following two main modules, biomas.agent (regrouping agents) and biomas.environment (which describes situated objects).

The environment is implemented as simple Java classes, but each agent is implemented as a set of Java classes, following the generic structure defined in the GEAMAS level. Each agent is then faithful to the structure defined in *Section 8.3*, and is then a micro-, medium-, or macro-agent: biomas is the macroagent, which describes the agents' society; ExploitationGroup is the medium agent; and breeding, culture, and conveying are described as microagents. These agents are simply inherited from the generic classes of the GEAMAS kernel, thanks to the user interface.

After defining Exploitation agents' roles in terms of offers and demands, negotiation between Conveying and Exploitation agents is quite simple. This scenario is illustrated in Figure 8.8.

Simulations have actually been performed by our team since the beginning of 1998. For further analysis, a graph plotter has been developed in Java and interfaced with GEOMAS outputs. For each simulation, the plotter prints graphs, and this is intended to quickly compare the results between different simulation methodologies. This application can be downloaded from our web site, www.univ-reunion.fr/~biomas/demo.

8.5 Summary

This chapter presents a generic platform to develop simulation applications of complex systems. The complexity of the systems tackled needs to consider the result of the program execution as provided by a set of interactions among agents. Knowledge division, which helps to reduce a design's intricacy when tackling complex systems, emphasizes the use of the agent paradigm. The twisting specifications of the platform involve representing complexity in individual elements, the system's dynamics as local interactions between agents, and the result of simulation as the emergence of phenomena by interpreting such local interactions. These challenges justify the need for an OMT approach to conduct a strong analysis and design. This software engineering point of view has led the project team to develop a specific architecture that allows distributing the complexity in independent and autonomous agents, as well as the focusing of a model of both the agents and the society.

This approach has proved to be very helpful in understanding and analyzing the behavior of geophysical or environmental simulations in life-sized contexts. Examples of such applications are presented in the chapter and are available from our Web pages. The global system behavior has been reproduced from a model of very simple micro-agents' behavior. This global behavior has previously been unattainable with more classical approaches. The architecture therefore validates both the methodology and the approach for complex systems modeling and simulation. We are now convinced that the architecture is appropriate for simulating other natural systems that exhibit similar behavior, and we actually aim to experiment with the approach in the social behavior framework.

8.6 References

[Coad-Yourdon 1991] Coad, P., and E. Yourdon. Yourdon Press Computing Series. Englewood Cliffs, NJ: Prentice Hall, 1991.

[Conte-Gilbert 1995] Conte R., and N. Gilbert. Introduction: Computer simulation for social theory. *Artificial Societies—The Computer Simulation of Social Life,* pp. 1–18. London, England: UCL Press, 1995.

[Marcenac-Calderoni 1997] Marcenac, P., and S. Calderoni. Self-organization in agent-based simulation. *Proceedings of Modeling Autonomous Agents in a Multi-Agent World (MAAMAW 1997).* Ronneby, Sweden, May 1997.

[Marcenac 1996] Marcenac, P. Emergence of behaviors in natural phenomena agent-simulation. *Complexity International Review,* 3, www.csu.edu.au/ci/vol3/cs964/cs964.html, 1996.

[Minar 1996] Minar, N., R. Burkhart, C. Langton, and M. Askenazi. The SWARM simulation system: A toolkit for building multi-agent simulations. Internal research report. www.santafe.edu/projects/swarm/, June 1996.

[Neimeyer-Peck 1996] Neimeyer, P., and J. Peck. *Exploring Java.* O'Reilly, 1996.

[Rumbaugh 1991] Rumbaugh, J., M. Blaha, W. Premerlani, F. Eddy, and W. Lorensen. *Object-Oriented Modeling and Design.* London: Prentice Hall, 1991.

[Stewart 1989] Stewart, I. *Does God Play Dice? The Mathematics of Chaos,* p. 141. Harmondsworth, Middlesex, England: Penguin Books, 1989.

[Zukowski 1997] Zukowski, J. *Java AWT Reference 1.1.* O'Reilly, 1997.

SIDEBAR 4
SOFTWARE AGENTS IN FRAMEWORKS

The ongoing development of communication technologies (such as the Internet and intranets) provides users with powerful distributed and concurrent systems. Because such systems are complex to design and implement, we can rely on object-oriented technology. Hence, these systems may be based on several cooperative objects that are gathered into *object-oriented application frameworks* [Cotter-Potel 1995; Fayad-Schmidt 1997]. Furthermore, in order to enable distributed and concurrent systems to perform in a coherent and efficient manner, *distributed artificial intelligence* (DAI) technology can be used. The aim of DAI is to study a broad range of issues related to the distribution and coordination of knowledge and actions in environments involving multiple entities. These entities, called *agents*, are viewed as complex objects [Shoham 1993]. A particular type of agent, the *software agent*, has recently attracted much attention. From this emerges the idea of substituting objects by software agents inside a framework [Maamar 1997]. The result is what we call *software agent-oriented frameworks*.

SB4.1 Object-Oriented Application Frameworks

When several objects evolve in the same environment, it is important to initially define their behaviors in order to avoid conflictual situations. Therefore, several questions have to be answered: How to create objects? What kinds of information can be exchanged by objects? What types of communication channels can handle these exchanges? And, how can objects be associated to achieve common goals?

Authors in [Cotter-Potel 1995; Fayad-Schmidt 1997; Lewis 1995] introduce the notion of object-oriented application frameworks. A *framework* is viewed as an organized environment for running a collection of objects. It is also defined as a set of related classes which a designer can specialize and/or instantiate to implement specific applications.

An environment can be based on several distributed object-oriented application frameworks. To set up such an environment, it is important to follow a design approach—that is, an approach that allows designers to identify and characterize the appropriate frameworks with regard to the domain to be analyzed and to the application to be developed. The proposed approach is to decompose a problem in such a way that a collection of frameworks can work together in order to provide the solution [Cotter-Potel 1995]. However, this seems too simple, because, in fact, several issues need to be addressed. These issues include how the needed frameworks (numbers, types, and localizations) are determined, how their objects are defined, how their responsibilities are assigned, and how their functionalities are specified. Moreover, it isn't easy for designers to develop such frameworks and to monitor their evolution, particularly in distributed and heterogeneous contexts. One solution to overcome these issues is to expand object-oriented frameworks through the use of software agents.

SB4.2 Software Agent-Oriented Frameworks

Designing software agent-oriented frameworks is a recursive activity that is applied in its turn to frameworks, teams of agents, and software agents [Maamar 1997].

A software agent-oriented framework offers a set of *services* that can be requested either by users or by other frameworks. If a framework cannot carry out a service on its own, it can require complementary services from other frameworks. A framework is based on a *supervisor* agent and one or several *teams* of software agents. A *bank* of software agents contains several agents having different functionalities that are specific to the application to be developed.

Teams of software agents are set up by the framework and are structured differently according to their responsibilities. A team is also characterized by a supervisor agent and a set of roles that agents must fulfill according to their abilities. To fulfill their goals, agents need to interact and exchange information.

Services provided by a framework satisfy specific users' needs, such as an information retrieval. When a service is invoked by a user, the framework's supervisor agent activates a *realization scenario* that specifies the interactions that are allowed between frameworks, teams of agents, and software agents and the operations required to carry out the service. According to this realization scenario, the framework supervisor creates teams that will play roles specified in the scenario. At their own level, team supervisor agents activate realization scenarios in order to coordinate the activities of their software agents.

A realization scenario is composed of the following elements: software agents' types and roles, scheduling sequences indicating in which order agents should perform their activities, the list of internal and/or external information resources that provide knowledge required by the agents to achieve their activities, and, finally, an evaluation procedure used by the supervisor agent to monitor the operations of the other agents.

SB4.3 Summary

Recall the main characteristics of software agent-oriented frameworks: The frameworks can interact in order to define a global behavior that is an outcome of such interactions. The frameworks can be adapted in terms of components (types of teams and agents to integrate) and functionalities (types of services to offer). The frameworks can play several roles according to the application to be developed. Finally, in the frameworks, software agents can be specified by knowledge structures and operating mechanisms. The first category defines agents' knowledge base and the second category describes agents' behavior.

Continues

SIDEBAR 4
SOFTWARE AGENTS IN FRAMEWORKS *(Continued)*

SB4.4 References

[Cotter-Potel 1995] Cotter, S., and M. Potel. *Inside Taligent Technology*. Reading, MA: Addison-Wesley, 1995.

[Fayad-Schmidt 1997] Fayad, M.E., and D. Schmidt. Object-oriented application frameworks. *Communications of the ACM,* 40(10), 1997.

[Lewis 1995] Lewis, T. *Object-Oriented Application Frameworks.* Englewood Cliffs, NJ: Manning Publications/Prentice Hall, 1995.

[Maamar 1997] Maamar, Z., and B. Moulin. Interoperability of distributed and heterogeneous systems based on software agent-oriented frameworks. *International Workshop on Cooperative Information Agents 1997 (CIA 1997)*, pp. 248–259, P. Kandzia and M. Klusch, editors. Lecture Notes in Artificial Intelligence 1202. Kiel, Germany: Springer-Verlag, February 1997.

[Shoham 1993] Shoham, Y. Agent-oriented programming. *Artificial Intelligence*, 60 , 1993: 51–92.

PART
Three

Specialized
Tool Frameworks

Implementers of programming tools often reuse concepts and code informally to build families of tools that support similar functionality. Part Four concentrates on tool frameworks, such as CSP++ and Luthier. This part consists of four chapters, Chapters 9 through 12.

Chapter 9, "CSP++: A Framework for Executable Specifications," uses one of the useful formalisms for designing concurrent systems, the process algebra called *communicating sequential processes* (CSP). CSP statements can be used to model a system's control and data flow in an intuitive way, constituting a kind of hierarchical behavioral specification. Furthermore, when coupled with simulation and model-checking tools, these statements can be executed and debugged until the desired behavior has been accurately captured. Certain properties (such as absence of deadlocks) can be proved, to help verify the correctness of the design. Chapter 9 discusses the development of OO framework that realizes the basic elements of CSP—processes, synchronizing events, and communication channels—in natural terms as C++ objects. CSP statements, thus re-expressed and compiled, form the control portion of a system, able to be linked with other software written in C++ that completes the functionality.

Chapter 10, "Applying Inheritance Beyond Class-Based Languages," presents a framework for systematically building a family of tools based on concepts from the domain of class-based inheritance itself. This chapter exploits the fact that many artifacts apparently unrelated to classes, such as compiled object modules and text fragments, are in fact classlike structures that can be reused via inheritancelike operations. This chapter also describes an implemented framework for building tools to manipulate such artifacts and explores two quite dissimilar completions of the framework in detail.

Chapter 11, "Luthier: Building Framework-Visualization Tools," presents Luthier, a framework designed to provide a flexible support for the construction of tools for object-oriented framework analysis and visualization, through reflective techniques based on metaobjects. Luthier is built as four subframeworks, which supply adaptable support to the four essential tasks that characterize both reverse engineering tools and visualization systems, that is, information gathering, information storing and structuring, abstraction analysis and recovery, and visualization and exploration. With these four subframeworks, Luthier supports the construction of different visualizations from analyzed examples, as well as navigation among different visual representations and textual documentation. Luthier introduces two main contributions, metaobject managers and abstractor objects.

Chapter 12, "Scalable Architecture for Reliable, High-Volume Datafeed Handlers," presents lessons learned and experience gained in building a family of datafeed handler systems in the domain of financial markets. These systems have been realized using (1) specification frameworks and components for structural stability, scalability, and reliability; and (2) implementation frameworks, patterns, and class hierarchies for customization and evolvability. The rationale and illustrative examples are presented at all levels of object orientation, namely, architecture, framework, components, patterns and classes. The singular emphasis and thesis of this chapter is that when coupled with sound engineering practice—in particular, understanding requirements, analysis, and design—the benefits of applying recent technical advances, such as frameworks, components, and patterns, are amplified and become durable over a generation of a family of products.

CHAPTER 9

CSP++: A Framework
for Executable Specifications

Executable specifications are something of a Holy Grail for system designers. We know from experience that in the usual course of transforming a specification into an implementation, each step of manual refinement presents a fresh opportunity to introduce undocumented design decisions and cause the end product to diverge from its specified behavior. The more steps required, the less likely the specs will ever be updated to reflect as-built status, and the less value they will have to future maintainers. If, on the other hand, the specification can somehow *become* the system, many pitfalls can be avoided. We call a specification *executable* when the tools exist to simulate it, reason about it, and, ideally, synthesize a realization using a chosen technology.

Among the many specification methodologies (some executable and some not), there is a category of methodologies called *formalisms* in that they have a mathematical basis. One of these, *communicating sequential processes* (CSP), is a process algebra that is particularly useful for designing concurrent systems. CSP specifications are executable in the sense that simulation and verification tools exist. We wish to extend this to the synthesis of software from CSP and have created an object-oriented (OO) framework for that purpose.

One technique for making something seemingly too abstract, such as formal specifications, executable in the synthesis sense, is to treat the areas requiring refinement or elaboration as blackboxes, encapsulating them with a standard component interface and pushing them to the side for the programmer to deal with separately. Then one can go ahead and synthesize code from the parts that do not need refinement. In our framework, the latter parts become a multitasking control program; the unrefined components—the semantics of events and communication channels in the target system that go beyond interprocess synchronization—are left for the programmer to fill in with custom C++ methods.

Figure 9.1 puts this technique into the context of our OO framework, named *CSP++*. To use the framework, a programmer supplies two sets of input: CSP specifications, which have been simulated and verified, and the custom C++ code that fills in the blackboxes, which will be invoked by the CSP portion. The framework supplies base classes for objects that correspond to the basic CSP statements, so it is straightforward to translate the CSP portion (by hand or with a tool) into C++ code that utilizes these classes. When the code is run, the effect is of executing the CSP statements, with the framework's methods creating concurrent threads and providing full CSP-style synchronization for the custom code.

The body of this chapter is organized as follows. First, in recognition that CSP, or formal methods in general, may not be familiar territory to OO readers, the chapter briefly introduces CSP, using a case study that can also be downloaded from this book's Web site. Then the CSP++ framework is described in terms of its class hierarchy and means of integrating user code. The translation of CSP input to executable C++ and runtime operation is lightly touched upon (details are available in the *Translation of CSP Statements to CSP++* sidebar). The chapter ends with a section on conclusions and future work.

9.1 CSP: Background and Case Study

The classic work on CSP was written by its inventor, Tony Hoare [Hoare 1985]. Recently, Michael Hinchey and Stephen Jarvis have contributed an excellent book

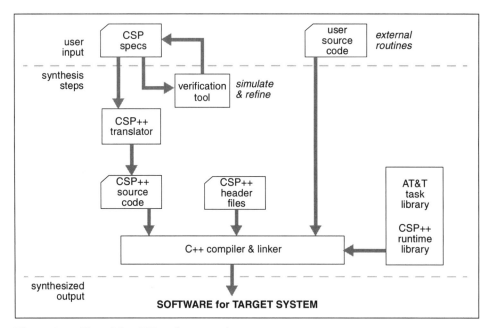

Figure 9.1 Use of the CSP++ framework.

TRANSLATION OF CSP STATEMENTS TO CSP++

Each CSP statement is an agent definition, and each must result in the creation of a distinct CSP++ code segment. Consider a CSP specification containing the following agent definitions:

```
P(0,_i) = ...
P(1,_i) = ...
```

These two must be translated into separate functions (typedef AgentProc), so they need different names, not simply *P*. AgentProcs will be named according to their argument *signature*. The two preceding would be P_c0v and P_c1v, where *c* indicates a constant argument (its value following) and *v* a variable argument. This allows the translator to set up the right invocation depending on the arguments used.

Static binding is the preferred way to match arguments with the appropriate signature. However, in the case of agents with constant argument definitions being invoked with variable arguments, runtime binding is required. That is, which signature preceding matches the invocation of P following?

```
Q = chan?_n→P(_n,0)
```

This depends on the value of *n*, which can be determined only at runtime. Thus, for agents requiring runtime binding, the translator must generate a table of argument descriptors for the binder (instance of AgentBinder class) to consult in such cases.

The details of translating each CSP construct can be found in [Gardner 1995]. Only a few key examples are given here:

Prefix. This is the basic invocation of actions via the arrow notation:

```
P(_x) = chan?_y→foo(_x+_y)→a→L(_x+2,1)
```

To translate, Actions are defined and AgentProcs are declared at the top of the program:

```
Channel chan("chan");
Atomic foo("foo",1);
AGENTDEF(L_b, "L", 2);
```

AGENTDEF is a macro for declaring a forward reference to an AgentProc. The ASCII names are for producing runtime diagnostics. The integers give the number of Atomic subscripts and AgentProc arguments. In this case, there must be several "L" agents with different signatures, because the AgentBinder L_b (not shown) is referenced.

Each prefix action becomes a separate C++ statement within a new AgentProc given its appropriate signature:

```
AGENTPROC( P_v )
    #define _x ARG(0)
    FreeVar _y;
    chan >> _y;
```

Continues

TRANSLATION OF CSP STATEMENTS TO CSP++ *(Continued)*

```
            foo(_x+_y);
            a();
            CHAIN2( L_b, _x+2, 1 );
            #undef _x
    }
```

The AGENTPROC macro includes code to establish the agent's identity as P for the sake of any diagnostics that may print out while it is executing. Here, _x is the 0th argument of agent P, and the #define allows the agent body to refer to it by that name. The ARG macro generates code to reference the 0th Lit in the Agent's argument array. A complementary #undef is needed to avoid interfering with any other uses of the symbol _x.

This statement has a single free variable _y, declared with class FreeVar at the start of the block. >> is Channel input; << is output. Variables in expressions are automatically converted to integers (there will be a runtime error if the Literal type is not Num). Unsubscripted Atomics take an empty function argument list.

Agent bodies often end with an agent constant. In this case, agent P can *chain* to L, which causes the resources of the present task to be reused and avoids a context switch. If the translator can determine which Agent's signature matches, it will code that directly (say, L_vc1) instead of resorting to the runtime binder.

Composition. This covers parallel composition (P‖Q), subordination (P//Q), and interleaving (P‖‖Q). The following sample starts S and T(2) in parallel, tells them to synchronize on Actions a(6) and b, and to hide name b from any parent context:

```
R = ( (S||T(2) )^{a(6),b} )\{b}
```

We translate from the outside in:

```
    AGENTPROC( R )
        static ActionRef r1(a(1,6)), r2(b);
        r2.hide();
        r1.sync();
        r2.sync();

        Agent::compose( 2 );

        Agent* a1=START0( S_, 0 );
        Agent* a2=START1( T_, 1, 2 );

        WAIT(a1);
        WAIT(a2);
    }
```

ActionRef objects are used to prepare Action names for pushing on the environment stack. An ActionRef for an Atomic must give the number of subscripts followed by their (integer) values. The names of these objects (r1, r2) are translator-generated temporaries.

Three classes which are not seen above, EnvHide, EnvSync, and EnvRename, are created and linked onto the stack of the current Agent when the hide, sync, and rename methods of ActionRef are invoked. An inverse method, Agent::popEnv, removes previously pushed environment objects; however, popping is not needed at the logical end of an agent body.

The Agent::compose(*m*) method prepares an *m*-way process fork. Each STARTn macro creates a new Agent task, and specifies the AgentProc signature (with *n* arguments) that it should start running. The second argument is a *branch number* (from 0 to *m* − 1) to associate with that new Agent. It will apply to any sync attempts originating in that branch of the dynamic process tree. The returned Agent* pointer allows the WAIT macro to suspend the present task until the descendent terminates. WAIT also deletes the Agent upon wakeup.

Deterministic Choice. Such choices are specified in terms of several alternative prefixes. The choice whose initial action succeeds first is taken, and the alternatives are abandoned. For example:

P = a?_x→Q(_x) | b→d→R | c!foo→S

This is the most elaborate construct in CSP++:

```
AGENTPROC( P )
    Agent::startDChoice( 3 );

    A > >_x;
    b();
    c << foo;

    switch( Agent::whichDChoice() )
    {
        case 0: CHAIN1( Q_v, _x );
        case 1: d(); CHAIN0( R_ );
        case 2: CHAIN0( S_ );
    }

}
```

The Agent::startDChoice(*n*) method prepares for an *n*-way choice. The initial actions of the *n* prefixes are tried in turn until one succeeds, either because synchronization with another agent is achieved on that action, or, for external actions, because the external routine returns a success code. When Agent::whichDChoice() is invoked, it checks to see whether any of the preceding actions have succeeded. If not, it suspends the Agent until some success is signaled. (The signaling Agent will also have cancelled any outstanding actions which were still waiting.) Finally it returns a choice number and the switch statement selects the corresponding case.

[Hinchey-Jarvis 1995] that features updated notation conventions. For a glance at CSP in comparison with other specification languages often used for embedded system design, [Gajski 1994] is recommended. A good starting point for exploring CSP on the Internet is Oxford University's CSP archive at www.comlab.ox.ac.uk/archive/csp.html.

Simply put, each statement in CSP is the description of a *process*. The process engages in a sequence of named *events*, which may include point-to-point communication with another process via a nonbuffered *channel*. The set of all events that a process may ever engage in is called its *alphabet*. These may correspond to real-world occurrences such as sensor input, device actuation, and so on.

Things get interesting when processes define themselves in terms of other processes, including several processes running in parallel. Then, the formalism provides for interprocess synchronization each time an event occurs that is in the processes' common alphabet. This also implies that processes synchronize around channel communication. CSP statements can thus be used to model a system's control and data flow in an intuitive way, constituting a kind of hierarchical behavioral specification.

An example will make this easier to follow. The simplified disk server is one to which we will return later. First consider Figure 9.2, which visually portrays the disk server subsystem (DSS) interacting with multiple clients C(*cl*). We write the CSP[1] for a two-client system starting from the complete system view:

```
SYS = (DSS || (C(1) ||| C(2)) )^{ds,ack(1),ack(2)}
```

This states that the system SYS is defined as the parallel composition of the disk server DSS and two client processes, C(1) and C(2). Parallel composition of concurrent processes is expressed with the symbol || plus an outer caret ^ that explicitly denotes the set of events on which the processes will synchronize. The synchronization set includes channel ds, over which a client communicates a request, and ack(*cl*), the acknowledge event to client *cl*. Strictly speaking, it should not be necessary to list these events, because CSP defines that any events in the common alphabet will implicitly cause synchronization. However, in practice it is difficult for simulators to derive the intersection of alphabets, and easy enough for the specifier to write it out. The clients are composed using the symbol for interleaving |||; that is, they run concurrently but they do not synchronize with each other.

The disk server is also defined as a number of subprocesses:

```
DSS = ( (DSched || DQueue)^{enq,deq,next,empty}
        || (DCtrl || Disk)^{dio,dint} )^{dc}
```

The disk request scheduler DSched is composed with the queue DQueue. Their synchronizing events concern the enqueuing and dequeuing of requests. The disk controller DCtrl is shown in this simplified model composed with a dummy process standing for the actual disk drive.

The scheduler DSched is drawn as a state machine, and these next statements show how CSP can accommodate this:

```
DSched = DS_idle
DS_idle = ds?req(_cl, _blk)→dc!start(_cl, _blk)→ DS_busy
DS_busy = dc?fini(_cl, _blk)→ack(_cl)→deq→DS_check
          | ds?req(_cl, _blk)→enq!req(_cl, _blk)→DS_busy
DS_check = empty→DS_idle
           | next?req(_cl, _blk)→dc!start(_cl, _blk)→DS_busy
```

---

[1]The CSP notation used here is that which is accepted by an in-house verification tool, csp12. It is mostly identical with the notation found in [Hinchey-Jarvis 1995]. csp12 was written in Prolog by M.H.M. Cheng, Department of Computer Science, University of Victoria, BC.

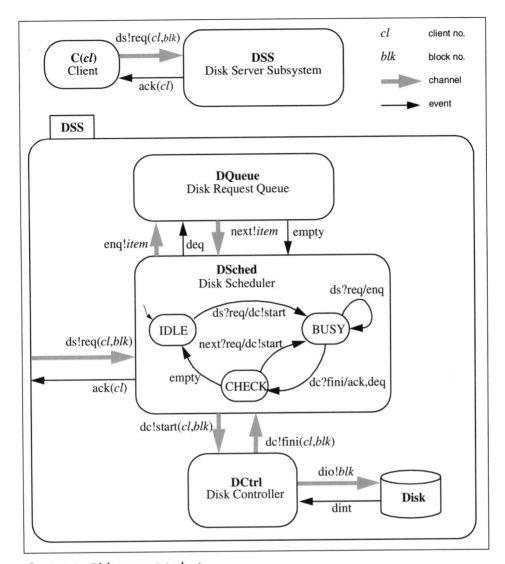

Figure 9.2 Disk server statecharts.

The specification for DS_idle illustrates two constructs. First, ds?req(_cl, _blk) means that the process waits for input on the channel ds. Input is denoted by the symbol "?" followed by a variable. Similarly, output is shown with "!" followed by a value. Here, channel ds receives the complex datum req which is made up of the client number and the block number. The names _cl and _blk function as local variables for the process. The right arrow is a transition to the next event in the process, the output of the start datum on the channel dc. After this, the DS_idle process continues as the process DS_busy, in effect performing a state transition to IDLE.

DS_busy illustrates deterministic choice, which works like this example:

```
P = a→Q | b→R
```

P has a choice. If event a occurs, P will continue as process Q, but if b occurs, it will continue as R. (If neither occurs, P will not proceed at all). Looking back to DS_busy, we see that if the scheduler hears from the controller that the disk has finished a request (the input dc?fini), it will acknowledge the appropriate client and enter the CHECK state. Otherwise, if it gets a fresh request from a client (ds?req) in this BUSY state, it will enqueue the request and remain BUSY.

The CSP for the controller and disk are simple sequences of events:

```
DCtrl = dc?start(_cl, _blk)→dio!_blk→dint→dc!fini(_cl,_blk)→DCtrl
Disk = dio?_blk→dint→Disk
```

DCtrl waits for a start request on its dc channel. The start datum contains the client number and disk block. The controller sends the block request on its output channel dio and then waits for an interrupt event dint. On the line below, the Disk process simulates inputting the request and outputting dint. Thereupon, DCtrl signals completion by sending the fini datum on channel dc. The process continues as itself (DCtrl=...→DCtrl), which specifies a loop.

The disk request queue (detail not shown in Figure 9.2) is more interesting and shows the last of the CSP notation to be introduced here:

```
DQueue = ( (DQ(0) || BUFF)^{left, right, shift} )\{left, right, shift}
DQ(_i) = enq?_x→left!_x→shift→DQ(_i+1)
           | deq→( ( if _i=0 then empty→DQ(0) )
                   + fix X.( right?_y→next!_y→DQ(_i-1)
                             | shift→X )
               )
BUFF = CELL |> CELL |> CELL
CELL = left?_x→shift→right!_x→CELL
```

The queue process is described as a buffer (here only three cells) composed with a subscripted process DQ_i, where i represents the number of items currently in the queue. Each CELL process receives a datum on its left channel and, after being told to shift, delivers it on its right channel, and then continues being a CELL. The symbol |> is a special kind of parallel composition, which can be defined in terms of other CSP operators, used only for pipelines. P |> Q has the effect of making P's right channel synchronize with Q's left channel, so that data is passed from P to Q. The entire BUFF pipeline has left and right channels to communicate with DQ_i, and can be told by DQ_i when to shift. The set of events prefixed by the backslash \ will be made local to this process DQueue, and will not be visible to any process with which it may have been composed at a higher level (this is called *hiding* or *concealment*).

As for DQ_i, when it gets input on enq it enqueues _x on BUFF's left channel and does a shift. When it gets a deq event, it faces a choice (+ is the general choice operator): If there are no items in the queue (shown by a subscript 0), the empty event occurs and the process continues as DQ_0. Otherwise, a subprocess X is declared (*fix* is a way of putting a process in line): If BUFF's right channel yields up an item _y, it is passed out through channel next and the process continues as DQ_{i-1}. Otherwise, a shift is ordered and the subprocess is repeated. Two observations: (1) The shift action in CELL is actually superfluous and is given to illustrate more CSP++ constructs; and (2) it is evident that CSP is hardly an optimal way of implementing a simple first-in, first-out (FIFO) buffer. Here, the strength of CSP in specifying control flow gives way to its weakness in manipulating data. An improvement would be to implement the buffer with a user-coded external action.

There are a few other CSP constructs that this example has not covered. These include event renaming, which is how pipelines are implemented, and nondeterministic choice, which is useful for keeping specifications at a high level of abstraction, but not for actual implementation. Furthermore, it should be noted that CSP notation has not been standardized, and that new operators can be invented. For example, the fix operator is a convenience notation supported by an in-house tool called csp12. Variants of CSP also exist, one of the most useful for real-time systems being timed CSP [Davies 1992], which adds timing constraints to the arrows between events.

Now that we have the specification, what's next? Because CSP specs are executable, we can turn to a simulation tool to run it. At the University of Victoria, csp12 will accept the preceding syntax. A more sophisticated simulation tool, Failure Divergence Refinement (FDR) [Roscoe 1994], is available commercially through Formal Systems of Oxford. It is industrial strength, and the FDR Web page (www.formal.demon.co.uk/FDR2.html) suggests that it can be used for "VLSI design, protocol development and implementation, networking and data distribution, control, signaling, fault-tolerant systems, telecommunications and man-machine interface," which is a good indication of the range of applications for which CSP seems suited.

These tools can also perform *model-checking*, which is a major virtue of formal methods having precise algebraic rules. In general, three properties can be checked, requiring various amounts of runtime depending on the complexity of the specification: deadlock, livelock (infinite loop), and equivalence. The last property means that if we have two specifications for a process or system (perhaps one, P', is intended to be a "better" version of P), we can prove whether they are indeed equivalent. See Chapter 3 of [Hinchey-Jarvis 1995] for details.

After we are satisfied with simulating and checking our specification, then it is time to turn it into executable code to constitute the control portion of our system. This is where our framework comes in, whose description follows.

9.2 The CSP++ Framework

There have been some efforts at making CSP specifications run as programs. Historically, the programming language occam has been derived from CSP, and Chapter 9 of [Hinchey-Jarvis 1995] shows how to convert from CSP to occam, but the authors also acknowledge that it is a "very specialized language intended for implementation on transputers." Our goal, therefore, is quite different: We wish to translate CSP into a popular language that will make it easy to combine with other code that fills out the functionality of the system. This has been done to some extent for the C language. The Channel Communication Sequential Processes (CCSP) tool [Arrowsmith 1994] provides a limited facility for translating a subset of CSP into C, but it does not directly support the key parallel composition operator ‖. Instead, each CSP process becomes a heavyweight UNIX process, and channels are implemented as UNIX sockets.

For Java enthusiasts it is worth noting that the Java Plug & Play (JavaPP) Project has created a set of classes called *Communicating Java Threads* (CJTs) [Hilderink 1997], which are designed to bring CSP-style synchronization and communication to Java programs. Again, this represents a different goal from ours, but does open up an avenue for converting CSP to Java.

For our attempt at creating an OO framework to run CSP, we set out three design goals: (1) runtime efficiency, (2) understandable code, and (3) portability. The first goal is intended to make CSP++ potentially useful for embedded real-time systems, which often run on platforms with limited hardware and OS support. As for the second goal, we knew that we would be hand translating from CSP to CSP++ initially. Therefore it was desirable to create a syntax that would be easy to code and debug. Finally, for our experimental implementation, we used version 3.0 AT&T (USL) C++ for the sake of its task library. It is compatible with a variety of architectures. The *Reflections on Design Goals* sidebar contains reflections on these goals in light of the implementation details given there.

9.2.1 Overview

Our purpose is to synthesize code from CSP specifications. In an OO implementation, that means creating objects. Following a typical OO design methodology, we choose classes directly corresponding to objects in the problem space—in this case, processes,

---

REFLECTIONS ON DESIGN GOALS

Many of our decisions can be explained by the design goals for our framework, which fall under three headings:

- **Runtime efficiency**
- **Understandable code**
- **Portability**

The first goal is intended to make CSP++ potentially useful for embedded real-time systems. Because these run on platforms with limited hardware and OS support, we tried to avoid constructs whose resource demands would make CSP++ too cumbersome. Therefore, we favored looping implementations over recursion (though CSP notation lends itself to the latter), and took a conservative approach to process creation, doing this only where control truly forks. We attempted to limit storage growth by utilizing automatic (stack) variables and putting heap variables under their control. This strategy enlists the C++ compiler to do storage management and avoids leakage. We also favored static versus dynamic binding, ruling out gratuitous use of virtual functions.

As for the second goal, we knew that we would be hand translating from CSP to CSP++ initially. Therefore, it was desirable to create a syntax that would be easy to code and debug. We did this by relying on C++ operator overloading to create a syntax similar to CSP where feasible, and we translated each CSP action as a fresh C++ statement for the benefit of symbolic debugging.

Finally, the AT&T C++ task library is compatible with a variety of architectures. If necessary, it can be ported by hand, retaining the public class definitions and substituting, for example, an interface to kernel-level thread management calls.

events, and data items. Our synthesis strategy is to statically analyze a set of CSP specifications to identify all of these occurrences, and then generate a source file having two sections: (1) compile-time definitions for all passive objects, that is, events and nontrivial data items; and (2) sequential code segments for all processes, packaged as one C++ function per process. Creation of active objects, that is, processes, is deferred until runtime to implement the dynamic occurrence of parallel composition operators || and |||. These processes, as their execution flows through the function bodies representing CSP statements, will invoke methods on event objects that cause interprocess synchronization and/or channel communication to take place.

The hierarchy of classes used to implement the above strategy is shown in Figure 9.3. The principal base classes are the following:

Agent. Embodies a process definition, subclassed from the AT&T task library task class (see Section 9.2.2), representing a schedulable thread of control.

Action. Encompasses two flavors of CSP events—*channel actions,* which pass data, and *atomic actions,* which do not.

Env. Declarative objects used to impose an Action reference (ActionRef) into the environment of a process in one of three roles—for synchronization (^{a,b,...}), hiding (\{a,b,...}), or renaming (#{a=b,c=d,...}).

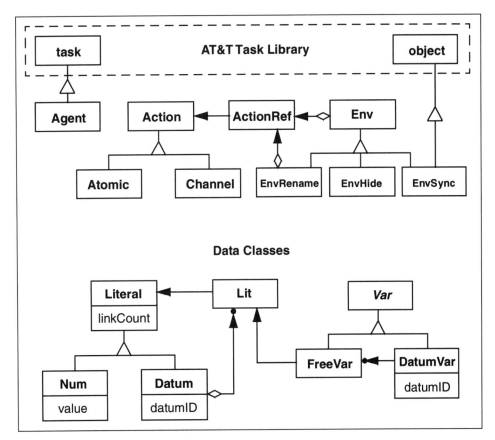

Figure 9.3   CSP++ class hierarchy.

The data classes are used to create Literal instances, which are passed between agents. The most primitive type is the integer-valued Num. The Datum, a complex datatype equivalent to csp12's label, consists of a symbolic DatumID optionally followed by a series of subscripts in parentheses. Each subscript is a Lit, which means it points to any type of Literal, possibly another Datum. For example:

```
request( client(10), block(5), flags( buff, eof, 10))
```

would be a valid Datum literal. Thus a Datum is an aggregate of Literal objects.

As a storage management technique, literals are all heap-based and have no public constructors. Lit is the corresponding container class. When a Lit is created, it (privately) allocates a new Literal of the appropriate subclass on the heap and stores a pointer to it. Each Literal keeps a *link count* of the Lit objects pointing to it, which when reduced to 0 invokes the ~Literal virtual destructor.

Lits, in turn, are in most contexts managed by the C++ compiler as automatic (stack) variables, the principle being that if the compiler manages the Lits (as blocks of code go in and out of scope), and the Lits manage the Literals (as the Lits are created, assigned, and destroyed), storage leaks should not be possible.

Turning from literals to variables, it is evident that Lit containers already function as variables, because they can point to any Literal. However, it is desirable to have a special datatype corresponding to the concept of *free variables* in CSP notation. These can be required in lexical contexts that demand receptacles, particularly Channel input. To this end, the FreeVar class is defined as containing a Lit* pointer and a DatumVar (by analogy to Datums), a labeled list of FreeVar* pointers. Both are derived from the abstract base class Var, so that either will work in a context requiring a variable.

A final note on data classes is that the Literal hierarchy is easily extensible: One need only create additional subclasses of Literal—say, String or Set—and appropriate operators to go with them. All the rest of the data-handling mechanisms should take them in stride without any modification.

The following section describes the two main nondata classes, Agent and Action, in more detail.

9.2.2 Agent Class

Because C++ does not contain the notion of concurrency, we have to provide it ourselves. The AT&T task library is based on a thread model. That is, the user's application runs as a single (heavyweight) Unix process under SunOS, but is free to spawn as many tasks—processes, in CSP parlance—as needed. Under this model, any object desiring to have a schedulable thread of control is derived from the class task. The thread body to be executed is none other than the object's constructor. Normally, in C++ the constructor is briefly given control when an object is created. What being a *task* means is that (1) execution of the constructor will be delayed until the task is dispatched for the first time, and (2) it will thereafter be suspended and resumed according to the operation of scheduling primitives (task methods). This is arguably an abuse of the philosophy of C++ constructors, but without concurrency in the language, such contrivances are expected.

This model might suggest that a unique subclass must be created for each agent so that it can have its own constructor. We avoid this class proliferation by making the Agent class, which is derived from task, a simple function-caller. As was previously mentioned, each CSP process definition is translated into an individual function (of type AgentProc). An argument to the Agent constructor designates which AgentProc the task is to run. When that finishes, its return code may designate another AgentProc to succeed it. This allows execution to chain from AgentProc to AgentProc until one ends with the special CSP SKIP process, which will terminate that Agent task and wake up its waiting parent (also an Agent task). Examples are provided in the *Translation of CSP Statements to CSP++* sidebar.

Combining inheritance with concurrent synchronization raises the specter of potential *inheritance anomalies* [Matsuoka 1993]. However, because our design utilizes a simple form of inheritance in which the task base class's synchronization methods are used as is (or, without being overridden in the Agent class or its subclasses), then according to [Reitzner 1997], this pattern of so-called *sequential inheritance* should not engender anomalies.

9.2.3 Action Class

The two subclasses, Atomic and Channel, correspond to the two types of actions available in CSP. Operators are defined to allow function-call syntax to invoke Atomic actions (for instance, foo(2)), and C++-style I/O to invoke Channel actions (for example, chan<<1 for chan!1 output, and chan>>x for chan?x input). This is similar, though not identical, to CSP syntax, and contributes to CSP++ source code readability.

The two subclasses are derived from the Action class, which provides common methods needed for invoking either kind of action. These include searching the agent environment for hiding, renaming, and sync orders; performing multiagent sync; handling deterministic choice situations; and printing traces. These are explained in the *Translation of CSP Statements to CSP++* sidebar.

9.2.4 Integration of User Code

The framework provides "hooks" for user code via CSP actions. To be specific, each Channel or Atomic action can *either* be used for internal synchronization (that is, with another CSP process) *or* it can be linked to an external routine. In the latter case, when the action is performed, the associated routine is invoked with arguments corresponding to the Atomic subscripts, Channel input variables, or Channel output values. The routine returns a status indicating whether the action was considered to succeed or not, for use when the action is being tried in the context of a choice.

This technique of integration is portrayed in Figure 9.4, which shows how a synthesized CSP program interacts with its external routines. Figure 9.4a shows how the two software components are prepared from the CSP specification and user source code, respectively, and how the latter interacts with the system's hardware components. Figure 9.4b shows processes communicating and synchronizing via internal actions (c1, a2, and a3). Other actions (a1, c2, and c3) are used to invoke the external routines.

In the disk controller case study, all actions shown in the preceding code are used for internal synchronization. To embed the CSP in a hardware environment, the dummy

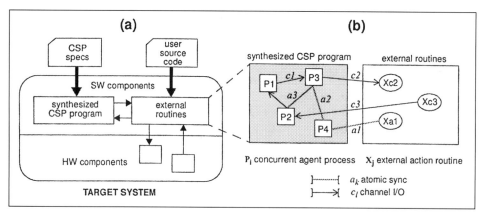

Figure 9.4   CSP and user code integration: (*a*) preparation of the software components, and (*b*) interaction of the user source code with the hardware components.

Disk process can simply be removed from the statement that defines DSS, leaving the following:

```
DSS = ( (DSched || DQueue)^{enq,deq,next,empty} || DCtrl )^{dc}
```

Now the dio and dint actions are available for external use. DCtrl will call the external routine associated with dio, which presumably starts the hardware I/O (nonblocking). The routine associated with dint will block awaiting a completion interrupt (hardware and OS dependent).

Summarizing this model, the CSP specification fully describes the control flow of the system in terms of concurrent processes. The user source code can be regarded as fleshing out the semantics of those actions which interact with hardware components. Furthermore, in a complex system, the external routines could well provide an interface layer to packaged software modules—supplied perhaps in the form of other C++ class libraries—such as a database subsystem or OS facilities. This layered concept is illustrated in Figure 9.5.

9.2.5 Translation of CSP Statements

The procedure for translating each CSP statement into CSP++ code, based on the classes just described , is relatively straightforward. It is, however, too detailed to give here. Interested readers should refer to the *Translation of CSP Statements to CSP++* sidebar for the translation of agent bodies and the prefix, composition, and deterministic choice constructions. Full details are available in a technical report [Gardner 1995] which may be downloaded from the book's Web site.

9.2.6 Runtime Operation

Execution of a C++ program commences at the main( ) function, which for CSP++ simply creates the SYS process. SYS, in turn, will spawn other processes, and these will

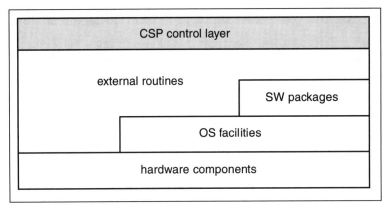

Figure 9.5 Layered system model.

invoke actions, including their associated external routines. In general, these processes (AT&T tasks) cannot be statically scheduled, because in CSP, exactly what happens when an action is executed depends not solely on the action's name, but on its environment. That environment is the accumulation of concealment, renaming, and sync orders that have been piled up by the immediate agent and all of its parents. Because agent descent (that is, parents creating child tasks) in CSP is dynamic, not static, a runtime stack is needed to keep track of the environment. This is explained in the *Runtime Operation of the CSP++ Framework* sidebar.

This functionality, and more, is provided in the infrastructure of the CSP++ framework. It is largely hidden from the user, who needs not understand how it works, but only how to write CSP statements.

9.2.7 Disk Server Revisited

In order to run a simulation, we need to specify the behavior of the client processes for test purposes. For example:

```
C(1) = ds!req(1,100)→moreone→ack(1)→SKIP
C(2) = ds!req(2,150)→moretwo→ack(2)→SKIP
```

This shows each client making a disk request, performing some additional activity asynchronously (moreone), waiting for acknowledgment from the server, and then terminating successfully (the special SKIP process in CSP).

The full translation of the DSS case study into CSP++ is given in the *Source Code of the DSS Case Study* sidebar. After compiling and linking the resulting C++ code, we can run it with the -t command line option. This instructs the framework to print on cerr (stderr) the trace of every action taken. Running the DSS system produces the following output (line numbers added). Each line starting with |= is part of the trace. The name of the agent producing the trace is printed first, followed by the action taken. (Because multiple agents are involved in a sync, we choose to print the name of the one that completes the sync.) As in csp12, $ denotes a synchronization of channel I/O, with the data value following.

RUNTIME OPERATION OF THE CSP++ FRAMEWORK

The environment stack is a branching stack. Each Agent has its own section of the stack, corresponding to whatever Env objects have been pushed while it is executing. In addition, each Agent object contains a pointer to its parent, so that stack searches can extend beyond the immediate Agent through all of its ancestors.

Whether an action is Atomic or Channel, the Action::execute method carries out these steps of processing until the action has been executed:

Check whether there is an *external routine* defined. If so, call it and then return.

Otherwise, start searching the environment stack, from this agent back through its parents.

If an Env object with a matching ActionRef is found in the stack, process according to the Env type:

EnvHide. Consider the action executed; it can have no further effect.

EnvRename. Do the substitution and resume searching.

EnvSync. Call Agent::doSync to attempt synchronization. After it succeeds, mark the action as executed. If we are the active party to the sync, resume searching.

The reason we resume searching after a sync is in case a renaming appears farther along the stack. If so, this should affect the name of the trace. To avoid duplicate traces, the convention is that the *active* party (defined as the last party to arrive at the sync) is responsible for printing the trace. The passive parties are silent.

Multiparty synchronization relies on EnvSync objects to be the nerve center. When one is pushed on the environment stack, it reserves a syncFlag for each party to a sync. Which syncFlag a particular Action will use is determined by which branch of the process tree it finds itself on (*branch number* in the preceding). When it wants to sync, it attempts to set its syncFlag. If all the flags are now set, the sync has just been completed. Otherwise, it calls a method to suspend its Agent task. The last party checking in for the sync has the duty to awaken the sleeping tasks that arrived at the sync before it.

Choice greatly complicates the picture painted here, because individual Actions are able to wait on their own for synchronization, thus suspending their Agents while they wait. In the context of multiple alternative actions, if any one were to wait, the following Actions could not be tried. So in order to allow *all* actions to wait in concert, it is necessary to add a try-then-back-out apparatus to the sync mechanism. This is too complex to explain here; see [Gardner 1995] for details.

SOURCE CODE OF THE DSS CASE STUDY

In the following C++ source code, the original CSP specifications (csp12 syntax) are shown on comment lines (//), followed by the CSP++ translation. Lines beginning with // % are csp12 comments. This file can be compiled (with AT&T cfront), linked, and executed.

In this sample, runtime binding is not actually needed. However, for demonstration purposes, Agent C(1) is invoked via AgentBinder C_b.

```
/* DSS.c   Disk Server Subsystem - Demonstration program */

// CSP++ class definitions
#include "Lit.h"
#include "Agent.h"
#include "Action.h"
#include "main.h"


AGENTDEF( BUFF_, "BUFF", 0 );
AGENTDEF( BUFF_s1, "BUFF", 0 );
AGENTDEF( BUFF_s2, "BUFF", 0 );
AGENTDEF( C_c1, "C", 1 );
AGENTDEF( C_c2, "C", 1 );
  static int C_x[] = {
        0, 1, AB_CALL,
        0, 2, AB_CALL,
        AB_END };
  static AgentProc* C_y[] = { C_c1, C_c2 };
  static AgentBinder C_b( C_x, C_y, "C", 1 );
AGENTDEF( CELL_, "CELL", 0 );
AGENTDEF( DCtrl_, "DCtrl", 0 );
AGENTDEF( Disk_, "Disk", 0 );
AGENTDEF( DQ_v, "DQ", 0 );
AGENTDEF( DQueue_, "DQueue", 0 );
AGENTDEF( DS_busy_, "DS_busy", 0 );
AGENTDEF( DS_check_, "DS_check", 0 );
AGENTDEF( DS_idle_, "DS_idle", 0 );
AGENTDEF( DSched_, "DSched", 0 );
AGENTDEF( DSS_, "DSS", 0 );
AGENTDEF( DSS_s1, "DSS", 0 );
AGENTDEF( DSS_s2, "DSS", 0 );
AGENTDEF( SYS_, "SYS", 0 );
AGENTDEF( SYS_s1, "SYS", 0 );


Atomic
        ack("ack", 1),
        comm("comm"),
        deq("deq"),
        dint("dint"),
        empty("empty"),
        moreone("moreone"),
        moretwo("moretwo"),
        shift("shift");

Channel
        dc("dc"),
        dio("dio"),
        ds("ds"),
```

Continues

SOURCE CODE OF THE DSS CASE STUDY *(Continued)*

```
            enq("enq"),
            left("left"),
            next("next"),
            right("right");


DATUMDEF( fini, 2 );
DATUMDEF( req, 2 );
DATUMDEF( start, 2 );


// %=============================
// % DQueue:  disk request queue
// %
// % Interface:
// %    enq!<item>        enqueue item
// %    deq               dequeue item, followed by:
// %      next?_x          next item returned, or
// %      empty            empty queue indication
// %=============================
//
// CELL ::= left?_x -> shift -> right!_x ->CELL.
//
AGENTPROC( CELL_ )
    FreeVar _x;

    left >> _x;
    shift();
    right << _x;
    CHAIN0( CELL_ );
}


// BUFF ::= CELL |> CELL |> CELL .       just 2 cells for now
// BUFF ::= (((CELL#{right=comm})||(CELL#{left=comm}))^{comm})\{comm}
//
AGENTPROC( BUFF_s1 )
    static ActionRef    r1(right),
                        r2(comm);

    r1.rename( r2 );
    CHAIN0( CELL_ );
}


AGENTPROC( BUFF_s2 )
    static ActionRef    r1(left),
                        r2(comm);

    r1.rename( r2 );
    CHAIN0( CELL_ );
}
```

```
AGENTPROC( BUFF_ )
    static ActionRef     r1(comm);

    r1.hide();
    {
        r1.sync();

        Agent::compose( 2 );
        Agent* a1 = START0( BUFF_s1, 0 );
        Agent* a2 = START0( BUFF_s2, 1 );
        WAIT( a1 );
        WAIT( a2 );

        Agent::popEnv( 1 );
    }
    Agent::popEnv( 1 );
    END_AGENT;
}

// DQueue ::= ((DQ(0)||BUFF)^{left,right,shift})\{left,right,shift}.
//
AGENTPROC( DQueue_ )
    static ActionRef     r1(left),
                         r2(right),
                         r3(shift);

    r1.hide();
    r2.hide();
    r3.hide();
    {
        r1.sync();
        r2.sync();
        r3.sync();

        Agent::compose( 2 );
        Agent* a1 = START1( DQ_v, 0, 0 );
        Agent* a2 = START0( BUFF_, 1 );
        WAIT( a1 );
        WAIT( a2 );

        Agent::popEnv( 3 );
    }
    Agent::popEnv( 3 );
    END_AGENT;
}

// DQ(_i) ::= enq?_x -> left!_x -> shift-> DQ(_i+1)
//          | deq -> ( (if _i=0 then empty -> DQ(0))
```

Continues

SOURCE CODE OF THE DSS CASE STUDY *(Continued)*

```
//                       + fix X.(right?_y -> next!_y -> DQ(_i-1)
//                                | shift -> X)
//                       ).
//
AGENTPROC( DQ_v )
#define _i ARG(0)
    FreeVar _x, _y;

    Agent::startDChoice( 2 );
        enq >> _x;
        deq();
    switch ( Agent::whichDChoice() ) {

        case 0:
            left << _x;
            shift();
            CHAIN1( DQ_v, _i+1 );

        case 1:
            if ( _i == 0 ) {
                empty();
                CHAIN1( DQ_v, 0 );
            }
            while ( 1 ) {
                Agent::startDChoice( 2 );
                    right >> _y;
                    shift();
                switch ( Agent::whichDChoice() ) {

                    case 0:
                        next << _y;
                        CHAIN1( DQ_v, _i-1 );

                    case 1:
                        continue;
                }
            }
    }
#undef _i
}


// %=============================
// % DCtrl: disk controller
// %
// % Interface:
// %    dc!start(_cl, _blk)     start operation on block <_blk> for
// %                            client <_cl>
// %    dc?fini(_cl, _blk)      operation finished
// %=============================
```

```
//
// DCtrl::=dc?start(_i,_blk)->dio!_blk->dint->dc!fini(_i,_blk)->DCtrl.
//
AGENTPROC( DCtrl_ )
    FreeVar _i, _blk;

    dc >> start(_i, _blk);
    dio << _blk;
    dint();
    dc << fini(_i, _blk);
    CHAIN0( DCtrl_ );
}


// %============================
// % Disk:  disk drive (simulated)
// %
// % Interface:
// %    dio!_blk                perform disk i/o on block _blk
// %    dint                    disk interrupt signalled
// %============================
//
// Disk ::=  dio?_blk -> dint ->Disk.
//
AGENTPROC( Disk_ )
    FreeVar _blk;

    dio >> _blk;
    dint();
    CHAIN0( Disk_ );
}


// %============================
// % DSched:  disk scheduler
// %
// % Interface:
// %    ds!req(_cl, _blk)       client <_cl> requests operation on
// %                            block <_blk>
// %    ack(_cl)                client's operation finished
// %============================
//
// DSched ::= DS_idle.
//
AGENTPROC( DSched_ )
    CHAIN0( DS_idle_ );
}


// DS_idle ::= ds?req(_cl, _blk) -> dc!start(_cl, _blk) -> DS_busy.
//
```

Continues

SOURCE CODE OF THE DSS CASE STUDY *(Continued)*

```
AGENTPROC( DS_idle_ )
    FreeVar _cl, _blk;


    ds >> req(_cl, _blk);
    dc << start(_cl, _blk);
    CHAIN0( DS_busy_ );
}


// DS_busy ::= dc?fini(_cl, _blk) -> ack(_cl) -> deq -> DS_check
//           | ds?req(_cl, _blk) -> enq!req(_cl, _blk) -> DS_busy.
//
AGENTPROC( DS_busy_ )
    FreeVar _cl, _blk;

    Agent::startDChoice( 2 );
        dc >> fini(_cl, _blk);
        ds >> req(_cl, _blk);
    switch ( Agent::whichDChoice() ) {

        case 0:
            ack(_cl);
            deq();
            CHAIN0( DS_check_ );


        case 1:
            enq << req(_cl, _blk);
            CHAIN0( DS_busy_ );
    }
}


// DS_check ::= empty -> DS_idle
//            | next?req(_cl, _blk)->dc!start(_cl, _blk) -> DS_busy.
//
AGENTPROC( DS_check_ )
    FreeVar _cl, _blk;

    Agent::startDChoice( 2 );
        empty();
        next >> req(_cl, _blk);
    switch ( Agent::whichDChoice() ) {

        case 0:
            CHAIN0( DS_idle_ );


        case 1:
            dc << start(_cl, _blk);
            CHAIN0( DS_busy_ );
    }
```

```
}

// %=============================
// % DSS:   disk server subsystem
// %
// % Interface: (see DSched)
// %=============================
//
// DSS ::= (   (DSched || DQueue)^{enq,deq,next,empty}
//         ||
//             (DCtrl || Disk)^{dio,dint}   )^{dc}.
//
AGENTPROC( DSS_s1 )
    static ActionRef      r1(enq),
                          r2(deq),
                          r3(next),
                          a4(empty);

    r1.sync();
    r2.sync();
    r3.sync();
    a4.sync();

    Agent::compose( 2 );
    Agent* a1 = START0( DSched_, 0 );
    Agent* a2 = START0( DQueue_, 1 );
    WAIT( a1 );
    WAIT( a2 );

    Agent::popEnv( 4 );
    END_AGENT;
}

AGENTPROC( DSS_s2 )
    static ActionRef      r1(dio),
                          r2(dint);

    r1.sync();
    r2.sync();

    Agent::compose( 2 );
    Agent* a1 = START0( DCtrl_, 0 );
    Agent* a2 = START0( Disk_, 1 );
    WAIT( a1 );
    WAIT( a2 );

    Agent::popEnv( 2 );
    END_AGENT;
```

Continues

SOURCE CODE OF THE DSS CASE STUDY *(Continued)*

```
}

AGENTPROC( DSS_ )
    static ActionRef      r1(dc);
    r1.sync();

    Agent::compose( 2 );
    Agent* a1 = START0( DSS_s1, 0 );
    Agent* a2 = START0( DSS_s2, 1 );
    WAIT( a1 );
    WAIT( a2 );

    Agent::popEnv( 1 );
    END_AGENT;
}


// SYS ::= (DSS || (C(1)|||C(2)) )^{ds,ack(1),ack(2)}.
//
AGENTPROC( SYS_s1)
    Agent::compose( 2 );
//    Agent* a1 = START1( C_c1, 0, 1 );
    Agent* a1 = START1( C_b, 0, 1 );        // use AgentBinder
    Agent* a2 = START1( C_c2, 1, 2 );
    WAIT( a1 );
    WAIT( a2 );

    END_AGENT;
}


AGENTPROC( SYS_ )
    static ActionRef      r1(ds),
                          r2(ack, 1, 1),
                          r3(ack, 1, 2);

    r1.sync();
    r2.sync();
    r3.sync();

    Agent::compose( 2 );
    Agent* a1 = START0( DSS_, 0 );
    Agent* a2 = START0( SYS_s1, 1 );
    WAIT( a1 );
    WAIT( a2 );

    Agent::popEnv( 3 );
    END_AGENT;
}


// %==============================
```

```
// % Demo
// %=============================
//
// C(1) ::= ds!req(1,100)->moreone->ack(1)->SKIP.
//
AGENTPROC( C_c1 )
    ds << req(1, 100);
    moreone();
    ack(1);
    END_AGENT;
}


// C(2) ::= ds!req(2,150)->moretwo->ack(2)->SKIP.
//
AGENTPROC( C_c2 )
    ds << req(2, 150);
    moretwo();
    ack(2);
    END_AGENT;
}

main( int argc, char* const* argv )
{
    MAIN( argc, argv, SYS_ );     // start first process SYS
}
```

```
[1]  |=C( 1 ) [ds$req( 1, 100 )]
[2]  |=C( 1 ) [moreone]
[3]  Action: moreone
[4]  |=DS_idle [dc$start( 1, 100 )]
[5]  |=DS_busy [ds$req( 2, 150 )]
[6]  |=DS_busy [enq$req( 2, 150 )]
[7]  |=DCtrl [dio$100]
[8]  |=C( 2 ) [moretwo]
[9]  Action: moretwo
[10] |=Disk [dint]
[11] |=DCtrl [dc$fini( 1, 100 )]
[12] |=DS_busy [ack( 1 )]
[13] |=DS_busy [deq]
[14] |=DQ [next$req( 2, 150 )]
[15] |=DS_check [dc$start( 2, 150 )]
[16] |=DCtrl [dio$150]
[17] |=Disk [dint]
[18] |=DCtrl [dc$fini( 2, 150 )]
[19] |=DS_busy [ack( 2 )]
[20] |=DS_busy [deq]
[21] |=DQ [empty]
[22] Agent::exit_fn: Program hung!  Dump printed on stdout.
```

From this we can observe how client C(1) submits a request for disk block 100 (line 1) and then continues about its business (line 2). "Action: moreone" (line 3) is the default output from an action that has no external routine provided, but neither is trapped in the environment for synchronization. These default actions are useful as *stubs* for external routines until they can be written and linked in. We observe the disk scheduler go from IDLE to BUSY with the first request, and then receive C(2)'s request for block 150 (lines 4 to 6). At that point, the disk controller orders the disk drive (via channel dio) to access block 100 (line 7), and we see C(2) continuing (lines 8 to 9).

After some time, the disk interrupts (action dint), the controller notifies the scheduler, and the scheduler acknowledges client C(1) (lines 10 to 12). We then observe them repeat the cycle with the second request (lines 13 to 19), which was enqueued while the server was busy (line 6). (The queue actions are not traced because the code ordered them hidden.)

Finally, things come to a halt when the disk scheduler checks the queue again and finds it empty (lines 20 to 21). Because there is no ready-to-run task, the AT&T task scheduler calls the exit function, which, by default, prints a dump of all the scheduled tasks (not shown). This kind of default idle termination can be suppressed when interrupts are expected.

9.3 Summary and Future Work

This chapter shows a proof of concept in extending the executability of CSP specifications to the synthesis of C++ source code by means of the CSP++ OO framework. The framework is designed for integration with user action code. This allows CSP to be used for the design of a target system's components for which it is most amenable, and standard C++ to be used for the rest of the components.

Future work will include automating the current manual translation, and in the process providing support for FDR-style syntax. This will give source-level compatibility with a commercial verification tool. It may also be practical to translate other similar process algebras into CSP++, such as calculus of communicating systems (CCS) [Milner 1989]. We would also like to elaborate the framework's infrastructure to give more support for user-coded actions, including a strictly prescribed protocol for participating in choices. More distant visions include support for timed CSP [Davies 1992], and translating CSP to VHDL for hardware synthesis. VHDL is an acronym that stands for VHSIC Hardware Description Language. VHSIC is another acronym which stands for Very High Speed Integrated Circuits. Under the heading of hardware/software codesign [DeMicheli 1996], it would be interesting to partition a CSP specification between the C++ and hardware domains, and then automatically synthesize the communication channels between processes in the two domains.

9.4 References

[Arrowsmith 1994] Arrowsmith, B., and B. McMillin. How to program in CCSP. Technical report CSC 94-20. Department of Computer Science, University of Missouri—Rolla, August 1994.

[Davies 1992] Davies, J., and S. Schneider. A brief history of timed CSP. Technical report PRG-96. Programming Research Group, Oxford University, April 1992.

[DeMicheli 1996] De Micheli, G., and M. Sami, editors. *Hardware/Software Co-Design*. NATO Advanced Science Institutes, vol. E310. Kluwer Academic Publishers, 1996.

[Gajski 1994] Gajski, D.D., F. Vahid, S. Narayan, and J. Gong. *Specification and Design of Embedded Systems*. Englewood Cliffs, NJ: Prentice Hall, 1994.

[Gardner 1995] Gardner, W.B. Synthesis of C++ software from CSP specifications. Technical report DCS-252-IR. Department of Computer Science, Victoria University, British Columbia, March 1995.

[Hilderink 1997] Hilderink, G., J. Broenink, W. Vervoort, and A. Bakkers. Communicating Java Threads. *Proceedings of the 20th World Occam and Transputer User Group Technical Meeting*, Enschede, The Netherlands, pp. 48–76.www.rt.el.utwente.nl/javapp/, 1997.

[Hinchey-Jarvis 1995] Hinchey, M.G., and S.A. Jarvis. *Concurrent Systems: Formal Development in CSP*. New York: McGraw-Hill, 1995.

[Hoare 1985] Hoare, C.A.R. *Communicating Sequential Processes*. Englewood Cliffs, NJ: Prentice Hall, 1985.

[Matsuoka 1993] Matsuoka, S., and A. Yonezawa. Analysis of inheritance anomaly in object-oriented concurrent programming languages. In *Research Directions in Concurrent Object-Oriented Programming*, pp. 107–150, G. Agha, P. Wegner, and A. Yonezawa, editors. Cambridge, MA: MIT Press, 1993.

[Milner 1995] Milner, R. *Communication and Concurrency*. Englewood Cliffs, NJ: Prentice Hall, 1995.

[Reitzner 1997] Reitzner, S. Splitting synchronization from algorithmic behaviour. Technical report TR-14-97-08. Computer Science Department, Friedrich-Alexander University, April 1997.

[Roscoe 1994] Roscoe, A.W. Model-checking CSP. In *A Classical Mind: Essays in Honour of C.A.R. Hoare*, pp. 353–378, A.W. Roscoe, editor. Prentice Hall International Series in Computer Science. Englewood Cliffs, NJ: Prentice Hall, 1994.

CHAPTER 10

Applying Inheritance beyond Class-Based Languages

Viewed abstractly, a class in object-oriented programming may be regarded simply as a collection of *names* associated with *bindings* of various types, such as constant values, references to objects, and methods implementing the behavior of the class. The latter kind of bindings, *methods*, may contain references back to other names in the class, via the use of constructs such as *self* or *this*. A class can thus be regarded as a *self-referential namespace*.

Class-based inheritance is a mechanism that supports reuse via incremental programming. That is, one can program by describing how a new software component differs from an existing one. A subclass is a *composition* of a superclass and a structure describing the incremental difference. Thus, when classes in object-oriented programming are viewed as self-referential namespaces, reuse via inheritance can be viewed as composition and adaptation of such namespaces.

The key insight of this chapter is that software artifacts other than classes, such as compiled object modules (for instance, ".o" files in Unix) and structured document fragments, can also be modeled as self-referential namespaces. Consequently, tools that are based on concepts underlying inheritance can be fruitfully applied to reuse such artifacts as well. Such tools will share concepts and code, and can thus be built as completions of a framework that embodies their commonality in the form of abstract semantics of inheritance. This chapter describes Etyma, a framework that captures an abstract semantics of inheritance and is designed for building tools that are based upon inheritance-based reuse.

The domain of class-based inheritance is captured in an abstract model we term *compositional modularity*. In this model, a self-referential namespace is known as a *module,* and operations on modules enable one to adapt and compose them in various ways. Compositional modularity supports a simple notion of modules along with a powerful notion of their composition, distilling and unifying many existing notions of modularity. The ultimate goal of compositional modularity is to enable maximal reuse of software components by breaking them down into small manageable units and reusing them effectively to build complex programs.

The next section describes the abstract model of compositional modularity in more detail. The section also shows how the model can be applied in four distinct and diverse settings. Following that, the abstract and concrete class structure of the Etyma framework is described. Two completions of Etyma are then described in detail. The chapter concludes by relating experience with building the framework and presenting a summary.

10.1 Compositional Modularity

In the model of compositional modularity (CM), a module is simply a collection of names, some of which are associated with bindings. These bindings may, in turn, contain references to names that are available either within the module itself or external to the module. Such modules can be adapted and composed in various ways to create other modules, which in turn make up entire systems, much like putting Lego pieces together.

Module manipulation in CM is performed using a suite of *operators*, each of which achieves an individual effect, such as combination, encapsulation, rebinding, or hierarchical nesting. The primary operators in this suite are shown in Table 10.1. These operators may be used together to achieve various composite effects of inheritance

Table 10.1 The Primary Operators of Compositional Modularity

OPERATOR	DESCRIPTION
merge m_1 m_2	Combine modules m_1 and m_2 without allowing conflicting attribute names.
override m_1 m_2	Combine modules m_1 and m_2 by choosing m_2's bindings for conflicting attribute names.
hide m a	Encapsulate the attribute *a* of module *m*.
rename m a_1 a_2	Rename the attribute a_1 of module *m* to a_2 and update all self-references.
restrict m a	Remove the attribute *a* from module *m*.
copy-as m a_1 a_2	Copy the binding of attribute a_1 in module *m* to an attribute with name a_2.
freeze m a	Statically bind self-references to attribute *a* in module *m*.
nest m_1 m_2 a	Nest the module m_1 within module m_2 as an attribute named *a*.

supported by modern object-oriented (OO) programming languages. This approach was originally proposed in [Bracha 1992] and developed further in [Banavar 1995a]; please see these sources for the precise semantics of the CM model.

A significant characteristic of the CM model is that it is *unifying* in scope. [Banavar 1995a] demonstrates in detail the expressive power of this model by emulating various existing models of inheritance in OO programming. Another significant characteristic of the model is that it is *abstract*. That is to say, the model can be presented and analyzed without committing to the nature of the actual values that are bound to names within modules. Thus, the model is independent of particular underlying computational paradigms. This property is used to advantage in developing the application framework presented in this chapter.

10.1.1 Applying CM

Compositional modularity is applicable within a wide range of systems, partly due to the simplicity of the model and partly due to the pervasiveness of modularity and namespace manipulation within software systems. There is indeed a wide range of software artifacts that can be modeled as self-referential namespaces. For instance, it is well known that recursive interface types can be viewed as self-referential namespaces [Canning 1989]. A traditional compiled object file can also be viewed as a self-referential namespace [Banavar 1995b]. Furthermore, structured document fragments can be modeled as self-referential namespaces. Even other artifacts, such as graphical user interface (GUI) components and file system directories can be regarded as recursive namespaces.

There currently exist many tools that manage the range of artifacts mentioned here. However, these tools are usually based on disparate, and often impoverished, underlying models. We argue that it is advantageous to manage these artifacts from the viewpoint of a well-understood model such as compositional modularity, and to build tools that are based on this viewpoint. The primary advantage of such an approach is that the underlying model of such tools can be significantly enriched, and reuse mechanisms akin to OO inheritance can be supported on the artifacts they manage. Moreover, the uniformity of the underlying model of such tools can be exploited to support better interactions between them.

The following sections describe four examples of systems that can profitably use a module system based on compositional modularity.

Module Composition in Scheme

In a conventional programming language such as Scheme [Clinger 1991], the notion of a module is that of an independent naming scope. A module comprises a set of identifiers bound either to locations (variables) or to any of the various Scheme values, including procedures. Procedures may contain references to other name bindings within the module. Furthermore, a first-class module value may itself be bound to an identifier, in a nested manner. In this way, a Scheme module may be modeled as a self-referential namespace.

Several module systems for Scheme have been proposed previously (for example, [Rees 1993]), but these systems mainly provide a facility for structuring programs via decomposition. However, the ability to compose first-class modules additionally supports design and implementation reuse akin to inheritance in OO programming. Furthermore, the notions of first-class modules and operations on them are consistent with the uniform use of first-class values and the expression-oriented nature of Scheme.

[Banavar 1996] describes the design of a CM-based module system for Scheme in detail and shows that the module system can emulate several composite inheritance idioms that are present in modern-day OO programming languages. This chapter later describes the design of an interpreter for the CMS language as a completion of our framework.

Object Module Composition

A separately compiled object file (such as an ".o" file generated from a C-language source file in UNIX) essentially consists of a set of symbols, some of which are associated with data or code and others of which are external references. This set of symbols is represented as a symbol table within the object module. Furthermore, internal references to these symbols are represented as relocation information within the object module. Thus, an object file can be modeled as a self-referential namespace.

The traditional notion of linking object files corresponds to a rudimentary notion of composition (it in fact corresponds to the semantics of the merge operator). However, the full power of compositional modularity made available via a programmable linker can significantly enhance the ability to manage and bind object modules. In particular, facilities such as function interposition, management of incremental additions of functionality to libraries, and namespace management can be made more principled and flexible. These effects are described in detail in [Banavar 1995b].

Interface Composition

An interface is essentially a naming scope, with labels bound to *types* instead of values. Type bindings of the interface can recursively refer back to the interface itself [Canning 1989]. For example, a Point interface containing attributes for coordinates x and y, a *move* method, and an *equal* predicate can be expressed as follows (where the keyword *selftype* represents recursion and *selftype.x* is abbreviated to x):

```
interface FloatPointType {
    float x, y;
    selftype move (x, y);
    boolean equal (selftype);
}
```

This interface can be extended to have a color attribute using the *merge* operation, as follows:

```
interface ColorType {
    color_type color;
}
interface ColorPointType = FloatPointType merge ColorType;
```

In this manner, an interface can be manipulated as a self-referential namespace. Explicit specification and composition of interfaces, as embodied in interface definition languages (IDLs)—for example, [CORBA 1991]—are becoming necessities in modern distributed systems. Composition of interface specifications as shown in the preceding examples can help in the reuse and evolution of interface specifications. Reuse facilitates the evolution of interfaces [Hamilton 1994] by ensuring that inheriting interfaces evolve in step with the inherited interfaces. It also simplifies maintenance by reducing redundant code. Again, details of interface composition can be found in [Banavar 1995a].

Document Composition

A document can be regarded as a naming scope consisting of section names, each associated with arbitrary text. Furthermore, there can be cross-references from within a textual body to other section names. Thus, a document fragment can be regarded as a self-referential namespace.

Document composition can be useful in enterprises where several document fragments are generated, edited, composed, maintained, and delivered in various ways. For example, document fragments for architectural specifications [Rossberg 1994] generated for one purpose (such as contractor plans) can be reused for other purposes (such as building permit applications). Another example is a report, such as a user manual, which can be composed from several document fragments, such as design documents. This chapter later describes an example of a document processing system, called *MteX*, for composing document fragments.

10.2 Structure of the Etyma Framework

This section describes the architecture of our framework, Etyma, which captures the basic concepts of compositional modularity. It begins by identifying the important abstractions and their relationships, then describes their organization.

Compositional modularity deals with modules, their instances, the attributes they are composed of, and the types of all the above. Thus, the primary concepts that must be captured by a reusable architecture for CM such as Etyma are those of *modules, instances, names, values, methods, variables,* and their corresponding types. Etyma is also a linguistic framework—that is, a framework from which language-processing tools will be designed. Thus, while modeling these concepts, we must not inadvertently omit abstractions and limit their generality. For example, a *method* is a specialization of the general concept of a *function*. Similarly, the concept of a *record* is closely related to those of a *module* and an *instance*. We must also be careful in determining the precise relationships between concepts. For example, a module abstracts over a record, whereas an instance is itself a record; thus, the concept of an instance is a subtype of the concept of a record, but neither of these concepts is subtype-related to the concept of a module.

The abstractions of Etyma form two layers. An abstract layer consists of abstract class realizations (partial implementations) of the concepts given here. These classes may be used as a whitebox framework (via inheritance) by completions. A concrete layer provides full implementations of the abstract classes that can be directly used as a blackbox framework (via instantiation) by completions. This layer, as is customary, is meant to increase the reusability of the framework. The following section describes the important classes in both layers—those corresponding to modules, instances, and methods. We utilize the notion of design patterns [Gamma 1995] to elucidate the structure of the Etyma framework.

10.2.1 Abstract Classes

Figure 10.1 shows an overview of the abstract classes of Etyma diagrammed using the OO notation in [Gamma 1995] extended to show protected methods under dashed lines within classes. Class Etymon is the abstract base class of all classes in Etyma, and classes TypedValue and Type represent the domains of values and their types respectively.

The abstract class Module captures the notion of a compositional module in its broadest conception. Its public methods correspond to the module operators introduced earlier in Table 10.1. Within this class, no concrete representation for module attributes is assumed. Instead, the public module operations are implemented as template method patterns in terms of a set of protected abstract methods such as insert, remove, and so on, which manage module attributes. Concrete subclasses of class Module are expected to provide implementations for these abstract protected methods. Two of these are abstract factory method patterns: create_instance, which is expected to return an instance of a concrete subclass of class Instance (described shortly), and create_iter, which is expected to return an instance of a concrete subclass

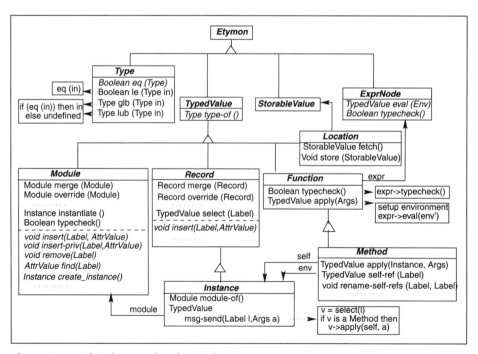

Figure 10.1   The abstract class layer of Etyma.

of class AttrIter, an iterator pattern for module attributes. Thus, the generality of class Module results from its use of a combination of the following patterns: *Template Method*, *Abstract Factory Method*, and *Iterator*.

Class Instance is a subclass of class Record; hence it supports record operations, implemented in a manner similar to those of class Module. In addition, it models the traditional OO notion of sending a message (dispatch) to an object by retrieving a method-valued attribute, invoking the method select, followed by invoking the method apply on it. This functionality is encapsulated by a template method pattern msg-send(Label,Args). Furthermore, class Instance has access to its generating module via its module data member.

The concept of a method is modeled as a specialization of the concept of a function. Class Function supports an apply method that evaluates the function body. Although class Function is a concrete class, the function body is represented by an abstract class ExprNode, a composite pattern. Because a method belongs to a class, class Method requires that the first argument to its apply method be an instance of class Instance, corresponding to its notion of self.

Type classes are an important part of this layer but are not detailed in Figure 10.1. Type classes corresponding to the value classes described are modeled as subclasses of class. Class Type supports methods for type equality (eq), subtyping (le), greatest common subtype (glb), and least common supertype (lub). (The latter two operations are required for merge and override operations.) Some of the important subclasses of class Type are the following:

Class UnitType (a singleton pattern). Represents a type that contains a single member.

Class NamedType. Models types that have identity.

Class Interface. Models the type of modules and contains methods that implement the typechecking rules for the operations in Table 10.1.

Class RecordType. Represents the type of records as well as the type of instances.

Class FunctionType. Models function types.

Type classes in the framework also support recursive typing. A constituent of a composite type may be a recursive type (such as the selftype construct given earlier) and is represented as an object of class RecType. Operations of class Type take recursive types into account when computing equality and subtyping, using algorithms such as those given in [Amadio 1993].

10.2.2 Concrete Classes

Some abstract classes in Figure 10.1 are subclassed into concrete classes to facilitate immediate reuse, as shown in Figure 10.2. Class StdModule is a concrete subclass of class Module that represents its attributes as a map. An attribute map (object of class AttrMap) is a collection of individual attributes, each of which maps a name (object of class Label) to a binding (object of class AttrValue). A binding encapsulates an object of any subclass of class TypedValue. This structure corresponds to a variation of the

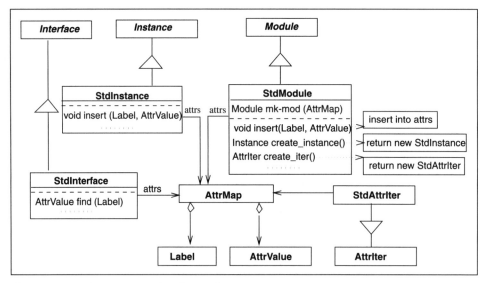

Figure 10.2   The concrete class layer of Etyma.

bridge pattern, which makes it possible for completions to reuse much of the implementation of class Module by simply implementing classes corresponding to attribute bindings as subclasses of class TypedValue.

Each of class StdModule's attribute management functions is implemented as the corresponding operations on the map. Furthermore, the factory method pattern create_iter of class StdModule returns an object of a concrete subclass of class AttrIter, class StdAttrIter. Similarly, the factory method pattern create_instance returns an object of the concrete subclass of class Instance, class StdInstance. The type of Std-Module objects is represented by objects of class StdInterface, a subclass of class Interface. Classes StdInstance and StdInterface are also implemented using attribute maps; thus, objects of class AttrValue hold either an object of class TypedValue or class Type.

10.3 Completions of Etyma

Architecturally, tools constructed as completions of Etyma have the basic structure given in Figure 10.3. The command input component reads in module manipulation programs that direct the composition engine. The data input component creates the internal representation (IR) of compositional modules by parsing module source data and instantiating appropriate framework and completion classes. The optional data output component transforms the IR into a suitable output format. The composition engine itself is derived from the Etyma framework, and comprises classes (data and composition behavior) corresponding to module-related entities. In the following sections, two tools derived from the Etyma framework in this manner are described.

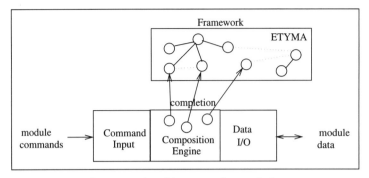

Figure 10.3   The general architecture of completions.

10.3.1 Building a Scheme Module System as a Completion

This section describes the implementation of an interpreter for an extension of Scheme, called CMS, that incorporates a module system based on CM. The CMS interpreter consists of two parts: a basic Scheme interpreter, written in the C language; and the module system, implemented as a completion of Etyma. The basic Scheme interpreter itself was extracted from a publicly available scriptable windowing toolkit called *STk* [Gallesio 1994]. The interpreter implementation exports many of the functions implementing Scheme semantics, thus making it easy to access its internals. Furthermore, the interpreter was originally designed to be extensible; that is, new Scheme primitives can be implemented in C/C++ and easily incorporated into the interpreter. For example, say we want to implement a new Scheme primitive new-prim that takes two input parameters and is implemented by a C function new_prim_in_C (...). This can be done by including the following C function call in the appropriate initialization routine of the interpreter and recompiling it:

```
add_new_primitive ("new-prim", tc_subr_2, new_prim_in_C);
```

Thus, in order to implement CMS, Scheme primitives implementing concepts of compositional modularity—for creating modules and instances, for self-reference, and for adapting and composing modules—were implemented in C++ and incorporated into the interpreter. More specifically, once the new CMS primitives were identified, subclasses of Etyma classes that support the primitives were designed and implemented. Furthermore, *glue* functions that extend the basic interpreter by calling the appropriate methods of the new subclasses were also implemented.

The overall architecture of the CMS interpreter is shown in Figure 10.4. The Scheme library shown on the left includes higher-level macros for OO programming, such as for defining new classes, as well as other support functions written in CMS, such as for emulating composite inheritance.

In order to extend Scheme with a new datatype corresponding to modules that contains other Scheme values, we must first model the Scheme value and type domains in the framework. Scheme consists of a uniform domain of first-class values that includes

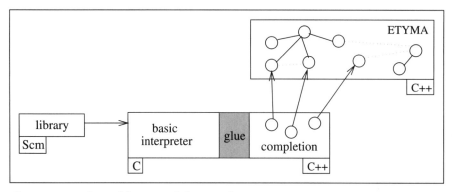

Figure 10.4 The architecture of the CMS interpreter.

primitive values and functions. (It is sufficient to consider these Scheme values for the purposes of this discussion.) Scheme variables are identifiers that are bound to locations, which, in turn, can contain any Scheme value. Scheme values are typed, but variables are not. An extension to Scheme must preserve Scheme's essential flavor and pragmatics; thus, module attributes should be designed to be untyped names. Furthermore, attributes can be bound to values, locations, or methods (functions). Hence, we should model all these notions—names, values, locations, and functions—using the framework.

The subclasses of framework classes comprising the completion are shown in Figure 10.5. The untyped nature of variables can be modeled using a singleton type represented by class UnitType in the framework. Scheme identifiers can be modeled with a subclass SchLabel of the framework class Label, with the notion of equality implemented using the corresponding method for Scheme names exported by the interpreter. Scheme values are modeled using class SchValue. Location bindings can be modeled with a subclass SchLocation of class Location and method bindings with a subclass SchMethod of class Method. Class SchMethod need not store the method body as a subclass of class ExprNode; instead, it can simply store the internal representation of Scheme expression as exported by the interpreter implementation. In addition, class SchMethod must define methods corresponding to the CMS primitives for self-reference, which call similar methods on the stored self object, an object of a subclass SchInstance of class StdInstance.

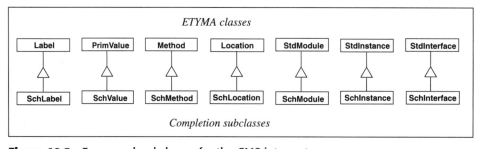

Figure 10.5 Framework subclasses for the CMS interpreter.

With the classes previously mentioned, the implementation of class StdModule can be almost completely reused for implementing CMS modules with class SchModule. However, methods to handle CMS primitives for creating modules and instances need to be added. The only modification required is to redefine the method create_instance of class StdModule to return an object of class SchInstance. Class SchInstance implements code for CMS primitives for attribute referencing and assignment. A subclass SchInterface of the framework class StdInterface also needs to redefine certain type-checking routines to reflect the fact that *abstract* attributes in CMS may be referenced but simply left undefined.

Table 10.2 shows several measures of reuse for the CMS module system implemented as a completion of Etyma. The percentages for class and method reuse give an indication of *design* reuse, because classes and their methods represent the functional decomposition and interface design of the framework. On the other hand, the percentages for lines of code give a measure of *code* reuse.

10.3.2 Building MTeX as a Completion

MTeX is a document manipulation system that takes as its input document fragments marked up with LaTeX commands [Lamport 1986] and composes them using module manipulation commands. An MTeX module instance is modeled as an ordered set of sections, each of which is a label bound either to a section body or to a nested module. The section label is a symbolic name that can be referenced from other sections. The section body is a tuple (H,B) where H is text corresponding to the section heading and B corresponds to the actual text body, which consists of textual segments interspersed with self-references to labels. Section bodies can have arbitrary text in them, including arbitrary LaTeX command sources.

The logical architecture of the MTeX document processing system is two-tiered. Physical modules are created with the syntax of LaTeX and parsed by the system. A Scheme-derived module language is then used to transform the physical files into first-class compositional modules and then compose them in various ways. For example, a mk-module primitive is used to read in a physical document module. Operators such as project (dual of restrict), nest, and override are then used to adapt and combine these first-class modules, which can be written back as files using the write-module primitive.

The implementation architecture of MTeX is shown in Figure 10.6. The STk-derived Scheme interpreter was used for MTeX in a manner similar to CMS. A yacc/lex parser reads in document modules, creates the appropriate framework classes, and returns a

Table 10.2   Reuse of Framework Design and Code for CMS Interpreter

REUSE PARAMETER		NEW	REUSED	PERCENT REUSE
Module system only	Classes	7	25	78
	Methods	67	275	80.4
	Lines of code	1,550	5,000	76.3
Entire interpreter	Lines of code	1,800	20,000	91.7

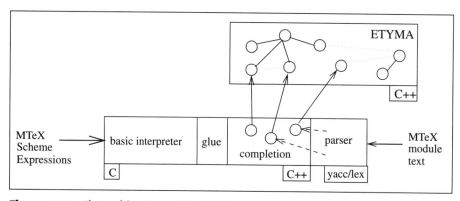

Figure 10.6 The architecture of the MTeX processor.

first-class MTeX module, an object of class TexModule (described following). These modules may then be manipulated using Scheme primitives via the interpreter.

In addition to the CM operators, metalevel introspective primitives are also useful while manipulating documents. For example, the operation self-refs-in returns a list of all the names referenced within a set of bindings. This function can be combined with the project operation (dual of restrict) to write a higher-level Scheme function that projects the closure of self-references from a set of sections. In fact, such a function, called *cl-project*, is included in the standard Scheme library associated with MTeX. MTeX script files can contain arbitrary Scheme code. Furthermore, because section order is crucial in documents, the user might wish to reorder sections using a primitive reorder.

A simple example of MTeX document composition follows. Say a document with three generic sections, *Introduction, Model,* and *Conclusions,* is stored in a file named *body.tex.* Imagine that another file *oo.tex* contains sections corresponding to the various concepts in OO programming. The following expression can be used to compose the two files:

```
(override
    (mk-module "body.tex")
    (nest (mk-module)
        "sec:model" "OO Concepts" (mk-module "oo.tex")))
```

This expression nests the module oo.tex with the section label sec:model into a freshly created empty module, which overrides the other module body.tex. The resultant module has a section labeled sec:model bound to a nested module, consisting of sections describing OO concepts. This module can be written out as a LaTeX file and instantiated into a .dvi file by running the LaTeX compiler.

The subclasses of Etyma created to construct the MTeX module engine are the following: TexLabel of Label, Section of Method, TexModule of StdModule, SecMap of AttrMap, and TexInterface of StdInterface. Also, a new class, Segment, which represents a segment of text between self-references, was created.

Approximate design and code reuse numbers for the MTeX implementation are shown in Table 10.3.

Table 10.3   Reuse of Framework Design and Code for Building MTeX

REUSE PARAMETER		NEW	REUSED	PERCENT REUSE
Module system only	Classes	6	20	77
	Methods	36	231	86.5
	Lines of code	1,600	4,400	73.3
Entire system	Lines of code	1,800	19,400	91.5

10.4 Experiences with Framework Construction

This section summarizes the evolution history of Etyma from its initial conception to its current form. The very first version of Etyma was almost fully concrete, and was designed to experiment with a module extension to the C language. It consisted only of the notions of modules, instances, primitive values, and locations, along with a few support classes. No front and back ends were constructed. The next incarnation of Etyma was used to build a typechecking mechanism for C-language object modules, described in [Banavar 1995a]. This experiment solidified many of the type classes of Etyma. However, at this point, Etyma was still primarily a set of concrete classes. The third incarnation was used to *direct* the reengineering of the programmable linker/loader Object and Meta Object Server (OMOS) introduced earlier (and described in [Banavar 1995b]). In this iteration, the framework was not directly used in the construction of OMOS (due to practical, not technical, constraints), but it evolved in parallel with the actual class hierarchy of OMOS. The design of OMOS classes followed that of Etyma closely. Also, much of the framework, including the abstract and concrete layers, developed during this iteration.

The fourth iteration of Etyma was the construction of CMS completion. There were few changes to the framework classes in this iteration; these were mostly to fix implementation bugs. However, some new methods for retroactive nesting were added. Nonetheless, the CMS interpreter was constructed within a very short period of time, which resulted in a high degree of reuse. The next iteration was to design and implement an IDL compiler front end. There were almost no modifications to the framework; additions included mechanism related to recursive types. The sixth, and most recent, iteration of Etyma has been to build the MTeX document composition system. There were no changes to the framework.

The first three iterations essentially evolved the framework from a set of concrete classes to a reusable set of abstract and concrete classes, thus crystallizing the reusable functionality of the framework. From the fourth iteration onward, the framework was mostly reused, with some additions but very few modifications. As the observed reusability of the framework increased, measurements were taken to record the reuse achieved, as shown in the tables given earlier.

10.5 Summary

This chapter describes a medium-sized framework for the domain of class-based inheritance itself. This framework, named Etyma, captures an abstract model of classes and inheritance known as *compositional modularity*. Etyma can be used to build tools for adapting and composing a diverse set of software artifacts, such as compiled object modules, interfaces, text fragments, and programming language modules. These artifacts share the common feature that they have an adaptable and composable self-referential structure similar to classes in OO programming.

A key point of this chapter is that an abstract understanding of a domain can bring seemingly dissimilar applications together. The abstract model of the domain and its implementation can then be realized as a unifying framework, and reused to build such applications—both anticipated and unanticipated. Furthermore, the complexity of the abstract model can be implemented once within the framework and reused efficiently in a number of contexts, thus significantly reducing development time.

10.6 References

[Amadio 1993] Amadio, R.M., and L. Cardelli. Subtyping recursive types. *ACM Transactions on Programming Languages and Systems,* 15(4), September 1993.

[Banavar 1995a] Banavar, G. An application framework for compositional modularity. Technical Report CSTD-95-011. University of Utah, Salt Lake City, UT, 1995.

[Banavar 1995b] Banavar, G., D. Orr, and G. Lindstrom. Layered, server-based support for object-oriented application development. *Proceedings of the Fourth International Workshop on Object Orientation in Operating Systems,* pp. 2–11, L.-F. Cabrera and M. Theimer, editors. Lund, Sweden, August 14–15. Los Alamitos, CA, IEEE Computer Society, 1995.

[Banavar 1996] Banavar, G., and G. Lindstrom. A framework for module composition tools. *Proceedings of the 10th European Conference on Object Oriented Programming,* Linz, Austria, July 8–12. *Lecture Notes in Computer Science 1098.* Springer-Verlag, 1996.

[Bracha 1992] Bracha, G., and G. Lindstrom. Modularity meets inheritance. *Proceedings of the International Conference on Computer Languages,* pp. 282–290, San Francisco, CA, April 20–23. Los Alamitos, CA, IEEE Computer Society, 1992.

[Canning 1989] Canning, P., W. Cook, W. Hill, and W. Olthoff. Interfaces for strongly-typed object-oriented programming. *Proceedings of the ACM Conference on Object-Oriented Programming, Systems, Languages, and Applications,* pp. 457–467, N. Meyrowitz, editor. Reading, MA: ACM Press, 1989.

[Clinger 1991] Clinger, W., and J. Rees. Revised 4 report on the algorithmic language Scheme. *ACM Lisp Pointers,* 4(3), 1991.

[CORBA 1991] Object Management Group. *The Common Object Request Broker: Architecture and Specification,* Revision 1.1. OMG Document. Framingham, MA: OMG December 1991.

[Gallesio 1994] Gallesio, E. *STk Reference Manual,* Version 2.1, 1993–1994 www.mips .unice.fr/Doc/Softs/STk/ or http://kaolin.unice.fr/STk/STk.html.

[Gamma 1995] Gamma, E., R. Helm, R. Johnson, and J. Vlissides. *Design Patterns: Elements of Reusable Object-Oriented Software.* Professional Computing Series. Reading, MA: Addison-Wesley, 1995.

[Hamilton 1994] Hamilton, G., and S. Radia. Using interface inheritance to address problems in system software evolution. *Proceedings of the Workshop on Interface Definition Languages,* pp. 119–128, J. Wing, editor, January 1994. Also in *ACM SIGPLAN Notices,* August 1994.

[Lamport 1986] Lamport, L. *LaTeX, a Document Processing System.* Reading, MA: Addison-Wesley, 1986.

[Rees 1993] Rees, J. Another module system for Scheme. Included in the Scheme 48 distribution, 1993. www.cs.hmc.edu/~fleck/envision/scheme48/module/module.html

[Rossberg 1994] Rossberg, W., E. Smith, and A. Matinkhah. Structured text system. U.S. Patent no. 5,341,469, August 1994.

CHAPTER 11

Luthier: Building Framework-Visualization Tools

Program comprehension is one of the most critical problems in the software life cycle. The success of activities such as debugging, maintenance, or reuse depends, to a large extent, on how easy it is for a programmer to understand a given program when it is necessary to correct an error or change its functionality. Object-oriented programs are, in general, more difficult to understand than traditional procedural systems (with functional architecture). The well-known problems of the dichotomy between the source code structure and the execution model, the distribution of functionality among classes, and the dynamic binding make object-oriented programs harder to understand [Wilde 1992].

In this context, software tools to help to reduce the complexity of object-oriented program comprehension are valuable. These tools aim to help a programmer to build a mental model of the program by providing mechanisms for analyzing, exploring, and visualizing information about the program at different levels of abstraction. Frequently, they provide different visual representations that synthesize relevant properties about the analyzed artifact, as well as mechanisms for filtering, organizing, and abstracting information, which allow the user to explore the information from different perspectives.

The construction of such tools, however, is not a simple task. The limitations of conventional mechanisms for data gathering and representation, combined with the dynamic model of object-oriented programs, complicates the flexible implementation of different mechanisms for program analysis and visualization. Most of the existing tools based on these techniques are oriented toward specific activities such as debugging, structural analysis, or visualization of dynamic behavior. In the general case, little support is provided to adapt them to different comprehension activities. Particularly, the dynamic nature of object-oriented programs makes data gathering one of the most problematic points. The huge amount of information that can be gathered in a single execution obliges one to build complex mechanisms to manage several thousands of objects or events generated within a few seconds. Conventional solutions also lead to complex mechanisms to coordinate visualizations with users' cognitive limitations, as well as representations with time and space tradeoffs. Furthermore, these mechanisms rarely provide a flexible structure that allows the gathering of both static and dynamic information at different levels of abstraction without a considerable programming effort.

In order to overcome some of these limitations, a framework for building tools for application analysis and visualization was developed. This framework, called *Luthier,* is characterized by the use of reflection techniques based on metaobjects. Luthier provides flexible support for building visualization tools that are adaptable to different analysis functionality, using a hyperdocument manager to organize the collected information. These mechanisms support the flexible construction of different visualizations from the analyzed examples, as well as navigation among different visual representations and textual documentation, through explicit support for editing documentation books. With this support, a prototype of a visual tool for framework comprehension, *MetaExplorer,* was developed. MetaExplorer provides both a rich set of visualizations and abstraction capabilities for subsystem analysis and Gamma design-pattern recognition. The tool provides two- and three-dimensional visualizations of the analyzed program information. Several two-dimensional visualizations are available for the different perspectives from which this information can be analyzed. The three-dimensional views provide several techniques for the visualization of the relationships among classes and design patterns [Gamma 1995] that attempt to integrate in a single view information corresponding to several two-dimensional visualizations.

The next sections describe the main characteristics of the Luthier design and an example of the instantiation of Luthier to build MetaExplorer. Also, experimental results of using MetaExplorer to understand the HotDraw framework and other Luthier applications are presented.

11.1 The Luthier Approach

Reverse engineering and software visualization systems are the lines of research that have made the most important contributions to the development of software comprehension support techniques. *Reverse engineering* is the activity through which relevant information about a program or system is identified, relationships are discovered, and abstractions are generated [Chikofsky 1990]. Tools to support this activity aim to provide automatic mechanisms to extract information from a program by analyzing its source code, and to deduce, or recognize, structural and behavioral abstractions not directly represented in such code. *Software visualization systems* (SVSs) aim to provide mechanisms to build visual representations of the program information, through which a user can analyze and comprehend the structure and behavior at a higher level of abstraction than the code. Within the wide spectrum of existing SVSs, algorithm animation systems, pioneered by BALSA [Brown 1984], TANGO [Stasko 1990], and so on, represent a particularly relevant class. These systems provide the support to build animation of the behavior of a program, which is especially useful to help users understand the way algorithms and complex programs behave at runtime.

Essentially, the two families of systems differ in the emphasis put on the aspects of abstraction analysis and recognition. However, they can be characterized by a basic sequence of four activities (see Figure 11.1): *data gathering, data representation, abstraction recognition,* and *presentation and exploration.* Luthier adopts a combination of techniques that enable the adaptation of these four essential mechanisms, as described here:

Data gathering. In contrast with annotative or parsing techniques commonly used by most current visualization tools, Luthier adopts a reflective approach based on Maes-style metaobjects [Maes 1988]. (Reflection is the ability of a system to make computations about its own computation [Maes 1988], that is, it is able to analyze and modify the entities defining its own behavior.) Basically, a metaobject is an object that can control, or observe, the behavior of an associated object (called a *base-level object*). Metaobjects offer a great level of flexibility to build libraries of reflective behavior that can be added transparently and nonintrusively (regard-

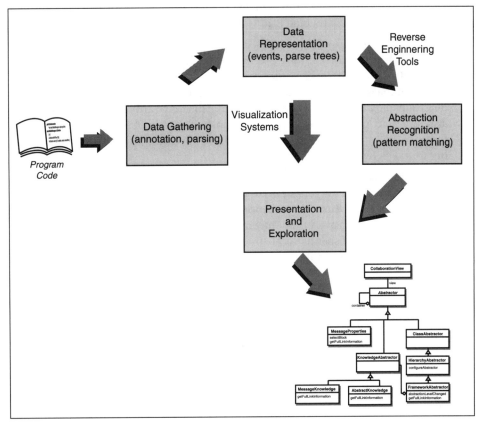

Figure 11.1   A comprehension tool's main activities.

ing source code) to a system either to extend its functionality or to monitor its runtime behavior. Metaobjects can dynamically be associated with application objects, so they represent an excellent vehicle to support analysis tools that are dynamically adaptable to different data-gathering functionality.

To support this functionality in a flexible way, Luthier introduces the concept of *metaobject managers.* A metaobject manager (MOM) is an object that determines how metaobjects are *associated* to base-level objects and how these metaobjects are *activated.* That is, a metaobject manager reifies the generic mechanisms that enable the implementation of specific metaobject protocols.

From a tool construction point of view, MOMs offer the advantage of providing a high-level interface to organize metaobjects independently of the functionality implemented by them. The separation of the association mechanism allows its specialization to implement specific management services adequate to the requirements of each particular tool. This ability is essential to enable an interactive substitution of metaobjects, which allows the comprehension tool to switch among different data-gathering functionalities. The ability to activate metaobjects enables a MOM to dynamically suspend and restart the reflection of messages of all the reflected objects, or just some of them. This capability allows, for example, the user to interactively determine whether a tool should activate metaobjects. Also, different functions of the metalevel can be activated or deactivated without accessing any specific metaobject.

Data representation. Luthier provides the support to define specific representations of the gathered information in terms of a hypertext model based on context objects [Casanova 1991]. The model supports classes of nodes and bidirectional links that make simpler the navigation through the complex web of information determined by an object-oriented program. This representation can be stored persistently as a part of documentation books. These books are implemented in terms of the same hypertext model, enabling the construction of design libraries organized as hyperdocuments.

Abstraction recognition. Luthier introduces the concept of *abstractor objects.* Abstractors represent a generic architectural component of tools, by which different analytical algorithms and selection criteria can be located, without the need of modifying either classes of the information representation or classes implementing visualizations. Essentially, abstractors behave as proxies of the objects of the data representation, controlling the access to these objects by visualization objects. In this way, abstractors can be hierarchically composed to provide independent control over each object contained in the model. Also, they can be dynamically composed to combine different functionality—for example, filtering on a specific selection of the program information. This powerful feature enables the combination and reuse of different algorithms for abstraction recognition with different visualization styles—for example, subsystem analysis, structural relationship analysis, or design pattern recognition.

Exploration and presentation. Adopting an advanced hyperdocument representation, the implementation of exploration mechanisms is almost trivial. On the other hand, as abstractors are able to decide which information will be visible, the detail level of the visualization can be controlled by abstractors in a simple way.

They allow the implementation of sophisticated mechanisms to gradually change the detail level, as continuous zooming of the visualization. This zooming can be controlled through the definition of *abstraction scales*. An abstraction scale is an ordered tuple naming the order in which constructions, such as subsystems, classes, methods, and so on, should be visualized. A scale can have its own user-interface control (usually a slider), through which the user can interactively vary the level of abstraction of the visualization (showing or dynamically hiding details). Visualizations, in turn, only have to worry about what must be shown according to the data that abstractors pass to them in the current abstraction level. For example, the following scale can be used to define the different detail levels in which a class can be shown:

```
(abstractMethods,hookMethods, templateMethods, baseMethods,
variables)
```

A selection of a level in this scale will define which information the visualization will receive to be graphically presented. That is, if the selected abstraction level is hookMethods, the visualization will receive only the information about abstract and hook methods. After that, if the user selects templateMethods, the same visualization will receive the same information plus the information about template methods.

Abstraction scales can also define inclusive levels of abstraction. A typical example is given by software structures. Subsystems are composed by packages or class hierarchies; these components, in turn, can be composed by procedures or classes, and so on. This hierarchy can be coded by an abstraction scale, as shown here:

```
(subsystem, abstractClasses, concreteSubclasses, methods)
```

Through this scale, it is possible to manage the degree of detail from a global perspective (for example, subsystems) adding gradually more information provided by the corresponding components (classes, methods, variables, and so on).

11.2 The Framework

The Luthier framework was designed and implemented in VisualWorks-Smalltalk. Luthier is constituted by four subframeworks, which provide adaptable support to the four tasks previously characterized: *LuthierMOPs,* for information gathering; *Luthier-Books,* for information representation; *LuthierViews,* for visualization and exploration of gathered information; and *LuthierAbstractors,* for abstraction analysis and recovery.

Figure 11.2 presents the generic structure of a visualization tool built using Luthier. A typical tool will be composed of a set of metaobjects monitoring the execution of an application, generating an abstract representation of the program information using a specific hyperdocument manager. The visualizations will request from the lower level the information to be visualized, which will be provided by *abstractor objects.* Abstractors are in charge of recognizing or building abstractions from the information contained in the hyperdocument representation.

The next sections describe the main design characteristics of each subframework. The descriptions include the overall class structures using OMT [Rumbaugh 1991] and

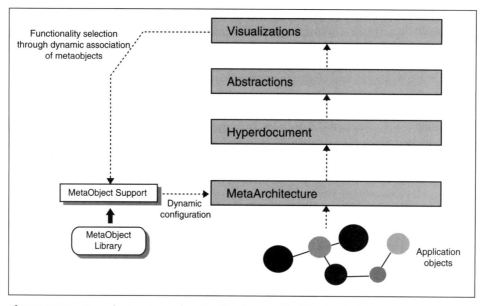

Figure 11.2   Generic structure of a visualization tool built using Luthier.

the specification of the generic collaborations among abstract classes using an extended version of the *contracts* notation presented in [Helm 1990]. Contracts are used because they offer a simple textual language to describe relationships at the object level, allowing expression of the relationship among hierarchically organized sets of objects.

Table 11.1 presents some of the extensions and conventions used to enhance the expressiveness of the original language.

The contracts presented were edited in order to give a brief and more comprehensible specification of the essential mechanisms of the framework. The complete specification can be found in [Campo 1997].

11.2.1 LuthierMOPs: Customizable Metaobject Protocols

A basic support for implementing a metaobject protocol must provide mechanisms for associating objects with metaobjects, activating such metaobjects, and intercepting the normal message flow among objects. Also necessary is a mechanism to access the static and dynamic information that defines the structure and behavior of the base program. To this end, LuthierMOPs defines four abstract classes (see Figure 11.3), which reify the different aspects involved in the implementation of such metaobject support:

MetaObjectManager. Provides the generic behavior to implement specific metaobject protocols and the interface to associate metaobjects with application objects.

MetaObject. Defines the generic protocol between managers and metaobjects.

Table 11.1   Extended Operators for the Contracts Notation

EXTENDED OPERATORS	USAGES
◊ (predicate | action)	Used to express actions that probably should be executed by abstract and hook methods. It intends to allow the expression of the design intent of the method.
φ	Empty method. It is used to specify services whose detailed specification is not relevant to the contract.
Current	Represents the current object or self.
Type(object)	Represents the type or class of an object.
Perform(operation)	Executes an operation of an object.
Intercepted selector	Represents any intercepted method through some interception mechanism.
Presents argument	Expresses that a view visually presents the values contained in its argument.

MessageInterceptor. Defines the general interface to intercept messages according to two interception mechanisms: *method-based interception* (ReflectedMethod subclass) and *object-based interception* (WrapperInterceptor subclass). The ReflectedMethod class provides the behavior to generate methods that substitute original methods to produce the reflection of the message to a manager. The WrapperInterceptor class allows the interception of messages directed to particular instances by wrapping the object and redirecting the messages to the associated manager.

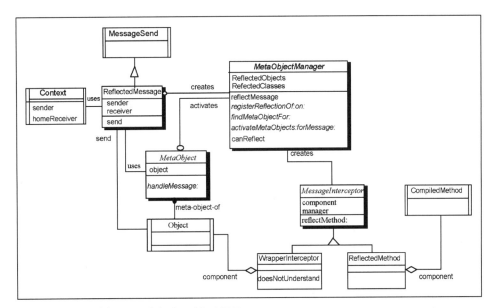

Figure 11.3   Object model of LuthierMOPs.

ReflectedMessage. Reifies a reflected message. It implements the interface to access the message data (selector, arguments, sender, and so on) and execute the original method.

When a reflected object receives a message, this message is deviated by the interception mechanism to the associated MOM. The MOM looks for metaobjects associated with the object that reflected the message (findMetaObjectsFor:) and decides whether to activate the selected metaobjects (activateMetaObjects:) by sending them the *handleMessage: manager:* message. When a metaobject is activated, it receives an instance of the ReflectedMessage class that contains all the information relative to the reflected message. The metaobject can execute the original method by sending to this instance the *send* message.

The following contracts describe two of the main functionalities provided by the subframework: interception of messages and metaobject activation when a message is reflected.

The generic relationship between a manager and a message interceptor is specified by the ReflectionServices contract. The MessageInterceptor participant must be extended for each interception method, that is, method-based or object-based interception. The MetaObjectManager participant provides the services to reflect classes and objects on specific metaobjects. The main hook provided is the registerReflectionOf: service. This service is supposed to encapsulate the specific implementation of the associations between objects and metaobjects (a Dictionary, aSortedCollection, and so on).

```
CONTRACT ReflectionServices
MetaObjectManager supports [
    reflectedObjects : Set(<Object,MetaObject>).
    unreflect(anObject:Object) ⇒ ΔreflectedObjects;
    registerReflectionOf(anObject:Object; aMetaObject:MetaObject) ⇒
            Δ reflectedObjects;

]


MessageInterceptor supports [
    component: Object.
    manager: MetaObjectManager.

    new(selectors:Set(Symbol);object:Object;manager:MetaObjectManager)
            ⇒ returns reflect(selectors;object;manager)

    reflect(aCollection:Set;anObject:Object;manager:MetaObjectManager)
            ⇒   {◊ (Δ component; Δ manager)}
]
END CONTRACT
```

The MethodReflectionServices contract refines the previous one for the case of a method-based interception mechanism. The participant MetaObjectManager provides services to reflect methods. The subcontract adds the Class participant, which provides services to alter the set of methods of a class. Some of these methods will be replaced by reflector methods, whose responsibilities are defined by the ReflectedMethod participant. This participant interacts with the compiler to generate the code that transfers the control to the manager when a method is activated.

```
CONTRACT MethodReflectionServices
refines ReflectionServices(Interceptor=ReflectedMethod)
    MetaObjectManager supports [

    reflectMethod(selector:String, class:Class) ⇒
      ReflectedMethod→new(oldMethod,selector,class,current);

    reflectMethodOn(selector:String;class:Class;
        metaObject:MetaObject)⇒ reflectMethod(selector, class);
]


Class supports [
    compiledMethods: Set(< String, CompiledMethod>).
....
]


ReflectedMethod supports [
    component: CompiledMethod.
    reflect(selectors: Set; class:Class; manager: MetaObjectManager)
        ⇒ r = transferMethodFor(selector,class, manager);
            r.component = method; returns r;

    transferMethodFor(selector:Symbol,class:Class,
        manager:MetaObjectManager) ⇒
            returns Compiler→compile('aManager→reflectMessage:
selector                    args: arguments forObject: current')
END CONTRACT
```

The second aspect of a metaobject protocol is the way metaobjects take control when a message is reflected. The following contract describes the generic protocol for this process. The contract involves four participants: the *message interceptor,* which activates the manager; the *manager,* which decides which metaobjects must be activated; the *metaobjects* to be activated; and the *reflected message,* which eventually will receive the *send* message to execute the original method.

```
CONTRACT MetaObjectActivation
Interceptor supports [
    manager: MetaObjectManager;

  // The intercepted selector transfers the control to the manager
    intercepted selector(args: List(Object)) ⇒
                managerreflect→Message(selector, args, current)
]
MetaObjectManager supports [
    reflectedObjects: Set(<Object, Set(MetaObject)>).

    // Implements the generic behavior of a MOP
    reflectMessage (selector:Symbol,args:Collection,object:Object) ⇒
            if findMetaObjectFor(object)= ∅
                then callBackMethod(selector, args, object)
                else activateMetaObjects(findMetaObjectFor(object);
                                    reflectedMessage).
```

```
findMetaObjectsFor(object: Object) ⇒
        returns listMetaObjects...

    activateMetaObjects(metaObjects: Set(MetaObject);
                        aMessage: ReflectedMessage) ⇒
        {◊ ⟨∀ mo:mo ∈ metaObjects:
                    mo→handleMessage(aMessage,current)⟩}.
]
MetaObjects Set(MetaObject) where each MetaObject supports [
    handleMessage(msg:ReflectedMessage,manager:MetaObjectManager)  ⇒
        { ◊ (msg→send) }
]

ReflectedMessage supports [
    send() ⇒ receiver→perform(selector, arguments)
]
END CONTRACT
```

According to this contract, customized metaobject management mechanisms can be implemented in subclasses of MetaObjectManager by providing specific implementations for the following methods:

findMetaObjectsFor:anObject. Use this to find those metaobjects associated with the message receiver.

activateMetaObjects:metaObjects withMessage. A ReflectedMessage used to activate the metaobjects found by the previous method. This method encapsulates the activation policy of the manager once the target metaobjects are selected.

11.2.2 LuthierBooks: Information Representation

LuthierBooks provides a generic support for hyperdocument management based on the Nested Context Model for hyperdocument modeling [Casanova 1991]. Contexts are the fundamental element for structuring a hypertext net composed of nested components. Through contexts, it is possible to represent aggregate nodes, whose association semantics can represent either a composition or a set relationship. Different contexts can define different associations among subsets of a given set of objects, according to different criteria of association. This capability allows considerable reduction of the net complexity, yet allows the use of links as a binary relationship and navigation mechanism.

The abstract class Component (see Figure 11.4) implements the generic behavior of objects stored in a repository. Component does not provide a specific implementation of this store, but the interface to access objects that can be persistently stored. Basically, each component of a hyperdocument will have a set of attributes, and one of them will be defined as the key attribute. *Context* class defines the generic behavior of aggregate or composite nodes. It provides services to add, remove, and locate components, which can be single nodes (defined by the Entity class), links, or contexts. A *link* is a component type that always relates two components. A link represents an associative entity because

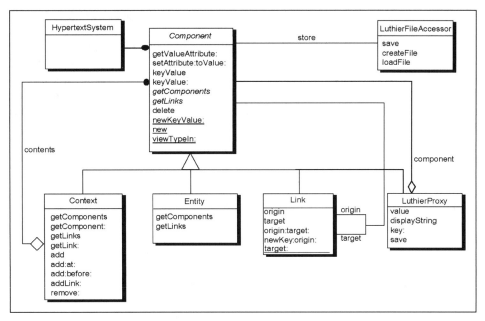

Figure 11.4   Object model of LuthierBooks.

it can only exist if the related components also exist. The class Link provides the generic behavior of links. *Single objects* are atomic entities defined generically by the Entity class.

The HypertextSystem class implements the interface to interact with a hyperdocument stored in a conceptual database. It also provides the functionality for creating and navigating links, as well as information about the different views that a given component can have associated in different visualizations. The services provided involve, for example, the recovery of the list of targets of a given link from a given origin, the list of links from a given component or to a given component, and so on.

Hyperdocument components are accessed through proxies implemented by the LuthierProxy class. A *proxy* holds the reference to the real component, summary information about its contents, and the necessary information to recover it from external storage. LuthierProxy implements a lazy recovering mechanism. A component is recovered from the external store only when information other than the summary is requested. In this way, recovering a context involves recovering just one object and its component proxies, increasing the efficiency of accessing information. The LuthierAccessor class encapsulates the storage method. Instances of this class are in charge of manipulating the external storage medium, that is, a single file or an external database. This separation allows the proxies to be independent from the storage medium.

11.2.3 LuthierViews: Information Exploration

The LuthierViews subframework is an extension of the MVC user-interface framework of VisualWorks. LuthierViews modifies, essentially, the mechanisms for handling mouse events and updating views. Figure 11.5 presents the object diagram of the classes composing LuthierViews.

Visualization built using the framework will be composed of a set of views organized as a double-linked hierarchy of views and subviews. The top of the hierarchy must be a (sub)instance of LuthierTopLevelView, which has an associated instance of LuthierEventController. This class converts the standard Smalltalk mechanism for treating mouse events to the mechanism of event transfer through the views implemented by LuthierViews.

The LuthierStrategyView subclass provides the support to implement visualizations with dynamically variable layout strategies. This type of view is composed of a *strategy* [Gamma 1995], LuthierLayoutStrategy, which encapsulates the algorithm that spatially distributes views in the visualization area. When a view receives its model, it creates the corresponding subviews to represent the information held by the model, through the *buildVisualPresentation* message. This method will have to create instances of subviews and add them to the composite view through the *addNode* message. This method delegates in the associated strategy the insertion of the new component at the corresponding place. LuthierTopLevelView implements a lazy mechanism for redistributing views when one of them changes its size. Before a display update, the strategy receives the *relayoutGraphFor:* message to reorganize the spatial distribution of the components, if necessary. After this process, the view propagates the *displayOn:* message among its subviews to effectively produce the display update.

The following contracts specify this interaction. The first one partially specifies the generic collaborations among views and their subviews for the lazy relayout and dis-

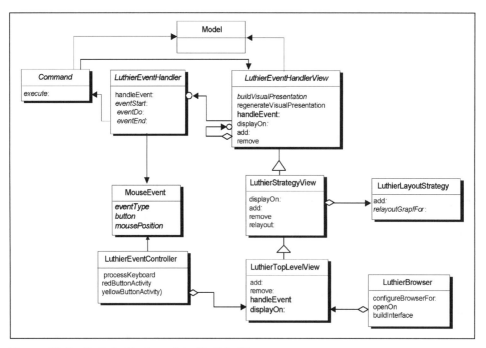

Figure 11.5 Partial object model of LuthierViews.

play functionality described previously. The next one refines the former for the case of the TopLevelView participant. Finally, the LayoutView-LayoutStrategy contract completes the specification of the whole generic collaboration for the case of views with associated layout strategies.

```
CONTRACT Superview-Subview
    Superview supports [
        subviews: Subviews.

        relayoutNeeded(subview) ⇒ φ
        displayOn() ⇒
            {⟨∀s:s ∈ subviews:if(includes(extent, s.extent))
                            then s→displayOn ⟩}.
    ]


    Subviews: Set(Subview) where each Subview supports [
        container:Superview.
        relayoutNeeded(subview) ⇒
            container→relayoutNeeded(subview).
        displayOn() ⇒ φ.
    ]
END CONTRACT


CONTRACT TopLevelView-Subview
    refines Superview-Subview(Superview=TopLevelView;Subview=Subview).

    TopLevelView supports [
        relayoutCollection: Subviews.
        displayOn ⇒ relayout.
        relayoutNeeded(subview) ⇒ Δ relayoutCollection;
        relayout() ⇒ Δ relayoutCollection;
                ⟨; s:s ∈ relayoutCollection:srelayout);
                {relayoutCollection = ∅}.
    ]
    Subviews: Set ( Subview ) where each Subview supports [
]
END CONTRACT


CONTRACT LayoutView-LayoutStrategy
    LayoutView supports [
        insert(classFigure:ViewType;position:Point;model:Component) ⇒
                layoutStrategy→insert(classFigure,position,model).
        relayoutGraphFor(anObject: Object) ⇒
                layoutStrategy→relayoutGraphFor(anObject).
    ]

    LayoutStrategy supports [
        clientObject: LayoutView.
        insert(type:ViewType; position:Point; model:Component) ⇒
                clientObject→addSubview(newNode).
        relayoutGraphFor(anObject: Object) ⇒
```

```
                        // Redistributes the views according to the corresponding
       layout algorithm
           ]
       INCLUDES
       Superview-Subviews(Superview = LayoutView; Subview = ComponentView ).
       END CONTRACT
```

Each view has an associated set of event handlers (LuthierEventHandler), which implement the typical mouse manipulations (click, drag, and so on). These manipulations can be dynamically associated with any view, allowing the addition of direct manipulation without the need of programming these behaviors for any particular view. When a user interacts with the mouse over a view, the controller associated with the top-level view sends to it the handleEvent: message with an instance of Luthier-MouseEvent as argument. This instance holds all the information relative to the event.

The event propagation mechanism is a double *chain of responsibility* [Gamma 1995] among views and handlers. The event is propagated from the lower levels of the view hierarchy to the upper ones, until some view has a handler interested in such event. If there is a handler interested in the event, the associated view transfers the control to that handler, which implements the manipulation (for example, dragging a figure). Once the manipulation is finished, the handler executes an associated command.

A *command* (class Command) encapsulates an operation to be applied over either the visualization or the data representation. Commands can be dynamically associated with event handlers, allowing the dynamic adaptation of the user-interface behavior. Commands respond to the *execute* message, which must be implemented for each specific operation.

The following contract specifies the generic mechanism of event propagation. Views propagate the *recognizeEvent* event message among their handlers. The first handler that recognizes an event treats it.

```
    CONTRACT View-EventHandler
        INCLUDES Superview-Subview(Subview = View).
    View supports [
        eventHandlers: Set (EventHandler).
        handleEvent(event:Event; point:Point) ⇒ returns result;
            {result =(∃ handler:handler ∈ eventHandlers:
                         handler→recognizeEvent(anEvent, current))}.

    ]
    EventHandler supports [
        handledEvent: Event.
        recognizeEvent(anEvent: Event; aView: View) ⇒
            {anEvent = handledEvent };
            returns handleEvent(anEvent).

        handleEvent(anEvent:Event) ⇒
            eventStart(anEvent);eventDo (anEvent); eventEnd (anEvent).

    requires subclass to support:
    eventStart (anEvent)
```

```
eventDo (anEvent)
eventEnd (anEvent)  ⇒ {◊ (execute)}
]
```
END CONTRACT

Subclasses of the abstract class LuthierEventHandler must implement the specific behavior of each manipulation, through the following methods:

eventStart: *anEvent.* Implements possible initialization actions. It must return *true* if the event can be treated by the handler.

eventDo: *anEvent.* Implements the continuous treatment of the event until a new mouse event occurs.

eventEnd: *anEvent.* Implements finish actions and/or executes an associated command.

11.2.4 LuthierAbstractors: Managing Software Abstractions

LuthierAbstractors provide, essentially, the generic functionality for the automatic management of semantic zoom mechanisms, based on symbolic abstraction scales. Also, they define the standard protocol through which visualizations request information to be visualized.

Figure 11.6 presents the object model of LuthierAbstractors. The abstract class Abstractor defines the generic behavior of abstractors. Each abstractor will have associated with it one instance of AbstractionLevel, which defines its current abstraction level; a view (generically represented by the class LuthierView); and a subject (generically represented by the class Subject). Any abstractor can be recursively composed by other abstractors, probably associated with components of the subject.

The AbstractionLevel abstract class defines the abstraction scale mechanism. Subclasses of this class provide support for comparing symbolic levels of abstraction

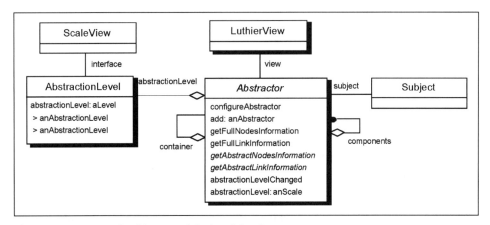

Figure 11.6 Generic object model of LuthierAbstractors.

according to the type of scale (discrete scale, inclusive scale, continuous scale, and so on). The ScaleView class implements the user interface of the scale (a slider is the default user-interface control). This control can be interactively manipulated by the user to dynamically increase or decrease the detail level of the visualization.

Abstractor instances are created through the message *on:aSubject*. This method creates the corresponding instance, sets the subject of the abstractor, and triggers the generic configuration mechanism (configureAbstractor method). The configuration mechanism allows the automatic construction of nested abstractors, which manage the individual abstraction levels corresponding to structured data.

The key idea behind the design of the abstractor support is the definition of a standard protocol, through which visualizations can ask their models for data to be visualized. Each view asks its model information to be visualized through two standard messages, *getNodes* and *getLinks*. The generic behavior of these messages implements the control mechanism of the current abstraction level. If this level is greater than the level represented by the abstractor, the complete information of the model is returned. Otherwise, only the corresponding abstract information is returned.

An abstractor can be enabled or disabled. When an abstractor is disabled, the default implementation of the protocol returns an empty list, indicating that there is no available information to be visualized. This functionality is very useful for visualizing the information resulting from a selection process. Enabling the abstractors associated with selected items eliminates those items not selected from the visualization, without programming special mechanisms for this behavior. The following contract specifies this functionality.

```
CONTRACT Abstractor-SubAbstractor
Abstractor supports [
    subject: Model.
    enabled: Boolean.
    components: Set(SubAbstractor).

    setSubject(object:Object) ⇒ configureAbstractor;

    configureAbstractor()⇒ φ { ◊ Δcomponents}
    enable()⇒ <|| c:c ∈ components:c→enable >.
    disable()⇒ <|| c:c ∈ components:c→disable >.
]
SubAbstractor supports [
    container: Abstractor.
    enable()⇒ Δ enabled.
    disable ()⇒ Δ enabled.
]
INVARIANT
SubAbstractor.container = Abstractor ⇔
        SubAbstractor ∈ Abstractor.components.
END CONTRACT
```

The contract Abstractor-View specifies the collaborations among abstractors and views. It defines the responsibility of each participant to obtain the information to be visualized, taking into account the current abstraction level of the visualization.

```
CONTRACT Abstractor-View
Abstractor supports [
    subject: Component
    components: Abstractor
    abstractionLevel: AbstractionLevel.

    getNodes() ⇒ if ¬enabled then return ∅;
              if(abstractionLevel > abstractionRepresented)
                        then return getFullNodesInformation;
                        else return getAbstractNodesInformation.
    getLinks()⇒ if ¬enabled then return ∅;
              if(abstractionLevel > abstractionRepresented)
                        then return getFullLinkInformation;
                        else return getAbstractLinkInformation.
    getAbstractNodesInformation ⇒ φ {◊( return ∅)}
    getAbstractLinkInformation ⇒ φ {◊( return ∅)}
    getFullNodesInformation() ⇒ return(components).
    getFullLinkInformation() ⇒ return(components).
]
View supports [
    buildVisualPresentation() ⇒
              {◊(model→getNodes() ∧ model→getLinks())}
]
END CONTRACT
```

When a user produces a change in the global abstraction scale, the *abstraction-LevelChanged* message is propagated to all the component abstractors to update their current abstraction levels. A change in the level of abstraction causes the top abstractor of the hierarchy to ask the visualization to update the global visualization, which is informed through the *regenerateVisualPresentation* message. This method triggers the buildVisualPresentation method described previously.

```
CONTRACT AbstractionLevelChange
Abstractor supports [
    level: AbstractionLevel.
    abstractionControl:ScaleInterface
    view: LuthierView.

    abstractionLevel(aLevel: Integer) ⇒ level→changeLevelTo(aLevel)
    interactiveAbstractionLevelChange ⇒
              abstractionLevel(abstractionControl.value);
              abstractionLevelChanged.
    abstractionLevelChanged ⇒ view→regenerateVisualPresentation.
]

AbstractionLevel supports [
    enabled: Boolean.
    abstractionScale: Set (Symbol).
    currentLevel: Integer.

    changeLevelTo (aLevel:integer) ⇒ Δ currentLevel;
```

```
            {currentLevel = max(aLevel, size(abstractionScale))}.
    ]


ScaleInterface supports [
    changed(newLevel: Integer) ⇒
        Abstractor→interactiveAbstractionLevelChange.
]


View supports [
    regenerateVisualPresentation()
]
END CONTRACT
```

11.3 MetaExplorer: Putting It All Together

This section presents a brief example of an instantiation of Luthier to build a visualization tool, called *MetaExplorer*. MetaExplorer was designed to help in the process of framework understanding. It provides a rich set of features that enables the analysis and visualization of a framework at different levels of abstraction from both architectural and instance behavior points of view.

MetaExplorer provides two-dimensional diagrammatic visualizations, as well as some experimental three-dimensional visualizations, built using an interface to an OPEN-GL library. For example, Figure 11.7 presents two snapshots of a three-dimensional visualization of design patterns. In this representation, a class is visualized as a volume composed of three semi-axes that represent the coordinate system. A concrete class is visualized as a sphere and an abstract class is visualized as a pyramid. Each axis represents a pattern category, that is, behavioral, creational, and structural. A distinctive polyhedral shape defined by specific mapping components represents each pattern.

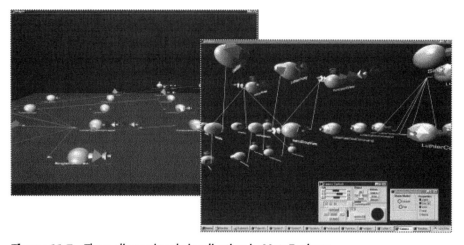

Figure 11.7 Three-dimensional visualization in MetaExplorer.

Through this representation, it is possible to simultaneously visualize the classes that compose the application, the way they are related by design patterns, and the methods that each pattern determines. This aspect is very important to facilitate the understanding of the global structure of a framework, because it integrates the information about which patterns are involved in the design of each class and which classes are related by each pattern.

11.3.1 Instantiating MetaExplorer

MetaExplorer provides a visual interface to reflect the classes to be inspected on a predefined set of metaobjects. An application or example developed with the target framework is executed, and, through a specially designed meta-architecture, an abstract representation of the framework is generated using an extension of LuthierBooks.

The meta-architecture is based on a special MetaObjectManager, *LayeredManager*. This MOM associates default metaobjects with each class that will be inspected. All the instances of an inspected class reflect on one of those default metaobjects. To implement that association, LayeredManager uses a dictionary that contains, for each reflected class, a collection of metaobjects. This collection is sorted by the decreasing order of the priority number of each metaobject. These priorities are used to specify the activation order of metaobjects. LayeredManager redefines the registerReflectionOf:on: method to add metaobjects to its dictionary, as shown in Figure 11.8.

When a message is reflected by an object, LayeredManager activates the metaobject of the class in the hierarchy where the method was found (if the object does not have its own metaobject). In this way, each metaobject deals only with the messages implemented by its associated class (that is, not the inherited ones). This means that a message received by

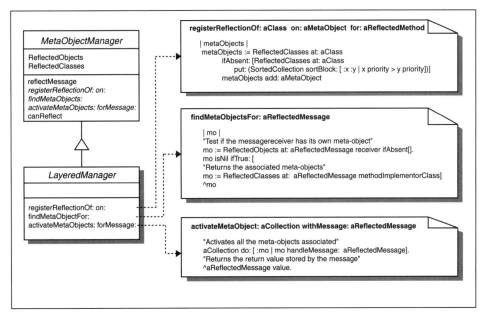

Figure 11.8 Instantiation of a specific metaobject manager.

a reflected object is intercepted by the metaobject associated with the class implementing the message. This simplifies the generation of the abstract model and avoids the analysis of the class hierarchy at every message exchange. The implementation of the abstract methods defined to locate and activate metaobjects is also shown in Figure 11.8.

MetaExplorer induces a two-phase exploration process oriented by the visualization of high-level architectural representations. From the visualizations provided, specific metaobjects can be dynamically associated with application objects to enable detailed analysis at the instance level (visualization of internal state changes, breakpoints on methods, and so on). This functionality allows the user to focus on specific points that require a detailed analysis of the involved instances, avoiding the collection of full information about instances. This is one of the most problematic points in object-oriented program visualization tools due to the huge amount of information that can be gathered in a single execution.

The example of Figure 11.9 shows the specialization of the MetaObject class for two metaobjects, one used in the phase of architectural analysis and the second used in the phase of instance analysis of MetaExplorer (note that these metaobjects use some of the Smalltalk reflective facilities to gather static information). The LayeredCollector metaobject is designed to recognize abstract components and their refinements, method categories, and inter- and intracomponent message flow. These metaobjects interact with the manager to build an abstract representation of the analyzed framework. The manager keeps count of the number of messages sent among objects, which is used to identify the sequence to which a given message belongs. The InstancesCollector metaobject is used to collect the instances that send or receive a given message. These metaobjects are dynamically installed when the user selects a message from an architectural view provided by the tool. The manager collects the messages through the registerSender method. This class of metaobjects extends the protocol defined by its associated class to open an instance browser on the collected instances.

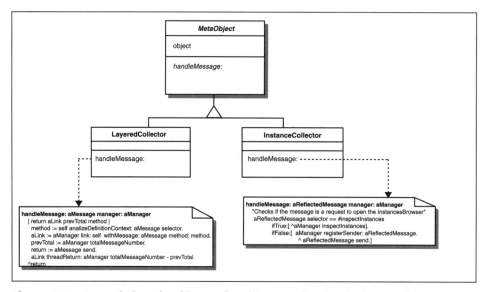

Figure 11.9 Instantiation of architectural and instance-level analysis metaobjects.

The abstract representation of the analyzed program is defined as a simple extension of LuthierBooks. Contexts, entities, or links represent each type of component of a program. For example, classes are represented by contexts that contain the information about methods and variables of the class. Messages between classes are represented by links from the sender method to the target method.

A visualization tool is built by creating a subclass of LuthierBrowser. This browser must create the visualization structure, specifying the subinstance of LuthierTop-LevelView to be used to visualize the information provided by a specific set of abstractors. The examples following show the partial instantiation of a LuthierBrowser for a class-based visualization. The browser is shown in Figure 11.10. Triangles represent class hierarchies and rectangles represent single classes. Colors suggest the relative sequence in which relationships are established at runtime. The semantics of these colors can be interactively selected by the user, to represent the first, the most frequent, or the last message that determines a relationship between two classes.

Figure 11.11 presents the partial instantiation of this visualization. RelationsView class implements a visualization of relationships among classes, asking its model for the nodes and links to be visualized when it receives the *buildVisualPresentation* message. This class has its own layout strategy, which is automatically requested by the framework through the *defaultLayoutStrategy* message when the view is opened. The classes ComponentView and KnowledgeView implement the visual appearance of the classes and relationships in the notation. These classes produce the graphical representation through the *displayOn* method defined by the MVC framework.

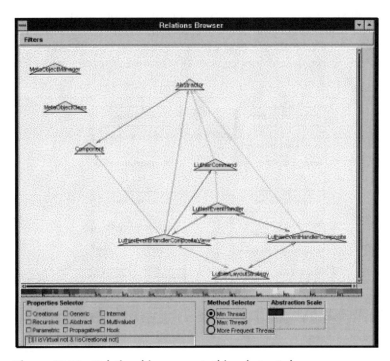

Figure 11.10   Relationship among Luthier abstract classes.

MetaExplorer provides a powerful direct-manipulation user interface, which allows, for example, a rubber-band selection and zooming of specific portions of diagrams using alternative notations, as well as the animation of the framework message flow (in message-flow-based visualizations) under the interactive control of the user [Campo 1996]. For example, RelationsView installs two handlers (existing in the Luthier library) in its *initialize* method as shown in Figure 11.12. In this case, the view installs a handler for dragging figures (DragHandler) and another to select visual components with rubberbanding (RubberBandHandler).

The following example shows the specialization for a drag handler. The *eventStart* method recovers the figure under the cursor and saves the point in which the mouse was pressed. The *eventDo:* method shows a rectangle using a primitive that follows the cursor movement during a specified time period. This method is called until the mouse button is released. When this release occurs, the *eventEnd:* method is called. It produces the effective movement of the figure to the location in which the button was released. The specialization for a rubberband handler redefines the eventEnd: method to execute the associated command. This command, a LuthierSelectionCommand, receives the selected region and recovers the models of the views inside the selected region. After that, it instructs its subject to open a new browser on a SelectionAbstractor that holds the selected information. The new browser will only show such information, as if its model contained only the selected data. In this way, abstractors facilitate the implementation of selection mechanisms through composition of orthogonal behaviors.

MetaExplorer visualizations are based on a rich set of abstractors that enables semantic zooming functionality and interactive filtering based on textual queries. Figure 11.13 presents some specializations of LuthierAbstractors used by MetaExplorer. A framework is represented by an abstractor (FrameworkAbstractor class), which is composed by abstractors representing the different class hierarchies of the framework (HierarchyAbstractor) and one abstractor (KnowledgeAbstractor) that generates the knowledge relationships among framework components according to the abstraction

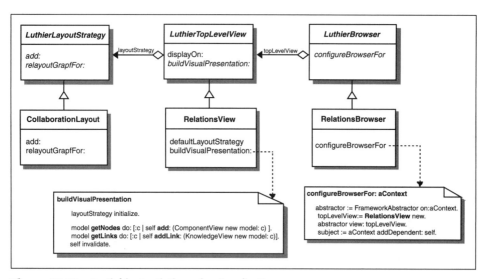

Figure 11.11   Partial instantiation of a visualization.

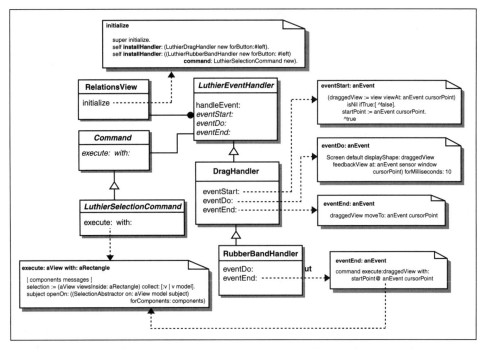

Figure 11.12   Association and instantiation of event handlers and commands.

level of the visualization. Hierarchy abstractors are composed of class abstractors. The figure shows an example of the *configureAbstractor* method redefinition of HierarchyAbstractor, which adds class abstractors on each class of the hierarchy contained by the subject. Each of these abstractors controls what data will be passed to the visualization, according to the current level of abstraction.

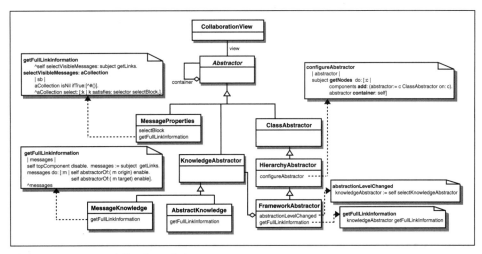

Figure 11.13   Specialization of abstractors.

The abstractionLevelChanged method of FrameworkAbstractor class presents an example of dynamic configuration of abstractors. When the level of abstraction changes, the abstractor sets the corresponding knowledge abstractor, on which the responsibility of returning the links will be delegated. For example, if the level is *abstractHierarchy,* an AbstractKnowledge abstractor will be in charge of computing the relationships among all the classes in each hierarchy and generating a relationship link that will be visualized. If the level is *allMethods,* a MessageAbstractor will be in charge of returning the messages among classes. As can be observed in the figure, this abstractor redefines the getFullLinkInformation method to disable all the abstractors and enable only those abstractors related by messages held by the model. In this way, only called and caller methods will be shown in the visualization.

The MessagePropertiesSelector class implements a selector abstractor that enables the selection of links according to a selection block specified as an argument. For example, the block

```
[:m| m originClass = LuthierProxy | m targetClass = LuthierProxy]
```

specifies the selection of messages sent or received by instances of the LuthierProxy class. This class specializes the protocol for returning links, as shown in Figure 11.13. The implementation calls a private method that applies the selection block to each link of the model. This abstractor can be a subject of another abstractor, enabling the visualization of only the selected information as if it were the real model. In this way, composing a FrameworkAbstractor with a MessagePropertiesSelector, it is possible to have both query and zooming capabilities by composition.

Figure 11.14 shows the results of applying the previous query to a class-based visualization combined with a change in the level of abstraction. This feature enables the analysis of dynamic relationships at the architectural level. Through these mechanisms, the tool provides a powerful mechanism to focus interesting aspects for the user, hiding irrelevant details.

MetaExplorer automatically recovers different potential abstractions, such as subsystems and Gamma design-patterns. Specific abstractors implement the algorithms for abstraction recovery. These abstractors provide the visualizations with the generated abstractions as normal data to be visualized. Figure 11.15 presents two snapshots of a

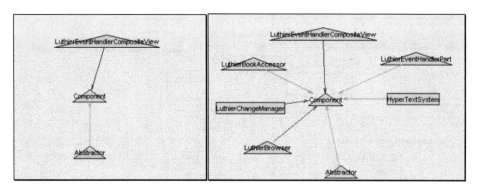

Figure 11.14 Example of a combined query and abstraction-level change in class-based visualization.

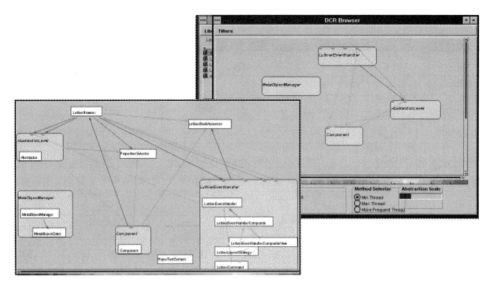

Figure 11.15 Example of an interactive change of abstraction level in a subsystem visualization.

visualization of the Luthier subsystems before and after an interactive change of abstraction level. In this case, subsystems are automatically recovered by a SubsystemAbstractor instance, which uses a simple closure algorithm that first groups classes by related names and next modifies the resulting sets by analyzing the message flow among classes. The resulting subsets are a good approximation of the candidate subsystems.

11.3.2 Experimental Results

In order to test the effectiveness of the approach and the tool, an experiment on framework utilization for building applications was carried out. This experiment does not precisely *demonstrate* the efficiency level of either the framework comprehension approach or the tools built to support it, but it gives a good idea of their advantages as well as their limitations. It consisted of building a Petri Net editor with typical editing functionality, using the framework HotDraw, for construction of graphical editors.

Three groups of well-trained students in a systems engineering course were used for the experiment: Two of them used MetaExplorer (groups GL1 and GL2), while the third group (GN) did not use the tool. The resultant applications were compared using a tool for metric collection built using Luthier, based on the metrics proposed in [Lorenz 1994]. The results obtained from the metrics (see Table 11.2) provide interesting suggestions about the relative differences among the three applications, which can be verified through a further analysis. The metrics highlighted in the table are those that, on average, are particularly suggestive regarding the framework reuse achieved by each application, as well as the design quality of each application compared with the others. For example, the specialization indexes of groups GL1 and GL2 are nearly equivalent, while the index of the GN group is significantly lower. This index shows a low level of method redefinition and reuse of the functionality provided by the frame-

Table 11.2 Metric Values

METRIC	GL1	GL2	GN
Totals			
Number of classes	16	12	32
Lines of code	1427	980	1854
Nesting level (max.)	7	7	8
Number of methods	178	148	281
Number of inherited methods	2040	1569	4082
Number of redefined methods	102	95	126
Number of Added Methods	76	53	155
Number of messages	815	781	1370
Number of class variables	0	0	16
Number of methods not called	51	25	115
Averages			
Number of inherited methods per class	127.50	130.75	127.56
Number of redefined methods per class	6.37	7.91	3.93
Number of added methods per class	8.56	4.41	6.85
Redefined/added proportion	0.63	1.55	0.61
Specialization index	3.47	3.20	2.36

work, as the number of new methods is high. On average, though, GL1 presents the greatest number of new methods per class and the highest nesting level. In this case, the specialization index is complemented for a great number of inherited methods. The relationship between redefined and added methods shows parity between groups GL1 and GN, while the value for GL2 is two times greater. The combination of both indexes suggests a better degree of reuse for group GL2. The complete result analysis can be found in [Campo 1997].

In order to determine which was the best solution, MetaExplorer was used to make a detailed analysis of the three applications. In this case, information similar to that provided by the metrics was extracted: The application developed by group GN presents the greatest problems related to the editor design, while the other two applications present little difference between them. Comparing the results in a general way, the main differences between the design decisions of the three applications are related to the design of the figures to be edited and the utilization of the constraints:

■ GL1 presents a better utilization of the constraint system, which allows easy resolution of some problems arising due to bad decisions about class specialization.

- GL2 presents the better structure, in terms of reuse of the framework functionality, due to an adequate selection of the classes to be specialized, but makes a weak utilization of the constraint system.

- GN presents problems with the reuse of behavior implemented by the framework and with aspects related to abstraction designs, as well as with the use of the constraint system.

11.4 Other Applications

LuthierMOPs and LuthierAbstractors have demonstrated Luthier's versatility in applications other than MetaExplorer. The next section briefly presents two applications developed using the subframeworks *CityVis* and *Brainstorm*.

11.4.1 CityVis

CityVis [Orosco 1997] was developed using an extension of Luthier, incorporating capabilities for city data visualization through specialized classes for the management of this kind of data. Its main goal is to support the exploration of city information, providing techniques to assist the user in this process. CityVis uses a specialized abstractor (a CityAbstractor class) for the global management of the city information to be shown, and different abstractors for the management of related information (topics such as hotels, apartments, map, and so on). In addition, there are other abstractors that manage information revealed during the exploration process. Abstractors greatly facilitate the construction of complex visualization techniques, such as layered or assistance techniques. These visualization techniques are used to compose different topics of information, based on the *transparent paper* metaphor. For example, in CityVis there are different layers for the city map, transports, hotels, restaurants, apartments, and so on. The user can manipulate these layers, adding and/or removing some of them at any time during the visualization, to display only the information relevant for the current task. CityVis implements a layering technique through different views for each layer, each with an associated abstractor (a TopicAbstractor) that determines the visible information in the layer. The management of visible topics at runtime is done automatically by the CityAbstractor (generally in response to user requests), which determines whether each TopicAbstractor is enabled. Figure 11.16 shows a snapshot of the CityVis layering, showing the city map, subway lines, restaurants, and hospitals layers.

11.4.2 Brainstorm

The Brainstorm metalevel architecture for agent-oriented programming [Amandi 1997] represents a good example of the flexibility provided by LuthierMOPs to build complex mechanisms of metaobject management. Brainstorm is based on a two-level meta-architecture and two MOMs, *PrimitiveManager* and *AgentManager*. The latter manager selectively activates metaobjects depending on the type of event that causes a message reflection (see Figure 11.17).

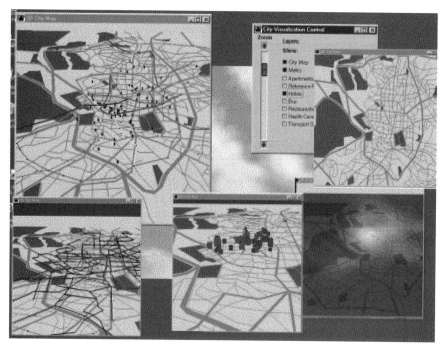

Figure 11.16 CityVis visualizations.

The first level of the meta-architecture is composed of *knowledge* metaobjects, *communication* metaobjects, and *perception* metaobjects. These metaobjects reflect their behavior on *reactor* and/or *deliberator* metaobjects, which define the second level of the meta-architecture. The latter two types of metaobjects use the knowledge metaobject.

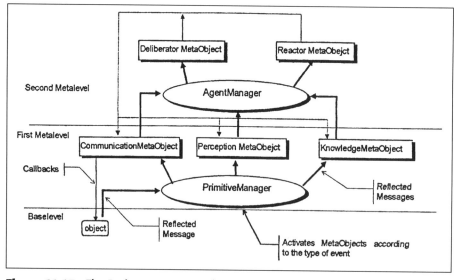

Figure 11.17 The Brainstorm meta-architecture.

Interaction among agents is established through messages or indirectly through perception. The messages received by an object are intercepted by the associated communication metaobject. This metaobject has the responsibility of treating messages by invoking a basic action defined in the object whenever necessary. The communication metaobject defines the communication protocol and is able to manage conversations. Perception metaobjects are responsible for managing the interaction among agents.

Reactor and deliberator metaobjects define the different ways that agents will act. Agents define their behavior by associating metaobjects of the reactor and/or deliberator types. If an agent has both types of behavior, AgentManager determines when an event involves reaction or deliberation. Reactors and deliberators intervene in all mechanisms that support the interaction process. When an agent perceives something (through some of its perception metaobjects) or receives a message (intercepted through its communication metaobject), the reactor and deliberator metaobjects intervene, reacting or deliberating. This behavior is implemented by AgentManager though the *activateMetaObject: withMessage:* method shown here:

```
activateMetaObjects: aCollection withMessage: aReflectedMessage
    "Verifies if the reactor metaobject is interested in the event
     represented by the message. If it is not interested, activates the
     deliberator metaobject"

    |reactorMetaObject  deliberatorMetaObject|

    reactorMetaObject:= aCollection  first.
    deliberatorMetaObject := aCollection at:2.
    reactorMetaObject isInterestedIn: aReflectedMessage
        ifTrue:[ ^reactorMetaObject handleMessage: aReflectedMessage]
        ifFalse:[ ^deliberatorMetaObject handleMessage:aReflectedMessage]
```

11.5 Summary

The previous section presents a brief description of the main architectural aspects of the Luthier framework and its use to build the comprehension tool MetaExplorer. Luthier offers a highly flexible infrastructure to build tools for object-oriented program analysis, dynamically adaptable to different analytical functionality.

The mechanisms introduced by Luthier allow the implementation of different visualization tools with little effort. The use of metaobject-based techniques centered on the concept of the metaobject manager enables the construction of sophisticated metaarchitectures, specially adapted to the requirements of each tool, in a simple and clear way. The concepts of abstractor objects and symbolic abstraction scales enable the construction, by composition, of complex filtering mechanisms that greatly simplify the implementation of visualizations. This aspect is often the more time-consuming task in the development of visualization systems.

Some relevant conclusions can be extracted from the previously described experiment regarding the utilization of the framework comprehension tool (although these conclusions cannot be considered definitive because of the small sampling size represented):

- The tool can help obtain much better results, in terms of the reuse of the functionality provided by the used framework and the quality of the final work.

- The tool can induce an exploration of details that are not necessarily relevant. Nevertheless, the comprehension of these details helped the group GL1 to use a very complex subsystem, such as the constraint system, very well.

- The tool does not necessarily help to reduce the development time.

Currently, based on the results of Luthier and MetaExplorer, the development of intelligent tools for framework instantiation based on smart cards, planning, and intentional logic is being explored.

11.6 References

[Amandi 1997] Amandi, A., and A. Price. Towards object-oriented agent programming: The Brainstorm metalevel architecture. *Proceedings of the First Autonomous Agents Conference Los Angeles*. New York: ACM Press, February 1997.

[Brown 1984] Brown, M., and R. Sedgewick. A system for algorithm animation. *ACM Computer Graphics*, 11(7), July 1984: 177–186.

[Campo 1996] Campo, M., and R. Price. A visual reflective tool for framework understanding. *Proceedings of Technology of Object-Oriented Languages and Systems, 17*, Paris. Londres, France: Prentice Hall, February 1996.

[Campo 1997] Campo, M. Visual understanding of frameworks through introspection of examples. Ph.D. thesis (in Portuguese). www.exa.unicen.edu.ar/~mcampo/luthier, 1997.

[Casanova 1991] Casanova, M., et al. The nested context model for hyperdocuments. *Proceedings of the Hypertext 1991 Conference*, Texas. New York: ACM Press, 1991.

[Chikofsky 1990] Chikofsky, E., and J. Cross. Reverse engineering and design recovery: A taxonomy. *IEEE Software*, 7(1), January 1990, 13–17.

[Gamma 1995] Gamma, E., R. Helm, R. Johnson, and J. Vlissides. *Design Patterns: Reusable Elements of Object-Oriented Design*. Reading, MA: Addison-Wesley, 1995.

[Helm 1990] Helm, R., I.M. Holland, D. Gangopadhyay. Contracts: specifying behavioral compositions in object oriented systems. *Proceedings of the OOPSLA 1990 Conference*, Ottawa, Canada. New York: ACM Press, 1990.

[Lorenz 1994] Lorenz, M., and J. Kid. *Object-Oriented Software Metrics: A Practical Guide*. Englewood Cliffs, NJ: Prentice Hall, 1984.

[Maes 1988] Maes, P. Issues in computational reflection. In *MetaLevel Architecture and Reflection*. Amsterdam: Elsevier Science, 1988.

[Orosco 1997] Orosco, R., M. Campo, and A. Teyseyre. Automatic abstraction management in information visualization systems. *Proceedings of the International Conference on Information Visualization*, London, England, August 1997.

[Rumbaugh 1991] Rumbaugh, J., M. Blaha, W. Premerlani, E. Eddy, and W. Lorensen. *Object-Oriented Modeling and Design*. Englewood Cliffs, NJ: Prentice Hall, 1991.

[Stasko 1990] Stasko, J. Simplifying algorithm animation with TANGO. *Proceedings of the IEEE Workshop on Visual Languages*, Stockie, IL. Los Alamos, NM: IEEE Press, 1990.

[Wilde 1992] Wilde, N., and R. Huit. Maintenance support for object-oriented programs. *IEEE Transactions on Software Engineering*, 18(12), December 1992.

CHAPTER 12

Scalable Architecture for Reliable, High-Volume Datafeed Handlers

In the financial markets, perhaps it is appropriate to say that the *haves* are those who have the capability to process information *at the earliest opportunity*, and the *have-nots* are those who pale in comparison. Today this capability is more than ever a direct measure of the robustness of the underlying information technology infrastructures and how well they are leveraged. In this context, information processing includes both of the following categories of activities:

Data communication and exchange–oriented activities, such as:

- Receiving data (from a single source)
- Gathering data (from multiple diverse sources)
- Transmitting and sending data (to a single consumer)
- Distributing data (to multiple diverse consumers)

Business-oriented activities, such as:

- Processing interest rate calculations, statistical analysis, and profit and loss calculations
- Processing workflow management
- Processing computations that perform myriad other business functions

Of these, data communication and exchange is the domain of interest in this chapter. The monetary consequences associated with gathering, distributing, and processing data in the financial domain are a question of survivability and profitability, not of a mere one-time economic reward. The ability to (1) gather and deliver new kinds of data, (2) leverage new networking technologies as they become available, and (3) process them over diverse platforms around the world is an essential ingredient for competitive advantage in this domain. This chapter presents our experience in designing and deploying high-availability infrastructures for market data communication and exchange under quite different operating environments. We refer to these infrastructures as *datafeed handlers* (DFHs).

This chapter focuses on application partitioning, architectural design, and customizable object-oriented software artifacts—such as frameworks, patterns, components, and classes—and the benefits thereof. Although important, we do not elaborate on other essentials of successful software projects, such as requirements gathering, joint application design, configuration management, and several other best software engineering practices. The remainder of the chapter is organized as follows: *Section 12.1* presents an overview of DFH; *Section 12.2* presents a reference (generic) component-based specification framework for handling continuous datafeed; and *Section 12.3* presents three different particular architectures to meet problem-specific requirements by systematic adaptation. *Section 12.4* presents an implementation framework employed in these systems. *Section 12.5* identifies patterns that were used in realizing these systems. *Sections 12.2* through *12.5* identify the role and illustrate the benefits of object orientation in building customizable, scaleable systems. *Section 12.6* discusses lessons learned from our experience.

12.1 Continuous Datafeed

Datafeeds in general are continuous and are valid only for a certain duration, a weak form of soft deadline. (A soft deadline in real-time systems specification denotes a deadline that cannot be exactly specified [Steinmetz 1995]. Datafeed deadlines are weaker than that except in the case where there is an impact on the revenue.) Examples include sports updates, weather updates, inventory-depletion feeds to suppliers, and, in the financial domain, *market-information feeds*. For example, Wal-Mart and Kmart stores all over the United States might send updates to suppliers telling them which stock items have sold at each store, much like efficient consumer response in the grocery store domain [United 1997] or just-in-time inventory management. Datafeed handlers manage datafeeds, and, as shown in Figure 12.1, there is a business need for the producers to disseminate the information to one or more consumers.

In this scenario, datafeed management or datafeed handlers must:

- Accept any unit of information submitted by a producer.

- Store or preserve all submitted information if necessary.

- Transform, embellish, or translate what is contributed to what is required by the consumers as necessary. (Converting from one protocol to another, adding time stamps, and sequences at the earliest or latest point of processing within the DFH are all examples of the transformation.)

- Forward or make that information available to all the consumers as per the exchange protocol, within security and performance constraints and in the order in which the submissions were received.

- Facilitate flexible (static or dynamic, on-demand) instrumentation—monitoring and logging as needed.

There is no restriction on the location of the producers or the consumers, the number of producers or consumers, the operating environment, and the business protocol between the producer and the consumers. The DFH system must necessarily be independent and external to both the producers and consumers and must be able to work under diverse conditions. In subsequent sections we will engineer a generic architecture for DFH and evolve it for three particular scenarios.

DFH systems are required to run *uninterrupted* for any given length of time and to distribute presented information *almost instantaneously* within the context of operating conditions. In other words, end-to-end delay introduced by DFH must be consistent, reasonable, and tolerable within the operating environment and must meet the customer's or client's business needs. Most important, no undue delay may be introduced by DFH systems. We carefully avoid the use of the term *real time* because in our application scenario, we do not have any (soft or hard) time constraints except that (1) data must be disseminated as soon as it is made available to the DFH system; and (2) when a deadline is missed or data items are not delivered, the producer and the consumer of the information must synchronize using an agreed-upon recovery protocol *without requiring human intervention*. Our datafeed service can then be characterized as a *best-effort* service. Market-information feeds may include expert commentary, summaries of what has happened in the market, and price feeds—price feeds being the most familiar. One exception to our disclaimer that datafeeds are not realtime is a steady flow of trades. Trades are the revenue-generating business transactions, in the simplest case an agreement between a trader and a consumer to buy or sell securities. In the case of trade feeds, missing a trade would be considered a hard system failure and undue delay would be considered a soft system failure, because missed trades mean lost revenue, not to mention irate customers. Delayed trades would mean inaccurate risk or exposure analysis and would also be considered a failure. For example, an organization might decide never to speculate on interest rate fluctuations for more than $25 million, given that if such a speculation for $15 million were not to be distributed instantaneously, other unsuspecting (so they could claim) traders might exceed the daily limit by further speculating in the same market. When trades, or any information that directly affects revenue or exposure, are involved, expediency is of the essence.

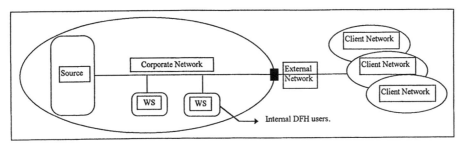

Figure 12.1   DFH application scenario.

In the most general sense, datafeeds may be characterized as a publisher-subscriber (consumer-producer) problem. In this type of problem, a message is produced somewhere in the network by one or more producers. Also known as a *logical data unit* (LDU), a message is the smallest unit of information that can be exchanged. On the other end are one or more consumers who subscribe to that information. The producer and/or the consumer may be a computing element or a human being. Of the datafeed management activities enumerated in the previous section, the central role of the datafeed handler is to accept messages as they are published and deliver all the messages in the order they are published to all the subscribers, as shown in Figure 12.2. In this simplified rendition, messages published by the set of producers (pub1 through pubN) are processed by a sequence of DFH resources (q processing elements), as in a linear bounded arrival process and are finally delivered to the set of subscribers (sub1 through subM).

In summary, the specification for datafeed handlers can be categorized into the following orthogonal profiles:

Consumer profile. Parameters such as the number of customers, if they can coexist (*simultaneity*), and do so without affecting each other (*independence*), are included in the customer profile.

Producer profile. Parameters such as number of producers, simultaneity, and independence are included in the producer profile, as well.

Messaging profile. Parameters such as message ordering requirements, data (content) format, and retransmission (history and message log) requirements are included in the messaging profile.

Protocol profile. Recovery, acknowledgment, replay, and security arrangements between the producer and the consumer are included in the protocol profile.

Network profile. Reliability, extent (LAN or WAN), reach (point to point or multicast), and the characteristics of the underlying network are included in the network profile.

Environment profile. Hardware and software platforms and media are included in the environment profile.

In closing, this section introduces the notion of datafeeds, and general-purpose datafeed handlers (DFHs) that manage such datafeeds. With this background, the next

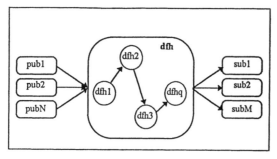

Figure 12.2   Datafeed handler.

section introduces a generic (reference) component-based architecture for any DFH and then evolves the reference architecture for three DFH application scenarios: (1) a price feed, (2) a page distribution system, and (3) a trade-processing system.

12.2 A Generic Component-Based DFH Architecture

The DFH presented here is a component-based architecture leveraging several different object-oriented concepts. There is much debate over the terms, including *object-orientation, architecture, framework, components, patterns, classes,* and so on. We use these terms with a specific intent. For a brief introduction, please refer to the *Objective Taxonomy* sidebar later in this chapter.

12.2.1 Partitioning the DFH Responsibilities

Optimal benefits of building a distributed application, such as concurrency, fault tolerance, isolation, and reliability, can be realized *if and only if* the distributed applications are designed using good principles, such as transparency and division of labor.

Division of labor, also known as *application partitioning,* is arguably the most important.

Application partitioning is a design activity—in particular, one of devising a functional architecture. Partitioning is a wicked science, in that there is no formula or rule for decomposing a given problem into the best partitioned architecture. However, there are guidelines regarding application partitioning:

Functional units (classes, patterns, components, and frameworks) must be cohesive. Such components, which fulfill a single-minded objective of the application, allow us to refine those distinct functions independently.

Intercomponent communication must be kept to a minimum so that the communication overhead is lowered. However, we should note that DFH is necessarily communication intensive.

Software architecture defines and lays the foundation for many desirable properties of software systems. There are cookbook models of application partitioning [Berson 1991]; for a basic introduction, refer to the primer on Architectural Evolution in the *Objective Taxonomy* sidebar. Our system is centered around distributed components; our primary motivation for adopting distributed object/component computing is "to simplify the development of flexible and extensible software" [Vinoski 1995]. Division of labor with well-defined separation of concerns is a direct consequence of this strategy.

We divide the DFH problem into a collection of cohesive, dependent, but autonomous components:

Source line reader (SLR). Manages communication with the source. Accepts input from contributors and transfers it to the data repository subsystem.

Subscription management (SM). Accepts subscription requests from clients. Accepts *publish* requests from a publishing agent and forwards them to all the subscribers.

Feed delivery agent (FDA). These agents handle client-specific activities. These components subscribe to the SM and process the feed as necessary and forward the processed data to the end client. Protocol conversion, data filter replay, and recovery management are client specific.

Data repository subsystem. Consists of two components, feed store server (FSS) and client query manager (CQM). FSS accepts data from a designated source and stores it in the repository. CQM handles refresh requests from client delivery agents. And a database management library (DB) interfaces with external database services.

Flexible instrumentation subsystem (FIS). Monitors data flowing through other components as needed, either in an obtrusive mode via an operating system service (OSS) library or in an unobtrusive mode using a component.

Data Management Subsystem. This subsystem facilitates message packing and unpacking service via a data parcel service (DPS) library, and transaction semantics via a transaction management (TM) library and a translation agent (XA) service component.

Selected ACE [Vinoski 1995] class libraries. Shared Memory and Semaphore classes from ACE class libraries are included in this library.

These components are *cohesive* in that each component is dedicated to a particular aspect of the feed handler. They are *dependent* in that each component depends on other components for the data. They are *autonomous* in that each component can execute and continue to be well behaved even in the absence of other components. These benefits are a direct consequence of the vertical decomposition (partitioning) employed here, as opposed to horizontal decomposition as in layering. The reference component-based architectural framework is shown in Figure 12.3.

We call this a *specification framework* because the architectural specifications are incomplete and are tailored to solve different problems in the datafeed handler domain by adding and removing the components. The following sections justify the architecture in terms of reliability, scalability, and business process transparency.

12.2.2 Reliability

Partitioning achieves a very high degree of fault isolation and containment. For example, if the end client fails, only the FDAs are affected. If the SLR is corrupted, the subscription list, data store, and all else remain functional until the SLR is resumed. SLR is a component that reads from a network device external to the DFH framework and writes to an internal network device managed by another DFH component. This scheme insulates the DFH from the data packaging, flow control, connection, and communication issues that may be peculiar to the external sources. We separate CQM (managing client requests) and FSS (populating the store) so that FSS is completely isolated and independent of client interactions. CQMs are transient components (short-lived UNIX processes) in that they are created as needed. But the FSS is always active, such that the repository is consistent with the feed history at all times. Failures in one client will not affect other clients or the integrity of the repository. Partitioning such cohesive activities provides for a higher level of reliability and fault isolation. FISs are

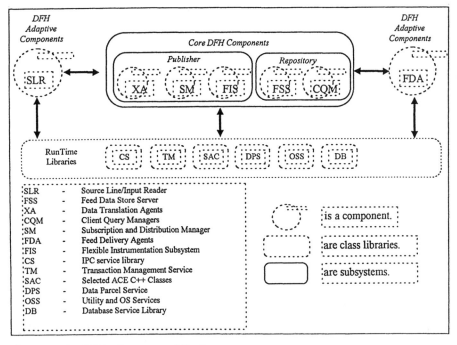

Figure 12.3 DFH reference architecture.

also components that provide unobtrusive instrumentation. FIS components attach to shared memory segments and read messages as they are processed. They are unobtrusive in that they are read-only clients and the shared memory servers do not observe any mutual exclusion strategy.

12.2.3 Scalability

As DFH instances are customized and deployed, the number of subscribers, number of messages from the source, and number of messaging protocols used are very likely to change over the lifetime of the deployment. The DFH architecture is elaborate in particular to handle such requirements.

Volume of Messages and Number of Data Sources

The SLR is isolated so that the source-to-DFH link and policies may be handled by the SLR component. The speed at which the input messages are accepted is independent of the number of subscribers at the other end of the DFH or other DFH activities, such as the storage subsystems or distribution. Furthermore, the subscription manager (SM) is oblivious to the number of input message sources by design. Thus, we achieve scalability in this dimension by providing for the SLR and by designing the SM to be independent of the number of sources.

Number of Clients and Messaging Protocols

The ability to provide access to data to a number of clients as required translates directly into revenue, and consequently is very desirable. The DFH architecture provides for scalability by separating the three responsibilities, namely: (1) subscription management through subscription managers (SMs); (2) client-specific translation through translation agents (XAs); and (3) history management through the feed store server (FSS). Additional subscription management may be deployed by subscribing to existing SMs (cascading SMs) or by deploying additional SMs in parallel. Because the client-specific protocols are captured in the transfer agent (XA), providing data to a new client with a very different messaging protocol is reduced to customizing the XA to handle the new protocol. Thus, DFH architecture can be customized to any number of protocols by deploying additional transfer or translation agents. Similarly, by isolating the history management to the FSS component, any number of clients can be engaged in this highly demanding *bursty* phase. Other important functions, including the line reader, subscription management, and transfer protocol, are left unhindered.

In summary, the reference DFH architecture presented here is designed to scale in data volume, number of sources, number of clients, and number of messaging protocols.

12.3 Adapting to Problem-Specific Requirements

Architectures facilitate structural stability at the level of abstraction they are devised and it is object orientation that facilitates evolvability shielding the architecture from instability at lower levels of abstraction. Fabricating a DFH solution to a particular problem is reduced to a problem of selecting the appropriate components, interconnecting and specializing them as needed. Architectures aid in selecting the components and interconnections. Object oriented techniques facilitate our ability to specialize without disrupting the stability afforded by the architecture.

We now demonstrate that the three business scenarios we presented can be (and most other business objectives in the domain of data feed services) achieved by a combination of at least one SLR, as many DFH core components as needed and one FDA. In this section we present the adaptation of the reference DFH architecture to three different very data feed scenario and the effectiveness of the OO techniques we have used.

12.3.1 Price-Feed Handler

The price-feed handler is a infrastructural service to distribute stock or other traded security prices from one trading entity to another. The topological requirement for our implementation is to distribute prices from a single mainframe to one or more sub-

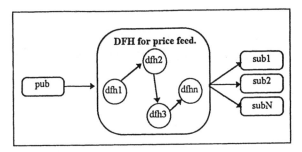

Figure 12.4   Price-feed handler.

scribers distributed over geographical distances, as shown in Figure 12.4. Some special requirements particular to price-feed systems include the following: (1) the protocol may include elaborate recovery and start-up protocols; (2) data may be delivered in bursts, especially during start-up and replay procedures; (3) subscribing customers and the network links can be patently unreliable; and (4) the two parties exchange a single message at a time, a price quote for a single security. Illustrative transactions supported by our implementation are shown in Table 12.1.

The particular architecture for the price-feed handler consists of several cooperative servers, as shown in Figure 12.5. The feed data server (FDS), an instance of the SLR, maintains a communication channel with the source, and the data is passed as is to the SM. The SM forwards the messages to the feed delivery agents (FDAs). The role of the FDS is to receive data as fast as the source can deliver and buffer the feed when the SM is busy forwarding. The separation between the receiver and the forwarder is necessary to avoid holding up the source. The FDAs are agents that customize the feed data according to particular customer requirements. The FSS is a special FDA that stores the entire feed in a persistent store so that all the messages can be replayed in the order they were generated at the source. The replay agent (RA) is a liaison between the FSS and the numerous FDAs. The RAs are transitory agents that request a feed replay from the FSS and feed it to the FDAs. The RAs are transitory in that they are created by the RA dispatch executive (RAX) whenever a FDA requests a replay, and they exit when the feed is completely played out. While the FSS is dedicated to storing the feed data, the RAs manage replay requests from any one of the FDAs representing a customer. The separation between RA and FSS is also essential so that replaying the messages to a particular customer does not affect the price feed or the storing of the feed into the database. Thus, FSS is isolated from communication errors and delays during replay. RAX is a dispatcher to provide concurrent RA service, and it creates one RA per replay request from the FDA. Notice that several FDAs can be activated (initiated) simultaneously, and—more important—exposure to a failure with a customer is limited to the FDA servicing that customer. DS is a simple lightweight directory service component that provides a higher degree of transparency and migratory capabilities for the components. For a discussion of the capabilities of the DS see [Kannan 1992]. DS is not integrated yet.

Table 12.1 Publisher-Subscriber Transactions for the Price-Feed DFH*

TRANSACTION ORIGINATOR	TRANSACTION	NOTES
Publisher	Start-of-day (SoD) process	Bursty message. 4000 or more messages in rapid succession. Elapsed end-to-end time, 2 to 6 minutes.
Publisher	End of start-of-day process	Database is complete. Regular interday message will begin.
Publisher	Price update	Fixed length.
Publisher	Security update	New security.
Publisher	Status update	Trading halted or resumed.
Subscriber	Start subscription	Is preemptive request in that it may arrive while the DFH is sending data. Overrides all other pending requests from that client. DFH must initialize a snapshot of the current status. Similar to start-of-day above. Results in burst.
Subscriber	Heartbeat	Subscriber is alive.
Subscriber	Retransmit range	Resend messages in range.
DFH 2 subscriber	Update messages	Same as above.
DFH 2 subscriber	Heartbeat	DFH is alive.
DFH 2 subscriber	Start-of-day message	Signals the beginning of database refresh.
DFH 2 subscriber	End of start-of-day message	Same as above.

*The transaction recipient is always the DFH, except when stated otherwise.

SMs and the FDAs together implement the feed delivery framework, and the interaction between them is realized using Publisher/Subscriber patterns. We present these patterns in a subsequent section. The price handler system has been in production on a variety of platforms for well over three years. During the start-of-day phase, a feed burst of up to 7000 messages is handled within a duration of 3 to 6 minutes over geographic distances. On any given trading day, this system transfers an average of 60,000 messages.

12.3.2 Page Distribution System

The page distribution system is a fundamentally different system. The unit information, a page, is fundamentally different from a price quote. Price quotes are transient,

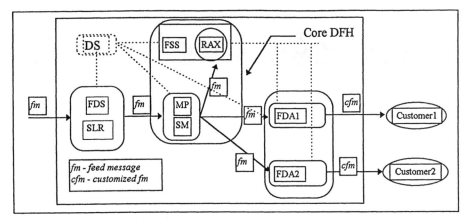

Figure 12.5   Price-feed handler architecture.

while pages are long-lived and are distinct. Content of the page may vary. Thus, in addition to distribution, storing and retrieving the pages are additional functional requirements of the system. Furthermore, because we now have more than one source, as shown in the component topology diagram in Figure 12.6, transferring the pages simultaneously to the page distribution system is consequently an additional requirement. The transactions supported by the page distribution system are presented in Table 12.2.

We first decompose the page distribution system into three major subsystems, as shown in Figure 12.7.

The page transfer subsystem (PTS) is a customization of the SLR component to receive two different kinds of input streams. One is a stream of pages and the other is an update to an existing page. A page is a represented as a file. The SLR(pg) component receives pages and stores them in the page repository subsystem (PRS) using a page replacement component, FSS(pg). When a page update is received, the corresponding page is updated in the page repository using the page update component,

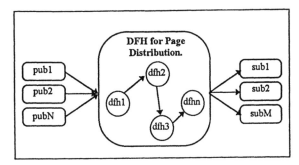

Figure 12.6   Page distribution.

Table 12.2 Publisher-Subscriber Transactions for the Page Distribution DFH*

TRANSACTION ORIGINATOR	TRANSACTION	NOTES
Publisher	Accept a page	A page has an immutable reference ID. Previous version of the same page is no longer valid. Forward to all subscribers.
Publisher	Accept a page fragment	Update the specified page and forward to all subscribers.
Subscriber	Start subscription	It may arrive while the DFH is sending data. Overrides all other pending requests from that subscriber and must not affect the input or other subscribers.
Subscriber	Heartbeat	Subscriber is alive.
Subscriber	Refresh a page	Send the specified page.
DFH 2 subscriber	Send a page fragment	DFH does not send a page at a time. The LDU between subscriber and DFH is a page fragment. Page fragments are interleaved.
DFH 2 subscriber	Heartbeat	DFH is alive.

*The transaction recipient is always the DFH, except when stated otherwise.

FSS(pu). The page repository is a customized feed store system. The architectural mismatch between the page repository and a record-oriented feed store are not trivial, and at this time a final (stable) solution is not in place. The page publisher subsystem (PPS) is, however, a direct descendant of the publisher subsystem of the reference architecture. Here the SM component does not know anything about the internal

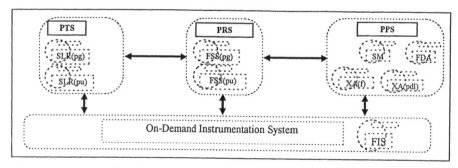

Figure 12.7 Page distribution architecture.

structure of the data units being exchanged. So we introduce a transaction agent (XA) to fragment pages and pass the fragments to the SM. The pages are submitted in a proprietary page description language (PDL). Because customers may require these pages to be delivered in other page description languages, we have an additional translation agent, XA(pdl).

12.3.3 Lazy Transaction Processing

Lazy transaction processing (LTP) receives trades which consist of one or more records. Each record represents a purchase or sale of securities or a cancellation of a previous record. Trades can be open, active, and closed. Trades can remain active for a long duration and only when a trade is closed the trade is committed to an external database that supports atomic, consistent, isolated, and durable (ACID) transaction semantics. Thus, we characterize this system as the lazy transaction processing system. The LTP configuration is different in that there is exactly one source and one client (external database), as shown in Figure 12.8, and it supports a different set of transactions, as shown in Table 12.3.

However, the reference model is consistent with this scaled-down version as well. As shown in Figure 12.9, we present the LTP architecture as comprised of two components: (1) TLR, which is a customized SLR(tr) with trade-processing abilities; and (2) DBMT, a database manager for trades. The difference is in data processing methods. We now have to preserve the state(s) of many trades that are exchanged between the source and the client. Furthermore, a trade or a record cannot be dropped even if the source or the client aborts. In the event that one of the systems does abort, LTP must recover from where it failed. Thus, we distribute the responsibilities over three components:

- A customized SLR(tr) receives trade records.
- A TM runtime library manages the trades in progress in a persistent store, with persistence to assure recoverability.
- A customized FDA(tr/db) posts completed trades to the database.

In our experience, we thus find that by adopting an architectural framework and by implementing the framework using components with well-defined roles (or parti-

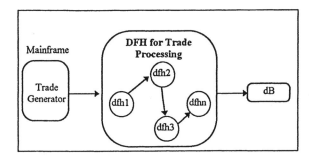

Figure 12.8 Trade-processing system.

Table 12.3   Provider-Consumer Transactions for the Trade-Processing DFH*

TRANSACTION ORIGINATOR	TRANSACTION	NOTES
Provider	Start trade feed	Expects a sequence number of the next trade expected by the DFH. Once each morning, DFH sends 000 to start the trade-processing system.
Provider	Begin a trade	A new trade.
Provider	Accept a trade record within a trade	DFH is to post this record into the appropriate trade container.
Provider	End a trade	Close an existing trade and commit it to the DB.
Consumer (DB)	None	Except for return (status) values of attempted returns, commercial DBs do not initiate a dialog with DFH. Transactions are pushed by the DFH onto the DB.
DFH 2 consumer (DB)	Open transaction	Atomic, consistent, isolated, and durable (ACID) properties.
DFH 2 consumer (DB)	Post a record	Insert, delete, or modify a DB record. SQL/DML.
DFH 2 consumer (DB)	Close transaction	Commit the transaction. Note that abort transaction is not a DFH primitive because of lazy evaluation.

*The transaction recipient is always the DFH, except when stated otherwise.

tions), the task of realizing a family of systems can be reduced to configuring the framework by including or excluding appropriate components as needed. In summary, specification frameworks facilitate evolution and customization at the level of components. The next section presents two implementation frameworks.

12.4 Implementation Frameworks

The DFH domain presents several opportunities to exploit traditional frameworks, which by definition are incomplete implementations for a specific problem. These partial implementations may be customized to realize working or complete systems. Two

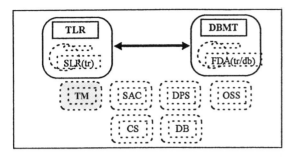

Figure 12.9 Lazy trade processor (LTP).

recurring responsibilities of a DFH are facilitating the exchange of information and transaction processing. The page distribution system receives data from one or more sources, while the price-feed server publishes the incoming messages to one or more subscribers. Thus, the communication can be achieved concurrently, and we implemented customizable frameworks—PAcceptor and Sconnector—which deliver messages concurrently. The details of these implementation frameworks are presented in [Kannan 1999]. Here we present yet another framework to implement flexible transaction processing strategies. In the LTR, both TLR and DBMT have to be aware of transactions but have to process them differently, while the communication aspects of both TLR and DBMT are rather straightforward. The TLR receives trade records and posts them to the persistent store, whereas the DBMT posts trades to the database. Thus, we implemented a TM framework in which some essential implementation details were left unspecified. Now we present the TransactionManager framework and the details of customization.

The benefit of frameworks is that they provide a convenient way of codifying the commonality within a family of problems and yet allow for independent customization for each problem within that family, so that the entire family of problems can be solved elegantly and economically without any compromise. The commonality between TLR and DBMT is that both subsystems have to detect when a trade is opened or closed and have to process records as they are received. The difference between them is that TLR stores the records in a persistent store, whereas the DBMT commits the transaction to an external database.

The framework consists of three classes: a *transaction manager*, a *transaction*, and *records* that make up a transaction, as shown in Figure 12.10. We wish to use these classes under different conditions. In other words, DBMT differs from TLR in two ways: (1) initialization and termination, to set up and dismantle database connectivity; and (2) what happens when an end_of_transaction is sensed—the records are committed to a commercial database, as opposed to a persistent file store. Figure 12.11 presents the implementation details.

It is under such conceptually similar but operationally different scenarios that frameworks are relevant, because the frameworks can be used to codify the conceptual simi-

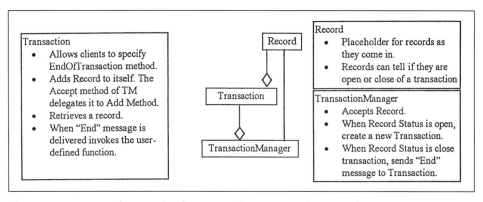

Figure 12.10   UML diagram for the TransactionManager framework.

larity, deferring the customization to a later phase. The following source listing presents relevant portions of the TransactionManager framework. Clients of the transaction manager can customize the trade processing but retain the transaction semantics. Note that runtime TransactionManager objects are instantiated with application-specific customization functions.

12.5 Patterns in Concert

Partitioning an application enables the analysis of components within a limited context. Isolated from other responsibilities of the entire problem at hand, it is easier to identify patterns that are candidate solutions to the particular problem being addressed by specific components. As the DFH evolved over the years, we discovered the applicability of numerous patterns, including the Publisher/Subscriber (Observer) pattern, the Header (Bridge) pattern, and the ParcelService (Façade) pattern.

The Publisher/Subscriber pattern, a customization of the Observer pattern [Gamma 1995], allows a continuous data generator to accept subscription requests, manage the subscription list, and maintain the datafeed to any number of consumers in a distributed environment with very little exposure to substrate system primitives and very high generality and reusability.

The Façade pattern from [Gamma 1995] provides a unified interface to a set of interfaces in a subsystem. Façade defines a higher-level interface that makes the subsystem simpler to use. In the DFH domain, a recurring problem is exchanging application objects between two processes. Exchanging application objects involves packing and unpacking these objects appropriately and managing the communication issues. Clients have to contend with two different abstractions, the *packaging abstraction* and the *ipc abstraction*. The packaging information includes both header information and the content of the package. To reduce the number of abstractions developers have to contend with, we implemented ParcelService, which is a domain-specific implementation of the Façade pattern [Gamma 1995].

```
// customizes the TransactionManager class
int record begins new trans(BasicRecord *rp)
{ return ( rp->Status()==START_OF_TRANS));}
int record is part of trans(BasicRecord *rp)
{ return (rp->Status()==PART_OF_TRANS));}
int record ends trans(BasicRecord *rp)
{
return ( rp->Status()==END_OF_TRANS));
}
// client specific end of transaction
// change this function to commit to DB
// at the DBMT
int end of transaction (char *tnamep)
{
 if ( /* communications links are functional */ )
  {// name of transaction in this case]
      Send Transaction Handle ;
      return (0);
  }
      // raise hell or exception
return (-1);
}
// global tmgrp
TransactionManager *tmgrp;
void ProcessRecord( BasicRecord *rp)
{
      if ( rp->WellDefined())
      return ( tmgrp->Accept(rp));
}
```

```
// TransactionManager Specification
class TransactionManager {
public:
TransactionManager(*is_new)(BasicRecord *),
int (*is_done)(BasicRecord *),
int (*is_active)(BasicRecord *)
char * (*extract_name)(BasicRecord *));
void SetEndOfTransactionProcessor(int (*ef)(char *))
  {
Transaction::SetEOTProcessor ( eot_processor );
  }
int Accept(COTS_BasicRecord *rp);
}; // lots of details omitted . . .
```

```
main (int argc, char *argv[])
{
// initialize the transaction manager and
// Tell TM how to find begin, end etc
  tmgrp = new TransactionManager(record begins new trans,
                  record ends trans,
                  record is part of trans,
                  message_txid);
// Tell TM what to do when end is detected
      tmgrp ->SetEndOfTransactionProcessor
          (end of transaction);

while (1)
{
      // Receive a Message
      rp = /* Convert it to a Record */;
      if ( ProcessRecord(rp)==Failed)
      {
      // long weekend . . . go home
      }
}}
```

Please note that only the bare essentials are presented here. The actual implementation fills in other details. The TM actually implements a bridge Pattern aka Cheshire cat.

```
//Transaction Implementation
int Transaction::End( )
{
  // users should be allowed to setup any kind of
  // CommitProtocol
  // we want to send the transaction over to the
  // next process which will process it further
  // for statistics we might want to keep track
  // of number of records and the time at which
  // the transaction ended.
  char buffer[64];

  CopyName(buffer);
  // OnEndOfTransaction is an external function
  // pointer that takes a buffer
// (or a handle to a transaction) and
  // does whatever it needs to do with it
  return ((*(OnEndOfTransaction))(buffer));}
```

```
int TransactionManager::Accept(BasicRecord *rp)
{
  Transaction *trp;

  // Extract Transaction Id from Record

  // Get the handle for the Transaction

  // If the record status is New
  trp = new Transaction(rp-> Name());
  // add this record to the transaction
  trp-> Add(rp);
  // If the record status is Done
  if  ( rp-> IsDone() )
          {      // ask the Transaction to End . . . .
          trp-> End ();
          }
  return (0);
}
```

Figure 12.11 Implementation framework.

OBJECTIVE TAXONOMY

Classes, patterns, components, frameworks, and architectures are all units of software artifacts (or tools) that help us manage complexity. In particular, they all help us divide and conquer and achieve a high degree of separation of concern. They vary in the degree of abstraction they afford. Subsystems and modules also deserve special mention. A module or a subsystem does not in itself violate any of the key characteristics of being object-oriented. Given how the subsystem is constructed, we can begin to characterize whether it is object-oriented or not. There is now some consensus on what constitutes being object-oriented; for basic concepts, please see [Booch 1994].

"A class is an implementation of abstract data types" as defined by James Coplien [Coplien 1992].

A design pattern consists of [Gamma 1995] "descriptions of communicating objects and classes that are customized to solve a general design problem in a particular context" [Gamma 1995].

Components are interpreted and defined in many different ways. Components are sometimes referred to as classes within a cohesive class library [Rogers 1997]. Others define a component as a unit of work and distribution [Orfali 1995]. We prefer to define components as units of work which are independent, with a well-defined context and interface, and which may even be executable, as prescribed in [Orfali 1995; Brown 1996].

Rogers [Rogers 1997] defines a framework as a partially completed software application that is intended to be customized to completion: "A framework is a class library that captures patterns of interaction between objects. A framework consists of a suite of concrete and abstract classes, explicitly designed to be used together. Applications are developed from a framework by competing the abstract classes." This definition of framework (a partial application that is completed by the developer or integrator) is also referred to as an *application framework* [Wallace 1996], as opposed to an *integration framework*, which refers to an infrastructure that is independent of application functionality [Wallace 1996]. Rogers differentiates a pattern from a framework in that patterns are prescriptions for a particular problem (need not include software), whereas frameworks are partial implementations for a problem. In other words, frameworks are implementations in a particular language and may employ one or more patterns, whereas patterns are problem-specific but language-independent prescriptions that may include illustrative implementations. See [Fayad-Schmidt 1997] for a comprehensive introduction to frameworks and the application of frameworks.

Objects, applications, and systems are all realizations (instances) of these concepts. An object is an instance of a class. A well-defined application is a realization of a framework. And if the applications are so devised that they execute independently and are configured to work in concert with other applications, such applications are components.

Mary Shaw and David Garlan, in [Shaw-Garlan 1996], offer an abstraction of architecture that includes, "description of elements from which systems are built, interactions among those elements, patterns that guide their composition, and constraints on these patterns." In [Garlan-Shaw 1993] they offer a simpler definition, that an architecture of a system defines the basic components of the system and their connections. *Components* ere refers to units of functionality.

Another common problem in the DFH domain is allowing clients to exchange in a manner transparent to the content of the message, including the header protocol used. The intent of the Bridge pattern [Gamma 1995] is to decouple the implementation from the interface. The Header class hierarchy in DFH implements the Bridge pattern to decouple the internal structure of the messages from the message-handling software.

The Publisher/Subscriber pattern is one of the prominent patterns employed in DFH. The Publisher/Subscriber pattern is a well-known pattern derived from the Observer pattern [Gamma 1995]. The relevance of the Observer pattern to our discussion here is that an Observer pattern is defined to be "used to decouple objects so that changes to one can affect any number of clients without requiring the changed object to know the details of the others" [Gamma 1995]. And in the DFH application scenario, the stream of messages generated by a source represents the *model,* and the customized stream of messages generated by the subscribing agents represents the *views.* The role of the distributor/publisher agent is to notify the list of subscribing agents when a new message arrives. Subscribers are observers.

The Publisher/Subscriber pattern has been used in numerous other implementations. In [Rogers 1997] the Subscriber/Publisher pattern is used to implement the CORBA Event Service Specification within the CORBA Object Service Specifications. Rogers [Rogers 1997] presents two concrete examples of the Observer pattern: (1) CORBA Event Notification Services, and (2) CORBA Security Alarm Reporting. Publisher/Subscriber is also discussed in [Buschmann 1996; Coad 1990] in this context. In [Pree 1995], example scenarios of the Subscriber/Publisher pattern are presented and a formal contract is specified. The earliest use of the Subscriber/Publisher pattern is perhaps within the Smalltalk Model-View-Controller (MVC) framework [Krasner-Pope 1988]. The MVC is a rather complex design construct, usually made up of several simple and cohesive design patterns; one of them is the Observer pattern.

12.6 Summary and Lessons Learned

Understanding the customer requirements and defining a conforming architecture are the very foundation of a successful software project. Real-world systems have real requirements and are naturally complex. Understanding the requirements and the business context is the first and foremost step toward automation. Unfortunately, it is neither inexpensive nor easy to achieve. It is time-consuming but quite rewarding over unusually long periods of time.

The next important endeavor toward a successful software project is the software architecture. We quote Barry Boehm [Boehm 1995] here:

> If a project has not achieved a system architecture, including its rationale, the project should not proceed to full-scale system development. Specifying the architecture as a deliverable enables its use throughout the development and maintenance phase.

From a system perspective, the DFH framework we have implemented is comprised of an architectural/specification framework and a realization/implementation framework. The architectural framework (DFH/AF) is independent of the realization framework (DFH/RF). DFH/AF merely stipulates how the components may be configured.

This guarantees stability (availability) and scalability. We present a reference architecture for datafeed handlers. Then we customize the reference architecture by (1) adding or removing problem specific components, (2) reconfiguring the interconnections between the components; and (3) introducing new components as needed.

The DFH/RF is a collection of classes (C++) that can be easily substituted with equivalent classes, and they provide the services to realize the capabilities of the components. We demonstrate the utility of object-oriented artifacts in the form of patterns and class categories. We present the details of the Publisher/Subscriber (Observer) pattern, the ParcelService (Façade) pattern, and the Header (Bridge) pattern. We also demonstrated the utility of components (SLR, FIS, and so on) and frameworks with the customizable TransactionManager framework.

From a domain perspective, the DFH is a collection of components (executable applications) that can collectively receive high volumes of arbitrary market data, maintain a history database, and disseminate the data as they are received to one or more customers. The DFH/AF explicitly addresses concerns regarding customization:

- Customer-specific data formats
- Application-level messaging protocols
- Customer faults
- History playback
- Data source characteristics
- Data processing characteristics

Most important, it accomplishes these requirements without affecting other customers who may also be receiving data at the same time.

The DFH has been in use to exchange U.S. Treasury Bond data, pages, and transactions over WANs and LANs involving commercial databases and other middleware toolkits. Our experience is that understanding the domain and the architecture are the most important aspects. Without the architectural stability and the evolvability due to object orientation, the level of customization we have achieved would not have been possible. Without understanding the domain, we could not have possibly satisfied customer requirements in such varied environments. The DFH system has evolved over four years, and the investment in the analysis and design phase has been truly rewarding.

12.7 References

[Berson 1991] Berson, A. *Client/Server Architecture*. New York: McGraw Hill, 1991.

[Boehm 1995] Boehm, B. Engineering context (for software architecture). Invited talk, First International Workshop on Architecture for Software Systems. Seattle, WA, April 1995.

[Booch 1994] Booch, D. *Object Oriented Analysis and Design with Applications*, 2d ed. Redwood City, CA: Benjamin/Cummings, 1994.

[Brown 1996] Brown, A., and K. Wallnau. Engineering of component based systems. In *Component Based Software Engineering: Selected Papers from the Software Engineering*

Institute, pp. 7–15, A. Brown, editor. Los Alamitos, CA: IEEE Computer Society Press, 1996.

[Buschmann 1996] Buschmann, F., H. Rohnert, P. Sommerlad, and M. Stal. *Pattern-Oriented Software Architecture: A System of Patterns.* New York: John Wiley & Sons, 1996.

[Coad 1990] Coad, P. Object-Oriented Patterns. *Communications of the ACM*, 33(9), September 1990.

[Coplien 1992] Coplien, J. *Advanced C++ Programming Styles and Idioms.* Reading, MA: Addison-Wesley, 1992.

[Fayad-Schmidt 1997] Fayad, M., and D. Schmidt. Object-oriented application frameworks. *Communications of the ACM*, 40(10), October 1997.

[Gamma 1995] Gamma, E., R. Helm, R. Johnson, and J. Vlissides. *Design Patterns: Elements of Reusable Object Oriented Software.* Reading, MA: Addison-Wesley, 1995.

[Garlan-Shaw 1993] Garlan, D., and M. Shaw. An introduction to software architecture. In *Advances in Software Engineering and Knowledge Engineering*, vol. 1. World Scientific Publishing Company, 1993.

[Kannan 1992] Kannan, R., et al. Software environment for network computing. *IEEE TCOS and Application Environment, Newsletter*,6(1), 1992. Also available as CERC-TR-RN-91-007, Concurrent Engineering Research Center, West Virginia University, Drawer 2000, Morgantown; Internet: cerc.wvu.edu, May 1992.

[Kannan 1999] Kannan, R. PAcceptor and SConnector frameworks: Combining concurrency and communication. *ACM Computing Surveys Symposium on Application Framework*, M.E. Fayad, editor, September 1999.

[Krasner-Pope 1988] Krasner, G.E., and S.T. Pope. A cookbook for using the model view-controller user interface paradigm in Smalltalk-80. *Journal of Object Oriented Programming*, August–September 1988: 26–49.

[Orfali 1995] Orfali, R., et al. Client server components: CORBA meets OpenDoc. *Object Magazine*, May 1995: 55.

[Pree 1995] Pree, W. *Design Patterns for Object-Oriented Software Development*, pp. 69–72, 88–94. Reading, MA: Addison-Wesley/ACM Press, 1995.

[Rogers 1997] Rogers, G. *Framework-Based Software Development in C++.* Upper Saddle River, NJ: Prentice Hall, 1997.

[Shaw-Garlan 1996] Shaw, M., and D. Garlan. *Software Architecture: Perspectives on an Emerging Discipline.* Englewood Cliffs, NJ: Prentice Hall, 1996.

[Steinmetz 1995] Steinmetz, R., and K. Nahrstedt. *Multimedia: Computing, Communications and Applications*, pp. 228–229. Englewood Cliffs, NJ: Prentice Hall, 1995.

[United 1997] Efficient consumer response. *Hemisphere* (United Airways in-flight magazine), May 1997.

[Vinoski 1995] Vinoski, S., and D. Schmidt. Comparing alternative distributed programming techniques. *C++ Report*, May 1995.

[Wallace 1996] Wallace, E., P. Clements, and K. Wallnau. Discovering a system modernization decision framework: A case study in migrating to distributed object technology. In *Component Based Software Engineering: Selected Papers from the Software Engineering Institute*, pp. 113–123, A. Brown, editor. Los Alamitos, CA: IEEE Computer Society Press, 1996.

PART Four

Language-Specific Frameworks

Part Four discusses issues related to programming languages and defines the impact of programming language constructs on component and application framework development. Part Four consists of seven chapters, Chapters 13 through 19.

Constraint satisfaction (CS) techniques are a powerful programming paradigm that distinguishes itself in that it allows the developer to state a computational problem in a declarative way. Chapter 13, "Hierarchical and Distributed Constraint Satisfaction Systems," presents an approach to the integration of the constraint programming (CP) paradigm with the object-oriented (OO) paradigm. The main contribution of this chapter is the description of an OO framework that has proven to be well suited to the development of hierarchical and distributed CS systems.

Chapter 14, "Modeling Collections of Changing Interdependent Objects," indicates that the modeling of changing interdependent objects is a major component of many large software systems. This modeling process requires a framework for capturing the application-important relationships between objects, as well as a mechanism for using these relationships when implementing the changing nature of the objects. Affective relations, relationships that capture important behavioral connections between objects, provide a framework for the first part of this process and can be used to build collections of interdependent objects in an object-oriented programming language. Data-driven rules integrated into the object-oriented programming language, such as those provided by R++, provide a mechanism for easily implementing changes to the collection of objects.

Chapter 15, "Oberon with Gadgets: A Simple Component Framework," presents a simple component framework that, in a nutshell, addresses many of the archetypal aspects of component-oriented software environments, with a particular emphasis on homogeneity and unified concepts. Some of the topics focused upon are a fully hierarchic notion of compound objects, persistent object representation, interactive and descriptive tools for object composition, and self-contained and mobile objects. Methodological highlights are (1) a novel kind of generic object interfaces in combination with a message protocol that strictly obeys the principle of parental control; (2) a multipurpose concept of indexed object libraries; and (3) an alternative approach (compared to the Java virtual machine) to portable code, accompanied by dynamic compilation. This framework is based on and integrated into Oberon, a language and system in the heritage of Pascal and Modula that runs both natively and on Intel-based PCs or on top of a commercial operating system.

Chapter 16, "Inheritance Management and Method Dispatch Framework," presents a framework that is usable by both compilers and runtime systems to provide table-based method dispatch, inheritance conflict detection, and compile-time method determination. The framework relies on a set of technique-independent algorithms for environment modification, which call technique-dependent algorithms to perform fundamental operations such as table access and index determination. The framework unifies all table-based method dispatch techniques into a cohesive whole, allowing a language implementor to change between techniques by changing the manner in which the dispatch table-based (DT) environment is instantiated. Incremental versions of all table-based techniques except the virtual function table (VTBL) have been implemented, all of which have low millisecond-per-invocation execution times. The framework provides a variety of new capabilities. The DT framework currently consists of 36 classes, 208 selectors, 494 methods, and 1081 meaningful class-selector pairs. When the DT framework is applied to a completely random ordering of itself, a selector colored compact table (SCCT)-based dispatch table is generated in 0.436 seconds. Because compiling the framework requires 390 seconds, even the slowest dispatch technique and input ordering produce a dispatch table in a negligible amount of time, relative to overall compilation time. The framework is available at ftp://ftp.cs.ualberta.ca/pub/ Dtf.

Chapter 17, "Constraint Satisfaction Problems Framework," discusses the relevance of the framework approach for building efficient and powerful constraint satisfaction programming environments. Constraint satisfaction programming is a paradigm for solving complex combinatorial problems. Integrating this paradigm with objects addresses two different objectives: (1) Objects may be used to implement constraint satisfaction algorithms efficiently, and (2) objects can be used to state and solve complex constraint problems more easily and more efficiently. This chapter argues that the framework approach is better adapted to the requirements of embedded object-oriented constraint satisfaction than is the language-based approach. This chapter proposes such a framework for stating and solving constraint problems involving objects and illustrates it with various examples.

Chapter 18, "Developing Frameworks to Support Design Reuse," proposes a generative methodology for the design and rapid prototyping of component-based systems, applicable in particular to the real-time distributed domain and hardware-software codesign. The approach commences with high-level support for structural reuse, ultimately leading to an application-specific framework supporting component reuse within an automated environment. In this context, a framework consists of a repository of formally defined structural patterns, or *styles*, a repository of components, and rules to instantiate a selected pattern from the style repository with components selected from the component repository. The approach addresses structural reuse on three abstraction levels and by different mechanisms: (1) the topological level, (2) the architectural level, and (3) the system level.

The *topological level* deals with the gross organization of a system as specified in terms of highly reusable, graph-theoretic constructions called *styles*. A style can specify a generic pattern, such as a *serial*, *parallel*, or *star* configuration of a set of components; or it can specify a more specific pattern, such as the complex topology of an ATM switch fabric, the topology of a canonical compiler, or that of a client-server system. Components are represented by *nodes,* and connections by *edges*. At this level, individual components are not assigned functionality. Within the topological level, structural reuse is supported by the ability to (1) compose more complex patterns from simpler styles, and (2) instantiate a variable or generic style into a specific pattern. The *architectural level* adds more detail: Interfaces are defined for components, and connections are refined into bindings between interface ports. Within this level, structural reuse is supported mainly by parametric architectures. The *system level* is where components are assigned their respective functionality in a target language. The system-level language can be an implementation, a specification, or a modeling language, and is independent of the two higher levels as long as it supports component-based development through a system-structuring method based on interface connection. Existing components stored in a repository are reused at this stage to further drive the design of the system. The methodology is demonstrated by a codesign example taken from the telecommunications domain.

Chapter 19, "Language Support for Application Framework Design," discusses the relationship between framework design and language constructs for two reasons: (1) Designing frameworks requires the ability to give the framework designer precise control over aspects of the framework extensions, and (2) the framework constraints should be specified such that they are statically checkable. Four existing language constructs are discussed: *generalized block structure, generalized inheritance, generalized virtuality,* and *singular objects*. The chapter discusses how these language constructs give precise means for controlling the framework extensions in statically checkable ways.

CHAPTER 13

Hierarchical and Distributed Constraint Satisfaction Systems

A constraint c is a relation which links a set of variables $X = \{x_1, x_2, \ldots, x_n\}$, each associated to a set of domain values $V = \{v_1, v_2, \ldots, v_n\}$ by means of arithmetic, logic, and functional operators. A constraint satisfaction (CS) problem is defined by (1) a set of logical variables which represent the characteristic parameters of a system for a given computational problem (for example, the position of a set of points in a graphical editor), and (2) a set of constraints between those variables which represent the invariant properties of the system (for example, the distances between the corners of a square). The solution to a CS problem is the set of variable assignments that satisfies all the defined constraints. A CS system is a computational environment, which provides the application developer with a set of tools to declare variables, specify constraints, and solve CS problems. A large number of problems in artificial intelligence and other areas of computer science can be specified as special cases of the CS problem (for a survey, see [Kumar 1992]). Some examples are machine vision, belief maintenance, scheduling, temporal reasoning, graph problems, and graphical interfaces. The strength of the approach is that CS systems allow a programmer to state in a declarative way a relation that has to be maintained between variables, rather than requiring him or her to write procedures specifically to do the maintenance.

However, traditional CS systems experience numerous problems. First, the abstraction level offered by these systems is often very low. Constraints can be defined only on variables with low-level domain values (integers, real numbers, and so on) even though it would be more natural and desirable to define constraints on more complex entities and data structures. Second, they do not support control structures such as iteration or recursion for constraint definition. Finally, few constraint systems recognize the fundamental importance of application reuse. All of these inconveniences have made the idea of combining the CP paradigm with other paradigms very attractive and interesting (see, for example, [Hyvonen 1995; Puget 1992]).

The aim of this chapter is to describe the Constraint Object-Oriented Programming (COOP) framework, which integrates the OO programming paradigm with the CP paradigm. The framework is provided with a set of classes written in C++, which allows the application developer to specify variables, constraints, and solving algorithms. The framework has proved to be well suited for applications that allow a seamless hierarchical and distributed decomposition of the CS problem to be carried out. The rest of the chapter is organized as follows. *Section 13.1* illustrates a case study in the Flexible Manufacturing Systems (FMS) domain. *Section 13.2* presents the framework and *Section 13.3* discusses related work, while *Section 13.4* draws some conclusions.

13.1 The Case Study

As a case study of the theory outlined in the following, the development of a production planning and scheduling system for a multistage, multiproduct manufacturing environment has been chosen. The generally accepted reference model for Flexible Manufacturing Systems (FMS), as specified by the U.S. National Bureau of Standards (NBS) is characterized by a hierarchical control architecture. The layers of the architecture are indicated as Facility, Shop, Cell, Workstation, Machine, and Equipment. Each layer contains control modules, which are the servers to a higher-level client and, in turn, are the clients of lower-level subservers [Brugali 1997]. Each Machine module controls a pool of resources (for example, a robot arm or a lathe machine) and performs a specific set of operations (such as cutting or drilling).

The production model is the store-and-forward type: At each layer of the hierarchy (according to the time-scale resolution considered) lots of parts flow from one control module to the next and wait in intermediary buffers according to the specific sequence of operations (called the *job*) to be performed [Croce 1993]. Each operation requires the exclusive use of the resources belonging to the corresponding control module and is characterized by a processing time, which depends from the specific lot to be processed. Each job must be completed within an interval specified by its release and due time. The production-planning problem (called *job-shop scheduling*) consists of defining a schedule that determines the starting time of each operation on each lot, so that all of the jobs are completed within their due dates.

The production-planning problem can be specified as a CS problem. It consists of a set of *temporal consistency* constraints and *resource consistency* constraints between a set of variables which represent the starting time and duration time of each operation on each lot.

A *temporal consistency* constraint between modules states that for a given lot, each operation can start only when the previous one is finished. Each lot might undergo a different sequence of operations. Let $start_{i,j}$ represent the start time of operation i on lot j, and $duration_{i,j}$ the duration of operation i on lot j. Formally, a temporal constraint can be stated as follows:

$$start_{i,j} + duration_{i,j} \leq start_{i+1,j}$$

A *resource consistency* constraint between lots states that a given operation can process only one lot at a time. In the general case, for each operation the processing order between lots is not fixed. This means that all the possible permutations between lots have to be evaluated in order to find a solution. Using the notation defined here, it is possible to write the following constraints:

$$\text{start}_{i,j} + \text{duration}_{i,j} \leq \text{start}_{i,j+1} \quad \text{or} \quad \text{start}_{i,j+1} + \text{duration}_{i,j+1} \leq \text{start}_{i,j}$$

13.2 The Framework

The framework integrates the OO and CP paradigms by objectifying the basic elements of a constraint (for example, variables and operators) and by allowing the developer to group constraints inside object definitions.

From the CP point of view, the framework makes it possible for the application developer to partition a CS problem into a collection of interdependent CS subproblems, each one specified inside an object definition.

From the OO point of view, the framework allows standard imperative object-oriented programs to be written without forcing any alteration of programming style. In the imperative portions of the program that do not use constraints, the programmer is allowed to create objects and to send messages to their interfaces without being aware of the fact that constraints are used inside.

Currently, the framework implements the solving algorithm described in [Hyvonen 1992], which uses interval arithmetic. Each constrained variable is associated with an initial interval domain, which contains values which may be not consistent with the defined constraints. The solving algorithm refines the initial interval domains as far as possible without losing possible exact solutions, and this is done so that the minimal consistent subinterval can be determined for each variable within its domain [Hyvonen 1992].

For the purpose of our case study, the main characteristic of interval arithmetic is the possibility of writing inequality constraints as equality constraints (see [APIC 1995] for a survey on interval computation).

13.2.1 Objectifying the Variables

Consider a manufacturing operation (for example, drilling) on two lots of parts (called i and $i + 1$). The starting time variables and duration constants of each job are represented by the vectors s_drilling[] and d_drilling[] of type DoubleI, the class provided by the framework that represents an interval between two real numbers. All the logical, arithmetic, and assignment operators of class DoubleI are redefined, so that the programmer is allowed to write the following resource consistency constraint in C++:

```
Constraint c = s_drilling[i] + d_drilling[i] == s_drilling[i+1];
```

The class Constraint internally represents a constraint as a tree structure. The instances of class Constraint are stored inside a collection and processed by the solving algorithm. The framework provides the abstract class Solver, which has to be specialized with specific solving algorithms (for example, the class DoubleISolver for interval arithmetic).

A CS system for an industrial manufacturing process may consist of hundreds of variables and constraints. Following the previous example, all the variables and constraints of an application would be defined in the same scope and solved simultaneously. In order to dominate the complexity of a real application, it is convenient to group decision variables according to the entities (objects) identified in the model of the system. For this purpose, the framework allows variables and constraints to be specified inside user-defined classes.

The framework provides the class ActiveVariable, which embeds a thread of control. ActiveVariable is the superclass of every class (such as Operation) that encapsulates constraints. The class ActiveVariable has a reference to an object of class Server, which has to be specialized inside each subclass of ActiveVariable. In this way, every subclass of ActiveVariable executes, through polymorphism, the solving algorithm that is best suited to the kind of constraints it encapsulates.

The class ActiveVariable encapsulates an object of class Collection that is used to store the constraints defined in the constructor of ActiveVariable subclasses. Constraints are inserted into the collection using the method addConstraints( ). The class ActiveVariable has the public method solve( ), which has to be explicitly invoked by a client object when the value of a constrained variable has been changed.

Consider the production-planning example. Each operation is conveniently modeled as an object of class Operation, which specializes the class ActiveVariable (see Figure 13.1). Each Operation object encapsulates the public vector start[ ] of starting time variables (one for each lot to be processed), the public vector and duration[ ] of duration constants (one for each type of lot), and a private set of resource constraints between starting time variables and duration constants. In order to solve resource consistency constraints, the framework implements a two-step algorithm (see the method solve( ) in Figure 13.1). For each operation, the first step selects one possible resource consistency constraint between lots, which corresponds to a specific ordering of the lot to be processed by an operation. The second step (the solving algorithm) evaluates a solution (if it exists) for the selected set of constraints. In the class Operation, the two-step algorithm makes use of the temporary variables t_st[ ] and t_dt[ ].

An important aspect of the active variable concept previously described is that active variables uniformly repeat themselves at different layers of the inclusion hierarchy of an application, and active variables may encapsulate and/or be encapsulated by other active variables, along with the constraints defined over them.

Supporting constraints over arbitrary objects in a general way presents a problem for constraint languages: User-defined datatypes do not usually contain enough semantic information for the built-in constraint solvers to reason about the constraints on them at their level of abstraction. In the current design of the framework, constraints on active variables are defined in terms of constraints on their public members.

In the production-planning example, manufacturing operations are grouped by the machines that support their execution. Using the framework, the class Machine, which specializes the class ActiveVariable, has been implemented. The class Machine encapsulates instances of class Operation and temporal consistency constraints between their public members start[ ] and duration[ ].

```
class Operation: public ActiveVariable {
   private:
      DoubleI t_st[LOTS], t_dt[LOTS];   // temporary variables
      Constraint *c;                    // pointer
   public:
      DoubleI start[LOTS];              // vector of start variables
      DoubleI duration[LOTS];           // vector of duration constants

      Operation() {
         solver = new DoubleISolver(); // solver is in ActiveVariable
         for(int i=0; i<LOTS-1; i++) {
            c = new Constraint(t_st[i] + t_dt[i] == t_st[i+1]);
            addConstraint(c);           // defined in ActiveVariable
         }
      }
      Boolean solve(){
         for( ; ; ) {                   // enumerates the variable
                                        // assignments
            t_st[i] = start[j];         // initializes the temporary
                                        // variables
            t_dt[i] = duration[j];
            ...
            if(solver->solve()){
               start[j] = t_st[i];      // updates the start variables
               ...
               return TRUE;
            }
         return FALSE;
      }
};
```

Figure 13.1 Constraint definition in the class Operation.

Figure 13.2 shows the implementation of the class Machine. It encapsulates two private members of class Operation, op1 and op2. It defines the public vectors start[] and end[], which represent start and end times of a machine to execute each lot. For each machine, start and end times are specified at the higher level of the control hierarchy by the Shop module.

Now consider the behavior of a Machine object. When the Shop module assigns new start and end times to one machine, the machine's solver is notified. It tries to reinforce the temporal constraints between the operations supported by the machine by assigning new values to their start times. In turn, each Operation object has to resatisfy its internal constraints. Because Operation objects are active variables, their solver can execute their constraints in parallel. In order to promote the parallel execution of the solvers, a two-step algorithm for the assignment operations of new values to the pub-

```
class Machine: public ActiveVariable {
   private:
      Operation op1, op2;            // operation objects
      Constraint *c;                 // pointer
   public:
      DoubleI start[LOTS];           // vector of start variables
      DoubleI end[LOTS];             // vector of end variables

      Machine() {
         solver = new DoubleISolver();
         for(int i=0; i<LOTS; i++) {   // temporal consistency
                                       // constraints
            c = new Constraint(op1.start[i]+op1.duration[i]
                              ==op2.start[i]);
            addConstraint(c);
         }
         c = new Constraint(op2.start[i]+op2.duration[i]==end[i]);
         addConstraint(c);
      }
      Boolean solve(){
         for( ; ; )(
            if(solver->solve()){
               if(op1.solve() && op2.solve())
                  return TRUE;
            }
            ...
         }
         return FALSE;
      }
};
```

Figure 13.2   Operation instances inside the Machine class.

lic members of an ActiveVariable has been defined. In the current example, the first step of the algorithm is the sequential evaluation of the new values for the public members start[] of each Operation object (that is, the machine's solver tries to reinforce its temporal consistency constraints). The second step is the parallel execution of the solvers of each operation.

Figure 13.3 shows the interaction diagram between the Shop, the Machine, and the operations op1 and op2. Two situations are possible. First, the parallel execution of each operation may succeed (see Figure 13.3*a*); that is, the starting time values calculated by the Machine may be compatible with the resource constraints of each operation. Or, the parallel execution may fail. The designer of a concrete application has to specify what happens when a parallel execution fails. One possibility is that the machine's solver iterates the sequential evaluation until a correct assignment is found,

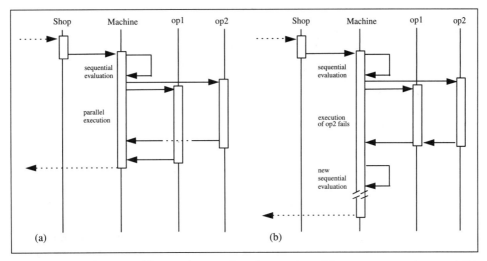

Figure 13.3 Shop, Machine, and operations interaction: (*a*) correct execution, and (*b*) execution failure.

or a specific condition is true. Another possibility is that the failure is propagated to the upper level in the hierarchy of ActiveVariable inclusion.

Active variables at adjacent levels in the hierarchy of inclusion communicate by direct method invocation and through events. An ActiveVariable client starts the solver of its private ActiveVariable members by invoking their public method solve( ). The solver of an ActiveVariable member notifies its client that its execution has been terminated by raising an event. Figure 13.4 shows the Specification Description Language (SDL) diagram [CCITT 1986] that represents the sequential evaluation and the parallel execution of an ActiveVariable.

Because active variables may be encapsulated by and may encapsulate other active variables, their solvers broadcast and listen to the same events. However, using the

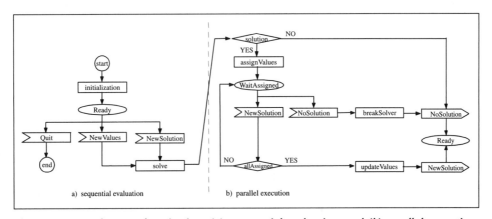

Figure 13.4 Solver synchronization: (*a*) sequential evaluation, and (*b*) parallel execution.

Broadcast/Listener mechanism [Aarsten 1996], it is possible to specify that a solver listens to specific events only if they are raised by the lower-level active variables. Figure 13.4 shows the event NoSolution, which notifies the upper level that the assignment operation has failed, and the event NewSolution, which notifies the upper level that all the parallel executions have succeeded.

When the solver is idle (that is, its current state is Ready), it listens to three events: (1) Quit is used for program termination; (2) NewValues is used to start the solver when the upper-level client invokes the solve( ) method; and (3) NewSolution is raised by a lower-level ActiveVariable to inform the client's solver that the value of some constrained variable has changed.

The last event is particularly meaningful in FMS applications. Consider a Machine that is performing some operations on a lot of parts according to a specific schedule. In the case of machine failure, the Machine has to notify the Shop module that the start times of some operations have been delayed; that is to say, their starting time variables have new values. The Shop module will then start a new sequential evaluation of its constrained variables. This new evaluation will require one or more Machines to execute their solvers in parallel and then execute the solvers of the Operation that they encapsulate.

13.2.2 Objectifying the Operators

The previous example shows how constraints are written over the public members of an active variable. In order to allow the designer to specify a CS problem on a higher level of abstraction, it should be possible to introduce problem-oriented dependencies between objects: The goal is to provide the programmer with the possibility of defining constraints on active variables and not on their public members.

The idea is to define new constraints as compositions of user-defined variables and user-defined operators. The framework provides the class MacroOperator, which has to be specialized for each user-defined operator. A macro-operator is an object that encapsulates one or more expressions defined on basic type variables. In particular, the expressions are defined on the public members of the active variable passed as parameters to the macro-operator constructor.

As an example, Figure 13.5 shows the implementation of the macro-operator END_OPERATION, which corresponds to the sum of the starting time and duration time of an operation. Implementation is based on the on-the-fly instantiation of the MacroOperator class. The infix notation has been adopted, so that macro-operators may even be nested inside other macro-operators in order to build every kind of expression. Figure 13.5 also shows the use of the END_OPERATION macro-operator in the implementation of the Machine class constructor of Figure 13.2.

There are several ways to define and use macro-operators in order to build constraints. For example, it is possible to define macro-operators that accept other macro-operators as parameters of their constructor or as right-hand-side parameters. It is also possible to define and use macro-operators using the powerful mechanism of recursion (for more details and examples, follow the link *Project* from www.cim .polito.it/).

```
class END_OPERATION: public MacroOperator {
   private:
      Operation left_op;              // operation object
      Constraint *c;                  // pointer
   public:
      END_OPERATION(Operation & op) {
         left_op = op;                // the = operator has been
                                      // overloaded

      }
      operator ==(Operation & right_op){
         for(int i=0; i<LOTS; i++){
            c = new Constraint(
              left_op.start[i] + left_op.duration[i] ==
                            right_op.start[i]);
            addConstraint(c);         // defined in MetaOperator
         }
      }
};

Machine::Machine()
   addConstraint(END_OPERATION(op1) == op2);
                      // Defined in ActiveVariable. It copies the
                      // constraints
                      // declared in the macro-operator inside the
                      // collection
                      // defined in ActiveVariable
}
```

Figure 13.5 Implementation and use of the END_OPERATION macro-operator.

13.3 Related Works

In recent years, several approaches to the integration of OO and constraint technologies have been proposed.

Kaleidoscope'93 [Lopez 1994]. The third generation of the Kaleidoscope approach offers the advantage that it supports the construct of object identity through constraints by means of object equality, thus providing a clean semantic of identity-based assignments. The construct requires the use of a number of nonstandard annotations—such as constraint duration *once, during,* and *always*—but it is implemented in such a way that a program that does not use constraints may use the standard assignment statements. The approach supports constraints on user-defined datatypes (which are split into constraints on their component parts), but does not allow the user to declare constraints inside objects. Kaleidoscope'93 is designed mainly to support the development of interactive graphical user interfaces.

NEMO-TEC [Shvetsov 1995]. This approach has the peculiarity of integrating subdefined (SD) models and constraint programming. SD models are based on the notion of subdefinite datatypes, which can be associated with a variable of any type and support both qualitative and quantitative information processing. The approach supports joint processing of values of different types and provides some capabilities for parallel computation. In the language of the NEMO-TEC system, the object-oriented approach is used only as a convenient way of describing complex notions; furthermore, because the *prototype-instance* approach was chosen and not the more traditional *class-instance* approach, the system does not seem to be practical for large applications. User-defined objects may be created via the inheritance mechanism or by constructing complex objects from simpler ones. All aspects of object interaction, as well as the principal functional semantics of user objects, are described by constraintlike dependencies realized by SD models: In fact a specific syntax has been introduced in the language.

ILOG Solver [Puget 1992]. The latest version of Solver embeds constraint satisfaction techniques in C++ libraries. The approach offers two means of defining new constraint types—by combining constraints using logical operators or by defining new classes of constraint. However, in the latter case, the meaning of a constraint is defined in a procedural way: The methods of the class describe how the constraint has to be satisfied. This approach has the advantage of allowing the user to specify certain kinds of strategic knowledge that deal with the way the problem should be solved. ILOG Solver has been used successfully to solve some real application problems.

13.4 Summary

This chapter presents a framework for the integration of the CP paradigm with the OO paradigm. It has two main characteristics: It adds expressiveness to the CP paradigm by supporting constraints over user-defined objects, and it adds expressiveness to the OO paradigm by allowing the developer to specify in a declarative way the invariant properties of an object. As Booch points out in [Booch 1991], the description of objects and their mutual relationships is characterized by two distinct and interlaced aspects: the class aspect and the instance aspect.

If an observer who is positioned on the boundary of an object looks inside, he or she will see the class that contains the object's internal description in terms of member variables (representing the object's state) and methods (representing the object's behavior). In the framework described in this chapter, that description may include a set of constraints between the public and private member variables. These constraints represent the invariant properties of that object's behavior.

Vice versa, if the observer looks outside, he or she will see the private environment offered by the class, which encapsulates an instance of that object. In this framework, that private environment interacts with that member object in a typical OO fashion through its interface.

13.5 References

[Aarsten 1996] Aarsten, A., D. Brugali, and G. Menga. Designing concurrent and distributed control architectures. *Communications of the ACM*, Theme Issue on Software Patterns, D. Schmidt, M.E. Fayad, and R. Johnson, editors, 39(10), October, 1996: 50–58.

[APIC 1995] Applications of Interval Computations (APIC). *Proceedings of the International Workshop on Applications of Interval Computations*, El Paso, TX, February 23–25, 1995.

[Booch 1991] Booch, G. *Object Oriented Design with Applications*. Redwood City, CA: Benjamin/Cummings, 1991.

[Brugali 1997] Brugali, D., G. Menga, and A. Aarsten. The framework life span. *Communications of the ACM*, Theme Issue on Object-Oriented Application Frameworks, M.E. Fayad and D. Schmidt, editors, 40(10), October 1997.

[CCITT 1986] The Consultative Committee for International Telegraph and Telephony (CCITT) *Specification and Description Language*. Recommendation Z.100, 1986.

[Croce 1993] Croce, D.F., G. Menga, R. Tadei, M. Cavalotto, and L. Petri. Cellular control of manufacturing systems. *European Journal of Operational Research*, 69, 1993: 498–509.

[Hyvonen 1992] Hyvonen, E. Constraint reasoning based on interval arithmetic: The tolerance propagation approach. *Artificial Intelligence*, 58, 1992: 71–112.

[Hyvonen 1995] Hyvonen, E., and S. De Pascale. C++ library family for interval computations. *Proceedings of the International Workshop on Applications of Interval Computations*, El Paso, TX, February 23–25, 1995.

[Kumar 1992] Kumar, V. Algorithms for constraint-satisfaction problems: A survey. *AI Magazine*, Spring 1992: 32–44.

[Lopez 1994] Lopez, G., B.N. Freeman-Benson, and A. Borning. Constraint and object identity. *Proceedings of the 1994 European Conference on Object-Oriented Programming (ECCOP 1994)*, Bologna, Italy, July 1994.

[Puget 1992] Puget, J. Object oriented constraint programming for transportation problems. *Proceedings of ASTAIR 1992*.

[Shvetsov 1995] Shvetsov, I. A. Semenov, and V. Telerman. Constraint programming based on subdefinite models and its applications. *Proceedings of the Post-Conference Workshop on Parallel Logic Programming Systems*, Portland, OR, December 8, 1995.

CHAPTER 14

Modeling Collections
of Changing
Interdependent Objects

In many domains it is necessary to create and maintain a model of a changing collection of interdependent objects. Such models need to be able to recognize and react to events that require changes in the model, propagating through the model and potentially triggering other changes. These events typically depend on data from several related objects in the model, so recognizing them is not just a simple matter of performing the change when a particular data member of an object is modified, but instead requires reacting to the condition of a number of objects in the model.

Although the importance of inter-object dependencies and the limitations of current object-oriented languages in this respect are well recognized, and various techniques [Helm 1990; Kilov-Harvey 1996] to solve this problem have lately emerged, there is still a lack of acceptance of various proposed solutions to specify and implement these dependencies in the context of object-oriented languages. In particular, lack of support for specifying and implementing these dependencies in commercial object-oriented languages has left the majority of object-oriented programmers to resort to object-oriented techniques to implement their own solutions, such as the Observer pattern [Gamma 1995]. Unfortunately, these are ad hoc solutions, and a systematic coverage without language support is the programmer's responsibility.

We propose a two-pronged framework for the creation and maintenance of models of changing collections of interdependent objects.

The first part of our framework is a collection of classes related to each other by means of *affective relations*—relationships between objects that *affect* one another in some application-important way [Crawford 1995]. The affective relation model does not capture the complete causal relationships between objects (in fact, it is much too weak for that). Instead, the model is a way to organize knowledge about the domain in a coherent way, replacing the use of ad hoc heuristics to determine which of the many domain relationships to include in the model with a small set of general principles for behavioral analysis from affective relations models.

The second part of our framework consists of data-driven object-centered rules that implement changes in the model using the R++ rule extension to C++ [Crawford 1996]. Using data-driven rules results in considerable savings over directly writing methods to implement changes, as there is an incredible amount of bookkeeping and coordination required to keep the model in correspondence with reality when changes can result in changes to other objects, which is often the case in collections of interdependent objects. The rules of R++ fit well within the framework, because these rules are directly integrated into the object hierarchy of C++.

Our framework has been used to implement a system to monitor and diagnose problems with the 4ESS telephone-switching system (the 4ESS handles most AT&T domestic long-distance calls). Unlike traditional device models, affective relations are easy to acquire from front-line experts such as operators and maintenance technicians, because they represent precisely the kind of knowledge that is needed to diagnose routine problems, particularly in complex self-checking devices. The data-driven rules are also easy to write and understand.

14.1 Affective Relations

Affective relations models are applicable to domains satisfying two basic criteria:

- There is a collection of changing objects such that the objects generally interact via known pathways.

- These pathways can be characterized by a small set of affective relationships between objects.

Modeling such a collection consists of creating a set of classes for the types of objects in the collection, in roughly the standard object-oriented manner. During the creation of these classes—in particular, during the creation of the data members of the classes— extra care is taken to seek out and identify the affective relationships, and to ensure that all such relationships have been identified.

There are two kinds of affective relationships. Some affective relationships are common to many domains, such as the whole/part relation. Other affective relationships are specific to particular domains or particular applications, such as the standby relationship in fault-tolerant devices.

The affective relationships in a model provide a skeleton for the reasoning that must be performed in an application using the model. Abstractly, reasoning with affective relationships proceeds by determining the state of key objects, and then propagating this information through the affective relationships to deduce the state of other objects. Actions are then performed based on external information and the states of the objects. The other half of our framework—data-driven object-centered rules—is used to effectively perform these propagations and actions.

To make affective relationships more concrete, the rest of this section presents an example of an affective relations model. In this example, the task is diagnosing a device made up of a collection of components.

14.1.1 Device Representation

The key elements of this device model are (1) a set of basic *classes* (such as Device), (2) a set of diagnostically motivated *affective relations* relating device components, (3) a set of relations relating other classes in the model, and (4) a set of properties and general relationships specifying the semantics of the relations, in other words, the knowledge that is implicit in any explicitly specified knowledge. See Figure 14.1 for a knowledge-level [Newell 1982] description of a portion of the device model. For a symbol-level description of a much larger portion of the device model, see [AT&T 1995].

Affective relations link components to other components in diagnostically useful ways. For example, *immediate-part-of* means that a direct subcomponent-component relationship exists between two devices. *Part-of* reflects direct as well as transitively closed subcomponent-component relations, while its inverse *subpart* reflects direct and transitive component-subcomponent relations. *Depends-on* means that the correct functioning of a device depends on the correct functioning of another device; *dependent* represents the inverse relation between the two devices. *Standby* means that if one device

Classes: **Device   Alarm   Boolean**

Affective relations, and their domain and range:

immediate-part-of	**Device, Device**	*depends-on*	**Device, Device**
part-of	**Device, Device**	*dependent*	**Device, Device**
subpart	**Device, Device**	*standby*	**Device, Device**

Other relations, and their domain and range:

self-alarm	**Device, Alarm**	*functional*	**Device, Boolean**
part-alarm	**Device, Alarm**	*simplex*	**Device, Boolean**
dependent-alarm	**Device, Alarm**		

Properties, and the affective relations they characterize:

Symmetric: *standby*
Transitive: *part-of, subpart*
Inverses: (*part-of, subpart*), (*depends-on, dependent*)

General relationships:

$\forall \mathbf{x} \forall \mathbf{y} [immediate\text{-}part\text{-}of(\mathbf{x},\mathbf{y}) \Rightarrow part\text{-}of(\mathbf{x},\mathbf{y})]$

$\forall \mathbf{x} \forall \mathbf{y} [part\text{-}alarm(\mathbf{x},\mathbf{y}) \equiv \exists \mathbf{z} (subpart(\mathbf{x},\mathbf{z}) \wedge self\text{-}alarm(\mathbf{z},\mathbf{y}))]$

$\forall \mathbf{x} \forall \mathbf{y} [dependent\text{-}alarm(\mathbf{x},\mathbf{y}) \equiv \exists \mathbf{z} (depends\text{-}on(\mathbf{z},\mathbf{x}) \wedge self\text{-}alarm(\mathbf{z},\mathbf{y}))]$

$\forall \mathbf{x} \forall \mathbf{y} [(depends\text{-}on(\mathbf{x},\mathbf{y}) \wedge functional(\mathbf{y},\mathbf{false})) \Rightarrow functional(\mathbf{x},\mathbf{false})]$

$\forall \mathbf{x} [simplex(\mathbf{x},\mathbf{true}) \equiv \forall \mathbf{y} (standby(\mathbf{x},\mathbf{y}) \Rightarrow functional(\mathbf{y},\mathbf{false}))]$

Figure 14.1   Device modeling with affective relations: A partial knowledge-level description.

fails, its standby partner will take over automatically; it also means that reliable operation is jeopardized if one device fails.

Other relations link devices to other classes in the model. *Self-alarm* means that a device is signaling an alarm. However, a problem with one device may not necessarily cause that device to itself signal an alarm; instead, the problem may affect a second device, causing *it* to signal an alarm. *Part-alarm* and *dependent-alarm* link devices to alarms signaled by other devices. *Part-alarm* relates a device to an alarm on another device when the alarming device is a subpart of the device; *dependent-alarm* relates devices to alarms based on depends-on. Devices are either *functional* or not. If a device depends on another device that is not functional, the dependent device is also not functional. If a device is in *simplex* mode, it means that none of the device's standbys are functional.

To illustrate the use of these relations, we examine in some detail a digital toll-switching system known as a 4ESS switch. A portion of the basic class hierarchy is shown in Figure 14.2. (To eliminate jargon, hardware component names have been replaced with ABC, and so on.) The class Device is broken down into a series of 4ESS-specific subclasses. Each major type of component of the 4ESS (down to the level of field-replaceable units) adds a class to the general device ontology shown in Figure 14.1.

Figure 14.3 shows how some of the key portions of the model of the 4ESS switch are instantiated using the general and domain-specific portions of the ontology shown in Figures 14.1 and 14.2, respectively. The actual 4ESS switch and its components are each defined as members of one of the device classes; for example, Device(4ESS) defines the switch 4ESS to be an instance of the type Device. Note that the model is *isomorphic* to the device: For each type of component in the device there is a class in the model, and for each component in the device there is one instance in the model. Affective relations are asserted between device instantiations—for example, immediate-part-of(Clock 0, 4ESS). Recall that the properties of and the general relationships between the affective relations (see Figure 14.1) specify the knowledge that is implicit in an explicitly defined model such as Figure 14.3. Thus, because of the first general relationship in Figure 14.1, immediate-part-of(Clock 0, 4ESS) entails part-of(Clock 0, 4ESS), which in turn entails the inverse relation subpart (4ESS, Clock 0). Similar inferences can be drawn from the other immediate-part-of assertions. Then, transitivity entails further subpart and part-of relations. The depends-on assertions entail a set of inverse dependent relations. Because standby is defined to be symmetric, standby(A-CNTL 0, A-CNTL1) entails standby(A-CNTL 1, A-CNTL0), and similarly for the other standby assertions.

Figure 14.4 pictorially represents the model. Each box represents a device. The immediate nesting of boxes depicts immediate-part-of relations. The labeled arrows depict some of the other explicit (for example, standby[A-CNTL 0, A-CNTL]) and implicit (for example, standby[A-CNTL 1, A-CNTL0]) affective relations linking devices.

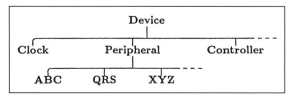

Figure 14.2 Partial taxonomy of 4ESS device types.

Device (4ESS)	depends-on(A-CNTL 0, Clock 0)	immediate-part-of(Clock 0, 4ESS)
Clock(Clock 0)	depends-on(A-CNTL 1, Clock 1)	immediate-part-of(Clock 1, 4ESS)
Clock(Clock 1)	depends-on(Q-CNTL 0, Clock 0)	immediate-part-of(ABC 6, 4ESS)
ABC(ABC 6)	depends-on(Q-CNTL 1, Clock 1)	immediate-part-of(A-CNTL 0, ABC 6)
Controller(A-CNTL 0)		immediate-part-of(A-CNTL 1, ABC 6)
Controller(A-CNTL 1)	standby(A-CNTL 0, A-CNTL 1)	immediate-part-of(SPC 0, ABC 6)
SPC(SPC 0)	standby(SPC 0, SPC 1)	immediate-part-of(SPC 1, ABC 6)
SPC(SPC 1)	standby(Q-CNTL 0, Q-CNTL 1)	immediate-part-of(QRS 0, 4ESS)
QRS(QRS 0)		immediate-part-of(Q-CNTL 0, QRS 0)
Controller(Q-CNTL 0)		immediate-part-of(Q-CNTL 1, QRS 0)
Controller(Q-CNTL 1)		

Figure 14.3 A portion of the device model of the 4ESS switch.

Note that affective relations among components are *not* traditional relations of structure, behavior, or function, except in some very abstract sense. Unlike typical behavioral models, the relations do not define or constrain the input/output behavior of components. Rather, affective relations express aspects of the design at a level of abstraction that expert human troubleshooters use to link symptoms to suspects. This is illustrated following. Furthermore, the use of the model for diagnostic reasoning not only motivates but also limits what must be explicitly represented in the model. We do *not* need to represent every type of component or every relationship between components, but only those that participate in an expert's causal analysis of alarms.

14.1.2 Diagnostic Reasoning from the Model

Our use of an explicit model of the components of a monitored device and affective relations between components brings many of the benefits of traditional model-based

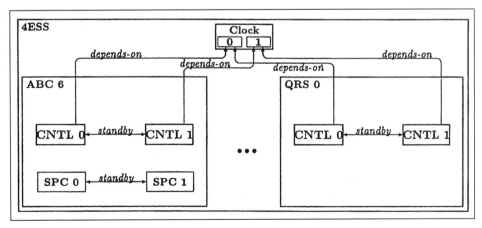

Figure 14.4 Pictorial representation of part of the 4ESS switch model.

reasoning to domains, such as 4ESS alarm monitoring, where conventional models are too costly to acquire. For example, one benefit is that the approach allows us to replace heuristic rules of first-generation expert systems with diagnostic rules that reason from the device model using general principles expressed in terms of the affective relations. This section informally contrasts our approach to diagnostic reasoning in the 4ESS domain with a previously developed heuristic approach.

In our domain, diagnostic reasoning involves real-time monitoring of alarms and other informational messages from the 4ESS switches—for example, to correlate alarm messages coming from the various components, ignore transient alarms, recognize chronic problems, run diagnostics, and signal problems requiring human attention. The monitoring system takes input in the form of alarm messages and produces output in the form of warning and action messages to field technicians. An expert system was originally developed for monitoring of the 4ESS switches in 1990. The system was designed as a conventional rule-based system using an OPS5-compatible language. It contained several hundred heuristics gleaned from many interviews with domain experts. Three example heuristics are shown here.

- If F-level alarms are occurring concurrently for more than one component in a peripheral device, add the number of alarms together and threshold on the sum.

- If a type-ABC component is in *normal* mode, perform thresholding of alarms, but if it is in *simplex* mode, ignore thresholding and alert on any F-level alarms.

- If F-level alarms are occurring on different type-ABC and -QRS components, but all alarms are on the same *controller* number, then suspect the *clock*.

Device representation and reasoning with affective relations allows us to replace such heuristics with diagnostic rules that reason from our device model using first principles. For example, one such general principle is the following:

Concurrent alarms on multiple components of a larger device indicate a problem at the device level.

We capture this principle by using part-alarm to link alarms on components to any larger devices the components are part of. We then threshold on the number of such links (looking for a device linked to a large number of alarms on different subparts). This subsumes the first heuristic rule and is clearly both simpler and more general. For example, the new rule covers all types of alarms and all levels of nesting in the part-of hierarchy. Of course, this reformulation is only possible because of the explicit representation of the immediate-part-of, part-of, and subpart relations between components. (Thresholds go up as one travels up the part-of hierarchy—for example, many alarms on many components are necessary before concluding that there is a problem with the 4ESS.)

We can also take advantage of the explicit encoding of standby. In the normal situation where a component is active and its standby is ready, alarms undergo thresholding before an alert is issued. However, if the standby is out of service, then *any* alarm should generate an immediate alert. By making standby explicit in our model, and defining simplex in terms of this affective relation, the second heuristic rule can be replaced with the following more general principle:

If a device's standby is not functional, then alert on any alarm.

Again, note that the new rule covers *all* devices that have a standby, not just ABCs, and similarly covers all types of alarms.

Finally, a dependency-based rule of monitoring allows us to recognize the failure of a device from alarms on the device's dependents. For example, if Clock 0 in Figure 14.4 is failing, this may be indicated by alarms on the dependent components CNTL 0 in ABC 6 and CNTL 0 in QRS 0. By making depends-on explicit in our model, the third heuristic rule (whose rationale for implicating the clock is particularly obscure) can be replaced with the following more general principle:

Concurrent alarms on multiple dependents of a device indicate a problem with that device.

This rule clarifies that diagnostic reasoning traces up a dependency chain to identify a common point of failure. Depends-on can also be exploited to propagate state information, as shown in the fourth general relationship of Figure 14.1.

14.2 Data-Driven Rules

Once a collection of classes has been modeled using affective relations, the next step in our process is to write data-driven rules that model the changes in the objects being modeled. Data-driven rules are ideal for this purpose because they hide the many details that need to be programmed if these changes are modeled directly in the object-oriented programming language.

For this step to be viable, we need a rule system that supports the classes of the model and the affective relations therein. Such a rule system thus has to be directly tied to an object-oriented programming language. This is a problem in that most rule systems do not integrate well with an object-oriented programming language, often requiring their own data structures. We have thus designed and implemented a data-driven rule extension to C++, called R++, that integrates data-driven rules directly into the C++ class and object hierarchy [Crawford 1996; Litman 1997].

R++ rules are associated with classes, just as data and functions are associated with classes, and directly with the objects that are instances of the class. In effect, we view rules as *member rules* of classes. Because rules are members of classes, they have class-specific names, just like data members and member functions. Also, rules follow the same access limitations as member functions.

R++ rules are different from member functions in that they cannot be called. Instead, a rule consists of a condition and an action. Whenever some change to object memory causes the condition of a rule to succeed, the action of the rule is executed. (There is, of course, more to be said about just when and how the action of rules are executed, but this is the basic idea.)

R++ rules are *path-based* in that their conditions must start with some root object and can reach other objects only by following paths of pointers (*access paths*), binding variables to objects on these paths as they go. Such path-based rules are not new, having appeared explicitly as *access-limited rules* in the Algernon implementation of access-limited logic [Crawford 1990; Crawford 1991]. The action of a path-based rule has access to the object bindings from its condition.

The association of rules with classes provides a type for the root object of a rule, namely that class with which the rule is associated. Further, the association provides a specification for when objects are brought to the attention of rules, namely that the *creation* of an instance of a class brings the object to the attention of the member rules of the class. The only way to remove an object from consideration by the rules of its classes is to destroy it. Therefore a rule associated with a class is active on all objects that belong to the class, which makes the rules easier to understand.

The restriction that R++ rules must follow access paths fits well into the affective relations modeling paradigm, as one result of the paradigm will be relationships between objects that affect one another. If rules could perform arbitrary joins of objects, as in most rule systems [Cooper 1988], they would not be following the affective relations modeling paradigm.

Rules can be overridden in subclasses, just as member functions can be. A subclass can have a rule with the same name as a rule in a superclass. Such a rule will override the rule in the superclass for instances of the subclass.

Because R++ rules work directly on all instances of a class, there is no need for a separate working memory nor even a mechanism to keep track of which objects are active in the rule system. The object-oriented paradigm provides all the control required, obviating any need for control of rules via explicit activation or deactivation of rules or via grouping of rules.

The conditions of R++ rules monitor data in various objects. Changes to this data may cause the condition of the rule to be satisfied, or to be satisfied in a different manner than before. Therefore, the conditions of rules are reevaluated whenever the data they inspect changes or when a new object of the appropriate type is constructed. We call these changes *relevant changes*. There is no need for any other mechanism for causing the conditions of rules to be evaluated—making changes to object data is the only mechanism required or allowed. The only priority mechanism for R++ rules is that rules on subclasses are run before rules on superclasses.

14.2.1 Rule Syntax and Semantics

R++ rules look and act as much like the rest of C++ as possible. Externally, R++ rules are declared and defined in a manner similar to C++ class members, as previously indicated, and as shown in the simplified rule syntax given in Figure 14.5.

The condition (left-hand side) of an R++ rule is a sequence of C++ boolean expressions interspersed with variable bindings. The boolean expressions and the expressions in the bindings can, of course, use the variables bound earlier, just as in C++.

The bindings in a condition look very much like C++ variable definitions. The first kind of binding, for example Person * mate = spouse, looks just like a C++ variable definition, and simply sets a variable to the value of an expression, succeeding if that value is non-null. The example binding declares a variable of type Person and sets it to the value of this->spouse, succeeding only if the value is non-null. The other kinds of bindings—for example, Person * child @ children—are similar to C++ variable definitions but use @ instead of =. These are branch bindings, where the @ should be read as *at* or *in*, and they bind a variable to elements of a set of values. The example branch binding says to iterate over all values in the children data member, which is declared to be a set of pointers to persons, succeeding for each element of the set.

A condition is evaluated in the obvious way. It succeeds for those successful bindings that make the boolean expressions evaluate to true.

```
<rule declaration> ::= rule <identifier> ;
<rule definition> ::= rule <class name>::<identifier> {
                          <condition> => <action>
                      }
<action> ::= <statement>⁺
<condition> ::= <binding> |
                <boolean expression> |
                <binding> && <condition> |
                <boolean expression> && <condition>
<binding> ::=
     <class name> * <identifier> = <expression> |
     <class name> * <identifier> @ <field> |
     <class name> * <identifier> @ <variable>-><field>
```

Figure 14.5 Simplified R++ Rule Syntax.

The action (right-hand side) of an R++ rule is just a sequence of C++ statements. In the action of a rule, the variables bound in its condition can be used as expected.

14.2.2 Rule Execution

As indicated earlier in this chapter, there are three parts to rule execution:

- Triggering of rules by relevant change
- Subsequent evaluation of the rule condition, possibly delayed if other rules have been triggered by the same change
- Execution of the rule action if the rule condition was satisfied

The conditions of R++ rules are evaluated only in response to relevant change (including relevant construction). However, the portion of the condition that is evaluated in response to a relevant change is unspecified, as is the order of evaluation. Thus, rule conditions are normally side effect–free.

The actions of R++ rules are executed only when their conditions successfully evaluate to true, and only on the data that caused the condition to evaluate to true. As a change to a data member can cause more than one rule condition to evaluate to true, the action of a rule may be delayed from the time of the change that caused its condition to evaluate to true. If the data that caused the condition to evaluate to true is changed in the meantime, the rule's action will not be executed.

R++ ensures that rules do not execute on old data, nor execute more than once on changed data. For example, if a relevant change (or construction) triggers two rules in a way that would satisfy both rule conditions, but the first rule to be evaluated and executed changes the original triggering data, thereby retriggering the same two rules, the second rule will eventually be evaluated on the newest data (and be executed only if its condition is satisfied). Although the second rule is triggered twice in this scenario, it will be executed at most once and only on the newest data.

The actions of R++ rules are executed whenever possible under these criteria. Thus, no rules are waiting to run if and only if there is no current collection of data that causes a rule's condition to evaluate to true for which the rule's action has not been run.

14.3 A Detailed Example

Our framework has been used to build a monitoring and diagnostic application in AT&T. This application monitors the activity of 4ESS switching systems in the AT&T long-distance telephone network and attempts to diagnose the problems that they encounter. The basic activity in the system is the analysis of alarms. Alarm messages from the switch, in conjunction with the semantics of the model, trigger the dynamic creation of and changes to relevant portions of the device model. From this model, general-purpose diagnostic rules determine the root cause of the alarm.

At start-up, the model of the 4ESS contains only a small set of core device types, associated instantiations, and immediate-part-of relations between the instantiations. This is because in a complex device such as the 4ESS, we have found it to be prohibitively difficult to build up a complete device configuration in advance. In general, device types, as well as the number and arrangement of actual components, vary among switching installations. Most devices and affective relations are thus dynamically created, in response to both the computation of the entailments of the model and to the rule-based processing of the alarms. For example, returning to the model of Figures 14.3 and 14.4, only 4ESS, Clock 0, Clock 1, and the two immediate-part-of relations relating the 4ESS and the clocks are initially asserted in the model.

An example of an alarm message from the switch is shown in the top portion of Figure 14.6. (We have simplified the alarm to enhance the clarity of this section.) The message assigns a unique identifier to the alarm, specifies the alarm type, and states that the alarm is occurring on the specified subunit of the specified unit of the 4ESS. That is, units link devices to the 4ESS as a component, while subunits link devices to units.

Processing of the alarm causes the device model to be updated as shown in the middle of Figure 14.6. Intuitively, a representation of the alarm is created and added to the model; the devices mentioned in the message are either found in the model or created and added to the model; and the alarm just created is related to the lowest-level device mentioned in the alarm. In particular, the first assertion in the figure creates an instantiation alarm1 and declares it to be a member of the class Alarm. (Alarms also have an internal structure which is not shown—for example, alarm1 has a slot *id* filled by *22257*, and so on.) The unit and subunit devices referred to in the alarm message will also be added to the model, along with the corresponding configurational relations between the 4ESS and the unit, and between the unit and the subunit. Thus, device ABC 6 is instantiated, declared to be a member of the class ABC, and linked to the device 4ESS (already instantiated at start-up) via immediate-part-of. Similar processing occurs for A-CNTL 0. Finally, a self-alarm assertion is added which relates A-CNTL 0, the device component that actually signaled the alarm, to alarm1.

As at start-up, the semantics of the model in conjunction with the immediate-part-of assertions will cause implicit part-of and subpart relations to be explicitly added to the model, as shown at the bottom of Figure 14.6. These assertions, in conjunction with the second general relationship in Figure 14.1, will in turn cause the assertions part-

New Alarm:
id:22257; type:F-LEV;
unit:ABC 6; subunit:A-CNTL 0

Assertions added to the device model:
Alarm(alarm1)
ABC(ABC 6)
immediate-part-of(**ABC 6, 4ESS**)
Controller(A-CNTL 0)
immediate-part-of(**A-CNTL 0, ABC 6**)
self-alarm(**A-CNTL 0, alarm1**)

Further implicit assertions:
part-of(**ABC 6, 4ESS**)
part-of(**A-CNTL 0, ABC 6**)
part-of(**A-CNTL 0, 4ESS**)
subpart(**4ESS, ABC 6**)
subpart(**ABC 6, A-CNTL 0**)
subpart(**4ESS, A-CNTL 0**)
part-alarm(**ABC 6, alarm1**)
part-alarm(**4ESS, alarm1**)

Figure 14.6 A simplified alarm message, and some device model additions.

alarm(ABC 6, alarm1) and part-alarm(4ESS, alarm1) to be added to the model. Thus, the alarm is propagated to other devices to which it is relevant, by adding a part-alarm relation between any devices the alarming device is a component of, and the alarm. In this case, it adds this relation between the two components that have A-CNTL 0 as a subpart (4ESS and ABC 6), and A-CNTL 0's alarm (alarm1). This captures the fact that a failure in 4ESS or in ABC 6 could have caused the alarm. At this point the computation of the implicit portions of the model is complete; initial processing of the alarm has resulted in dynamic construction of a portion of the model shown in Figures 14.3 and 14.4, and incorporation of the alarm into the model. Although not illustrated here, other relations in the model—for example, depends-on and standby—can also be dynamically created. This is done by supplementing the general relationships shown in Figure 14.1 with domain-specific relationships—for example, for all devices of type controller, the device depends-on the clock device having the same number. Thus, when an alarm causes a controller to be created, the appropriate depends-on assertion from the controller to a clock is entailed.

Once our model is created, diagnostic rules of inference determine the root cause of the alarms by reasoning from the model. In particular, creation of the relations self-alarm, part-alarm, and dependent-alarm between devices and alarms triggers the diagnostic rules. For example, the following rule formalizes the first example from the diagnostic reasoning section (*Section 14.1.2*):

For all x and for all y, part-alarm(x,y) and part-threshold(x,true) implies functional(x,false).

(In reality, a warning is sent and further evidence is obtained before inferring nonfunctional.)

The rule is an example of a thresholding rule that determines when a nonalarming component is not functional, based on thresholding of the part-alarm relations in which it is involved. The domain-specific relation part-threshold holds if there are a sufficient number of alarming devices that are components of the device x. When a threshold is met and a device is asserted to be nonfunctional, a warning message can be sent to a technician.

Assume part-threshold is defined to be true when a device has at least two alarming components. The rule would thus not be satisfied for any device after the first alarm. If the switch then generated an alarm on another component of ABC 6, say self-alarm(SPC 0, alarm1), part-alarm(ABC 6, alarm2) would be among the newly entailed relations, and part-threshold(ABC 6, true) would now be satisfied. This would entail functional(ABC 6, false), and an operator could be sent a warning message. Again, this example illustrates how our approach supports reasoning from the device model using general principles involving affective relations.

14.4 Summary

We believe that the combination of affective relations and data-driven object-centered rules is an effective framework for modeling interdependent collections of changing objects. Our experience with using this framework in a diagnostic application has produced considerable benefits, including a more capable system and approximately 50 percent cost savings by reducing development and software maintenance time [Mishra 1996].

14.5 References

[AT&T 1995] AT&T Bell Laboratories. *R++ User Manual.* www.research.att.com/sw/tools/r++/UserManual.ps, 1995.

[Cooper 1988] Cooper, T.A., and N. Wogrin. *Rule-Based Programming with OPS5.* San Mateo, CA: Morgan Kaufmann, 1988.

[Crawford 1990] Crawford, J.M. Access-limited logic—A language for knowledge representation. Ph.D. thesis, Department of Computer Sciences, University of Texas, Austin, 1990. Also published as Technical Report AI 90-141, Artificial Intelligence Laboratory, University of Texas, Austin.

[Crawford 1991] Crawford, J.M., and B. Kuipers. Negation and proof by contradiction in access-limited logic. *Proceedings of the Ninth National Conference on Artificial Intelligence*, pp. 897–903. Menlo Park, CA, American Association for Artificial Intelligence, 1991.

[Crawford 1995] Crawford, J.M., D. Dvorak, D. Litman, A. Mishra, and P.F. Patel-Schneider. Device representation and reasoning with affective relations. *Proceedings of the Fourteenth International Joint Conference on Artificial Intelligence*, pp. 1814–1820. International Joint Committee on Artificial Intelligence, 1995.

[Crawford 1996] James Crawford, Daniel Dvorak, Diane Litman, Anil Mishra, and P.F. Patel-Schneider. Path-based rules in object-oriented programming. *Proceedings of the Thirteenth National Conference on Artificial Intelligence*. Menlo Park, CA, American Association for Artificial Intelligence, 1996.

[Gamma 1995] Gamma, E., R. Helm, R. Johnson, and J. Vlissides, *Design Patterns: Elements of Reusable Object-Oriented Software*. Reading, MA: Addison-Wesley, 1995.

[Helm 1990] Helm, R., I.M. Holland, and D. Gangopadhyay. Contracts: Specifying behavioral compositions in object-oriented systems. *Proceedings of the OOPSLA 1990 Conference on Object-Oriented Programming Systems, Languages, and Applications*. Reading, MA: ACM Press, 1990.

[Kilov-Harvey 1996] Kilov, H., and V. J. Harvey, editors. *Fifth Workshop on Specification of Behavioral Semantics, OOPSLA 1996*, San Jose, CA. Reading, MA: ACM Press, 1996.

[Litman 1997] Litman, D., P.F. Patel-Schneider, and A. Mishra. Modeling dynamic collections of interdependent objects using path-based rules. *Proceedings of the OOPSLA 1997 Conference on Object-Oriented Programming Systems, Languages, and Applications*. Reading, MA: ACM Press, 1997.

[Mishra 1996] Mishra, A., J.P. Ros, A. Singhal, G. Weiss, D. Litman, P.F. Patel-Schneider, D. Dvorak, and J. Crawford. R++: Using rules in object-oriented designs. *Addendum to the Proceedings of the OOPSLA 1996 Conference on Object Oriented Programming Systems, Languages, and Applications*. Reading, MA: ACM Press, 1996.

[Newell 1982] Newell, A. The knowledge level. *Artificial Intelligence*, 18, 1982: 87–127.

CHAPTER 15

Oberon with Gadgets: A Simple Component Framework

Perhaps the most important conceptual cornerstone of today's hardware industry is its pervasive *component culture*. Devices are typically composed of functional components of all kinds and granularities that have been developed and fabricated by highly specialized teams from possibly different locations. Interestingly, no similar culture has been able to establish itself in the software industry, probably for lack of both a well-defined and globally accepted notion of interface and a corresponding market.

In [Cox 1986], Brad Cox considers a more advanced component culture as paramount for future stages of software development and use. From this perspective, we have developed an experimental component-oriented framework that, in a nutshell, deals with many of the archetypal aspects of component orientation. Our framework integrates smoothly with the original Oberon language and system as described in [Wirth 1988, 1989, 1992] but goes beyond the ordinary object-oriented level in three respects: (1) persistent representation of individual objects in their current state outside of the runtime environment, (2) construction and composition of individual objects, and (3) object mobility.

To put it differently: While the underlying object-oriented language provides both a compositional framework for object *classes* (allowing the derivation of specialized classes) and a production factory for generic object *instances*, our component-oriented framework in addition supports the construction, maintenance, organization, and reuse of individual, prefabricated *components*. The following example may illustrate our point.

Figure 15.1 shows a snapshot of the Oberon display screen. The multimedia panel in the upper left quarter is a persistent composition of a number of components: a main panel, a movie subpanel, two captions, two sliders, and two text fields. The movie subpanel is itself a composition of a scaling panel (autoscaling its components), a video pad, two pushbuttons, and a text field. It is important in this connection to point out again the conceptual difference between generic objects, such as a fresh and empty panel, a fresh caption, a fresh slider, a fresh text field, and so on, that can be obtained directly from the system's class library by instantiation and prefabricated objects such as the movie subpanel and the multimedia panel itself.

The example reveals the two-dimensional structure of the space of software construction in a component culture whose axes represent development of generic components and object construction and composition, respectively. From a methodical view, the two axes are orthogonal. Developing generic components is *class-centered*. It essentially amounts to object-oriented programming within a given framework of classes—that is, deriving subclasses from existing classes. In contrast, object composition is *instance-centered* and is primarily a static matter of design specification. For example, a generic scaling panel is defined by a subclass *ScalingPanel* that has been derived from class Panel by adding some programmed autoscaling functionality, while the specific movie subpanel is an individual composition of a generic scaling panel, a video pad, two buttons and a text field.

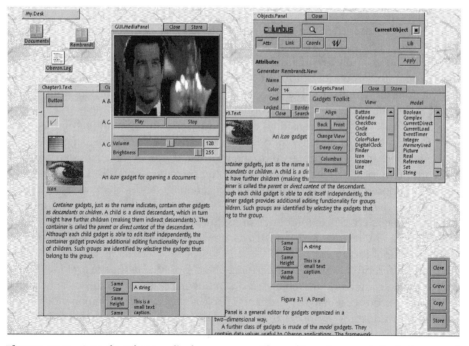

Figure 15.1 Sample Oberon display screen with multimedia panel, text document views, gadgets tool, and Columbus inspector on a desktop.

15.1 A Lightweight Component Framework

A variety of component-oriented software systems are available today. Among the most prominent are Microsoft's COM/OLE/ACTIVE-X [Brockschmidt 1993] and Sun's JavaBeans [Feghhi 1997]. In addition, technologies such as OpenDoc [OpenDoc 1993] and OMG's CORBA [Ben 1995] address related aspects such as compound documents and standardized client-server communication, respectively.

The following sections present an alternative *lightweight* component framework. We will focus our presentation according to four topics that we consider to be essential to the field of component software in general, helpful for building the conceptual base, and the connecting glue of our framework. These topics are (1) message protocol in compound objects; (2) object databases, that is, persistent representation of object collections; (3) object construction tools; and (4) self-containedness and mobility.

15.1.1 A Message Protocol for Compound Objects

The concept of *compound object* is fundamental in every component architecture. In favor of a concrete terminology, we restrict ourselves to compound objects of *container* types that are particularly popular as units in graphical user interfaces. Looking at Figure 15.1 again, we recognize an entire hierarchy of nested containers and a terminating atomic object: desktop => media panel => movie subpanel => pushbutton. Figure 15.2 shows an excerpt of this hierarchy, called a *display space*, in terms of a data structure. We emphasize that our rigorous hierarchic view pays in terms of a highly uniform object model, wherein coarse-grained objects such as desktops, medium-grained objects such as panels, and fine-grained objects such as pushbuttons are completely unified.

The Principle of Parental Control

The role of containers is characterized in our framework by the single postulate of *parental control*, imposing on containers both full authorization and full responsibility for the management of their contents. This postulate has far-reaching consequences. First of all, it basically rules out any message traffic to content objects that bypasses their container. In other words, parental control indispensably implies readiness of containers for message dispatching and request brokering in the small.

The term *message traffic* needs clarification. As in every object-oriented environment, messages are used in our framework to specify and answer requests. However, static object interfaces as they are commonly provided by object-oriented languages are incompatible with the principle of parental control, at least in combination with generic containers that are prepared to include contents of potentially unknown (future) types and, correspondingly, to dispatch potentially unknown messages.

For this reason we make use of a novel kind of *generic object interface* that relies on a built-in interpreter which is able to interpret and dispatch arbitrary arriving messages appropriately. Technically, if Message is the base type of messages accepted by

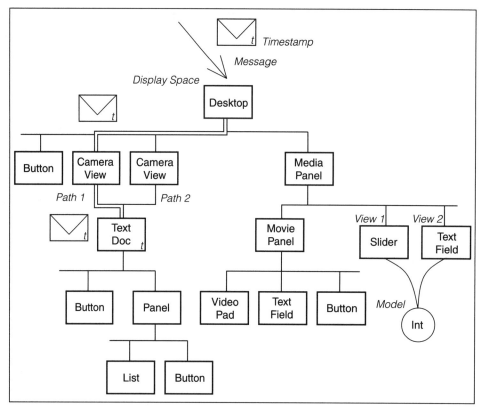

Figure 15.2   Data structure of the sample display space.

instances of some given object type, and MessageA and MessageB are subtypes of Message, then the structure of the dispatcher is as follows:

```
PROCEDURE Dispatch (me: Object; VAR M: Message);
BEGIN (* common preprocessing *)
  IF M IS MessageA THEN (* handle message of subtype MessageA *)
  ELSIF M IS MessageB THEN (* handle message of subtype MessageB *)
  ELSE (* default handling *)
  END
END Dispatch;
```

Note in particular that the dispatcher (1) is able to perform some common preprocessing, (2) makes use of Oberon's safe runtime type test IS for message discrimination, (3) calls some default handler to handle common cases, and (4) is extensible with respect to message subtypes without any need to change its interface.

For the sake of uniformity, we use generic interfaces for atomic (that is, noncontainer) objects as well. In that case, message processing in the display space manifests itself in a hierarchic traversal of the structure, directed by dispatchers of the kind just described. The ordinary case is target-oriented dispatching, where the target object is specified as part of the message. Typical examples of target-oriented messages are requests to get, set and enumerate *attributes* (properties) of a certain object. However, interesting strategic variations of message dispatching exist. For example, universal notifications without a specific target are typically *broadcast* within the display space or within any one of its subspaces. Other options concern incremental processing (incremental contributions to message handling by individual dispatchers) and context-dependent behavior (behavior depending on the path the message arrives from). The subsequent sections present applications.

Camera Views

The MVC scheme [Krasner 1988] is a fundamental design pattern and an integral aspect of every object architecture that provides a conceptually clean separation of the concerns of modeling, viewing, and controlling objects. In our case, a very general interpretation of MVC is applied. A simple case is one or more visual objects (with a representation in the display space) serving as *view* of some abstract object. Examples of this kind are (1) a checkbox view of a Boolean object, (2) a slider view or text-field view (or both) of a Integer object, and (3) a color palette view of a color vector (red, green, and blue).

A more intricate case is given by views of views, here called *camera views*. Camera views are useful for a number of purposes. They provide a conceptual frame for multiple views on one and the same visual document on one or several display screens. For example, Figure 15.1 depicts a double view on a text document with integrated visual objects. An interesting variant of camera views is functional views that are combined with some specific functionality. For example, in addition to ordinary user views, special *developer views* can be offered for the support of interactive editing and construction of a visual object or GUI in situ.

Camera views are implemented as special kinds of visual objects that are able to display visual models. As a desirable consequence, common parts of the data structure representing the display space are automatically shared by camera views and unnecessary duplication is avoided, as shown in Figure 15.2. Obviously, this adds both complexity and flexibility to message processing in the display space. Messages may now arrive at objects along different paths and therefore need to be *time-stamped* for detection of multiple arrivals. On the other hand, context-sensitive processing is now possible and can be used beneficially—for example, to implement the previously mentioned developer views.

The following simplified examples of message processing in compound objects in general and in the display space in particular may promote a better understanding of the concepts discussed in this section and of their combination.

Update Notifications

Update notifications are sent by models or controllers (in the case of smart bundling) to notify potential views of a state change. They are always addressed to the display space as a whole with an implicit broadcast request. Affected views then typically reestablish consistency with their model after querying its actual state. Message broadcasting is simpler and more generic than alternative methods such as callback lists, but it claims an efficiency penalty that, however, has proved to be not noticeable in practice. Optimizations could easily be implemented—for example, by adding knowledge to critical containers. We emphasize that generic message interfaces are absolutely essential for this broadcast method to be applicable within a strongly typed framework.

Display Requests

This type of message is used to request a visual target object to display itself in the display space. For example, a display request would be issued by a reorganized container for every one of its content objects or by the recipient of an update request to adjust its own display. Display requests are again addressed to the display space as a whole. They require incremental processing while traversing the container hierarchy in two respects: successive accumulation of relative coordinates and successive computation of overlap masks. If camera views are involved, multiple paths may lead to the target object, so that it must be prepared for multiple arrivals of a message. All arrivals are handled in the same manner, albeit with different absolute coordinates and overlap masks.

Copy Requests

Copying or *cloning* is an basic operation on objects. Nevertheless, in the case of compound objects, it is quite intricate. Obviously, a generic copy operation on objects is equivalent to an algorithm to copy any arbitrary and truly heterogeneous data structure. Moreover, different possible variants of copies exist. For example, a *deep copy* of a compound object consists of a real copy of both the original container and its contents, while a *shallow copy* typically would include just new views on the original contents.

Our implementation of the copy operation is again based on message broadcasting. This time, multiple arrivals at an object must be handled with more care. The following is a rough sketch of copy message handling by a container:

```
IF first arrival of message THEN create copy of container;
  IF deep copy request THEN
    pass on message to contents; link copy of contents to copy of
container
  ELSE (* shallow copy request *)
    link contents to copy of container
  END
END;
RETURN copy of container
```

Note as a fine point that recipients in fact have some freedom in the handling of a copy request. For example, a heavyweight object receiving a *deep copy* message could decide to merely return some new view on itself or even to return itself (leading to copy by reference) instead of a genuine copy.

15.1.2 Object Libraries as a Versatile and Unifying Concept

Object persistence is a trendy expression for a facility that allows individual objects to be stored on some external device (typically a disk) in their current state. The essential part of every such facility is two transformation methods called *externalizer* and *internalizer*, respectively. Externalizers are used to transform objects from their internal representation into an invariant, linear form, while internalizers are used for the inverse transformation. The problems of externalizing and internalizing are similar in their generic nature to the copy problem just discussed. However, there is one additional aspect to be considered: invariant representation of *pointer links*.

Our approach to invariant pointer links is based on an institution of indexed sets of objects called *object libraries*. The idea is to implement object linearization by recursively registering components in some object library, thereby replacing pointers with reference indexes. With that, externalization and internalization become *distributed* two-pass processes that again rely on broadcasting messages within the desired object.

The Externalizing Algorithm

The externalizing algorithm is used to transform objects from their internal representation into an invariant of linear form. The externalizing algorithm is described here:

```
Externalize(object X) = {
  Create(library L); Register(X, L); Externalize(L) }

Register (object X, library L) = {
  WITH X DO
    * FOR ALL components x of X DO Register(x, L) END
  END;
  IF X is unregistered THEN
    assign index and register X in L
  END }

Externalize (library L) = {
  WITH L DO
    FOR index i := 0 to max DO
      WITH object X[i] DO store generator of X[i];
        * replace pointer links with index references
          and externalize descriptor of X[i]
      END
    END
  END }
```

Obviously, acyclicity of the relation of containment is a precondition for this algorithm. Further note that the statements marked * must be implemented as object methods because they are type specific.

The Internalizing Algorithm

The internalizing algorithm is used to inverse the transformation of the externalizing algorithm. The internalizing algorithm is described here:

```
Internalize (library L) = {
  WITH L DO
    FOR index i := 0 to max DO
      load generator of X[i]; generate descriptor of X[i]
    END;
    FOR index i := 0 to max DO
      * internalize descriptor of X[i]
      and replace index references with pointer links
    END
  END }
```

Note that internalizing a library is a potentially recursive process, because indexes in internalized object descriptors may refer to foreign libraries. And again, the statement marked * must be implemented as an object method.

Object libraries represent a surprisingly versatile and thereby unifying concept. The spectrum of their application is much wider than one would perhaps expect. Beyond supporting externalization and internalization of individual objects, they are simple object databases that serve the purpose of organizing any local or distributed space of objects. Some typical manifestations are: (1) a collection of logically connected reusable components, (2) a collection of public objects shared by a set of documents, and (3) a set of objects private to some document.

Objects Flowing in Text

Another unifying application of the concept of object libraries is *generalized text*. A simple reinterpretation of ordinary (multifont) text as sequences of references to character patterns (where the reference numbers are ASCII codes) leads the way to a far-reaching generalization. By allowing references to arbitrary object libraries instead of just to fonts, we immediately get to text with integrated objects of any kind, including pictures, links, formatting controls, entire functional panels, and other units that are similar to Java applets. Additional flexibility is provided by the possibility of embedding both private objects (collected in the so-called *private library* of the text) as well as public objects (belonging to some public library). Such a high degree of integration of text with objects has proved to be incredibly useful, mainly in the area of documentation. Thanks to it, functional units of any complexity and granularity that have been developed anywhere can simply be copied to and integrated with their textual documentation. An illustrative example is the chapter of the electronic Oberon book shown in Figure 15.1.

15.1.3 Object Construction Tools

In principle, two different kinds of methods for object construction and composition exist: *interactive* and *descriptive*. Interactive methods are based on direct editing, in contrast to descriptive methods, which typically rely on some formal language and a corresponding interpreter. In most cases, the two methods are interchangeable. However, while the interactive method is more suitable for the construction of visual GUI objects, the descriptive method is preferable for the construction of regular layouts and is indispensable for program-generated objects (such as property sheets and so on) and for nonvisual (model) objects. The following list summarizes:

KIND OF OBJECT	SUITABLE CONSTRUCTION METHOD
Visual GUI	Interactive
Regular layout	Descriptive
Program generated	Descriptive
Nonvisual model	Descriptive

Independent of the construction method, components can be acquired alternatively from (1) generators for atomic objects, (2) generators for container objects, and (3) prefabricated object libraries.

Interactive Construction

Our framework supports interactive construction on different levels. On the tool level, the Gadgets toolkit [Gutknecht 1994; Marais 1994; Fischer 1998] and the Columbus inspector tool shown in Figure 15.1 offer functionality for the following purposes:

- Generating new instances of an existing type
- Calling prefabricated instances from an object library
- Aligning components in containers
- Establishing model-view links
- Inspecting and altering the state, attributes, and properties of objects
- Binding Oberon commands to GUI objects

On the view level, the previously mentioned developer views enable editing of visual objects. On the object level, support for in-place editing is provided by built-in local editors. Mouse event messages are tagged with a pair of absolute mouse coordinates and undergo a location-oriented dispatching in the display space. Because mouse events should be handled differently in user and developer contexts, most mouse event handlers make beneficial use of context-dependent message processing.

Descriptive Construction

Descriptive construction requires a formal description language as a basis. Because layout specification is functional, we decided in favor of a functional language with a LISP-like syntax.

We basically distinguish two modes of processing of a functional object description: compilation and direct interpretation. Separate descriptions are compiled into an object library, while descriptions that are embedded in some document context (for example, in a HTML page) are typically interpreted and translated directly into an inline object. Figure 15.3 visualizes the compiling mode. Note that generic objects are retrieved by the compiling composer from the class library by cloning, while prefabricated objects are imported from any object library either by *cloning* or by *reference*.

The subsequent commented example of a functional description of the multimedia panel in Figure 15.1 may suffice to give an impression of the use of descriptive construction in our framework.

```
(LIB GUI
  (FRAME MediaPanel (OBJ Panels.NewPanel)
    (Volume (OBJ BasicGadgets.NewInteger (Value 100)))
    (Brightness (OBJ BasicGadgets.NewInteger (Value 200)))
    (GRID 2:50 1:* @ 1:25% 1:50% 1:25%) (PAD 2 @ 2)
    (FRAME (POS 1 @ 1) (OBJ TextFields.NewCaption) (Value "Brightness"))
    (FRAME (POS 1 @ 2) (OBJ BasicGadgets.NewSlider) (Max 255)
      (Model Brightness) (Cmd "Movie.SetBright #Value Movie"))
    (FRAME (POS 1 @ 3) (OBJ TextFields.NewTextField)
      (Model Brightness) (Cmd "Movie.SetBright #Value Movie"))
    (FRAME (POS 2 @ 1) (OBJ TextFields.NewCaption) (Value "Volume"))
    (FRAME (POS 2 @ 2) (OBJ BasicGadgets.NewSlider) (Max 255)
      (Model Volume) (Cmd "Movie.SetVol #Value Movie"))
    (FRAME (POS 2 @ 3) (OBJ TextFields.NewTextField)
      (Model Volume) (Cmd "Movie.SetVol #Value Movie"))
    (FRAME (POS 3 @ 1:3) (OBJ Movies.MoviePanel) (SIZE 296 @ 246))))
```

Comments

The following list brings forth several key observations and comments about the formal description language that describes the functional specifications of the multimedia panel.

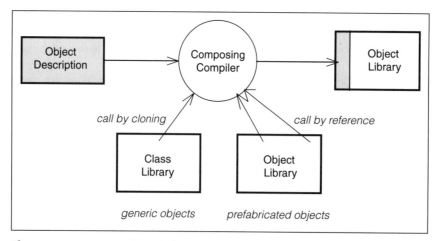

Figure 15.3 Construction of objects by compilation of a functional description.

- A (compound, visual) object is generally specified as a nested hierarchy of frames, where each frame may optionally use the OBJ clause to define a carrier object.

- The compilation of this declaration results in an object library file called *GUI* containing an instance of the constructed object called *MediaPanel*.

- Frames may optionally declare local objects that are typically used as models. In the example, two such model objects are declared, one for volume control and one for brightness control.

- Within the OBJ construct, the first identifier specifies either a generator procedure Module.Procedure (representing the class of the desired object) or a prefabricated object Library.Object that is imported by reference or copy from an object library.

- Visual objects typically specify a *grid* of type rows @ columns. In our case, the grid consists of three rows and three columns, respectively. The heights of the first 2 rows are 50, while the height of the third row is generic, that is, determined by the contents. Column widths are indicated in percents, where the total width is again generic. The first two rows from the bottom represent brightness and volume control, respectively. Each row consists of a caption, a slider, and a text field, where the slider and the text field are coupled by a local model. The third row has a column span of three and displays a prefabricated object called *MoviePanel* that is imported from a library called *Movies*.

We should note that the functional object description tool just discussed is only the leaf-end of a much more general experimental system called *PowerDoc* that allows the descriptive construction of arbitrarily general documents that may include any kind of passive or active objects (*applets*) and datastreams.

15.1.4 From Persistent Objects to Mobile Objects

In the previous discussion, we have developed our component architecture to a state that includes a mechanism for an external, linear representation of general objects. So far, we have used this facility for object persistence on secondary store only. However, there is a second potential application: *mobility*. In this case, the linear representation must obviously be accompanied by self-containedness and portability. These notions are the topics of this and the next section.

The essential request to self-contained objects is their completeness in terms of resources used. Thanks to our highly unified architecture, only two types of resources exist: object libraries and program modules (units of the class library). Unfortunately, it is impossible for any central authority to find out the entirety of resources used by some general object. The reason is that resources are frequently specified implicitly by an inconspicuous name string. For example, Module.Procedure command names typically hide in attribute strings of pushbuttons, and Library.Object object names may well occur within any scrolling list.

Our solution to the resource detection problem consists of two new ingredients: a resource query message used to collect resources and a resource-management object acting as a *shrinkwrapper* for self-contained objects. If *X* is any self-contained object and *M* is a resource-management object, the shrink-wrapped composition *MX* is then externalized like this:

```
Externalize self-contained object MX = {
  Send resource query message Q to X asking X to report its resources;
  Externalize M; Externalize X }
```

In the case of containers, the broadcast strategy is again used beneficially for the dispatch of resource query messages:

```
Receive resource query message Q = {
  Pass on Q to contents; Report own resources to resource manager }
```

In combination with mobility, there are some significant areas of problems behind the apparent simplicity of this algorithm. Among them are (1) scoping of resource names and (2) protection of the target system from malicious or erroneous program code. We now briefly touch on the first problem, while we postpone a short discussion on the second problem to the next section.

Mobile objects are developed in general without any global coordination. As a consequence, they define their own scope of resources that, in case of a migration, need to be mapped to a separate space on the target system. However, it is reasonable to distinguish some global set of kernel resources that are assumed to be identically available as a plug-in on every target system. Obviously, kernel resources need not be transported with every individual object but need to be checked for consistency, perhaps with the help of fingerprints [Crelier 1996].

We emphasize that our approach to mobile objects is generic in the sense that any persistent object can be made mobile in principle. The spectrum of potential mobile objects therefore covers an impressive range—from simple buttons and checkboxes to control panels and documents and finally to desktops representing an entire Oberon system.

15.1.5 An Effective Approach to Portable Code

The final aspect of mobile objects that merits consideration is cross-platform *portability* of their implementation code. As mobile objects are expected to long outlive their creation environments and all currently existing hardware architectures, the choice of a software distribution format should be guided less by the present-day prevalence of specific processor families but rather by more fundamental considerations. While it might be a smart tactical decision at this moment to distribute mobile objects in the form of i80386 binary code that can be executed directly on the vast majority of computers currently deployed (and interpreted on most of the others), this would be a bad choice in the long run. A future-oriented software distribution format needs to meet three primary requirements: (1) It must be well suited for a fast translation into native code of current and future microprocessors; (2) it must not obstruct advanced code optimizations required for tomorrow's superscalar processors; and (3) considering the anticipated importance of low-bandwidth wireless connectivity in the near future, it should be highly compact.

Our concept of portable code incorporates a distribution format called *Slim Binaries* [Franz 1997] that satisfies all of these requirements. In contrast to approaches like p-code [Nori 1981] and Java bytecode [Lindholm 1996] that are based on an underlying virtual machine, the slim-binary format is an adaptively compressed representation of syntax trees. In a slim-binary encoding, every symbol describes a subtree of an abstract syntax tree in terms of the subtrees preceding it. Roughly speaking, the encoding process proceeds by successively externalizing subtrees and simultaneously steadily extending the vocabulary that is used in the encoding of subsequent program sections.

This format has the obvious disadvantage that it cannot be decoded by simple pointwise interpretation. The semantics of any particular symbol in a slim-binary-encoded datastream is revealed only after all the symbols preceding it have been processed. Random access to individual instructions as it is typically required for inter-preted execution is impossible.

However, in return for giving up the possibility of pointwise interpretation (whose value is limited due to low efficiency anyway), we gain several important benefits. First of all, our software distribution format is exceptionally compact. For example, it is more than twice as dense as Java bytecode, and it performs significantly better than standard data compression algorithms such as LZW applied to either source code or object code (for any architecture). This is an advantage that cannot be overestimated. In fact, experience has shown that on-the-fly code generation can be provided at almost zero cost if a highly compact program representation is chosen, because the additional computational effort can be compensated almost completely by a reduction of I/O overhead [Franz 1994].

Second, the tree-based structure of our distribution format constitutes a consider-able advantage if the eventual target machine has an architecture that requires advanced optimizations. Many modern code-optimization techniques rely on struc-tural information that is readily available on the level of syntax trees but is more diffi-cult to extract on the level of bytecodes.

Third, we can make use of our slim-binary technology to optimize code across mod-ule boundaries. Such global optimizations as, for example, procedure inlining and interprocedural register allocation, pay particularly well in a software component environment that is made up of a large number of relatively small and separate pieces of code. When a piece of slim-binary code is initially loaded into the system, it is trans-lated into native code in a single burst, trading code efficiency for compilation speed. After its creation, the piece of code is immediately subject to execution and optimiza-tion in the background. After completion of the optimization step, the previous gener-ation of code is simply exchanged for the new one. Obviously, in conjunction with runtime profiling, this procedure can be iterated continually to produce ever-better generations of code.

Fourth, unlike most other representations, slim-binary encoding preserves type and scope information. It thus supports the detection of violations by malicious or faulty code that potentially compromise the integrity of the host system. For example, it is easy to catch any kind of access to private variables of public objects that may have been allowed by a rogue compiler. In the case of bytecode, a corresponding analysis is more difficult.

15.2 Applications

Our framework has been used in numerous projects. Three substantial interdisciplinary applications are a computer aided control system design (CACSD) environment [Qiu 1998], a generic robot controller architecture [Roshardt 1994], and a real-time audio- and video-stream service in a local switch-based network. Noteworthy technical highlights in the CACSD environment are matrix and plot gadgets that are connected behind the scenes with a Matlab engine and powerful tree-node objects that abstract control system design actions in an action tree. In the robot controller project, object libraries are beneficially used for a persistent but decoupled representation of I/O objects (sensors, actuators, and so on). Another interesting facility is *remote views*—views that display state models of the robot on the development system (connected to the robot via the Internet). Finally, in the stream-server project, a new kind of visual objects that display remotely supplied contents (video streams bypassing the client's memory) have been integrated smoothly into the Gadgets system.

15.3 Summary

Building on the original version of the Oberon language and system, we have developed a component framework that, strictly speaking, splits into three interacting subframeworks:

- A framework of user interface components that can be configured interactively or descriptively
- A framework for externalizing and internalizing object structures
- A framework for shrink-wrapping object structures in a self-contained way

The subframeworks are connected by two universal and unifying facilities: a software bus in the form of a generic message protocol obeying the principle of parental control and an object database in the form of a hierarchy of indexed object libraries.

In contrast to COM and CORBA, the emphasis in our system is on homogeneity rather than on platform independence. In fact, Oberon components are not viable in any environment apart from Oberon, with the important exception of a HTML context with an Oberon plug-in. On the other hand, the range of Oberon components covers the whole bandwidth from simple character glyphs to entire documents and desktops.

Our architecture further distinguishes itself by a clear decoupling of object composition from component development. While generic components (both atomic and container) are represented by Oberon classes and are programmed in Oberon (essentially by implementing the message protocol of parental control), compound objects are created interactively through usage of built-in in situ editors or descriptively in a LISP-like notation. Unlike, for example, Microsoft's Visual Basic and Developer Studio wizards or Borland's Delphi and Sun's JavaBeans, the Oberon composer tools do not map compound objects to classes and constructors, but directly create data structures of the DAG type that are able to externalize to identifiable instances of some object library. Each compound object can therefore be called and used alternatively by reference or by cloning.

The system runs on bare Intel PC platforms. Versions hosted by Windows and Macintosh platforms are also available. In its current state, it includes all of the previously mentioned local facilities, numerous applications, and an advanced navigator that is designed to handle compound Oberon documents and HTML hypertexts uniformly. Mobile objects and dynamic recompilation are currently under development. Plans eventually aim at an Oberon in a gadget paradigm.

Several substantial projects have made intensive use of our component framework. They have demonstrated not only its power and limits but also an ample potential for further generalizations.

15.4 References

[Ben 1995] Ben-Natan, R. *CORBA: A Guide to Common Object Request Broker Architecture.* New York: McGraw-Hill, 1995.

[Brockschmidt 1993] Brockschmidt, K. *Inside OLE.* Redmond, WA: Microsoft Press, 1993.

[Cox 1986] Cox, B.J. *Object-Oriented Programming: An Evolutionary Approach.* Reading, MA: Addison-Wesley, 1986.

[Crelier 1996] Crelier, R. Extending module interfaces without invalidating clients. *Structured Programming,* 16(1), 1996: 49–62.

[Feghhi 1997] Feghhi, J. *Web Developer's Guide to Java Beans.* San Mateo, CA: Coriolis Group Books, 1997.

[Fischer 1998] Fischer, A., and H. Marais. *The Oberon Companion: A Guide to Using and Programming Oberon System 3.* Zürich, Switzerland: vdf Hochschulverlag AG an der ETH Zürich, 1998.

[Franz 1994] Franz, M. Code-generation on-the-fly: A key to portable software. Doctoral dissertation no. 10497, ETH Zurich. Zürich, Switzerland: Verlag der Fachvereine, 1994.

[Franz 1997] Franz, M., and T. Kistler. Slim binaries. *Communications of the ACM,* 40(12), December 1997: 87–94.

[Gutknecht 1994] Gutknecht, J. Oberon system 3: Vision of a future software technology. *Software—Concepts and Tools,* 15, 1994: 26–33.

[Krasner 1988] Krasner, G.E., and S.T. Pope. A cookbook for using the Model-View Controller user interface paradigm in Smalltalk-80. *Journal of Object-Oriented Programming,* 1(3), August 1988: 26–49.

[Lindholm 1996] Lindholm, T., F. Yellin, B. Joy, and K. Walrath. *The Java Virtual Machine Specification.* Reading, MA: Addison-Wesley, 1996.

[Marais 1994] Marais, J.L. Towards end-user objects: The Gadgets user interface system. In *Advances in Modular Languages,* P. Schulthess, editor. Technology Transfer Series, vol. 1. Ulm, Germany: Universitätsverlag Ulm, September 1994.

[Nori 1981] Nori, K.V., U. Ammann, K. Jensen, H.H. Nägeli, and C. Jacobi. Pascal-P implementation notes. In *Pascal: The Language and Its Implementation,* D.W. Barron, editor. Chichester, England: John Wiley & Sons, 1981.

[OpenDoc 1993] The OpenDoc Design Team. *OpenDoc Technical Summary.* Apple Computers, October 1993.

[Qiu 1998] Qiu, X., W. Schaufelberger, J. Wang, and Y. Sun. Applying O3CACSD to control system design and rapid prototyping. *The Seventeenth American Control Conference (ACC 1998)*, Philadelphia, June 24–26, 1998.

[Roshardt 1994] Roshardt, R. Modular robot controller aids flexible manufacturing. International Federation of Robotics, *Robotics Newsletter*, 16, December. 1994.

[Wirth 1988] Wirth, N. The programming language Oberon. *Software—Practice and Experience*, 18(7), 1988: 671–690.

[Wirth 1989] Wirth, N., and J. Gutknecht. The Oberon system. *Software—Practice and Experience*, 19(9), 1989: 857–893.

[Wirth 1992] Wirth, N., and J. Gutknecht. *Project Oberon*. Reading, MA: Addison-Wesley, 1992.

CHAPTER 16

Inheritance Management and Method Dispatch Framework

Most object-oriented frameworks are motivated by industry, and are developed for a particular application domain, such as user interfaces or database management. The framework presented here is somewhat unusual in that the framework is used to implement object-oriented languages. We make a distinction between the framework *client* (the software that invokes the framework) and the framework *users* (the people who are implementing the object-oriented language in question). In some ways, the dispatch table (DT) framework presented here is a metaframework, as it provides a framework within which a fundamental object-oriented concept can be implemented by language developers.

Object-oriented languages have two special properties: (1) *polymorphism*, which allows the same name to be used to refer to two or more different executable methods, and (2) *inheritance*, which hierarchically relates the types in the programming environment to one another. These properties provide object-oriented languages with the highly desirable concepts of abstraction, modularity, and code reuse. However, these same properties have an impact on execution performance.

To see why this is the case, consider a function call. The invocation of a function involves specifying a function name and a list of arguments on which that function operates. Each argument has a *type* (a set of legal values) which restricts it. *Function dispatch* is the process of determining the address of the function code to execute. In most non-object-oriented languages, only the name of the function is needed, because a one-to-one correspondence between names and addresses exists. Some non-object-oriented languages allow polymorphic functions in which the *static* type of function arguments are used in conjunction with the function name to identify the function address. In either case, the function address for a particular function call is determinable at compile time, so the compiler can generate an appropriate JSR statement, or even inline the function code within the caller.

Unfortunately, in object-oriented languages the compiler does not always have sufficient information to determine the method (function address) associated with a particular selector (function name). This is because inheritance introduces a distinction between the static type of expressions and the dynamic type of values. Inheritance generates a hierarchical ordering on the types in the environment, so if a certain type T' is below another type T in the inheritance hierarchy, T' is said to *be* a T, and thus instances of type T' can be used wherever instances of type T can be used. Thus, it is legal, under the rules of inheritance, to assign an object of type T' to a variable of type T. The reason this type substitutability poses problems is that all object-oriented languages use the *dynamic type* of at least one method argument (the receiver), in conjunction with the selector, to determine which method to invoke. Because the dynamic type of an argument can be different than the static type, a compiler can not always establish the correct method to execute. Instead, the compiler must often generate code that will compute the appropriate address at runtime. The process of computing the method address at runtime is known as *method dispatch*. The code generated by the compiler, along with the information this code relies on, makes up a specific *method dispatch technique*.

There has been a variety of published method dispatch techniques for languages that use only the receiver's dynamic type. Such techniques are divided into two primary categories: cache-based and table-based. *Cache-based* techniques use lookup and caching during runtime, and require a minimum of precalculated information, while *table-based* techniques calculate all addresses before dispatch occurs, so that dispatch consists of a single table access (although memory accesses may be necessary to compute table indexes). Traditionally, the table-based techniques have only been applicable in *nonreflexive languages*, where no new types or methods can be added at runtime. A later section demonstrates how all single-receiver table-based dispatch techniques can be generalized to *reflexive languages*, wherein methods and types can be added at runtime.

There are two separate but related components in a method dispatch technique: (1) the actions required at each call site in order to establish an address, and (2) the maintenance actions that allow the call-site-specific actions to work. For the most part, the cache-based techniques place emphasis on the call-site actions, while the table-based techniques place emphasis on the maintenance actions.

The DT framework is a general framework for both compile-time and runtime inheritance management and table-based method dispatch. It applies to a broad category of object-oriented languages: *reflexive, nonstatically typed, single-receiver* languages with type/implementation-paired multiple inheritance. Within this chapter, we refer to this collection of languages as Ψ. A *reflexive* language is one with the ability to define new methods and classes at run-time. A *nonstatically-typed* language is one in which some (or all) variables and method return values are unconstrained, in that they can be bound to instances of any class in the entire environment. A *single-receiver* language is one in which a single class, together with a selector, uniquely establishes a method to invoke (as opposed to multimethod languages, discussed in *Section 16.5*). *Type/ implementation-paired inheritance* refers to the traditional form of inheritance used in most object-oriented languages, in which both the definition and implementation of inherited selectors are propagated together (as opposed to inheritance in which these two concepts are separated, as discussed in *Section 16.5*). Finally, *multiple inheritance* refers to the ability of a class to inherit selectors from more than one direct superclass. Note that nonstatically typed languages are a superset of statically typed languages, and multiple inheritance is a superset of single inheritance.

Any compiler or runtime system for a language in Ψ can obtain substantial code reuse by deriving its dispatch code from the DT framework. In this chapter, we refer to compilers and runtime systems as *DT framework clients*. For our purposes, a language that can be compiled is inherently nonreflexive, and *compilers* can be used on such languages (such as C++). By *runtime system* we mean language support existing at runtime to allow new types or methods to be added.

The DT framework relies on a fundamental data structure that extends the concept of a dispatch table. In addition to method addresses, it maintains information that provides efficient incremental inheritance management, inheritance conflict detection, and dispatch table modification. The algorithms that perform these actions are general enough to be used in conjunction with any table-based dispatch technique. This provides a complete framework for inheritance management and maintenance of dispatch information that is usable by both compilers and runtime systems. The algorithms provided by the framework are incremental at the level of individual *environment modifications*, consisting of any of the following: adding a selector to a class, adding one or more class inheritance links (even adding a class *between* two or more existing classes), removing a selector from a class, or removing one or more class inheritance links.

The following capabilities are provided by the framework:

Inheritance conflict detection. In multiple inheritance, it is possible for inheritance conflicts to occur when a selector is visible in a class from two or more superclasses. The framework detects and records such conflicts at the time of method definition.

Dispatch technique independence. The framework provides end users with the ability to choose which dispatch technique to use. Thus, an end user could compile a C++ program using virtual function tables, or selector coloring, or any other table-based dispatch technique.

Support for reflexive languages. Dispatch tables have traditionally been created by compilers and are usually not extendable at runtime. Therefore, reflexive languages cannot use such table-based dispatch techniques. By making dispatch table modification incremental, the DT framework allows reflexive languages to use any table-based dispatch technique, maintaining the dispatch table at runtime as the environment is dynamically altered. The DT framework provides efficient algorithms for arbitrary environment modification, including adding a class between classes already in an inheritance hierarchy. Even more important, the algorithms handle both additions to the environment *and* deletions from the environment.

Separate compilation. Of the five table-based dispatch techniques discussed in *Section 16.1.2*, three require knowledge of the complete environment. In situations where library developers provide object files, but not source code, these techniques are unusable. Incremental dispatch table modification allows the DT framework to provide separate compilation in all five dispatch techniques.

Compile-time method determination. It is often possible (especially in statically typed languages) for a compiler to uniquely determine a method address for a specific message send. The more refined the static typing of a particular variable, the more limited is the set of applicable selectors when a message is sent to the object referenced by the variable. If only one method applies, the compiler can generate a function call or inline the method, avoiding runtime dispatch. The method-node data structure maintains information to allow efficient determination of such uniqueness.

The rest of this chapter is organized as follows. *Section 16.1* summarizes the various method dispatch techniques. *Section 16.2* presents the DT framework. *Section 16.3* discusses how the table-based method dispatch techniques can be implemented using the DT framework. *Section 16.4* presents some performance results. *Section 16.5* discusses related and future work, and *Section 16.6* provides a summary.

16.1 Method Dispatch Techniques

In object-oriented languages, it is often necessary to compute the method address to be executed for a class/selector pair $<C, \sigma>$ at runtime. Because message sends are so prevalent in object-oriented languages, the dispatch mechanism has a profound effect on implementation efficiency. In the discussion that follows, C is the receiver class and σ is the selector at a particular call-site. The notation $<C, \sigma>$ is shorthand for the class/selector pair. It is assumed that each class in the environment maintains a dictionary that maps native selectors to their method addresses, as well as a set of immediate superclasses. We give only a very brief summary of the dispatch techniques in this chapter. For detailed descriptions, see [Driesen 1993], and for a comparison of relative dispatch performance, see [Driesen 1995b].

16.1.1 Cache-Based Techniques

There are three basic cache-based dispatch techniques. All of them rely on the dynamic technique called *Method Lookup* (ML) [Goldberg 1983], the default dispatch technique in Smalltalk-80, as their cache-miss technique. In Method Lookup, method dictionaries are searched for selector σ starting at class C, going up the inheritance chain until a method for σ is found or no more parents exist. This technique is space efficient but time inefficient. The three cache-based techniques are called *Global Lookup Cache* (LC) [Goldberg 1983; Krasner 1983], *Inline Cache* (IC) [Deutsch 1994], and *Polymorphic Inline Cache* (PIC) [Holzle 1991]. Because the DT framework is based on table-based techniques, this chapter does not discuss these approaches.

16.1.2 Table-Based Techniques

The table-based techniques provide a mapping from every legal class/selector pair to an executable address that is precomputed before dispatch occurs. These techniques have traditionally been used at compile-time, but the DT framework shows how they can be used at runtime. In each technique, classes and selectors are assigned numbers that serve as indexes into the dispatch table. Whether these indexes are unique or not depends on the dispatch technique:

STI (selector table indexing). Uses a two-dimensional table in which both class and selector indexes are unique. This technique is not practical from a space perspective and is never used in implementations [Cox 1987].

SC (selector coloring). Compresses the two-dimensional STI table by allowing selector indexes to be nonunique. Two selectors can share the same index as long as no class recognizes both selectors. The amount of compression is limited by the largest complete behavior (the largest set of selectors recognized by a single class) [Dixon 1989; Andre-Royer 1992].

RD (row displacement). Compresses the two-dimensional STI table into a one-dimensional master array. Selectors are assigned unique indexes so that when all selector rows are shifted to the right by the index amount, the two-dimensional table has only one method in each column [Driesen 1995a].

VTBL (virtual function tables). Has a different dispatch table for each class, so selector indexes are class-specific. However, indexes are constrained to be equal across inheritance subgraphs. Such uniqueness is not possible in multiple inheritance, in which case multiple tables are stored in each multiderived class [Ellis 1990].

CT (compact selector–indexed dispatch tables). Separates selectors into one of two groups. *Standard selectors* have one main definition and are overridden only in subclasses. Any selector that is not standard is a *conflict selector*. Two different tables are maintained, one for standard selectors, the other for conflict selectors. The standard table can be compressed by *selector aliasing* and *class sharing*, and the conflict table by class sharing alone. *Class partitioning* is used to allow class sharing to work effectively [Vitek 1996].

16.2 The DT Framework

The DT framework provides a collection of abstract classes that define the data and functionality necessary to modify dispatch information incrementally during environment modification. From the perspective of the DT framework, environment modification occurs when selectors or class hierarchy links are added or removed.

The primary benefit of the DT framework is its ability to incrementally modify dispatch table information. Table-based dispatch techniques have traditionally been static, and efficient implementations usually rely on a complete knowledge of the environment before the dispatch table is created. However, dispatch techniques that rely on complete knowledge of the environment have two disadvantages: (1) they cannot be used by reflexive languages that can modify the environment at runtime, and (2) they preclude the ability of the language to perform a separate compilation of source code. One of the fundamental contributions of the DT framework is a collection of algorithms that provides incremental dispatch table updates in all table-based dispatch techniques. An implementation of the DT framework exists, and detailed runtime measurements of the algorithms are presented in *Section 16.4*.

The DT framework consists of a variety of special-purpose classes. This discussion presents the conceptual names of the classes, rather than the exact class names used in the C++ implementation. Figures 16.1 through 16.4 show the class hierarchies. In addition, there are three singleton classes, called *Environment, Selector,* and *Class.* We describe the data and functionality that each class hierarchy needs from the perspective of inheritance management and dispatch-table modification. Clients of the framework can specify additional data and functionality by subclassing some or all of the classes provided by the framework.

The Table hierarchy describes the classes that represent the dispatch table, and provides the functionality to access, modify, and add entries. The MethodNode hierarchy represents the different kinds of addresses that can be associated with a class/selector pair (that is, messageNotUnderStood, inheritanceConflict, or user-specified method). The SIS and CIS hierarchies implement methods for determining selector and class indexes. Although these concepts are components of Tables, they have been made classes to allow the same table to use different indexing strategies.

16.2.1 The DT Classes

The Environment, Class, and Selector classes have no subclasses within the DT framework, but the MethodNode, Table, SIS, and CIS classes are subclassed. However, clients of the framework are free to subclass any DT class they choose, including Environment, Class, and Selector.

Environment, Class, and Selector

The DT Environment class acts as an interface between the DT framework client and the framework. However, because the client can subclass the DT framework, the interface is a whitebox, not a blackbox. This interface serves as an API for the language implementor that provides inheritance and method dispatch operations.

Each client creates a unique instance of the DT Environment class, and as class and method declarations are parsed (or evaluated at runtime), the client informs the Environment instance of these environment modifications by invoking its interface operations. These interface operations are *Add Selector, Remove Selector, Add Class Links,* and *Remove Class Links.* The environment also provides functionality to register selectors and classes with the environment, save extended dispatch tables, convert extended

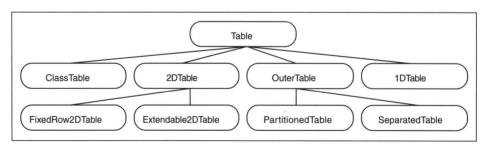

Figure 16.1   The Table hierarchy.

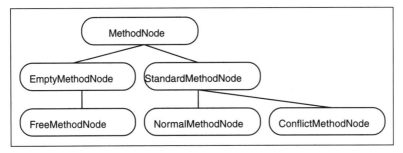

Figure 16.2 The MethodNode hierarchy.

dispatch tables to dispatch tables, merge extended dispatch tables together, and perform actual dispatch for a particular class/selector pair.

Within the DT framework, instances of class Selector need to maintain a name. They do not maintain indexes, because such indexes are table specific. Instances of Class maintain a name, a set of native selectors, a set of immediate superclasses (parent classes), a set of immediate subclasses (child classes), and a pointer to the dispatch table (usually, a pointer to a certain starting point within the table, specific to the class in question). Finally, they need to implement an efficient mechanism for determining whether another class is a subclass (for example, by using bit vectors or hierarchical encoding schemes [Vitek 1996].

Method Nodes

The Table class and its subclasses represent extended dispatch tables, which store *method-node* pointers instead of addresses. Conceptually, a method node is the set of all classes that share a method for a selector. However, this set of classes is not explicitly maintained because it can be computed using a few basic pieces of information. Within each method node, only one class C has a native definition for the selector σ. This class is called the *defining class*. For a method node M representing class/selector pair <C, σ>, the defining class is C and the dependent classes of M consist of all classes that inherit selector σ from class C, including class C itself. Furthermore, each selector σ defined in the environment generates a *method-node inheritance graph*, which is an induced subgraph of the class inheritance hierarchy, formed by removing all classes

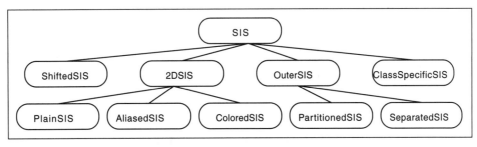

Figure 16.3 The SelectorIndexStrategy (SIS) hierarchy.

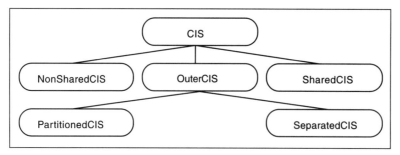

Figure 16.4 The ClassIndexStrategy (CIS) hierarchy.

that do not natively define σ. Method-node hierarchy graphs allow the DT framework to perform compile-time method determination. These graphs can be maintained by having each method node store a set of child method nodes. For a method node M with defining class C and selector σ, the child method nodes of M are the method nodes for selector σ and classes C_i immediately below C in the method-node inheritance graph for σ. Figure 16.5 shows a small inheritance hierarchy and the method-node hierarchies obtained from it for selectors α and β.

The MethodNode hierarchy is in some ways private to the DT framework, and language implementors that use the DT framework will not usually need to know anything about these classes. However, method nodes are of critical importance in providing the DT framework with its incremental efficiency and compile-time method determination. By storing method nodes in the tables, rather than simple addresses, the following capabilities become possible:

- Localized modification of the dispatch table during environment modification so that only those entries that need to be will be recomputed

- Efficient inheritance propagation and inheritance conflict detection

- Detection of simple recompilations (replacing a method by a different method) and avoidance of unnecessary computation in such situations

- Compile-time method determination

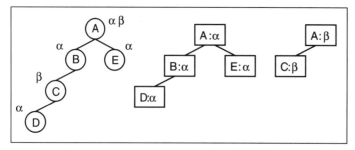

Figure 16.5 An inheritance hierarchy and its associated method-node hierarchies.

In fact, each entry of an extended dispatch table represents a unique class/selector pair, and contains a MethodNode instance, even if no user-specified method exists for the class/selector pair in question. Such empty entries usually contain a unique instance of EmptyMethodNode, but one indexing strategy uses a FreeMethodNode instance, which represents a contiguous block of unused table entries. Instances of both of these classes have a special methodNotUnderstood address associated with them. Nonempty table entries are StandardMethodNodes, and contain a defining class, selector, address and a set of child method nodes. The NormalMethodNode subclass represents a user-specified method address, and the ConflictMethodNode subclass represents an inheritance conflict, in which two or more distinct methods are visible from a class due to multiple inheritance.

Tables

Each Table class provides a structure for storing method nodes, and maps the indexes associated with a class/selector pair to a particular entry in the table structure. Each of the concrete table classes in the DT framework provides a different underlying table structure. The only functionality that subclasses must provide is that which is dependent on the structure. This includes table access, table modification, and dynamic extension of the selector and class dimensions.

The 2DTable class is an abstract superclass for tables with orthogonal class and selector dimensions. For example, these tables are used for selector coloring. The rows represent the selector dimension, and columns represent the class dimension. The Extendable2DTable class can dynamically grow in both selector and class dimensions as additional elements are added to the dimensions. The FixedRow2DTable dynamically grows in the class dimension, but the size of the selector dimension is established at time of table creation, and cannot grow larger.

The concrete 1DTable class represents tables in which selectors and classes share the same dimension. For example, these tables are used for row displacement. Selector and class indexes are added together to access an entry in this table. This table grows as necessary when new classes and selectors are added.

The OuterTable class is an abstract superclass for tables that contain subtables. For example, these tables are used in compact selector-indexed dispatch tables. Most of the functionality of these classes involves requesting the same functionality from a particular subtable. For example, requesting the entry for a class/selector pair involves determining (based on selector index) which subtable is needed, and requesting table access from that subtable. Individual selectors exist in at most one subtable, but the same class can exist in multiple subtables. For this reason, class indexes for these tables are dependent on selector indexes (because the subtable is determined by the selector index). For efficiency, selector indexes are *encoded* so as to maintain both the subtable to which they belong and the actual index within that subtable. The PartitionedTable class has a dynamic number of FixedRow2DTable instances as subtables. A new FixedRow2DTable instance is added when a selector cannot fit in any existing subtable. The SeparatedTable class has two subtables, one for standard selectors and one for conflict selectors. A *standard selector* is one with only one root method node (a new selector is also standard), and a *conflict selector* is one with more than one root method node. A *root method node* for <C, σ> is one in which class C has no superclasses that define σ. Each of these subtables can be an instance of either Extendable2DTable or PartitionedTable. Because PartitionedTables are also outer tables, such implementations express tables as subtables containing subsubtables.

Selector Index Strategy (SIS)

Each table has associated with it a selector index strategy, which is represented as an instance of some subclass of SIS. The OuterTable and 1DTable classes have one particular selector index strategy that they must use, but the 2DTable classes can choose from any of the 2D-SIS subclasses.

Each subclass of SIS implements the algorithm DetermineSelectorIndex, which provides a mechanism for determining the index to associate with a selector. Each SIS class maintains the current index for each selector, and is responsible for detecting selector index conflicts. When such conflicts are detected, a new index must be determined that does not conflict with existing indexes. Algorithm DetermineSelectorIndex is responsible for detecting conflicts, determining a new index, storing the index, ensuring that space exists in the table for the new index, moving method nodes from the old table locations to new table locations, and returning the selector index to the caller.

The abstract 2D-SIS class represents selector index strategies for use with 2D-Tables. These strategies are interchangeable, so any 2D-Table subclass can use any concrete subclass of 2D-SIS in order to provide selector index determination. The PlainSIS class is a naive strategy that assigns a unique index to each selector. The ColoredSIS and AliasedSIS classes allow two selectors to share the same index as long as no class in the environment recognizes both selectors. They differ in how they determine which selectors can share indexes. AliasedSIS is applicable only to languages with single inheritance and places certain restrictions on selectors for which indexes can be computed.

The ShiftedSIS class provides selector index determination for tables in which selectors and classes share the same dimension. This strategy implements a variety of auxiliary functions that maintain doubly-linked freelists of unused entries in the one-dimensional table. These freelists are used to efficiently determine a new selector index. The selector index is interpreted as a shift offset within the table, to which class indexes are added in order to obtain a table entry for a class/selector pair.

The ClassSpecificSIS assigns selector indexes that depend on the class. Unlike the other strategies, selector indexes do not need to be the same across all classes, although two classes that are related in the inheritance hierarchy *are* required to share the index for selectors understood by both classes.

The PartitionedSIS class implements selector index determination for PartitionedTable instances. When selector index conflicts are detected, a new index is obtained by asking a subtable to determine an index. Because FixedRow2D subtables of PartitionedTable instances are not guaranteed to be able to assign an index, all subtables are asked for an index until a subtable is found that can assign an index. If no subtable can assign an index, a new subtable is dynamically created.

The SeparatedSIS class implements selector index determination for SeparatedTable instances. A new index needs to be assigned when a selector index conflict is detected or when a selector changes status from standard to conflicting, or vice versa. Such index determination involves asking either the standard or the conflict subtable to find a selector index.

Class Index Strategy (CIS)

Each table has associated with it a class index strategy, which is represented as an instance of some subclass of CIS. The OuterTable and 1DTable classes have one particular class index strategy that they must use, but the 2DTable classes can choose from either of the 2D-CIS subclasses.

Each subclass of CIS implements the algorithm DetermineClassIndex, which provides a mechanism for determining the index to associate with a class. Each CIS class maintains the current index for each class, and is responsible for detecting class index conflicts. When such conflicts are detected, a new index must be determined that does not conflict with existing indexes. Algorithm DetermineClassIndex is responsible for detecting conflicts, determining a new index, storing the index, ensuring that space exists in the table for the new index, moving method nodes from old table locations to new table locations, and returning the class index to the caller.

The NonSharedCIS class implements the standard class index strategy, in which each class is assigned a unique index as it is added to the table. The SharedCIS class allows two or more classes to share the same index if all classes sharing the index have exactly the same method node for every selector in the table.

The PartitionedCIS and SeparatedCIS classes implement class index determination for PartitionedTable and SeparatedTable, respectively. In both cases, this involves establishing a subtable based on the selector index and asking that subtable to find a class index.

16.2.2 The DT Algorithms

Although the class hierarchies are what provide the DT framework with its flexibility and the ability to switch between different dispatch techniques at will, it is the high-level algorithms implemented by the framework that are of greatest importance. Each of these algorithms is a *template method* describing the overall mechanism for using inheritance management to incrementally maintain a dispatch table, detect and record inheritance conflicts, and maintain class hierarchy information useful for compile-time optimizations. They call low-level, technique-specific functions in order to perform fundamental operations such as table access, table modification, and table dimension extension. This section provides a high-level description of the algorithms. A detailed discussion of the algorithms and how they interact can be found in [Holst 1996].

The following notation is used. C is a class, σ is a selector, M is a method node, and ϕ is an empty method node. G represents a set of classes, index(C) is the numeric index for class C, index(σ) is the numeric index for selector σ, and T[index(σ), index(C)] contains a method node which in turn establishes the address to execute for class C and selector σ.

The Interface Algorithms

In general, framework users do not need to know anything about the implementation details of the framework. Instead, they create an instance of the DT Environment class and send messages to this instance each time an environment modification occurs. There are four fundamental *interface* algorithms for maintaining inheritance changes in the Environment class: algorithms *AddSelector*, *RemoveSelector*, *AddClassLinks*, and *RemoveClassLinks*. In all four cases, calling the algorithm results in a modification of all (and only) those table entries that need to be updated. Inheritance conflict recording, index conflict resolution, and method-node hierarchy modification are performed as the table is updated. Most of this functionality is not provided directly by the interface algorithms; instead, these algorithms establish how two fundamental inheritance management algorithms (ManageInheritance and ManageInheritanceRemoval) should be invoked.

In addition to the four interface routines for modifying the inheritance hierarchy, there are also registration routines for creating or finding instances of classes and selectors. Each time the language parser encounters a syntactic specification for a class or selector, it sends a *RegisterClass* or *RegisterSelector* message to the DT environment, passing the name of the class or selector. The environment maintains a mapping from name to instance, returning the desired instance if already created, and creating a new instance if no such instance exists. Note that the existence of a selector or class does not in itself affect the inheritance hierarchy; in order for the dispatch tables to be affected, a selector must be associated with a class (AddSelector) or a class must be added to the inheritance hierarchy (AddClassLinks).

Figure 16.6 shows algorithm AddSelector, which is invoked each time a selector is defined in a particular class and algorithm.

```
Algorithm AddSelector (inout σ: Selector, inout C : Class,
      in A : Address, inout T: Table)
 1  if index(σ) = unassigned or (T[index(σ), index(C)] > φ and
       T[index(σ), index(C)].σ > σ) then
 2     DetermineSelectorIndex(σ, C, T)
 3  endif
 4  M_C := T[index(σ), index(C)]
 5  if M_C.C = C and M_C.σ = σ then
 6     M_C.A := A
 7     remove any conflict marking on M_C
 8  else
 9     insert σ into selectors(C)
10     M_N := NewMethodNode(C, σ, A)
11     AddMethodNodeChild(M_C, M_N)
12     ManageInheritance(C, C, M_N, nil, T)
13  endif
end Algorithm
```

Figure 16.6 Algorithm AddSelector.

Lines 1 to 3 of algorithm AddSelector determine whether a new selector index is needed and, if so, call algorithm DetermineSelectorIndex to establish a new index and move the method node if appropriate.

Lines 4 to 7 determine whether a method recompilation or inheritance conflict removal has occurred. In either case, a method node already exists that has been propagated to the appropriate dependent classes, so no repropagation is necessary. Because the table entries for all dependent classes of $<C, \sigma>$ store a pointer to the same method node, assigning the new address to the current method node modifies the information in multiple extended dispatch table entries simultaneously.

If the test in line 5 fails, algorithm AddSelector falls into its most common scenario, lines 8 to 12. A new method node is created, a method node hierarchy link is added, and algorithm ManageInheritance is called to propagate the new method node to the child classes.

Algorithm AddClassLinks updates the extended dispatch table when new inheritance links are added to the inheritance graph. Rather than having algorithm Add-ClassLinks add one inheritance link at a time, we have generalized it so that an arbitrary number of both parent and child class links can be added. This is done because the number of calls to algorithm ManageInheritance can often be reduced when multiple parents are given. For example, when a conflict occurs between one or more of the new parent classes, such conflicts can be detected in algorithm Add-ClassLinks, allowing for a single conflict method node to be propagated. If only a single parent were provided at a time, the first parent specified would propagate the method node normally, but when the second (presumably conflicting) parent was added, a conflict method node would have to be created and propagated instead. Algorithm AddClassLinks accepts a class C, a set of parent classes G_P, and a set of children classes G_C. We have omitted the code for the algorithm for brevity [Holst 1997b].

Algorithms for Inheritance Management

Algorithm ManageInheritance, and its interaction with algorithms AddSelector and AddClassLinks, forms the most important part of the DT framework. Algorithm ManageInheritance is responsible for propagating a method node provided to it by algorithm AddSelector or AddClassLinks to all dependent classes of the method node. During this propagation, the algorithm is also responsible for maintaining inheritance conflict information and managing selector index conflicts. Algorithm ManageInheritanceRemoval plays a similar role with respect to algorithms RemoveSelector and RemoveClassLinks.

Algorithms ManageInheritance and ManageInheritanceRemoval are recursive. They are applied to a class, then invoked on each child class of that class. Recursion terminates when a class with a native definition is encountered, or no child classes exist. During each invocation, tests are performed to determine which of four possible scenarios is to be executed: *method-node child update*, *method-node reinsertion*, *conflict creation* (conflict removal, in ManageInheritanceRemoval) or *method-node insertion*. Each scenario either identifies a method node to propagate to children of the current class, or establishes that recursion should terminate. Due to inheritance conflicts, a recursive call may not necessarily propagate the incoming method node, but may instead propagate a new conflict method node that it creates.

These algorithms have gone through many refinements, and the current implementations provide extremely efficient inheritance management, inheritance conflict detection, index conflict resolution, and method-node hierarchy maintenance. An in-depth discussion of how these algorithms are implemented, the optimal tests used to establish scenarios, and how the method-node data structure provides these tests is available in [Holst 1996].

The algorithms are implemented in the abstract Table class, and do not need to be reimplemented in subclasses. However, these algorithms do invoke a variety of operations which do need to be overridden in subclasses. Thus, algorithms ManageInheritance and ManageInheritanceRemoval act as template methods [Gamma 1995], providing the overall structure of the algorithms, but deferring some steps to subclasses. Subclasses are responsible for implementing functionality for determining selector and class indexes, accessing and modifying the table structure, and modifying method-node hierarchies.

Algorithm Inheritance Manager, shown in Figure 16.7, has five arguments:

C_T. The current target class.

C_B. The base class from which inheritance propagation should start (needed by algorithm DetermineSelectorIndex).

M_N. The new method node to be propagated to all dependent classes of $<C_B, \sigma>$.

M_P. The method node in the table for the parent class of C_T from which this invocation occurred.

T. The extended dispatch table to be modified.

Algorithm ManageInheritance can be divided into four distinct parts. Lines 1 to 4 determine the values of the test variables. Note that $M_C = \phi$ when $M_N.\sigma$ is not currently visible in C_T. We define $\phi.C = nil$, so in such cases, C_I will be nil.

Lines 5 to 9 test for a selector index conflict and, if one is detected, invoke algorithm DetermineSelectorIndex and reassign test variables that change due to selector index modification. Algorithm DetermineSelectorIndex assigns selector indexes, establishes new indexes when selector index conflicts occur, and moves all selectors in an extended dispatch table when selector indexes change. Note that selector index conflicts are not possible in STI and VTBL dispatch techniques, so the DT Tables classes used to implement these dispatch techniques provide an implementation of algorithm ManageInheritance without lines 5 to 9 for use in these cases. Furthermore, due to the manner in which algorithm DetermineSelectorIndex assigns selector indexes, it is not possible for more than one selector index conflict to occur during a single invocation of algorithm AddSelector or AddClassLinks, so if lines 6 to 8 are ever executed, subsequent recursive invocations can avoid the check for selector index conflicts by calling a version of algorithm ManageInheritance that does not include these lines. These are two examples of how the framework uses polymorphism to optimize the implementation of dispatch support.

Lines 10 to 22 apply the action-determining tests to establish one of the four actions. Only one of the four actions is performed for each invocation of algorithm ManageInheritance, but in each action, one of two things must occur: The action performs an immediate return, thus stopping recursion and not executing any additional code in the algorithm; or the action assigns a value to the special variable D. If the algorithm reaches

```
Algorithm ManageInheritance(in C_T: Class, in C_B: Class,
        in M_N: MethodNode, in M_P: MethodNode, inout T : Table)
"Assign important variables"
1   σ := M_N.σ
2   C_N := M_N.C
3   M_N := T[index(σ), index(C_N)]
4   C_I := M_C.C
"Check for selector index conflict"
5   if M_C > φ and M_C.σ > M_N.σ then
6       DetermineSelectorIndex (M_N.σ, C_B ,T)
7       M_C := T[index(σ), index(C_T)]
8       C_I := M_C.C
9   endif
"Determine and perform appropriate action"
10 if (C_T = C_I) then method-node child update
11     AddMethodNodeChild(M_N, M_C)
12     RemoveMethodNodeChild(M_P, M_C)
13       return
14 elsif (C_T = C_I) method-node re-insertion
15       return
16 elsif (π = true) then conflict creation
17     M := RecordInheritanceConflict (σ, C_T, {M_N, M_C})
18 else method-node insertion
19     M := M_N
20 endif
"Insert method-node and propagate to children"
21 T[index(σ), index(C_T)] := M
22 foreach C_I ∈ children (C_T) do
23     ManageInheritance (C_I, C_B, M, M_C, T)
24 endfor
end ManageInheritance
```

Figure 16.7   Algorithm ManageInheritance.

the fourth part, variable M represents the method node that should be placed in the extended dispatch table for C_T and propagated to child classes of C_T. It is usually the method node M_N, but during conflict creation this is not the case. In line 11, algorithm AddMethodNodeChild adds its second argument as a child method node of its first argument. In line 12, algorithm RemoveMethodNodeChild removes its second argument as a child of its first argument. In both cases, if either argument is an empty method node, no link is added. The test π = true in line 16 establishes whether an inheritance conflict exists, and has an efficient implementation that is discussed in [Holst 1996].

When the DT algorithms are used on a language with single inheritance, conflict detection is unnecessary and multiple paths to classes do not exist, so the conflict-creation and method node reinserting actions are not possible. In such languages, algorithm ManageInheritance simplifies to a single test: If $C_T = C_I$, perform method-node child updating, and if not, perform method-node inserting.

Finally, lines 21 to 24 are executed only if the action determined in the third part does not request an explicit return. It consists of inserting method node M into the extended dispatch table for $<C_T, \sigma>$ and recursively invoking the algorithm on all child classes of C_T, passing in the method node M as the method node to be propagated. It is important that extended dispatch table entries in parents be modified before those in children, in order to commute π efficiently.

Algorithms for Selector and Class Index Determination

Each selector and class instance is assigned an index by the DT framework. The indexes associated with a class/selector pair are used to establish an entry within the table for that class/selector pair. An *index strategy* is a technique for incrementally assigning indexes so that the new index does not cause index conflicts. An *index conflict* occurs when two class/selector pairs with different method nodes access the same entry in the table. Because it is undesirable for an entry to contain more than one method node [Vitek 1996, 1994], we want to resolve the conflict by assigning new indexes to one of the class/selector pairs. Note that because indexes are table specific, and each table has a single selector index strategy and class index strategy, it is the index strategy instances that maintain the currently assigned indexes for each selector and class, rather than having each selector and class instance maintain multiple indexes (one for each table they participate in).

Given a class/selector pair, algorithm DetermineSelectorIndex, shown in Figure 16.8, returns the index associated with the selector. However, before returning the index, the algorithm ensures that no selector index conflict exists for that selector. If such a conflict does exist, a new selector index is computed that does not conflict with any other existing selector index, the new index is recorded, the selector dimension of the associated table is extended (if necessary), and all method nodes representing the selector are moved from the old index to the new index. Algorithm DetermineClass-Index performs a similar task for class indexes. Algorithm DetermineSelectorIndex is provided by classes in the SIS inheritance hierarchy, and algorithm DetermineClass-Index by classes in the CIS inheritance hierarchy.

In line 3, algorithm IndexFreeFor is a dispatch-technique-dependent algorithm that obtains an index that is not currently being used for any class that is currently using σ, as well as those classes that are dependent classes of σ. The algorithm is responsible for allocating any new space in the table necessary for the new index.

In line 5, if the old index is unassigned there are no method nodes to move, because no method nodes for s currently exist in the table. Otherwise, the method nodes for σ have changed location, and must be moved. The old locations are initialized with empty method nodes.

16.2.3 How the DT Framework Is Used

Recall that users of the DT framework are implementors of object-oriented language compilers and/or interpreters. Such individuals can provide their languages with table-based method dispatch and inheritance management as follows. During the

```
Algorithm DetermineSelectorIndex(inout σ : Selector, in C :
Class,
        inout T : Table)
1   L_old := index(σ)
2   if L_old is unassigned or a selector index conflict exists
3     L_new := IndexFreeFor(ClassesUsing(σ) ∪ DependentClasses(C, σ))
4     index(σ) := L_new
5     if L_old > unassigned then
6       for C_i ∈ ClassesUsing(σ) do
7         T[L_new, C_i] := T[L_old, C_i]
8         T[L_old, C_i] := φ
9       endfor
10    endif
11    extend selector dimension of table to handle L_new
12    index(σ) := L_new
13 endif
end DetermineSelectorIndex
```

Figure 16.8 Algorithm DetermineSelectorIndex.

implementation of an object-oriented language, the native language must provide some data structures to represent the classes and selectors defined within the language being implemented. In order to use the DT framework, these data structures should be subclasses of Selector and Class, as provided by the framework. The DT framework implementation of these classes provides only the state and behavior that is required for inheritance management and method dispatch. Clients are free to extend the state and functionality depending on their own requirements.

Having created appropriate subclasses of Selector and Class, the DT framework client then creates a single instance E of the DTEnvironment. This instance acts as a whitebox interface between the client and the DT framework, because the environment provides the functionality for registering new selectors and classes with the environment, associating methods with classes, and associating inheritance links between classes. Each time the compiler or interpreter encounters a class or selector definition, the appropriate interface routines of the DT environment instance are called to record the information.

16.2.4 How Clients Extend the DT Framework

Extending the DT framework means developing a new table-based method technique. Depending on the technique developed, one or more of the following may need to be created: a new table class, a new selector-indexing class, a new class-indexing class, and a new method-node class. In some techniques, there is a one-to-one mapping from table to selector- and class-indexing strategies, while in other techniques, a single table can use one of a variety of indexing strategies, and multiple tables can use the same indexing strategies.

To create a new table class, the implementor creates a new subclass of Table and implements the virtual access and change methods. These methods get and set entries within the table when given various combinations of selector, class, selector index, and class index.

To create a new selector-indexing strategy, the implementor subclasses the SelectorIndexStrategy class and implements algorithm Determine Selector Index. This method establishes whether a new index is required, and, if so, finds one that does not conflict with existing indexes. The algorithm is also responsible for recording the newly determined index and allocating additional (dynamic) space in the table if the new index exceeds the current maximum size of the table. Creating a new class-indexing strategy is very similar, except that algorithm DetermineClassIndex is implemented instead.

16.3 Incremental Table-Based Method Dispatch

As discussed in *Section 16.1.2*, there are five existing single-receiver table-based dispatch techniques. However, published implementations of all techniques except STI and SC have assumed *nonreflexive* environments. However, the DT algorithms are technique-independent algorithms for *incremental* modification of dispatch tables. Thus, not only does the framework allow us to implement all of the dispatch techniques by combining various table, SIS, and CIS subclasses, it also provides the first *incremental* versions of these algorithms.

The exact dispatch mechanism is controlled by parameters passed to the DT Environment constructor. The parameters indicate which table(s) to use, and specify the selector and class index strategies to be associated with each of these tables.

Selector table indexing (STI). Uses Extendable2DTable, PlainSIS, and NonSharedCIS.

Selector Coloring (SC). Uses Extendable2DTable, ColoredSIS, and NonSharedCIS.

Row displacement (RD). Uses 1DTable, ShiftedSIS and NonSharedCIS.

Virtual function tables (VTBL). Uses ClassTable, ClassSpecificSIS and NonSharedCIS.

Compact tables (CT). Uses a SeparatedTable with two PartitionedTable subtables, each with FixedRow2DTable subsubtables. The selector index strategy for all subsubtables of the standard subtable is AliasedSIS, and the strategy for all subsubtables of the conflict subtable is PlainSIS. All subsubtables use SharedCIS.

Incremental compact tables (ICT). Identical to CTs, except that the standard subtable uses ColoredSIS instead of AliasedSIS.

Selector colored compact tables (SCCT). Identical to table CTs, except that both standard and conflict subtables used ColoredSIS (instead of AliasedSIS and PlainSIS, respectively).

The last two techniques are examples of what the DT framework can do to combine existing techniques into new hybrid techniques. For example, ICT dispatch uses selector coloring instead of selector aliasing to determine selector indexes in the standard table, and is thus applicable to languages with multiple inheritance. Even better, SCCT uses selector coloring in both standard and conflict tables (remember that the CT dispatch effectively uses STI-style selector indexing in the conflict table).

In addition to providing each of these dispatch techniques, the framework can be used to analyze the various compression strategies introduced by CT dispatch in isolation from the others. For example, a dispatch table consisting of a PartitionedTable, whose FixedRow2DTable subtables each use PlainSIS and SharedCIS indexing strategies, allows us to determine how much table compression is obtained by class sharing alone. Many variations based on SeparatedTable and PartitionedTable, their subtables, and the associated index strategies are possible.

16.4 Performance Results

The previous sections describe a framework for the incremental maintenance of an extended dispatch table, using any table-based dispatch technique. This section summarizes the results of using the DT framework to implement STI, SC, RD, ICT, and SCCT dispatch and to generate extended dispatch tables for a variety of object-oriented class libraries [Holst 1997a].

To test the algorithms, we modeled a compiler or runtime interpreter by a simple parsing program that reads input from a file. Each line of the file is either a *selector definition*, consisting of a selector name and class name, or a *class definition*, consisting of a class name and a list of zero or more parent class names. The order in which the class and selector definitions appear in this file represent the order in which a compiler or runtime system would encounter the same declarations.

In [Driesen 1995a], the effectiveness of the nonincremental RD technique was demonstrated on 12 real-world class libraries. We have executed the DT algorithms on this same set of libraries in order to determine what effects dispatch technique, input order, and library size have on per-invocation algorithm execution times and on the time and memory needed to create a complete extended dispatch table for the library in question.

The cross product of technique, library, and input ordering generates far too much data to present here. Of the 15 input orderings we analyzed, we present three: a nonrandom ordering that is usually best for all techniques and libraries, a nonrandom ordering that is the worst of all nonrandom orderings, and our best approximation of a natural ordering. Parcplace1 was chosen because it is a large, robust, commonly used single-inheritance library. Geode was chosen because it is even larger than Parcplace1 and it makes extensive use of multiple inheritance, with an average of 2.1 parents per class. In addition, both of these libraries were used in [Driesen 1995a, 1995b]. Finally, BioTools was chosen because it is a real application with a real sequence of reflexive environment modifications. It represents one of many possible *natural* orderings, where a natural ordering is one that is typical of what a real programmer would use. We obtained the natural order from the Smalltalk change log that records every class and selector defined, in the correct order. Because the Parcplace and Geode libraries are predefined class libraries, we used a completely random ordering of the classes and selectors instead of a natural ordering.

Table 16.1 presents some useful statistics for the class libraries, where C is the total number of classes, S is the total number of selectors, M is the total number of legitimate class/selector combinations, m is the total number of defined methods, P is the average number of parents per class, and B is the size of the largest complete behavior [Driesen 1995a].

Tables 16.2 and 16.3 present the total time and memory requirements for each of the class libraries from Table 16.1, for each of the table-based dispatch techniques on the best, worst, and natural input orderings. The framework is implemented in C++, was compiled with g++-O2, and was executed on a SPARC-Station 20.

Overall execution time, memory usage, and fill rates for the published nonincremental versions are provided for comparison. We define *fill rate* as the percentage of total table entries having user-defined method addresses, including addresses that indicate inheritance conflicts. Note that for CT, this definition of fill rate is misleading, because class sharing allows many classes to share the same column in the table. A more accurate measure of fill rate is possible, but it is not relevant to this chapter. Therefore, to avoid confusion, we do not describe CT fill rates here.

In [Andre-Royer 1992], the incremental algorithm for SC took 12 minutes on a Sun 3/80 when applied to the Smalltalk-80 Version 2.5 hierarchy. That hierarchy is slightly smaller than the Smalltalk Parcplace1 library presented in Tables 16.2 and 16.3. The DT framework, applied to all classes in this library, took 113 seconds to complete on a Sun 3/80. No overall memory results were reported in [Andre-Royer 1992] (DT uses 2.5 Mb), but their algorithm had a fill rate within 3 percent of optimal (the maximum total number of selectors understood by one class is a minimum on the number of rows to which SC can compress the STI table). Using the best input ordering, the DT algorithms have a fill rate within 1 percent of optimal.

In [Driesen 1995a], nonincremental RD is presented, and the effects of different implementation strategies on execution time and memory usage are analyzed. Our current DT implementation of RD is roughly equivalent to the implementation strategies DIO and SI as described in that paper. Implementing strategies DRO and MI, which give better fill rates and performance for static RD, requires complete knowledge of the environment. Their results were run on a SPARC-Station 20/60, and were 4.3 seconds for Parcplace1, and 9.6 seconds for Geode. Total memory was not presented, but detailed fill rates were. They achieved a 99.6 percent fill rate for Parcplace1 and 57.9 percent for Geode (using SI). Using the input ordering that matches their ordering as closely as possible, our algorithms gave fill rates of 99.6 and 58.3 percent. However, fill rates for the natural ordering were 32.0 and 20.6 percent, respectively.

Table 16.1 Statistics for Various Object-Oriented Environments

LIBRARY	C	S	M	M	P	B
BioTools	493	4,052	11,802	5,931	1.0	132
Parcplace1	774	5,086	178,230	8,540	1.0	401
Geode	1,318	6,549	302,709	14,194	2.1	795

Table 16.2 Timing Results for the DT Framework, in Seconds

LIBRARY	ORDER	STI	SC	RD	ICT	SCCT
BioTools	Best	5.7	3.5	5.7	6.7	10.7
	Worst	11.4	7.0	10.9	11.4	11.6
	Natural	18.3	13.8	20.2	21.9	22.5
Parc1	Best	8.6	7.2	9.3	16.9	18.3
	Worst	23.4	30.5	126.0	37.2	34.9
	Natural	24.2	28.0	1064.0	73.2	77.3
Geode	Best	25.3	27.1	133.1	61.4	68.4
	Worst	59.9	84.3	937.0	125.7	133.4
	Natural	67.4	75.7	6032.0	157.7	174.1

In [Vitek 1996], nonincremental CT is presented, with timing results given for a SPARC-Station 5. A timing of about 2 seconds for Parcplace1 can be interpolated from the data, and a memory consumption of 1.5 Mb. Results for Geode were not possible because Geode uses multiple inheritance. In the DT framework, we use selector coloring instead of selector aliasing, which removes the restriction to languages with single inheritance. On a SPARC-Station 5, the DT algorithms run in 21.1 seconds using 1.9 Mb when applied to Parcplace1, and run in 70.5 seconds using 4.8 Mb when applied to Geode.

We have also estimated the memory overhead incurred by the incremental nature of the DT framework. The data maintained by the Environment, Class, and Selector classes is needed in both static and incremental versions, and only a small amount of the memory is taken by table overhead, so the primary contributor to incremental overhead is the collection of MethodNode instances. The total memory overhead varies with the memory efficiency of the dispatch technique, from a low of 15 percent for STI to a high of 50 percent for RD and SCCT.

Table 16.3 Space Requirements for the DT Framework, Mb

LIBRARY	ORDER	STI	SC	RD	ICT	SCCT
BioTools	Best	10.6	1.2	1.0	1.3	1.0
	Worst	11.3	1.2	1.2	1.3	1.0
	Natural	10.7	1.1	1.1	1.8	1.0
Parc1	Best	20.1	2.7	2.6	1.9	1.6
	Worst	20.6	3.0	4.2	2.2	1.8
	Natural	20.1	3.1	5.6	2.6	2.1
Geode	Best	44.5	8.7	7.0	4.8	4.3
	Worst	44.8	8.9	11.8	5.6	5.0
	Natural	44.3	9.0	13.9	8.3	6.8

16.4.1 Invocation Costs of the DT Algorithms

Since we are stressing the incremental nature of the DT framework, the per-invocation cost of our fundamental algorithms, AddSelector, AddClassLink, and InheritanceManager, are of interest. Rather than reporting the timings for every recursive call of InheritanceManager, we report the sum over all recursive calls from a single invocation from AddSelector or AddClassLinks. The per-invocation results for the Parcplace1 library are representative, so we summarize them here. Furthermore, SC, ICT, and SCCT techniques have similar distributions, so we present only the results for SC and RD dispatch. In Parcplace1, algorithm AddSelector is always called 8540 times, and algorithm AddClassLinks is called 774 times, but the number of times ManageInheritance is invoked from these routines depends on the input ordering. Per-invocation timings were obtained using the getrusage( ) system call and taking the sum of system and user time. Note that because Sun 4 machines have a clock interval of 0.01s, the granularity of the results is 10 ms.

For SC dispatch, each algorithm executes in less than 10 ms for more than 95 percent of its invocations, for all orderings. The differences occur only for the other 5 percent of the invocations. For algorithm AddSelector, the maximum (average) per-invocation times were 30 ms (0.7 ms) for optimal order, and 120 ms (0.6 ms) for natural order. For algorithm AddClassLinks, they were 10 ms (0.1 ms) and 4100 ms (27.3 ms), and for algorithm ManageInheritance, 30 ms (0.2 ms) and 120 ms (0.25 ms).

The results are similar for RD dispatch. However, the timing variations between different natural orderings can be as much as 100 percent (the maximum time is twice the minimum time). For algorithm AddSelector, maximum (average) per-invocation times were 80 ms (0.9 ms) for optimal order, and 1970 ms (6.7 ms) for natural order. For algorithm AddClassLinks, they were 10 ms (0.1 ms) and 52,740 ms (12,763 ms), and for algorithm ManageInheritance, 70 ms (0.2 ms) and 3010 ms (24.5 ms).

16.4.2 Effects on Dispatch Performance

In [Driesen 1995b], the dispatch costs of most of the published dispatch techniques are presented. The costs are expressed as formulae involving processor-specific constants like load latency L and branch miss penalty B, which vary with the type of processor being modeled. This section observes how the incremental nature of our algorithms affects this dispatch speed.

At a particular call site, the method selector and the class of the receiver object together uniquely determine which method to invoke. Conceptually, in object-oriented languages, each object knows its (dynamic) class, so we can obtain a class index for a given object. This index, along with the index of the selector (which is usually known at compile time), uniquely establishes an entry within a global dispatch table. In this scheme, we do a fair amount of work to obtain an address: get the class of the receiver object, access the class index, get the global table, get the class-specific part of the table (based on class index), and get the appropriate entry within this subtable (based on selector index).

This dispatch sequence can be improved by making a simple observation: If each class explicitly stored its portion of the global dispatch table, we could avoid the need to obtain a class index. In fact, we would no longer need to maintain a class index at all (the table replaces the index). In languages where the size of the dispatch table is known at compile time, it is even more efficient to assume that each class *is* a table, rather than assuming that each class contains a table. This avoids an indirection, because we no longer need to ask for the class of an object, then obtain the table from the class; we now ask for the class and immediately have access to its table (which starts at some constant offset from the beginning of the class itself). Thus, all of the table-based dispatch techniques must do at least the following (they may also need to do more): (1) get table from receiver object, (2) get method address from table (based on selector index), and (3) call method.

We want to determine how much dispatch performance degrades when using the DT framework, with its incremental nature, dynamic growing of tables as necessary, and the use of extended dispatch tables instead of simple dispatch tables. Note that during dispatch, indirections may incur a penalty beyond just the operation itself due to load latency (in pipelined processors, the result of a load started in cycle i is not available until cycle $i + L$). In the analysis of [Driesen 1995b], it is assumed that the load latency L is 2. This implies that each extra indirection incurred by the DTF algorithms will slow down dispatch by at least one cycle (for the load itself) and by at most L cycles (if there are no other operations that can be performed while waiting for the load).

Figure 16.9 shows a conceptual version of the internal state of the fundamental DT classes. Rather than showing the layout of all of the Table subclasses, we have chosen Extendable2DTable as a representative instance. The only difference between this table and the other tables is the nature of the Data field. This field, like many other fields in Figure 16.9, is of type Array, a simple C++ class that represents a dynamically growable array. The Data field of the Array class is a pointer to a contiguous block of bytes (usually containing indexes or pointers to other DT class instances). Such Arrays have more space allocated than is actually used (hence the Alloc and Size fields), but this overhead is a necessary part of dynamic growth.

In Figure 16.9, each Class object also has a Data field (another growable array), which in turn points to a block of dynamically allocated memory. Each entry in this block is a pointer to a MethodNode instance, which contains a pointer to the method to execute. Note that in Figure 16.9, Class instances are not considered to be dispatch tables, but instead contain a growable array representing the class-specific portion of the global dispatch table.

Given this layout, two extra indirections are incurred during dispatch, one to get the table from the class, and one to get the method node from the table. Thus, dispatch speeds in all table-based techniques will be increased by at most $2 \times L$ cycles. Depending on the branch-miss penalty B of the processor in question (the dominating variable in dispatch costs in [Driesen 1995b]), this results in a dispatch slow-down of between 50 percent ($B = 1$) and 30 percent ($B = 6$) when $L = 2$.

Given these performance penalties, the DT framework appears not to be desirable for use in production systems. However, it is relatively easy to remove both of the indirections mentioned, one by using a modest amount of additional memory, and the other by relying on implementations of object-oriented languages that do not use

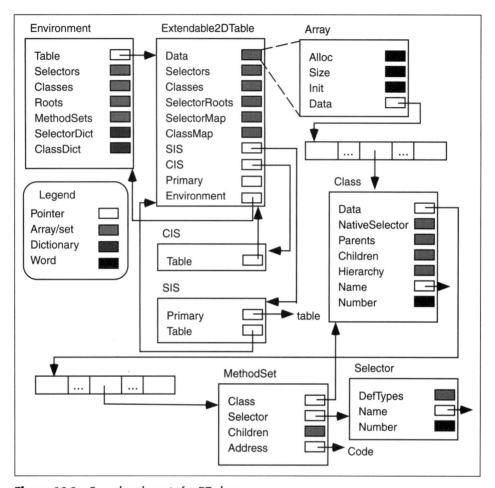

Figure 16.9 C++ class layouts for DT classes.

object tables. By removing these indirections, the DT framework has exactly the same dispatch performance as nonincremental implementations.

We can remove the extra indirection needed to extract the address from the method node by using some extra space. As is shown in Figure 16.10, each table entry is no longer just a pointer to a MethodNode instance; it is instead a two-field record containing both the method address and the MethodNode instance (the address field within the method node itself becomes redundant and can be removed). This slightly decreases the efficiency of incremental modification (it is no longer possible to change a single MethodNode address and have it be reflected in multiple table entries), but optimizing dispatch is more important than optimizing table maintenance. Furthermore, the amount of inefficiency is minimal, given how quickly algorithm AddSelector executes. Finally, the extra space added by effectively doubling the number of table entries is not necessarily that expensive, especially in techniques such as RD and CT.

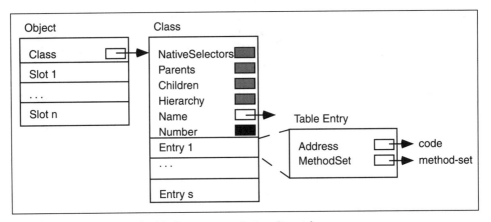

Figure 16.10   Improved table layout to optimize dispatch.

For example, in RD, the space for the table is about 25 percent of the total memory used, so doubling this table space increases the overall space used by 25 percent.

The other extra indirection exists because in Figure 16.9, classes *contain* tables instead of *being* tables. In the nonincremental world, the size of each class-specific dispatch table is known at compile time, so at runtime it is possible to allocate exactly enough space in each class instance to store its table directly. At first glance, this does not seem possible in the DT framework because the incremental addition of selectors requires that tables (and thus classes) grow dynamically. The reason this is difficult is because dynamic growth requires new memory to be allocated and data to be copied. Either we provide an extra indirection, or we provide some mechanism for updating every variable pointing to the original class object, so that it points to the new class object. Fortunately, this last issue is something that object-oriented language implementations that do not use object tables already support, so we can take advantage of the underlying capabilities of the language implementation to help provide efficient dispatch for the language. For example, in Smalltalk, indexed instance variables exist (Array is an example), which can be grown as needed. We therefore treat classes as *being* tables, rather than *containing* tables, and avoid the second indirection. Figure 16.10 shows the object, class, and table layouts that allow the DT framework to operate without incurring penalties during dispatch.

16.5 Related and Future Work

This section discusses work that is related to the research discussed in this chapter and describes future directions for the DT framework.

16.5.1 Related Work

[Driesen 1995b] presents an analysis of the various dispatch techniques and indicates that in most cases, IC and PIC are more efficient than STI, SC, and RD, especially on highly pipelined processors, because IC and PIC do not cause the pipeline stalls that the table indirections of STI, SC, and RD cause. However, even if the primary dispatch technique is IC or PIC, it may still be useful to maintain a dispatch table for cases where a miss occurs, as a much faster alternative to using method lookup (ML) or global cache (LC) and ML together. Especially in reflexive languages with substantial multiple inheritance, ML is extremely inefficient, because each inheritance path must be searched to detect inheritance conflicts.

[Dean 1995] discusses static class hierarchy analysis and its utility in optimizing object-oriented programs. The researchers introduce an *applies-to* set representing the set of classes that share the same method for a particular selector. These sets are represented by our concept of dependent classes. Because each method node implicitly maintains its set of dependent classes, the DT algorithms have access to such sets, and to the compile-time optimizations provided by them.

[Andre-Royer 1992] presents an incremental approach to selector coloring. However, the algorithm proposed often performs redundant work by checking the validity of selector colors each time a new selector is added. The DT algorithms demonstrate how to perform selector color determination only when absolutely necessary (that is, only when a selector color conflict occurs), and have applied this technique to a variety of table-based approaches. [Driesen 1995a] presents selector-based row displacement (RD) and discusses how to obtain optimal compression results. [Vitek 1996] presents the compact selector indexed table (CT), expanding on previous work in [Vitek 1994].

Predicate classes, as implemented in Cecil [Chambers 1993], allow a class to change its set of superclasses at runtime. The DT framework provides an efficient mechanism for implementing predicate classes using table-based dispatch.

Another framework that is used to implement a programming language is shown in [Adl-Tabatabai 1996], which produces optimizing retargetable compilers for ANSII C.

16.5.2 Future Work

The DT framework provides a general description of all work that needs to be performed to handle inheritance management and method dispatch in reflexive, non-statically typed, single-receiver languages with multiple inheritance. A variety of extensions are possible.

First, the framework as presented handles methods, but not internal state. A mechanism to incrementally modify object layout is a logical, and necessary, extension. Second, multimethod languages such as Tigukat [Ozsu 1995], Cecil [Chambers 1992], and CLOS [Bobrow 1988] have the ability to dispatch a method based not only on the dynamic type of a receiver, but also on the dynamic types of all arguments to the selector. Multimethods extend the expressive power of a language, but efficient method dispatch and inheritance management is an even more difficult issue in such languages. Extending the DT framework to handle multimethod dispatch is part of our continued research in this area. Third, the framework currently assumes that inheriting the interface of parent classes implies that the implementation associated with the interface is inherited also. A more general mechanism for inheritance management that separates these concepts is desirable. We are using the DT framework to implement all three of these concepts in Tigukat [Ozsu 1995], an object-oriented database language with massive schema evolution (reflexivity), multimethod dispatch, multiple implementation types, and many other extensions to the object-oriented paradigm.

Fourth, although the DT framework provides a general mechanism for handling table-based method dispatch, it is really only one component of a much larger framework that handles all method dispatch techniques. The DT framework can be extended so that framework clients call interface algorithms each time a call site is encountered, similar to the manner in which the environment is currently called, when class and selector definitions are encountered. This would extend the DT framework to encompass caching techniques as well as table-based techniques.

Fifth, the DT framework allows various compression techniques, such as selector aliasing, selector coloring, and class sharing, to be analyzed both in isolation and in interaction with one another. More research about how these techniques interact, and about how SCCT dispatch can be optimized, is necessary.

16.6 Summary

This chapter presents a framework that is usable by both compilers and runtime systems to provide table-based method dispatch, inheritance-conflict detection, and compile-time method determination. The framework relies on a set of technique-independent algorithms for environment modification, which call technique-dependent algorithms to perform fundamental operations such as table access and index determination. The framework unifies all table-based method dispatch techniques into a cohesive whole, allowing a language implementor to change between techniques by changing the manner in which the DT environment is instantiated. Incremental versions of all table-based techniques except VTBL have been implemented, all of which have low millisecond-per-invocation execution times.

The framework provides a variety of new capabilities. The various table-based dispatch techniques have different dispatch execution times and memory requirements. Because the framework allows any table-based dispatch technique to be used, a particular application can be optimized for either space or dispatch performance. Furthermore, the DT framework allows table-based dispatch techniques to be used in reflexive languages. In the past, reflexive languages necessitated the use of a non-table-based technique. One reason that C++ uses virtual function tables is that they allow for separate compilation, unlike other table-based dispatch techniques. The DT framework now allows all table-based dispatch techniques to work with separate compilation. Finally, the framework introduces a new level of software verification in reflexive languages by allowing inheritance conflicts to be detected immediately when they occur, rather than during dispatch.

The framework has been used to merge SC and CT method dispatch into a hybrid dispatch technique with the advantages of both. The CT dispatch technique is limited by its restriction to single inheritance. By replacing selector aliasing with selector coloring, we obtain a dispatch technique that works with multiple inheritance and that benefits from the class sharing made possible by CT class partitioning. Furthermore, SCCT dispatch provides better compression because the conflict table can be colored, unlike in CT dispatch, where it remains uncompressed.

The DT framework currently consists of 36 classes, 208 selectors, 494 methods, and 1081 meaningful class/selector pairs. When the DT framework is applied to a completely random ordering of itself, a SCCT-based dispatch table is generated in 0.436 s. Because compiling the framework requires 390 s, even the slowest dispatch technique and input ordering produce a dispatch table in a negligible amount of time, relative to overall compilation time. The framework is available at ftp://ftp.cs.ualberta.ca/pub/Dtf.

16.7 References

[Adl-Tabatabai 1996] Adl-Tabatabai, A.-R., T. Gross, and G.-Y. Lueh. Code reuse in an optimizing compiler. *Proceedings of the OOPSLA 1996 Conference on Programming Systems, Languages, and Applications.* San Jose, CA, ACM SIGPLAN Notices 31(10), Reading, MA: ACM Press, October 1996.

[Andre-Royer 1992] Andre, P., and J.C. Royer. Optimizing method search with lookup caches and incremental coloring. *Proceedings of the OOPSLA 1992 Conference on Programming Systems, Languages, and Applications.* ACM SIGPLAN Notices 27(10), Reading, MA: ACM Press, October 1992.

[Bobrow 1988] Bobrow, D.G., L.G. DeMichiel, R.P. Gabriel, S.E. Keene, G.Kiczales, and D.A. Moon, *Common Lisp Object System Specification.* X3J13 Document 88-002R. June 1988.

[Chambers 1992] Chambers, C. Object-oriented multi-methods in Cecil. *Proceedings of the 1992 European Conference on Object-Oriented Programming (ECOOP 1992).* Utrecht, The Netherlands, June/July 1992, O. Lehrmann Madsen, editor, LNCS 615, Springer-Verlag, 1992.

[Chambers 1993] Chambers, C. Predicate classes. *Proceedings of the 1993 European Conference on Object-Oriented Programming (ECOOP 1993).* Kaiswealautern, Germany, July 1993, O. Nierstrasz, editor, LNCS 707, Springer-Verlag, 1993.

[Cox 1987] Cox, B. *Object-Oriented Programming: An Evolutionary Approach.* Reading, MA: Addison-Wesley, 1987.

[Dean 1995] Dean, J., D. Grove, and C. Chambers. Optimization of object-oriented programs using static class hierarchy analysis. *Proceedings of the 1995 European Conference on Object-Oriented Programming (ECOOP 1995).* Aarhus, Denmark, August 1995, W. Olthoff, editor, LNCS 952, Springer-Verlag, August 1995.

[Deutsch 1994] Deutsch, L.P., and A. Schiffman. Efficient implementation of the Smalltalk-80 system. In *Principles of Programming Languages.* Salt Lake City, UT, 1994.

[Dixon 1989] Dixon, R., T. McKee, P. Schweizer, and M. Vaughan. A fast method dispatcher for compiled languages with multiple inheritance. *Proceedings of the OOPSLA 1989 Conference on Programming Systems, Languages, and Applications.* New Orleans, Louisiana, ACM SIGPLAN Notices 24(10), Reading, MA: ACM Press, October 1989.

[Driesen 1993] Driesen, K. Method lookup strategies in dynamically typed object-oriented programming languages. Master's thesis, Vrije Universiteit Brussel, Brussels, Belgium, 1993.

[Driesen 1995a] Driesen, K., and U. Holzle. Minimizing row displacement dispatch tables. *Proceedings of the OOPSLA 1995 Conference on Programming Systems, Lan-

guages, and Applications. Austin, Texas, ACM SIGPLAN Notices 30(10), Reading, MA: ACM Press, October 1995.

[Driesen 1995b] Driesen, K., U. Holzle, and J. Vitek. Message dispatch on pipelined processors. *Proceedings of the 1995 European Conference on Object-Oriented Programming (ECOOP 1995).* Aarhus, Denmark, August 1995, W. Olthoff, editor, LNCS 952, Springer-Verlag, August 1995.

[Ellis 1990] Ellis, M.A., and B. Stroustrup. *The Annotated C++ Reference Manual.* Reading, MA: Addison-Wesley, 1990.

[Gamma 1995] Gamma, E., R. Helm, R. Johnson, and J. Vlissides. *Design Patterns: Elements of Reusable Object-Oriented Software.* Reading, MA: Addison-Wesley, 1995.

[Goldberg 1983] Goldberg, A., and D. Robson. *Smalltalk-80: The Language and its Implementation.* Reading, MA: Addison-Wesley, 1983.

[Holst 1996] Holst, W., and D. Szafron. Inheritance management and method dispatch in reflexive object-oriented languages. Technical Report TR-96-27, University of Alberta, Edmonton, Canada, 1996.

[Holst 1997a] Holst, W., and D. Szafron. A general framework for inheritance management and method dispatch in object-oriented languages. *Proceedings of the 1997 European Conference on Object-Oriented Programming (ECOOP 1997).* Jyväskylä, Finland, June 1997.

[Holst 1997b] Holst, W., and D. Szafron. Incremental table-based method dispatch for reflexive object-oriented languages. *TOOLS 1997 Conference Proceedings*, Santa Barbara, CA, July/August 1997.

[Holzle 1991] Holzle, U., C. Chambers, and D. Ungar. Optimizing dynamically-typed object oriented languages with polymorphic inline caches. *Proceedings of the 1991 European Conference on Object-Oriented Programming (ECOOP 1991).* Geneva, Switzerland, July 1991, P. America, Editor, LNCS 512, Springer-Verlag, 1991.

[Horspool 1997] Horspool, R.N., A. Krall, and J. Vitek. Near optimal hierarchical encoding of types. *Proceedings of the 1997 European Conference on Object-Oriented Programming (ECOOP 1997).* Jyväskylä, Finland, June 1997.

[Krasner 1983] Krasner, G. *Smalltalk-80: Bits of History, Words of Advice.* Reading, MA: Addison-Wesley, 1983.

[Ozsu 1995] Ozsu, M.T., R.J. Peters, D. Szafron, B. Irani, A. Lipka, and A. Munoz. Tigukat: A uniform behavioral objectbase management system. *VLDB Journal,* 1995: 100–147.

[Vitek 1994] Vitek, J., and R.N. Horspool. Taming message passing: Efficient method lookup for dynamically typed languages. *Proceedings of the 1994 European Conference on Object-Oriented Programming (ECOOP 1994).* Bologna, Italy, July 1994, M. Tokoro and R. Pareschi, editors, LNCS 821, Springer-Verlag, 1994.

[Vitek 1996] Vitek, J., and R.N. Horspool. Compact dispatch tables for dynamically typed programming languages. *Proceedings of the International Conference on Compiler Construction,* 1996.

CHAPTER 17

Constraint Satisfaction Problems Framework

Constraint satisfaction programming (CSP) is a powerful paradigm for solving combinatorial problems, which was initially seen as an *algorithmic* issue [Laurière 1978; Mackworth 1977]. The first proposals for integrating constraints in a language were developed within the community of logic programming. Constraint logic programming (CLP) was primarily designed to deal with specific computation domains such as integer numbers. Its best-known representatives are Prolog III [Colmerauer 1990], Chip [Hentenryck 1989], and CLP(FD) [Codognet 1996].

Using CSP from within a programming language is a definitive advantage, compared to the situation where the user must call an external system. Depending on what the language offers to the user, the integration of CSP may take the three forms reviewed here: *library, language constructs,* or *framework.*

Library of generic constraints approach. In this approach, the objective is to identify generic constraints that can be used in a wide range of applications, for example, global constraints in Chip [Beldiceanu 1994]. This approach is adapted to classical problems, and in this case the only task is to formulate the problem in terms of the predefined constraints. This can be summed up by the phrase *constrain and solve*. For specific problems, because constraints are complex and domain independent, this formulation may be hard to find.

Language construct approach. This approach is illustrated by Claire [Caseau 1996], a language for building constraint solvers. Claire does not propose any predefined resolution mechanisms, but integrates general and efficient low-level constructs that can be used to build specific solvers (such as save/restore and forward chaining rule mechanisms). This approach can be seen as the opposite of the library approach: The user has a lot to do, but ends up with a efficient algorithms. This is well suited to hard problems not identified as instances of well-known classes of problems.

Framework approach. The framework approach is an intermediary position. It comes from works aiming at integrating *object-oriented languages* with constraints. Rather than providing specific computation domains as for CLP, the interest of integrating constraints and objects is to provide extensible and flexible implementations of CSP (for example, Cool [Avesani 1990], IlogSolver [Puget 1995], and Laure [Caseau 1994]). Besides, objects provide facilities for *domain adaptation*. One particularly efficient way to achieve domain adaptation is to provide *frameworks* [Fayad 1997] in which the general control loop and mechanisms are coded once for all, and adaptation to specific problems can be achieved easily. More than a class library, a framework is a semicomplete application containing integrated components collaborating to provide a reusable architecture for a family of applications. The following sections outline the features of such a framework.

17.1 From Theory to Practice

This section introduces briefly the basic concepts underlying constraint satisfaction as defined in the technical and theoretical literature. For the sake of simplicity, these theoretical works are based on a simplified model of constraint satisfaction, both from a technical and a conceptual viewpoint. We emphasize the fact that this simplified model is not adapted to the context of real-world applications, and argue in favor of a nonrestrictive model of CSP. The following section addresses the implementation of this richer model of CSP using the object-oriented framework approach.

17.1.1 Finite-Domain Constraint Satisfaction: Basic Notions

Stating a combinatorial problem as a CSP amounts to characterizing a priori what properties a solution should satisfy. A finite-domain constraint satisfaction problem is defined by a set of *variables*, each variable taking its value in a finite set, its *domain*; and by a set of *constraints*, defining the properties of the solutions. A *solution* is an instantiation of all the variables satisfying every constraint.

A naive resolution mechanism may be described as shown in Figure 17.1 (see, for instance, [Prosser 1993]). This procedure yields all the solutions of the problem, and is the core of all complete algorithms for finite-domain constraint satisfaction. Of course, this basic algorithm is very inefficient. The following sections review the main improvements of these basic algorithms as they are described in the literature.

1. **Choose a non-instantiated variable *V* of the problem.**

2. **Instantiate *V* with a value of its domain, and save the current state of the problem.**

3. **Check all instantiated constraints. If a constraint is violated, then backtrack to a previously saved state of the problem.**

4. **If all the variables are instantiated, then a solution has been found.**

   a. **Yield the solution.**

   b. **Go backward to a previously saved state.**

5. **Go to 1.**

Figure 17.1 The basic enumeration algorithm (BEA) for constraint satisfaction problems.

Arc Consistency

In the BEA, a constraint is used once all its variables are instantiated. The following example shows that constraints can also be used, actively, to anticipate dead ends. Consider for instance two variables X and Y whose domains are {1, 2, ..., 10}, and the constraint $X > Y$. If X is instantiated with 3, the constraint can be used right away to reduce the domain of Y to {1, 2}. This domain reduction prevents the algorithm from checking 3, 4, ..., 10 for Y. Note that *this domain reduction does not discard any solution*.

Domain reduction is the main tool for pruning branches of the search tree developed by BEA. The maximum amount of "safe" domain reduction is determined by the property of *arc consistency* [Bessière 1994; Mackworth 1977]—a binary constraint C holding on variables X and Y, is arc consistent if, and only if:

$\forall x \in$ dom $(X); \exists y \in$ dom (Y) such that $C(x, y) =$ true

and

$\forall y \in$ dom $(Y); \exists x \in$ dom (X) such that $C(x, y) =$ true

Informally, a constraint is arc consistent if every value of the domain of a variable appears in at least one consistent tuple of the constraint. This definition generalizes easily to nonbinary constraints. A constraint can be made arc consistent by removing values in the domains of its variables. More precisely, arc consistency, for a constraint C that involves variables X and Y, can be enforced as follows:

While C is not arc consistent, do

$\forall x \in$ dom $(X); [\forall y \in$ dom $(Y), C(x, y) =$ false $\Rightarrow$ dom $(Y) \leftarrow$ dom $(Y) \backslash \{y\}]$

$\forall y \in$ dom $(Y); [\forall x \in$ dom $(X), C(x, y) =$ false $\Rightarrow$ dom $(X) \leftarrow$ dom $(X) \backslash \{x\}]$

A CSP is said to be arc consistent if all its constraints are arc consistent. As previously noted, a constraint can be made arc consistent by reducing the domains of its variables, and arc consistency is safe, in the sense that it does not discard any solution. Therefore, arc consistency can be used during the execution of an enumeration algo-

1. Choose a noninstantiated variable *V* of the problem.

2. Instantiate *V* with a value of its domain, and save the current state of the problem.

3. *Enforce arc consistency for the whole problem.*

If a variable domain is wiped out, then backtrack to a previously saved state of the problem.

4. If all the variables are instantiated, then a solution has been found (stop).

5. Go to 1.

Figure 17.2 Real full look-ahead algorithm.

rithm to speed up the search by reducing the problem. This idea leads to much more efficient algorithms, as the next section explains.

Arc-Consistency-Based Algorithms

The most efficient algorithms for solving CSPs are based on the BEA, augmented with arc consistency, which is used to reduce the problem during the search. The main difference between these algorithms lies in the *amount* of arc consistency enforced. For instance, the algorithm called *real full look-ahead* [Nadel 1989] reduces the problem using arc consistency as much as possible (see Figure 17.2). Of course, enforcing arc consistency of the whole problem requires a considerable amount of computation time. One could say that this method slowly explores a small search space.

In the algorithm called *forward checking* [Haralick 1980] (see Figure 17.3), the reduction consists of enforcing arc consistency only for constraints involving the last instantiated variable. Compared to real full look-ahead, this method prunes fewer branches of the search tree, but it spends less time during the domain reduction phase: This algorithm quickly explores a large search space.

Many other algorithms have been devised that fit in with this scheme. Differences concerns the amount of propagation performed and the backtracking strategies applied. The following section reviews several limitations of this basic model in the context of real-world constraint satisfaction problems.

1. Choose a noninstantiated variable *V* of the problem.

2. Instantiate *V* with a value of its domain, and save the current state of the problem.

3. *Enforce arc consistency for the constraints involving V.*

If a domain is wiped out, then backtrack to a previously saved state of the problem.

4. If all the variables are instantiated, then a solution has been found (stop).

5. Go to 1.

Figure 17.3 Forward-checking (FC) algorithm.

17.1.2 Restriction to Binary Problems

A binary CSP is a problem whose constraints hold on at most two variables. A theoretical result is that, for every CSP, there exists an equivalent binary CSP [Dechter 1987] *Equivalent* here means that there exists a one-to-one mapping between the solutions of the two problems. Based on this equivalence, most of the theoretical and technical works limit themselves to the study of binary CSPs, assuming that the equivalent binary CSP retains all the properties of the original CSP.

This limitation is very restrictive, as illustrated both by the following problem and its statement as a binary CSP:

In the addition SEND+MORE=MONEY, replace each letter by a number between 0 and 9 so that:

- S and M are positive.

- S, E, N, D, M, O, R, and Y are pairwise different.

- The numeric addition obtained after replacing each letter by the associated number is correct.

There is only one solution to this problem: 9567 + 1085 = 10,652.

If one has to define this problem as a binary CSP, the resulting statement will look like the following:

Variables: s, e, n, d, m, o, r and y whose domain is $\{0, 1, \ldots, 9\}$.
Constraints: $s \neq e; \quad s \neq n; \quad s \neq d; \quad \ldots etc\ldots \quad r \neq y$

Variables: se, nd, mo, re, on and ey whose domain is $\{0, 1, \ldots, 99\}$
Constraints: $nd \equiv d$ (10) "nd equals d modulo 10"
$[nd/10] = n$ "where [.] denotes the integer part of a real number"
$se \equiv e$ (10) and $[se/10] = s$
$re \equiv e$ (10) and $[re/10] = r$
$mo \equiv o$ (10) and $[mo/10] = m$
$on \equiv n$ (10) and $[on/10] = o$
$ey \equiv y$ (10) and $[ey/10] = e$

Variables: $send, more$ and $oney$ whose domain is $\{0, \ldots, 9\ 999\}$
Constraints: $send \equiv nd$ (100) and $[send/100] = se$
$more \equiv re$ (100) and $[more/100] = mo$
$oney \equiv ey$ (100) and $[oney/100] = no$

Variable: $money$ with domain $\{0,\ldots,99\ 999\}$
Constraints: $money \equiv oney$ (1,000) and $[money/1,000] = m$

Variable: $sendmore \in \{(0,0),(0,1),\ldots,(0,9999),(1,1),\ldots,(1,9999),\ldots,(9999,0),\ldots,$
$(9999,9999)\}$
Constraints: $sendmore1=send$ and $sendmore2=more$

Variable: $sendplusmore$ whose domain is $\{0,\ldots,19\ 998\}$
Constraint: $sendplusmore = (sendmore1 + sendmore2)$

This representation is very cumbersome: It requires 49 binary constraints, 20 variables, and 100 million domain values. *Section 17.1.3* a more compact representation using nonbinary constraints.

17.1.3 Intension versus Extension

A constraint can be seen as a boolean relation holding between variables. In the case of finite-domain CSP, this relation can be expressed either in *extension* or in *intension* [Puget 1992]. Defining a constraint in extension consists of providing the set of consistent tuples of values (see example following). Defining a constraint in intension consists of providing a formula of satisfaction.

For instance, the constraint C holding on two variables X and Y, which requires that the value of X should be greater than the value of Y, can be defined either in intension, by the formula $X > Y$, or in extension, by the set $ext(C) = \{(x, y) \in dom(X) \times dom(Y) \mid C(x, y) = true\}$. For instance, assuming that X and Y have domain $\{1, 2, 3\}$, the extension of constraint $X > Y$ is $\{(2, 1), (3, 1), (3, 2)\}$.

The extensional representation of constraints is motivated by the desire to interpret CSP in the context of set theory. Indeed, it is relatively easy in an extensional context to describe algorithms, and to prove various properties. However, in practice, the extensional representation of constraints raises several issues:

- It requires an important memory space, especially for nonbinary constraints, because the size of the Cartesian product of the domains grows exponentially with the number of variables.

- In many cases, constraints are more naturally expressed in intension than in extension. In addition, evaluating a formula is often more efficient than checking that a tuple belongs to a set.

- Representing constraints in extension is well suited to brute combinatorial reasoning, but is not adapted for higher-level reasoning, such as formal reasoning.

17.1.4 Arc Consistency versus Constraint Filtering

As *Section 17.1* shows, arc consistency is used during the resolution to reduce the size of the domains after each instantiation. Unfortunately, enforcing arc consistency for a constraint is expensive because it requires computing the cartesian product of the domains. To address this issue, arc consistency is, in practice, replaced by a weaker concept—*constraint filtering*. Filtering a constraint consists of performing only domain reductions that are reasonably computable.

Constraint filtering ranges within two extremes. On the one hand, the upper limit for constraint filtering consists of enforcing strict arc consistency, because enforcing more than arc consistency leads to discarding solutions. On the other hand, the lower limit for constraint filtering consists of checking satisfiability once all the variables are instantiated, with no domain reduction. Indeed, this is a limit because otherwise the solver would provide solutions that do not satisfy every constraint.

Just checking satisfiability $\leq$ constraint filtering $\leq$ arc consistency

The main idea behind filtering is that it depends on the constraint considered. For instance, for the constraint $X > Y$, arc consistency is enforced, because only lower and upper bounds have to be considered. The corresponding implementation using the BackTalk solver is given in *Section 17.2.3*.

Conversely, for the constraint $X + Y = 0$, enforcing arc consistency is very expensive, because all possible values for X and Y have to be considered. In this case, a good filtering method consists of considering only the bounds of X and Y. This is a good filtering because it realizes almost full arc consistency; and it is efficient, because only the bounds are considered, instead of the whole cartesian product dom $(X) \times$ dom (Y).

Consequently, one of the most important issues of constraint solving is to define filtering methods that are efficient and as close as possible to full arc consistency. Of course, these two properties are conflicting, so the real issue is to find the right compromise.

17.1.5 Enumeration Algorithms

There is a profusion of solving algorithms [Dechter 1994; Nadel 1989; Prosser 1993]. Each of them is adapted to specific situations, and none is always better than the others. For instance, full look-ahead is especially efficient when the filtering of a constraint is cheap and when there are strong dependencies between variables. Forward checking is interesting for weakly constrained problems, especially when constraints are hard to filter. Unfortunately, these criteria are hard to specify formally and, thus, to automate. In practice, what is needed is to adapt an existing algorithm to specific problems.

Another problem with the profusion of published algorithms is that they are usually described in the scope of binary CSP, and it is not easy to adapt them to our context. Trying to implement an exhaustive library of algorithms is therefore unrealistic, because there are virtually as many algorithms as there are problems. This situation led us to design a single resolution mechanism (see *Section 17.2*), with support for implementing specific resolution algorithms adapted to specific problems.

17.1.6 No Utilization of Knowledge on Variable Values

Several works explore the possibility of exploiting the properties of domains seen as specific types (for example, order-sorted domains [Caseau 1991]). However, resolution algorithms implicitly assume no particular properties on the domain *values*. Values are considered as reducible to atomic entities.

Note that because no hypothesis on the domain values is made, solving CSPs in which domains are collections of arbitrary objects does not raise any technical issue, as long as a language with pointers is used. However, in our case, we claim that the structure and properties of objects involved in real-world problems can be exploited by the resolution process to compute solutions faster and to state problems more easily.

For instance, CSP techniques have been used to produce musical harmonization automatically. Such applications developed to date do not take advantage of the properties of the musical structures handled. More precisely, complex musical structures, such as chords and melodies, are handled as mere collections of atomic values. We have shown that such an approach leads to building inefficient and bloated applications. We claim that objects can be used to represent the structures of the problem explicitly as values for the variables, and that doing so improves the efficiency as well as the design of the resulting application. This point constitutes the main motivation in integrating objects with constraint satisfaction; it is developed in *Section 17.2,* and an illustration is presented in *Section 17.3.3.*

To summarize, we outline five restrictions of the standard theoretical constraint satisfaction model, in the context of practical, real-world object-oriented problems, which are:

- Restriction to binary constraints
- Constraints defined in extension
- Complexity of arc consistency
- Profusion of algorithms
- No utilization of knowledge on variable values

These limitations motivated the design of the BackTalk framework, which the following section describes. As outlined in the introductory section, BackTalk is considered from two viewpoints: *Section 17.2* examines the technical aspects (points 1 to 4); *Section 17.3* considers point 5 and discusses the statement of problems involving objects.

17.2 BackTalk: The Framework Approach for Implementing Constraints

BackTalk [Roy 1997] is a framework for constraint satisfaction. It consists of a library of classes representing the concepts of variables, domains, constraints, problems, and solving algorithms, linked together by a propagation mechanism. The requirements expressed in the preceding section prevailed throughout the design of BackTalk, which provides predefined high-level nonbinary constraints and implements a sophisticated filtering mechanism as well as a resolution algorithm adaptable to specific cases.

17.2.1 Integration of BackTalk in the Host Language

BackTalk was designed as a traditional Smalltalk framework, with no modifications of the virtual machine. In other words, BackTalk is implemented *without kernel support*, so that it can be run on any platform supported by Smalltalk, as advocated for the backtrack mechanism of [Lalonde 1988]. Moreover, BackTalk introduces no syntactic extension to Smalltalk: Stating and solving problems is done using standard mechanisms, class instantiation and message sending.

17.2.2 Overall Design

BackTalk is implemented as a library of related classes, which we can classify into three main clusters: *variables, constraints,* and *solving algorithms.*

Three main hierarchies provide constrained variables, constraints, and algorithms. Constraints, algorithms, and variables are linked together by demons that are used to implement propagation mechanisms efficiently, as shown in Figure 17.4.

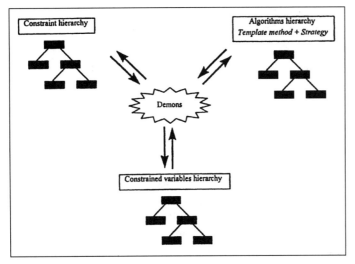

Figure 17.4   The overall design of the BackTalk system.

Constrained Variables

Constrained variables are the basic building blocks of the framework. They represent the notion of an unknown value, to be computed by the solver. Practically, it is the responsibility of constrained variables to inform the solver of domain modifications. A variable is defined by a *domain*, a *value* within the domain, and a *label* for display purposes. The behavior of constrained variables depends heavily on the nature of their domain; therefore, we reified variables into classes, and organized them into the hierarchy:

```
BTVariable ('domain' 'constraints' 'valueDemons' ...)
    BTBooleanVariable ()
    BTIntegerVariable ('min' 'max' 'minEvent' 'minDemons' ...)
        BTRealVariable ('precision')
    BTObjectVariable ('domainDictionary' 'actualDomain' ...)
        BTOrderedObjectVariable ('minEvent' 'minDemons' ...)
```

It is important to note that the user does not have to be aware of this class hierarchy: BackTalk automatically chooses the most adapted class to instantiate, depending on the domain provided. We give below examples of BackTalk expressions, with their evaluation (V is short for BTVariable), illustrating the behavior of constrained variables.

```
"Creation of an integer variable, from the bounds of an interval"
x := V label: 'x' from: 1 to: 10 => ['x' int[1..10]]

"Modifying the bounds of the domain of an integer variable"
x min: 3; max: 4 => ['x' int[3..4]]

"Creation of an Integer Variable from a collection of integers"
V label: 'Var' domain: #(1 6 7 8 9),#(2 3 18 0 -5) => ['Var' int[-5 0..3
6..9 18]]
```

```
"Creation of an Object Variable from the collection of all Points"
V label: 'obj' domain: (Point allInstances) => ['obj' (0@0 0@1 142@274
0@4 etc...)]
```

Constrained variables are also responsible for a part of the resolution mechanism (the demon mechanism).

Expressions and Constraints

In the intensional model of constraint, constraints may be seen as *links* between several variables (instead of sets of consistent tuples). Moreover, constraint filtering depends on the nature of the constraint considered, which leads naturally to the idea of organizing constraints into a hierarchy of classes. The root of this hierarchy is an abstract class, BTConstraint. This class implements a default filtering algorithm, which enforces arc consistency. This default filtering is redefined in subclasses to implement specific methods, achieving a better compromise between reduction and efficiency.

To define a new class of constraint in BackTalk one needs to create a subclass of class BTConstraint or of any of its subclasses. Because all constraints are defined in intension in BackTalk, the new class will redefine the formula of satisfaction.

Of course, defining specific filtering methods is not necessary because of inheritance. Indeed, when the user defines a new constraint class, it benefits automatically from the filtering method defined in its superclass. In the less interesting cases, the default filtering mechanism will be used by the newly defined constraint class. Specific filtering methods are used only to implement more efficient filtering mechanisms.

Hierarchy of Constraints

Predefined BackTalk constraints include arithmetic constraints, cardinality, difference, and logical constraints. There are also particular predefined constraints, dedicated to using specific object-oriented mechanisms, that are presented in following sections. One important aspect of organizing constraints in such a hierarchy is to provide the user with many ready-to-use constraints. Moreover, the user does not have to know anything more than the class of the constraint to instantiate and the appropriate creation method. For instance, the constraint $X \neq Y$ is stated by the following class instantiation message, where X and Y denote constrained variables:

```
BTAllDiffCt on: X and: Y
```

Other constraints are created similarly, using, as far as possible, the same creation interface. For instance, the constraint $X + 2Y - 5Z \geq 0$ is stated by the following class instantiation message, where X, Y, and Z denote constrained variables:

```
BTLinearGreaterOrEqualCt
    on: (Array with: X with: Y with: Z)
    coefficients: #(1 2 -5)
    value: 0
```

Figure 17.5 shows an excerpt of the hierarchy of constraints in BackTalk.

```
BTConstraint ('isPersistent' 'isStatic' 'owner')
    BTBinaryCt ('x' 'y')
        BTBinaryExtensionCt ('relation')
        BTComparatorCt ()
            BTGreaterOrEqualCt ()
            BTGreaterThanCt ()
        BTEqualCt ()
        BTPerformCt ('expression')
        BTUnaryOperatorCt ()
            BTAbsCt ()
            BTOppositeCt ()
            BTSquareCt ()
    BTGeneralCt ('variables' 'arity')
        BTAllDiffCt ('remainingVars')
        BTBlockCt ('block')
        BTIfThenCt ('ifBlock' 'thenBlock')
        BTLinearCt ('expression' 'constant' ...)
            BTLinearEqualCt ('min' ...)
            BTLinearGreaterOrEqualCt ('max' 'maxList')
        BTNaryLogicalCt ('expression' 'leftVariablesNumber')
            BTAndCt ('trueVariablesNumber')
            BTOrCt ('falseVariablesNumber')
            BTXOrCt ('falseVariablesNumber')
```

Figure 17.5   Excerpts of the hierarchy of predefined constraint classes in BackTalk.

Expressions

BackTalk provides another means of stating constraints, which is, in some cases, even simpler to use than explicit instantiation messages. The idea is to let the user state constraints using the syntax of standard arithmetical and logical expressions. BackTalk transforms these Smalltalk expressions into constraint creation messages automatically.

This notion of expression is purely syntactical. The idea is only to spare the user the explicit creation of constraints. In practice, this is realized by introducing a language of expressions, which is implemented as messages sent to constrained variables. For instance, messages making up arithmetic expressions (such as + and *) are implemented in the class of constrained variables, and yield particular expression objects. These expressions, in turn, understand these same messages to yield more complex expressions on the fly. Finally, these expressions indeed behave like variables in the sense that they can be constrained using the usual arithmetic operators (such as =, <, and >). These operators, in turn, are implemented in the expression classes to generate corresponding BackTalk constraints.

Consider, for instance, the constraint $x + 2y - 5z \geq 0$. Instead of using the following syntax:

```
BTLinearGreaterOrEqualCt
        on: (Array with: x with: x with: z)
        coefficients: #(1 2 -5)
        value: 0
```

the constraint can be stated using the following Smalltalk expression:

```
x + (2*y) -(5*z) >= 0.
```

Example

Because problems are stated to be eventually solved, there is no point in differentiating problems and solvers. Problems and solving algorithms are therefore represented in BackTalk by a single class, BTSolver. A problem basically consists of a collection of variables and a collection of constraints. The protocol for creating problems is illustrated here on the following cryptogram: "send + more = money."

First, a problem is created by instantiating the class BTSolver. Then variables and constraints are stated. Finally, the problem is initialized by sending the message "pbm variablesToInstantiate: letters," which specifies that solving this problem amounts to instantiating all eight of the letters. The *print:* messages sent to the problem define how solutions will be printed.

```
sendMoreMoney
    | letters s e n d m o r y send more money pbm |
    "The problem is created by instantiating class BTSolver"
    pbm := BTSolver new: 'send + more = money'.
    "Constrained variables creation.  The domains of s and m are
    restricted to 1..9 as required in problem statement"
    (letters := OrderedCollection new: 8)
        add: (s := V from: 1 to: 9); add: (e := V from: 0 to: 9);
        add: (n := V from: 0 to: 9); add: (d := V from: 0 to: 9);
        add: (m := V from: 1 to: 9); add: (o := V from: 0 to: 9);
        add: (r := V from: 0 to: 9); add: (y := V from: 0 to: 9).
    "Arithmetic expressions that are to be used to declare the
    actual constraints"
        send := (1000*s + (100*e) + (10*n) + d).
        more := (1000*m + (100*o) + (10*r) + e).
        money := (10000*m + (1000*o) + (100*n) + (10*e) + y).
    "Constraints statement"
        (send + more - money) @= 0.
        BTAllDiffCt on: letters.
    "Pattern used to display the eventual solution"
        pbm    print: s; print: e; print: n; print: d; print: '+';
            print: m; print: o; print: r; print: e; print: '=';
            print: m; print: o; print: n; print: e; print: y.
    "The resulting problem"
    ^pbm variablesToInstantiate: letters
```

Once created, such a problem can be sent solving messages (for example, printFirst-Solution, printAllSolutions, printNextSolution, and allSolutionsDo: aBlock) as follows:

```
pbm printFirstSolution
(send + more = money) 0.002sec ; 1 bt ; 2 choices
9567+1085=10652
```

```
pbm printAllSolutions
SOL 1: (send + more = money) 0.002sec ; 1 bt ; 2 choices
9567+1085=10652
```

```
No more solutions.
(send + more = money) 0.004sec ; 4 bt ; 3 choices
```

The message printFirstSolution (resp. printAllSolutions) triggers the computation of the first solution (resp. of all solutions). For each solution, information related to the resolution is printed, as well as the solution itself. Information printed includes the name, the resolution time, the number of backtracking (bt) and the number of branches developed (choices).

Solving Algorithm

As previously noted, a wealth of algorithms has been developed for solving constraint satisfaction problems. Their respective efficiency is highly dependent of the nature of the problem to be solved, so none can be considered better than the others. More generally, as claimed in [Caseau 1991], "no constraints solver to our knowledge holds all the techniques that we have found necessary to solve [particular problems]." This speaks for the design of a general and extensible solving algorithm, which can be augmented, if necessary, with specific mechanisms.

A second remark is that enumeration algorithms are based on the same basic idea: combining a propagation mechanism with a more or less sophisticated backtracking strategy [Nadel 1989]. As argued in *Section 17.1.5*, we propose to unify all these algorithms into a single control loop, and use inheritance to adapt the control loop to specific cases, using Strategy [Gamma 1995]. This control loop implements the following general scheme:

General Solving Algorithm (GSA)

1. Choose a noninstantiated variable V and a value x of dom (V).

2. Instantiate V with x, and save the current state of the problem.

3. Filter constraints to reduce the domains of the remaining problem variables.

4. If there is an empty domain, then backtrack to a previous state.

5. If instantiation is complete, then:

   If a solution is found, then stop. Else backtrack to a previous state.

6. Go to 1.

In this algorithm, point 1 is generally undertaken by heuristics. Point 3 is the core of the algorithm. Depending on the actual algorithm considered, point 3 ranges from doing nothing (algorithm BEA, described in *Section 17.1.1*) to enforcing arc consistency on all constraints. Point 4 triggers a backtracking to a previous state of the problem.

The strategy used for choosing this previous state is an important characteristic of the algorithm.

This general algorithm is implemented in class BTSolver, and represents the default solving procedure. The main job of this default control loop is to implement an efficient and robust save/restore mechanism, which takes into account the modifications of domains performed by filtering methods. It also handles arbitrary modifications of the problem during the resolution, such as dynamic constraint creation or suppression.

The algorithm is described in Figure 17.6. We use here the Template Method pattern [Gamma 1995]: The algorithm is decomposed into several methods, each representing a part of the algorithm. It uses the methods *forward* and *backward*, which are redefined in subclasses.

This solving mechanism, which is close to a real full look-ahead method, is implemented in class BTSolver. Using the Template Method and Strategy design patterns, one can subclass BTSolver to implement other algorithms by redefining some of the five methods listed previously and as shown in Figure 17.7.

```
firstSolution
    "goes forward until a solution is found"
[self solutionFound] whileFalse: [self moveForward].
    ^self solution


moveForward
"goes forward until a failure occurs, which triggers a backtracking"
    [self domainWipedOut] whileFalse: [self forward].
    self backward


forward
"saves the state of the problem and chooses an instantiation to
enforce"
    self saveContext.
    self makeAChoice


backward
    "chooses a previously saved state of the problem and restores it
| context |
    context := self choosePreviousAContext.
    self restoreContext: context


makeAChoice
"chooses a variable to instantiate and a value for this variable. Then
performs the instantiation and triggers constraint propagation"
    currentVar := self chooseAVar.
    currentVal := currentVar nextValue.
    self propagateInstantiationOf: currentVar
```

Figure 17.6   The basic control loop for enumeration algorithms. Parts of this control loop are redefined in concrete subclasses, following the Template Method pattern.

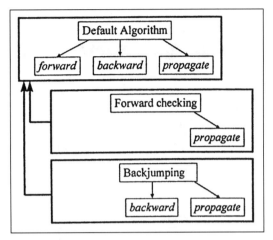

Figure 17.7 A graphical representation of the library of algorithms, which are represented as classes, following the Strategy pattern.

Three classes are represented in Table 17.1: *Forward checking* and *backjumping* are subclasses of the *default algorithm* class that implements three key methods, following the Template Method pattern. Subclasses redefine some of these methods, and inherits the others.

17.2.3 Constraint Propagation

This section aims to present the mechanism implemented for constraint filtering in BackTalk, as defined in *Section 17.1.4*. It examines how we implement constraint filtering in the BackTalk framework. The main idea is to implement filtering as a set of special methods, called *demons,* that will be triggered automatically by the solving algorithms at the right time. This demon mechanism allows us to specify filtering methods in a modular and efficient way. The next section shows that this mechanism can also support the definition of higher-level global constraints.

The Demon Mechanism: Filtering According to Events

The main idea is to decompose the filtering procedure for a given constraint into a set of independent methods that take charge of only a part of the filtering procedure. This allows us to define a more efficient propagation mechanism and to define the filtering methods more easily by decomposing them into several elementary methods. The key idea is that the domain of a variable can undergo (1) the suppression of one of its elements, (2) the suppression of several elements, (3) the modification of its lower or upper bound, and (4) its reduction to a singleton (that is, an instantiation). We propose to implement the filtering procedure of a constraint with at most five methods, one for each event. Note that a constraint does necessarily respond to all the four events.

Table 17.1   Resolution Times of BackTalk on Well-Known Numeric Problems, Compared to IlogSolver, One of the Most Efficient Commercial Solvers, Written in C++

PROBLEM INSTANCE	BACKTALK	ILOGSOLVER
Send + more = money	0.016	0.01
Donald + gerald = robert	0.252	0.4
8 queens	0.021	0.01
40 queens	0.181	0.1
100 queens	1.813	0.5
Magic square 4 x 4	0.129	0.01
Magic square 5 x 5	7.490	0.5
Magic square 6 x 6	821.045	50.0
AUTOMATIC HARMONIZATION*	**BACKTALK**	**ILOGSOLVER**
Harmony: 12-note melody	1 s	180 s
Harmony: 16-note melody	1.5 s	240 s

* The automatic harmonization problem is described in *Section 17.3.3*, where the results presented here are explained.

Technically, when a constraint C is created, the solver declares a set of demons associated with each variable involved in C. Each demon corresponds to a specific domain reduction event (value, min, max, remove, or domain changes). When a variable undergoes a domain reduction, the corresponding demon will trigger the execution of the corresponding filtering method implemented in the class C.

For instance, the constraint $X > Y$ has to be filtered when the upper (resp. lower) bound of X (resp. Y) is decreased (resp. increased). Therefore, when such a constraint is created, the following methods declare the two corresponding demons:

```
postDemons
    "Defines the demons constraint 'self' has to respond to.   In this
case,
    self is filtered when the maximum bound of x is changes (i.e.
decreased)
    and when the minimum bound of y increases"

    x addMaxDemonOn: self.
    y addMinDemonOn: self
```

the corresponding filtering methods follow:

```
max: v
    "Here v is necessarily x since no maxDemon is defined for y."
    y max: v max; remove: v max
```

```
min: v
    "Here v is necessarily y because no minDemon is defined for x"
    x min: v min; remove: v min
```

As mentioned in *Section 17.1.4* to ensure the correctness of the solver, constraint filtering has at least to test that a constraint is satisfied once all its variables are instantiated. This is done in BackTalk by a method called *minimalFiltering,* which is automatically executed when a variable is instantiated to check that no constraint is violated; otherwise, a failure is raised that provokes a backtracking.

High-Level Constraint Definition

The demon mechanism previously described can support the definition of high-level constraints (see Figure 17.8). This is a typical use of BackTalk as a blackbox framework, following the terminology of [Johnson 1988]—that is, by composition of existing components, instead of inheritance.

The algorithm performs reduction messages on its variables. The variables propagate these reductions as events to their demons (a variable can have one to five demons, corresponding to its instantiation, the modification of its bounds, the suppression of a value, and an arbitrary modification of its domain). Then, the demons forward the events to the constraints associated with them. Depending on the event it receives, each constraint will trigger the execution of one of its filtering methods, which causes new modifications to the domains of its variables.

Using Dynamic Constraint Management to Control the Resolution

BackTalk was designed in such a way that constraints can be dynamically created or removed during the resolution of a problem. When a constraint is removed during the resolution, it is restored when the system backtracks. Thanks to this save/restore mechanism, dynamically created constraints can be used to define high-level constraints without implementing new classes.

Consider a constraint that has to be satisfied depending on some condition. For instance, if the variable $x = 1$, then variables y and z should be equal; otherwise, they should be different. To implement such a constraint class, we need to write filtering

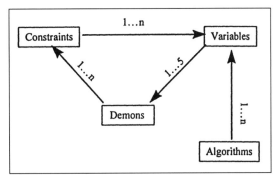

Figure 17.8   A diagram of the demon mechanism.

methods as shown in the previous section, which can be discouraging. Instead, Back-Talk allows us to *compose* the existing filtering methods for each of the constraints appearing in the conditional statement automatically.

Conditional constraints are instances of the class BTIfThenElseCt, which composes existing constraints. An instance of BTIfThenElseCt holds three blocks representing the components of a conditional statement: ifBlock, thenBlock, and elseBlock. For example:

```
x := V from: 1 to: 2. y := V from: 1 to: 2. z := V from: 1 to: 2.
BTIfThenElseCt on: x
    if: [x value = 1]
    then: [y @= z] else: [BTAllDiffCt on: y and z].
                            SOL 1: x = 1; y = 1; z = 1
                            SOL 2: x = 1; y = 2; z = 2
                            SOL 3: x = 2; y = 1; z = 2
                            SOL 4: x = 2; y = 2; z = 1
```

Following is the filtering method value: for conditional constraint. Evaluation of the ifBlock yields either true, false, or nil, triggering the evaluation of thenBlock, the else-Block, or nothing, respectively.

```
value: aVar
    ifBlock value == nil ifTrue: [^self]."nothing to do"
    self remove.    "restored after backtrackings"
    Condition    ifTrue: [thenBlock value]
            ifFalse: [elseBlock value]
```

Disjunctive Constraints

A similar example of using BackTalk as a blackbox framework is given by the definition of *disjunctive* constraints. Disjunctive constraints are often needed—for instance, in scheduling problems, to specify that a resource must be used by at most one process at a time. BackTalk provides a general mechanism for creating disjunctive constraints from existing ones, which uses a class called BTDisjunctiveCt:

```
"The constraint states that tasks t1 and t2 are not simultaneous"
BTDisjunctiveCt    either: [t1 precedes: t2] or: [t2 precedes t1]
```

17.2.4 The Resulting Framework

To summarize, the BackTalk framework is essentially made up of four distinct class hierarchies, which entertain complex relationships. As far as the user is concerned, defining a constraint problem amounts to the definition of a small number of sub-classes and, for each of them, a limited number of methods. The difficult parts of constraint satisfaction processes are reused, mainly by inheritance. In this respect, BackTalk is a whitebox framework [Johnson 1988]. The only composition mechanism offered by BackTalk is the ability to define higher-level constraints by composition, as seen in the previous section.

Efficiency is an important issue, and the design of BackTalk was strongly influenced by efficiency objectives. Table 17.1 shows the performance of BackTalk on several well-known combinatorial problems, and compares it with the IlogSolver system.

The difference between the performance of BackTalk and IlogSolver, renowned for its efficiency, is constant (BackTalk is 15 times slower). This means that the complexities are the same. This difference of efficiency is due to the host language, Smalltalk, which is known to be slower than C++. On problems involving objects (the last three lines of the table), BackTalk is more efficient. This is due to the way it can be used to state and solve such problems [Pachet 1995].

The following section examines the other side of BackTalk: What are the benefits gained by combining objects and constraints for defining and solving constraint satisfaction problems?

17.3 BackTalk: Objects for Stating Constraint Problems

The previous section considers object orientation as a means of designing and implementing a constraint satisfaction solver. This section addresses the opposite issue; that is, how can our framework be used for stating and solving object-oriented constraint satisfaction problems? We show that there are two radically different ways to constrain objects. We also examine how to mix, as much as possible, the natural mechanisms of object-oriented programming with constraints.

17.3.1 Constraining Objects: Two Approaches

As previously noted, constraint satisfaction is based on the notion of constrained variables, which represent unknown values to be computed by the solver. In the previous sections, these values were implicitly considered as atomic (that is, numerical) values. When solving problems whose unknown values are complex structures, it becomes necessary to represent the concept of *unknown objects*. The purpose of this section is therefore to answer the following question: What happens when unknown values become objects?

Two different approaches can be used to address this issue: whether constraints are put *inside* objects or *outside* objects. The choice of one of these approaches is of the utmost importance as to reusability, ease of use, and efficiency. The following sections introduce these two approaches.

Constraints within Objects: Constraining Partially Instantiated Objects

A natural way to constrain objects is to consider attributes as constrained variables, thus leading to the notion of *partially instantiated objects*. A partially instantiated object is an object whose attributes are constrained variables instead of being *fully fledged objects*. This approach, called the *attribute-based approach*, corresponds to the following idea: Constraining an object amounts to expressing a property holding onto its attributes.

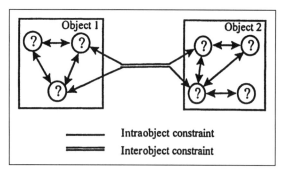

Figure 17.9 Graphical illustration of the attribute-based approach for constraining objects. Instance variables are considered as constrained variables. Constraints are therefore *inside* objects.

Figure 17.9 illustrates the attribute-based approach. Circled question marks represent constrained variables, which are indeed the instance variables of the objects, and square boxes represent partially instantiated objects. Simple arrows are internal constraints, also called *structural constraints,* which express properties of the objects. The double arrow represents an external constraint.

Constraints outside Objects: Constraining Fully Fledged Objects

The orthogonal approach consists of putting the constraints outside objects that need to be constrained. This *class-based* approach aims to handle fully fledged rather than partially instantiated objects. The idea is to use classes as natural domains for constrained variables by putting objects in the domains. Figure 17.10 illustrates the class-based approach. Question marks represent the variables, and boxes represent fully fledged objects. In this case, objects are in the domains of the constrained variables.

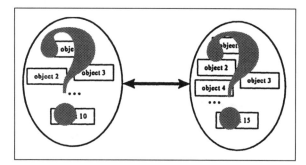

Figure 17.10 Graphical illustration of the class-based approach for constraining objects. Objects are in the domains of constrained variables. Constraints are therefore *outside* objects.

Illustrating the Two Approaches

Given a set of rectangles with their sides parallel to the axis, consider the problem of finding two squares that do not overlap each other. We assume that a rectangle is determined by the coordinates of its upper left and lower right vertices (that is, left, right, top, and bottom). Let us express this problem using both attribute-based and class-based approaches.

Using the attribute-based approach, one would define partially instantiated rectangles, say R1 and R2, whose attributes are the constrained variables of the problem. In this case, the constraint *being square* and the nonoverlapping constraint would be defined as arithmetical relations between these constrained attributes. The problem statement would look as follows:

```
"R1 is a square"
(R1 top) - (R1 bottom) = (R1 right) - (R1 left)
"R2 is a square"
(R2 top) - (R2 bottom) = (R2 right) - (R2 left)
"R1 and R2 do not overlap"
(R1 right < R2 left)
OR (R1 top > R2 bottom)
OR (R1 left > R2 right)
OR (R1 top < R2 bottom)
```

Defining this problem following the class-based approach would lead to state variables R1 and R2, whose domains contain fully fledged rectangles, and to defining constraints directly between these variables. The following problem statement illustrates this point:

```
"R1 is a square"
R1 isASquare
"R2 is a square"
R2 isASquare
"R1 and R2 do not overlap"
R1 doNotOverlap: R2
```

It is to be understood that isASquare (resp. doNotOverlap:) messages state constraints holding on the R1 (resp. R1 and R2) constrained variable(s).

Comparison of the Two Approaches

Intuitively, the attribute-based approach answers the question of what happens when unknown values become partially instantiated objects, while the class-based approach answers the question of what happens when unknown values become fully fledged objects. The two preceding problem statements illustrate the fundamental differences between them, which are concerned with predefined class reuse, constraint definition, problem structure, and efficiency, as well.

As for class reuse, when using the attribute-based definition, one has to deal with partially instantiated rectangles that cannot be instances of predefined Smalltalk classes.

In other words, the attribute-based approach forces one to define ad hoc classes. Conversely, the class-based approach allows predefined classes to be reused as is. The idea is that the class-based approach does not depend on class implementation (encapsulation is not jeopardized by class-based statements, while it is by attribute-based statements).

As for constraint definition, in the attribute-based case, arithmetical constraints are used to state the problem. Conversely, the class-based definition uses constraints that directly hold on the Rectangle constrained variables. The question that arises here is how to define these class-based constraints. *Section 17.3.2* addresses this issue.

The structures of the two problems are radically different both in terms of variables and of constraints. The attribute-based problem is a numerical CSP, whose objects are mere collections of variables, while fully fledged object structures are used in the class-based problem as values for variables. This leads to dramatic efficiency differences (see *Section 17.3.3* and [Roy 1997]).

17.3.2 Defining Class-Based Constraints

Recall that the central question here is what happens when unknown values become fully fledged objects. As the previous section notes, using the class-based approach for stating problems involving objects leads to the statement of constraints holding directly on object variables (that is, constrained variables whose domain contains fully fledged objects).

Numerical problems involve constraints that are generally combinations of basic operators (for example, $+$, $-$, $*$, $/$, $=$, $\neq$, $>$, $<$, $\leq$, $\geq$, and X^Y). Of course, other constraints have to be considered for specific problems, such as graph theory constraints (for example, cycle constraint in Chip) or set theory constraints (for example, cardinality and distribution constraints [Régin 1996]). However, these constraints generally have well-known semantics and are limited in number.

On the contrary, when stating problems involving objects using the class-based approach, as illustrated in the previous section, we need to define constraints expressing arbitrary properties of objects. The general idea is that any boolean expression involving objects is likely to be used as a constraint. For instance, in *Section 17.3.1*, one can assume that class Rectangle implements a method, say isASquare, for testing if a rectangle is a square. In this case, our purpose is to use this method in order to create a constraint. BackTalk provides two different means of stating such constraints.

A General Mechanism: Block Constraints

The simpler and most general way to use methods directly to state constraints is to use *block constraints*, which allow defining constraints by way of any Smalltalk BlockClosure whose evaluation yields a boolean.

For instance, consider two constrained variables, R1 and R2, whose domain contains instances of class Rectangle. A constraint requiring that the two rectangles do not overlap can be defined as follows, as long as the method doNotOverlap: is defined in class Rectangle:

```
BTBlockCt
    on: R1 and: R2
    block: [:a :b | a doNotOverlap: b]
```

The block has one argument for each variable involved in the constraint. These arguments are not the constrained variables, but rather possible values for these variables. Indeed, during the resolution of the problem, these arguments will be assigned values of the domain of the corresponding variable. In other words, the block can use the language of the values in the domains (that is, the methods defined in their class). For instance, in the block constraint just defined, argument a (resp. b) is assigned a value picked up in the domain of R1 (resp. R2) when the block is evaluated.

To give another example, consider two variables, C1 and C2, whose domain contains Smalltalk classes. The following block constraint forces the value of variable C2 to be a subclass of the value of C1:

```
BTBlockCt
    on: C1 and: C2
    block: [:a :b | b inheritsFrom: a]
```

However, block constraints are useful for many problems because they allow complex relations to be stated as constraints. For instance, we used such constraints to implement a simple application that finds design patterns in a standard Smalltalk image, which is not reported here due to space limitations.

Block constraints are a general means of defining arbitrary constraints on arbitrary objects. Of course, because of this generality, the filtering method implemented in class BTBlockCt is not efficient; it enforces arc consistency by computing, in the worst case, the cartesian product of the domains of the variable, according to the definition given in [Mackworth 1977].

Block constraints are particularly well adapted to prototyping applications rapidly, although they are often replaced by user-defined constraints in the final application for efficiency reasons.

An Efficient Mechanism: Perform Constraints

Block constraints, introduced in the preceding section, are the most general type of class-based constraints provided in BackTalk. These constraints cannot be efficiently implemented in their full generality, because nothing is known about the semantics of the corresponding block. However, there exist families of class-based constraints for which an efficient filtering method can be provided. One of them is the family of constraints defined by a single Smalltalk message, which is the purpose of *perform constraints*.

Perform constraints are used to specify that there is between two variables X and Y a relation defined by a method selector m; that is, the value Y is the image of the value X by the method named m. Note that a perform constraint C holding on variables X and Y and whose message is m can be stated as the following block constraint:

```
BTBlockCt on: X and: Y block: [:a :b | (a perform: m) = b]
```

A perform constraint is made up of two constrained variables, say X and Y, and an arbitrary Smalltalk selector (possibly with arguments), and it means that variable Y is deduced from variable X by applying it to the associated selector. Consider, for instance, a variable X whose domain contains Smalltalk rectangles and a variable Y whose domain contains integer numbers. Stating a perform constraint between X and Y associated to selector area will ensure that the value of Y (a number) is the area of the value of X (a rectangle).

The following BackTalk session illustrates the creation of perform constraints, and how consistency is maintained between variables linked by a perform constraint. When variable y is assigned value false, the perform constraint is used right away to remove every vowel from the domain of x. Conversely, removing all the vowels of the domain of variable y would cause variable x to be assigned the value false.

```
x := V label: 'x' domain: #(a b c d e f).      => ['X' (#a #b #c #d #e
                                                   #f)]
y := (x btPerform: #first) btPerform: #isVowel. => ['X first isVowel'
                                                   (t f)]
y value: false.                                 => ['X first isVowel'
                                                   (f)]
x                                               => ['X' (#b #c #d #f)]
```

Using Methods for Constraints: Choosing the Right Approach

Block and perform constraints are implemented using second-order abilities of Smalltalk. Their purpose is to put the language of objects at the user's disposal. This is a sine qua non to allow the statement of constraint satisfaction problems involving fully fledged objects. Moreover, these particular constraints favor the reusability of predefined classes, because their methods can be used straightforwardly to define constraints.

An important thing to note is that when stating constraint problems involving complex objects using the class-based approach, complex constraints can be defined by way of perform and block constraints from methods implemented in the corresponding classes. On the contrary, when using the attribute-based approach, constraints expressing relations between complex objects have to be stated in terms of rock-bottom objects (that is, attributes of complex objects). This implies an overhead in the problem's statement, and is very often less efficient, as argued in *Section 17.3.3*.

17.3.3 Stating Problems Involving Objects: A Case Study in Automatic Harmonization

This section reports the design of a system that solves harmony exercises. It illustrates the points discussed in the previous sections because harmony exercises, or automatic harmonization problems (AHPs), are particularly representative of object

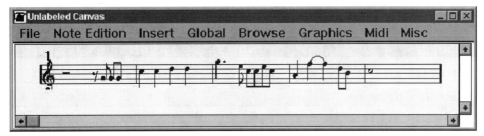

Figure 17.11 Initial melody for harmonization of the first 18 notes of the French national anthem.

plus constraint problems. Solving a harmony exercise consists of finding the harmonization of a melody—for example, the melody shown in Figure 17.11—or, more generally, any *incomplete* musical material that satisfies the rules of harmony. The standard exercise is to harmonize four voices (see Figure 17.12 for a solution of the melody).

The constraints needed to solve the AHP can be found in any decent treatise on harmony [Schoenberg 1978]. The problem is an interesting benchmark because it involves many complex objects (that is, chords). Moreover, there are various types of constraints that interact intimately: (1) horizontal constraints on successive *notes* (for example, "two successive notes should make a consonant interval"), (2) vertical constraints on the notes making up a *chord* (for example, "no interval of augmented fourth, except on the 5th degree" or "voices never cross"), and (3) constraints on *sequences of chords* (for example, "two successive chords have different degrees").

Figure 17.12 A solution proposed by BackTalk from the initial melody of Figure 17.11.

Table 17.2 Performance of Our Solution Compared with Previous Attempts to Solve the AHP Using CHP

SOURCES	11 NOTES	12 NOTES	16 NOTES
Tsang (CLP)	60 s	?	?
Ballesta (IlogSolver)	?	180 s	240 s
BackTalk + MusES	1 s	1 s	1.5 s

Previous Attempts at Solving Harmony Exercises with Constraints

Harmonization of a given melody naturally involves the use of constraints, because of the way the rules are stated in the textbooks. Indeed, several systems have proposed various approaches to solve the AHP using constraints. The pioneer was Ebcioglu [Ebcioglu 1992], who designed BSL, a constraint logic programming language, to solve this problem. His system not only harmonizes melodies (in the style of J.S. Bach), but is also able to generate chorales from scratch. Although interesting, the architecture is difficult to transpose in our context because constraints are used passively, to reject solutions produced by production rules.

More recently, [Tsang 1991] proposed to solve the AHP by using CLP, a constraint extension to Prolog [Jaffar 1987]. The results are poor: More than 1 min and 70 Mb of memory are required to harmonize an 11-note melody (see Table 17.2). Ovans [Ovans 1992] was the first to introduce the idea of using arc consistency techniques to solve the AHP, but his system is poorly structured and imposes an unnatural bias on the representation of musical entities. The system proposed by Ballesta [Ballesta 1998] is much more promising. Ballesta uses IlogSolver to solve the AHP, and uses both objects and constraints.

All these systems are based on a representation of musical structures as atomic variables and structural constraints. In other words, they follow the attribute-based approach. For instance, in Ballesta's system, 12 attributes are defined to represent one interval. Nine constraints are then introduced to state the relations that hold between the various attributes.

As a result, constraints have to be defined using a low-level language, thus requiring a translation of harmonic and melodic properties, given in harmony treatises, in terms of numbers. The constraint representing the rule that parallel fifth relations between two successive chords are forbidden is shown in Figure 17.13 as it is expressed in Ovan's system.

```
parallel-fifth(c_i,m_i,c_{i+1},m_{i+1})⇔¬perfect(c_{i+1},m_{i+1})∨(c_i-c_{i+1}).(m_i-m_{i+1})≤0
where
perfect(c_i,m_i)⇔|c_i-m_i|∈{7,19}
```

Figure 17.13 The constraint corresponding to the parallel fifth rule, as expressed in Ovan's system, based on CLP.

Moreover, the attribute-based approach leads to stating a huge amount of constraints and variables. For instance, to state the AHP on an n-note melody in Ballesta's system, $126 \times n - 28$ variables are defined.

Our Approach for Solving Harmony Exercises

The poor performance of existing systems (see Table 17.2) led us to experiment with a radically different approach. The drawbacks of these systems can be summed up as follows: First, there are too many constraints. The approaches proposed so far do not structure the representation of the domain objects (intervals and chords). When such a structure is proposed, as in Ballesta's system, objects are treated as passive clusters of variables. Second, the constraints are treated uniformly, at the same level. This does not reflect the reality: A musician reasons at various levels of abstraction, working first at the note level, and then on the chords. The most important harmonic decisions are actually made at the chord level. This separation could be taken into account to reduce complexity.

These thoughts led us to reconsider the AHP in the light of the class-based approach for object + constraint problems—that is, with a viewpoint the reverse of our predecessors'. Rather than starting from the constraints, and devising object structures that fit well with the constraints, we start from the objects, and fit the constraints to them. Indeed, a lot of properties of the domain objects may be more naturally described as methods rather than constraints.

To do so, we reuse an object-oriented library, the MusES system [Pachet 1994], which contains a set of approximately 90 classes that represents the basic elements of harmony—notes, intervals, scales, and chords. In our application, the domains contain musical objects provided by MusES. The constraints hold directly on these high-level objects, using the methods defined in the corresponding classes. These constraints are instances of block and perform constraints, introduced in *Section 17.3.2*.

The main idea here is to consider high-level objects of the problem, namely chords, as possible values for constrained variables. In other words, domains contain fully fledged chords, which are instances of MusES class Chord. As a consequence of reifying chords as values for variables, the resulting system is very much understandable, because constraints can be stated using the language of chords directly. For instance, the rule forbidding parallel fifth is simply defined by the following BackTalk expression:

```
BTConstraint
on: chord and: nextChord
block: [:c1<:c2 | c1 (hasParallelFifthWith: c2) not]
```

Moreover, the problem to solve is much smaller, because for an n-note melody, only $5 \times n$ constrained variables are created (compared to the $126 \times n - 28$ variables in Ballesta's system). This improves efficiency in a dramatic way, as shown in Table 17.2, which gives the performance of our application compared with the systems of Ballesta and Tsang. Ovan's work is not reported here because it addresses a simpler problem, namely two-voice rather than four-voice harmony exercises.

17.4 A Complete Application: Crossword Puzzle Generation

Crossword puzzle generation is a highly combinatorial problem that can be solved by procedural approaches [Ginsberg 1990; Jensen 1997; Mazlack 1979]. Addressing this problem with a declarative approach generally leads to inefficient systems [Berghel 1989; Wilson 1989]. The reason is that a standard puzzle contains about 30 word slots, leading to a huge search space of about 10^{100} combinations if the dictionary contains approximately 150,000 words.

The problem consists of finding a crossword, given an initial empty puzzle with open and closed cells and a list of words. Standard CSP techniques are not able to cope with this problem. This section shows how domain-specific knowledge can be expressed using BackTalk's full range features of to solve this problem. This knowledge is threefold: *topologic* knowledge, *lexical* knowledge, and knowledge of *letter distribution*.

17.4.1 Choosing the Right Algorithm

The crossword problem is a typical example of a weakly constrained problem. Intuitively, the idea is that instantiating a variable with a given word will have a limited impact on the variables not directly crossing it. This is explained by the fact that the distribution of letters in words is quite uniform, except for special letters (such as *q*, see *Section 17.4.3*). Therefore, we chose the forward-checking algorithm. Exceptional cases due to nonuniform distribution of letters are examined in *Section 17.4.3*.

17.4.2 A Filtering Method for Intersection Constraints

The crossword problem, in its basic form, contains only intersection constraints. Knowledge of intersection can be used to devise an efficient filtering method for these constraints. The method is as follows:

```
filter intersection between X and Y:
(i, j) := intersection of X and Y.
Compute possibleLetters (X,i) = the set of possible letters at position
i for X.
Remove from domain(Y) words that don't contain one of possibleLetters
(X,i) at j.
Compute possibleLetters (Y,j) = the set of possible letters at position
j for Y.
If possibleLetters(Y,j) ⊄ possibleLetters (X,i) then remove from
domain(X) words that don't contain one of possibleLetters (Y,j) at
position i.
```

It is easy to show that this procedure achieves full arc consistency for the intersection constraint. The complexity is linear, compared to the quadratic complexity of the default filtering method!

17.4.3 Exploiting Knowledge of Letter Distribution

A particular knowledge is that all letters are not distributed uniformly in words. A typical example is that the letter *q* is almost always followed by the letter *u* (at least, in English and French). There are numerous examples of this kind of rule, such as "no word starts by the same consonant twice," "*j* is never repeated twice," "letters are rarely repeated three times," and so forth. These regularities are not always true, but only give strong indications on letters not yet found.

It is possible to express this piece of knowledge in terms of constraints and variables, by considering a *virtual constraint* between two parallel words *v* and *v'*, only when certain conditions are satisfied (here, when the letter *q* appears). Of course, it would be awkward to actually add this virtual constraint to the problem dynamically, because this virtual constraint is already represented by the constraint *u* between *v'* and *w* (see Figure 17.14).

A way to implement this virtual constraint is to define a conditional constraint, called *LetterDependencyCt*. The statement of this constraint consists of a condition on values of variables and a set of intersection constraints to filter when the condition is satisfied:

```
BTIfThenCt
    on: wordVariableList
    if: [there exists a variable v, whose value contains a 'q']
    then: [filter intersection between v', parallel to v, and w
(perpendicular to v at position of letter 'q')]
```

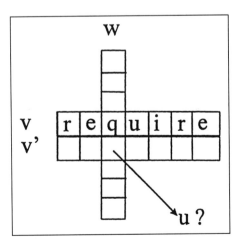

Figure 17.14 The letter *q* implicitly creates a relation between *v* and *v'*, which corresponds to the intersection between *v'* and *w*.

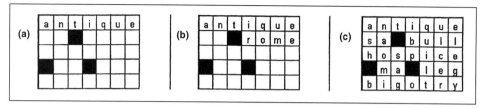

Figure 17.15 The resolution of a crossword. (*a*) Word *antique* is fixed before the resolution. (*b*) Without rule $q \rightarrow u$, word *rome* is tried, which leads to the development of a useless search tree. (*c*) With rule $q \rightarrow u$, the variable parallel to *antique* is instantiated only with words having a *u* in the second position.

17.4.4 Results

We conducted a series of experiments on crosswords, with and without these three kinds of knowledge.

Figure 17.15 illustrates the effect of exploiting knowledge of letter distribution.

These experiments show clearly that our approach allows reducing the domains of word variables, thereby reducing the number of backtracks. Table 17.3 gives execution times and number of failures when combining the various knowledge representations described in this section. As expected, the best strategy is achieved when combining all three types of knowledge with forward checking.

17.5 Summary

The framework paradigm offers a smooth and efficient integration of CSP with objects. One way to assess the relevance of this approach, as opposed to the language-based approach, is to compare it with two extreme cases: Chip and Claire. The main difference with Chip is that because BackTalk provides the relevant concepts of CSP as classes, it allows redefining them by inheritance, thus gaining flexibility. The difference with Claire is that BackTalk imposes the main control loop, whereas Claire leaves this responsibility to the user. Because Claire has all the abilities of a complete hybrid language, it is suitable for highly specific applications.

Table 17.3 Execution Times and Number of Failures

SPECIALIZED FILTERING	FIRST FAIL HEURISTIC	KNOWING $Q \rightarrow U$	CPU TIME, S	FAILS
No	No	No	> 3,600	> 5,000
Yes	No	No	545	10,546
Yes	No	Yes	166	3,396
Yes	Yes	No	23	268
Yes	Yes	Yes	6	36

Table 17.4 Three Approaches in Proposing CSP Mechanisms to a User

APPROACH	MAIN CHARACTERISTICS	EXAMPLES
Library	Parameterized high-level constraints	Chip
Framework	Control loop, simple constraints	BackTalk, IlogSolver
Language	Low-level language constructs	Claire

Table 17.4 illustrates the position of the framework approach.

The framework approach is claimed to be more comfortable for standard applications because it provides relevant predefined abstractions. By hiding the difficult mechanisms of CSP techniques from the user, while allowing the user to redefine parts of it, BackTalk achieves a desirable feature of frameworks—that is, a good compromise between efficiency and complexity. This echoes Steve Jobs' opinion concerning interface builder frameworks: "Simple things should be simple, complex things should be possible."

17.6 References

[Avesani 1990] Avesani, P., A. Perini, and F. Ricci. COOL: An object system with constraints. *Proceedings of the TOOLS USA1990 Conference,* pp. 221–228, Santa Barbara, CA, July/August 1990.

[Ballesta 1998] Ballesta, P. Contraintes et objets : clefs de voûte d'un outil d'aide à la composition? *Recherches et applications en informatique musicale,* P. Ballesta, editor. Paris: Hermès, 1998

[Beldiceanu 1994] Beldiceanu, N., and E. Contejean. Introducing global constraints in CHIP. *Journal of Mathematical and Computer Modelling,* 20(12), 1994: 97–123.

[Berghel 1989] Berghel, H., and C. Yi. Crossword compiler-compilation. *Computer Journal,* 32(3), June 1989: 276–280.

[Bessière 1994] Bessière, C. Arc consistency and arc consistency again. *Artificial Intelligence,* 65(1), 1994: 179–190.

[Caseau 1991] Caseau, Y. Abstract interpretation of constraints over an order-sorted domain. *International Logic Programming Symposium,* pp. 435–454, San Diego, CA, 1991

[Caseau 1994] Caseau, Y. Constraint satisfaction with an object-oriented knowledge representation language. *Journal of Applied Intelligence,* 4, 1994: 157–184.

[Caseau 1996] Caseau, Y., and F. Laburthe. *Introduction to the CLAIRE Programming Language.* Paris, 1996.

[Codognet 1996] Codognet, P., and D. Diaz. Compiling constraints in clp(FD). *Journal of Logic Programming,* 27(3), 1996: 185–226.

[Colmerauer 1990] Colmerauer, A. An introduction to Prolog-III. *Communications of the ACM,* 33(7), 1990: 69.

[Dechter 1987] Dechter, R., and J. Pearl. Network-based heuristics for constraint satisfaction problems. 34(1), 1987: 1–38.

[Dechter 1994] Dechter, R., and I. Meiri. Experimental evaluation of preprocessing algorithms for constraint satisfaction problems. *Artificial Intelligence,* 68, 1994: 211–214.

[Ebcioglu 1992] Ebcioglu, K. An expert system for harmonizing chorales in the style of J.-S. Bach in understanding music with AI: Perspectives on music cognition, KEOL, M. Balaban, editor. CA: AAAI Press, 1992.

[Fayad 1997] Fayad, M.E., and D. Schmidt. Object-Oriented Application Frameworks, *Communications of the ACM,* Special Issue on Object-Oriented Application Frameworks, 40(10), October 1997.

[Gamma 1995] Gamma, E., R. Helm, R. Johnson, and J. Vlissides. *Design Patterns.* Reading, MA: Addison-Wesley, 1995

[Ginsberg 1990] Ginsberg, M.L., M. Frank, M.P. Halpin, and M.C. Torrance. Search lessons learned from crossword puzzles. *Proceedings of the 8th National Conference on AI,* pp. 210–215, Boston, 1990.

[Haralick 1980] Haralick, R., and G. Elliot. Increasing tree search efficiency for constraint satisfaction problems. *Artificial Intelligence,* 14, 1980: 263–313.

[Hentenryck 1989] Hentenryck, P. Van. *Constraint Satisfaction in Logic Programming.* Cambridge, MA: MIT Press, 1989.

[Jaffar 1987] Jaffar, J., and J.L. Lassez. Constraint logic programming. *Proceedings of the IEEE 4th International Conference on Logic Programming,* Melbourne, Australia, May 25–29, 1987.

[Jensen 1997] Jensen, S.C. Design and implementation of crossword compilation programs using serial approaches. Master's thesis, Department of Mathematics and Computer Science, Odense University, Odense, Denmark, 1997.

[Johnson 1988] Johnson, R., and B. Foote. Designing reusable classes. *Journal of Object-Oriented Programming,* 1(2), 1988: 22.

[Lalonde 1988] Lalonde, W., and M. Van Gulik. Building a backtracking facility for Smalltalk without kernel support. *Proceedings of the OOPSLA 1988 Conference on Object-Oriented Programming Systems, Languages, and Applications,* pp. 10–123, San Diego, CA, 1988. New York: ACM Press, 1988.

[Laurière 1978] Laurière, J.L. A language and a program for stating and solving combinatorial problems. *Artificial Intelligence,* 10(1), 1978: 29–127.

[Mackworth 1977] Mackworth, A.K. Consistency in networks of relations. *Artificial Intelligence,* 8(1), 1977: 99–118.

[Mazlack 1979] Mazlack, L.J. Computer construction of crossword puzzles using precedence relationships. *Artificial Intelligence,* 7(1), 1976: 1–19.

[Nadel 1989] Nadel, B.A. Constraint satisfaction algorithms. *Computational Intelligence,* 5, 1989: 188–224.

[Ovans 1992] Ovans, R. An interactive constraint-based expert assistant for music composition. *Proceedings of the Ninth Canadian Conference on Artificial Intelligence,* University of British Columbia, Vancouver, Canada, 1992.

[Pachet 1994] Pachet, F. The MusES system : An environment for experimenting with knowledge representation techniques in tonal harmony. *Proceedings of the First Brazilian Symposium on Computer Music (SBC&M), pp. 195–201,* Caxambu, Minas Gerais, Brazil, August 1994.

[Pachet 1995] Pachet, F., and P. Roy. Integrating constraint satisfaction techniques with complex object structures. *Proceedings of the 15th Annual Conference of the BCS Specialist Group on Expert Systems,* pp. 11–22, Cambridge, England, December 1995.

[Prosser 1993] Prosser, P. Hybrid algorithms for the constraint satisfaction problem. *Computational Intelligence,* 9, 1993: 268–299.

[Puget 1992] Puget, J.F. PECOS: A high level constraint programming language. *Proceedings of the SPICIS 1992 Conference,* Singapore, 1992.

[Puget 1995] Puget, J.F., and M. Leconte. Beyond the glass box: Constraints as objects. *Proceedings of the International Logic Programming Symposium (ILPS 1995),* pp. 513–527, Portland, OR, December 1995.

[Régin 1996] Régin, J.C. Generalized arc consistency for global cardinality constraint. *Proceedings of the 13th National Conference on Artificial Intelligence,* Portland, OR, 1996.

[Roy 1997] Roy, P., and F. Pachet. Reifying constraint satisfaction in Smalltalk. *Journal of Object-Oriented Programming,* 10(4), 1997: 51–63.

[Schoenberg 1978] Schoenberg, A. *Theory of Harmony.* Berkeley, CA: University of California Press, 1978.

[Tsang 1991] Tsang, C.P., and M. Aitken. Harmonizing music as a discipline of constraint logic programming. *Proceedings of the ICMC 1991 Conference,* pp. 61–64, Montréal, Canada, 1991.

[Wilson 1989] Wilson, J.M., Crossword compilation using integer programming. *Computer Journal,* 32(3), June 1989: 273–275.

CHAPTER 18

Developing Frameworks to Support Design Reuse

Design complexities and shortened time-to-market pressures dictate the need for environments that can help designers construct computer-based systems at an abstract level, long before software-hardware partitioning is attempted. By allowing the designers to conceptualize their systems as early as possible in a product's life cycle, such codesign environments can expedite design activities—for example, specification, simulation, design space exploration, and verification. By the same token, to be more effective, application frameworks should facilitate the reuse of abstract, generic design elements. Frameworks support application development by allowing large-grain designs—involving both components and structure—to be reused. Component or object reuse has been the traditional approach to reuse. However, *structural reuse*, a relatively new concept, promises more options in the composition of abstract designs. Unfortunately, frameworks often do not take advantage of structural reuse at an abstraction level high and versatile enough to be conducive to rapid prototyping. A unified, multilevel approach to framework development can address both structural and component-based reuse from this perspective.

This chapter proposes a generative methodology for the design and rapid prototyping of component-based systems, applicable in particular to the realtime distributed domain and hardware-software codesign. The approach commences with high-level support for structural reuse, ultimately leading to an application-specific framework supporting component reuse within an automated environment. In this context, a framework consists of the following:

- A repository of formally defined structural patterns, or *styles*

- A repository of components

- Rules to instantiate a selected pattern from the style repository with components selected from the component repository

The methodology addresses structural reuse on two abstraction levels and by different mechanisms. The highest abstraction level is the *topological* level. Here the gross organization of a system is specified in terms of highly reusable, graph-theoretic abstractions called *styles*. A style can specify a generic pattern, such as a *serial, parallel,* or *star* configuration of a set of components, or a more specific pattern, such as the complex topology of an ATM switch fabric, the topology of a canonical compiler, or that of a client-server system. Components are represented by *nodes,* and connections by *edges*. At this level, individual components are not assigned functionality. Within the topological level, structural reuse is supported by the ability to compose more complex patterns from simpler styles and instantiate a variable style into a specific pattern.

The next level is the *architectural* level, where more detail is added: Interfaces are defined for components, and connections are refined into bindings between interface ports. Within this level, structural reuse is supported mainly by parametric architectures.

The lowest abstraction level considered is the *system* level, where components are assigned their respective functionality in a target language. The system-level language can be an implementation or a specification language, and is independent of the two higher levels. Existing components stored in a repository are reused at this stage to further drive the design of the system.

Figure 18.1 illustrates the application of the methodology. To generate a specific system, the user first selects a style from the style repository of an application-specific framework. If the selected style is a variable style, then it must be first instantiated into a particular topology. Subsequently, the result is mapped into an architecture. To do this, the user either defines a set of refinement rules or selects one such set that is supplied by the style repository. Finally, the resulting architecture is translated into the notation of the system-level language by pulling in the specified components from the component repository and interconnecting them according to the generated architecture.

The main goal of this chapter is to demonstrate that structural reuse can be supported formally and independent of the target language to complement component reuse. The reuse concepts introduced are applied to the construction of a framework that allows easy generation of system prototypes for a specific application domain. The actual mechanisms of reuse and the levels of abstraction at which such reuse may occur are of particular interest. Other important problems, such as how to search, identify, and retrieve reusable artifacts, are beyond the scope of the chapter.

The rest of the chapter is organized as follows. The next section first elaborates upon the various definitions of reuse. This is followed by an introduction to the methodology. The three different abstraction levels of the methodology are subsequently discussed in more detail with small illustrative examples. In addition, a larger example taken from the telecommunications domain is progressively carried through each of

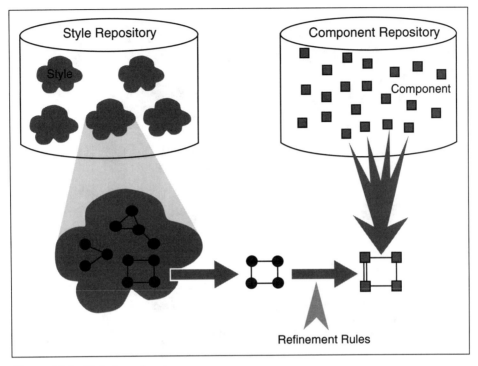

Figure 18.1   Style-based reuse.

the sections. The example develops a framework for the design and rapid prototyping of ATM switches. It uses a realtime object-oriented modeling language as the system-level language. The chapter concludes with a substantial review of relevant work, followed by a summary and a discussion of future activities in this area.

18.1 Methodology

Figure 18.2 illustrates the three abstraction levels of the development methodology. After a discussion of the concept of design reuse, we give the motivation for these abstraction levels. Then we elaborate on the characteristics of the languages that support them.

18.1.1 Design Reuse

Reuse is the process of creating new artifacts out of existing ones. The importance of reuse in the design and development of computer-based systems, software in particu-

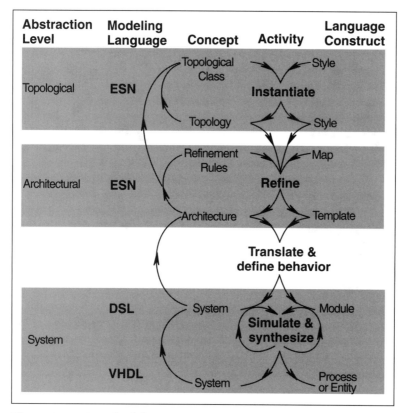

Figure 18.2 A methodology to support component and structural reuse.

lar [Batory-O'Malley 1992; Krueger 1992; Parnas 1983], has long been recognized. In this context, it is possible to distinguish between two kinds of reuse that are complementary to each other, component reuse and structural reuse. Whereas *component reuse* [Batory-O'Malley 1992; Biddle-Tempero 1996] has been studied extensively and is well supported in modern programming languages and design environments, the notion of *structural reuse* is still relatively new and thus poorly understood.

Component reuse is possible when an artifact recurring in system descriptions can be isolated and encapsulated as a unit of abstraction. Then the artifact in question can conveniently be incarnated on demand by a simple reference to the corresponding unit of abstraction. These artifacts, which can be assembled to produce systems of arbitrary size and complexity, are referred to as *components*. In software systems, components may represent computations, data, or both. In hardware systems, they represent functional units.

In the notion of structural reuse (sometimes called *context reuse*), the objects of reuse are the *contexts* in which these artifacts are embedded, rather than those that make up a system description. Structural reuse is based on the identification, isolation, and exploitation of organizational patterns recurring across system descriptions. An organizational pattern is expressed in terms of configurations of *abstract* components that serve as placeholders for real, or *concrete*, components. Such patterns are often parameterized, making them generic—and thus more amenable to reuse.

A generic pattern must first be specialized to a fixed pattern before a particular system description can be obtained from it. Two levels of reuse are possible here. Reuse is *extensional* if smaller reusable patterns are combined to form larger reusable patterns. It is *intentional* if either a generic pattern is instantiated into a specific pattern, or a given fixed pattern is instantiated with the proper *concrete* components to produce the desired system. The jigsaw diagrams in Figure 18.3 illustrate these two kinds of structural reuse in comparison with component reuse [Biddle-Tempero 1996].

Reusable artifacts are often grouped into repositories. Within such repositories, reuse is intentional. When a component from a repository is reused, it is instantiated once and this instance is final. Only one level of intentional reuse takes place in this case. The situation is slightly different for structural reuse based on repositories of reusable organizational patterns: When a pattern is reused from such a repository, first it must be retrieved and instantiated in the same way that a component is retrieved

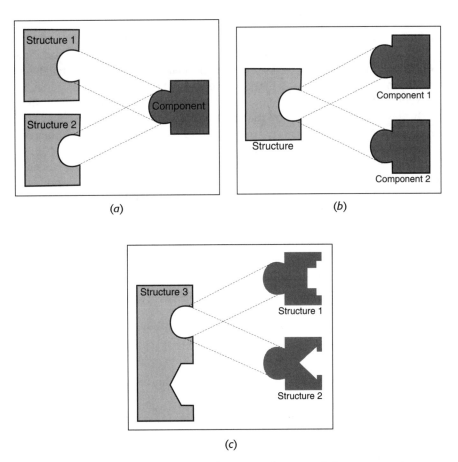

Figure 18.3 Component reuse and structural reuse: (*a*) component reuse, (*b*) intentional structural reuse, and (*c*) extensional structural reuse.

from a component repository and instantiated. The result is a fixed pattern, but this does not constitute the required final artifact because it still is expressed in terms of abstract components for which concrete counterparts must be substituted. Therefore, a second level of instantiation is also necessary. Following the terminology of the software architecture literature, we use the term *style-based reuse* to refer to this two-stage intentional reuse. Figure 18.1 shows an example of style-based reuse.

The identification and formal specification of organizational patterns may constitute a significant investment on the part of the framework developer. Such investment would be worth the effort in cases where the underlying complexity is nontrivial, the systems described manifest a high degree of internal replication (have many identical components), or the patterns can be reused sufficiently many times.

Today, a large number of concurrent and distributed systems possess a degree of organizational complexity that requires effective management, and with the proliferation of rapid prototyping environments, support for structural reuse is becoming increasingly important.

18.1.2 Levels of Design Abstraction

Structural reuse should start with a clear separation of structure from functionality or behavior. This separation is critical to deal with organizational complexity—and indirectly with behavioral complexity, because organizational complexity ultimately leads to behavioral complexity. The idea is that at some high level of abstraction, it may be desirable to concentrate exclusively on the purely structural organization of a system family. At this level, the emphasis is on the types of the components involved and the relationships among those components, making component functionality irrelevant. Thus, components are completely abstract and serve merely as placeholders (stubs). Also, the details of component connectivity are overlooked at this level: The focus is rather on whether some connectivity relationship exists between any two components. This very high-level of abstraction is referred to as the *topological level*.

The next level is the so-called *architectural level*, where, although more detail can be added, components are still not assigned a particular functionality. A blurry line separates the topological and architectural levels; however, the distinction is maintained for two reasons. First, by subdividing the structural specification into two levels, the underlying complexity becomes more manageable. Second, by raising the level of abstraction, reuse is facilitated: The more general a structural specification is, the more reusable it becomes.

In moving from a topological to an architectural description, component interfaces and connectivity relations may be refined as illustrated in Figure 18.4a. Such refinement involves the following:

- Mapping *abstract* components with single-point interfaces to *concrete* components with multipoint interfaces

- Mapping connectivity relations between abstract components to *bindings* between the associated multipoint interfaces

Note that this process preserves topological properties; hence, the architectural level encompasses the topological level.

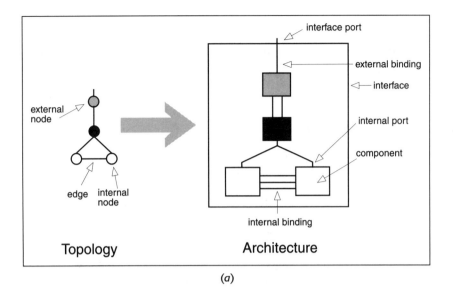

Topology

Architecture

(a)

* Topological Level (Styles)
    abstract components
    single-point interfaces
    component-to-component connections

* Architectural Level (Templates)
    concrete components
    multi-point interfaces
    point-to-point connections

* System Level (Modules)
    behaviors for lowest-level components

potential for reuse

structural reuse

extensional

style-based

extensional

intentional

language independent

language dependent

(b)

Figure 18.4 (a) Topology versus architecture. (b) Reuse within and across different levels of abstraction.

The third and the lowest level of abstraction considered is the *system level*, where each concrete component is assigned functionality in terms of a behavioral description. The transition from the architectural to the system level involves mapping the architectural specification to an executable model. In the executable model, bindings can be implemented by standard communication protocols or by a supported communication regime (such as rendezvous, message passing, mailboxes, communication by first-in, first-out [FIFO] queues, or remote procedure call). The system level preserves architectural properties, so that it encompasses the architectural level in the same manner as the architectural level encompasses the topological level. Figure 18.4*b* summarizes the properties of the three levels and illustrates how structural reuse is addressed within and across these levels.

18.1.3 Language Support

As shown in Figure 18.2, two formal languages, ESN and DSL, are utilized to support the three abstraction levels. We now briefly touch upon some important characteristics of these languages.

Extended Style Notation (ESN) is an interpreted language whose formal semantics are based on a graph algebra and a box-and-line-type architectural model. ESN supports activities that take place at and across the topological and architectural levels. It allows formal specification of system topologies using a graph-algebraic notation, and synthesis of architectural templates from such topologies using refinement rules. The relevant features of ESN are illustrated in the context of several examples, following.

To support system level activities, the behavioral modeling capability of *Design Specification Language* (DSL) [Tanir 1997] is used. Note that other languages or techniques that support the *interface connection model* [Luckham 1995] to structure system specifications would be equally suitable for this purpose, depending on the application considered. DSL supports object orientation. A realtime distributed system is specified as a hierarchical network of interconnected components called *modules*. A distinguishing feature of DSL is its integrated simulation and synthesis environment. The DSL simulator does not require specifications to be complete: Partial specifications can be executed, and the missing parts—including timing information and necessary communication protocols, as well as new bindings and ports—synthesized during simulation. This activity is referred to as *design space exploration*. The capability provides the designer with a great deal of flexibility when working on higher abstraction levels, alleviating overspecification and avoiding the consideration of many low-level issues and their impact too early in the design. Once a complete design specification has been obtained and the simulation results are satisfactory, DSL can also automatically generate VHDL code, giving the designer the choice to implement the final design in hardware. Component reuse is supported through a robust library mechanism that allows replaceable components to be grouped into classes.

18.1.4 Example: A Framework for ATM Switch Architectures

This chapter uses a progressive example to illustrate the methodology. The example concerns the development of a framework for rapid prototyping of asynchronous transfer mode (ATM) switch architectures. In this example, ESN is used to specify structure and DSL is used as the system-level (target) language in which the executable prototypes are produced. The framework consists of the following components:

- A base style repository that contains highly reusable, generic patterns
- An application-specific style repository that contains the patterns for generating switch architectures
- An application-specific component repository to store the required DSL components

The reader is referred to [Awdeh-Mohftah 1995; Tanir 1997] for more comprehensive discussions of the ATM technology. This exercise concentrates exclusively on high-level architectural issues in order to demonstrate the proposed approach.

Separate ESN packages are defined for the two style repositories:

- The package BASE encapsulates the definitions that can be reused across many application domains. This package represents the base style repository.
- The package ATMS encapsulates the definitions particular to the application domain. This package represents the application-specific style repository.

The public styles of the BASE package provide examples of extensional reuse. The ATMS package frequently refers to these styles for defining the private, application-specific styles of this second package. The private styles of the ATMS package are reused intentionally within that package only. They permit the synthesis of static architectural templates for subsequent translation to DSL modules. The DSL application-specific component repository provides behavioral descriptions for the lowest-level components.

The ATMS package is organized into four system layers, as shown in Figure 18.5. This chapter concentrates on the Switch and Switch Fabric layers and shows how each of these layers are tackled with respect to the three abstraction levels of the methodology, starting from the topological level in *Section 18.2.2,* then moving to the architectural level in *Section 18.3.3,* and finally to the system level in *Section 18.4.2.*

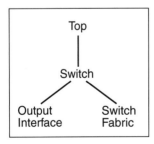

Figure 18.5   Logical organization of the ATMS package into four system layers.

18.2 Topological Level

The highest level of abstraction addressed by our approach is the topological level. A topological specification provides a highly reusable structural view of a system. In terms of the detail provided, we place it above the architectural level, which the next section discusses. Unlike the architectural level, the topological level provides only a flat view of a specific system layer, and as such, does not support hierarchical specifications.

At the topological level, a node with a singular interface represents an abstract component. The interface may admit several aliases. We call this interface the *external name* of that node. An edge (connection) between two components expresses only the existence of some relationship or interaction between components—hence a single connection is semantically equivalent to multiple connections (see the sidebar titled *A Formal Model of Topologies* for more details.) A single edge, however, can be refined into several bindings at the more detailed architectural level. Similarly, a node can be refined into one or more interface ports. This way, it is possible to obtain several different architectures from a common topology.

The only other information associated with a node (abstract component) is its type. Node types are uninterpreted. We also allow the edges to be typed as a mechanism to refer to them in groups. However, the type of an edge does not alter its semantics.

18.2.1 Styles to Represent Topologies

The ESN construct that specifies topologies is the *style*. A style may specify a single topology as well as a class of related topologies. When it specifies such a class, a particular topology—an *instance* of the style—must be explicitly selected when the style is evaluated. Graph-algebraic constructs form styles (or style expressions). Table 18.1 summarizes the main style constructs.

Consider the following simple parameterized style that specifies the topology of a multiple-client/single-server system with a central node representing the server component and *N* satellite nodes representing identical clients:

```
def style ClientServer[int N] is
  \s node \Server    \* server node is named \s; typed \Server *\
  rep j from 1..N in
    \c node \Client \* client nodes are named \c; typed \Client *\
  end rep
  edge \CtoS <\s, \c>   \* client-to-server connections *\
  hide \c               \* hide client nodes *\
end def;
```

The topology of a five-client system can be obtained by instantiating this style as:

```
style ClientServer[5];
```

The following equalities give the sets of external names, node types, and edge types of the resulting instance:

A FORMAL MODEL OF TOPOLOGIES

Formally, we define a topology as a finite graph consisting of a set of abstractly typed nodes linked with featureless, binary edges. Each node is designated either as an *external* (visible or accessible) node or as an *internal* (invisible or inaccessible) node, depending on whether it is allowed to participate in an edge within a larger topology. Nodes and edges respectively represent components and connections of a subsystem. An external node has a singular interface, which can be refined into several interface ports at the architectural level (see Figure 18.4a). An external node (the singular interface of an external node) is referenced by at least one *name*, which provides access to that node. Node names need not be unique, making it possible both for a single name to collectively refer to a group of nodes and for a single node to be associated with multiple names (aliases) which refer to it.

topology ::= ⟨nodes, edges⟩

nodes ::= finite_set_of(node)

edges ::= finite_set_of(edge)

edge ::= {node, node}

types_of: nodes → node_types

names_of: nodes → names

The set of *external nodes* and the set of *external names* of a topology are defined as follows:

external_nodes = {n ∈ nodes | (∃ a ∈ names_of(n))}

external_names = {a ∈ names | (∃ n ∈ nodes)(a ∈ names_of(n))}

The set of nodes of a topology can be partitioned in two ways: (1) by node types into disjoint sets, where each set consists of all nodes of a particular type; and (2) by external names into possibly overlapping sets, where each set consists of all nodes accessible through a particular external name. In the name-based partition, it is possible for a single node to belong to more than one set of the partition, as well as for a node to belong to none of the sets of the partition (as in the case of an internal node).

A semantic model for topologies can be obtained by defining an equivalence on their graphs. Two topologies are considered *equivalent* if there exists an isomorphism between the nodes of the graph of the first topology and those of the second. This isomorphism must preserve the edges (graph isomorphism) as well as the partitioning of the nodes.

```
externals style ClientServer[5] seteq {\s}
edges style ClientServer[5] seteq {\CToS}
types style ClientServer[5] seteq {\Server, \Client}
```

Note here that whereas the client nodes are not externally accessible, the central server node is accessible through the (external) name \s. This allows the resulting topology to be extended by additional clients, as follows:

Table 18.1 Main ESN Style Constructs: Naming Binds Strongest, Followed by Grouping, and then the Postfix Constructs Connection, Hiding, and Renaming

NAME OF CONSTRUCT	SYNTAX	PURPOSE
Node Creation	node nameExpr	Creates a new node whose type is specified by nameExpr.
Naming	name styleExpr	Adds the name specified by nameExpr to the set of (external) names of each node of the style styleExpr. After the naming operation, nameExpr becomes an external name of style.
Grouping	styleExpr1 styleExpr2	Forms a larger style out of styleExpr1 and styleExpr2 by taking the union of their nodes and edges.
Semantic Renaming	styleExpr ren nameExpr1 as nameExpr2	Substitutes external name nameExpr2 for external name nameExpr1 in the style specified by styleExpr. Note that semantic renaming is different from simple syntactic substitution.
Hiding	styleExpr hide nameExpr	Hides the external name specified by nameExpr in the style specified by styleExpr. After hiding, nameExpr is no longer an external name of styleExpr.
Connection	styleExpr edge nameExpr \<nameExpr1, nameExpr2>	Introduces an edge of type nameExpr between each pair of nodes m and n of style styleExpr such that m has external name nameExpr1 and n has external name nameExpr2.

Choice	choice
	  choice tag1 is
	    styleExpr1
	  ...
	  choice tagN is
	    styleExprN
	end choice
		Defines a variable style, or a topological class, formed by taking the union of styleExpr1 to styleExprN. The tags (which may be parameterized) are used to identify specific instances or substyles of a variable style (e.g., aStyle@tag[K]).

```
style ClientServer[5]
\aNewClient node \Client
edge \CtoS <\s, \aNewClient>
hide \aNewClient;
```

This style expression is semantically equivalent to the instance style ClientServer[6].

To illustrate how styles can be based one upon another to support extensional reuse, consider the topology of a canonical compiler as an instance of a predefined library style with the following signature:

```
style Pipeline[int, name, name seq, name seq]
```

The parameterized *pipeline* style takes an integer parameter, say *M*, and creates a pipeline of length *M*. The name parameter specifies the type of the pipe edges that connect two consecutive nodes in the pipeline. The types and external names of the nodes in the pipeline are specified by the two sequence parameters (of size *M* each), respectively. The topology of a canonical compiler can then be specified as a pipeline of length 4 with nodes of type \L (lexer), \P (parser), \S (semantic analyzer), and \C (code generator), plus an additional memory node of type \M (representing the symbol table) connected to the lexer, parser, and code generator nodes. This topology is shown in Figure 18.6. The first node of the pipeline is an external node accessed by the name \i (for *input*) and the last node is another external node accessed by the name \o (for *output*):

```
def style Compiler is
   style Pipeline[4, \FF, <\L, \P, \S, \C>, <\i, \x, \x, \o>]
   \m node \M           \* symbol table node *\
   edge \FM <\x, \m>    \* \P- and \S-nodes can access the \M-node *\
   edge \FM <\o, \m>    \* \C-node can access the \M-node *\
   hide \x hide \m      \* \P-, \S-, and \M-nodes are internal *\
end def;
```

Note that the compiler style forbids access to the nodes of type \P (parser), \S (semantic analyzer), and \M (symbol table) by hiding the names \x and \m, thus leaving only the nodes of type \L (\lexer) and \C (code generator) as external nodes.

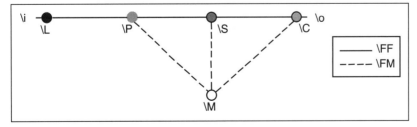

Figure 18.6   Canonical compiler topology.

18.2.2 ATM Example Revisited: Topological Level

The ATMS package relies on a number of utility definitions from a library package called BASE. They include two parametric styles that are reused extensively within the ATMS package. These styles are not discussed in detail here; however, we provide their signatures and briefly explain their purpose.

The first widely reused definition is that of a generic *parallel* style with the signature:

```
style Parallel[int, style, name seq, int seq]
```

This definition accepts another style as one of its parameters, generates M displaced replicates of it, and returns the grouping (or concatenation) of these replicates. The first parameter specifies the number of replicates (the value of M); the second specifies the style that is to be replicated. The third and last parameters are respectively a one-dimensional name sequence and a one-dimensional integer sequence of equal size such that if \a is an element of the name sequence, and m is an element of the integer sequence occupying the same position as \a, then \a<0> to \a<m-1> must be among the external names of the style to be replicated (this is a precondition of the *parallel* style). When the kth instance (replicate) of the argument style is generated, the indices of its external names are displaced appropriately not to clash with those of the existing $k-1$ instances. The process is equivalent to composing M instances of the style parameter in parallel. An example of this kind of composition is illustrated in Figure 18.7a.

The second relevant definition of the BASE package specifies a class of *star* topologies, a more general version of the client-server style of the previous section. It admits the signature:

```
style Star[name, name, int seq, name seq, name seq, name seq]
```

When instantiated with actual parameters, this definition returns a topology consisting of a central node and K types of satellite nodes. The type of the central node is specified by the first name parameter and is accessed through the external name specified by the second name parameter. The integer sequence (of size K) specifies the number of nodes for each type of satellite node. The first name sequence specifies the node types themselves for the satellite nodes. The second name sequence specifies the common prefix of the external names for each type of satellite node, and the last name sequence specifies how the edges between the satellite nodes and the central node are to be named. An instance of this style is shown in Figure 18.7b.

We can now discuss some of the styles of the ATMS package. All of these styles are specified in the same form:

```
private def style StyleName[int N1, ... , int Nk]
  is
    ... /* body of style definition */
  pre
    ... /* preconditions on the Ni */,
  post
    types style this seteq ... ,      /* node types of the result */
```

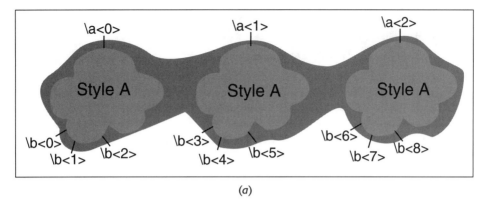

(a)

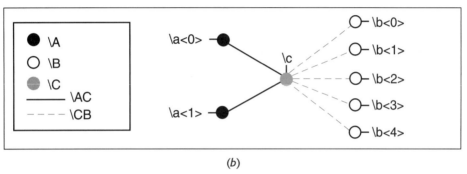

(b)

Figure 18.7   (*a*) Composition of topologies using the *parallel* style. Here the instance style Parallel[3, style A, <\a, \b>, <1, 3>] is illustrated. (*b*) Visualization of style Star[\c, \C, <2, 5>, <\A, \B>, <\a, \b>, <\AC, \CB>], an instance of the parameterized star style.

```
      externals style this seteq ... , /* external names of the result */
      edges style this seteq ...        /* edge names of the result */
end def;
```

Note that these are *private* definitions, and thus are not visible outside the ATMS package. Here, for each style, the k integer parameters (optional) specify the size of the desired instance in the case where a size has to be specified when the style is instantiated. If a size is not associated with the style, the style is not parameterized, and it effectively has a single instance. The preconditions specify the constraints on the size parameters. The postconditions stipulate that the resulting instance have the specified sets of external names, edge types, and node types.

The styles of the Top, Switch, and Output Interface layers of the ATMS package are based on the star style of the BASE package, whereas the styles of the Switch Fabric layer take advantage of both the *star* style and the *parallel* style. We treat only the Switch and Switch Fabric layers here.

Figure 18.8 illustrates the Switch layer. The underlying topology is specified by the style given in Figure 18.8*a*. An instance of this style is depicted in Figure 18.8*b*. The central \F-node in the switch topology represents the fabric component; the \I- and \O-

```
private def style Switch[N]
  is
    (style NStar[\F, \f, <N, N>,
      <\I, \O>, <\i, \o>, <IF, \FO>] *
    \r node \R
    edge \RF <\r, \f>)
    rep k from 0..N-1 in
      edge \IR <\i<k>, \r>
    end rep
    hide \r hide \f
  pre
    N gt 0
  post
    types style this seteq
{\I, \O, \F, R},
    externals style this seteq
      {\i<0...N-1>, \o<0...N-1>},
    edges style this
      seteq {\IF<0...N-1>,
        \FO<0...N-1>, \IR<0...N-1>, \RF}
end def
```

(a)

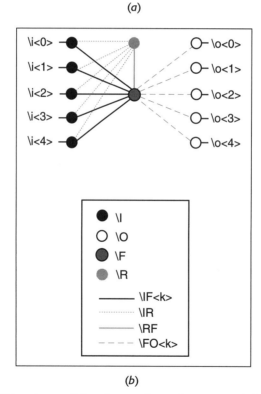

(b)

Figure 18.8 (*a*) ESN code specifying the topology of an ATM switch. (*b*) Visualization of style Switch[5].

nodes represent the input interface units (where incoming cells are accepted) and output interface units (where outgoing cells are transmitted), respectively; and the \R-node represents the control component. The \I- and the \O-nodes are external nodes accessed by the names \i and \o, respectively.

The Switch Fabric constitutes the most complex layer. It admits several alternative topologies. We consider two different topologies—namely, Banyan and Knockout—but discuss only the Banyan topology in detail. The topology of an $n \times n$ Banyan network, where n is a positive power of two, consists of n^2 binary switch elements. In the corresponding style each switch element is represented by a node of type \E, of which $2n$ are external nodes. There are two kinds of external nodes: The first n are named from \a<0> to \a<N-1> and designated as entry nodes, and the remaining n are named from \b<0> to \b<N-1> and designated as exit nodes. Such a network can be constructed recursively using two $n/2 \times n/2$ Banyan networks organized in parallel and an additional entry stage of n parallel elements, as illustrated in Figure 18.9*a*. Figure 18.9*b* shows an example, and Figure 18.10 gives the corresponding ATMS style.

The topology of the fabric of a Knockout switch is simpler. An $M \times M$ Knockout network consists of M parallel streams, where the kth stream consists of a central node of type \K representing the concentrator component, M nodes of type \I<k> representing the address filter components (entry nodes), and an \O-node representing the shared buffer component (exit node). An example is shown in Figure 18.11. Note that it is impossible to compose the M streams using the *parallel* style of the BASE package because the index k in the \I<k>-nodes is different for each stream. Each stream can easily be generated using the star style.

18.3 Architectural Level

The term *architecture* is often overused. Although no widely accepted definition exists and opinions abound as to what kind of information an architectural specification is supposed to convey, it is generally agreed that at the architectural level of abstraction, the key issue is the gross decomposition of a system into components and the relationships among those components [Shaw-Garlan 1996]. Different definitions arise from placing the focus on different aspects of system design at the architectural level. In [Tanir 1997], this level falls somewhere between the conceptual and algorithmic levels of design, where a system is described as a hierarchical network of interacting components. Because components are assigned behaviors, this also encompasses the system level, which is treated separately here. For the purposes of this chapter, at the architectural level, functional and extrafunctional properties are abstracted away. That is, the focus is purely on structure.

Note that intent is implicit in architecture; thus, we consider architecture not as an artifact that is extracted from an existing system, but rather as something that is deliberately defined for the system. See the sidebar titled *Notions of Architecture* for similar and alternative views of architecture.

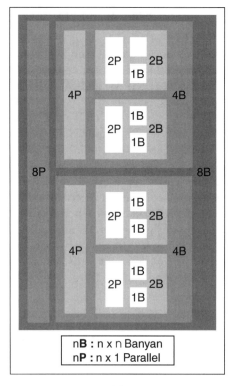

2P   2B
      1B

4P   4B

      1B
2P   2B
      1B

8P   8B

      1B
2P   2B
      1B

4P   4B

      1B
2P   2B
      1B

nB : n x n Banyan
nP : n x 1 Parallel

(a)

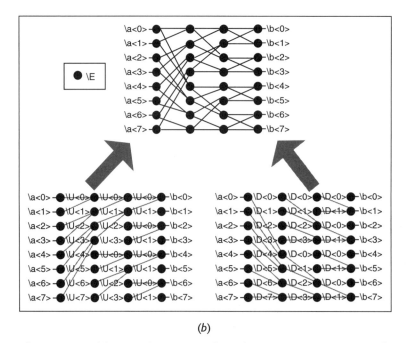

(b)

Figure 18.9 (a) Recursive construction of an 8 × 8 Banyan network, where nB represents an n × n Banyan and nP represents an n × 1 stage of parallel elements. (b) Visualization of an 8 × 8 Banyan topology and its decomposition into *up* (\U) and *down* (\D) edges.

```
private def style Banyan[int N]
  is
    let
      int M be N div 2,
      style E be \a<0> \b<0> node \E,
      style Stage[int L, name a, name b] be
        style Parallel[int L, style E,
          <~a, ~b>, <1, 1>],
      style B[int M] be
          style Banyan[M]
          rep k from 0..N-1 in
            ren \a<k> as \xa<k>
          end rep
    in
      branch
        case if N = 1 then
          style Stage[1, \a, \b]
        otherwise
          style Stage[N, \a, \xb]
          style Parallel[2, style B[M],
            <\xa, \b>, <N, N>]
          rep k from 0..N-1 in
            edge \U<k> <\xb<k>, \xa<k>>
            edge \D<k> <\xb<k>, \xa<k div 2+M>>
          end rep
          rep k from 0..N-1 in
            hide \xa<k> hide \xb<k>
          end rep
      end branch
    end let
  pre
    cond PowerOf2[N]
  post
    types style this seteq {\E},
    externals style this seteq
      {\a<0..N-1>, \b<0..N-1>},
    edges style this seteq
      {\U<0..N-1>, \D<0..N-1>}
end def
```

Figure 18.10 ESN code specifying the topology of an $M \times M$ Banyan network.

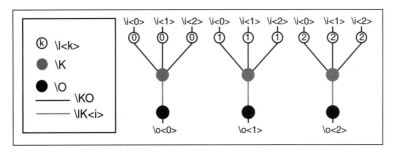

Figure 18.11 Topology of a Knockout network. Here the visualization of the instance style Knockout[3] is shown.

NOTIONS OF ARCHITECTURE

Software Architecture

In the software engineering literature, several different definitions of architecture can be found. In this context, the vocabulary invariably refers to the notions of *component*, *connection*, and *configuration*, where components represent computational entities, connections represent relationships or interactions between these entities, and configurations represent the overall organization of a system in terms of the constituent components and connections.

Often architecture specifies structure alone as the permitted set of connections among components. This purely structure-oriented view is also adopted in [Dean-Cordy1995].

The architecture description language Rapide [Luckham 1995] defines architecture as a "plan of a distributed object system showing what types of modules are components of the system, how many components of each type are there, and how its components interact." An architectural plan, besides serving as a template for guiding the construction of a system, is also used to "prototype its behavior before effort is put into building the components." This statement implies that some degree of behavioral modeling is required at the architectural level. The definition of [Perry-Wolf 1992] goes further: They consider an architecture as being composed of—in addition to components and connections—constraints and a rationale, which together may address not only topological and functional (behavioral) properties (such as data and control flows, communication protocols, and synchronization), but also extrafunctional aspects (such as performance, reliability, security, and modifiability). [Shaw-Garlan 1996] also adopt a similar extended definition. They state that "in addition to specifying the structure and topology of the system, the architecture shows the intended correspondence between the system requirements and elements of the constructed system. It can additionally address system-level properties such as capacity, throughput, consistency, and component compatibility." Finally, according to [Perry-Wolf 1992], architecture is not merely a one-dimensional view of the high-level organization of a system, but a collection of one or more useful complementary views that are consistent with each other.

Software versus Hardware and Network Architectures

[Perry-Wolf 1992] point out some important differences between software, hardware, and network architectures. In hardware systems, architecture is typically characterized by a relatively small number of component types (design elements), and scale is primarily achieved by replication. In network architectures, the emphasis is on the topology (nodes and connections), and a few such topologies are considered.

By contrast, in software systems architectural scale is typically achieved by having a large number of component types. In software architecture, many different topologies are possible, and those topologies may not be distinguishable from one another in any useful way. Thus, we are led to believe that a notion of architecture based on the multiplicity of possible topologies may not convey any useful information as far as software systems are concerned. This observation shifts the emphasis away from topological properties. However, with the growing emphasis on distribution and the current trend toward component-based development, it is still possible to benefit from using both hardware and network architecture as a metaphor for software architecture. For component-based distributed systems, especially in the real-time domain, the stated differences are becoming increasingly blurry. Thus the ideas developed in this chapter are equally applicable to architectural-level modeling of distributed and component-based software systems as well as software-based prototyping of hardware systems and networks.

Another important aspect distinguishes hardware architectures from their software and network counterparts: Hardware architectures are static in nature, whereas network and software architectures are often dynamic; that is, they may evolve at execution time by the introduction of new and removal of existing components and connections [Luckham 1995]. The dynamic aspect is not addressed here, but is worth considering given the trend toward open distributed processing and the adoption of related standards such as CORBA and DCOM.

The Interface Connection Model of Architecture

Then precisely what kinds of architectures does this chapter address? Will it be possible to model, for example, architectures of systems developed in common object-oriented languages such as C++, Smalltalk, or Java? If not, how are the architectures of interest characterized, and how do they differ from other kinds of architectures? Luckham and others [Luckham 1995] provide the sought characterization. The primary focus of this chapter is on the so-called *interface connection architectures*, for such architectures can be defined *before* their components are implemented, thus effectively separating implementation from structure. This notion can be explained best by an analogy taken from [Luckham 1995]: An interface connection architecture is like "a printed circuit board, in which interfaces play the role of sockets into which component chips may be plugged and connections play the role of wires between the sockets." For example, hardware description languages, such as VHDL, and object-oriented modeling techniques for real-time distributed systems, such as ROOM [Selic 1994], SDL-92 [Sarma 1996], and DSL [Tanir 1997], all support the interface connection model.

By contrast, in *object connection architectures*—typical of systems in traditional object-oriented languages such as C++, where components are objects and connections arise from one object calling the methods of another in its implementation—the architecture of the resulting system is dependent on the implementation of the underlying object classes.

18.3.1 Templates to Represent Architectures

In ESN, the language construct *template* is used to specify architectures. A template consisting only of an interface represents the architecture of a primitive, or atomic, system. For example, the following parameterized primitive template defines a simple filter component to be used in a pipe-and-filter system:

A FORMAL MODEL OF ARCHITECTURES

Adopting the purely structural view, we formally define an architecture as being composed of an interface, an internal structure, and a set of external bindings. Thus:

architecture ::= <interface, internal_structure, external_bindings>

For a primitive system, the architecture consists only of an interface, and both the internal structure and the set of external bindings are empty. In a composite system, the internal structure, and usually the set of external bindings, are nonempty.

An interface consists of a finite set of interaction points, called *ports*. The interface allows an instance of a subsystem to be connected with instances of other subsystems:

interface ::= finite_set_of(port)

Internal structure is defined in terms of a finite set of components and a finite set of internal bindings between these components:

internal_structure ::= <finite_set_of(component),

finite_set_of(internal_binding)>

A component is an instance of some subsystem, called the component's *parent*. The interface and architecture of the component are inherited from the parent. Each component is distinguished by a unique identifier.

component ::= <component_id, system>

An interface port of a component is referred to as an *internal port*. Hence, each internal port is identified by a component and an interface port of the component's parent.

internal_port ::= <component, port>

A *binding* models a physical or logical connection between two components. An *internal binding* involves a pair of internal ports. Because order (direction) is not important, it is formally defined as a two-element set:

internal_binding ::= {internal_port, internal_port}

An *external binding* involves an internal port and an interface port:

external_binding ::= <internal_port, port>

In a composite system, the set of external bindings relates the internal structure to the interface. Note that in this model, bindings are neither directed nor typed, and they are *not* first-class entities. In ESN, bindings may be typed so that they can be explicitly identified; however, this does not alter their semantics.

```
def temp Filter[name T] is
  spec temp
    interface \in, \out
  end spec
end def;
```

Similarly, templates to represent memory components and a variant of the simple filter component with memory access could be specified as:

```
def temp Memory[name T] is
  spec temp
    interface \read, \write
  end spec
end temp;

def temp FilterWithMemAccess[name T] is
  spec temp
    interface \in, \out, \read, \write
  end spec
end def;
```

Then the architecture of a canonical compiler [Dean-Cordy 1995], shown in Figure 18.12, may be specified as a composite template with a memory component and two kinds of filter components as follows:

```
def temp COMPILER is
  spec temp
    interface \source, \object
    components
      \L is 'temp Filter[\Lexer]',
      \P is 'temp FilterWithMemAccess[\Parser]',
```

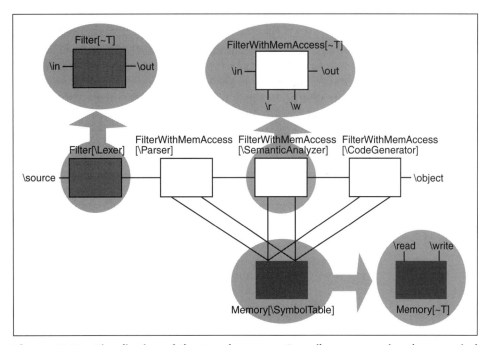

Figure 18.12 Visualization of the template temp Compiler, representing the canonical architecture of a compiler.

```
           \S is 'temp FilterWithMemAccess[\SemanticAnalyzer]',
           \C is 'temp FilterWithMemAccess[\CodeGenerator]',
           \M is 'temp Memory[\SymbolTable]'
        internal bindings
           \L.\out to \P.in, \P.\out to \S.in, \S.\out to \C.in,
           \P.\r to \M.\read, \P.\w to \M.\write,
           \S.\r to \M.\read, \S.\w to \M.\write,
           \C.\r to \M.\read, \C.\w to \M.\write
        external bindings
           \in to \L.\in, \out to \C.out
     end spec
  end def;
```

18.3.2 Mapping Topologies to Architectures

It is possible to refine a topological description (a style) into an architectural description (a template). In ESN, the construct *map* specifies the rules governing such refinement. A map consists of three parts:

- A set of rules for refining external nodes to an interface (possibly with several ports) and the associated external bindings

- A set of rules for refining the abstract components (nodes) to concrete architectural components (templates)

- A set of rules for refining connectivity relations (edges) to internal bindings

For a formal model of maps, see the sidebar titled *A Formal Model of Maps*.

The application of a map to an instance of a style (or a topology) results in a fixed architecture (template). For example, it is possible to generate the composite *compiler* template of *Section 18.3.1* (see Figure 18.12) by applying the following map to the topology specified by the *compiler* style of *Section 18.2.1* (see Figure 18.6):

```
def map Compiler_to_COMPILER is
   spec map
      interface
         \i to \in as \source, \o to \out as \object
      components
         \L to 'temp Filter[\Lexer]',
         \P to 'temp FilterWithMemAccess[\Parser]',
         \S to 'temp FilterWithMemAccess[\SemAnalyzer]',
         \C to 'temp FilterWithMemAccess[\CodeGenerator]',
         \M to 'temp Memory[\SymbolTable]'
      bindings
         \FF to <\out, \in>,
         \FM to <\w, \write>, \FM to <\r, \read>
   end spec
end def;
```

A FORMAL MODEL OF MAPS

A *map* consists of interface, component, and binding rules:

map ::= ⟨finite_set_of(interface_rule), finite_set_of(component_rule),

finite_set_of(binding_rule)⟩

A *component rule* maps a given node type to a particular architectural component in the target architecture:

component_rule ::= ⟨node_type, component⟩

An *interface rule* involves an external name and an external binding:

interface_rule ::= ⟨name, external_binding⟩

If a component rule ⟨T, C⟩ maps each node of type T to an instance of component C; n is an external node of type T with external name b; and p is an interface port of C; then the interface rule ⟨b, ⟨⟨C, p⟩, q⟩⟩ maps b to q by adding a port named q to the interface of the target architecture and creates an external binding between q and the interface port p of C. Note that port p becomes an internal port of the resulting architecture. This process roughly corresponds to interface refinement in [Moriconi 1994].

A *binding rule* maps an edge to an internal binding.

binding_rule ::= ⟨edge, internal_binding⟩

If component rules ⟨T, C⟩ and ⟨U, D⟩ map nodes of type T and U to components C and D, respectively; e is an edge; p is an interface port of C; and q is an interface port of D; then the binding rule ⟨e, ⟨⟨C, p⟩, ⟨D, q⟩⟩⟩ creates an internal binding between ports p and q in the target architecture. Note that both p and q become internal ports of the target. This roughly corresponds to connector refinement in [Moriconi 1994].

Here the different sections of the map specification give the interface, binding, and component rules. In the interface and binding rules, external and internal bindings are specified without the associated components. Instead, the components are inferred from the interface ports and component rules. For example, from the interface rule \i to \in as \source, ESN infers that the external name \i is mapped to port \in of the component of type \L (the lexer), and this port is bound to the interface port \source of the resulting composite template. Similarly, from the binding rule \FF to <\in, \out>, it can be inferred that the \out port of each filter is to be bound to the \in port of the subsequent filter in the compiler pipeline: For example, the \out port of the component of type \L (the lexer) gets bound to the \in port of the component of type \P (the parser).

18.3.3 ATM Example Revisited: Architectural Level

Returning back to the ATM switch example, we define for each of the four system layers a *synthesized* composite template representing the architecture of the associated subsystem. Applying the refinement rules specified by a proper map to an instance of the underlying style accomplishes this mapping. The instantiation of a private style of the ATMS package into a fixed topology to produce an architectural template for the corresponding subsystem is an example of the intentional reuse of the style in question.

As with styles, where applicable, each template may be parameterized to specify the *size* of the desired instance. With this convention in mind, a primitive template of the ATMS package is specified as follows:

```
def temp TempName[int N1, ... , int Nk, ... ]
  is
    spec temp
      interface  ...
    end spec
  translations
    ...
end def;
```

A synthesized template is specified as follows:

```
def temp TempName[int N1, ... , int Nk, ... ]
  is
    apply map MapName[...] to style StyleName[...]
  post
    interface temp this seteq { ... }
  translations
    ...
end def;
```

Here the *apply* construct applies a map to a topology represented by an instance of a style to produce a synthesized composite template. The postcondition (*post*) specifies the expected interface of an instance of the synthesized template explicitly. The *translations* section of a template definition is reserved for the translation rules related to the target system language. These rules permit automatic translation of an instance of the synthesized template to a corresponding system-level description in the target language. *Section 18.4* addresses this topic.

We proceed bottom-up this time, so first consider the Switch Fabric layer of the ATMS package. The fabric of a Banyan switch is composed of only one type of component—the *switch element*. This component is represented at the architectural level by a primitive template:

```
def temp BE
  is
    spec temp
      interface \x<0>, \x<1>, \y<0>, \y<1>
    end spec
  translations
    ...
end def;
```

Thus, each node of the Banyan topology is to be refined into an architectural component with four interface ports. The map given in Figure 18.13 specifies the refinement. We omit the templates associated with the Knockout fabric.

The map in Figure 18.13 specifies how the external names and edges of a Banyan topology should be refined into interface ports and bindings in an architectural description. Care must be taken with the bindings, because up (\U) and down (\D) edges with even and odd indexes are treated differently.

The architecture of a generic switch fabric can then be defined as a *variable* synthesized template, which makes it possible to choose between a Banyan and a Knockout fabric on the fly. This is illustrated in Figure 18.14. Here the *choice* construct expresses the variability of the template. The interface port \r is added (by the *extend* construct) in case the switch fabric needs a synchronization or a clock message from the control component within the switch. The system level will determine whether such synchronization is indeed necessary. Therefore, in the architectural specification, this port is not bound to any internal port within the switch fabric. The necessary internal bindings and the missing ports of the switch components may be added later at the system level.

```
private def map Banyan_to_BANYAN[int M]
   is
     let
       name x[k] be if cond Even[k] then
             \x<0>
          else
             \x<1>
          end if
     in
        spec map
          interface
            enum k from 0..M-1 in
              \a<k> to \x<0> as \i<2*k>,
              \a<k> to \x<1> as \i<2*k+1>,
              \b<k> to \y<0> as \o<2*k>,
              \b<k> to \y<1> as \o<2*k+1>
            end enum
          components \E to 'temp BE'
          bindings
            enum k from 0..M-1 in
              \U<k> to <\y<0>, ~x[k]>,
              \D<k> to <\y<1>, ~x[k]>
            end enum
          end map
       end let
     pre
        cond Powerof2[M]
end def
```

Figure 18.13   ESN code for mapping a Banyan topology to a Banyan architecture.

To generate the architecture of a 4×4 Banyan fabric with input ports \i, output ports \o, and a synchronization port \r, we instantiate the template of Figure 18.14 as follows:

```
temp SF[4]@BANYAN;
```

Note that to generate an $M \times M$ switch, an $M/2$ by $M/2$ topology is used. This is because an \E-node in a Banyan topology is mapped into the primitive template temp BE, which has four interface ports: \x<0> and \x<1> for incoming cells, and \y<0> and \y<1> for outgoing cells. Accordingly, each of the external names \a<k> and \b<k> is mapped to two internal ports: the \a<k> to \x<0> and \x<1>; and the \b<k> to \y<0> and \y<1>. The fabric architecture of a 16×16 Banyan switch is depicted in Figure 18.15*a*.

The fabric architecture of a Knockout switch may be generated in a similar fashion, except that for a Knockout switch, an internal concentration factor must also be specified as a parameter. For example, the following would generate the architecture of a 4×4 Knockout fabric with an internal concentration factor of 3:

```
temp SF[4]@KNOCKOUT[3];
```

Figure 18.15*b* illustrates the resulting composite template.

```
def temp SF[M]
  is
    extend
      choose
        choice BANYAN is
          let L be M div 2 in
            apply map Banyan_to_BANYAN
              to style Banyan[L] preserve
          end let
        choice KNOCKOUT[N] is
          apply map Knockout_to_KNOCKOUT[M, N]
            to style Knockout[M]
        end choose
    with
      interface \r
    end extend
  pre
    M gt 0
  post
    interface temp this seteq
      {\i<0...M-1>, \o<0...M-1>, \r}
  translations
    ...
end def
```

Figure 18.14 ESN code specifying the variable architecture of an ATM switch fabric.

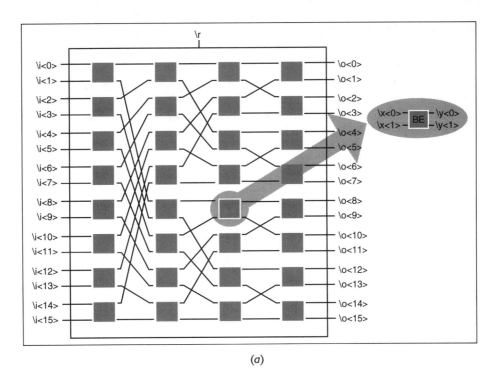

(a)

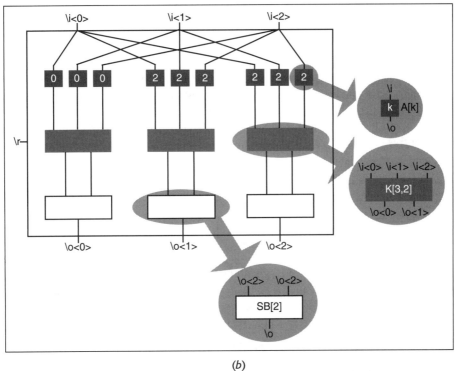

(b)

Figure 18.15 (*a*) Visualization of a 16 × 16 Banyan fabric architecture represented by the template temp SF[16]@BANYAN. (*b*) Visualization of the architecture of a 4 × 4 Knockout switch fabric with an internal concentration factor of 3, represented by temp SF[4]@KNOCKOUT[3].

Now consider the Switch Layer. A generic $M \times M$ ATM switch consists of an $M \times M$ *fabric component*, *M output interface units*, *M input interface units*, and a *control component*. Among these, the switch fabric and the output interface units (not discussed here) are synthesized components. The control component and the input interface units are primitive, and thus each is associated with a primitive template:

```
def temp R \* Control Component *\
  is
    spec temp
      interface \i, \o, \f
    end spec
  pre M gt 0
  translations
    ...
end def;

def temp IIU \* Input Interface Unit *\
  is
    spec temp
      interface \i, \f, \ri, \ro
    end spec
  translations
    ...
end def;
```

The refinement rules of the switch are straightforward, and easily specified by the map given in Figure 18.16. We need pay particular attention only to the refinement of the \IR edges: Each such edge is refined two bindings, one connecting an \ri port to an \i port, and the other an \ro port to an \o port. Figure 18.17a gives the ESN code specifying the synthesized architecture of an $M \times M$ switch, and Figure 18.17b depicts an instance of this template.

18.4 System Level

We define a *system* (or *subsystem*) as an artifact that performs a particular function with a well-defined interface. Much like classes in object-oriented programs, systems are reusable abstractions. Their *instances* can serve as *components* (subsystems) in larger systems, giving rise to a *part-of* hierarchy. Depending on whether it is composed of such instances, a system is called *primitive* or *composite* (see the sidebar titled *Formal Basis of System Level*).

18.4.1 Instantiation of Architectures in a Target Language

An architectural description must ultimately be mapped into a system-level description in a target language. At the system level, a primitive template is assigned

```
private def map Switch_to_SWITCH[M]
  is
    spec map
      interface
        enum k form 0..M-1
          \i<k> to \i as \i<k>,
          \o<k> to \o as \o<k>
        end enum
      components
        \I to 'temp IIU',
        \O to 'temp OIU',
        \F to 'temp SF[M]',
        \R to 'temp R',
      bindings
        enum k from 0..M-1 in
          \IF<k> to <\f, \i<k>>,
          \IR to <\ri, \i>,
          \IR to <\ro, \o>,
          \FO<k> to <\o<k>, \f>,
          \RF to <\f, \r>
        end enum
      end spec
    pre
      M gt 0
end def
```

Figure 18.16 ESN code for mapping a switch topology to a switch architecture.

a behavior and a composite template is translated into a corresponding description in the target language's notation using the composition mechanism of that language.

ESN can accommodate more than one system-level language by specifying the translation rules for each of these languages in the translations section of a template definition. Eligible target languages must support interface connection architectures and possess a library or repository mechanism to store sets of related reusable components. Assume that the basic unit of abstraction (and of composition) of the target language is called a *module*. Thus, the module is the analogue of an ESN template in the target language's vocabulary. As templates, modules are interconnected through their interface ports.

For each primitive ESN template defined, the component repository must contain a suitable module that implements the behavior of the corresponding component. Then a composite ESN template (for example, an instance of a synthesized template obtained by applying an ESN map to an instance of an ESN style) can be *translated* into a composite module description using the target language's interface connection (composition) model.

```
def temp SWITCH[M]
  is
    apply map  Switch_to_SWITCH[M]
      to style Switch[M]
  pre
    M gt 0
  post
    interface temp this seteq
      {\i<0...M-1>, \o<0...M-1>}
  translations
    ...
end def;
```

(a)

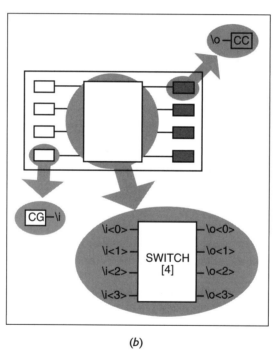

(b)

Figure 18.17 (*a*) ESN code specifying the architecture of an ATM switch as a synthesized template. (*b*) Visualization of temp SWITCH[4], an instance of the template given in (*a*).

The ESN abstract machine does not interpret the translation rules when a template expression is evaluated. These rules are interpreted by a language-specific translator that is invoked through an export statement:

```
export 'TempExpr' to Target:LANG using ModuleRepository;
```

Here TempExpr is a template expression (for example, an instance of a synthesized composite template); Target is the name of the target repository or file where the result

FORMAL BASIS OF SYSTEM LEVEL

A primitive system constitutes a leaf node in the part-of hierarchy. It is defined in terms of an *interface* and its *internal behavior.* The internal behavior describes how the functionality of the system is implemented. A composite system, on the other hand, is defined in terms of an *architecture.*

   system ::= primitive_system | composite_system

   primitive_system ::= ⟨interface, internal_behavior⟩

   composite_system ::= architecture

Two important functions are defined on systems: The first one extracts the *external behavior* and the second one the *architecture.* The external behavior gives the blackbox functionality of the system, whereas the architecture gives the structure as described in the sidebar titled *A Formal Model of Architectures.*

   external_behavior_of: systems → external_behaviors

   architecture_of: systems → architectures

Since the concept of systems is based on external functionality, a semantic model of systems is one of external behaviors. Therefore, two systems are considered equivalent if and only if their external behaviors are equivalent in some respect. The literature on such semantic models is extremely rich and diverse. However, the topic is well beyond the scope of this chapter.

of the translation is to be stored; LANG specifies the target language; and ModuleRepository specifies a component repository of the target language where the system-level implementations of the primitive templates are stored.

18.4.2 ATM Example Revisited: System Level

We use DSL as the target language at the system level to specify the components of the switch system. This section demonstrates how the architectural templates of *Section 18.3.3* are translated into DSL modules. See the sidebar titled *DSL Overview* for more information on DSL.

As mentioned in the previous section, for each primitive template of *Section 18.3.3,* the application-specific DSL component repository must contain a corresponding DSL module that implements the associated component. We call this repository *ATMS_Components.* The translations section of a primitive template specifies the association of the primitive template with a DSL module. This information permits the automatic translation of composite templates to their corresponding DSL module descriptions.

In DSL, the analogous notion for an ESN composite template is the *higher-order module.* Thus, a composite template is translated to a corresponding higher-order DSL module. The translation is accomplished by the ESN-to-DSL translator, which is invoked by an export statement, as explained earlier.

Again, we examine only the Switch and Switch Fabric layers. Consider the Switch Fabric layer first. This layer involves several primitive templates related to the two variant fabric architectures. One of these is the template BE (see *Section 18.3.3*), representing the switch element component of a Banyan fabric (the only component type for this kind of switch fabric). Suppose in the DSL repository ATMS_Components, this component is to be implemented by a primitive DSL module called *binary_switch_elmt*, which is defined as follows:

```
module(binary_switch_elmt, [
  (atm_cell(VPI, VCI, D, [Bit | Rest]) :-
    delay(BE_delay),
    send(_, y(Bit), atm_cell(VPI, VCI, D, Rest)))
]).
```

This module accepts incoming ATM cells through a parameterized message atm_cell, stores them for a fixed amount of time, and routes them to one of its two output ports. The last parameter of the atm_cell message determines the output port address of the switch (that is, the output interface unit) to which the cell is destined. Upon receiving an atm_cell message, the module removes the most significant bit of the output port address, and uses this bit to route the cell either to its y(0) or y(1) port.

The correspondence between the switch element component and the defined DSL module is specified in the DSL translation rules of the template BE as follows:

```
def temp BE
  is

    ...

  translations
    with DSL use "binary_switch_elmt" where
      \x<0> is "x(0)",
      \x<1> is "x(1)",
      \y<0> is "y(0)",
      \y<1> is "y(1)"
    end with
end def;
```

The translation rules state that an instance of this primitive template is to be mapped to the DSL module binary_switch_elmt whenever such an instance is generated as a component of an exported composite template. The interface port \x<0> of the template is mapped to the input port x(0) of binary_switch_elmt, and the interface port \y<0> is mapped to the output port y(0). Note that the input ports are not referenced in the definition of the module because in DSL, input ports of primitive modules are created dynamically at execution time (see the sidebar titled *DSL Overview*).

The synthesized template SF of *Section 18.3.3* represents the switch fabric. The translation rules for this template are defined as follows:

```
def temp SF[int M]
  is

    ...
  translations
    with DSL use "generic_fabric(%(M))" where
      enum k from 0 .. M-1 in
        \i is "cell_in(%(k)))",
        \o is "cell_out(%(k)))"
      end enum,
      \r is "synch_in"
    end with
end def;
```

Because SF is a composite template, the module generic_fabric is a synthesized, higher-order module—it does not come from the DSL repository ATMS _Components. Note that the module is parameterized by a variable M whose value is determined by the actual parameter of the template SF. The ports cell_in and cell_out are parameterized as well. The description of the module generic_fabric is generated automatically by the ESN-to-DSL translator. For example the following export statement generates the DSL description for the fabric component of a 16×16 Banyan switch:

```
export 'temp SF[16]@BANYAN' to ATMS_hoModules:DSL
  using ATMS_Components;
```

Moving to the Switch layer, we can now give the translation rules for the switch, which was defined by another synthesized template SWITCH in *Section 18.3.3:*

```
def temp SWITCH[int M]
  is

    ...
  translations
    with DSL use "atm_switch(%(M))" where
      enum k from 0..M-1 in
        \i is "cell_in(%(k))",
        \o is "cell_out(%(k))"
      end rep
    end enum
end def;
```

Again, because the switch is a synthesized component, atm_switch is a higher-order module that is automatically generated by the ESN-to-DSL translator. For a 3×3 switch, the translator will generate the DSL description given in Figure 18.18 in response to the following export statement:

```
export 'temp SWITCH[3] ' to ATMS_hoModules:DSL
  using ATMS_Components;
```

```
ho_module(atm_switch(3), [c(X)]).
ho_module(c(0), []).
module(c(1), []).
ho_module(c(2), []).
module(c3), []).
ho_module(c(4), []).
module(c(5), []).
ho_module(c(6), []).
ho_module(c(7), []).
isa(c(0), generic_fabric(4)).
isa(c(1), generic_input_interface).
isa(c(2), output_interface_unit).
isa(c(3), generic_input_interface).
isa(c(4), output_interface_unit).
isa(c(5), generic_input_interface).
isa(c(6), output_interface_unit).
isa(c(7), generic_control).
path(c(1), c(0), [cell_out, cell_in(0)]).
path(c(0), c(2), [cell_out(0), cell_in]).
path(c(3), c(0), [cell_out, cell_in(1)]).
path(c(0), c(4), [cell_out(1), cell_in]).
path(c(5), c(0), [cell_out, cell_in(2)]).
path(c(0), c(6), [cell_out(2), cell_in]).
path(c(7), c(0), [synch_out, synch_in]).
```

Figure 18.18 DSL higher-order module description for a 3×3 ATM switch, generated by the ESN-to-DSL translator in response to an export statement.

Note that the higher-order module description of Figure 18.18 refers to modules generic_fabric and output_interface_unit as components. Both are synthesized higher-order modules, and as such, are not defined in the component repository ATMS _Components. The other components—generic_input_interface and generic_control— are retrieved from the component repository. These modules are specified in the translations part of the primitive templates R and IIU of *Section 18.3.3* as the DSL modules implementing these components.

DSL OVERVIEW

DSL is the specification language of the Design Analysis and Synthesis Environment (DASE), a rapid prototyping and synthesis tool that was developed at McGill University and Bell Canada. DSL is based on Prolog, in which DASE is implemented.

The basic construct in DSL is the module. Modules are the primitive building blocks of a system, the unit of abstraction and of composition. A module has a parametric *name*, a set of possible *behaviors*, and, usually, a set of *resources*. The name of a module uniquely identifies that module. Modules react to external events. Resources act like local variables, and as such can contribute to the local state of a module.

The *behaviors* of a module define the actions that the module must perform when an external event occurs. This happens whenever a *message* is sent from one module to another. When a new message arrives, it is pattern-matched with a module's message name list. When a match is found, the destination module then attempts to execute the behavior associated with that message. Message names can be parameterized just as module names can.

Within each behavior, optional *conditions* can serve as guards. If each condition is evaluated to be true, then the *actions* following the conditions are executed in the given sequence. An action may initiate a communication with other modules, update local resources, or suspend the module for a specified time period.

Each DSL behavior can be viewed as a Prolog clause. The head of the clause consists of the behavior name, a unary or *n*-position predicate. The body consists of a series of conditions and actions, which represent compound subgoals of that clause. More precisely, a DSL condition is a Prolog subgoal to be satisfied. An action is a subgoal that is always satisfied, but may result in some desired side effects (such as message generation and resource manipulation).

Intermodule communication is realized using a send construct. The construct takes advantage of an optional output port name from which the message is to be sent. Another parameter specifies a *destination*, which is either (1) the name of a single destination module, (2) a set of destination modules, (3) a wild-card expression implying that the message is to be sent to all modules connected to the module's specific port, or (4) undefined. In the last case, the message will be sent to the first module connected to a port capable of interpreting the message. If a port is not specified, one will be synthesized during simulation. The DSL simulator creates the data structures necessary for communication, and takes care of internal queuing of incoming and scheduling of outgoing messages.

DSL permits hierarchical specifications through composition of modules into *higher order (ho)* modules. Connections between the constituent modules of a ho module are specified through *path* statements. A path statement connects an interface port of one module to that of another module. Note that because ports are not typed, any message can be sent from or received at any port. A module's behavior refers only to output ports, not input ports. Before execution time, the port in which a particular incoming message will be received is unknown. This is determined only at execution time by the DSL simulator, depending on the result of the incoming message pattern match. Path statements are optional because the DSL simulator is able to synthesize connections between ports on demand at execution time.

DSL has a special library mechanism to better support component reuse. This mechanism allows *on-the-fly* exploration of the design space during simulation (at execution time). A DSL library module is not to be confused with an ordinary module stored in a flat component repository. It differs from a nonlibrary module in several ways: (1) It may be more generic than a nonlibrary module; (2) its interface is well defined in that both input and output ports are explicitly specified; (3) it may be associated with a set of constraints related to the configuration of its components (for ho modules) or execution time properties; and (4) it may be replaced by another library module belonging to the same class if a constraint is violated during

Continues

> **DSL OVERVIEW** *(Continued)*
>
> simulation. For example, for a library module, it is possible to constrain the synthe-
> sis of new ports and paths at execution time, thus ensuring that the interface of the
> module and its initial configuration will be preserved throughout the simulation.
> DSL library modules are organized into *classes*. Modules belonging to the same
> class can be substituted for each other by the DSL simulator when a constraint is
> violated or an execution time error occurs. If a nonlibrary module is to be replace-
> able in this way, a dummy library module with the same name and parameters (that
> is, signature) must be created, and the name of this module must be included in the
> appropriate class definition. In this way, the full power of the DSL library mecha-
> nism can be exploited.

18.5 Relevant Work

The idea of reusing structure in the development of computer-based systems is not
new. Hardware description languages such as VHDL provide mechanisms for both
intentional and extensional reuse of structure. In software, successful application of
structural reuse goes as far back as the automatic generation of parsers for compilers
and syntax-directed editors for programming languages. Application generation technologies of today, most notably design environments for developing graphical user
interfaces, similarly rely on the concept of structural reuse.

As early as in the mid-1970s, Parnas [Parnas 1976] suggested the notion that families
of software systems can be realized systematically by reusing predefined organizational patterns. In the same spirit, module interconnection languages (MILs) [Prietro-
Diaz 1986] provided mechanisms for the specification of software families in order to
support version control. This idea was formalized and applied elegantly by [Goguen
1986] in the Library Interconnection Language (LIL). LIL was proposed for realizing
Ada programs from repositories of interconnection structures and plug-in components. It supports structural reuse through powerful parametric mechanisms, which
give rise to generic packages with substitutable components.

More recent and relevant work on the subject has been centered on object-oriented
design patterns, frameworks, style-based formalisms of software architecture, domain-
specific architectures, and architecture description languages. These and other techniques that address structural reuse are reviewed in more detail.

18.5.1 Design Patterns and Frameworks

Design patterns [Coad 1992; Beck 1996; Gamma 1995; Schmidt 1996] aim to capture
design idioms that are commonly encountered in object-oriented software development in terms of problem-solution pairs. Reuse here involves structure and behavioral
patterns, rather than preexisting components. It takes place on an informal level,

although sometimes a blend of ad hoc and more formal techniques is used. As such, the reuse mechanisms cannot be easily automated. Design patterns are more concerned with providing a means for communicating complex (and usually relatively low-level) concepts effectively between designers and for recording and encouraging the reuse of proven design practices. They are not intended to capture and document system architectures as formally reusable artifacts, and their focus has been mostly on microlevel design problems. A philosophical discussion of design patterns in the context of software architecture can be found in [Coplien 1997].

Design patterns are closely related to frameworks, which can be considered as a generative technology [Biddle-Tempero 1996] in the same spirit as the application generation technologies of the late 1970s. Recent works on frameworks have concentrated on pattern languages as informal documentation mechanisms. A pattern language is similar to a recipe that describes how to generate a particular type of application by reusing existing structures and components. Thus, unlike design patterns, application development using frameworks can involve reuse of preexisting or packaged components.

18.5.2 Architectural Styles

In software architecture, the term *architectural style* [Shaw-Garlan 1996] refers to the structure of a family of related systems. Architectural styles can be used to specify reference architectures or common high-level idioms and organizational patterns—such as pipeline, pipe-and-filter, client-server, layered, and blackboard—which underlie software systems. Like design patterns and frameworks, an architectural style can be reused to construct specific instances of a system family. [Monroe 1997] provides a comparison of architectural styles and design patterns. The approach presented in this chapter derives largely from the body of research on the style-based approach to software architecture. For examples, see [Dean-Cordy 1995; Moriconi 1995; Shaw-Garlan, 1996].

ESN supports style-based reuse based on separation of behavior from structure and generation of architectural descriptions through the instantiation of an underlying pattern. This kind of instantiation often involves refinement of interfaces and connections, such as discussed in [Moriconi 1995]. In ESN, the potential for reuse is greater than other style-based approaches because reuse takes place at a higher level.

18.5.3 Domain-Specific Software Architectures

Research in domain-specific software architectures (DSSAs) has been closely linked to related research in design patterns, frameworks, and architectural styles. A DSSA focuses on architectural support for a particular application domain (such as avionics, mobile robots, and command and control), again from a design reuse perspective [Tracz 1994]. The goal is the generation of a domain-specific application through the instantiation of a *reference architecture*.

A reference architecture defines the organization of a family of systems for a specific application area. A frequently cited example is the organization of a compiler into a lexer, parser, typer, optimizer, and code generator [Perry-Wolf 1992]. Because the applications targeted are constrained to a particular domain, reuse is limited, while being more amenable to formalization and automation.

Automated tools and environments have been implemented to aid in the development of applications conforming to a particular architectural style or reference architecture. An example is Honeywell's MetaH environment for building real-time embedded avionics systems. This environment can also be considered as an application framework.

18.5.4 Functional Programming Languages

In functional programming languages, sophisticated type systems and higher-order features provide powerful linguistic support for structural reuse. The typical example is SML [Milner 1990], with its parametric module facility. Modules in SML, called *structures*, are packaged collections of types, variables, functions, and other structures. A structure's type is determined by its *signature*. Parametric structures can be defined through the *functor* mechanism. Functors are essentially functions from signatures to signatures, applicable to structures. Combined with parametric types, they can be used effectively to specify generic modules. A generic module can be based upon others, supporting extensional reuse. Intentional reuse is also supported by means of the functor mechanism: A specific module conforming to a given signature and with the desired components can be generated through the application of a functor to a particular structure.

ESN is also an interactive, strongly-typed language like SML, but does not enjoy higher-order features. The basic unit of specification in ESN is the *definition*, which is analogous to a function. However, definitions cannot be parameterized by other definitions. Unlike SML, ESN has a simple type system that does not support parametric types. Although generic system structures can conveniently be defined through parameterization, this is not necessary in ESN to address extensional reuse.

18.5.5 Hardware Description Languages

Hardware description languages such as VHDL and Verilog also have parametric features similar to those found in ESN and SML. Parametric architectures in VHDL give rise to generic structure descriptions that can be built one upon another. This mechanism supports both extensional and intentional reuse. For example, *configuration specifications* allow abstract components specified by *component* declarations in an architecture to be instantiated to concrete components specified by *entity* declarations (and their respective architectures), supporting intentional reuse. ESN also has linguistic facilities for easy generation of system configurations (topological and architectural specifications) similar to those found in VHDL. An example is ESN's repetition (*rep*) construct, which roughly corresponds to VHDL's generate statement (*for-generation* schemes).

Reuse in ESN occurs at a much higher level than it does in a hardware description language. At this level, the exact semantics of connections and components are unknown, and it may not be clear or even relevant whether the individual components will be implemented in software or hardware.

18.5.6 Languages for Concurrent and Distributed Systems

In specification languages and formalisms for concurrent and distributed systems, and for tools based on these, support for structural reuse has been largely nonexistent. This is the case for SDL [Turner 1993], Modechart [Jananian-Mok 1994], Estelle [Turner 1993], and Lotos [Turner 1993]. The emphasis in these languages has been on other aspects, such as the ability to generate implementation code, expression of realtime properties, formal verification, and controlling mathematical tractability to facilitate formal verification. Some exceptions are noted next.

Although the original version of SDL did not support structural reuse, the situation has been addressed in SDL-92 [Sarma 1996] with the introduction of object orientation and parametric types. The unit of composition and modularity in SDL is the *block*. The designer may specify a type for a block that is then used to generate instances of that type. The real flexibility is achieved through parametric types that allow a block to be instantiated with different processes or other blocks. In this case, parameters serve as placeholders, and the type defines a structural context. Thus, the type facility of SDL-92 supports intentional reuse. Because types may be based upon other types, extensional reuse is also supported.

In DSL [Tanir 1997], generic system configurations with varying numbers of components and connections may be specified as *constraints* for library modules by taking advantage of Prolog's imperative features. However, this mechanism does not provide sufficient flexibility in terms of intentional reuse, because DSL constraints can only specify system configurations with fixed component types. In addition, configuration rules may turn out to be quite cumbersome to specify.

In ROOM [Selic 1994], a realtime object-oriented modeling technique, components are modeled by *actors*. Actors and ports can be replicated to generate multiple instances of an actor or a port of an actor at once. Replication permits specification of some standard system configurations. Another relevant feature is that of a *replaceable* actor. Systems with replaceable actors can serve as contexts, or templates, where another actor with a compatible interface may be substituted for a replaceable actor. Replaceable actors and replication together support intentional reuse in a limited sense. Extensional reuse is supported through the ability to compose replaceable actors.

In process algebra [Milner 1989], system specifications are structured as a parallel composition of a set of communicating sequential processes. Generic process interconnection structures can be specified as parametric process expressions. These expressions are actually derived process algebraic operators that are often referred to as *contexts*. A context can be instantiated by substituting particular processes for the unknown parameters, and hence supports intentional reuse. This mechanism, however, is not offered in most languages based on process algebra. For example, for Lotos, it would turn the language into a higher-order one, giving it the expressive power of a mobile calculus in which processes and connections may change locales. In the near future, Lotos is expected to remain first order, resolving the tradeoff between expressive power and mathematical tractability in favor of the latter. The style sublanguage of ESN has been inspired by process algebra. Although ESN does not possess any higher-order features either, it can effectively specify generic interconnection structures, which can be instantiated and translated into static process interconnection structures as done in [Hinterplattner 1990].

18.5.7 Architecture Description Languages

Another important line of research has been centered on architecture description languages (ADLs). An ADL places the emphasis upon large-scale design, and as such has a more general scope than that of traditional specification or programming languages. Naturally, support for structural reuse is brought into the foreground in an ADL. Strong connections exist between ADLs, architectural styles, and DSSAs.

In comparison with ESN, four such languages are mentioned: Aesop, Rapide, Wright and ACME. All of these languages follow the interface connection model of architecture based on the standard *component-connection-configuration* paradigm, and support style-based reuse. The following discussion omits other ADLs, such as UniCon, as well as earlier work on module interconnection languages (MILs). UniCon [Shaw 1995] has a more low-level focus than these ADLs, and as such does not support style-based reuse. Similarly, MILs—which were predecessors of ADLs—had been developed before style-based models of software architecture emerged, and hence do not address structural reuse from that perspective. MILs are discussed in [Prietro-Diaz 1986].

PCL [Sommerville-Dean 1996], a language for developing multiversion computer-based systems, also evolved from MILs, but is not discussed in the ADL literature. PCL supports style-based reuse in a limited way. The variable parts of a system family can be specified using conditional structure expressions. Version descriptions can be used to remove this variability, allowing the instantiation of a system family into a particular system (a version). Again, this mechanism supports intentional reuse, but only system families with a small number of members can be specified in this way.

In Aesop [Garlan 1994], an architectural style is defined through subtyping, or by specializing a base style's ontology (vocabulary of connector and component types, connection rules, and semantic interpretation) and object model. These specializations give rise to environments called *fables* to aid in the development of individual instances of the underlying style. Aesop relies on a generative technology. In this sense, a fable is akin to a framework. Extensional reuse is supported by the ability to combine a set of different styles in producing a new fable.

Wright [Allen-Garlan 1994] supports developing general, style-based theories for families of system architectures. Topological and other structural properties that a family of systems must satisfy can be expressed as constraints in a style's definition. This is done using a notation based on set theory and predicate logic, similar to [Moriconi 1995]. Styles are analogous to types for architectures, and conformance of a particular architecture to its specified style can thus be type-checked. Connectors, components, and interfaces are also typed. Additional flexibility is provided through parametric types, as in SML and Rapide. This feature allows for the specification of generic configurations of components and connectors.

Rapide [Luckham 1995] is similar to Wright, but provides features that are more powerful for structural reuse. It comprises several different sublanguages to address different aspects of system architecture. Unlike ESN and the previously mentioned ADLs, Rapide permits specification of dynamic architectures whose components and connections may vary during execution time. Rapide combines the higher-order features of SML—an advanced type system and parametric specifications—with the flexible configuration features of VHDL, in excellent support of structural reuse, both extensional and intentional.

The ACME language [Garlan 1997] is a more recent initiative and is still under development at this writing. It provides an interchange format between different ADLs and ADL-based tools. ACME does not define an execution model, but allows architectural specifications to be annotated with language-specific information that can be passed uninterpreted to a tool capable of understanding it. Style-based reuse is supported by a simple, extensible macrolike facility called *template* and a type facility called *style*. ACME templates are first order. Parametric templates can define generic components, connectors, and configurations, which can be grouped together to define a style. As such, an ACME style specifies the common vocabulary of a family of systems. Templates are expanded (or instantiated) in place to produce specialized descriptions. This is analogous to the instantiation of a style into a particular topology in ESN. However, the template facility does not provide the same level of flexibility as the intentional reuse mechanisms of Rapide, Wright, or ESN.

18.6 Summary

This chapter presents a language-independent methodology to support both structural and component reuse. The approach relies on the formal specification of structural patterns for families of systems at a very high level, allowing easy composition of abstract design elements. These patterns are stored in a style repository to support structural reuse. The actual components are stored separately in a component repository implemented in a target system-level language. The methodology is particularly applicable to the hardware-software codesign of real-time distributed systems, but it can also be adapted to software design in general—for example, by using an object-oriented programming language at the system level with back-end support for object connection architectures; or for a component technology such as JavaBeans or ActiveX. Currently, the back end supports only those languages whose system structuring method is based on the interface connection model.

Reuse of structure is supported at two different levels of design, topological and architectural. The topological level provides a higher level of abstraction with more potential for reuse than the architectural level by focusing on abstract components and relationships among these components. The architectural level is more detailed, in that it defines multipoint interfaces for components, as well as multiple bindings that represent more refined forms of component interaction. At the architectural level, components can be defined hierarchically, whereas at the topological level, a component is represented as an atomic *node* which cannot be expanded further. It is shown that architectural descriptions can be obtained from topological specifications through a set of refinement rules.

The approach supports both extensional and style-based, intentional reuse. In extensional reuse, an artifact is reused to create another reusable artifact, whereas in intentional reuse, an artifact is reused to produce a final artifact. Extensional reuse is supported by allowing the specification of a reusable pattern to be based on other reusable patterns. In style-based reuse, a generic pattern is first instantiated, and then, in the resulting instance, abstract components serving as placeholders are replaced by their concrete counterparts. This idea is applied in the generation of architectural descriptions from higher-level, topological specifications.

Extended Style Notation (ESN) is proposed as a common high-level language for design activities at the topological and architectural levels. ESN is representative of the kind of facilities needed in such a language. (For a comparative overview of ESN, see the sidebar titled *ESN Overview*.) System-level descriptions can be obtained using the proposed methodology in a variety of target languages. The Design Specification Language (DSL) is used for this purpose in a realistic, incremental example. Besides DSL, two other object-oriented specification languages for real-time distributed systems—ROOM and SDL—would be good candidates. (SDL blocks and composite actors in ROOM are analogous to DSL higher-order modules.)

The untyped nature of DSL and the synthesis capability of its simulator pose a problem. The DSL simulator does not require complete or consistent specifications: Inconsistencies can be detected and missing information—including new paths and ports—can be generated at execution time. In addition, using its library mechanism, different library modules can be substituted for components that are found to be unsatisfactory. This means that the final synthesized system may no longer be faithful to the original architectural specification. The problem can be addressed in two ways. First, the simulator can be instructed explicitly to remain faithful to the original architecture, thereby overriding its synthesis capability. Second, the architectural changes that are introduced at execution time can be recorded, and the results can be reflected back to the original architectural specification along with meaningful feedback to the user. The latter alternative requires automated support for the upward feedback arrows of Figure 18.4. However, it is not entirely clear how to synchronize the topological, architectural, and system-level specifications so that they remain consistent with each other throughout the design life cycle.

As a last remark, we touch on visualization issues. It would be highly desirable to supply a formal graphical notation for the style and template sublanguages of ESN. For the style sublanguage, this task is particularly challenging, especially for parametric, variable, and recursively defined styles. Although specific instances that represent fixed topologies of a style are best visualized graphically (as is done throughout the chapter), the generic versions are most easily defined algorithmically using graph-algebraic and generative constructs. It is in principle possible to represent some of these algorithmic specifications in a graph-grammar-like formalism and produce effective visualizations for them. Unfortunately, a full generalization seems inherently difficult. A prototypical implementation of ESN, including a visualization component, has been developed at NRC, and can be obtained by writing to the authors.

ESN OVERVIEW

ESN is a strongly typed language based on a graph algebra and a standard architectural model. It is intended as a front end for a variety of modeling and specification languages to enhance their structural reuse capabilities.

Level of Abstraction

ESN supports structural reuse *at* and *across* two distinct levels of abstraction, topological and architectural. The separation of the topological level from the architectural level is novel. The topological level is above the architectural level in terms of its ability to describe structural detail. For this reason, it offers more potential for reuse. ESN has different sublanguages to express system topologies and classes of topologies (the *style* sublanguage), refinement rules (the *map* sublanguage), and system architectures (the *template* sublanguage).

System Structuring Model

ESN adopts the interface connection model for architectural specifications. The model is based on the familiar *component-connection-configuration* paradigm. In contrast to the architectural models suggested in [Dean-Cordy 1995; Perry-Wolf 1992], and of Wright, UniCon, and Rapide, connections in ESN are not first-class entities; they are represented by featureless relationships between components. In other architectural models, connectors are often distinct elements, or different types of connections are distinguishable from one another with respect to their semantics in an underlying execution model. ESN's architectural model is compatible with specification techniques having a uniform module interconnection mechanism, such as SDL [Sarma 1996], DSL [Tanir 1997], Modechart [Jananian-Mok 1994], ROOM [Selic 1994], and Lotos and Estelle [Turner 1993]. At the level of abstraction at which ESN operates, the notion of connectors as first-class objects is redundant because typed components are sufficient to model connectors.

Execution Model Independency

ESN does not define an underlying execution model. In ACME's terminology, it has an *open semantic framework* [Garlan 1997]. This implies complete separation of behavior from structure, and contrasts with some other ADLs, such as Rapide and Wright, which allow behavioral properties to be associated with components and connectors. In ESN, all behavioral modeling takes place at a lower level (system level) in the target language's notation. Static system architectures can be synthesized in ESN and the results can be translated automatically to the target language's notation, where behavioral specifications are provided only for the lowest-level components. For example, in addition to DSL higher-order modules, it would in principle be possible to generate complex Lotos process interconnection structures or SDL block structures from composite ESN architectures.

Continues

ESN OVERVIEW *(Continued)*

Types of Reuse

ESN does not possess the higher-order features found in SML, Rapide, or Wright. The type system of ESN is simple, and there are no parametric types or higher-order functional abstractions. Special types (style and template) are used to represent patterns of system structures at two distinct abstraction levels. Both style-based (intentional) and extensional reuse are supported by first-order methods only. The mechanisms used vary.

At the topological level, the graph-algebraic constructs (the style sublanguage) of ESN allow larger structural patterns to be defined by composing smaller structural patterns. This capability supports extensional reuse. Structural descriptions can also be composed through special "stylistic" constructs to form families and express variability of components. (The idea of describing system families through variable components is also suggested by [Battory-O'Malley 1992; Prietro-Diaz 1986; Sommerville 1996].) A generic pattern can then be instantiated into a particular member structure (a topology). This mechanism constitutes the first kind of intentional reuse possible in ESN. Families of structural patterns can also be defined using parametric abstractions (as in generic styles), which can be instantiated by specifying actual values for the formal parameters. This mechanism constitutes the second kind of intentional reuse. Once an instance representing a fixed topology is obtained, it must be mapped into an architectural description (called a *template*). This is accomplished by selecting a concrete component for each abstract component (node), defining an external interface, and refining the connectivity relations into connections (bindings) between concrete components. Such mapping of topologies to architectures constitutes a third form of intentional reuse that is distinct from the first two. Both instantiation and refinement are involved here because of a leap to a lower, and thus more detailed, level of abstraction. In addition, component reuse is supported because concrete components are selected from an existing system-level repository using the translation rules embedded in the definition of primitive templates.

The architectural level also supports extensional reuse through parametric abstractions (generic templates). This combination of reuse mechanisms is unique to ESN.

18.7 References

[Allen-Garlan 1994] Allen, R., and D. Garlan. Beyond definition/use: Architectural interconnection. *Proceedings of the Workshop on Interface Definition Languages*, Portland, OR, January 20, 1994.

[Awdeh-Mohftah 1995] Awdeh, R.Y., and H.T. Mohftah. Survey of ATM switch architectures. *Computer Networks and ISDN Systems*, 27, 1995: 1567–1613.

[Batory-O'Malley 1992] Batory, D. and S. O'Malley. The design and implementation of hierarchical software systems with reusable components. *ACM Transactions on Software Engineering Methodology*, 1(4), October 1992.

[Beck 1996] Beck, K., James O. Coplien, Ron Crocker, Lutz Dominick, Gerard Meszaros, Frences Paulisch, and John Vlissides. Industrial experience with design patterns.

Proceedings of ICSE 1996, 18th IEEE International Conference on Software Engineering, Berlin, Germany, March 1996.

[Biddle-Tempero 1996] Biddle, R., and E. Tempero. Understanding the impact of language features on reusability. *Proceedings of the Fourth International Conference on Software Reuse,* Orlando, FL, April 1996.

[Coad 1992] Coad, P. Object-oriented design patterns. *Communications of the ACM,* 35(9), 1992: 153–159.

[Coplien 1997] Coplien, J. Idioms and patterns as architectural styles. *IEEE Software,* January 1997.

[Dean-Cordy 1995] Dean, T.R., and J.R. Cordy. A syntactic theory of software architecture. *IEEE Transactions Software Engineering,* 21(4), April 1995: 303–313.

[Gamma 1995] Gamma, E., R. Helm, R. Johnson, and John Vlissides. *Design Patterns: Elements of Reusable Object-Oriented Software.* Reading, MA: Addison-Wesley, 1995.

[Garlan 1994] Garlan, D., R. Allen, and J. Ockerbloom. Exploiting style in architectural design environments. *Proceedings of SIGSOFT 1994, Second International ACM SIG-SOFT Symposium on Foundations of Software Engineering,* December 1994. New York: ACM Press, 1994.

[Garlan 1997] Garlan, D., R.T. Monroe, and D. Wile. ACME: an architectural interchange language. *Proceedings of ICSE 1997, 19th IEEE International Conference on Software Engineering, Boston, MA, May 1997,* Los Alamitos, CA: IEEE Computer Press 1997.

[Goguen 1986] Goguen, J. A. Reusing and interconnecting software components. *IEEE Computer,* February 1986.

[Hinterplattner 1990] Hinterplattner, J., H. Nirschl, and H. Saria. Process topology diagrams. *FORTE 1990, Proceedings of the Third International Conference on Formal Description Techniques,* 1990.

[Jananian-Mok 1994] Jananian, F., and A. Mok. Modechart: A specification language for real-time systems. *IEEE Transactions on Software Engineering,* 21(12), December 1994.

[Krueger 1992] Krueger, C.W. Software reuse. *ACM Computing Surveys,* 24(2), June 1992: 131–183.

[Luckham 1995] Luckham, D.C., John. J. Kenney, Larry A. Augustin, James Vera, D. Bryan, and Walter Mann. Specification and analysis of system architecture using Rapide. *IEEE Transactions on Software Engineering,* 21(6), April 1995.

[Milner 1989] Milner, R. *Communication and Concurrency.* Englewood Cliffs, NJ: Prentice-Hall, 1989.

[Milner 1990] Milner, R., M. Tofte, and R. Harper. *The Definition of Standard ML.* Cambridge, MA: MIT Press, 1990.

[Monroe 1997] Monroe, R.T., Andrew Kompanek, Ralph Melton, and David Garlan. Architectural styles, design patterns, and objects. *IEEE Software,* January 1997.

[Moriconi 1994] Moriconi, M., X. Qian, and R.A. Riemenschneider. Correct architecture refinement. *IEEE Transactions on Software Engineering,* 21(4), April 1994.

[Parnas 1976] Parnas, D.L. On the design and implementation of software families. *IEEE Transactions on Software Engineering,* 2(1), 1976: 1–9.

[Parnas 1983] Parnas, D.L., P.C. Cements, and D.M. Weiss. Enhancing reusability with information hiding. *IEEE Proceedings of the Workshop on Reusability in Programming,* Los Alamitos, CA: IEEE Computer Press, 1983.

[Perry-Wolf 1992] Perry, D.E., and A.L. Wolf. Foundations for the study of software architecture. *Software Engineering Notes*, 17(4), October 1992.

[Prietro-Diaz 1986] Prietro-Diaz, R., and J.M. Neighbors. Module interconnection languages. *Journal of Systems and Software*, 6(4), November 1986: 307–334.

[Sarma 1996] Sarma, A. Introduction to SDL-92. *Computer Networks and ISDN Systems*, 28(12), June 1996: 1603–1615.

[Schmidt 1996] Schmidt, D., M.E. Fayad, and R. Johnson. Software patterns. *Communications of the ACM*, 39(10), October 1996: 36–40.

[Selic 1994] Selic, B., G. Gullekson, and P.T. Ward. *Real-Time Object-Oriented Modeling*. New York: John Wiley & Sons, 1994.

[Shaw 1995] Shaw, M., R. DeLine, D.V. Klein, T.L. Ross, D.M. Young, and G. Zalasnik. Abstractions for software architecture and tools to support them. *IEEE Transactions on Software Engineering*, 21(6), April 1995.

[Shaw-Garlan 1996] Shaw, M., and D. Garlan. Software *Architecture—Perspectives on an Emerging Discipline*. Upper Saddle River, NJ: Prentice Hall, 1996.

[Sommerville-Dean 1996] Sommerville, I., and G. Dean. PCL: A language for modeling evolving system architectures. *Software Engineering Journal*, 11(2), March 1996: 111–121.

[Tanir 1997] Tanir, O. *Modeling Complex Computer and Communication Systems: A Domain-Oriented Design Framework*. New York: McGraw-Hill, 1997.

[Tracz 194] Tracz, W. Domain-specific software architecture (DSSA) frequently asked questions (FAQ). *ACM Software Engineering Notes*, 19(2), April 1994: 52–56.

[Turner 1993] Turner, K., ed. *Using Formal Description Techniques: An Introduction to ESTELLE, LOTOS, and SDL*. New York: John Wiley & Sons, 1993.

CHAPTER 19

Language Support for Application Framework Design

A framework encapsulates a reusable, stable design, provides hooks for extending and varying this design, and is *planned* for reuse. Its whole reason for existence is to be reused in different applications. A framework realizes a coherent software architecture, consisting of classes and objects with well-defined structural and behavioral properties [Fayad-Schmidt 1997]. The framework is intended to be varied in given ways; a well-designed framework will allow these variations to be easy to write correctly, and at the same time will provide sufficient flexibility in varying the design. Good language support will allow a framework designer to use the language to set up rules for the intended use of the framework. For example, it is desirable to have precise control over how framework classes may be specialized.

This chapter focuses on the role of language constructs for the design of frameworks with emphasis on support for encapsulation of the stable part of the design, and on support for capturing its intentions in a precise and preferably statically checkable way.

Framework design is a balance between flexibility and safety. However, in order for frameworks to be industrially acceptable, the structural and behavioral properties of a framework must be enforceable (mostly statically). Such enforcement can be supported by mechanisms external to the language, as suggested in [Hedin 1997; Minsky-Pal 1997], but it is better if the language is able to directly enforce these framework properties. We show that well-known static language constructs offer strong support for industrial framework design, providing that they are generalized. Our starting point is to look at current object-oriented languages that are both safe and flexible, exemplified by Eiffel [Meyer 1992], BETA [Madsen 1993], and Java [Arnold-Gosling 1996]. These languages are all based on mainly static type checking and garbage collection, which we find to be basic prerequisites for designing safe frameworks. We discuss the role of four generalized language mechanisms in supporting framework design: *generalized block structure, generalized inheritance, generalized virtuality,* and *singular objects*. These mechanisms are all available in BETA, and partly in several other languages. BETA was developed as a successor to Simula [Dahl 1970]. Simula frameworks are discussed in another chapter in Volume 1 [Vaucher 1999]. This chapter is partly based on previous works, as reported in [Hedin-Knudsen 1999].

19.1 General Block Structure

Most programming languages exhibit some form of block structure, where block constructs such as classes, records, procedures, and functions can be nested within each other. By *general block structure*, we mean the possibility to nest any kind of block construct within any other kind of block construct to an arbitrary nesting depth. General block structure also implies that each instance of a block (activation record or object) will exist in the context of an instance of its enclosing block and will have access to all attributes (variables, methods, and classes) of that enclosing instance. This was pioneered in Algol, whose block constructs are the procedure and statement block, which could be nested arbitrarily and to any depth. Some function-oriented languages are also built on general block structure, most notably Scheme [Abelson 1985].

For object-oriented languages, the general tendency has unfortunately been *not* to provide general block structure, and to have severe restrictions on how blocks may be nested. Typical block constructs in object-oriented languages are class and method constructs. For most object-oriented languages, classes may contain methods, but classes cannot contain local classes, and methods cannot contain local classes or methods. In contrast, Simula (which was designed as an extension to Algol) kept the general block structure and allows arbitrary nesting of classes and methods to any depth. However, there are certain restrictions in Simula for how nested classes may be used and how nested classes may inherit from other classes. These restrictions are removed in BETA. C++ [Stroustrup 1997] allows a limited form of nested classes, because a nested class can access only static members of its outer class. (In C++, an instance of an inner class is not automatically linked to an instance of the outer class, and it can therefore not access ordinary nonstatic members of the outer class.) Java has recently adopted the BETA style of allowing classes to be nested (called *inner classes* in Java) [Sun 1996].

General block structure is useful in frameworks because it supports the notion of what we may call *nested hooks*. A hook is a location in the framework that can be specialized by the application programmer. Normally, a hook is an abstract class that can be specialized by subclassing, and that contains abstract methods (hook methods) which can be specialized by providing overriding methods in the subclasses [Pree 1994]. This normal kind of hook is thus a two-level nested entity. However, by utilizing general block structure it is possible to support *nested hooks*: A hook (class or method) may contain any number of local hooks (other classes or methods), each of which may contain any number of local hooks, and so on to any suitable depth. This provides the framework designer with excellent possibilities for describing precisely what can be extended and specialized in a framework.

19.1.1 Nested Class Hooks

The use of general block structure is omnipresent in the BETA frameworks [Knudsen 1993]. As an example of nested hooks using classes within classes, consider a GUI framework with a window class, defined in Figure 19.1. (The language used in this chapter is similar in syntactic structure to the Java language to ease the reading of the code examples. The language constructs are all found in the BETA language, and there is a one-to-one mapping between the syntax used here and the syntax of the BETA language.) Here, the outermost class Window contains an instance variable wCanvas, a method setTitle, and a local class Button. Class Button contains a virtual method onMouseUp (a hook method) and two nonvirtual methods, drawAt and draw. Because of the class nesting, a Button object will exist in the context of a Window object, and can access attributes and operations in that Window object. For example, the draw method draws the button on the enclosing window's canvas. The framework in this case uses three levels of hooks: a Window hook, containing a Button hook, containing an onMouseUp hook.

An application may use the framework to implement a calculator tool, as shown in Figure 19.2. Here, the framework is extended at all three hook levels: CalcWindow is a subclass to Window; plusButton and minusButton are defined as instances of the local class Button; and their onMouseUp methods are given appropriate implementations. (The plusButton and minusButton are defined as *singular objects*, a concept discussed in *Section 19.4*.) Because of the class nesting, the plusButton and minusButton objects will exist in the context of a CalcWindow object. This allows their implementations of onMouseUp to access, for example, theCalculator (an object defined in CalcWindow) and setTitle (a method in CalcWindow).

The example in Figure 19.2 shows how the framework imposes a structure where a Button is viewed as something local to a Window; that is, it can exist only in the context of a Window. This allows Button objects to easily access attributes and operations of their window. This imposed structure makes application programming much easier than if the connection between buttons and windows had to be handled explicitly.

```
Window: class {
    wCanvas: Canvas;
    void setTitle(t: text) { ... };
    Button: class {
        void onMouseUp() virtual;
        void drawAt(c: Canvas) { ... };
        void draw() { drawAt(wCanvas) };
    }
}
```

Figure 19.1 Window framework with local Button class.

```
CalcWindow: class Window {
    theCalculator: instance Calculator;
    plusButton: instance Button {
        void onMouseUp() extended {
            theCalculator.plus();
            setTitle(theCalculator.result());
        };
    };
    minusButton: instance Button {
        void onMouseUp() extended {
            theCalculator.minus();
            setTitle(theCalculator.result())
        };
    };
    ...
}
```

Figure 19.2   Application using the Window framework.

Refactoring Nested Classes

Local classes are particularly useful when the local class is meaningful only inside the context of its enclosing class. However, if parts of it are also meaningful outside this context, it may be advantageous to refactor the framework to define those parts outside the enclosing class. This structure is shown in Figure 19.3. The parts of Button that are not dependent on Window are factored out into a new top-level class, which may be reused in contexts other than Window. This refactoring thus achieves both the reusability of non-nested classes and the tight coupling of nested classes.

Simulating Nested Classes

In a language without nested classes, the nesting can be simulated by declaring the local class at the same level as the outer class, and giving the local class an explicit con-

```
Button: class {
    void onMouseUp() virtual;
    void drawAt(c: Canvas) { ... };
};
Window: class {
    wCanvas: Canvas;
    void setTitle(t: text) { ... };
    WindowButton: class Button {
        void draw() { drawAt(wCanvas) };
    };
};
```

Figure 19.3   Refactored Window framework.

text reference to an object of the outer class, as shown in Figure 19.4. For a framework, this has several drawbacks, however. First, the context reference needs to be explicitly administered by the application. Second, the context reference will be qualified by the outer class in the framework. This has the effect that extensions of the local class cannot safely access attributes and operations in extensions of the outer class, but have to resort to casting.

The use of general block structure thus allows the framework to capture more of the architecture of the system, and allows safer and easier application programming.

Nested Method Hooks

General block structure also allows methods to be nested within methods. For frameworks, this allows a hook method to contain a finer structure of local hook methods. *Section 19.2* discusses this in more detail, because the full advantages of this method build on the notion of method inheritance.

19.1.2 The Framework as a Class

General block structure allows the framework itself to be described as a class. In most object-oriented languages, a framework is a collection of classes that forms some kind of package or library. However, general block structure allows the framework itself to be described as a class. The framework class can then contain local classes and methods, some of which may be hooks.

Framework Specialization Hierarchy

Modeling the framework as a class is useful because it allows a specialization hierarchy of frameworks to be defined, with the general framework at the root of the hierarchy and the very application-specific frameworks at the leaves of the hierarchy. An

```
NESTED CLASSES                SIMULATED IMPLEMENTATION
OuterClass: class {           OuterClass: class {
    v: Type;                      v: Type;
    InnerClass: class         };
{
        void m( ...)          InnerClass: class {
{                                 context:
            ... v ...         OuterClass;
        };                        void m(...) {
    };                                ... context.v
};                            ...
                                  };
                              };
```

Figure 19.4   Nested classes versus simulated implementation.

example of this is Simula's standard class Simulation, which is a general framework for discrete-event simulation. It contains a local class Process for modeling processes in a simulation and maintains a queue of such processes, as sketched in Figure 19.5.

More specialized simulation frameworks can be built by subclassing the Simulation framework and introducing more specialized local classes. Figure 19.6 shows an example of such framework specialization, taken from the Simula documentation from 1970 [Dahl 1970].

Multiple Framework Instantiation

Modeling the framework as a class allows data global to the framework to be modeled as ordinary instance variables. For example, in class Simulation, the process queue reference SQS is an instance variable. Languages without general block structure usually have special language constructs for global variables—for example, *static* variables in C++ and Java. However, in contrast to such framework packages, a framework class can be instantiated more than once. Each instance of the framework will then obtain its own set of data local to the framework, but freely accessible (as global data) to the local classes in the framework. Such multiple framework instantiation is often useful. For example, in an instance of a simulation framework it is possible for an individual process to have its own instance of the framework in order to perform a local simulation. This technique is used, for example, by Islo [Islo 1994].

19.2 General Inheritance

Inheritance is often described as an *incremental modification mechanism* [Wegner-Zdonik 1988], allowing individual instance variables and operations to be added in subclasses.

```
Simulation: class {
    SQS: list of Process;

    Process: class {
        ...
    };

    Process current() { ... };

    void hold(T: double) { ... };
    void activate(... X: Process ...) { ... };
    void passivate(...) { ... };
    ...
}
```

Figure 19.5 The framework as a class: Simula's class Simulation.

```
JobShop: class Simulation {
    Crane: class Process {
        ...
    };

    Machine: class Process {
        ...
    };
}
```

Figure 19.6 A specialized simulation framework for job-shop analysis.

However, the possibility of adding or overriding operations gives fairly coarse-grained incremental modification. Fine-grained incremental modification can be achieved by also supporting inheritance for methods; that is, a method can have submethods in analogy to a class having subclasses. BETA supports inheritance for methods in the following way: The supermethod may contain a statement *inner* which causes the code of the submethod to be executed. Submethods may declare additional input and output parameters (return values). The inner construct originates from Simula, and combining submethods with the inner mechanism was originally proposed in [Vaucher 1975].

If inheritance is supported for all kinds of block constructs in a language, we say that the language has *general inheritance*. The fine-grained incremental modification that can be obtained in languages with general inheritance is important in framework design because it gives the framework designer the possibility of capturing more of the common architecture in the framework.

By using method inheritance, a hook in the form of an inner statement can be added directly into a control structure in the framework, allowing the application programmer to extend the behavior directly in the context of the hook.

19.2.1 Method Inheritance

As an example of when method inheritance is beneficial, consider the construction of a framework for concurrent programming, including a class for *monitors* [Hoare 1974], which provides mutually exclusive access to its encapsulated data by means of *entry methods*. (This example is taken in part directly from the original paper by Vaucher [Vaucher 1975], and in part directly from [Madsen 1993].) Each entry method must first lock the monitor (possibly involving waiting for the lock to become available), then access data, and finally unlock the monitor. This common behavior for entry methods can be captured in the framework by an abstract method entry, as shown in Figure 19.7. A Semaphore object is declared in the Monitor class and is used by the entry method to lock and unlock the monitor (mutex.P, mutex.V). In applications of the framework, application-specific monitors can be defined by subclassing Monitor and providing suitable access methods as submethods to entry. The access methods will extend the behavior of entry at the point of INNER, thereby ensuring that the access to the monitor data is done while the monitor is locked.

```
Monitor: class {
    mutex: instance Semaphore;
    void entry() { mutex.P(); INNER entry; mutex.V() }
}
```

Figure 19.7   A framework for concurrent programming.

Figure 19.8 shows an example application defining a FIFOqueue using the Monitor class in the framework. The FIFOqueue contains a list of elements L, the encapsulated data. Two access methods, put and get, are defined as submethods of entry. These methods extend entry both by providing additional parameters (put provides an input parameter and get a return value), and by extending the code of the method (by actual accesses to the encapsulated list).

In executing a method—for example, put—which is a submethod of some other method—for example, entry—the execution starts in the most general method (in entry in this case), and methods are combined top-down in the method inheritance hierarchy. At the place of an INNER, the code of the immediate submethod is executed. Figure 19.9 shows the full behavior of the put method when super- and submethods are combined.

This example shows that subclassing and submethoding allows the framework to factor out all that is specific to monitors as such: the monitor encapsulation and the locking and its implementation using a semaphore. The application defines an application-specific monitor, with data to encapsulate and access methods to that data, much as if a built-in language construct for monitors were available.

19.2.2 Implementation of Rendezvous Communication with Method Inheritance

The framework for concurrent programming can be extended by adding facilities for synchronous communication similar to *rendez-vous* in Ada [USDoD 1980]. We do this by adding a Port concept, as shown in Figure 19.10.

By combining block structure and method inheritance, this framework offers elegant support for rendezvous communication. Figure 19.11 illustrates an application of

```
FIFOqueue: class Monitor {
    L: list of Element;
    void put(e: element) entry { L.insertLast(e) };
    Element get() entry { return L.removeFirst() };
}
```

Figure 19.8   Application using the Monitor class in the framework to define a FIFOqueue.

```
// transfer input parameters (e in this case)
mutex.P()
L.insertLast(e)
mutex.V()
//transfer return values (none in this case)
```

Figure 19.9 Full behavior of put after method combination.

the framework, using the rendezvous facilities for synchronizing web browsers with a shared network server. Browser1 and browser2 both utilize the shared server theHTTPServer. All three objects run in separate threads. Assume that both browsers at the same time wish to download a web document. They will then at the same time execute essentially theHTTPServer.getURL(url). Because the getURL operation in HTTPServer is a submethod of entry, the very first thing that happens in both browsers in this case will be the execution of mutex.P() on the mutex semaphore instance in theHTTPServer. Their execution will therefore be postponed until theHTTPServer accepts a call of one of the entry operations in the port HTTPport by executing HTTPport.accept(). As soon as this has been executed, one of the two browsers will be allowed to continue its execution, whereas the second browser is still awaiting the mutex semaphore, and theHTTPServer is awaiting the sync semaphore (see the code of the accept operation in Port). Just before the first browser has finished the server.getURL operation, it will release the sync semaphore, which, in turn, will release the theHTTPServer, making it possible for theHTTPServer to continue execution. TheHTTPServer will then execute another HTTPport.accept(), thereby allowing the second browser to download a web document. This synchronization behavior is totally encapsulated, and controlled by the port framework, made possible by the two language construct's generalized block structure and generalized inheritance (especially inheritance for methods).

More extensive examples of defining and using concurrency constructs are given in [Madsen 1993], including definition of monitors with conditions and more advanced ports. These examples all show that by the use of subclassing and submethoding, mechanisms can be built in a framework where other languages require built-in language constructs to give the same degree of support for the application programmer.

```
Port: class {
    mutex, sync: Semaphore;
    void entry() { mutex.P(); INNER entry; sync.V() };
    void accept() { mutex.V(); sync.P() }
}
```

Figure 19.10 Port framework for concurrent programming.

```
HTTPserver: class {
    CommPort: class Port {
        HTMLdocument getURL(url: text) entry {
            ... // get the document from WWW
        };
        void putURL(url: text; doc: HTMLdocument) entry {
            ... // download "doc" at location "url"
        };
    };
    HTTPport: instance CommPort;

    while (true) {
        HTTPport.accept()
    }
}
Browser: class {
    server: HTTPserver;
    void connectToServer(WEBserver: HTTPserver) {
        server = WEBserver; ...
    }

    ... when the user clicks a link ...
        server.getURL(linkURLaddress);
    ...
};


theHTTPServer: instance HTTPserver;
browser1, browser2: instance Browser;


...
browser1.connectToServer(theHTTPServer);
browser2.connectToServer(theHTTPServer);
...
```

Figure 19.11 Application of Port framework: An HTTP communication example.

19.2.3 Further Illustration of Method Inheritance

We can further illustrate method inheritance by extracting the common behavior of the different buttons in the CalcWindow class of Figure 19.2 and using method inheritance to reuse this generalized behavior in all CalcWindow buttons, as illustrated in Figure 19.12. This shows the use of method inheritance to factor out common behavior in methods, analogous to how class inheritance is often used to factor out common behavior in classes. Other examples of the use of submethoding include the definition of control structures such as iterators for generic data structures. We return to this issue in *Section 19.3*.

```
CalcWindow: class Window
    {
        theCalculator: instance Calculator;
        UpdatingButton: class Button
            { void onMouseUp() extended
                { INNER onMouseUp; setTitle(theCalculator.result) };
            };
        plusButton: instance UpdatingButton
            { void onMouseUp() extended { theCalculator.plus() } };
        minusButton: instance UpdatingButton
            { void onMouseUp() extended { theCalculator.minus() } };
        ...
    }
```

Figure 19.12   CalcWindow example.

19.2.4 Top-Down Combination of Virtual Methods

The two previous examples show how the inner mechanism is used to combine methods in submethoding. In BETA, the inner mechanism is used also to combine implementations of virtual methods. The inner mechanism combines virtual method implementations top-down, starting execution in the method implementation in the most general class. This is opposite to the *super* mechanism in Smalltalk [Goldberg-Robson 1983] and Java, which combines virtual method implementations bottom-up. The top-down combination means that virtual methods are never overridden—they can only be extended. For frameworks, such a top-down combination is appropriate because it gives the framework control over how methods are extended, which is essential in order to ensure that invariants in the framework are not broken by the application programmer. In contrast, bottom-up combination and free method overriding is suitable for *unplanned* reuse, where an application programmer reuses an implementation in order to recast it to some other purpose than originally intended. (To support frameworks better, many languages with bottom-up method combination have other facilities to give the framework more control. For example, in C++ it is possible to declare nonvirtual methods, and in Java it is possible to declare methods as *final*, meaning that they cannot be overridden in subclasses.)

We now discuss three different examples of top-down method combination in relation to frameworks.

Virtual Method Extension

When an application programmer defines a subclass to a framework class, it is common that the methods of the class should be extended as well. For example, consider a GUI framework supporting the *Decorator* design pattern that allows the functionality of an object to be extended dynamically [Gamma 1995]. In the GUI framework a window can be decorated with, for example, scrollbars and borders. A decorator keeps track of its component to which it forwards all messages. In addition, the decorator may perform some extra behavior. For example, when a decorator receives the message draw it will first draw its component and then draw itself. Figure 19.13 shows an example of the framework code for draw in Decorator, capturing the common behavior of forwarding the message to the component. An INNER is placed last in draw to allow subclasses of Decorator to perform their extra behavior.

The GUI framework may provide some standard decorators, like scrollbars and borders, but it is also possible to define specialized decorators in the application. For example, if the application programmer is not satisfied with the standard scrollbars, a new specialized decorator for narrow scrollbars can be defined, as shown in Figure 19.14. The extension of the virtual method draw simply implements the drawing of the scrollbar. The application programmer does not have to worry about forwarding the message to the component; this is already taken care of in the framework. This solution for the Decorator pattern differs from the standard implementation using bottom-up method combination, where the application would typically need to remember to call super.

The need for virtual method extension is particularly apparent for operations that in some way deal with the *complete* set of data in an object—for example, initialization methods, clone methods, print methods, and so on. Here top-down combination makes sure that the framework can perform all its actions without the risk of these actions being overridden by application code. Another use of virtual method extension is in the instrumentation of framework code—for example, in order to animate computations taking place in the framework.

Preconditions

Checking of preconditions for methods is common practice, in order to make sure that framework operations are called by the application when in an appropriate state and with appropriate arguments, thereby supporting safe use of the framework. Top-down method combination allows preconditions of virtual methods to be checked at the declaration of the virtual method rather than having to be repeated in each implementation of the method. Of course, a special language mechanism for preconditions, such as in Eiffel, serves the same purpose.

```
Component: class {
    draw() virtual { INNER draw };
};


Decorator: class Component {
    myComponent: instance Component;
    draw() extended { myComponent.draw; INNER draw };
};
```

Figure 19.13 GUI framework with support for the Decorator pattern.

```
NarrowScrollbarDecorator: class Decorator{
    draw() extended {
        ... // draw the scrollbar
    };
};
```

Figure 19.14 Application of GUI framework defining specialized decorator.

Default Behavior

It is common that virtual methods in a framework define default behavior that is *intended* to be overridden if desired in the application. In this case, the usual style of overriding virtual methods works fine. If top-down method combination is used, as in BETA, the framework method implementing the default behavior needs to check whether the method is extended. In BETA this can be done by means of so-called *pattern variables* (variables holding the class value of an object or analogously for methods). If the method is not extended, the default behavior will be executed. While this is not as straightforward for the framework application as in traditional method overriding, the application program will be the same in both cases. In addition, the top-down method combination allows default behavior to be combined with preconditions, as previously discussed.

19.2.5 Comparison of Top-Down Method Combination with Other Techniques

We have argued that top-down method combination using inner is more appropriate for frameworks than the usual bottom-up method combination using super. The use of super leads to informal programming conventions, such as "when overriding this method, you must call super at the start of the method." In contrast, top-down combination using inner gives the framework precise control over how methods may be extended and/or overridden, thus supporting planned reuse and supporting the intention that framework invariants are not broken by the application.

The inner construct is somewhat similar to the call-next-method construct for around methods in CLOS [Keene 1988]. However, CLOS combines actions bottom-up, so it is always possible for an application programmer to override both around methods and the ordinary primary methods defined in the framework, thus possibly destroying the semantics of the framework.

Top-down method combination for virtual methods can be simulated by using the design pattern Template Method, which factors out sub-behavior of a template method to virtual hook methods [Gamma 1995]. This can be used to replace INNER with a call to a virtual procedure. However, this leads to a proliferation of virtual methods. For example, for a virtual method init which is extended at each level in a hierarchy of classes A, B, and C, there would be a need to introduce three new virtual methods—called, for example, *initInnerA, initInnerB,* and *initInnerC.* While this is possible, it is cumbersome and error prone, and leads to a more complex framework specialization interface.

Note, however, that inner can be simulated by the Template Method pattern only in the case of *virtual* methods. Submethoding, as discussed in *Section 19.2.1,* cannot be simulated by the Template Method. For example, if INNER in the entry method was replaced by a virtual method entryInnerMonitor, this would not help because put and get are not virtual implementations, but *submethods* of entry. The best we could do with the Template Method would be to define two template methods put and get in class Monitor, and let them call virtual methods putInner and getInner. These virtual methods would then be implemented by the application in subclasses to Monitor. However, this would restrict the monitor functionality to monitors with exactly two entry methods, and would furthermore make it necessary to decide on the number and types of parameters for these methods already in the framework. In contrast, in a framework based on submethoding, applications can define monitors with any number of entry methods and with parameters decided by the application.

19.3 General Virtuality

The virtual methods concept is well understood in object-oriented programming: A class defining a virtual method gives incomplete information about the implementation of that method. The complete information is, in general, not known until runtime. By taking a more general view on virtuality, we can define it as a mechanism for supplying incomplete information about an entity at a given level of abstraction. With this view, we can see that virtuality in mainstream object-oriented languages is limited to virtual methods. By *general virtuality* we mean that virtuality can be applied to *all* kinds of block constructs in the language.

19.3.1 Virtual Classes

In BETA, the unification of methods and classes has led to the notion of *virtual classes* [Madsen 1989], analogous to virtual methods. A class defining a local virtual class declares that the local virtual class must be a subclass of some specific class. However, the exact subclass may not be known until runtime. Virtual classes correspond to a kind of type parameters (bounded polymorphism), and the mechanism can be used as an alternative to parameterized classes in Eiffel, or templates in C++. A recent proposal shows how virtual classes can be added to Java [Thorup 1997].

Consider a simple example of a framework with a bounded polymorphic list datatype, as shown in Figure 19.15. (<<listLib: attributes>> is inserted in Figure 19.15 for future reference. We later add some operations to this List class. To reduce space, we do not repeat the entire List declaration, but just give the declaration of the new operations. Just think of these new operations as being inserted textually at this place in the List class declaration.) The List class contains a class ElementType, which is the class of the elements in the list. ElementType is *virtual*, meaning that at this level we

```
List: class {
    ElementType: virtual class Object;
    Node: class {
        element: ElementType;
        next, previous: Node
    };
    first: Node;
    <<listLib: attributes>>
}
```

Figure 19.15 Framework with polymorphic list datatype.

don't know exactly which class ElementType is—we know only that it is at least Object (that is, either Object or a subclass of Object). The List is implemented using a local class Node with next and previous references.

In an application of the framework, we can describe a list of houses, as shown in Figure 19.16. The virtual class ElementType is now *extended* to House, meaning that it is ensured to be at least House (that is, either House or a subclass of House). This implies that all elements in a HouseList will be at least House objects, and when accessing attributes of an element we can safely access, for example, the taxRate attribute, as shown in Figure 19.16. The method getElement() here symbolizes any operation in List that returns an object of ElementType. Because aHouseList is of type HouseList where ElementType is bound to House, the expression aHouseList.getElement() has the type House and the access to taxRate can be statically type checked.

```
House: class {
    taxRate: float;
    void display() { ... };
    ...
};

HouseList: class List {
    ElementType: extended class House;
    <<HouseListlib: attributes>>
}

// access to element in a HouseList

aHouseList: instance HouseList;
...
print (aHouseList.getElement().taxRate);
```

Figure 19.16 Application defining specialized list.

19.3.2 Virtual Classes and Method Inheritance

The combination of virtual classes with method inheritance is very powerful because it allows abstract methods specified in a framework to be parameterized by types using the virtual class mechanism. We illustrate this by extending the List class in the framework with a number of operations. Figure 19.17 shows scan, an abstract method iterating over all the elements in the list. (--- listLib: attributes --- in Figure 19.17 specifies that this new scan operation is to be inserted at the <<listLib: attributes>> place in the List class declaration in Figure 19.15.) Scan calls INNER for each element in the list (see *Section 19.2.1* on method inheritance), and current is a reference denoting the current element in the iteration.

The scan method can be specialized by the application—for example, to display all houses in a HouseList, as follows:

```
--- HouseListLib: attributes ---
void print() scan { current.display() }
```

Note that the virtual extension of ElementType in HouseList ensures that it is statically known that current is of type House, and, therefore, that current.display() is legal. We can also modify the attributes of the objects through the current reference in scan, as illustrated by the following raiseTax method, which will raise the tax rate of all houses in the HouseList by 1 percent:

```
--- HouseListLib: attributes ---
void raiseTax() scan {
    current.taxRate = (current.taxRate*1.01)
}
```

Submethoding can be used to define more advanced operations on List in the framework. Figure 19.18 shows the definition of an operation select, which is a submethod of scan, and operations find and remove, which are submethods of select.

```
--- listLib: attributes ---
void scan() {
    // Iterates over all elements in List
    pos, next: Node; current: ElementType

    pos = first;
    while (posnull) {
        current = pos.element; next = pos.next;
        INNER scan;
        pos = next
    }
}
```

Figure 19.17   Extension of the framework List class.

```
--- listLib: attributes ---
void select() scan {
// iterates over all elements in List which
// satisfies the predicate
    boolean predicate() virtual { INNER predicate }

    if (predicate) { INNER select }
}

ElementType find() select {
// returns the first element in List which satisfies
// the predicate
    INNER find; return current; leave find;
}

void remove() select {
// removes all elements in List which satisfy the
// predicate
    if (pos.nextnull) {
        pos.next.previous = pos.previous
    } else {
        pos.next.previous = null
    }
    if (pos.previousnull) {
        pos.previous.next = pos.next
    } else {
        pos.previous.next = null
    }
    if (pos=first) { first = pos.next }
    pos.next = null; pos.previous = null
}
```

Figure 19.18   Operations implemented as submethods of scan in the framework List class.

The select method also shows the use of general block structure for methods. It defines a local method predicate, which is virtual and is used to decide which elements to include in the iteration. The select method can be used in the application to display all houses with a tax rate of more than 10 percent, as illustrated by the printExpensive method:

```
--- HouseListLib: attributes ---
void printExpensive() select {
    void predicate() extended { return current.taxRate>0.1 }

    current.display()
}
```

The find method in Figure 19.18 is a submethod of select that returns the first element satisfying the predicate. If no such element is found, the method will return null. (The return statement sets the return value of a method but does not alter the execution control. The leave statement is a structured goto statement that returns control to the caller. We can now find the first house in the list with a tax rate of more than 25 percent by the findHighTaxed method:

```
--- HouseListLib: attributes ---
void findHighTaxed() find {
        void predicate() extended { return current.taxRate>0.25 }
}
```

The remove method in Figure 19.18 is also defined as a submethod of select and removes all elements satisfying predicate. We can use this operation to remove all houses with a 0 percent tax rate by the removeZeroTaxed method:

```
--- HouseListLib: attributes ---
void removeZeroTaxed() remove {
    void predicate() extended { return current.taxRate=0.0 }
}
```

The preceding discussion illustrates the elegance and powerful static constraints that can be encapsulated in a framework when the framework design is supported by strong, static language mechanisms such as general block structure, general inheritance, and general virtuality.

19.3.3 Virtual Classes in Frameworks

Virtual classes are very powerful when combined with general block structure. They allow virtuals (or incomplete information) to be described at any level in the program. This is very useful in framework design, because it allows incomplete descriptions to appear at any level in the design. For example, the framework may itself contain a virtual class. This will then serve as a type parameter to the entire framework, provided as a single point for specialization by the application programmer. The alternative using ordinary mainstream parameterized classes would be for the application programmer to consistently parameterize all abstract classes in the framework (or give special instantiation operations for these abstract classes, such as by using the factory patterns [Gamma 1995]) that make use of this virtual class. This is cumbersome and error prone for the application programmer, leading to possible structural or behavioral problems in the usage of the framework.

We illustrate this with the framework for business applications shown in Figure 19.19. This framework defines a set of cooperating classes, each implementing aspects of the business, such as the financial aspects (Accounting), the advertising and so on (Marketing), and the order and shipment handling (Operations). Important for the proper cooperation of these classes within the framework is that they share the same understanding of the concept of a customer. This is expressed in this framework by defining one common definition of Customer as a virtual class. Customer is virtual in

```
BusinessFramework: class {
    Customer: virtual class Object;
    CustomerDatabase: class Database {
        ObjectType: extended class Customer
    };
    theDatabase: instance CustomerDatabase;
    Accounting: virtual class {
        void invoice(c: Customer) virtual {
            ... INNER invoice ...
        }
        ... functionalities for accounting ...
    };
    Marketing: virtual class {
        ... functionalities for marketing ...
    };
    Operations: virtual class {
        ... functionalities for operations ...
    };
}
```

Figure 19.19   Business framework.

BusinessFramework, because it should be possible to create specialized business frameworks in which there is a specialized understanding of the concept of a customer.

A specialized business framework ITbusiness is shown in Figure 19.20. Here, the Customer class is extended to include, for example, information about the customer's favorite operating system. The local classes for Accounting and so on are extended to make use of that information, for example, in the invoice method.

```
ITbusiness: class BusinessFramework {
    Customer: extended class {
        void favoriteOS() {
            ...
        }
    };
    Accounting: extended class {
        void invoice() extended {
            ... c.favoriteOS; ...
        }
    };
    ... similar extensions for marketing and operations ...
}
```

Figure 19.20   Specialized framework for ITbusiness.

Figure 19.21 shows how we can go even further by specializing this ITbusiness framework into a framework for security software. This specialization is done in a similar way by extending the definitions of Customer, Accounting, and so on.

The preceding business framework example illustrates the power of combining virtual classes with general block structure: A virtual class (Customer) provides a single point of type parameterization for a complete framework of different classes (such as Accounting, Marketing, and Operations). In a system with traditional type parameters such as C++ templates or Eiffel parameterized classes, one would model Accounting, Marketing, and so on as templates, each with a Customer type parameter. These templates would then have to be individually instantiated to classes, providing a Customer subclass as a parameter.

The example further illustrates how virtual classes can be extended in several steps: The virtual classes Customer and Accounting defined in the general BusinessFramework are extended in the ITbusiness framework (a subclass of BusinessFramework) and again in ITsecurity (a subclass of ITbusiness). Such stepwise extension is not possible in traditional type parameterization.

19.3.4 Virtual Classes and Covariance

Virtual classes lead to what is known as a *covariant* type system: Consider a class C with a local variable v of the virtual class T, and a subclass D that extends T. This leads to a situation where the type of v will be more special in a D object than in a C object. In other words, the types of v and its enclosing class vary in the same direction (hence the term *co*-variance). The usefulness of covariance in frameworks is illustrated in *Section 19.3.1*, where List is specialized to HouseList and local references to elements are specialized from Object to House using the virtual class ElementType. This allows a framework to capture general aspects of a system without fixing the types of the entities described in the framework.

Many papers have discussed type problems for covariant type systems—for example, [Cook 1989]—but they have usually taken a type system based on type redefinition

```
ITsecurity: class ITbusiness {
    Customer: extended class {
        securityLevel: integer;
        ...
    };
    Accounting: extended class {
        void invoice() extended {
            ... c.securityLevel; ...
        }
    };
    ... similar extensions for marketing and operations ...
}
```

Figure 19.21 Further specialized framework.

as a starting point where argument types may be redefined, and there is no distinction between a virtual class and an ordinary class. In contrast, the use of virtual classes allows the use of covariance without type problems. Figure 19.22 shows the difference between covariance in a type system based on redefinition and in a type system based on virtual classes.

In the ordinary type system, the argument e to insert is thought of as having the type Object, and a call to aList.insert(new Object) would seem to be correct. But the type system will break if aList happens to be a HouseList object that redefines the argument type to House. In the virtual class type system, the argument e does not have the type Object. Instead, e has the type ElementType, and the meaning of ElementType is (in general) not known until runtime because it is a virtual class. Therefore, a call to aList.insert(new Object) will (in general) result in a runtime check, checking the type of e against the value of ElementType for aList. However, in many cases, runtime checks are unnecessary because the value of ElementType can be determined at compile time. In the following example, aHouseList is a constant reference and its value of Element-Type is House, which can be determined at compile time. Thus, no runtime check is needed at insert(new House).

```
aHouseList: instance HouseList;
aHouseList.insert(new House); // statically typesafe
```

Another possibility of allowing the value of ElementType to be statically determined is to use *final extensions* of virtual classes. A final extension of a virtual class is an extension that prohibits further extension in subclasses. If ElementType in HouseList was defined as a final extension, this would disallow subclasses to HouseList—for example, SummerHouseList—to further extend ElementType. A SummerHouseList would have to accept any House in its list. This would allow calls to insert to be also statically type checked for dynamic references qualified by HouseList. Figure 19.23 shows an example of this. At the call to insert, the runtime type of aHouseList is not known: It could be HouseList or any subclass of HouseList. But because ElementType is defined as a final extension in HouseList, we know its value for aHouseList at compile time, namely House, and there is no need for a runtime check at the call to insert.

TYPE SYSTEM BASED ON REDEFINITION	TYPE SYSTEM BASED ON VIRTUAL CLASSES

`List: class {`
`    Void insert(e: Object)`
`        { ... }`
`};`
	`List: class {`
	`    ElementType: virtual class Object;`
	`    void insert(e: ElementType)`
	`        { ... }`
	`}`

`HouseList: class List {`
`    Void insert (e: House)`
`}`
	`HouseList: class List {`
	`    ElementType: extended class House;`
	`}`

Figure 19.22   Covariance in different type systems.

```
HouseList: class List {
    ElementType: final class House; // Final extension
}


aHouseList: HouseList;
... // aHouseList is assigned to an object
aHouseList.insert(new House); // Statically typesafe
```

Figure 19.23   Statically checkable covariance using final extensions.

The covariant properties of general virtuality thus give an elegant separation of the statically available information, defined in the abstraction, and the dynamically available information, defined in the specializations—in contrast to type systems based on redefinition, which mix these issues. Covariance and virtual classes are treated in more detail in [Madsen 1990].

19.4 Singular Objects

In traditional object-oriented languages, objects are always instances of previously defined classes. In framework design, and especially framework usages, this imposes an extra burden on the application programmer, because in order to create an object that is not just a plain instance of a framework class, the programmer needs to define a subclass of this framework class, and then instantiate the object from this new class.

An elegant solution to this problem is to allow class specialization and object instantiation to be done in the same declaration, as shown in Figure 19.24. An object s defined in this way is called a *singular object*. The class of s is an anonymous subclass of the class C used in the declaration. The right column in Figure 19.24 shows a traditional implementation where the class of s has to be named (sClass) and declared explicitly. The use of singular objects thus leads to substantially simpler application code.

Singular objects were originally introduced in BETA and are now also available in Java (where they are called *anonymous classes*). We have already seen the use of singular objects in *Section 19.1.1,* where plusButton and minusButton in the calculator are defined as singular objects. Without singular objects, the application programmer

```
SINGULAR OBJECT          | TRADITIONAL IMPLEMENTATION
s: instance C {          | sClass: class C {
    void v( ...) { ... }  |     void v( ...) { ... }
}                        | }
                         |
                         | s: instance sClass;
```

Figure 19.24   Singular objects versus traditional implementation.

would have had to first define two classes, PlusButtonClass and MinusButtonClass, containing the respective implementations of onMouseUp, and then define the two objects plusButton and minusButton as instances of these classes.

Note that singular objects should not be confused with *singletons*—classes of which there is only one global instance [Gamma 1995]. Singular objects are not necessarily globally defined, and if their definition is nested in some other block, there may be several instances of the singular object—one for each instance of the enclosing block. For example, plusButton and minusButton are singular objects, but if we create several CalculatorWindow objects, there will be one plusButton and one minusButton for each of the windows.

19.4.1 Singular Objects as Adapters

There is often a need to *adapt* framework classes to work together with classes defined in an application. As an example, consider a Model/View/Controller (MVC)-like framework [Krasner-Pope 1988] with general View classes for displaying information in window panes. To build an interactive tool in an application, different View classes are adapted to work together with application-specific model classes. One example of a View class is ListView, implementing a pane containing a scrollable list with a current selection. The specialization interface to ListView contains three hook methods, as shown in Figure 19.25. To use a ListView in an application, we need to adapt it to fill in these hooks. Singular objects provide a very elegant solution to this adaptation.

As an example, consider an application implementing a music tool. One of the panes in the tool should be a scrollable list displaying a number of different music styles—reggae, jazz, classical, and so on. An application class MusicModel contains the data to be displayed in the list pane. The tool can be constructed by attaching instances of the framework class ListView to a MusicModel instance. Figure 19.26 shows how this is done using singular objects.

The object LV in Figure 19.26 is an *adapter*: It adapts the behavior of a framework class (ListView) to work with a class in the application (MusicModel). This way to implement adapters is an alternative to the more traditional implementation techniques discussed in [Gamma 1995]. The implementation relies on block nesting: The object LV is nested inside the object musicTool. Because LV is a (specialized) instance of

```
ListView: class {
    List getList() virtual;
        // Should answer list of alternatives to display
    integer getCurrentSelection() virtual;
        // Should answer current selection to display
    void changeModelSelection(index: integer) virtual;
        // Should change the current selection.
        // Called when the user performs a new selection.
}
```

Figure 19.25   MVC framework: Specialization interface for ListView.

```
MusicModel: class Subject {
    selection: integer;
    musicList: List = ("reggae", "jazz", "classic");

    List getMusicList() { return musicList };
    integer getMusicSelection() { return selection };
    void setMusicSelection(index: integer) {
        selection := index;
        ...
    };
    ...
};

// Code creating music tool:
musicTool: instance MusicModel {
    LV: instance ListView {
        List getList() { return getMusicList(); };
        integer getCurrentSelection() {
            return getMusicSelection();
        };
        void changeModelSelection(index: integer) {
            setMusicSelection(index);
        };
    };
    ...
};
```

Figure 19.26 Application of MVC framework: A music tool.

ListView, it has direct access to the information in *both* of two classes that need to be connected: to ListView by subclassing and to MusicModel by block nesting. This makes it straightforward to define the adaptation: Virtual methods in ListView can be implemented directly to call appropriate methods in MusicModel.

This use of singular objects as adapters is omnipresent in applications using the BETA frameworks. The key motivation for the introduction of class nesting and singular objects in Java (called *inner classes* and *anonymous classes* in Java) was to support this implementation of adapters.

19.4.2 Singular Objects versus Pluggable Objects

Singular objects are an alternative to so-called *pluggable objects,* as introduced in the Smalltalk MVC framework [Krasner-Pope 1988]. A pluggable class is a framework class that can be adapted by the application by providing parameters rather than by subclassing. The goal is to avoid having to write trivial subclasses in the application. Typically, many of the parameters to a pluggable class are method names, and the framework class will call these methods by using the Smalltalk perform mechanism. In the MVC framework there are, for example, pluggable View and Controller classes which can be instantiated and attached to an application model without the need for subclassing these framework classes. Figure 19.27 shows the Smalltalk instantiation interface of a pluggable version of the ListView discussed in *Section 19.4.1*. The figure also shows the use of the perform mechanism in the implementation of PluggableListView.

A problem with Smalltalk's pluggable object technique is that it is a fairly complex technique for the application programmer to understand, relying on many informal programming conventions. For example, the framework assumes a certain signature for each of the methods whose names are passed in the creation message, but these signatures are not a formal part of the framework interface. Figure 19.28 shows a Smalltalk application program for constructing the music tool discussed in *Section 19.4.1*, using the pluggable ListView class.

Comparing the solution using singular objects in Figure 19.26 with the solution using pluggable objects in Figure 19.28, we see that the size of the application code is practically the same. The main technical difference is in static checkability. In the Smalltalk solution, the framework uses perform to invoke methods in the application model. This call can go wrong if the application programmer provides the wrong arguments in the instantiation of the PluggableListView. For example, it is not statically checkable that anObject actually has a method with the name given by setSelectionSel. Even if there is such a method, it is not statically checkable if it has the right number of arguments. In contrast, in the solution using singular objects, all this information is statically checkable. Singular objects provide an alternative solution to pluggable objects which also avoids explicit trivial subclasses, but which provides a safer interface, not relying on passing method names as arguments, and which includes the signatures of all methods as part of the framework interface.

19.4.3 Whitebox versus Blackbox Frameworks

In the Smalltalk community, frameworks are often characterized as being mainly *blackbox* (meaning that classes are instantiated rather than specialized) or mainly

```
PluggableListView

// class methods for creation

    on: anObject list: getListSel selected: getSelectedSel
            changeSelected: setSelectionSel

// instance methods ...

    ... anObject perform: setSelectionSel with: index
```

Figure 19.27 Smalltalk instantiation interface to PluggableListView.

```
MusicModel // (the same as in Figure 19.26)

// Code creating music tool:
| aMusicModel, aLV |
aMusicModel <- MusicModel new.
aLV <- PluggableListView
    on: aMusicModel
    list: getMusicList#
    selected: getMusicSelection#
    changeSelected: setMusicSelection#.
. . .
```

Figure 19.28 Smalltalk implementation of music tool using pluggable objects.

whitebox (meaning that classes are intended to be specialized) [Johnson-Foote 1988]. The introduction of pluggable objects is seen as a way of making a framework more blackbox [Roberts-Johnson 1998]. However, these definitions of blackbox and whitebox frameworks may be suitable for Smalltalk, where there are very weak possibilities for controlling specialization. For languages where static checkability is of prime importance, we find it desirable that frameworks can also provide blackbox interfaces for specialization—that is, that parts of a framework class can be encapsulated and not be used or affected by the subclasses in the application. Many languages have information-hiding constructs, such as private, hidden, and so on, that support this. Another very important aspect is the potential for the framework to control where overriding may take place. This can be done by such mechanisms as the nonvirtual methods in Simula, BETA, and C++; by the inner mechanism in BETA; or using the final construct in Java.

As shown in *Section 19.4.1*, the specialization interface is clear, and singular objects make it easy to use. In contrast, the use of pluggable objects to turn a specialization interface into an instantiation interface may lead to an interface that is both unsafe and difficult to understand.

19.4.4 Singular Method Specialization

By building on method inheritance, as discussed in *Section 19.2.1*, the idea of singular objects can also be applied for methods. Whereas singular instances of classes are normally declared as attributes of another object or class, a singular instance of a method can be used to specialize a method call.

Section 19.3.2 defines a class HouseList and a series of special purpose methods: print, raiseTax, printExpensive, findHighTaxed, and removeZeroTaxed. If we assume that these methods are to be used only once, we could avoid having to define these auxiliary methods, and could invoke the methods as singular specializations of the original list operations. And further, if we assume that we need only one house list, we could avoid the auxiliary HouseList class definition. We could then define aHouseList as follows:

```
aHouseList: instance List {
    ElementType: final class House; // Final extension
}
```

With this definition, instead of defining the auxiliary methods, we could just invoke the singular method specialization shown in Figure 19.29. This shows how method specialization and singular objects can be combined and used to effectively define new control abstractions in the framework that can be used in the application. And it should be noted that the singular object aHouseList and the singular method specializations are equally as subject to static type checking as the HouseList class and the auxiliary methods defined in *Section 19.3.2*.

19.5 Summary

Advanced and mission-critical frameworks impose modeling and safety requirements on the programming languages to be used. In particular, there is a growing need for providing flexibility in a statically checkable, type-safe manner. The traditional object-oriented language constructs of classes, inheritance, and virtual methods provide the basic mechanisms for constructing frameworks. This chapter shows how generalizing these language constructs can provide the framework designer with greater possibilities for encapsulating the stable parts of a design in a type-safe way, giving the framework

```
// print
aHouseList.scan { current.display() }

// raiseTax
aHouseList.scan { current.taxRate = (current.taxRate*0.01) }

// printExpensive
aHouseList.select {
    void predicate() extended { return current.taxRate>0.1 }

    current.display()
}

// findHighTaxed
theHouse =
    aHouseList.find {
        void predicate() extended { return current.taxRate>0.25 }
    }
// removeZeroTaxed
aHouseList.remove {
    void predicate() extended { return current.taxRate=0.0 }
}
```

Figure 19.29   Singular method specialization.

designer fine-grained possibilities for controlling how the framework can be varied, and providing a very high degree of flexibility in applying the framework. The generalized language constructs discussed here are not new; they have been realized and tested in real languages for many years, most notably in the BETA language. This chapter illustrates precisely how these generalized constructs give support in framework design and application. We hope this illustrates how these generalized constructs give support for *planned reuse,* where the framework controls how it can be extended and where framework invariants can be encapsulated so they cannot be compromised by the application. This is somewhat in contrast to mainstream object orientation, where the focus is on how an application can freely override and replace parts of the framework.

The introduction of new languages, or the adoption of new language constructs into existing languages, is a difficult process which takes a very long time. Recall that classes and inheritance were introduced by Simula in 1967, and it took 15 to 20 years before these constructs came into widespread use through Smalltalk and C++. All of the generalized language constructs presented in this chapter have been in use for many years in BETA, and we are happy to see that several of these language constructs are beginning to make their way into popular programming languages, such as Java.

19.6 References

[Abelson 1985] Abelson, H., G.J. Sussman, and J. Sussman. *Structure and Interpretation of Computer Programs.* Cambridge, MA: MIT Press, 1985.

[Arnold-Gosling 1996] Arnold, K., and J. Gosling. *The Java Programming Language.* Reading, MA: Addison-Wesley, 1996.

[Cook 1989] Cook, W.R. A proposal for making Eiffel type safe. *Proceedings of the European Conference on Object-Oriented Programming (ECOOP 1989),* Nottingham, July 1999, S. Cook, editor. Cambridge, England: Cambridge University Press, 1989.

[Dahl 1970] Dahl, O.J., B. Myhrhaug, and K. Nygaard. *SIMULA 67 Common Base Language.* NCC Publication S-22. Oslo, Norway: Norwegian Computing Centre, 1970.

[Fayad-Schmidt 1997] Fayad, M.E., and D.C. Schmidt. Object-oriented application frameworks. *Communications of the ACM,* 40(10), October 1997.

[Gamma 1995] Gamma, E., R. Helm, R. Johnson, and J.O. Vlissides. *Design Patterns: Elements of Reusable Object-Oriented Software.* Reading, MA: Addison-Wesley, 1995.

[Goldberg-Robson 1983] Goldberg, A., and D. Robson. *Smalltalk 80: The Language.* Reading, MA: Addison-Wesley, 1983.

[Hedin 1997] Hedin, G. Attribute extension: A technique for enforcing programming conventions. *Nordic Journal of Computing,* 4, 1997: 93–122.

[Hedin-Knudsen 1999] Hedin, G., and J.L. Knudsen. On the role of language constructs for framework design. *Symposium on Object-Oriented Application Frameworks.* ACM Computing Surveys Symposium on Application Frameworks, M.E. Fayad, editor, September 1999.

[Hoare 1974] Hoare, C.A.R. 1974. Monitors: An operating system structuring concept. *Communications of the ACM,* 17(10), October 1974:549–557.

[Islo 1994] Islo, H. Simulation models built on nested quasi-parallel systems. *Proceedings of the 20th Conference of the ASU (Association of Simula Users),* pp. 80–95, Prague, 1994.

[Johnson-Foote 1988] Johnson, R.E., and B. Foote. Designing reusable classes. *Journal of Object-Oriented Programming*, 4(2), June/July 1988: 22–35.

[Keene 1988] Keene, S.E. *Object-Oriented Programming in Common Lisp: A Programmer's Guide to CLOS*. Reading, MA: Addison-Wesley, 1988.

[Knudsen 1993] Knudsen, J.L., M. Löfgren, O.L. Madsen, and B. Magnusson, eds. *Object-Oriented Environments: The Mjølner Approach*. Englewood Cliffs, NJ: Prentice Hall, 1993.

[Krasner-Pope 1988] Krasner, G.E., and S.T. Pope. A cookbook for using the Model-View-Controller user interface paradigm in Smalltalk-80. *Journal of Object-Oriented Programming*, 1(3), August/September 1988: 26–49.

[Madsen 1989] Madsen, O.L., and B. Møller-Pedersen. Virtual classes: A powerful mechanism in object-oriented programming. *OOPSLA 1989, ACM SIGPLAN Notices*, 24(10), October 1989: 397–406.

[Madsen 1990] Madsen, O.L., B. Magnusson, and B. Møller-Pedersen. Strong typing of object-oriented languages revisited. *ECOOP/OOPSLA 1990, ACM SIGPLAN Notices*, 25(10), October 1990: 140–150.

[Madsen 1993] Madsen, O.L., B. Møller-Pedersen, and K. Nygaard. *Object Oriented Programming in the BETA Programming Language*. New York: ACM Press, 1993.

[Meyer 1992] Meyer, B. *Eiffel: The Language*. Englewood Cliffs, NJ: Prentice Hall, 1992.

[Minsky-Pal 1997] Minsky, H., and P. Pal. Law-governed regularities in object systems. *Journal of Theory and Practice of Object Systems*, 3(2), 1997.

[Pree 1994] Pree, W. Meta patterns: A means for capturing the essentials of reusable object-oriented design. *Proceedings of the 1994 European Conference on Object-Oriented Programming (ECOOP 1994), Bologna, Italy, July 1994*. Lecture Notes in Computer Science 821. M. Tokoro and R. Pareschi, editors. Springer-Verlag, 1994: 150–162.

[Roberts-Johnson 1998] Roberts, D., and R. Johnson. Patterns for evolving frameworks. In *Pattern Languages of Program Design 3*. Reading, MA: Addison-Wesley, 1998: 471–501.

[Stroustrup 1997] Stroustrup, B. *The C++ Programming Language*, 3d ed. Reading, MA: Addison-Wesley, 1997.

[Sun 1996] Sun Microsystems. *Inner Classes Specification*. http://java.sun.com/products/jdk/1.1/docs/guide/innerclasses, 1996.

[Thorup 1997] Thorup, K.K. Genericity in Java with virtual types. *Proceedings of the 1997 European Conference on Object-Oriented Programming (ECOOP 1997), Jyväskylä, Finland, June 1997*. Lecture Notes in Computer Science 1241. Springer-Verlag, 1997: 389–418.

[USDoD 1980] U.S. Department of Defense. *Ada Reference Manual*. Washington, DC: U.S. Government Printing Office, 1980.

[Vaucher 1975] Vaucher, J. Prefixed procedures: A structuring concept for operations. *INFOR*, 13(3), October 1975.

[Vaucher 1999] Vaucher, J., and B. Magnusson. SIMULA frameworks: The early years. In *Building Application Frameworks: Object-Oriented Foundations of Framework Design*, M.E. Fayad, R. Johnson, and D. Schmidt, editors. New York: John Wiley & Sons, 1999.

[Wegner-Zdonik 1988] Wegner, P., and S. Zdonik. Inheritance as an incremental modification mechanism. *Proceedings of the 1988 European Conference on Object-Oriented Programming (ECOOP 1988), Oslo, August 1988*. Lecture Notes in Computer Science 322. S. Gjessing and K. Nygaard, editors. Springer-Verlag, 1988: 55–77.

PART

Five

System Application Frameworks

Part Five describes several system application frameworks, such as Tigger (Chapter 20), Déjà Vu (Chapter 21), Graphics Recognition (Chapter 22), Cryptographic Protocols (Chapter 23), and Component User Interface (Chapter 25). Part Five has six chapters, Chapters 20 through 25.

Chapter 20, "Tigger: A Framework for Supporting Distributed and Persistent Objects," discusses Tigger design, in which instantiations of the framework should be able to support different object models so that a range of object-oriented languages for distributed or persistent programming can be supported without unnecessary duplication of effort. The principal contribution of this work is the design of a framework for language runtime systems that allows a wide range of object-oriented programming languages for distributed or persistent programming to be supported in a way that does not impose particular constructs and models on the language. Moreover, where an existing language is to be supported, the design does not necessarily require changes to its compiler nor to its native object reference format or local invocation mechanism.

Chapter 21, "The Déjà Vu Scheduling Class Library," shows how an application framework can be designed for modern production scheduling applications, the basic techniques underlying the Déjà Vu scheduling class library, and how to reuse and to extend the framework for a new application. The motivation of designing and realizing the framework was twofold: to support the development of industrial scheduling systems as well as academic research in scheduling theory. The contribution is a sound architecture for the domain of interactive intelligent production scheduling. From the scheduling point of view, the framework is characterized by the capability to express multicriteria objective functions and the applicability of heuristic search functions, as well as iterative improvement procedures such as tabu search, simulated annealing, or similar techniques.

Chapter 22, "A Framework for Graphics Recognition," discusses an object-oriented application framework for graphics recognition applications, which is a problem domain of increasing interest. The technical concept is that the recognition applications of all graphic objects could follow a similar procedure. The goal of the graphics recognition framework is to abstract and model such similar procedures and supply generic code for graphics recognition algorithms to be used as ready-made and easily extendible components in the graphics recognition systems being developed in the future. In addition to the generic graphics recognition process model, the framework consists of reusable classes of graphic objects that appear in engineering drawings as well as in other classes of line drawings. The new graphic class may inherit from the available graphic classes in the framework or be totally independent as long as its interface conforms to the framework's. Applications to several graphic classes are also discussed.

Chapter 23, "A Java Beans Framework for Cryptographic Protocols," presents a Java Beans–compatible framework well suited for the implementation of telecommunications protocols in general and cryptographic protocols in particular. This framework is based on experience gained in building several earlier frameworks, including CVOPS, OVOPS, and Conduits+. The framework is relatively independent of the actual cryptosystems used and relies on the Java 1.1 public key security API. Future work will include Java 1.2 support, and utilization of a graphical Beans editor to further ease the work of the protocol composer.

Chapter 24, "Dynamic Database Instance Framework," illustrates a framework that enables rapid development of high-performance object-relational applications and infrastructure services. It detects changes in the underlying relational or object database at runtime and adapts to changing database schemas or configurations without additional customization, configuration, or recompiles. The Dynamic Database Instance framework has been deployed as an intermediate tier linking object-oriented applications and relational databases, as an object-oriented translation layer between multiple relational databases, and (in modified form) as a lightweight ODMG 93 object database engine. Key objectives in each of these initiatives were (1) rapid time to market, (2) high performance, and (3) ability to automatically adapt at runtime to changing relational and object database schemas without reconfiguration. The framework achieves these objectives using a specialized set of runtime objects and design patterns.

Chapter 25, "Component User Interfaces Framework," indicates that the most recent development on the user interface front can be seen as a merger of more traditional, graphical user interfaces and compound documents. The key idea is that all user interface elements are modeled as elements of compound documents: A dialog box is seen as a document displayed in a specific mode and containing various controls. This unification holds great promise, as it finally reunites the intuitively close concepts of documents and forms, as known from the paper-based office.

Implementing graphical user interfaces without guidance is hard; application frameworks came to the aid, as illustrated in several other chapters of this volume. Implementing software components for compound documents is even harder, as it is generally harder to build component software than it is to build monoliths. Traditional application frameworks—with their largely whitebox-reuse-oriented approach—do not significantly help to tackle the chore of building software components that, in their instances, live and manifest themselves in compound user interfaces and in compound documents as a special case. This chapter introduces the BlackBox component framework; a framework that emphasizes components and blackbox reuse and that specifically targets compound documents. Some selected aspects are studied in detail, including the message propagation mechanism provided to flexibly couple component instances and allow them to interact. Beyond the scope of BlackBox itself, the presented solutions can serve as a general repository of ideas and approaches in the domain of compound user interfaces.

CHAPTER 20

Tigger: A Framework Supporting Distributed and Persistent Objects

Many different object models for distributed or persistent programming have been proposed [Cahill 1997]. This is hardly surprising because different object models are likely to be appropriate for different application domains. *Shared data object models*, in which objects are passive and accessed by active threads of control, are often used to support cooperative applications concerned with access to shared data in domains such as computer-aided design, office automation, and software engineering. In contrast, realtime and process control applications may employ *reactive object models* in which objects are active and autonomous but react to events raised by other objects. Although these particular models represent different positions in a spectrum of possible object models, a key observation is that an important feature of any flexible object-support system should be the ability to support a number of different object models without duplication of effort, if not necessarily simultaneously.

Even where the same object model is appropriate to different applications, the non-functional requirements of those applications may vary significantly. Requirements in areas such as support for security, heterogeneity, reliability and fault tolerance, allowable memory usage, and realtime behavior may differ. Thus, any flexible object-support system should be capable of supporting the same object model in different ways, depending on the way in which the applications to be supported are to be deployed.

In keeping with these observations, the Tigger project (after A.A. Milne's famously bouncy character [Milne 1928]) undertook the design of a family of language runtime systems supporting distributed and persistent objects whose members can be customized for use in a variety of different application domains. The two primary goals of this design were:

- To allow members of the family to support a number of different object models, in order to allow a range of different object-oriented programming languages for distributed and persistent programming to be supported without unnecessary duplication of effort.

- To allow the same object model to be supported in different ways subject to differing nonfunctional requirements.

To support customizability, the design is captured as a framework that can be instantiated to implement the individual members of the family. The framework is sufficiently general so as to allow a set of possible instantiations that is capable of supporting a wide range of object-oriented programming languages for distributed or persistent programming and that is suitable for use in a wide range of application areas exhibiting different nonfunctional requirements. In addition, the Tigger framework has been designed to be extensible so that new functionality can be supported when required.

The major abstractions supported by the Tigger framework are distributed or persistent objects, threads, and extents (that is, protected collections of objects). A given Tigger instantiation may support only distributed objects, only persistent objects, or both. Of course, different instantiations will support these abstractions in different ways (for example, in order to accommodate different object models) by employing different mechanisms and policies.

Individual Tigger instantiations may support additional abstractions, such as activities (for example, distributed threads) and object clusters as required. Moreover, all of these abstractions are based on lower-level abstractions such as address spaces and endpoints (for example, communication channels) that are not normally expected to be used directly by supported languages or individual applications.

The remainder of this chapter describes the Tigger framework in some detail with special emphasis on the way in which it provides support for distributed and persistent programming languages. For a complete description of the framework see [Cahill 1996].

20.1 Related Work

This section introduces a number of previous systems that have particularly influenced Tigger: the Amadeus object-support system and the Choices and Peace object-oriented operating systems.

Amadeus [Horn-Cahill 1991] was a general-purpose platform for distributed and persistent programming targeted at application domains, such as office automation and software engineering. A major feature of Amadeus was that it was designed to support the use of a range of existing object-oriented programming languages. A language could be extended to support a set of (interrelated) properties including distribution, persistence, and atomicity for its objects by using the services of the Amadeus Generic Runtime Library (GRT), while maintaining its own native object reference format and invocation mechanism [Cahill 1993]. The Amadeus GRT provided a range of mechanisms from which the language designer could choose those appropriate for the intended use of the extended language. Extended versions of C++ and Eiffel, which were known as C** [DSG 1992] and Eiffel** [McHugh 1993] respectively, and an implementation of the E persistent programming language [McEvoy 1993] were supported by Amadeus.

Other major features of Amadeus included language-independent support for atomic objects and transactions [Mock 1992; Taylor 1994a] based on the use of the ReLaX transaction manager and libraries [Kröger 1990], and a novel security model supporting access control for objects at the level of individual operations as well as isolation of untrustworthy code [Ooi 1993].

Experience with the design and implementation of Amadeus has obviously had a major influence on Tigger. Tigger shares the goal of language independence and has adopted several of the key features of Amadeus, including the idea of a GRT and the basic security model. However, the goal of Tigger is to allow the implementation of a variety of language runtime systems providing more or less functionality as required, rather than a single general-purpose system, as was the goal of Amadeus.

Apart from Amadeus, Tigger has been most influenced by Choices [Campbell 1992], which developed a C++ framework for the construction of operating systems for distributed and shared memory multiprocessors, and Peace [Schröder-Preikschat 1994], which addressed the use of object-oriented techniques in the construction of a family of operating systems for massively parallel computers. The Peace family encompasses a number of different members, ranging from one supporting a single thread of control per node to one supporting multiple processes per node.

20.2 Overview

Tigger is a framework for the construction of a family of language runtime systems. Every instantiation of the framework is a runtime system to which one or more object-oriented programming languages are bound in order to provide an application programming interface. Tigger instantiations typically provide support for features such as creation of distributed or persistent objects, access to remote objects, object migration, access to stored persistent objects, dynamic loading of objects on demand, dynamic loading and linking of class code, and protection of objects.

In fact, the heart of any Tigger instantiation is a generalized object-access mechanism that allows local, remote, stored, protected, or unprotected objects to be accessed in a uniform manner. This mechanism provides support for all aspects of locating the target object, loading the object and its class into memory, and forwarding the access request to the object as required. In fact, this basic mechanism subsumes much of the functionality provided by the Tigger framework and provides the basis for supporting a high degree of network transparency for object access. Of course, the details of what this mechanism does, and how it does it, are subject to customization and will differ from one Tigger instantiation to another.

It is important to understand two points about the nature of the functionality provided by a Tigger instantiation. First, a Tigger instantiation, in cooperation with the runtime libraries of supported languages, *only* provides the necessary support for the use of objects by applications. The semantics and function of the objects that they support are opaque to Tigger instantiations. A particular object might implement a spreadsheet, one cell in a spreadsheet, a file, or a file server. The distinction is not visible to Tigger instantiations.

The second major point to be understood is that the functionality provided by a Tigger instantiation is intended to be used by object-oriented programming languages to provide programming models based on distributed or persistent objects to their application programmers. Thus, the main interface provided by a Tigger instantiation is that provided for the language implementer. The interface used by an application developer is that provided by a supported language. Moreover, a Tigger instantiation provides only basic support for distribution or persistence that is intended to be supplemented by each language's runtime library in order to implement the programming model of the language. How support for distribution or persistence is made available in any language—whether transparently to application programmers, via a class library, or even via the use of particular language constructs—is not mandated by the Tigger framework. Likewise, the degree of network transparency provided by the language is a function of the programming model supported by the language. The framework has, however, been designed to support languages that provide a high degree of network transparency.

20.2.1 Software Architecture

Tigger instantiations are intended to support both conventional object-oriented programming languages that have been extended to support distributed or persistent programming as well as object-oriented languages originally designed for that purpose. Moreover, this is intended to be done in a way that does not impose particular constructs and models on the language and, where an existing language is being extended, that does not necessarily require changes to its compiler nor to its native object reference format or local invocation mechanism. In this way, the language designer is free to choose the object model to be provided to application programmers independently. Supporting existing (local) object reference formats and invocation mechanisms allows the common case of local object invocation to be optimized. Finally, where an existing language is to be supported, this approach facilitates the reuse and porting of its existing compiler and runtime libraries.

In order to achieve these goals, every Tigger instantiation provides one or more GRTs providing common runtime support for one or more languages supporting distributed or persistent programming that have similar requirements on their runtime support. A more precise characterization of a GRT is given in [Cahill 1996]. Suffice it to say here that a GRT is *generic* in the sense that it provides only that part of the support for distribution or persistence that is independent of any language. Every GRT is bound to a *language-specific runtime library* (LSRT) for each language to be supported. The LSRT provides language-dependent runtime support. Each GRT provides an interface to the language implementer that has been designed to interface directly and easily to an LSRT. Thus, the interface to a Tigger instantiation seen by a language implementer is that of one of the GRTs that it provides.

This basic approach to language support is derived from the Amadeus project. Unlike Amadeus, which provided a single GRT supporting a (fairly limited) range of mechanisms that could be used by supported languages, the Tigger framework allows

GRTs to be customized depending on the object model and intended use of the language(s) to be supported. For example, GRTs supporting remote object invocation (ROI) and/or distributed shared memory (DSM) style access to distributed objects, GRTs supporting the use of different object fault detection or avoidance schemes, and GRTs supporting the use of eager, lazy, or no swizzling can all be instantiated from the framework. A given Tigger instantiation can support one language or several similar languages with one GRT, or a number of different languages with several GRTs. For example, Figure 20.1 shows one possible scenario in which one Tigger instantiation provides two different GRTs: One GRT is being used to support the C** and Eiffel** programming languages while the other is being used to support the E programming language. Both C** and Eiffel** support distributed and persistent objects using ROI and eager swizzling respectively, whereas E is a nonswizzling persistent programming language. Figure 20.1 depicts a scenario in which one application is written using some combination of two supported languages. While such interworking between languages may be facilitated when the languages involved have some of their runtime support in common, it should be noted that it cannot be implemented completely at this level—additional mechanisms are still required at higher levels to, for example, support interlanguage type checking.

20.2.2 Logical Model

The classes making up the Tigger framework are divided into five subframeworks. Each of these subframeworks is responsible for supporting some subset of the fundamental abstractions provided by the Tigger framework, as follows:

The GRT subframework, known as Owl. Supports distributed and persistent objects and optional clusters, and provides the main interface to supported languages. An instantiation of Owl corresponds to a GRT as previously described, and a single Tigger instantiation may include multiple Owl instantiations.

The threads subframework, known as Roo. Supports threads and related synchronization mechanisms, and may support activities. Supported languages (that is, their LSRTs) and applications may use Roo directly.

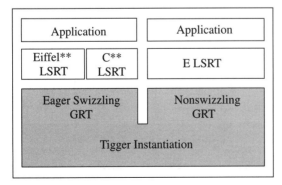

Figure 20.1   A Tigger instantiation.

The communications subframework, known as Kanga. Supports endpoints. Again, supported languages and applications may use Kanga directly.

The storage subframework, known as Eeyore. Supports containers (that is, secondary storage volumes) and storage objects (that is, segments), which can be used to store persistent objects and clusters. Supported languages are not expected to use Eeyore directly; hence, its main client is Owl.

The protection subframework, known as Robin. Supports extents and related abstractions.

Figure 20.2 illustrates the preceding subframeworks and their dependencies. Note that all the other subframeworks may use both Owl and Roo. In the case of Roo, this reflects the fact that all the components of a Tigger instantiation are expected to be thread-aware. In the case of Owl, this reflects the fact that components of a Tigger instantiation may use distributed or persistent objects.

Although Owl is specialized, depending primarily on the needs of the language(s) to be supported, the other subframeworks can also be specialized to support different mechanisms and policies. In particular, different instantiations of Robin determine whether the Tigger instantiation of which it is a part supports only a single extent or multiple extents, as well as whether it supports one or more address spaces. Other responsibilities of Robin include supporting cross-extent object invocation and unique object identification. Decisions made about the implementation of Robin are therefore of fundamental importance for the overall structure of a Tigger instantiation.

The Robin and Owl subframeworks are described in detail in [Cahill 1996]. For a description of Kanga, see [Burke 1996]. Eeyore is based on the Amadeus persistent object store (POS) framework described in [O'Grady 1994]. The remainder of this chapter gives an overview of the Owl class category.

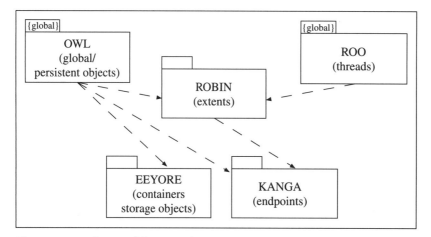

Figure 20.2 Tigger subframeworks.

20.3 Object-Support Functionality

This section considers how the functionality required to support distributed and persistent objects can be divided between an LSRT and a GRT. An important goal of Tigger is that Owl should provide as much of this functionality as possible. Only where a service is clearly language specific or is intimately connected with the code that is generated by the language's compilation system should that service be assigned to the LSRT.

In reading the following sections, it should be borne in mind that a particular Owl instantiation (that is, a GRT) might support only persistent objects, only distributed objects, or both. Hence, not all of these services will need to be supported by all Owl instantiations. Furthermore, the list presented here is not exhaustive; Owl can be extended to support other services.

Object layout and naming. Unless the compilation system is to be seriously constrained by the use of a GRT, the LSRT should be able to dictate the layout of objects in memory, the format of internal and local references used by such objects, and the mapping from such an object reference to the address of a collocated object. To reflect this fact, internal and local references are referred to as *language references,* or LREFs, from here on.

A GRT, on the other hand, should be responsible for the provision of globally unique object identifiers (OIDs) suitable for identifying every object in the system. (In the Tigger framework, responsibility for the format and allocation of OIDs actually rests with Robin rather than Owl.) A GRT should also be responsible for the provision of external and global references (referred to simply as *global references,* or GREFs, from here on). A GRT should also implement the mapping from a GREF for an object to the location of that object in the system.

Where the language to be supported already supports distribution or persistence, its LSRT will already support its own form of OIDs and GREFs. Moreover, its LREFs and GREFs may be the same. Owl does not support all possible existing GREF formats, but only those that support an Owl-defined protocol. Owl instantiations may, however, use (virtual) addresses as GREFs. Owl also supports languages in which GREFs and LREFs are the same as long as the GREFs support the required protocol.

Object access, binding, and dispatching. Each language is free to determine how objects may be accessed by their clients. However, it is important to realize that this decision has important repercussions for the choice of object fault avoidance or detection mechanisms that are available and for the ways in which object faults can be resolved. Typically, the choice of possible object fault avoidance, detection, or resolution mechanisms is constrained by the form of access to objects allowed. For example, the use of proxies to represent absent objects is not appropriate where direct access to the instance data of an object by its clients is allowed.

Because the means of binding code to objects and of dispatching invocations (including the layout of parameter frames) is usually intrinsic to the compilation system, these must continue to be implemented in the LSRT. Thus, a GRT need not be involved in local object invocation. However, this also means that when

ROI is used to access remote distributed objects, the marshaling and unmarshaling of ROI requests, as well as the dispatching of incoming requests to their target objects, must be done by or in cooperation with the LSRT.

Object allocation and garbage collection. Owl only supports allocation of objects on the heap or embedded in other (heap-allocated) objects. Moreover, Owl is responsible for management of the heap and hence provides the routines to allocate (and where supported, deallocate) objects.

Object fault detection and avoidance. Detection or avoidance of object faults is the responsibility of the LSRT because it depends on the type of access to objects supported, and the mechanisms used may need to be tightly integrated with the compilation system. For example, if presence tests are used to detect absent objects, the language compiler or preprocessor will usually be required to generate the code necessary to perform these tests before any access to an object proceeds.

Owl does, however, provide underlying support for a number of common object fault detection mechanisms (for example, presence tests and proxies) as well as support for object fault avoidance. Other object fault detection mechanisms may be implemented entirely at the language level.

Object fault resolution. Where object fault detection is used, Owl provides the underlying means of resolving object faults, including locating the target objects, mapping objects, transferring ROI requests to objects, and/or migrating threads as appropriate. The choice of object fault resolution policy is, however, constrained by the LSRT.

In the case of ROI requests, the formatting of the request must be carried out by the LSRT, because only it understands the format of parameter frames. Owl does, however, support the marshaling and unmarshaling of LREFs and values of basic types. The translation of LREFs to the corresponding GREFs and vice versa must be carried out in cooperation with the LSRT. Similar comments apply to migration of objects. On the remote side, the LSRT must be prepared to accept incoming ROI requests from the GRT, unmarshal the parameters, dispatch the request in the language-specific manner, and, once the request has been completed, marshal the reply. Note that the dispatching of the request must be carried out by the LSRT, because only it understands the dispatching mechanism to be used.

Object loading, unloading, and migration. Owl provides the basic support for the loading and unloading of persistent objects, as well as the migration of distributed objects.

During loading or migration, Owl supports the conversion of objects to local format where heterogeneity is supported; no, lazy, and eager swizzling of references as required; and binding of code to recently loaded objects. In each case, these actions require language- (and indeed type-) specific information. Hence, while Owl supports each of these, it does so in cooperation with the LSRTs of supported languages.

Where swizzling is used, the GRT must be able to translate a GREF to the appropriate LREF (whether or not the target object is located in the current address space). This, again, requires cooperation with the LSRT, depending on the object faulting strategy in use.

Likewise, binding of code to a recently loaded object must be done in a language-specific way. However, Owl provides the underlying support for dynamic linking where this is required, including supporting the storage and retrieval of class code.

Clustering. Owl supports the use of both application-directed and transparent clustering as required.

Directory Services. Finally, Owl provides a (persistent) name service (NS) that can be used to attach symbolic names to object references.

20.4 An Overview of the Owl Subframework

A GRT supporting one or more specific languages is instantiated by providing appropriate implementations of (a subset of) the classes that constitute the Owl subframework. The process of instantiating a GRT from Owl is obviously driven by the requirements of the language(s) to be supported, but it is also constrained by the model of a GRT and of GRT-LSRT interaction embodied in the design of Owl. This section describes the abstract model of a GRT, and of its interaction with an LSRT, that underpins the design. The next section describes the organization of the Owl subframework in more detail.

20.4.1 GRT Model

Some GRTs support only distributed objects and others only persistent objects, whereas some support both. In fact, distributed or persistent objects can be seen as specializations of abstract GRT objects supported by Owl. Every GRT supports at least the following services for GRT objects (the term object is hereafter used as a synonym for GRT object unless otherwise noted):

- Object creation
- Location-independent object naming
- Object faulting
- Object loading and unloading
- Directory services

Together, these services constitute the basic runtime support that must be provided for any distributed or persistent programming language. Depending on how each is implemented, the resulting GRT can support distributed or persistent objects using various policies and mechanisms. A given GRT can also provide additional services, such as object deletion or garbage collection, object clustering, or marshaling and unmarshalling of ROI requests. The Owl class category described in the remainder of this chapter includes classes providing a number of these additional services. Moreover, Owl has been designed to be extensible so that support for further services—for example, transaction management—can be provided in the future.

Typically, each of these services is invoked by a *downcall* from the LSRT to the GRT and makes use of *upcalls* from the GRT to the LSRT when a language-specific action has to be performed or language-specific information has to be obtained.

Every GRT provides exactly one form of GREF and one swizzling policy as dictated by the language(s) to be supported. A GRT may support either object fault avoidance or object fault detection. In the case of object fault detection, the actual detection of object faults is the responsibility of the LSRT. A given GRT may support the LSRT in using a number of different techniques for object fault detection, or the object fault detection technique used may be completely transparent to the GRT. A GRT supporting object fault detection may provide a number of different interfaces for object fault reporting. Each object fault reporting interface implies a set of allowable object fault resolution techniques that the GRT can apply.

20.4.2 Object Model

Abstractly, at the language level, an *object* is an entity with identity, state, and behavior [Booch 1994]. Every language object is assumed to have an associated *type* that specifies the interface to the object available to its clients.

On the other hand, a GRT object can be viewed as being essentially a container for one or more language objects that can be uniquely identified and to which code implementing the interface to the contained object(s) can be bound dynamically by the appropriate LSRT. Distributed or persistent language objects must be mapped, in a way specific to their language, onto appropriate GRT objects. The most obvious mapping is to use a single GRT object for each dynamically allocated language object. Other mappings are also possible. For example, an array of language objects could be contained within a single GRT object, or a language object might be embedded within another language object that is contained within a GRT object. The main consequence of supporting arrays of language objects or embedded language objects is that LREFs may map to arbitrary addresses within a GRT object rather than just the start address of the object.

In any case, both the internal structure of a particular GRT object and the semantics implemented by the contained language objects are dictated by the language level. Such information can be acquired by the GRT if necessary only by making upcalls to the LSRT. In particular, a set of upcall methods, which are implemented by the appropriate LSRT and which the GRT can call when required, must be bound to every GRT object in a way defined by Owl.

Object Allocation and Layout

New GRT objects are created dynamically in the GRT's heap by explicitly calling the GRT. Neither static allocation of GRT objects in some per-address space data segment nor stack allocation of GRT objects is supported.

Every GRT object has a header that is used to store information required by the GRT to manage the object. Depending on the GRT instantiation, this header may be allocated contiguously with the GRT object in memory or separately (perhaps to allow GRT objects to be moved within memory while loaded). In normal operation, an object's GRT header is transparent to the language level, although it may be accessed by upcall code provided by the LSRT.

Language objects are expected to be contiguous in memory but may have contiguous or noncontiguous headers containing information required by their LSRTs. In order to support LSRTs that use noncontiguous object headers, a GRT may be specialized to allow GRT objects to be split into (at most) two memory regions, resulting in the four possible GRT object layouts being supported.

Object Naming

GRT objects are uniquely identified by their OIDs. GRTs may assign OIDs to objects either eagerly (that is, when they are created) or lazily. A GRT that supports lazy OID allocation may, for example, allocate OIDs to objects only when they become known outside of the address space in which they were created, or, if clustering is supported, when they become known outside of their initial cluster.

Supporting lazy OID allocation requires that the GRT can detect when an object reference is about to be exported from an address space or cluster as appropriate. This means that lazy OID allocation is possible only if the GRT supports swizzling, and it may additionally require an address space scan [Sousa 1993].

A GRT object to which no OID has been allocated is known as an *immature* object. When allocated an OID, an object is said to be *promoted* to being a *mature* object.

The GREFs provided by a GRT serve not only to allow the referenced object to be located; they are also used to support object fault handling mechanisms. For example, besides providing the target object's OID or storage identifier, a GREF might contain information to allow a proxy for the object to be created when required.

In addition, because most GRTs will support embedded language objects within a GRT object, a GREF may refer to a particular offset within a GRT object. This is useful when a GREF is to be converted to an LREF, referring to such an embedded language object rather than its enclosing language object.

Code Management

The code to be bound to each language object is provided by its LSRT as a *class*. A given type may be represented by one or more classes. For example, if the LSRT uses proxies for object fault detection, then every type may be represented by a real class bound to language objects of that type and a proxy class bound to proxies for objects of that type. Each class consists of *application code*, which implements the methods required by the object's type, and *upcall code*, which implements the upcall methods to be bound to GRT objects containing objects of that type. In fact, upcall code may be specific to one type or shared between different types. As mentioned previously, the upcall code is bound to the appropriate GRT object by the GRT, whereas the application code is bound to the language object in a language-specific way by its LSRT, usually in response to an upcall from the GRT. Note, however, that only a single set of upcall methods can be associated with each GRT object.

Each class is represented by a *class descriptor* and named by a *class identifier* that acts as an index for the class descriptor in the GRT's *class register* (CR).

Objects and Representatives

A distributed or persistent language object can have *representatives* in many address spaces. The representatives of an object might be used to implement an object and its proxies, the replicas of a replicated object, or the fragments of a fragmented object. The mapping of a distributed or persistent language object onto a set of representatives is thus language-specific. Moreover, depending on the object model supported by the language, the existence of multiple representatives of an object in the system may or may not be transparent to application programmers.

To support this model, a GRT object can likewise have representatives in many address spaces. The representatives of a GRT object share its identity. However, the representatives may be different sizes and may or may not have application code bound to them. Moreover, the code bound to each representative may be the same or different. All representatives of a GRT object do, however, have GRT object headers and all have (possibly different) upcall code bound to them. If, when, and how representatives for GRT objects are created depends on the GRT instantiation. For example, to support a language that uses proxies for object fault detection, a GRT might be instantiated that creates representatives for absent GRT objects that are the same size as the real object and have proxy application code bound to them. If the language uses descriptors to represent absent objects, the GRT instantiation might create representatives for absent objects that are smaller that the actual object and have no application code bound to them.

When the GRT creates or maps an object or a representative for an object, such as a proxy, the GRT will ask the LSRT to *prepare* the object or representative for possible accesses by its clients by making an upcall to the object or representative. This upcall allows the LSRT to carry out any appropriate language-specific actions necessary to make the object or representative ready to be accessed. Typically, this will include binding application code to the object or representative, but it may also involve initiating swizzling or doing other format conversions that are necessary prior to the object or representative being accessed. Thus, initiating swizzling is the responsibility of the LSRT and not the GRT. When exactly the GRT makes this upcall depends on the particular GRT instantiation.

20.5 The Organization of the Owl Subframework

A GRT consists of a number of major functional components that can be individually customized to implement a GRT providing some required set of object-support mechanisms and policies. The six major components of all GRTs are illustrated in Figure 20.3, along with one optional component.

The main interface between an LSRT and a GRT is provided by an instance of Owl-GRT$_{sc}$. (The notation ClassName$_{sc}$ is used to denote subclasses of ClassName; that is, ClassName$_{sc}$ can be read as "one of the subclasses of ClassName.") Subclasses of Owl-GRT provide the major GRT methods related to object (and cluster) management callable from LSRTs and are also responsible for the translation between LREFs and GREFs that takes place at the LSRT-GRT interface.

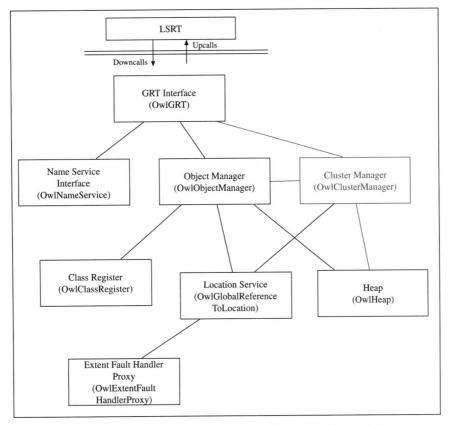

Figure 20.3 The major components of a GRT and their main associations.

Every GRT has a heap in which objects are created and loaded as required. A GRT's heap is implemented by an instance of OwlHeap$_{sc}$ that provides the methods to allocate and deallocate memory from the heap. Higher-level methods, such as those to create objects and clusters within the heap or those to load and unload objects and clusters into and out of the heap, are provided by a heap manager—an instance of OwlManager$_{sc}$. Heap managers come in two varieties, object managers (OMs) and cluster managers (CMs). OMs—instances of OwlObjectManager$_{sc}$—provide methods related to the creation, loading, and unloading of objects; whereas CMs—instances of OwlClusterManager$_{sc}$—provide methods related to the creation, loading, and unloading of clusters. Every GRT has an OM. A GRT that supports application-directed clustering will also have a CM. Thus, as indicated by the shaded lines in Figure 20.3, a CM is an optional component of a GRT. The OM or CM is also the component of the GRT that interacts with the POS to store and retrieve objects or clusters respectively when required.

Although heap managers are responsible for control of the heap, the location and—where necessary—forwarding of access requests to absent objects (be they persistent objects stored in the POS or distributed objects located in another address space or on another node) is encapsulated within the location service (LS) component of the GRT, which is implemented by an instance of OwlGlobalReferenceToLocation$_{sc}$. The LS implements the GRT's mapping from the GREF for an object to its current location in the (possibly distributed) system. In a GRT supporting distribution, the LS is a distributed component, and it uses Kanga for communication between its distributed parts.

A CR is a repository for class descriptors and code. Every GRT uses a CR—an instance of OwlClassRegister$_{sc}$—to obtain the class code for new and recently loaded objects when required. A CR is normally persistent and may also be remotely accessible. Likewise, the objects that it uses to store classes and their code would normally be expected to be persistent. Thus, a CR represents a good example of a service provided by the Tigger framework that is itself implemented using distributed and persistent objects. The design of the Tigger framework assumes that there is a single CR in each system, which is shared between all the GRTs in that system.

Finally, every GRT also provides an NS to supported languages via an instance of OwlNameService$_{sc}$. Although instances of OwlNameService$_{sc}$ are local volatile objects that are private to one GRT, the directories to which they refer are typically implemented by distributed persistent objects.

20.5.1 Interactions between GRT Components

Figure 20.4 shows the main interactions that occur between the major components of a GRT. For the sake of generality, the GRT in question is assumed to support both distribution and persistence; hence, it is distributed over multiple nodes and makes use of a POS instantiated from Eeyore.

The LSRTs of supported languages usually invoke methods provided by the GRT interface. This will typically result in the GRT interface invoking one of the other com-

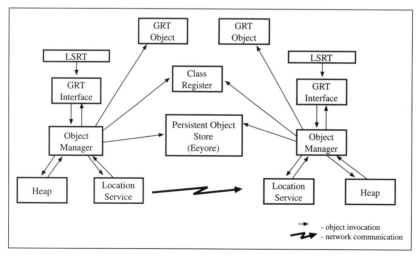

Figure 20.4 The interactions between the major components of a GRT.

ponents of the GRT, normally the NS or OM. In the case in which the request from the LSRT is related to object management (for example, requests to create or delete objects and requests related to object faulting), the GRT interface calls the OM. The OM will typically use the services of the LS, the heap, or the POS to carry out the request. During object fault handling, the request is typically forwarded to the LS. The LS may indicate that the object should be retrieved from the POS and loaded locally, return the object immediately, or forward the request to the OM at the node where the object is located. In handling the request, the LS will typically communicate with its remote peers, who may, in turn, need to upcall their local OMs. Thus, an OM typically provides a downcall interface for use by the GRT interface and an upcall interface for use by the LS during object fault handling. Like the interface to the GRT, the interfaces to both the OM and the LS must be specialized, depending on the approach to object faulting supported. In addition, as a heap manager, the OM also provides an upcall interface for use by the heap when heap space is exhausted. This interface typically causes the OM to try to unload some objects. The OM may use the CR to load class code for newly created objects or objects that have been loaded recently and is also the component that most commonly makes upcalls to GRT objects. Finally, the OM may upcall the GRT interface—usually to convert a GREF to an LREF, or vice versa.

Figure 20.5 shows the interactions that occur between the major components of a GRT that supports application-directed clustering. Such a GRT has an additional component, its CM, which is interposed between the OM and other components such as the heap, LS, and POS. Requests related to clusters (for example, requests to create or delete clusters) are passed by the GRT interface directly to the CM, whereas requests related to objects are still passed to the OM. A request concerning some object might

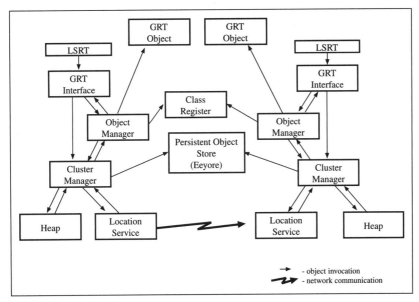

Figure 20.5 Interactions between components of a GRT supporting application-directed clustering.

result in the OM making a corresponding request to the CM for that object's cluster. Because the unit of location, loading, and unloading is a cluster rather than an individual object, the CM is responsible for interacting with the LS, POS, and heap to resolve the request in much the same way as the OM is in a GRT that does not support application-directed clustering. Resolving the request might require that a CM make an upcall to its local OM. Like the interfaces to the GRT interface, OM, and LS, the interface to the CM is also specialized depending on the approach to object faulting supported.

20.6 Implementing the Tigger Abstractions

Having looked briefly at the major components of a GRT and the ways in which they typically interact, this section describes the design of the Owl subframework in more detail. In particular, the organization of the various class hierarchies that make up Owl is described, as well as the opportunities that exist for specializing these classes in order to implement GRTs providing different mechanism and policies.

20.6.1 GRT Objects

The basic structure of GRT object headers, the methods on GRT object headers available to all GRTs, and the minimal set of upcalls that must be provided for all objects are all described by class OwlObject. The latter are defined as sets of pure virtual functions on GRT objects that are expected to be implemented for each class of global or persistent language object and bound to the GRT objects containing instances of those classes.

A basic GRT object header includes fields giving information such as the object's GREF (which also allows its OID to be obtained), its class identifier, the size of its body, and its state. The basic methods provided by OwlObject allow the mandatory information stored in a GRT object header to be retrieved and/or modified. Because GRT object headers are typically not constructed but are instead allocated by a GRT as part of allocating the GRT objects to which they belong, OwlObject provides a method to initialize the mandatory fields of a GRT header. In addition, OwlObject provides the GRT with the method ::bindUpcalls to cause the appropriate upcall code to be bound to the object.

OwlObject also describes the set of upcalls that is required by all GRTs and, hence, must be provided by all LSRTs. This minimum set of upcalls includes the following:

::onCreate. Upcalled on every GRT object when created; allows the associated LSRT to perform any language-specific actions that may be required, including binding code to the contained language objects in the language-specific manner, making language-level object table entries for the contained objects, or even executing application-specific initialization code.

::onPrepare. Upcalled whenever an object or representative is prepared by the GRT; depending on the language, this upcall may bind class code or initiate swizzling.

::onMap. Upcalled on an object when it is prepared after being migrated from another node or loaded from the POS.

::onUnmap. Upcalled on an object just before it is migrated to another node or stored to the POS.

Subclasses of OwlObject introduce additional upcalls that must be provided in different situations. Such additional upcalls are required to support the following functions:

Swizzling. To allow a GRT to locate references to be swizzled or unswizzled within an object.

Garbage collection. Also to allow references contained within an object to be located.

Different fault-handling mechanisms. Different sets of upcalls are required by different fault-handling mechanisms—for example, in a GRT supporting ROI, an upcall to dispatch incoming ROI requests to objects is required.

Access control. To allow method-based (and hence type-specific) access control lists to be used to control accesses to objects.

The resulting class hierarchy is best viewed as consisting of a number of layers, as shown in Figure 20.6. The top two layers of the class hierarchy provide the OwlUpcall and OwlObject classes and describe the minimum set of upcalls required. The third layer provides the OwlSwizzlingObject class, which describes the extra upcalls required by GRTs that support eager or lazy swizzling. The fourth layer of the hierarchy introduces classes describing the upcalls required to support different fault-handling policies. These may be derived from any of the classes in the second or third layers as required. Thus, OwlRPCObject (derived from OwlObject) and OwlRPCSwizzlingObject (derived from OwlSwizzlingObject) both add the ::dispatch upcall used to dispatch an incoming ROI request to its target object. Following a similar pattern, OwlPinObject and OwlPinSwizzlingObject introduce upcalls to maintain a per-object pin count for use in E-like object fault avoidance. Because a GRT may support multiple approaches to object fault handling, these sets of upcalls can also be combined in a single class when necessary. Finally, the fifth layer of the hierarchy adds the ::checkAccess upcall to support method-based access control.

Although subclasses of OwlObject providing different combinations of these sets of upcalls could have been defined by using multiple inheritance to combine appropriate mixin classes with OwlObject, the use of multiple inheritance would make the binding of upcall code to GRT objects more complex and was rejected.

20.6.2 Language References

The only meaningful methods on an LREF, from the GRT point of view, are those to obtain a GREF given an LREF, and vice versa. These conversions are performed by the OwlGRT class hierarchy. However, OwlLanguageReference is provided as a placeholder for classes describing the format of LREFs to be supported by a particular GRT and on which other classes depend. In particular, OwlLanguageReference is necessary because a number of other Owl classes have methods that take or return LREFs and, hence, have a dependency on the size of an LREF.

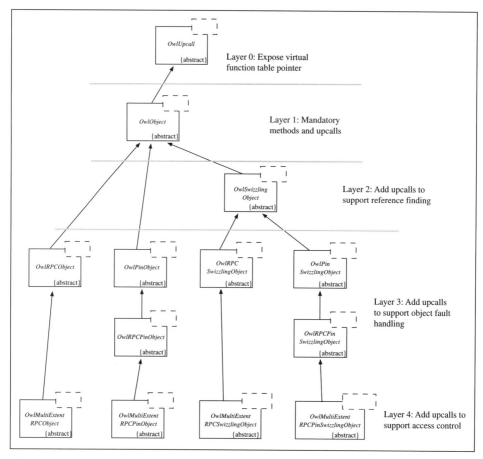

Figure 20.6 The structure of the OwlObject class hierarchy.

20.6.3 Global References

The OwlGlobalReference class hierarchy describes the format of and protocol supported by GREFs. The base class, OwlGlobalReference, describes the most basic form of GREF supported—that is, one that simply allows the referenced object to be identified, and hence located, anywhere in the distributed system.

OwlGlobalReference can be specialized to provide any additional information required by a GRT to allow it to access absent objects as well as to support different object fault detection strategies. For GRTs supporting persistence, OwlLoadableGlobalReference provides an additional method, ::getStorageIdentifier, to return the target object's storage identifier.

OwlOProxiableGlobalReference provides a method, ::getClassIdentifier, to return the target object's class identifier as required when proxies are used to represent absent objects. Likewise, OwlOProxiableLoadableGlobalReference combines the protocols of

OwlLoadableGlobalReference and OwlOProxiableGlobalReference for GRTs that use proxies to represent absent persistent objects.

Further subclasses of OwlGlobalReference could be derived to support different fault detection or resolution strategies or combinations thereof.

20.6.4 Clusters

The format of cluster headers and the basic methods on clusters available to the GRT are described by OwlCluster. Clusters, when supported, act as mini–persistent heaps in which objects can be allocated and deallocated as required. Thus, the header of a cluster is mainly expected to include the data structures required to manage the cluster space and will be specialized depending on the policies implemented by the GRT. In any case, every cluster header will contain at least the cluster's identifier and the total size of the cluster.

Because cluster headers, like GRT object headers, are not constructed but are allocated in the GRT's heap as part of the cluster, OwlCluster provides a method to initialize the header of a new cluster, as well as methods to extract information from the header.

Most of the methods to be provided by clusters are concerned with object management, including the allocation and deallocation of space for objects within the cluster's heap, as well as methods used to inform a cluster that an object has migrated into or out of the cluster.

Because OwlCluster has virtual functions, code must be bound to every cluster's header when it is loaded. Because cluster classes do not have class identifiers, binding of code to a cluster cannot be done in the same way that, for example, upcall code is bound to GRT object headers. The only viable alternative relies on knowing the actual name of the cluster class and using a dummy binding constructor provided by the class to cause the virtual function table pointer to be set up.

20.6.5 Cluster Identifiers

The OwlClusterIdentifier class hierarchy describes the format of and protocol supported by cluster identifiers. Essentially, cluster identifiers are used by GRTs that support application-directed clustering to identify a cluster and retrieve it from the POS; that is, a cluster identifier contains at least a storage identifier. The protocol supported by cluster identifiers basically allows cluster identifiers to be compared (including with some designed null cluster identifier) and hashed as a basis for table lookups based on cluster identifier. OwlClusterIdentifier might be specialized to provide additional information required for cluster fault handling.

For practical reasons, such as the need to minimize their size and to avoid the overhead of binding code to them when loaded into an address space, instances of OwlLanguageReference$_{sc}$, OwlGlobalReference$_{sc}$, and OwlClusterIdentifier$_{sc}$ cannot have virtual functions. If other Owl classes are to be able to use different implementations of each of these classes, they must be designed as template classes that take these classes as template parameters. Thus, these class hierarchies specify the public interfaces that can be used by the template classes of which they are parameters. A particular GRT instantiation fixes the types of these template parameters, and invocations of methods on objects of these types are then statically bound. This means that every GRT instantiation uses exactly one type of LREF, one type of GREF, and, if required, one type of cluster identifier.

20.6.6 The GRT Interface

The OwlGRT class hierarchy provides the main (downcall) interface between a GRT and an LSRT. Most of the GRT methods concerned with object (or cluster) management that are intended to be callable from an LSRT are provided as methods on an appropriate instance of $OwlGRT_{sc}$. The few exceptions include the methods provided to marshal and unmarshal values into and out of messages and a few methods on GRT objects that are available to upcall code provided by an LSRT. Encapsulating the GRT-LSRT interface in a single class makes writing the code necessary to interface an existing LSRT to a GRT straightforward.

The OwlGRT class hierarchy is also responsible for performing the conversion between the LREFs used by supported languages and the GREFs used internally by the GRT, thus making the rest of the GRT independent of how this conversion is performed.

The interface to a GRT can be divided into a number of sets of methods, some of which are provided by all GRTs and others of which are provided only by specific GRTs. The main sets of methods that may be provided are as follows:

- Methods concerned with the interface to the GRT's NS
- Methods concerned with object creation and deletion
- Methods concerned with conversions between memory addresses, LREFs, and GREFs
- Methods concerned with object fault avoidance or resolution
- Methods concerned with swizzling
- Methods concerned with application-directed clustering
- Methods concerned with interaction between extents

Every GRT provides the first four sets of methods. In addition, a GRT that supports eager or lazy swizzling will provide methods to initiate swizzling and unswizzling of objects or references. A GRT that supports application-directed clustering will provide additional methods to create and manage clusters, whereas a GRT that is part of a multiextent Tigger instantiation will typically provide additional methods supporting, for example, cross-extent object invocation. A GRT may provide any of a number of possible object fault avoidance or resolution interfaces. Moreover, because the decisions concerning whether or not to provide support for swizzling, application-directed clustering and/or multiple extents are orthogonal to each other, any GRT may support any combination of these features.

The result of supporting such a large number of possible GRT types is a rather complicated class hierarchy that exhibits the layered structure illustrated in Figure 20.7. The top layer—that is, OwlGRT—provides the methods that are common to all GRTs. The next layer adds classes supporting different swizzling policies (only one such

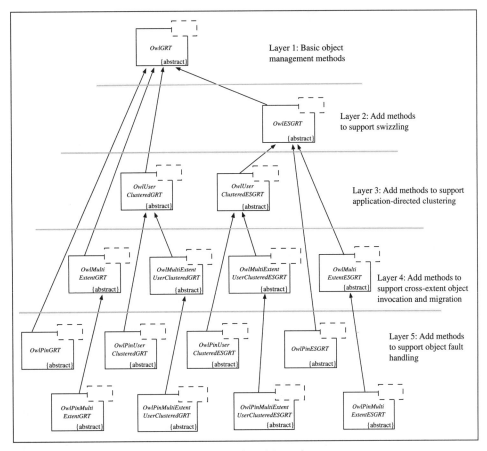

Figure 20.7   The structure of the OwlGRT class hierarchy.

class, supporting eager swizzling, is shown in the diagram). For each class in any previous layer, the third layer adds a class supporting application-directed clustering. Likewise, the fourth layer adds a class supporting interaction between multiple extents. The final layer adds classes supporting different fault avoidance or resolution interfaces (only classes supporting one such interface, object fault avoidance by means of pin and unpin methods, are shown in the diagram).

Because support for application-directed clustering, multiple extents, and particular object fault handling mechanisms can be seen as options applicable to any GRT, these interfaces could again have been provided by means of mixin classes. However, although these interfaces are orthogonal to each other, the implementations are unlikely to be. For example, the implementation of a pin/unpin type object fault avoidance interface will depend critically on whether clustering is supported. Hence, while the mixin style approach may appear natural for the interface definition, the class hierarchy as defined more closely reflects the required implementation hierarchy.

Converting between LREFs and GREFs

The knowledge that a GRT has about the format of LREFs is encapsulated within the methods ::languageToGlobalReference and ::globalToLanguageReference. In the simplest case of a nonswizzling GRT, where LREFs are the same as GREFs, these will be empty methods. Where the LREF and GREF for an object differ, these methods must be specialized to perform the required conversions, depending on factors such as the format of LREFs and the layout of objects in memory.

To support the conversion from an LREF to a GREF, the GRT provides an ancillary method, ::addrToObject, that returns a pointer to an object's GRT header, given an address for the object. Depending on whether LREFs can refer to embedded objects, ::addrToObject can be specialized to accept only the start address of the object's body or any address within its body. Clearly, ::addrToObject can be used only if the object is represented in the current address space, but it must work even if the target object is not loaded in the address space, thereby introducing a dependency on the way in which absent objects are represented.

Where the LSRT uses addresses as object references, ::languageToGlobalReference can use ::addrToObject to locate the target object's header and then extract the required GREF and update its offset field if the LREF refers to an embedded object. The reverse conversion, from a GREF to an address, is usually straightforward, because the GRT maintains a mapping from the GREFs of GRT objects to their addresses, to which any offset in the GREF can then be added.

If the LSRT uses something other than addresses as LREFs, then some means for ::languageToGlobalReference to obtain an object's address given an LREF will have to be provided in the LSRT. This will not be difficult for most LSRTs, because this mapping must be implemented by the LSRT in any case. However, ::globalToLanguage-Reference requires that the LSRT provide a means of obtaining an LREF given the address of an object. Supporting this mapping may require additional work within the LSRT.

GRT Support for Swizzling

Support for different swizzling policies is provided by classes in layer two of the Owl-GRT class hierarchy. These classes describe the additional methods provided by GRTs that support either lazy or eager swizzling.

OwlESGRT and its subclasses support eager swizzling by providing the methods ::swizzleObject and ::unswizzleObject to swizzle or unswizzle a specified object. In fact, overloaded versions of these methods are provided to support swizzling in place and copy swizzling respectively. In the case of copy swizzling, the responsibility for determining the location to which the object will be copied belongs to the caller, and ::un/swizzleObject copies the entire object, including its header and nonreference data.

Swizzling is expected to be initiated by LSRTs rather than by a GRT. In particular, LSRTs are expected to swizzle objects as they are prepared by calling ::swizzleObject from the ::onPrepare upcall.

::swizzleObject works by repeatedly upcalling the target object in order to locate its GREFs, calling the OM's OwlObjectManager::processReference method (see *Section*

20.6.8) for each GREF found, and storing the LREF returned into the object. Similarly, ::unswizzleObject upcalls the object to locate the LREFs stored in the object and calls ::languageToGlobalReference for each before storing the GREF obtained into the object.

OwlLSGRT and its subclasses support lazy swizzling by providing ::swizzleReference to swizzle a single reference and the overloaded method ::unswizzleObject to unswizzle any swizzled references within a specified object. ::swizzleReference takes a GREF supplied by the LSRT and returns the corresponding LREF returned by OwlObjectManager::processReference, which the LSRT can then store in an object. On unmapping, ::unswizzleObject is called, as usual, by the GRT. However, in this case, the responsibility for distinguishing swizzled from unswizzled references rests with the LSRT. In fact, an LSRT that uses lazy swizzling need not use ::swizzleReference. Because LREFs subsume GREFs in a system that supports lazy swizzling (all GREFs are, by definition, also valid LREFs), the swizzled form of a reference can be obtained as a side effect of using one of the object fault handling interfaces described following. For example, if using the ROI interface, the LSRT might pass an unswizzled LREF (that is, a GREF) to the GRT, which, if the object is subsequently loaded, will then return the address of the object to the LSRT. The LSRT can then use this address to update the LREF.

OwlNSGRT is provided to support GRTs that, although they do not support swizzling, allow the GREFs contained within an object to be processed in some way when the object is loaded. For example, consider a GRT that uses virtual addresses as GREFs and needs a protected memory page or object descriptor to be allocated for any address representing an absent object when the containing object is loaded. OwlNSGRT provides an interface that allows an object to declare its references to the GRT when it is loaded, thereby giving the GRT the opportunity to set up representatives for the objects to which they refer, using OwlObjectManager::processReference, without actually swizzling the references.

Supporting Application-Directed Clustering

A GRT that supports application-directed clustering must provide an interface that allows applications to create and delete clusters, as well as to create objects in specified clusters and to move objects between clusters. Such an interface is provided by the classes in layer three of the OwlGRT class hierarchy and their subclasses.

The decision as to whether support for application-directed clustering is provided is independent of the decision as to which approach to swizzling should be supported. Thus, a layer 3 class supporting application-directed clustering can be derived from any of the classes supporting different swizzling interfaces in layer 2 of the GRT hierarchy, as well as directly from OwlGRT. Such classes provide the minimal set of additional methods required to allow applications to control clustering.

::createCluster takes a size and container identifier as parameters and asks the CM to create a cluster of the specified size in the specified container. ::deleteCluster simply asks the CM to delete the specified cluster under the assumption that it is owned by the calling extent and that it contains no objects. An overloaded version of ::createObject allows an application to choose the cluster in which the new object should be created. Finally, ::moveObject simply asks the OM to migrate the object to the specified cluster in the same extent.

Object Fault Handling

The lowest layer of the OwlGRT class hierarchy adds interfaces for object fault avoidance and/or reporting. Numerous such interfaces can be conceived; hence, rather than all of the classes making up this level introducing the same additional interface, different classes may introduce different interfaces. Typical object fault handling interfaces provide the LSRT with the ability to:

- Avoid object faults by loading and storing objects explicitly

- Avoid object faults by pinning and unpinning objects in memory

- Initiate ROI requests in response to detected object faults (perhaps resulting in the target object being loaded locally or a ROI being carried out)

- Generate a memory protection fault in response to an object fault (resulting in the target object being loaded locally)

Other interfaces are also possible. It should be clear that not all combinations of these interfaces with the other facilities that might be provided by a GRT are meaningful. For example, if the GRT supports application-directed clustering, then a fault avoidance interface that explicitly loads and stores single objects is not meaningful (although one that pins objects would be if it is understood that pinning an object might cause further objects to be loaded). Likewise, a system that supports object fault avoidance is unlikely to employ swizzling (although it might). Finally, whatever interface is provided for the LSRT, a GRT supporting interworking between extents always provides a ROI-based fault-reporting interface.

Marshaling Support

OwlMarshalStream provides an interface for marshaling and unmarshaling messages that is intended primarily for use by supported LSRTs. An instance of OwlMarshalStream is created to marshal or unmarshal data into or out of a message. Messages themselves are essentially untyped but have headers that are described by subclasses of OwlRequestDescriptor and that vary in size depending on the request type. Thus, OwlMarshalStream is a template class that must be instantiated for each type of request that it is to handle because it must know the size of the request header.

The methods of OwlMarshalStream allow values of basic types to be inserted into or extracted out of a message and can be specialized to support encoding of values in a canonical format for transmission between heterogeneous nodes as required. Among the basic types that can be supported are object references. Inserting an LREF into a message requires that it be converted to a GREF for transmission using OwlGRT::languageToGlobalReference. Extracting an LREF from a message involves converting the GREF that will have been contained in the message to the appropriate LREF using OwlObjectManager::processReference, possibly resulting in a representative for the target object being created in the receiving address space.

OwlRequestDescriptor is the base class for the headers of messages transmitted between parts of a GRT. Classes derived from OwlRequestDescriptor describe the headers of different types of messages. For example, OwlRPCDescriptor describes the header of a ROI request message. Such a message must include the GREF of the target object for use by the receiving GRT and will also contain LSRT- and application-specific data inserted by the LSRT that are not interpreted by the GRT.

20.6.7 Heaps and Heap Managers

A heap describes a memory region into which objects (and their representatives) or clusters can be loaded. In principle, there can be many heaps in a single address space, and a single heap can be distributed over several address spaces if the GRT of which it is a part supports DSM. In addition, a heap may be persistent. The interface provided by a heap simply provides for the allocation and deallocation of space within the heap.

Every heap has a manager that is responsible for management of the space allocated to the heap. In particular, the heap's manager is the component that requests the allocation and deallocation of memory within the heap and must react to exhaustion of the heap space when necessary—typically by releasing some memory that it has previously allocated. OMs and CMs are examples of heap managers.

The class OwlHeap describes the interface provided by a heap and simply provides methods to allocate and release space within the heap. In addition, every heap has a reference to its manager, which is an instance of OwlManager. OwlManager introduces the method ::needSpace, which is intended to be called by instances of OwlHeap when they are unable to satisfy further allocation requests. The implementation of ::needSpace in a particular OM or CM would therefore typically cause object or cluster unloading to be initiated, depending on the policy implemented by the GRT.

Subclasses of OwlHeap may support distributed or persistent heaps. A distributed heap is required when the GRT supports DSM. In this case, instances of the appropriate subclass of OwlHeap might cooperate to partition the available memory space. Thus, these local instances would communicate directly with their remote peers to manage the heap. Most likely, their managers would also need to cooperate to maintain a common view of which objects or clusters have been loaded in the heap. A persistent heap might be required when the GRT implements a single-level store; that is, when memory is allocated to a persistent object for its lifetime. In this case, the data structures describing the allocation of memory must also be made persistent.

20.6.8 Object Managers

OMs are responsible for most aspects of object management within a single address space, and, in particular, implement the creation, deletion, loading, and unloading of objects within their heap. OMs act as heap managers and are thus responsible for determining when an object may be unloaded (in the absence of support for application-directed clustering, in which case the CM acts as the heap manager). OMs are also responsible for local garbage collection where supported.

Like the GRT interface, the interface to an OM can be divided into a number of sets of methods, some of which are common to all OMs and some of which are specific to particular OMs. The main sets of methods that may be provided by an OM are as follows:

- Methods supporting object creation and deletion
- Methods supporting object loading and unloading

- Methods supporting reference swizzling
- Methods supporting application-directed clustering
- Methods supporting object promotion
- Methods supporting object migration between extents

Every OM provides the first three sets of methods, although the methods provided to load objects into the heap may be overloaded to support different object fault resolution strategies. An OM that supports application-directed clustering provides additional methods to support creation of objects in clusters, as well as migration of objects between clusters. An OM for a GRT supporting lazy promotion will provide a method to promote an immature object. Finally, an OM for a GRT that is part of a multiextent Tigger instantiation may provide additional methods to support object migration between extents. As a result, the OwlObjectManager class hierarchy exhibits a layered structure that is similar to that of the OwlGRT class hierarchy, as illustrated in Figure 20.8.

OwlObjectManager itself describes the methods that are provided by all OMs, essentially those to create and delete, as well as to load and unload, objects into and out of the heap.

Two overloaded versions of ::createObject are provided to create GRT objects. One version takes a class identifier as input and returns a pointer to the header of the newly created object. The other version supports the creation of GRT objects that are to contain arrays of language objects and takes an additional parameter specifying the number of language objects (of the specified type) that are to be contained in the array. In both cases, ::createObject takes care of allocating space for the new object, including its GRT header, as well as allocating an OID for the object and making a GREF referring to it as necessary. ::createObject also initializes the object's header, including binding the required upcall code to the object. At object creation, the OM uses the ::onCreate upcall to allow language-specific actions to be carried out; this might include binding the application code to the object in a language-specific manner, making an LSRT object table entry for the new object, or just executing application-specific initialization code (the latter is particularly useful when remote creation is supported).

::deleteObject is provided to delete an object and may be called directly from the GRT interface or by the OM's garbage collector in a GRT supporting garbage collection. ::deleteObject is basically responsible for freeing up any heap and/or secondary storage space occupied by the object, as well as for informing the LS that the object has been deleted if necessary.

The basic method used by a GRT to load an object into its local heap is ::mapObject, which takes the GREF of the required object as a parameter and tries to load the object locally. The main steps involved in loading an object include using the LS to locate the object (possibly obtaining a copy of it from a remote address space), allocating local heap space for the object, and, in a GRT supporting persistent objects, retrieving the object from the POS. In addition, when an object is loaded into an address space, ::mapObject is responsible for binding its upcall code to the object and making the ::onPrepare and ::onMap upcalls to the object to allow any necessary language- or application-specific actions to take place.

Unloading of objects from the heap is carried out using ::unmapObject. The steps that are typically involved in unloading an object include writing the object to the POS,

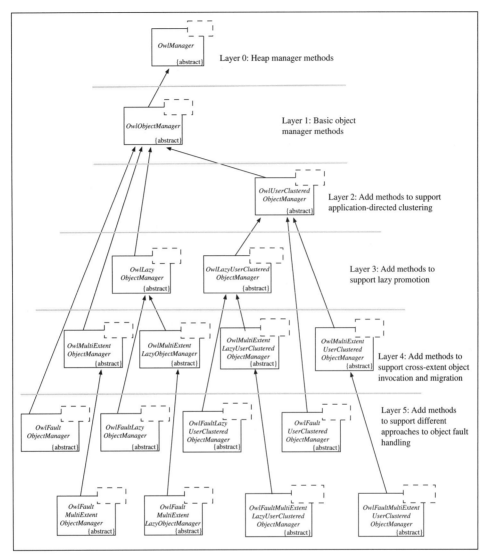

Figure 20.8   The structure of the OwlObjectManager class hierarchy.

releasing the heap space that was occupied by the object or leaving behind an appropriate representative for the now absent object, and informing the LS that the object is no longer loaded in that address space. Of course, before unloading the object, its ::onUnmap upcall is invoked to allow any language- or application-specific actions required to be carried out.

The OM also provides the method ::processReference that is responsible for taking a GREF to be swizzled and returning the corresponding LREF, possibly resulting in the creation of a local representative for the target object if none is already present. For example, ::processReference might create a local proxy, descriptor, or language-level object table entry for the target object, depending on the object fault handling policy of the language.

Supporting Application-Directed Clustering

Supporting application-directed clustering requires only modest extensions to the interface exported by OwlObjectManger. In fact, OwlUserClusteredObjectManager adds only two additional methods. One of these is simply an overloaded version of ::createObject that takes an extra parameter identifying the cluster in which the new object should be created.

The other method introduced by OwlUserClusteredObjectManager is ::moveObject, which implements migration of objects between clusters. The main steps involved include the loading of both the source and destination clusters of the migration and the actual migration of the object between the clusters concerned, using the overloaded OwlCluster::migrateObject methods of the two clusters concerned. A major issue here is whether the target object can actually be copied between the clusters at the time of the migration or whether this must be postponed, typically until the destination cluster is being unloaded. This depends primarily on whether supported languages can tolerate an object moving while it may be accessed. Thus, ::moveObject is typically specialized depending on whether objects can be copied during migration.

Supporting Other Fault-Reporting Interfaces

The OM can be further specialized to support different fault-handling interfaces. In particular, the ::mapObject method can be overloaded to take inputs other than a GREF to identify the target of an object fault and allow the requested access to be carried out. Different overloaded versions of ::mapObject are introduced by different subclasses in the fifth layer of the OwlObjectManager class hierarchy. Such classes can potentially be derived from any of the classes in the previous layers of the hierarchy and might introduce interfaces supporting the use of ROI or DSM to access absent objects.

20.6.9 Cluster Managers

The CM is an optional component of a GRT that is responsible for most aspects of cluster management in GRTs supporting application-directed clustering. In particular, the CM implements the creation, deletion, loading, and unloading of clusters within the local heap. When present, the CM interacts closely with the OM during object loading and unloading. An OM supporting application-directed clustering will use the CM to load the clusters that it requires to service the requests to load objects and to migrate objects between clusters that it receives. The CM also acts as the heap manager in a system supporting application-directed clustering in which clusters are the units of loading and unloading. Thus, the CM is responsible for determining when a cluster can be unloaded. During cluster unloading, the CM will typically upcall the OM as part of unloading each cluster. Thus, there is both a downcall and an upcall interface between the CM and the OM.

OwlClusterManager provides methods to create, delete, load, and unload clusters. The ::createCluster method is responsible for cluster creation and takes the required size of the cluster and the identifier of the container in which the cluster is to be created as parameters. In general, creating a cluster involves allocating space for the cluster in the heap, allocating an identifier for the new cluster (including allocating a storage identifier for it), initializing the cluster's header, and, finally, informing the LS that the new cluster is loaded at the current node. Allocating space for the cluster in the heap may result in a callback to the CM's ::needSpace method if there is insufficient space available in the heap. This may result in cluster unloading being initiated.

The ::deleteCluster method is responsible for implementing cluster deletion and simply takes the identifier of the cluster to be deleted as input. A cluster can be deleted only if it contains no objects. Thus, this method will fail if called for a cluster that still contains objects. In this case, the onus is on the application to respond to this failure by either explicitly deleting those objects (if possible) or migrating them to a different cluster before retrying the deletion. In order to check that the cluster is empty (by means of the OwlCluster::isEmpty method), deleting a cluster requires that it first be loaded in the current address space. Once loaded and found to be empty, deletion of the cluster simply requires that the space it occupies in the POS (if any) be released, the LS be notified that the cluster is no longer loaded (if required), and the heap space assigned to the object be released. Releasing the heap space allocated to a cluster may be complicated by the fact that objects that have recently been migrated out of the cluster (and are, therefore, not considered to belong to the cluster) may still be located in the memory region allocated to the cluster if they could not be immediately copied to their new cluster. In this case, deallocation of the heap space occupied by the cluster must be postponed until these objects are actually copied—typically when the cluster to which they now belong is unloaded.

The basic interface for loading a cluster given its identifier is provided by ::mapCluster. ::mapCluster is typically called by an OM supporting application-directed clustering where object fault avoidance is used or in response to an object fault that is to be resolved by loading the target object locally. Essentially, ::mapCluster uses the LS to ensure that the required cluster is not loaded elsewhere (thereby allowing it to be loaded locally), uses the POS to obtain the size of the cluster, allocates space for the cluster in the local heap, and retrieves the cluster from the POS.

Unloading of individual clusters is implemented by ::unmapCluster, which takes a pointer to the header of the cluster to be unloaded and an indication of whether the address space is terminating as input. The latter allows certain optimizations to be implemented when the address space is terminating; for example, it may not be necessary to inform the LS about the unloading of each cluster individually. ::unmapCluster asks the cluster to prepare itself to be unloaded by calling OwlCluster::onUnmap, which will, in turn, call one of the overloaded versions of OwlObjectManager::unmapObject for every prepared object in the cluster (including objects that are migrating into the cluster). The effect of this call should be to unswizzle each object and copy it to the cluster as required. The cluster can then be written to the POS and the local heap space that was occupied by the cluster can be reclaimed. If necessary, the LS can then be informed that the cluster has been unloaded.

Supporting Different Object Fault Handling Interfaces

Subclasses of OwlClusterManager are introduced to support different object fault resolution strategies. In particular, subclasses of OwlClusterManager typically overload the ::mapCluster method to support the different object fault reporting interfaces that might be provided by a GRT, as well as to support different strategies for object fault resolution. In addition, subclasses of OwlClusterManager may introduce new methods required to support the object fault resolution strategy supported. Thus, OwlFaultClusterManager supports object fault detection based on trapping virtual memory protection faults and typically resolves the fault by loading the required cluster page(s) locally. OwlRPCClusterManager supports GRTs providing ROI-based object fault reporting interfaces and allows the fault to be resolved either by loading the cluster locally or by performing a ROI to the target object.

OwlFaultClusterManager overloads ::mapCluster to take an address (rather than a cluster identifier) as input and tries to resolve the implied page fault by mapping the required cluster page locally. As in the case of OwlClusterManager::mapCluster, this may result in the cluster being retrieved from the POS, or, if global objects are supported using DSM, it may result in the required page being fetched from a remote node by the LS.

OwlRPCClusterManager overloads ::mapCluster to take a ROI request as input and tries to resolve the implied object fault either by loading the target cluster locally or by performing a ROI to the target object remotely. To support ROI, OwlRPCClusterManager also adds another method, ::remoteMapCluster, which is intended to be upcalled from the LS on the remote side of a ROI request.

20.6.10 The Name Service

The GRT NS allows mappings between symbolic names and object references to be established and persistently recorded. More particularly, the primary responsibility of the NS is to record mappings between Unix-style path names and GREFs. The only major complication in the design arises because the NS must be able to store entries containing different types of GREFs corresponding to the different types of GRTs provided by the instantiation of which it is a part. One consequence of this is that an attempt to retrieve an NS entry inserted by a GRT of one type might be made by a GRT of a different type—in particular, one supporting a different GREF format. However, NS entries should really be retrieved only by GRTs that are of the same type as the GRTs that originally made those entries and that are capable of interpreting the GREFs contained therein. Thus, the NS interface component of each GRT has been designed to detect when an NS entry retrieved was made by a different type of GRT. In addition, the NS interfaces for recording and looking up object references take a class identifier parameter, and every NS entry stores the class identifier of the object to which it refers. On lookup, this allows the application to dynamically check that the reference retrieved is of the type expected (because the possibility of retrieving object references from an NS may break the type safety of any language).

The NS is made up of an arbitrary graph of directories. A directory typically contains a set of references to other directories or NS entries in which each NS entry contains a single GREF. Directories are instances of OwlNSDirectory$_{sc}$, whereas NS entries are instances of OwlNSEntry$_{sc}$, both of which are derived from the common base class OwlNSDirectoryEntry. Thus, an instance of OwlNSDirectory$_{sc}$ contains a set of references to instances of OwlNSDirectoryEntry$_{sc}$.

In fact, OwlNSEntry is a template class that depends on the format of GREFs supported by the GRT of which it is a part. Thus, every type of GRT introduces its own form of NS entry, all of which are derived from the common base class OwlNSDirectoryEntry. Entries made by different types of GRT can be stored in the same directories. An instance of OwlNSEntry$_{sc}$ contains a GREF (of the appropriate type) for some object and the class identifier of the object, as well as the name under which the entry is stored in its containing directory. In general, the content of an instance of OwlNSEntry (other than its name) is not interpreted by the other components of the NS and is interpreted only by the GRT that retrieves the entry.

20.6.11 The Location Service

The OwlGlobalReferenceToLocation class hierarchy encapsulates the GRT's LS. As such, subclasses of OwlGlobalReferenceToLocation have a number of different responsibilities. First and foremost, they are responsible for implementing the mapping from a GREF for an object to its location in the distributed system. They are also responsible for determining whether such an object can be loaded into some address space. In addition, rather than simply returning an indication of the location of some object given a GREF referring to it, OwlGlobalReferenceToLocation can be specialized to support different object fault resolution policies that can benefit from close integration with the LS component of the GRT. For example, OwlGlobalReferenceToLocation can be specialized to forward ROI requests to their target objects in a GRT that supports ROI. Likewise, OwlGlobalReferenceToLocation can be specialized to implement a single distributed address space in a GRT supporting DSM-style access to objects.

Each GRT has a single instance of OwlGlobalReferenceToLocation$_{sc}$ in each of the address spaces in which it is running. These instances must cooperate with each other in order to locate objects and support object fault resolution according to the policy implemented by the GRT of which they are a part. In a GRT supporting distribution, communication between remote instances of OwlGlobalReferenceToLocation$_{sc}$ forms the basis for the implementation of access to remote objects and, hence, explicitly uses Kanga endpoints rather than ROI.

In order to be able to locate and support the resolution of faults on objects, instances of OwlGlobalReferenceToLocation$_{sc}$ must collectively track the location of every object that is currently loaded into some address space. Subclasses of OwlGlobalReferenceToLocation are free to implement any policies and algorithms to support object location and object fault resolution, including the activation of new address spaces when required. Neither the way in which the instances of OwlGlobalReferenceToLocation$_{sc}$ communicate nor the way in which they coordinate their activities is mandated by Owl, and several different approaches are possible.

In a *centralized* approach, one instance, the *controller*, is responsible for keeping track of the location of every loaded object and supporting the resolution of object faults. If an object fault occurs at a node other than that at which this instance is located, the instance of OwlGlobalReferenceToLocation$_{sc}$ in the faulting address space forwards the request to the controller. The controller determines whether the object is loaded and, if so, where. Resolution of the fault will depend on the policy implemented by the GRT and will typically involve further communication between the controller and other instances of OwlGlobalReferenceToLocation$_{sc}$. For example, in a ROI-based system, the ROI request would be forwarded to the node where the object was loaded. In a DSM-based system, the page or pages containing the object would be migrated from their current location to the required node. When the object is not already loaded, the controller can simply arrange to have the object loaded from the POS, and the required access take place at an appropriate node.

This scheme requires that the instance of OwlGlobalReferenceToLocation$_{sc}$ in each address space has an endpoint for communication with the controller and that the controller can communicate with each of its peers. Thus, each instance of OwlGlobalReferenceToLocation$_{sc}$ creates an endpoint on which to receive messages from its peers. The controller advertises its address in the NS, and each peer retrieves its controller's address from the NS when created and sends its address to the controller in a registration message. In order for the controller to keep an accurate record of which objects are loaded, and where, it must also be informed of object creation and unloading.

In a *distributed* approach, instances of OwlGlobalReferenceToLocation$_{sc}$ cooperate to determine the location of objects. For example, on an object fault, instances might multicast a request for the target object's current location to their peers. If the object is discovered not to be loaded at any node, it can be retrieved from the POS. One possibility is for the instances of OwlGlobalReferenceToLocation$_{sc}$ to form a multicast group. Assuming a ranking on the members of the group according to the order in which they joined, and notification of membership changes to all the members, the controller can be chosen to be the highest-ranked member of the group, and all members can maintain a common view of the current controller. Object fault resolution requests can be multicast to all the members of the group using an appropriately ordered multicast protocol provided by Kanga.

The base class of the OwlGlobalReferenceToLocation class hierarchy describes an LS suitable for a nondistributed GRT. This class simply provides methods to record (::insert), remove (::remove), and query (::apply) the current location of an object identified by a GREF. Given that this class is not intended to support distribution, the ::apply interface can be used to determine whether the target object is loaded.

Subclasses of OwlGlobalReferenceToLocation add interfaces required by GRT instantiations supporting multiple extents, distribution, and different fault resolution interfaces. OwlDistributedGlobalReferenceToLocation describes the interface to an LS suitable for a GRT that supports distribution. As such, it adds additional interface-supporting interaction between the distributed instances of its subclasses in the various address spaces in which the GRT is running. It provides a method (::dispatch) to be used to dispatch incoming messages from its peers to the correct method or component of the GRT. It also provides a number of methods that are expected to be called in instances on receiving a message from one of their remote peers. ::resolve is to be called at a remote instance in response to an invocation of ::apply on the instance of OwlDistributedGlobalReferenceToLocation in some address space. Likewise, ::remoteInsert and ::remoteRemove may be called at remote instances in response to a call to ::insert or ::remove on some instance. ::reg and ::unreg are expected to be used by instances to keep track of their peers.

As an example of specializing the LS to support different object fault resolution strategies, OwlRPCDistributedGlobalReferenceToLocation describes an LS suitable for a GRT that supports distribution and provides a ROI interface to supported LSRTs. It extends OwlDistributedGlobalReferenceToLocation by overloading ::apply to accept a ROI request that can be forwarded to the appropriate target object in the appropriate address space—possibly having created the address space if necessary.

Finally, any of the different variations of OwlGlobalReferenceToLocation$_{sc}$ can be further specialized to support DSM-style access to objects by overloading ::apply to take an address input and supporting an appropriate protocol between the instances of OwlGlobalReferenceToLocation to resolve the implied object fault, as exemplified by, for example, OwlFaultDistributedGlobalReferenceToLocation.

20.7 Summary

To date, the design of the first complete version of the framework has been completed, and a number of simple instantiations have been implemented. [Taylor 1994b] describes the first Tigger instantiation implemented. The so-called T1 instantiation supports an extension to C++ for distributed and persistent programming inspired by Panda/C++ [Assenmacher 1993]. T1 is a single-extent Tigger instantiation layered above Unix that implements a single distributed and persistent address space and supports DSM-style access to global and persistent objects. Object faults are detected as memory protection faults. No swizzling is employed, and virtual addresses are used as GREFs. In addition, T1 supports application-directed clustering. Another Tigger instantiation supporting a prototype of a novel object model providing application-consistent DSM [Judge 1996] has also been implemented.

The majority of existing runtime systems designed to support distributed and persistent objects can support only a single language or else severely constrain the way in which different languages can be supported—in particular, by supporting only a single object model. In contrast, Tigger provides a framework for the construction of runtime systems supporting distributed and persistent objects that can be tailored for use in a variety of different application domains. The two primary goals of this design are to allow instantiations of the framework to support a number of different object models and to allow the same object model to be supported in different ways subject to differing nonfunctional requirements.

An important contribution of this work is the design of a framework for language runtime systems that allows a wide range of object-oriented programming languages for distributed or persistent programming to be supported in a way that does not impose particular constructs and models on the language. Moreover, when an existing language is being supported, the design does not necessarily require changes to its compiler nor to its native object reference format or local invocation mechanism. Although framework technology is well established and the use of frameworks to implement customized operating systems is not new, the use of a framework as the basis for implementing customized object-support systems is novel. The Tigger framework provides a common basis for the implementation of a range of object-oriented programming languages for distributed and persistent programming that encompass different nonfunctional requirements, such as heterogeneity or protection.

20.8 References

[Assenmacher 1993] Assenmacher, H., T. Breitbach, P. Buhler, V. Huebsch, and R. Schwarz. PANDA: Supporting distributed programming in C++. *Proceedings of the 1993 European Conference on Object-Oriented Programming (ECOOP 1993).* Lecture Notes in Computer Science 707. Springer-Verlag, 1993: 361–383.

[Booch 1994] Booch, G. *Object-Oriented Analysis and Design with Applications.* Redwood City, CA: Benjamin/Cummings, 1994.

[Burke 1996] Burke, G. Kanga: A framework for building application specific communication protocols. Master's thesis, Department of Computer Science, Trinity College, Dublin, Ireland, 1996.

[Cahill 1993] Cahill, V., S. Baker, G. Starovic, and C. Horn. Generic runtime support for distributed persistent programming. *Proceedings of the OOPSLA 1993 Conference on Object-Oriented Programming Systems, Languages and Applications,* Washington, DC. New York: ACM Press, 1993:144–161.

[Cahill 1996] Cahill, V. On the architecture of a family of object-support operating systems. Ph.D. thesis, Department of Computer Science, Trinity College, Dublin, Ireland, 1996.

[Cahill 1997] Cahill, V., P. Nixon, B. Tangney, and F. Rabhi. Object models for distributed or persistent programming. *Computer Journal,* 40(8), 1997: 513–527.

[Campbell 1992] Campbell, R., N. Islam, and P. Madany. Choices, frameworks and refinement. *Computing Systems,* 5(3), 1992: 217–257.

[DSG 1992] Distributed Systems Group. *C** Programmer's Guide (Amadeus v2.0).* Technical Report TCD-CS-92-03. Department of Computer Science, Trinity College, Dublin, Ireland, 1992.

[Horn-Cahill 1991] Horn, C., and V. Cahill. Supporting distributed applications in the Amadeus environment. *Computer Communications,* 14(6), July/August 1991: 358–365.

[Judge 1996] Judge, A. Supporting application-consistent distributed shared objects. Ph.D. thesis, Department of Computer Science, Trinity College, Dublin, Ireland, 1996.

[Kröger 1990] Kröger, R., M. Mock, R. Schumann, and F. Lange. RelaX: An extensible architecture supporting reliable distributed applications. *Proceedings of the IEEE Ninth Symposium on Reliable Distributed Systems,* pp. 156–165, Los Alamitos, CA, IEEE Computer Society, 1990.

[McEvoy 1993] McEvoy, J.E. Porting the E database language to Amadeus. Master's thesis, Department of Computer Science, Trinity College, Dublin, Ireland, 1993.

[McHugh 1993] McHugh, C., and V. Cahill. Eiffel: An implementation of Eiffel on Amadeus, a persistent, distributed applications support environment. *Proceedings of the 10th Technology of Object-Oriented Languages and Systems Conference (TOOLS 10),* pp. 47–62, 1993.

[Milne 1928] Milne, A.A. *The House at Pooh Corner.* London: Methuen, 1928.

[Mock 1992] Mock, M., R. Kröger, and V. Cahill. Implementing atomic objects with the RelaX transaction facility. *Computing Systems,* 5(3), 1992: 259–304.

[O'Grady 1994] O'Grady, D. An extensible, high-performance, distributed persistent store for Amadeus. Master's thesis, Department of Computer Science, Trinity College, Dublin, Ireland, 1994.

[Ooi 1993] Ooi, J.L. Access control for an object-oriented distributed platform. Master's thesis, Department of Computer Science, Trinity College, Dublin, Ireland, 1993.

[Schröder-Preikschat 1994] Schröder-Preikschat, W. *The Logical Design of Parallel Operating Systems*. London: Prentice Hall, 1994.

[Sousa 1993] Sousa, P., M. Sequeira, A. Zúquete, P. Ferreira, C. Lopes, J. Pereira, P. Guedes, and J. Alves Marques. Distribution and persistence in the IK platform: Overview and evaluation. *Computing Systems,* 6(4), 1993: 391–424.

[Taylor 1994a] Taylor, P. *The T1 Cub.* Tigger document T16-94. Distributed Systems Group, Department of Computer Science, Trinity College, Dublin, Ireland, 1994.

[Taylor 1994b] Taylor, P., V. Cahill, and M. Mock. Combining object-oriented systems and open transaction processing. *Computer Journal,* 37(6), 1994: 487–498.

CHAPTER 21

The Déjà Vu Scheduling Class Library

Modern production management has to face considerable organizational problems due to the shifting from mass production to more specialized small-lot-size production. The production of smaller lot sizes and the requirements for fast reactions to market demands pose a manifold of constraints on the usage of available resources on the shop floor level. To be competitive in the global market, companies must especially solve the efficient coordination in their production to avoid as much as possible of the hidden costs.

The adequate coordination of all activities that have to be performed to fulfill customers' orders is a key process to eliminate these costs. Due to the diversity of products as well as the diversity of required resources, such as human resources, machines, energy, and others, it becomes impossible to realize such scheduling systems with standard software. Each production unit is unique and requires dedicated solutions; moreover, it will change due to new production technologies and changing market demands.

Thus, a promising software engineering technique is application frameworks that offer reusable semicomplete applications that can be specialized to produce custom applications [Fayad-Schmidt 1997]. An application framework is based on a domain analysis that states the basic assumptions on a number of related applications. The input to such a domain analysis is due to several sources, such as literature, existing implementations, customer surveys, and more [Prieto-Díaz 1990]. For the domain of production scheduling, there exists a huge body of theory [Bazewicz 1993; Conway 1967; French 1982] and a lot of dedicated journals; however, all these theories have an idealized view of scheduling applications. They abstract from real-world problems. Software developers are expected to reuse the design of such theories (mainly algorithms). How production data is gathered, how information is displayed to a user, and how the user can participate in the solution are not treated in these approaches. Typically, these interfaces are the most tedious development work.

As a consequence, high-level scheduling languages were devised to improve the efficiency of developing scheduling systems. Systems such as ISIS [Fox 1994], OPIS [Smith 1994], or SONIA [Le Pape 1994] offer a constraint-based language to the developer to express scheduling problems. The architecture of the system is predefined, and the scheduling algorithm is more or less fixed; the user can only tune the applied heuristics. There have also been attempts to build application generators for scheduling systems—for example, the Protos-System [Sauer 1993]—but the success of such generators in industrial practice was small. Today, several research groups see the limited reusability of both approaches. For example, the Robotics Institute of Carnegie Mellon University, a very well known group for intelligent scheduling systems, has also just started to design a scheduling framework (OZONE/DITOPS Project, www.cs .cmu.edu/afs/cs/project/ozone/www/DITOPS/ditops.html).

The Déjà Vu scheduling class library is such an application framework for modern production scheduling. Based on a broad domain analysis and the development of two industrial scheduling systems, we started to develop this framework in 1995. This chapter describes the basic assumptions that led to the design of the scheduling framework and describes how dedicated applications can be produced with Déjà Vu.

21.1 Design Principles of Déjà Vu

Déjà Vu is a framework of C++ classes to support developers in the construction of scheduling systems for industrial production processes. The design of the framework was directed by the following criteria:

- The scheduler's evaluation of a schedule is based on the evaluation of individual constraints and their weighted aggregation.

- The user has the full control over the scheduling process, with the ability to experiment with different settings.

- The scheduler applies iterative improvement methods to optimize solutions.

- The framework should be extendible and refinable.

The goal is to support the construction of dedicated scheduling systems for a specific application rather than to develop a system capable of scheduling different applications.

21.1.1 Constraint-Based Representation of Schedules

Scheduling is an activity controlled by constraints and guided by several objective functions. Usually, scheduling is described as a problem of satisfying temporal constraints. However, temporal constraints, such as processing times or due dates, and objectives, such as minimization of the makespan or of the mean flow time, are often insufficient to represent industrial problems. The Déjà Vu framework supports further constraints and objectives, such as compatibility constraints (chemical and format), idle time constraints, minimization of substitutable resources, restricted capacity, or equilibrium loads of sharable resources. These constraint types have been derived from several scheduling problems in the steel industry. Other constraint types for new domains can be generated by deriving constraint types from existing types with minimal effort due to the general approach to represent them.

From a software engineering point of view, we achieve this by defining a standard interface for constraints. Thus, it is possible to call constraint methods in other components without knowing which constraints are defined for a certain application. If a new kind of constraint must be defined for an application, only the new constraint class must be defined. An application-specific class can then call the constructor method without any further manipulations.

Many constraints of industrial production environments are soft and can be relaxed. Moreover, constraints may be contradictory, and a tradeoff between constraints must be found for a good solution. Déjà Vu meets these requirements as follows: A constraint is a relation between two or more scheduling objects. The relation is mapped on a satisfaction degree that evaluates how well this constraint is satisfied in the actual schedule. Different constraint types obtain a domain-dependent weight reflecting the constraint's importance. A schedule is evaluated by a weighted aggregation of all satisfaction degrees. Further, for each constraint type, a threshold can be specified to decide whether the constraint violation is hard. The constraint's weight and threshold can be modified in a scheduling session to experiment with different settings.

21.1.2 Interactive Scheduling

An automatic scheduler cannot consider all aspects relevant to the evaluation of a schedule, because the environment of industrial scheduling systems is too complex and many quantities cannot be measured. The complexity also comes from the ever-changing production environment: New machines are erected, new production techniques and objectives are regularly developed, and the demand for products changes. The software must, therefore, be adaptable and under full control of the user to overrule outdated system rules. Although production control and planning software should support human personnel as far as possible, the responsibility should remain in human hands. Mixed-initiative scheduling is a paradigm that solves the described problem best. The user always has either the ability to let the system schedule automatically or to perform some scheduling tasks manually. The user should always be able to change the schedule that was constructed by the system, but the system should show new conflicts effected by this change to the user. Furthermore, the user should have the ability to freeze some part of the schedule and let the system improve the remaining part. Déjà Vu supports mixed-initiative scheduling by defining *scheduling tasks* for schedule alterations that provide a common interface with methods for undoing, redoing, evaluating, and so on.

21.1.3 Iterative Improvement Methods

An iterative improvement method is an optimization technique that starts with an initial solution and tries to find better solutions by local modifications. The initial schedule can be constructed randomly, by some constructive method, or by a heuristic method. It can also be created by a human or by another computer process. To modify given schedules, scheduling tasks are used to transform a schedule into a new and similar schedule. A scheduling task can be, for example, the exchange of two adjacent jobs, or the move of an operation from one machine to another machine having the same capabilities. Scheduling tasks always construct legal schedules that do not violate hard constraints. If several tasks are applicable, a procedure must choose the task to be applied. This selection can be made randomly or with some look-ahead, allowing the task leading to the best neighbor to be performed. To determine whether an improvement can be achieved by a task, the comparison of schedules by an evaluation function must be possible. The most efficient look-ahead is achieved when the schedule evaluation can be determined locally.

A simple hill-climbing algorithm would accept only schedules that evaluate better. Unfortunately, scheduling problems usually have many solutions that differ in their quality, and good solutions are not direct neighbors. Therefore, a search method based on local improvements can easily be trapped in a local optimum. An important feature of all iterative improvement methods, therefore, is the capability to escape from local optima. However, with this ability, it becomes more likely to search in cycles, and some kind of control to avoid repetition is needed.

Déjà Vu allows the user to select between different improvement methods (tabu search, simulated annealing, iterative deepening, and genetic algorithms) and to set different parameters of these algorithms individually. Furthermore, if a combination of techniques seems to be appropriate (for example, tabu search with some stochastic technique), this can easily be realized by derived classes, because the optimization algorithms are also designed as classes that can be inherited. Experimental comparisons of these algorithms with data from the VA Stahl Linz LD3 plant are described in [Dorn 1996], and important design issues for iterative improvement methods are described in [Dorn 1995a].

21.1.4 Reusability of the Scheduling Framework

The design criteria mentioned so far have led to a software architecture that should be applicable to a wide range of scheduling applications. The main principle to support the reusability of the developed framework is the object-oriented design with the support of some well known design patterns [Gamma 1995], such as the following:

The abstract factory. Create a domain-dependent schedule object without specifying its concrete class.

The factory method. Create domain-dependent orders in the domain-independent order director class.

Chain of responsibility. Give the most specific or selected user interface element the first chance to react to a user action and to pass it to its supervisor if the element does not know how to react.

Command. Encapsulate a user action as an object that has a common interface for undoing or redoing the action.

Iterator. Provide a way to access elements of an aggregate object, such as a list of constraints, sequentially, without knowing its implementation.

Observer. When an object such as a schedule changes, all dependents should be notified without being called by the scheduling object.

More design patterns will be partly explained later.

However, the critical task in designing reusable software (or reusable classes) is always to foresee the potential extensions and problems of new applications. A good practice is to implement existing theoretical frameworks, because they are based on abstractions of many practical applications. Especially in scheduling, there is a large amount of theoretical work offering many forms for such a design. Objects such as *order, job, operation, resource, allocation,* and *schedule,* or their synonyms, exist in almost every theoretical investigation. Also, the associations between these objects are obvious. Unfortunately, this theoretical work does not integrate user interaction with schedule optimization. As previously mentioned, the user of complex industrial applications should be capable of modifying a proposed solution of the system.

Our approach to support the reuse is as follows: The core of Déjà Vu is a framework of classes realizing basic scheduling theory. Furthermore, basic forms for the representation of constraints are realized by abstract classes. For example, many constraints, such as due dates or release dates, refer to attributes of a job. Thus, we have defined an abstract class for job constraints.

The abstract core enables an application and platform-independent definition of the following tasks and entities:

Schedule evaluation. All constraints stored in a constraint list are evaluated and aggregated.

Scheduling tasks. Exchange of operations on a resource, exchange of jobs, and so on.

Algorithms. Apply and compare applicable scheduling tasks to find better schedules.

Graphic entities. Windows, panes, and text fields, for example, to represent scheduling objects on the user's desktop.

On top of this core we have implemented common specialization as a job-shop or flow-shop schedule and several optimization algorithms. A further derivation layer consists of specific classes for subdomains. At the moment, there exists one subdomain for steel-making applications, and we are just designing another subdomain for computer scheduling.

21.2 The Scheduling Core

The main scheduling object is a schedule. It stores the temporal allocation of operations for all resources. There may be different instances of a schedule because the optimization algorithm must store intermediate schedules, and the user will be able to experiment with different settings, thus constructing different schedules. The user must be able to return to schedules produced earlier. A schedule object consists of three conceptual parts:

- A list of resources with scheduled allocations
- A list of jobs with their operations
- A list of constraints

The main design criteria for a schedule are the following:

- The representation should be as flexible as possible to enable the representation of schedules of different applications with different resources and jobs.
- Support of scheduling tasks should be initiated either by a user or an iterative improvement method.
- Scheduling tasks must be very efficient to provide users with immediate feedback and to fasten the optimization algorithms.
- A schedule should be an object that can be copied easily (especially optimization techniques such as Genetic Algorithms that rely heavily on an efficient technique to produce new schedules).

Flexibility and efficiency are two potentially conflicting objectives for which a tradeoff must be found. To achieve this, we use a high degree of pointer arithmetic for the core schedule instead of pure object-oriented representation. Thus, the lists are realized as pointer arrays based on the template mechanism of C++. The lists can be extended dynamically and store only pointers, because we do not know in advance how much storage is needed for the objects. A resource points to a double-linked list of allocations that store time points when operations are performed on the resource. A job points to a double-linked list of allocations describing the operations of the job.

The dynamic links between allocations support the algorithm that checks and enforces temporal consistency of all allocated operations. Each time an allocation is moved in the schedule, the start and end points of the adjacent allocations must be adjusted. The adjustment of another allocation will be propagated. This consistency mechanism is complete because only simple temporal algebra is used. The efficiency of the mechanism relies strongly on the linkage structure.

The sequence of the jobs in the list of all jobs also represents the sequence of jobs in the schedule. When this sequence is changed by a scheduling task, this change is further propagated to each resource on which this job is also scheduled to move the allocation accordingly. Figure 21.1 illustrates the *core* schedule representation.

An abstract root schedule class already realizes many methods sufficient for handling schedules. Its main service provided to other classes is the temporal consistency-enforcing mechanism that ensures that specified temporal relations between allocations hold. However, a schedule is specialized to reflect certain characteristics of job shops, flow shops, and schedules consisting of only one machine. For a certain application, we may further specialize to represent in this class application-specific information and to overload general methods by more efficient domain-dependent strategies. For example, a schedule has a method that generates a set of scheduling tasks that can be applied to find a neighbor. The basic abstract schedule class does not define this method because

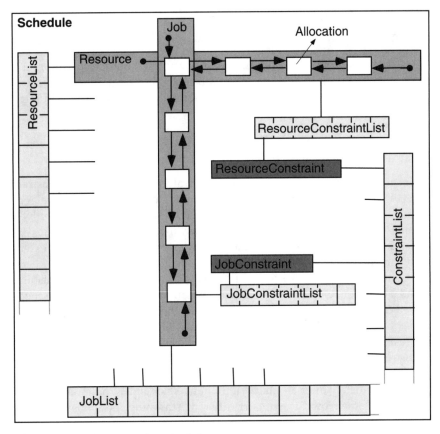

Figure 21.1   Structure of a schedule.

the differences between a flow shop and a job shop are too great. The flow-shop schedule realizes a very general version that generates many tasks, and the schedule class for a dedicated application may generate a smaller set by applying heuristics, which results in a more efficient search through the neighborhood.

Methods dependent on the schedule type are the methods that realize different scheduling tasks. The efficiency of scheduling tasks is supported if inverse scheduling tasks can be defined. In this case, whole schedules do not have to be copied. Moving a job from one position to another in a flow shop is more efficient, because its operations are in the same sequence for both jobs and its inverse task can be defined easily by storing the old position. In a job shop, it is not clear what an exchange of two jobs means. The jobs may be allocated on different resources that cannot be used for the other job. Moreover, two jobs may be scheduled simultaneously. We can define the move, but for the inverse task we must return to the old schedule by copying the old schedule. For a flow shop, the move of single operations is not useful. Each schedule type has its own method for deciding which scheduling tasks are applicable and how they are performed, if possible.

21.2.1 Temporal Reasoning Component

Temporal reasoning is an inference that occurs in every scheduling application and should always be reusable. The developer should be able to select different characteristics of how temporal reasoning is applied in different applications. Two different types of temporal knowledge must be supported:

- Quantitative time (Monday, 10 P.M.)

- Qualitative temporal relations (operation 1 must start before operation 2)

A *time point* is the basic class to represent temporal knowledge. It is an abstract datatype with overloaded operators and access methods. Currently, two temporal representations are supported: Time can be represented by a simple long integer, or by a week time consisting of the number of the week, a day, an hour, and minutes. The representation is selected by a simple class variable. The design also allows an easy extension for fuzzy time points.

Time points are used to define *time intervals* consisting of a starting and a finishing time point and a duration. Other classes, such as allocation, operation, job, and schedule, are derived classes, which means that each object of these classes has a starting and finishing time point, and, of course, they reuse the methods defined for intervals.

Temporal relations are hard temporal constraints on the sequence of intervals. Simple sequencing relations, such as before or after, occur in almost every application. Furthermore, we define a *meets* relation and its inverse relation, which constrain two intervals to be immediately after another without any slack time. These relations are defined as a class of their own to support different reasoning mechanisms. In the future, we also want to support the full expressiveness of Allen's interval calculus [Allen 1983] with 13 different relations. Whether we can support the same propagation as Allen is still under investigation, because its combinatorial complexity is intractable.

21.2.2 Orders and Jobs

An *order* contains a description of one or more *products* to be produced and a process plan that describes how to produce these products. The *process plan* contains the required operations and their prescribed sequences. Furthermore, an order may have attributes, such as a priority, and constraints, such as the release and the due dates. A *job* describes the performance of an order in the shop floor. A job may be scheduled to produce several orders. However, the main conceptual difference is the specification of the planned starting and finishing times for the scheduled operations. In contrast, the order describes only the requirements.

In some domains (especially flow-shop domains), the order does not need to have an explicit process plan to describe the required operations and their temporal dependencies because the sequence is the same for all jobs. In this case, a job is generated from an order by following predefined rules of application. A process plan is then constructed for the job.

When a job is generated from an order, some attributes, such as the release and the due dates, are copied into the job. However, a job also has a pointer to its order to enable computations dependent on the produced goods that are not represented in the job object. A job points to its first and last allocations, which are linked in the allocation network. For a simple job in a flow shop, the chain of allocations describes a sequence of operations. If a more complex temporal dependency must be described, interval relations are used [Dorn 1995b]. Jobs have a unique identifier to enable pointing to the same job in two schedules. Furthermore, a job maintains its own list of *job constraints*. If certain operations of a job are modified, the job updates these constraints accordingly. If, for example, the last operation is moved, the tardiness constraint must be updated if it exists.

21.2.3 Capacitive Reasoning Component

Operations to be performed require prescribed resources. These resources have typically restricted capacity. There are resources that can handle only one operation at a time (for example, a machine) and there are resources (for example, a stock) that have restricted capacity but that several operations may use at the same time.

A *resource* object stores the operations that are to be performed on it. For the set of all resources, an array of unlimited length is used because the schedule class will not already be restricted to a certain application with a predefined number of resources. The resources and the array are generated from a description of the application in a derived class of the *scheduler* class. If an additional resource is to be considered in the schedule, no modification of the scheduler class is necessary. Pointers to resources are stored instead of the resources themselves, because the usage of different resources requiring different memory space will be supported. Resources maintain their own list of *resource constraints*, and they have a list of so-called *working zones*, which are time intervals that describe time periods when the resource is usable. Therefore, if a machine is broken down or in maintenance, these periods are not included.

Different kinds of resources are distinguished; from the resource abstract class the nonsharable resource, sharable resource, and resource group classes are derived.

Allocations

An *allocation* assigns an operation that is part of a job to a resource. Simple allocations are used for resources that can perform only one operation at a time and, thus, cannot overlap. Allocations on a resource are linked forwards and backwards. For the basic type of allocation, this sequence also means a temporal sequence, but the derived *capacitive allocation* may overlap. An allocation is assigned a number, making it unique to a resource. This is necessary because we store a pointer to an allocation in a *scheduling task* to exchange two allocations, for example. We need a unique identification to point to the same allocation in two schedules. To find the job and the resource object to which the allocation belongs, two pointers to these objects are stored. Further pointers to the next and to the previous allocations of the job exist. If a predecessor allocation exists on the resource, one or more *allocation constraints* may be stored for this allocation. Another derived class is defined for allocations having a sequence that is constrained by compatibility constraints.

Nonsharable Resources

On a *nonsharable resource,* operations are allocated that are required for a job. These allocations are stored in a double-linked list, whereby the sequence in the list also reflects the temporal sequence. The link structure is also more efficient for scheduling tasks such as swapping allocations or moving an allocation to another place. A nonsharable resource has a pointer to the first and the last allocations of the resource.

A nonsharable resource knows how to perform scheduling tasks such as allocating an operation, swapping an allocation, moving an allocation to another place on the resource, or deleting an allocation. It may have defined attributes such as minimal idle time or required setups. If the nonsharable resource allocates operations or modifies the allocations, it maintains the constraints derived from the idle time and the setup attributes accordingly.

Sharable Resources

A *sharable resource* can be used by several jobs simultaneously. An example is the space to store products. This space is often limited, but several products produced in different jobs may be stored at the same time. Another example is a group of workers that may handle several jobs simultaneously. Because such resources are limited and different operations may require different amounts of the resource, a capacitive allocation is used to incorporate additional attributes for size and amount. Scheduling tasks such as moving or shifting an allocation must be realized for sharable resources. The maximal capacity of a sharable resource is a hard constraint, but a soft constraint that could be considered is the equilibrium load. A typical example is energy consumption, which has an upper limit. For a cheap production, however, it is important to distribute the energy consumption as much as possible over the whole production period, because peaks of high energy consumption are often expensive.

Resource Groups

A *resource group* is used to represent a group of almost identical resources. For the production process it makes no difference which of them is used, because all have the same capabilities. Yet, objectives such as minimizing the number of used resources and constraints on subsequent allocations may constrain the usage of the group. The only scheduling task a resource group must support is the move of an operation from one of its resources to another. Other tasks are deferred to the individual resources. A special method of a resource group is that which finds the best resource for an allocation. The resource group will return the first resource that is free for the desired interval. Derived classes will overload this method with more sophisticated heuristics.

21.3 Schedule Evaluation

The evaluation of schedules in Déjà Vu is based on the evaluation of individual *constraints.* Constraint types are differentiated and we define, for example, tardiness and makespan constraints. If all tardiness constraints of a schedule are evaluated, the tardiness of jobs is a *measure* of the schedule. For a certain application, different constraint types or measures can be defined. In a preference-setting dialog, the user can select which of the defined measures shall be evaluated for the next schedule construction process. These settings can be assigned to a schedule, thus constructing schedules with different evaluation settings, which are used to support what-if games in the sense that a user neglects some constraints to see whether this leads to a better schedule.

21.3.1 Constraint Evaluation

A constraint is a relation between two or more scheduling objects or attributes of scheduling objects mapped on a satisfaction degree that evaluates how well the constraint is satisfied in the actual schedule. A typical example of such a relation is the tardiness of a job. A due date indicates when a certain job should be completed, which is related to the scheduled finishing time. The relation is mapped on a satisfaction degree that evaluates how well this constraint is satisfied. If the finishing time equals the due date, the satisfaction of this constraint is considered to be very good; otherwise, it is considered to be poor. A relaxed form in which a too-early completion is also considered to be good is realized by a *tardiness constraint*. In Figure 21.2, the satisfaction of a tardiness constraint is used as a prototype to illustrate how the satisfaction of a constraint may be specified and how it is computed for a given relation.

If a job has a defined due date, and the tardiness measure has been selected by the user, the job class creates a tardiness constraint in its constructor having two parameters, OptimalDeviation and LeastAcceptableDeviation. If the deviation between due date and finishing time is smaller than the optimal deviation, the constraint evaluates to 1.0. If it is larger than the least acceptable deviation, it evaluates to 0. Otherwise, it is computed as follows:

$$\text{Satisfaction }(J_i) = \frac{(\text{LeastAcceptableDeviation} - |\,\text{DueDate }(J_i) - \text{FinishingTime }(J_i)\,|)}{(\text{LeastAcceptableDeviation} - \text{OptimalDeviation})}$$

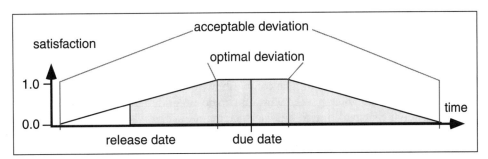

Figure 21.2 Satisfaction degree of a tardiness constraint.

21.3.2 Constraint Types

Below the abstract constraint class, four further abstract constraint classes are defined describing relations between different scheduling objects. An *allocation constraint* is a relation between an allocation and its predecessor on a resource. If this sequence or the distance to the predecessor is changed, the allocation updates this constraint. A *job constraint* is a relation over different attributes of a job. If one of these attributes is changed, the constraint is updated by the job. A *resource constraint* describes a relation between different objects and attributes of this resource. The update is initiated by the scheduling object if all changes on this resource are finished. The fourth kind is a form for constraints relating objects of the whole schedule. The *schedule constraint* is maintained by the schedule. The four described abstract classes support the construction of new constraint types by defining a common interface and a predefined mechanism to create and update them. Only the scheduling objects know this interface, and the allocation can update a constraint without knowing which actual constraint type it is. If a new allocation constraint type is defined, a derived class of an allocation has to insert this constraint, but no further changes need to be made.

All constraints defined below the four classes are concrete classes. These constraint types describe actual relations between scheduling objects. After being updated, they will have a satisfaction degree, which is used to evaluate a schedule. To reflect that different constraint types have different importance for the application, constraint types are associated with a weight factor between 0 and 1. The sum for all types is defined as 1. If several constraint types are defined, a weight of .4, for example, means that the constraint type has a great influence on the evaluation function. Another attribute describes a threshold to differentiate soft and hard constraint violations. A constraint satisfaction below this threshold indicates that the constraint must be repaired to get a legal schedule. If the threshold is set to 0, no repair will be necessary.

A special constraint that should be elaborated upon is the *compatibility constraint*, with its two specializations, *chemical constraint* and *format constraint*. A compatibility constraint is a relation between subsequent operations that assigns a value to this pair of operations, reflecting how optimal it is to schedule each after the other. In the process industry, resources are often infiltrated with residuals of the produced goods, which may spill subsequent products. This infiltration can either be accepted (if small enough), or some cleaning operation must be scheduled as well. A compatibility constraint can represent the cost of a cleaning operation or the quality loss due to the infiltration. For some processes, such as steelmaking, cleaning operations are either not possible or are too expensive. Therefore, it is important to find sequences that incorporate only small infiltrations. Thus, the threshold cannot be 0. Similar constraints exist for some machines, such as, for example, rolling mills, on the format or size that can be described by a format constraint. The compatibility constraints can be seen as a prototype of the manner in which new constraints can be integrated into the framework. For allocations having such a compatibility aspect, the *compatible allocation* class is derived from an allocation. When certain conditions hold, the allocation creates a compatibility constraint. Compatibility constraints and the way they are handled are explained in more detail in [Dorn-Slany 1994].

21.4 User Interaction

The design of Déjà Vu is user oriented, which means that the user always has control over the scheduling activities. The system supports the user as far as possible: The user shouldn't be unnecessarily restricted, although senseless actions should be prevented. The system should disable actions that violate hard constraints. For example, the system does not allow an operation to be moved to a resource that is not capable of performing the operation. On the other hand, the user should be capable of examining solutions that are evaluated poorly by the system. An inexperienced user should be supported by indicating the possible actions; an experienced user should be able to perform the manipulation of the schedule with as few keystrokes or mouse actions as possible.

21.4.1 The Supervision Hierarchy

User actions are context dependent. The system must know which actions are allowed in a certain context, and which modifications must be made if an allowed action is performed. To determine this, one has to model which part of the user interface is active. Typically, the frontmost window is active and only actions manipulating this window are enabled. A window itself may contain different panes, of which one pane may be active (or selected). Then, only commands for this pane or commands that change the status (deactivate this pane and activate another) are allowed. However, if a pane of the window is active, there are still commands associated with the enclosing window or with the whole application. To model this flexible behavior, two control hierarchies are defined:

Supervision hierarchy. If the pane has no command handler or its command handler does not handle the actual command, the command is given to its supervisor.

Visual enclosure hierarchy. If a mouse click cannot be handled by the pane, it is deferred to its enclosing view.

An object that can handle a user action is called a *bureaucrat*. Each bureaucrat has a *supervisor*, which is again a bureaucrat. If the bureaucrat cannot handle the command itself, it is deferred to its supervisor. The topmost supervisor, having no other supervisor, is the scheduler itself. The scheduler also defines the principal course of a scheduling session by internal states that decide which commands are to be enabled. Therefore, the user can first open a list of orders, which are visualized in an *order window*. Then, these orders may be scheduled and visualized either by a gantt chart in the *schedule window* or by a simple list chart in a *resource window*. The user may then change the schedule interactively or start an optimization search that can be stopped at any time.

A static variable of the scheduler, theExpert, always points to the most specialized bureaucrat that is in the focus of the last action. For example, if the user clicks into an *allocation pane* that visualizes an allocation in the gantt chart, then commands manipulating single allocations are enabled. If the user clicks on the menu bar, the actual supervision hierarchy, from the expert up to the application object, is responsible for deciding which menus and which menu items are enabled. Each bureaucrat informs the menu bar which commands it allows.

If the user selects (for example, by a mouse click) some visual object in a window, this object becomes the expert (for example, the allocation pane). If a new window is created, either its supervisor—a *director*—may become the expert, or some subview may become the expert. This expert is the first in the supervision hierarchy to react to a user command and the last one in the chain of this hierarchy to enable commands.

User actions can be classified into five basic categories:

- Selecting a visual object (with a mouse-click or a special key, such as an arrow key)

- Typing characters with the keyboard

- Calling a menu command either by mouse or a command sequence

- Moving the mouse

- Tracking an object with the mouse

The basic techniques to perform these user actions are a mouse click, a key stroke, and moving the mouse. For the first type, the system decides to which part of the display the mouse points. Three main parts are differentiated with their associated classes: the menu bar, a window, or the desktop. A message to process the mouse click is sent to the appropriate class object, either TheMenubar, TheDesktop, or an instance of the window class.

If the user clicks on the menu bar, a menu shows all possible commands. A command item can be dimmed to reflect that the command is disabled in the actual context. To establish the menu according to the actual context, all command items are first disabled, then an update method is sent to the expert to enable all the commands that are allowed in the context of this bureaucrat. Before the bureaucrat enables commands, it allows its supervisor to enable commands by calling the update method of its supervisor. Thus, the expert can also disable a command that was enabled by its supervisor, and it can overwrite the text of a command.

If a window is not active, it is activated by a mouse click. If it is already active, the window class differentiates which part of the window the mouse points to. If the mouse click is inside the window, the subview of the window in which the click was performed is determined. The click can be processed by a method of the visual object (also a bureaucrat). If the object does not define this method, the system looks upward in the visual hierarchy to determine whether another object can process the click. The *visual hierarchy* is a hierarchy of enclosing views. If a new visual object is defined, such as a pane, its constructor is called with an argument representing its enclosing view. This reference is also used to define the position of the new subview by specifying relative coordinates. The enclosing view appends the new view in its list of subviews.

21.4.2 Scheduling Tasks

Scheduling tasks are a paradigm for the coupling of automatic scheduling with user actions and are derived from concepts in model-based knowledge acquisition [Bylander 1988]. In principle, each action that a user can perform is modeled as a scheduling task. A scheduling task is described by a class that provides all types of tasks in a uniform interface. If a new task is to be defined, all methods of this interface must be realized. If a task is initiated by the user, all necessary data is stored to enable an undo or a redo. The definition of an inverse task also supports the iterative improvement methods. In such a search method, a scheduling task is applied to check whether a task leads to an improvement. To evaluate the schedule, we must usually adjust the operations and the jobs of the schedule. If we want to check for other alternatives, we must return to the old schedule. For complex applications, it is more efficient to have an inverse task that undoes the last change, rather than copying a whole schedule. In cases in which no inverse task can be specified, the whole schedule must be stored before performing the task. In addition, for tabu search the inverse tasks are used as a tabu criterion, thus forbidding cycles during search.

The realization of scheduling tasks is dependent on the schedule type. The performance in a job shop and in a flow shop can thus differentiate, and some tasks are not applicable in all schedule types. For example, the move of an operation in a flow shop and the exchange of a job in a job shop are not allowed. The following scheduling tasks are defined:

- Allocate a job as early as possible.
- Allocate a job after another job.
- Allocate a job at a certain time.
- Remove a job (back into the list of orders).
- Exchange two adjacent jobs.
- Move a job to another position.
- Exchange an operation with an adjacent operation.
- Move an operation to another place on the resource.
- Move an operation to another resource.
- Shift an operation.

This set can be extended easily if other tasks become necessary for an application.

21.4.3 Graphical Schedule Visualization

Figure 21.3 shows the different available views on a schedule of the Böhler application. The main schedule window in the background (lower part on the left side) shows the whole schedule in a gantt chart that can be scrolled. Resources and their allocations are shown below each other. The topmost resource in the window is an electric arc furnace (EAF), followed by a group of ladles, a horizontal continuous caster (HCC), and a BEST (Böhler Edelstahl Slack Topping) unit. The allocations on these resources are depicted by small boxes (allocation panes). The last two resources are sharable resources describing the space requirements in the teeming bay and the load of the workers in the teeming bay.

Two panes in the bottom window show the total evaluation and, in this case, the mean chemical compatibility. With a pop-up menu, other measures can also be selected.

By clicking the panes in the window, the user can select allocations and jobs in order to move them to other places in the schedule. If an allocation or a job is selected, menu commands can also be applied to the selected object.

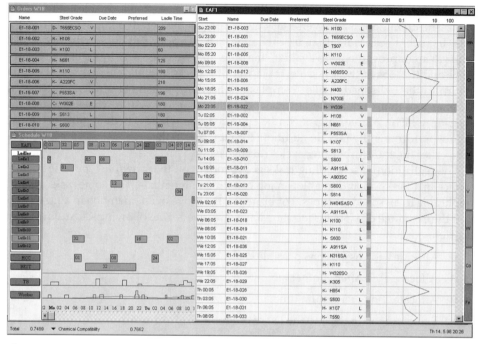

Figure 21.3   GUI of the Böhler application.

The information shown in the schedule window is sometimes insufficient. With a double-click on the resource name's pane, a resource window that shows the sequence of its allocations as a list is created. Figure 21.3 shows a window for the electric arc furnace. On the right side is a logarithmic diagram that visualizes the chemical content of subsequent orders on the furnace.

21.5 Reusability of Déjà Vu

The general Déjà Vu class library consists of about 150 classes, of which one-third implement the user interface. On top of this framework we have built about 20 classes (user interface and scheduling theory) for steelmaking applications that address particularly the problem of compatibilities. At the top of our application for the Böhler Kapfenberg steelmaking plant are 10 domain-specific classes. Figure 21.4 shows the architecture of the Déjà Vu class library.

The scheduler for the Böhler company in Kapfenberg, Austria, schedules heats in a steelmaking plant. This application (described in detail in [Dorn-Shams 1996]) is a prototype for industrial applications, characterized by a lot of domain-dependent data that users want to see on their computer desktop. Moreover, a lot of preferences and heuristics for solving several subproblems must be applied. These domain-dependent features are realized by new derived classes. For example, the existing order class with 10 attributes must be specialized to read more attributes (about 30). However, tech-

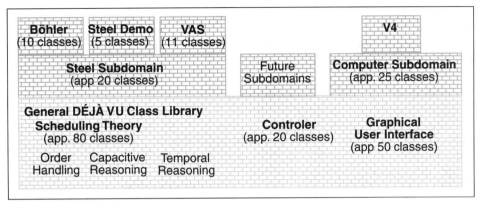

Figure 21.4   Architecture of the Déjà Vu class library.

niques such as presenting an order graphically, deleting it, or scheduling it must not be reimplemented. Furthermore, we had to define one new scheduling task and two new constraint types. However, these modifications have no effect on the interaction classes or on the algorithms that need the evaluation and scheduling tasks. We have defined a derived schedule class in order to realize improved domain heuristics for scheduling jobs. Altogether, we estimate that only about 10 percent new code has been developed for the application. Of course, during the development of the framework we had the application in mind. A second application for a different steel plant (VAS) has been used as a further test bed, which shows that about the same effort is required here. A simplified application, the SteelDemo application, needs only five extra classes because of its simplification. (A documentation of the scheduling class library, as well as further information and the SteelDemo application, is publicly available at: www .dbai.tuwien.ac.at/proj/DejaVu/ document/docu .htm.)

At the moment, a totally different application is being developed. This scheduler has to schedule operations on distributed computer hardware. Although we again identify objects such as orders, jobs, and resources, an own subdomain for computer scheduling has to be defined. And there are several other application types, such as job-shop scheduling or roster scheduling, that are not yet sufficiently supported by our framework. Therefore, it is very likely that changes in the architecture may also become necessary in the future.

21.6 Future Extensions

To improve the reusability of Déjà Vu for new applications, it seems important to define an order description language from which the system can automatically generate the order class and the class that is used to display an order. Although the logic behind this class is simple, the construction is error prone.

The framework is available at the moment for Windows NT and MacOS. The transformation to other platforms should be relatively simple, because the differences in the operating systems are already isolated. Thus, in the near future a transformation to Unix is expected.

At the moment, only a very simple temporal logic is used to describe how operations of one job have to be performed. Because we use only before and after relations, we cannot express any possible constellation of operations. The temporal consistency mechanism that is incorporated is based on this simple model. To use the full expressiveness of Allen's interval algebra [Allen 1983] for the consistency mechanism would be computationally too expensive (NP–complete), but it seems possible to use it to describe the temporal relations of process plans.

The most important extension, however, will be the introduction of reactive scheduling. The main problem for the application at Böhler, as well as for most industrial problems, is the daily work with the adaptation of the schedule to react to unexpected events such as new rush orders, machine breakdowns, destroyed products, or others. Based on [Dorn 1995c], we have already built a reactive scheduling prototype for Böhler, which is now being integrated in Déjà Vu. Because this prototype has worked in a simulation model, we must now test it in a real domain.

21.7 Summary

This chapter shows how an application framework can be designed for modern production scheduling applications, what the basic techniques underlying the Déjà Vu scheduling class library are, and how to reuse and extend the framework for a new application. The motivation of designing and realizing the framework is twofold, to support the development of industrial scheduling systems as well as academic research in scheduling theory.

The contribution is a sound architecture for the domain of interactive intelligent production scheduling. The difficulty here is that on one hand, there is a huge body of scheduling theory that should be able to be integrated into one framework to give developers of scheduling systems as much support as possible. On the other hand, scheduling theory does not treat interactive scheduling and interfacing to legacy software, which is unavoidable in practical scheduling. The existing Déjà Vu framework already realizes various scheduling algorithms, and with its so-called scheduling tasks, it supports the integration of scheduling theory with interactive scheduling. Initial experiments and a fielded system have shown that the framework can easily be reused for different problems.

From the scheduling point of view, the framework is characterized by the capability to express multicriteria objective functions and the applicability of heuristic search functions, as well as iterative improvement procedures such as tabu search, simulated annealing, or similar techniques.

21.8 References

[Allen 1983] Allen, J.F. Maintaining knowledge about temporal intervals. *Communications of the ACM*, 26(11), 1983: 823–843.

[Bazewicz 1993] Bazewicz, J., K. Ecker, G. Schmidt, and J. Węglarz. *Scheduling in Computer and Manufacturing Systems*. Springer-Verlag, 1993.

[Bylander 1988] Bylander, T., and B. Chandrasekaran. Generic tasks in knowledge-based reasoning: The "right" level of abstraction for knowledge acquisition. In *Knowledge Acquisition for Knowledge-Based Systems*, B. Gaines and J. Boose, editors. London: Academic Press, 1988: 65–77.

[Conway 1967] Conway, R.W., W. Maxwell, and L.W. Miller. *Theory of Scheduling*. Reading, MA: Addison-Wesley, 1967.

[Dorn 1995a] Dorn, J. Iterative improvement methods for knowledge-based scheduling. *AICOM Journal*, March 1995: 20–34.

[Dorn 1995b] Dorn, J. Case-based reactive scheduling. In *Artificial Intelligence in Reactive Scheduling*, R. Kerr and E. Szelke, editors. London: Chapman & Hall, 1995: 32–50.

[Dorn 1995c] Dorn, J., R.M. Kerr, and G. Thalhammer. Reactive scheduling: Improving the robustness of schedules and restricting the effects of shop floor disturbances by fuzzy reasoning. *International Journal on Human-Computer Studies*, 42, 1995: 687–704.

[Dorn 1996] Dorn, J., M. Girsch, G. Skele, and W. Slany. Comparison of iterative improvement techniques for schedule optimization. *European Journal on Operational Research*, 1996: 349–361.

[Dorn-Shams 1996] Dorn, J., and R. Shams. Scheduling high-grade steel making. *IEEE Expert*, February 1996: 28–35.

[Dorn-Slany 1994] Dorn, J., and W.A. Slany. Flow shop with compatibility constraints in a steel making plant. In *Intelligent Scheduling*, Monte Zweben and Mark S. Fox, editors. Morgan Kaufmann, 1994: 629–654.

[Gamma 1995] Gamma, E., R. Helm, R. Johnson, and J. Vlissides. *Design Patterns: Elements of Reusable Object-Oriented Software*. Reading, MA: Addison-Wesley, 1995.

[Fayad-Schmidt 1997] Fayad, M.E., and D.C. Schmidt. Object-oriented application frameworks. *Communications of the ACM*, 40(10), 1997: 32–38.

[Fox 1994] Fox, M.S. ISIS: A retrospective. In *Intelligent Scheduling*, Monte Zweben and Mark S. Fox, editors. Morgan Kaufmann, 1994.

[French 1982] French, S. *Sequencing and Scheduling: An Introduction to the Mathematics of the Job-Shop*, Chichester, England: Ellis Horwood, 1982.

[Le Pape 1994] Le Pape, C. Scheduling as intelligent control of decision-making and constraint propagation. In *Intelligent Scheduling*, Monte Zweben and Mark S. Fox, editors. Morgan Kaufmann, 1994: 67–98, 1994.

[Sauer 1993] Sauer, J. Meta-scheduling using dynamic scheduling knowledge. In *Scheduling of Production Processes*, J. Dorn and D. Froeschl, editors. Chichester, England: Ellis Horwood, 1993: 151–162.

[Smith 1994] Smith, S.F. OPIS: A methodology and architecture for reactive scheduling. In *Intelligent Scheduling*, Monte Zweben and Mark S. Fox, editors. Morgan Kaufmann, 1994: 29–66.

[Prieto-Díaz 1990] Prieto-Díaz, R. Domain analysis: An introduction, *ACM SIGSOFT Software Engineering Notes* 15(2), 1990: 47–54.

CHAPTER 22

A Framework
for Graphics Recognition

As a domain of engineering, software engineering strives to establish standard, well-understood building blocks, which are expected to be developed and stored in libraries for common use and as a basis for extensions and modifications in the spirit of the reusability concept. Although software reuse had existed in software development processes since software engineering began as a research field in 1969, it was not until 1978 that the concept of reusability was clear in the minds of people as a solution to the software crisis. Currently, software reuse is getting a great deal of attention for its potential in increasing productivity, reducing costs, and improving software quality, and quite a few reuse techniques have been proposed.

The advent of object-oriented techniques makes the reuse technology even more powerful. Framework [Johnson 1988], as an object-oriented reuse technique, is playing an increasingly important role in contemporary software development [Fayad-Schmidt 1997]. Although people are developing and utilizing frameworks, the definitions of frameworks vary. [Johnson 1997] lists two common definitions of frameworks as follows:

- A framework is a reusable design of all or part of a system that is represented by a set of abstract classes and the way their instances interact.

- A framework is a skeleton of an application that can be customized by an application developer.

Although it is hard to define frameworks formally and clearly, there are several common features of frameworks:

- A framework is for reuse (in the development of applications in some specific problem domain).

- A framework is a skeleton program that can be extended to a complete application by being filled with necessary components at hot spots, the implementations of which vary from application to application of the framework.

- A framework is customizable to fit the applications being developed.

- A framework predefines some interfaces of the filling components as the framework contract so that the components fit each other and fit into the framework.

- A set of abstract classes is usually used to describe the behaviors of frameworks.

- A corresponding concrete class should be implemented as the filling component when extending the framework to applications.

From the these features, we can see that framework is a design reuse technique for developing new applications. There are a lot of advantages in using frameworks in application development. Rather than developing an application from scratch, extending and customizing an appropriate framework to cater to the need of the application will save much effort and therefore speed up the development process. Another important advantage is that the quality guarantee of the framework as a product also assures the quality of its applications.

[Fayad-Schmidt 1997] categorizes the existing frameworks into three scopes: *system infrastructure frameworks, middleware integration frameworks,* and *enterprise application frameworks.* Frameworks can also be classified as *whitebox* and *blackbox frameworks* by the technique used to extend them. Whitebox frameworks are extended to applications by inheriting from some base classes in the frameworks and overriding their interface methods, whereas blackbox frameworks are extended by customizing new components according to particular interfaces defined by the frameworks and plugging them into the frameworks. However, the whitebox and blackbox reuse techniques frequently coexist in one framework [Johnson 1988], because some common abstractions among many blackbox components (object classes) within the same problem domain may also be expressed and implemented using inheritance and overriding.

This chapter presents a framework for graphics recognition applications. It is an enterprise application framework in the problem domain of graphics recognition. The recognition of graphic objects from files of scanned paper drawings, known as *graphics recognition*—which is a part of engineering drawing interpretation and document analysis and recognition (DAR)—is a topic of increasing interest in the field of pattern recognition and computer vision. Although many algorithms and sytems have been developed, the result is not satisfactory due to the complex syntax and semantics these drawings convey, and more powerful algorithms and systems are strongly needed. To reduce the effort involved in developing basic algorithms for such systems, we have developed the graphics recognition framework. After comprehensive domain analysis, the design of the graphics recognition framework was inspired by the observation that all classes of graphic objects consist of several or many primitive components, and the algorithms for recognizing them can employ an incremental, stepwise recovery of the primitive components.

The framework is implemented using a C++ template class with the graphic class used as a parameter. It is a blackbox framework, whose application can be easily generated by instantiating the template class with a concrete graphic class that conforms to the framework contract. Some common graphic classes are also defined in a preliminary inheritance hierarchy so that new concrete graphic classes can also inherit from some appropriate class in the hierarchy. The framework has been successfully used in developing the applications of arc detection [Liu-Dori 1998b], leader and dimension set detection [Liu-Dori 1998a], and general line detection [Liu-Dori 1998c].

The rest of the chapter is organized as follows. *Section 22.1* describes the domain analysis process. *Section 22.2* presents the design of the framework. *Section 22.3* presents the implementation and applications of the framework. *Section 22.4* presents a summary.

22.1 Domain Analysis of Graphics Recognition

Like other domain frameworks, the graphics recognition framework is a vertical reuse component [Hooper 1991] in the problem domain of graphics recognition. The first step in developing such a framework is domain analysis, in which the common knowledge is identified, captured, and organized. In order to clearly present the domain analysis, *Section 22.1.1* briefly introduces the graphics recognition problem and the solution approaches.

22.1.1 The Graphics Recognition Problem and Its Solutions

Graphics recognition is an important basic problem in the engineering drawing interpretation area of document analysis and recognition, interest in which is constantly increasing as more research and development of experimental and commercial systems to solve this problem are conducted. The entire task is detailed here.

The engineering drawing interpreter accepts as input the raster image of a scanned drawing. Vectorization, or raster-to-vector conversion, is applied to the raster image, yielding coarse bars and polylines. Extra processing yields fine bars and polylines in complex and noisy drawings. After vectorization, the coarse bars and polylines are input to the extraction of text, arcs, dashed lines, and other forms of higher-level graphic objects. We refer to this procedure as *graphics recognition*.

We define the problem of graphics recognition as grouping the raw wires resulting from the vectorization according to certain syntax rules, recognizing these groups as types of graphic objects, and determining their attribute values. The low-level graphic objects include bars, polylines, and arcs. Higher-level graphic objects include characters and text, arrowheads and leaders, dashed lines, entities (geometric contours), hatched areas, and dimension sets.

Traditional algorithms (such as in [Dori 1995]) recognize each class of graphic objects by clustering all the potential constituent segments at once before determining their type and attributes. This blind search procedure tends to introduce inaccuracies in the grouping of the graphic primitive components that constitute the graphic objects, which ultimately account for inaccurate graphics recognition. [Liu 1995] proposes an incremental, stepwise approach, which is more flexible and adaptive as it constantly checks the syntactic and semantic constraints of the graphic object while gradually grouping its primitive components.

22.1.2 Graphic Objects and the Graphic Database

The graphic objects that appear in engineering drawings include solid straight lines, solid arcs, solid polylines, dashed straight lines, dashed arcs, dashed polylines, dash-dotted straight lines, dash-dotted polylines, dash-dot-dotted straight lines, dash-dot-dotted arcs, dash-dot-dotted polylines, character boxes, character string boxes, logic text boxes, filled arrowheads, hollow arrowheads, straight leaders, angular leaders, entities (close geometric contours), hatched areas, longitudinal dimension sets, angular dimension sets, radial dimension sets, diametric dimension sets, and so on. Graphics recognition includes the recognition of these classes of graphic objects. The intermediate and final recognized objects are stored in a graphic database. Based on observations and analysis of these classes of graphic objects, we have found that all of them are composed of several or many vector-form primitive components. Even a bar may consist of several coarse line segments. This common feature can be generalized and modeled in the Unified Modeling Language (UML) class diagram [Rational 1997] shown in Figure 22.1. The repository of graphic objects and primitive objects is called *GraphicsDatabase* and can be modeled in the UML class diagram shown in Figure 22.2.

22.1.3 The Generic Graphics Recognition Process

The incremental, stepwise approach proposed in [Liu 1995] can be applied to the recognition of all these classes of graphic objects. The algorithm consists of two main phases, based on the hypothesis-and-test paradigm. The first step is hypothesis generation, in which the existence of a graphic object of the class being detected is assumed by finding its first key component from the GraphicsDatabase. The second

Figure 22.1 Generic model of the composition of graphic objects.

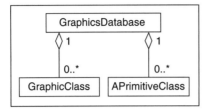

Figure 22.2 The GraphicsDatabase model.

step is hypothesis testing, in which the presence of such a graphic object is proved by successfully constructing it from its first key component and serially extending it to its other components. In the second step, an empty graphic object is first filled with the first key component found in the first step. The graphic object is further extended as far as possible in all possible directions in the extension process—a stepwise recovery of its other components. In the extension procedure, an extension area is first defined at the current extension direction. All candidates of possible components that are found in this area and pass the candidacy test are then inserted into the candidate list, sorted by their nearest distance to the current graphic object being extended. The nearest candidate undergoes the extendibility test. If it passes the test, the current graphic object is extended to include it. Otherwise, the next nearest candidate is taken for the extendibility test, and so on until some candidate passes the test. If no candidate passes the test, the extension process stops. If the graphic object is extended, it is added to the graphic database. The algorithm can be modeled using the UML sequence diagram [Rational 1997] shown in Figure 22.3, which outlines the framework and shows the hot spots of the recognition process of all graphic classes. The recognition of any graphic class requires only the implementation of these hot-spot functions.

22.2 Design of the Graphics Recognition Framework

The design of the graphics recognition framework is done in two subsequent steps: designing an initial whitebox framework that evolves into a blackbox framework. These steps are described in the following sections.

22.2.1 Initial Whitebox Framework

The inheritance feature among the classes of graphic objects listed in *Section 22.1.2* is obvious, and it is necessary to organize them in a class inheritance hierarchy, which is shown in Figure 22.4.

At the root of the hierarchy is the class Primitive, which abstracts all features of all graphic objects. At the second level of the hierarchy, there are several abstract classes. The class Line abstracts the most common features of all line classes. Lines are classi-

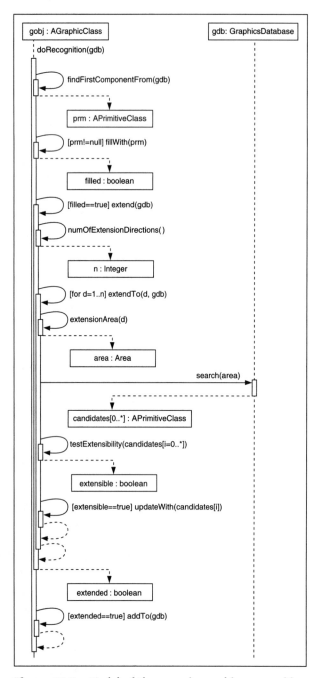

Figure 22.3 Model of the generic graphics recognition algorithm of [Liu 1995].

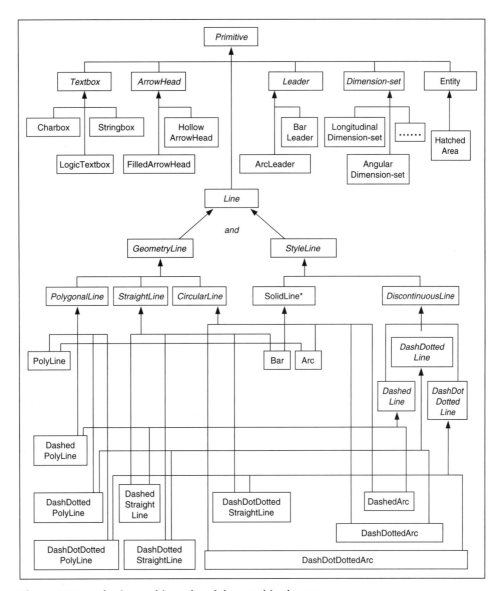

Figure 22.4   Inheritance hierarchy of the graphic classes.

fied into types by two attributes, geometry (shape) and style (continuity). The three line-geometry classes are straight, circular, and polygonal. The four line-style classes are solid, dashed, dash-dotted, and dash-dot-dotted. However, each concrete line class should be specified by geometry and style simultaneously. Parallel inheritance can therefore be used to depict this feature. Textbox is inserted into the hierarchy to generalize the features of the classes Charbox, Stringbox, and LogicTextbox. ArrowHead generalizes the classes FilledArrowHead and HollowArrowHead. Leader generalizes

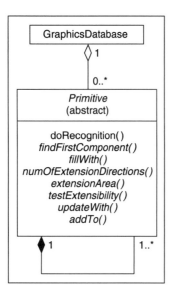

Figure 22.5 Abstract model of graphic objects and the graphic database.

the classes BarLeader and ArcLeader. Both Entity and HatchedArea are concrete classes, but HatchedArea can be considered as a subclass of Entity. DimensionSet can be used to generalize all kinds of dimension sets.

Based on the class generalization shown in Figure 22.4, the generic composition model of graphic objects shown in Figure 22.1 and the GraphicDatabase model in Figure 22.2 can be abstracted and combined, as shown in Figure 22.5. The recognition process can be extracted and implemented inside Primitive by the member function doRecognition(gdb), which can be considered as a whitebox framework. In the framework, the hot spots, which are also abstracted to the top abstract class Primitive as abstract member functions, can be delegated to be implemented in some lower-level abstract or concrete graphic classes. In this case, a hot spot may be divided into several smaller hot spots that vary in different descendant classes. For example, the extensionArea( ) function for all line classes can be implemented inside Line, whereas the implementation of endPoint( ) and tangetAngle( ) are delegated further to the descendant classes. The subframework of extensionArea( ) for all line classes is shown in Figure 22.6.

22.2.2 Blackbox Framework Architecture

Following the framework evolution guideline of [Roberts 1997], we update the generic graphics recognition framework from a whitebox one to a blackbox one, so that it can be applied to any graphic class, regardless of whether the graphic class inherits from Primitive. The blackbox framework is depicted as a parameterized class in Figure 22.7. In the framework, the parameter class AGraphicClass is the overall hot spot and the contract object, which can be easily plugged into the framework. It can be replaced

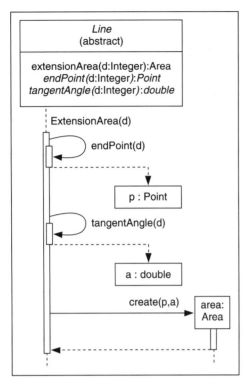

Figure 22.6 Subframework of extension-Area( ) for line classes.

with any class as long as the class meets the framework contract (the relationship among objects in the framework) depicted in Figure 22.7. However, the graphic class is preferred to inherit from the classes in Figure 22.4 in order to fully reuse the framework. Figure 22.8 shows three possible recognition applications of Recognizer-Of<DashedArc>, RecognizerOf<CharBox>, and RecognizerOf<HatchedArea> by instantiating the parameterized class RecognizerOf<AGraphicClass>, using arguments of DashedArc, CharBox, and HatchedArea separately.

22.3 Implementation and Applications of the Framework

We implement the graphics recognition framework using a C++ template class, as shown in the code in Figure 22.9. The application of the framework to a specific graphic class is as simple as the following line of code:

```
(new RecognizerOf<AGraphicsClass>())->runWith(gdb);
```

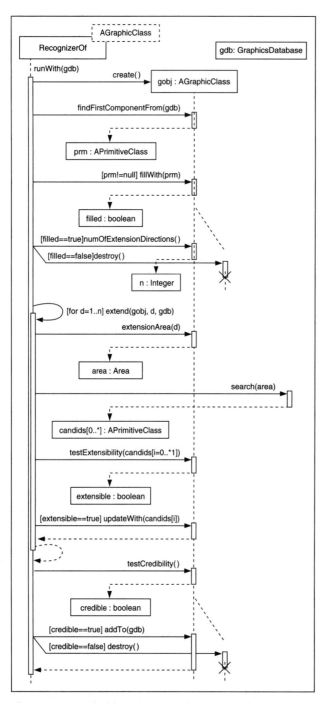

Figure 22.7 Blackbox framework for recognition of any class of graphic objects.

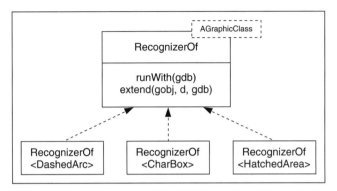

Figure 22.8 Blackbox graphics recognition framework architecture and three possible applications.

The graphics recognition framework is used as the kernel of the Machine Drawings Understanding System (MDUS) [Liu-Dori 1996]. The framework has been applied to arc segmentation [Liu-Dori 1998b], leader and dimension set detection [Liu-Dori 1998a], and generic line detection [Liu-Dori 1998c]. We have tested the graphics recognition framework with MDUS using real-world drawings of various complexity levels. Experiments show that it is very successful in detecting many classes of graphic objects in engineering drawings.

22.4 Summary

This chapter presents the domain analysis, design, implementation, and applications of an object-oriented application framework for developing graphics recognition systems. It is based on the generic graphics recognition algorithm developed in [Liu 1995]. The interfaces of the framework and potential filling components are defined in an abstract class, Primitive, which contains a set of pure virtual member functions. Some common graphic classes are organized into an inheritance hierarchy deriving from Primitive. New concrete graphic classes can inherit from Primitive, either directly or indirectly, and implement these member functions so that they can be plugged into the framework. However, the application framework is also a blackbox framework that can take as input any independent but well-defined graphic class component. It is implemented using a C++ template class, with the graphic class used as a parameter. Applications can be easily generated by instantiating the template class with a real graphic class whose interface conforms to the framework contract. The applications of the framework to several classes of graphic objects have shown great success.

```
template <class AGraphicClass>
class RecognizerOf
{
    RecognizerOf() {}
    void runWith(GraphicDataBase& gdb) {
        while (1) {
            AGraphicClass* gobj = new AGraphicClass();
            Primitive* prm = gobj->findFirstComponentFrom(gdb);
            if (prm == null)
                return;
            if (!gobj->fillWith(prm))
                continue;
            for (int d=0; d<=gobj-> numOfExtensionDirections();
                    d++)
                while (extend(gobj, d, gdb));
            if (!gobj->isCredible())
                delete gobj;
            else gobj->addTo(gdb)
        }
    }
    boolean extend(AGraphicClass* gobj, int direction,
                        GraphicDataBase& gdb) {
        Area area = gobj->extensionArea(direction);
        PrimitiveArray& candidates = gdb.search(area);
        for (int i=0; i < candidates.getSize(); i++) {
            if (!gobj->extensible(candidates[i]))
                continue;
            gobj->updateWidth(candidates[i]);
            break;
                }
        if (i < candidates.getSize())
            return true;
        return false;
        }
};
```

Figure 22.9 Outline of the C++ implementation of the generic graphics recognition algorithm.

22.5 References

[Dori 1995] Dori, D. Vector-based arc segmentation in the Machine Drawing Understanding System environment. *IEEE Transactions on Pattern Analysis and Machine Intelligence (PAMI)*, 17(11), 1995: 959–971.

[Fayad-Schmidt 1997] Fayad, M.E., and D.C. Schmidt. Object-oriented application frameworks. *Communications of the ACM*, 40(10), October 1997: 32–38.

[Hooper 1991] Hooper, J.W., and R. Chester. *Software Reuse: Guidelines and Methods.* New York: Plenum Press, 1991.

[Johnson 1988] Johnson, R.E., and B. Foote. Designing reusable classes. *Journal of Object-Oriented Programming,* 1(5), 1988: 22–35.

[Johnson 1997] Johnson, R.E. Frameworks = (components + patterns). *Communications of the ACM,* Theme Issue on Object-Oriented Application Frameworks, M.E. Fayad and D. Schmidt, editors, 40(10), October 1997: 39–42.

[Liu 1995] Liu, W., D. Dori, L. Tang, and Z. Tang. Object recognition in engineering drawings using planar indexing. *Proceedings of the First International Workshop on Graphics Recognition,* pp. 53–61, Pennsylvania State University, State College, August 1995.

[Liu-Dori 1996] Liu, W., and D. Dori. Automated CAD conversion with the Machine Drawing Understanding System. *Proceedings of the Second IAPR Workshop on Document Analysis Systems,* pp. 241–259, Malvern, PA, October 1996.

[Liu-Dori 1998a] Liu, W., and D. Dori. Genericity in graphics recognition algorithms. *Graphics Recognition: Algorithms and Systems,* K. Tombre and A. Chhabra, editors. Lecture Notes in Computer Science 1389. Springer-Verlag, 1988: 9–21.

[Liu-Dori 1998b] Liu, W., and D. Dori. Incremental arc segmentation algorithm and its evaluation. *IEEE Transactions on Pattern Analysis Machine Intelligence,* 20(4), 1998: 424–431.

[Liu-Dori 1998c] Liu, W., and D. Dori. A generic integrated line detection algorithm and its object-process specification. *Computer Vision and Image Understanding,* 70(3). 1998: 420–437.

[Rational 1997] Rational. *UML Semantics and UML Notation Guide,* v1.1. www.rational .com/uml, 1997.

[Roberts 1997] Roberts, D., and R.E. Johnson. Evolving frameworks: A pattern language for developing frameworks. In *Pattern Languages of Program Design 3,* D. Riehle, F. Fuschmann, and R.C. Martin, editors. Reading, MA: Addison-Wesley, 1997.

A JavaBeans Framework
for Cryptographic Protocols

Designing and implementing telecommunications protocols has proven to be a very demanding task. Building secure cryptographic protocols is even harder, because in this case we have to be prepared not just for random errors in the network and end systems but also for premeditated attacks on any weaknesses in the design or implementation [Anderson 1995; Simmons 1994]. During the last 10 years or so, much attention has been focused on the formal modeling and verification of cryptographic protocols (for example, [Nikander 1997]). However, the question of how to apply these results to real design and implementation has received considerably less attention [Abadi 1994; Anderson 1994; Mao-Boyd 1994]. Recent results in the area of formalizing architecture-level software composition and integrating it with object-oriented modeling and design seem to bridge one section of the gap between the formal theory and everyday practice [Allen-Garlan 1997; Zremski 1997].

In our work, we are focusing on a framework for secure communications protocols that has the following properties:

- The framework is made to the needs of today's applications based on the global infrastructure that is already forming (Internet, WWW, Java).

- The framework allows us to construct systems out of our own trusted protocol components and others taken from the network. These systems can be securely executed in a protocol "sandbox," where they cannot, for example, leak encryption keys or other secret information.

- Together they allow us to relatively easily implement application-specific secure protocols, securely download the protocol software over the Internet, and use it without any prior arrangements or software installation.

We have implemented the main parts of our vision as an object-oriented protocol component framework called *Java Conduits*. It was built using JDK 1.1 and is currently being tested on the Sun Solaris operating system. The framework itself is pure Java and runs on any Java 1.1–compatible virtual machine.

Our goal is to provide a sound practical basis for protocol development, with the desire to create higher-level design patterns and architectural styles that could be formally combined with protocol modeling and analysis. The current focus lies in utilizing the *gang-of-four* (GoF) object-level design patterns [Gamma 1995] to create a highly stylistic way of building both cryptographic and noncryptographic communications protocols. Our implementation experience has shown that this approach leads to a number of higher-level design patterns—protocol patterns—that describe how protocols should be composed from lower-level components in general.

As a detail, we would like to allow application-specific secure protocols to be built from components. The protocols themselves can be constructed from lower-level components, called *conduits*. The protocol components, in turn, can be combined into complete protocol stacks.

Our framework encourages building protocols from simple standard components. Most of the components can be used as blackboxes. In several cases, the actual protocol-specific behavior is supplemented with separate strategy objects. Typically, there is only one instance of each strategy object (according to the Singleton pattern). In addition to other benefits, this allows the framework to strictly control object creation, making it possible to port the framework into environments where dynamic object management and garbage collection are not possible due to performance or other reasons.

The rest of this chapter is organized as follows. *Sections 23.1.1* through *23.1.3* introduce our assumptions behind our framework and its relationship to existing work. *Section 23.2* describes the architecture and components of developed framework. *Section 23.3* delves into implementation details and experience gained while building prototypes of real protocols. *Section 23.4* describes in detail the implementation of our Internet Security (IPSEC) protocol prototype. *Section 23.5* presents an outline of some future work, and *Section 23.6* presents a summary.

23.1 Assumptions and Existing Work

This section covers the underlying assumptions for building the JavaBeans framework and discusses the existing work.

23.1.1 Underlying Assumptions

In our view, the world for which we are building applications consists of the following main components: the *Internet*, the *World Wide Web* (WWW), the *Java programming language and execution environment*, and an *initial security context* (based on predefined trusted keys). Our vision is based on these four cornerstones.

The worldwide Internet has established itself as the dominating network architecture that even the public switched telephone network has to adapt to. The new Internet protocol Ipv6 will solve the main problem of address space, and together with new techniques, such as resource reservation and IP switching, will provide support for new types of applications, such as multimedia on a global scale. As we see it, the only significant threats to the Internet are political, not technical or economic. We regard the Internet, as well as less open extranets and intranets, as an inherently untrustworthy network.

The World Wide Web (WWW) has been the fastest-growing and most widely used application of the Internet. In fact, the WWW is an application platform that is increasingly being used as a user interface to a multitude of applications. Hypertext Markup Language (HTML) forms and the Common Gateway Interface (CGI) make it possible to create simple applications with the WWW as the user interface. More recently, we have seen the proliferation of executable content.

The Java programming language extends the capabilities of the WWW by allowing us to download executable programs, Java applets, with WWW pages. A Java virtual machine has already become an essential part of a modern web browser and we see the proliferation of Java as being inevitable. We are basing our work on Java and the signed applets security feature of Java 1.1.

In order to communicate securely, we always need to start with an initial security context. In our architecture, the minimal initial security context contains the trusted keys of our web browser, which we can use to check the signatures of the downloaded applets and other JavaBeans.

23.1.2 Component-Based Software Engineering

Attention has shifted from basic object-oriented (OO) paradigms and frameworks toward combining the benefits of OO design and programming with broad-scale architectural viewpoints [Allen-Garlan 1997; Meyer 1997]. Component-based software architectures and programming environments play a crucial role in this trend.

For a long time, it was assumed that object-oriented programming alone would lead to software reusability. However, experience has shown this assumption to be false [Meyer 1997]. On the other hand, non-object-oriented software architectures, such as Microsoft OLE/COM and IBM/Apple OpenDoc, have shown modest success in creating real markets for reusable software components. Early industry response seems to indicate that the JavaBeans architecture may prove more successful.

There are a number of basic viewpoints to component-based software. However, common to all these is the desire to promote software reuse. Other desires include empowering end users; creating a global market for software components; and allowing software testing, distribution, and maintenance to be performed piecemeal, that is, one component at a time [Wu 1997].

The JavaBeans component model we are using defines the basic facets of component-based software to be *components*, *containers*, and *scripting* [Hamilton 1997]. That is, component-based software consists of component objects that can be combined into larger components using containers. The interaction between the components can be controlled by scripts that should be easy to produce, allowing less sophisticated programmers and users to create them. This is achieved through *runtime interface discovery*, *event handling*, *object persistence*, and *application builder support* [Wu 1997].

Java as a language provides natural support for runtime interface discovery. A binary Java class file contains explicit information about the names, visibility, and signatures of the class and its fields and methods. Originally provided to enable late loading and to ease the fragile superclass problem, the runtime environment also offers this information for other purposes, such as for application builders. Java 1.1 provides a reflection application program interface (API) as a standard facility, allowing any authorized class to dynamically find and access the class information.

The JavaBeans architecture introduced a new event model for Java 1.1. The model consists of *event listeners*, *event objects,* and *event sources*. The mechanism is very lean, allowing basically any object to act as an event source, event listener, or even the event itself. Most of this is achieved through class- and method-naming conventions, with some extra support through manifestational interfaces.

Compared to other established component software architectures, such as OLE/ COM, CORBA, and OpenDoc, the JavaBeans architecture is relatively lightweight. Under Java 1.1, nearly any object can be turned into a JavaBean. If a Java class supports Bean properties by naming access functions appropriately, if the class has event support added (with a few lines of code), and if all references to the enclosing environment are marked transient, the instances of the class can be considered Beans.

On the other hand, the JavaBeans architecture, as it is currently defined, does not address some of the biggest problems of component-based software architectures any better than its competitors do. These include the mixing and matching problem that faces anyone trying to build larger units from the components. Basically, each component supports a number of interfaces. However, the semantics of these interfaces are often not immediately apparent, nor can they be formally specified within the component framework. When the components are specifically designed to cooperate, this is not a problem. However, if the user tries to combine components from different sources, the interfaces must be adapted. This may, in turn, yield constructs that cannot stand but collapse due to semantic mismatches.

In the protocol world, the mixing and matching problem is reflected in two distinct ways. First, the data transfer semantics differ. Second, and more important, the information content needed to address the intended recipient(s) of a message greatly differs. In our framework, the recipient information is always implicitly available in the topology of the conduit graph. Thus, the protocols have no need to explicitly address peers once an appropriate conduit stream has been created.

It has been shown that secure cryptographic protocols, when combined, may result in insecure protocols [Heintze 1994]. This problem cannot be easily addressed within the current JavaBeans architecture. We hope that future research, paying more attention to the formal semantics, will alleviate this problem.

23.1.3 Related Work

The study and application of communication protocol frameworks began well before the design patterns emerged into general knowledge. The early frameworks were based on procedural languages such as Pascal or C [Karila 1986; Malka 1998]. Unfortunately, the majority of the newer frameworks, even though based on object-oriented concepts and languages (typically C++), seem to lack patterned solutions or explanations [Birman 1991; Heinilä 1997; van Renesse 1996].

Our framework is heavily based on ideas first presented with the x–Kernel [Hutchinson 1991; O'Malley 1992; Orman 1994], Conduits [Zweig-Johnson 1990], and Conduits+ [Hueni 1995] frameworks. Some of these ideas, especially the microprotocol approach, have also been used in other frameworks, including Isis [Birman 1991], Horus/Ensemble [van Renesse 1996], and Bast [Garbinato 1997]. However, Isis and Horus concentrate more on building efficient and reliable multiparty protocols, whereas Bast objects are larger than ours, yielding a whitebox-oriented framework instead of a blackbox one.

Compared to x–Kernel, Isis, and Horus, our main novelty is in the use and recognition of design patterns at various levels. Furthermore, our object model is more fine-grained. These properties come hand-in-hand—using design patterns tends to lead to collections of smaller, highly regular objects.

The Horus/Ensemble security architecture is based on Kerberos and Fortezza. Instead, we base our architecture on the Internet IPSEC architecture [Atkinson 1995]. Kerberos does not scale well and requires a lot of trusted functionality. Fortezza has been developed mainly for U.S. government use, and is not expected to be generally available. On the other hand, we expect the IPSEC architecture to be ubiquitously available in the same way as the Domain Name System (DNS) is today.

Most important, our framework is seamlessly integrated into the Java security model. It utilizes both the language-level security features (packages and visibility) and the new Java 1.1 security functionality. A further difference is facilitated by the Java runtime model. Java supports code and object mobility. This allows application-specific protocols to be loaded or used on demand.

Another novelty lies in the way we use the JavaBeans architecture. This allows modern component-based software tools to be used to compose protocols. The introduction of the Protocol class, or the metaconduit (see *Section 23.2.1*), which allows composed subgraphs to be used as components within larger protocols, is especially important. The approach also allows the resulting protocol stacks to be combined with applications.

23.2 The Implementation Framework

Java Conduits provides a fine-grained object-oriented protocol component framework. The supported way of building protocols is very patterned, on several levels. The framework itself heavily utilizes the gang-of-four object design patterns [Gamma 1995]. A number of higher-level patterns for constructing individual protocols are emerging. At the highest level, we envision a number of architectural patterns to surface, as users will be able to construct protocol stacks that are matched to application needs.

23.2.1 Basic Conduits Architecture

The basic architecture of Java Conduits is based on that of Conduits+ by Hueni, Johnson, and Engel [Hueni 1995]. The basic kinds of objects used are *conduits* and *messages*.

Messages represent information that flows through a protocol stack. A conduit, on the other hand, is a software component representing some aspect of protocol functionality. To build an actual protocol, a number of conduits are connected into a graph. Protocols, moreover, are conduits themselves, and may be combined with other protocols and basic conduits into larger protocol graphs, representing protocol stacks.

A conduit has two distinct sides, *side A* and *side B*. Each of its sides may be connected to other conduits, which are its neighbor conduits. Basically, a conduit accepts messages from a neighbor conduit on one side and delivers them to the conduit on the opposite side. The conduit is bidirectional, so both of its neighbors can send information to it.

All conduits have two basic interfaces:

- An interface that connects the conduit to its neighbors and accesses those neighbors

- An interface that handles incoming messages

There are five kinds of conduits, as shown in Figure 23.1: *Session, Mux, ConduitFactory, Adaptor,* and *Protocol*. All conduits have one neighbor on their A side. A Mux can have many neighbors on its B side; an Adaptor does not have any B side; and a Session and a ConduitFactory have exactly one neighbor on their B sides.

Sessions are the basic functional units of the framework. A session implements the finite state machine of a protocol, or some aspects of it. The session remembers the state of the communication and obtains timers and storage for partial messages from the framework. The session itself does not implement the behavior of the protocol but delegates this to a number of state objects, using the State design pattern.

The Mux conduits are used to multiplex and demultiplex protocol messages. In practical terms, a Mux conduit has one side A that may be connected to any other conduit. The side B[0] of the Mux is typically connected to a ConduitFactory. In addition, the Mux has a number of additional side B[i] conduits. Protocol messages arriving from these conduits are multiplexed to the side A conduit, and vice versa.

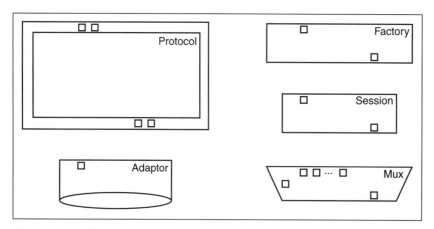

Figure 23.1 The five types of conduits.

If the Mux determines, during demultiplexing, that there is no suitable side B[i] conduit to which a message may be routed, the Mux routes the message to the side B[0], where a ConduitFactory is typically attached. The ConduitFactory creates a new Session (or Protocol) that will be able to handle the message, installs the newly created Session to the graph, and routes the message back to the Mux (see Figure 23.2).

Adaptors are used to connect the conduit graph to the outside world. In conduit terms, Adaptors have only side A. The other side, side B, or the communication with the outside world, is beyond the scope of the framework, and can be implemented by whatever means is feasible. For example, a conduit providing the TCP service might implement the Java socket abstraction.

A Protocol is a kind of metaconduit that encapsulates several other conduits. A Protocol has sides A and B. However, the explicit endpoints—that is, sides A and B—are typically used only for delivering interprotocol control messages. That is, the actual data connections usually stretch directly from and to the conduits that are located inside the Protocol.

In practice, a Protocol is little more than a conduit that happens to delegate its sides independently, to other conduits. The only complexity lies in the building of the initial conduit graph for the Protocol. Once the graph is built, it is easy to frame it within a

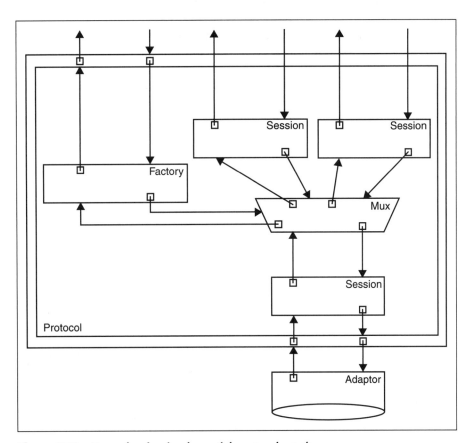

Figure 23.2   Example of a simple partial protocol graph.

protocol object. The protocol object can then be used as a component in building other, more complex Protocols or protocol stacks.

The Session

Sessions are the basic functional units of the framework. They are used both for connection-oriented protocols, in which case there is typically at least one session for each connection, and for connectionless protocols, in which case there may be just one session handling all the protocol communication.

Most communication protocols are defined as or can be represented as finite state machines. A typical session implements the finite state machine of a protocol. In the Session conduit, protocol messages are produced and consumed. The session remembers the state of the communication, and obtains counters, timers, and storage for partial protocol messages from the framework. A Session has exactly one neighbor conduit on both of its sides.

Sessions are implemented using the State pattern [Gamma 1995], which means that each state of the Session is represented by a separate object. Sessions delegate their behavior to their state objects, thus letting the session change its behavior when its state changes (see Figure 23.3). A session changes its state by replacing its old state object with a new one.

The Java Conduits framework uses one version of the State pattern [Hueni 1995]. This makes the Session conduit more reusable than the State pattern in [Gamma 1995].

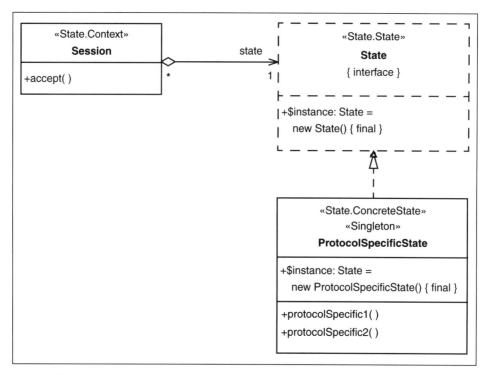

Figure 23.3 The State and Singleton patterns in the Session conduit.

The session offers just one method, a method to accept messages. The message interacts with the state object, usually invoking session-specific operations on it. Thus, State offers a relatively broad interface to messages, but the Session has a narrow interface.

Each Session requires a new State class hierarchy with a new derived class for each state in the finite state machine. Because there will always be at most one instance of such a State class, it makes sense to use the Singleton pattern [Gamma 1995] for all State classes. Thus, there will be exactly one instance of each State class, and they will not have to be dynamically created or destroyed.

The Mux and the ConduitFactory

The Mux conduits multiplex and demultiplex messages. In practical terms, a Mux conduit has one A side, which may be connected to any other conduit. The default B side of the Mux, or side B[0], is typically connected to a ConduitFactory. In addition to these, the Mux has a number of *additional* B side conduits. Messages arriving from these conduits are multiplexed to the A side conduit, and vice versa.

In the Java Conduits framework, Muxen are used as blackboxes. The Mux itself does not know how to encode information about where the message arrived from, nor how to decode which side B conduit a message (which arrived from side A) should be demultiplexed to. A separate Accessor class is used to perform the encoding and decoding functionality (see Figure 23.4).

The Accessor

The Accessor is used as a whitebox. It is assumed that the protocol implementor will create an accessor class that knows the structure of the messages flowing through the mux. By interacting with the message, the Accessor can determine where to route the message, or encode the source of the message.

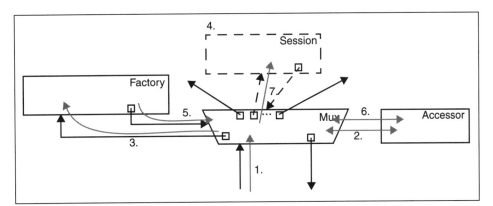

Figure 23.4 The Mux, the ConduitFactory, and the Accessor in concert. (1) A message arrives at the A side of a Mux. (2) The Mux asks the Accessor to look up proper routing for the message. (3) No route is found; the message is delivered to the Factory. (4) The Factory creates a new Session, and attaches it to the Mux. (5) The message is returned to the Mux. (6) The Mux again asks the Accessor to route the message. (7) This time a route is found, and the message is passed to the newly created Session.

Separating an algorithm from the object that uses the algorithm is implemented according to the Strategy pattern [Gamma 1995]. The intent of the Strategy pattern is to let the algorithm, or strategy, vary independently of the clients that use it. The Mux is the context of the strategy, and the Accessor plays the role of the strategy (see Figure 23.5). Accessors abstract out the difference between different Mux objects on different layers in a protocol stack, so that the relatively complex Mux class need not be subclassed. Instead, a Mux is given a reference to its Accessor when it is created.

The ConduitFactory

If the Mux finds out that there is no suitable side B[i] conduit to which a message may be routed, the Mux routes the message to the ConduitFactory attached to its side B[0]. The ConduitFactory creates a new Session (or Protocol) that will be able to handle the message, installs the newly created Session to the Mux, and routes the message back to the Mux.

The Adaptor

An Adaptor is a conduit that has no neighbor conduit on its B side. Thus, only its A side is connected to another conduit. The Adaptor conduit is used to interface the framework to some other software or hardware. Its B-side implementation is usually specific to a particular software or hardware environment. The Adaptor converts messages to and from an external format. The Adaptor conduit is an implementation of the Adapter pattern [Gamma 1995].

The Protocol

A Protocol, in the Java Conduits framework, is a MetaConduit that encapsulates several other conduits. A Protocol has sides A and B. However, these typically are conduit

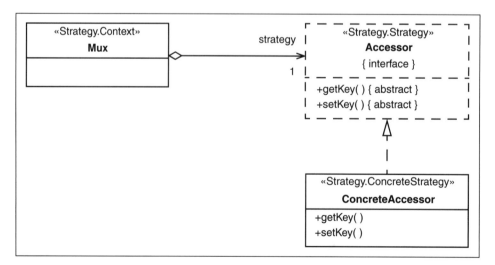

Figure 23.5 The Strategy pattern in Accessor, as used by the Mux.

connections that are mainly used for the delivery of various kinds of interprotocol control messages. The actual data connections typically stretch directly between the conduits that are located inside some protocols.

Figure 23.6 illustrates a simple protocol in two different states. Initially, the protocol is connected to a low-level Adaptor—a hardware plug-and-play controller—and to some upper-level conduit (not shown). Later, when a couple of plug-and-play adaptors are activated, and when connections are built to the upper-layer protocols, we can see how the additional connections cross the protocol boundaries without touching them.

A number of alternative designs were also considered. Most of them circulated around the idea of making a Protocol act like a double Mux—that is, a conduit having several distinct side A and side B connections. However, it appears that most communication protocols initially provide and require just a single service access point, or they can easily be modeled in such a way. That is, a protocol initially wants generic services from the lower layer, or a lower-layer controller. Similarly, it initially offers just a single control connection to the upper-layer protocols. Using this control connection, the upper-layer protocols can request a separate, identified connection. Similarly, in the case of routing or other downward demultiplexing, the control connection can be used to request connections to the available lower-layer protocols.

The main benefit of the design of the Protocol class is simplicity. A Protocol is little more than a Conduit that happens to delegate its sides, side A and side B, indepen-

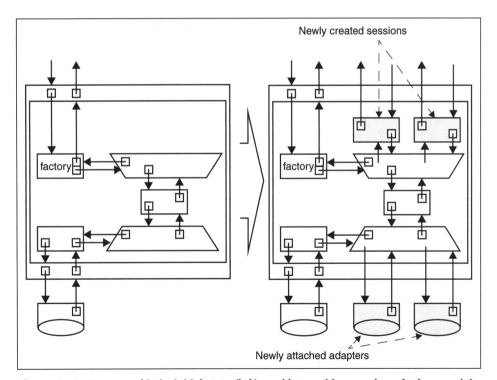

Figure 23.6 A protocol in its initial state (left), and later, with a number of other conduits connected (right).

dently to other conduits. The complexity of building the initial conduit graph for the protocol lies beyond the scope of the actual class. Once the graph is built, it is easy to frame it within a Protocol object. The Protocol object can then be used as a component in building other, more complex graphs. The Protocol conduit can be considered to be a manifestation of the Proxy pattern [Gamma 1995].

23.2.2 Using Java to Build Protocol Components

Java 1.1 provides a number of features that facilitate component-based software development. These include *inner classes, Bean properties, serialization,* and *Bean events.* These all play an important role in making the development of protocols easier.

A basic protocol component—a conduit—usually has two sides. Whenever a message arrives at the protocol component, it is important to know where the message came from, in order to be able to act on the message. On the other hand, it is desirable to view each conduit as a separate unit, having its own identity. Java inner classes, and the way the JavaBeans architecture uses them, provide a neat solution for this problem.

Each conduit is considered to be a single JavaBean. Internally, the component is constructed from a number of objects: the conduit itself, sides A and B, and, typically, also some other objects depending on the exact kind of conduit. The Conduit class itself is a normal Java class, specialized as a Session, Mux, ConduitFactory, or such. On the other hand, the side objects, A and B, are implemented as inner classes of the Conduit class. In most respects, these objects are invisible to the rest of the object world. They implement the Conduit interface, delegating most of the methods back to the conduit itself. However, their being separate objects makes the source of a message arriving at a conduit immediately apparent.

Because the conduits are attached to each other, the internal side objects are actually passed to the neighbor conduits when constructing the conduit graph. Now, when the neighboring conduit passes a message, it will arrive at the receiving conduit through some side object. This side object uniquely identifies the source of the message, thereby allowing the receiving conduit to act appropriately.

The JavaBean properties play a different role. Using the properties, the individual conduits may publish runtime attributes that a protocol designer may use through a visual design tool. For example, the Session conduits allow the designer to set the initial state, as well as the set of allowed states, using the properties. Similarly, the Accessor object connected to a Mux may be set up using the Bean property mechanism.

Java 1.1 provides a generic event facility that allows Beans and other objects to broadcast and receive event notifications. In addition to the few predefined notification types, the Beans are assumed to define new ones. Given this, it is natural to map conduit messages onto Java events.

23.2.3 Information Embedded within the Graph Topology

One important lesson learned, although possibly obvious once stated, is that *there is important information embedded in the topology of the protocol graph.* For example, consider transmission control protocol (TCP). The endpoint of a TCP connection is represented as a socket to a typical application. In conduit terms, a socket is an Adaptor that allows nonconduit applications to communicate through the TCP, implemented as conduits. Once created, the socket adaptor itself has no notion of the identity of the attached application, nor of the port numbers of IP addresses that identify the TCP connection. The information about the port numbers and IP addresses are embedded into the two Muxen and their Accessors that are part of the TCP implementation (see Figure 23.7). That is, the information about how a certain message can reach the designated application is embedded into the Accessor of the conduit graph, and in the fact that the application is connected to that particular socket adaptor. This information is *not available anywhere else.*

Section 23.4 considers cryptographic protocols. It notes that the graph topology also represents *security-relevant information.* For example, when a message is flowing upward at a certain point on a graph, we may know that the message has passed certain security checks. Because the only path for a message to arrive at that point goes through some Session that makes security checks, the message *must* be secure.

23.2.4 Protocol Messages

In Java Conduits, a protocol message is composed of three or four objects: a *message carrier*, a *message body*, possibly some *out-of-band data*, and a *message interpreter* (see Figure 23.8).The message carrier extends the java.util.EventObject class, thereby declaring itself as a Bean event. The carrier includes references to the message body that holds

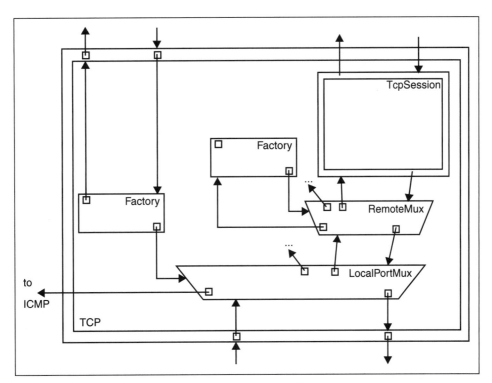

Figure 23.7   The structure of the TCP prototype (simplified).

the actual message data, a message interpreter that provides protocol-specific interpretation of the message data, and an optional out-of-band data object. The message interpreters are called *Messengers,* and they act in the role of a command according to the Command pattern [Gamma 1995].

Messages are passed from one conduit to the next one using the Java event delivery mechanism. By attaching to a conduit, the next conduit registers its internal side object as an event listener that will receive messages in the form of Java events.

The actual message delivery is synchronous. In practice, the sending conduit indirectly invokes the receiving conduit's accept method, passing the message carrier as a parameter. The receiving conduit, depending on its type and purpose, may apply the Messenger to the current protocol state, yielding an action in the protocol state machine, replace the Messenger with another one, giving new interpretation to the message, or act on the message independent of the Messenger. Typically, the same event object is used to pass the message from conduit to conduit until the message is delayed or consumed.

Java Conduits use the provider/engine mechanism offered by the JDK 1.1 security API. Because the encryption/decryption functionality and its interface specification were not available outside the United States, we created a new engine class, java.security.Cipher, along the model of the java.security.Signature and java.security.MessageDigest classes (see Figure 23.9).

The protocols use the cryptographic algorithms directly through the security API. The data carried in the message body is typically encrypted or decrypted in situ. When the data is encrypted or decrypted, the associated Messenger is typically replaced to yield new interpretation for the data.

23.2.5 Running Protocols

Whereas Conduits represent the static (but changing) structure of a protocol stack, Messages represent the dynamic communication that happens between the protocol

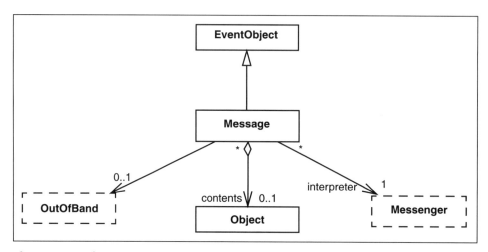

Figure 23.8 The structure of messages.

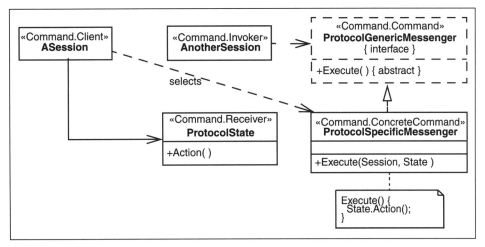

Figure 23.9   The Command pattern as used in the message.

parties. Following the model of Conduits+, each message is represented as an aggregation of two larger (aggregate) objects in runtime: a Visitor and a Message. The Message itself contains subparts (the carrier, the body, and so on), as previously mentioned. A Visitor (and its subclass Transporter) is an object that is conscious of the existence of conduits and that is able to navigate appropriately through the conduit graph. A Message (and its parts), on the other hand, is an object that does not know anything about the conduit graph, but carries the actual data and is able to communicate with the actual protocol state machines (see Figure 23.10).

In other words, Visitors and Conduits are deeply bound together, providing a means to construct graphs and perform controlled graph traversal. Similarly, Messages, States, and Accessors are bound together, but in an application-dependent way, and without any consent or even need to be aware of the existence of the conduit graph.

The Visitor and the Transporter

Visitor is a Java interface that acts in concordance to the Visitor pattern ([Gamma95], pp. 331–344) with respect to the conduit graph. The Visitor itself is the abstract «Visitor» of the pattern, whereas Conduit acts as the abstract «Element» of the pattern. The classes that implement the Visitor interface (Transporter and its subclasses) act in the role of «ConcreteVisitor»s, and the conduit types—Adaptor, ConduitFactory, Mux, and Session—are the «ConcreteElement»s of the pattern.

(The Protocol class does not take part in the Visitor pattern. It acts as a Proxy: Whenever a Visitor enters a Protocol, the Protocol immediately passes the Visitor to the conduit inside without the Visitor's involvement.)

All Visitors traverse the conduit graph carrying *something*. The basic difference between various visitors is in the *way, or algorithm*, according to which they traverse.

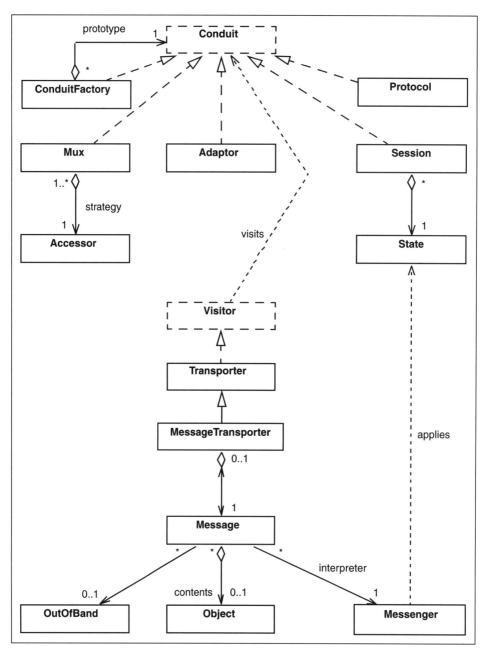

Figure 23.10 An overview of the classes in the framework.

A Transporter traverses the graph using a simple default algorithm. Every time it arrives at a conduit, it continues at the other side of the conduit. In a Mux, it calls the Mux's muxing function, leaving the mux by an appropriate demultiplexed or multiplexed channel. In a way, the purpose of a transporter is to traverse from one side of a graph to the other. This direction may be redirected by Conduits; the Transporter just walks blindly.

MessageTransporter is a subclass of Transporter that carries Messages. There is one slight difference between the traversal algorithms of a generic Transporter and a MessageTransporter: The MessageTransporter activates a State to handle a Message whenever it encounters a Session (see Figure 23.11).

The Conduits architecture is centered around the idea of a conduit graph that is traversed by protocol messages. The graph is the local representation of a protocol stack. The messages represent the protocol messages exchanged by the peer protocol implementations. This aspect of a graph and graph traversal is abstracted into a Visitor pattern [Gamma 1995]. The pattern is generalized in order to also allow other kinds of visitors to be introduced on demand. These may be needed, for example, to pass interprotocol control messages or to visualize protocol behavior.

A protocol message or other visitor arrives as a Java event at an internal side object of a conduit. The side object passes the message to the conduit itself. The conduit invokes the appropriate overloaded at(ConduitType) method of the message carrier, allowing the message to decide how to act, according to the Visitor pattern.

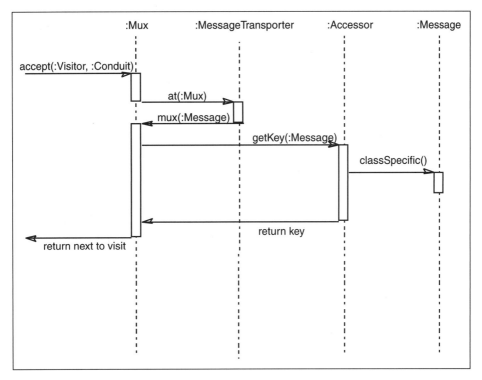

Figure 23.11   A Message arrives at a Mux (simplified).

CryptoSession: An Example

Consider the situation when a protocol message arrives at a Session that performs cryptographic functions (see Figure 23.12). The execution proceeds in steps, utilizing a number of design patterns.

The message arrives at the Session according to the Visitor pattern.

The message is passed to the Session's internal side as a JavaBeans visitor event. The event is passed to the session, which invokes the message's at(Session) method. Because the visitor in hand is a message, it calls back the Session's apply(Message) method.

- The Session gets the message, and applies it according to the Command pattern.

- The Session uses the Messenger command object, and asks it to be applied on itself, using the current state and message.

- The Messenger command object acts on the session, state, and message (second half of the Command pattern).

This behavior is internal to the protocol. Typically, all states of the protocol implement an interface that contains a number of command methods. The Messenger calls one of these, depending on the message's type. In the example situation, where a message arrives and should be sent encrypted, the Messenger invokes the protocol state's encrypt(Session, Message) method.

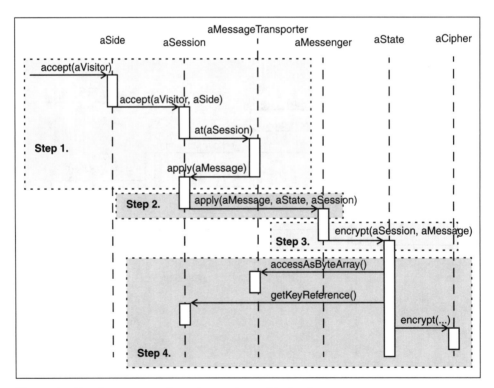

Figure 23.12   A message arrives at a cryptographic Session.

The current State object acts on the Session and Message.

This, again, depends on the protocol. The State may replace the current state at the Session with another State (according to the State pattern), modify the actual data carried by the message, or replace its interpretation by changing the Messenger associated with the message. In our example, the State encrypts the message data. A reference to a Cipher has been obtained during the State initialization through the Java 1.1 security API. The key objects are stored at the Session conduit.

23.2.6 Protocol Design Patterns

Our experience with the framework has shown that protocol-independent implementation patterns do arise. That is, there seem to be certain common ways that the different conduits are connected to each other when building protocols. This section shows how the use of encryption tends to be reflected as a conduit topology pattern.

A cryptographic protocol handles pieces of information that are binary encoded and cryptographically protected. Usually the whole message is signed (or otherwise integrity protected), encrypted, or both. This yields a highly regular conduit structure in which three sessions are stacked on top of each other (see Figure 23.13). The uppermost session (FSM) receives messages from upper protocols or applications, and maintains the protocol state machine, if any. Directly below lies a session that takes care of the binary encoding and decoding of the message data (Coder). The lowermost session within the protocol takes care of the actual cryptographic functions (Cipher).

According to the conduit architecture, the actual cryptographic keys are stored into the cryptosession. Thus, the information about what key to use is implicitly available from the conduit graph topology. However, this is not always feasible.

In the case of the IPSEC Authentication Header (AH) protocol we resorted to storing the keying information as additional, out-of-band information within the outgoing protocol message. Similarly, the incoming messages are decorated with information about the security associations that actually were used to decrypt or to check the message integrity. These are then checked further up in the protocol stack to ensure security policy.

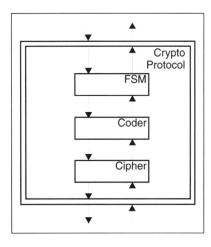

Figure 23.13   A cryptographic protocol pattern.

23.3 Building Protocols with Java Conduits

This section and the following one, *Section 23.4,* show how we have applied the framework to real-world protocols. The implementations we have are working, but often partial, prototypes. Therefore, it is probable that there will be slight changes in the implementation strategies as more functionality is added. In particular, currently both our IPv4 and IPv6 support only one physical network interface.

23.3.1 Lower-Layer Protocols versus Upper-Layer Protocols

According to our experience, there seems to be a clear distinction between the strategies that are suitable when implementing lower-layer protocols versus implementing upper-layer protocols. Here, the term *lower-layer protocol* applies to most of the OSI Layers 2 to 5, whereas the term *upper-layer* applies to application-layer and control-plane protocols.

A characteristic feature of what we call lower-layer protocols is that they carry some payload, received from some upper layer, which is considered opaque or binary format. Upper-layer protocols, on the other hand, may or may not carry data that belongs to some layer still further upward, but if so, the data is not considered binary encoded but has some semantic structure. For example, in the case of protocol stacks that rely on ASN.1, most layers below the ASN.1 representation layer can be considered lower layers, whereas the ones above it are upper-layer protocols (see Figure 23.14).

When applied to the basic TCP/IP stack, all of Ipv4, Ipv6, ICMP, UDP, and TCP fall under the category of lower-layer protocols. Some application-layer protocols, such as SMTP and NFS, are clearly upper-layer protocols. Some, on the other hand, fall somewhere between in implementation terms. Such hybrids might be, for example, FTP, in which the control connection would probably be best implemented according to the upper-layer strategies, whereas the data connections can be considered a lower-layer-carried protocol; and HTTP, which is able to transfer binary blobs in addition to HTML and other structured data.

23.3.2 Building Lower-Layer Protocols

A characteristic feature of lower-layer protocols is that they have a strict, built-in binary representation of their messages. Usually, any upper-layer data carried is copied verbatim into the lower-layer message, prepending it with a binary header carrying the data needed for the operation of the lower-layer protocol.

Lower-layer protocols are usually not specified in terms of distinct protocol primitives. Instead, the protocol header typically carries various fields and flags that together determine the intended behavior of the party on receipt. This makes usage of the Messenger Command pattern hard or, sometimes, impossible.

Another aspect is performance. Object creation and destruction are not cheap. Thus, if we can reserve a single data buffer along with the enclosing objects high on the protocol stack, and reuse them by prepending lower layer data, much unnecessary overhead is avoided.

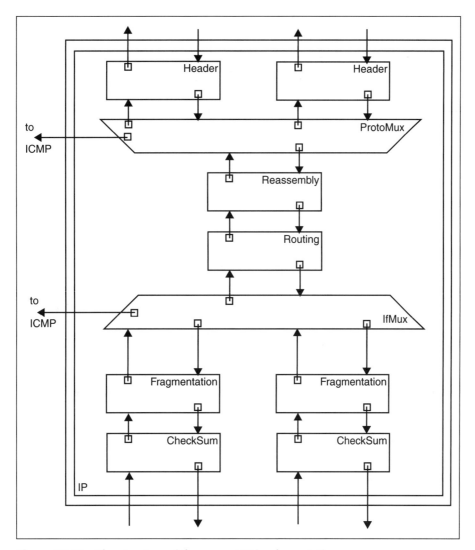

Figure 23.14   The structure of the current IP implementation.

In our implementation work an easy way to implement lower-layer protocols emerged. This is perhaps not the most compact nor best-performing way of implementing low-level protocols such as IP or TCP, but it makes the implementation straightforward to understand and easy to modify. The basic structure of this pattern is shown in Figure 23.15.

The actual protocol implementation is surrounded with simple, stateless Sessions. A separate session object is placed on all links leading up or down from the protocol. The sessions on the lower link convert the binary header representation of upcoming messages into a separate, protocol-specific header message. Accordingly, they encode the separate protocol header message into the binary message when a message traverses downward. On the upper link, on the other hand, the sessions either add or strip the

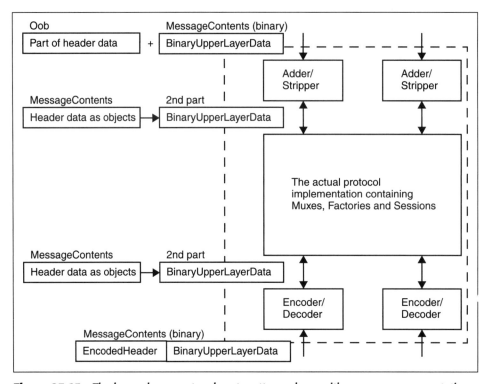

Figure 23.15 The lower-layer protocol metapattern, along with message representations.

separate header messages. The stripped header is usually simply discarded; the upper-layer protocol should not be interested in it (although in the case of TCP/IP this is not altogether possible, because both TCP and UDP use information from the IP message in computing and checking checksums). Accordingly, the added header message is usually empty, and is filled by the protocol.

23.3.3 Building Upper-Layer Protocols

Typical upper-layer protocols are quite different from lower-layer protocols. Instead of having a rigid, predefined binary message format, the messages are usually defined in terms of some kind of abstract syntax. The CCITT and ISO protocols tend to use the ASN.1 syntax; the situation is somewhat different in the case of Internet protocols. Some TCP/IP-based protocols do use some kind of abstract syntax. For example, NFS and other SunRPC-based protocols use the XDR to define the message formats. The TCP/IP-based CORBA protocol, IIOP, has its own abstract syntax defined. Actually, the ASCII-based control messages of most older TCP/IP application-level protocols, such as SMTP, NNTP, and FTP, may be considered to have a kind of abstract representation layer, as well.

Having an abstract syntax (of some sort) makes it natural to represent protocol messages as objects. Each protocol message type may be represented as a separate class. The Visitor and Builder patterns can be used to encode and decode messages at the presentation layer. As an alternative, the messages and classes may themselves know how to encode and decode their contents (refer to the Memento pattern).

Due to the representational difference, it is easy to apply another change. Instead of viewing the messages as dump data blocks (DataMessages in our terminology), they can be made intelligent, or Messengers instead of messages. This difference becomes apparent when the messages arrive at Sessions. The Session has delegated the responsibility of handling messages to states. Now, when an intelligent Messenger arrives at a State, the State may allow the Messenger to read the message, or call an appropriate method, instead of decoding the message itself.

23.4 Integrating Cryptography into Java Conduits

As mentioned in the introduction, one of the fundamental goals of our work is to provide an environment—a framework—where the implementation of cryptographic protocols is easier than it would otherwise be and yields fewer implementation-specific security errors on the average. In the long term, we also hope to be able to provide some implementation means and design patterns that are suitable for large numbers of cryptographic protocols.

23.4.1 Implementing Cryptographic Protocols

From a protocol implementation point of view, cryptographic protocols are communication protocols with a number of additional features. Like noncryptographic protocols, they are represented by means of protocol messages and protocol state machines. They may contain multiplexing aspects, though often in a format somewhat different from most protocols. And they certainly are embedded in a protocol framework that does perform multiplexing, even though the cryptographic protocol itself might not.

There are a number of typical extra operations performed by a cryptographic protocol:

- A protocol message may contain a signature or a keyed secure hash over itself and possibly some protocol state data. The protocol engine must be able to correctly create this data and check its validity on receipt.

- A protocol message or parts of it may be encrypted. The protocol engine must be able to encrypt and decrypt data as appropriate.

- A protocol message may include one or more digital certificates. The protocol engine must have some means to interpret the meaning of these certificates, and to check the validity of the signature of the certificate.

- To ensure freshness, or timeliness, some protocols require that a protocol party be able to generate random numbers. The protocol engine must include a cryptographically strong random-number generator.

- A protocol must be able to detect when it is offered a replay of an old message as a new message. This property is tightly integrated into the concept of freshness.

In general, it is impossible to detect a single replay unless all previous messages are stored and remembered. However, a good cryptographic protocol uses nonces (that is, random numbers) and the principles of message freshness to ensure liveness of communication.

In addition to these extra operations, there are also a couple of differences in the generic design guidelines. Specifically, the following principles are important:

- Malformed messages should be recognized as soon as possible. Failing to do this not only sacrifices performance, but may open new denial-of-service threats.

- The usual "be liberal in what you accept and strict in what you generate" does not always apply to cryptographic protocols. Usually, one has to be very strict in what to accept, or inadvertent vulnerabilities may be introduced.

- The role of redundancy at the message level is different from other protocols. If the integrity of a message is important, the message *must* contain enough redundancy, or else it may be easy to forge its signature or message authentication code. On the other hand, if the confidentiality of the message contents is important, the encrypted portion should contain as little redundancy as possible, in order to make cryptanalysis harder.

25.4.2 Representing Cryptographic Transformations as Conduits

There are a number of fundamental properties of cryptography that make it somewhat hard to embed cryptography into the conduit framework. First, cryptography is intrinsically bound to the binary representation of data. One cannot just encrypt or sign some arbitrary objects. The objects must first be converted into some predefined binary representation, and only then can be encrypted or signed. Second, because the purpose of cryptography is to make the system secure, we must pay extra attention to the security of the underlying framework.

The data representation requirements force us to sometimes explicitly encode some aspects of a session state, or some contents of a forthcoming message, into a binary representation. This is such a usual occurrence that we have been trying to identify some kind of design pattern for this; unfortunately, one hasn't emerged yet. On occasion we have encoded both the state information and the message contents in the graph, generated a digital signature, and passed this as an object along with the message to the lower layers. Typically, the message content is encoded again at some lower layer, yielding both performance problems and potential compatibility problems. If the encoding differs, it is possible that the peer protocol entity will not accept the message. As an alternative, elsewhere we have passed the relevant portions of the state information downward along with the message. This seems more promising, because the encoding needs to be performed only once. However, it has its own drawbacks, too. First, the messages are decorated with information that is otherwise not needed and that semantically does not belong to the lower layer. Second, we cannot simply pass references to the state data but must copy it, because sometimes the state may change before the encoding is performed.

A similar dilemma can be found in the handling of received messages. It would seem to be useful to check signatures or other integrity data simultaneously with the decoding of the message. Unfortunately, this is not always possible, or would violate protocol layering, because all the information needed for the integrity check may not be available before some of the decoded data is interpreted.

23.4.3 Using Java's Language-Level Security Features

Java offers a number of language-level security features that allow a class library or a framework to be secure and open at the same time. The basic facility behind these features is the ability to control access to fields and methods. In Java, classes are organized in packages. A well-designed package has a carefully crafted external interface that controls access to both blackbox and whitebox classes. Certain behavior may be enforced by making classes or methods final and by restricting access to the internal features used to implement the behavior. Furthermore, modern virtual machines divide classes into security domains based on their class loader. There are numerous examples of these approaches in the JDK itself. For example, the java.net.Socket class uses a separate implementation object, belonging to a subclass of the java.net.Socket-Impl class, to provide network services. The internal SocketImpl object is not available to the users or subclasses of the socket class. (Actually, other classes within the same package can access the SocketImpl object. Classes outside the package can't.) The java.net.SocketImpl class, on the other hand, implements all functionality as protected methods, thereby allowing it to be used as a whitebox.

The Java Conduits framework adheres to these conventions. The framework itself is constructed as a single package. The classes that are meant to be used as blackboxes are made final. Whitebox classes are usually abstract. Their behavior is carefully divided into user-extensible features and fixed functionality.

The combination of blackbox classes, fixed behavior, and internal, invisible classes allows us to give the protocol implementor just the right amount of freedom. New protocols can be created, but the framework conventions cannot be broken. Nonetheless, liberal usage of explicit interfaces makes it possible to *extend* the framework, but again, without the possibility of breaking the conventions used by the classes provided by the framework itself.

All this makes it possible to create *trusted protocols*, and to combine them with untrusted, application-specific ones. This is especially important with cryptographic protocols. The cryptographic protocols need access to the user's cryptographic keys. Even though the actual encryption and other cryptographic functions are performed by a separate cryptoengine, the current Java 1.1 security API does not enforce key privacy. However, it is easy to create, for example, an encryption/decryption microprotocol that encrypts or decrypts a buffer, but does not allow access to the keys themselves.

23.4.4 IPSEC: An Example

The Internet Protocol Security Architecture (IPSEC) [Atkinson 1995; Thayer 1997; Timo 1996] is an extension to Ipv4 and an essential part of Ipv6. It provides us with authenticated, integral, and confidential channels for transparent exchange of information between any two hosts, users, or programs on the Internet. Designed to be used everywhere, it will be implemented on most host and workstation operating systems in the near future. The flexible authentication schemes, provided by its key management layer, make it possible to individually secure single TCP connections and UDP packet streams.

In practical terms, IPSEC is implemented with two subprotocols, Authentication Header (AH) and Encapsulated Security Payload (ESP). Their location in IP headers is shown in Figure 23.16.

Our IPSEC prototype is designed to work with both IPv4 and IPv6. So far, it has been tested only with IPv6. It is designed to be policy neutral, allowing different kinds of security policies to be enforced.

Conceptual Model

Figure 23.17 shows the conceptual security model of the IPv6-IPSEC. The IPSEC itself can be thought of as consisting of some kind of security control, a number of security mechanisms, and a number of security variables. The security variables act as an interface to Security Management. Security Management updates and maintains the variables [Sahlin 1997].

An externally defined security policy defines the goals and bounds that the IPSEC attempts to establish. Security Management is responsible for converting the policy into a concrete implementation—that is, to set up and update the security variables in

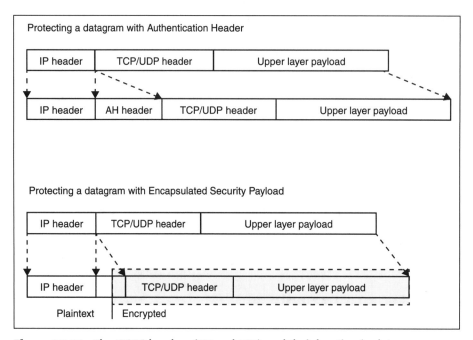

Figure 23.16 The IPSEC headers (AH and ESP) and their location in datagrams.

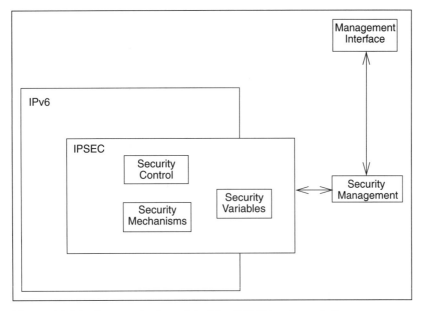

Figure 23.17 A conceptual model of the IPSEC implementation.

an appropriate way. Currently, the implementation does not directly support policy management; the security variables are simply read from a flat text file.

A basic IP protocol stack, including IPSEC, is shown in Figure 23.18. In this configuration, the IPSEC is located as a separate protocol above IP. The IP functions as usual, forwarding packets and fragments and passing upward only the packets that are addressed to the current host. IPSEC receives complete packets from IP. The example configuration initially accepts packets that either have no protection, are protected with AH, or are protected with AH *and* ESP. It does not accept packets that are protected with ESP only or with double AH, for example. This is one expression of policy. Furthermore, the conduit graph effectively prevents denial-of-service attacks with multiply encrypted packets.

During input processing, the AH and ESP protocols decorate the packet with information about performed decryptions and checks. Later, at the policy session, this information is checked to ensure that the packet was protected according to the desired policy. We have also experimented with an alternative configuration, in which the policy is checked immediately after every successful decryption or AH check. This seems to be more efficient, because faulty packets are typically dropped earlier. However, the resulting conduit graph is considerably more complex.

During output processing, the policy session and the policy mux together select the right level of protection for the outgoing packet. This information may be derived from the TCP/UDP port information or from tags attached to the message earlier in the protocol stack.

A different IPSEC configuration, suitable for a security gateway, is shown in Figure 23.19. In this case, instead of being on top of IP, IPSEC is integrated as a module within the IP protocol. Because the desired functionality is that of a security gateway, we want

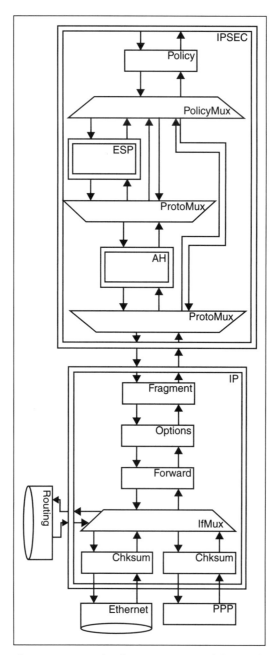

Figure 23.18 The host IPSEC conduit graph (simplified).

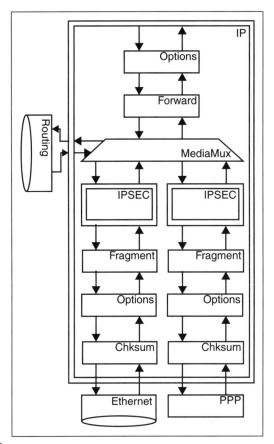

Figure 23.19 The security gateway IPSEC conduit graph (simplified).

to run all packets through IPSEC and filter them appropriately. Because IPSEC is always applied to complete packets, all incoming packets must be reassembled. This is performed by the Fragment session, which takes care of fragmentation and re-assembly.

Once a packet has traveled through IPSEC, passing the policy decisions it applies, it is routed normally. Packets destined to the local host are passed to the upper layers. Forwarded packets are run again through IPSEC, and a separate outgoing policy is applied to them. In this case, it is easier to base the outgoing policy on packet inspection rather than on separate tagging.

Our current IPSEC prototype runs on top of our IPv6 implementation, also built with Java Conduits, on Solaris. We use a separate Ethernet adaptor, which is implemented as a native class on top of the Solaris DLPI interface. We have not yet applied JIT compiler technology; therefore, the current performance results are modest.

23.5 Future Work

There are a number of future projects that we are planning to start. Due to our limited resources, we have not been able to work on all the fronts simultaneously.

The use of security services and features is usually mandated by security policies. The management of security policies in global networks has become a major challenge. We have recently started a project to design and implement an Internet Security Policy Management Architecture (ISPMA) based on trusted Security Policy Managers (SPM). When users contact a service, they need to be authorized. Authorization may be based on the identity or credentials of the user. Having obtained the necessary information from the user, the server asks the SPM if the user can be granted the kind of access that has been requested. Naturally all communications between the parties need to be secured.

A graphical JavaBeans editor could make the work of the implementor much more efficient than it currently is. This would also make it easier to train new average programmers to develop secure applications. In a graphical editor, the building blocks of our architecture would show as graphical objects that can be freely combined into a multitude of applications. The amount of programming work in developing such an editor is quite large, and there certainly are lots of ongoing projects in the area of graphical JavaBeans editors. Our plan is to take an existing editor and integrate it into our environment.

So far, our work has been focused on the design and implementation of secure application-specific protocols. Our long-term goal is to create an integrated development environment for entire secure applications. This environment would also include tools for creating the user interface and database parts of the applications.

23.6 Summary

This chapter presents a JavaBeans-compatible framework for generic telecommunications protocols and for cryptographic protocols in particular. The framework consists of structural elements called *conduits,* and of dynamic elements called *visitors* and *messages*. There are five kinds of conduits: Adaptors, ConduitFactories, Muxen, Protocols, and Sessions. There are currently two different Visitors, namely (generic) Transporters and MessageTransporters. However, the usage of the Visitor pattern allows easy addition of new Visitor types. The Messages themselves do not know anything about the static protocol structure; the Visitors insulate the Conduit graph and the Messages from each other.

When a protocol programmer uses the framework to implement a protocol, there are typically two major phases in the process. Initially, the protocol is divided into tiny pieces that match various kinds of conduits. Patterns for doing this seem to emerge. Second, the pieces are implemented by subclassing specific conduit and other classes. Typically, a small protocol will be implemented as one or more Session classes, a number of State classes, a number of Messenger classes, and possibly some Accessors as well. Finally, the Protocol class is subclassed to contain the resulting structure.

23.6.1 Design Patterns in the Framework

The framework itself has numerous examples of using Gang of Four (GoF) design patterns [Gamma 1995]. The major patterns include the following:

- The Visitor pattern insulates the Messages from the conduit graph, and allows other kinds of graph operations to be performed on the graph.

- The State pattern is applied in the Sessions in order to implement protocol state machines.

As examples of other kinds of usage of patterns, the following are worth mentioning:

- The actual encoding/decoding aspect of the Muxen is delegated to separate Accessor objects using the Strategy pattern.

- The State objects are designed to be shared between the Sessions of the same protocol. In order to encourage this behavior, the base State class implements the basic details needed for the Singleton pattern.

- The ConduitFactories are used as blackboxes in the framework. Each Conduit-Factory has a reference to a Conduit that acts as its prototype, following the Prototype pattern.

- The Adaptor conduits, obviously, act according to the Adapter pattern, with respect to the world outside the conduit framework.

- The Protocol conduits act according to the Proxy pattern, with respect to the Visitor pattern, delegating actual processing to the conduits encapsulated within the protocol [Schmidt 1995].

In addition to the use of the GoF patterns in the framework, the actual building of protocols is highly patterned, as already mentioned. Both of these shorten the time needed to learn how to use the framework, and to understand how others have implemented protocols when using the framework.

23.6.2 Availability

The current framework prototype is available at www.tcm.hut.fi/~pnr/jacob/. The actual protocol prototypes and the protocol sandbox prototype are available directly from the authors. An integrated JDK 1.2–based release is expected to be published some time in late 1998.

23.7 References

[Abadi 1994] Abadi, M., and R. Needham. *Prudent Engineering Practice for Cryptographic Protocols.* Research report 125. Systems Research Center, Digital Equipment Corporation, June 1994.

[Allen-Garlan 1997] Allen, R., and D. Garlan. A formal basis for architectural connection. *ACM Transactions on Software Engineering and Methodology*, 6(3), July 1997.

[Anderson 1994] Anderson, R.J. Why cryptosystems fail. *Communications of the ACM*, 37(11), November 1994: 32–40.

[Anderson 1995] Anderson, R.J. Programming Satan's computer. In *Computer Science Today: Recent Trends and Developments*. Lecture Notes in Computer Science 1000. Springer-Verlag, 1995: 426–440.

[Atkinson 1995] Atkinson, R. *Security Architecture for the Internet Protocol*. RFC1825. Internet Engineering Task Force, August 1995.

[Birman 1991] Birman, K., and R. Cooper. The ISIS project: Real experience with a fault tolerant programming system. *Operating Systems Review*, April 1991: 103–107.

[Gamma 1995] Gamma, E., R. Helm, R. Johnson, and J. Vlissides. *Design Patterns: Elements of Reusable Object-Oriented Software*. Reading, MA: Addison-Wesley, 1995.

[Garbinato 1997] Garbinato, B., and R. Guerraoui. Using the Strategy design pattern to compose reliable distributed protocols. *Proceedings of the Third Conference on Object-Oriented Technologies and Systems (COOTS 1997)*, pp. 221–232, Portland, OR, June 16–20, 1997.

[Hamilton 1997] Hamilton, G. *JavaBeans*. Sun Microsystems, http://java.sun.com:81/beans/docs/spec.html, 1997.

[Heinilä 1997] Heinilä, P. OVOPS Home Page. Lappeenranta University of Technology, www.lut.fi/dep/tite/labs/dc/ovops/index.html, 1997.

[Heintze 1994] Heintze, N. and J.D. Tygar. A model for secure protocols and their compositions. *Proceedings of the 1994 IEEE Computer Society Symposium on Research in Security and Privacy*. Los Alamitos, CA: IEEE Computer Society Press, May 1994: 2–13.

[Hueni 1995] Hueni, H. , R. Johnson, and R. Angel, A framework for network protocol software, *Proceedings of the OOPSLA 1995 Conference on Object-Oriented Programming Systems, Languages and Applications*. New York: ACM Press, 1995.

[Hutchinson 1991] Hutchinson, N.C., and L.L. Peterson, The x–kernel: An architecture for implementing network protocols. *IEEE Transactions on Software Engineering*, 17(1), January 1991: 64–76.

[Karila 1986] Karila, A. Portable protocol development and run-time environment. Licentiate's thesis, Helsinki University of Technology, Helsinki, Finland, 1986.

[Malka 1998] Malka, J., and E. Ojanperä. *CVOPS User's Guide*. Technical Research Center of Finland, www.vtt.fi/tte/tte22/cvops/, 1998.

[Mao-Boyd 1994] Mao, W., and C.A. Boyd. Development of authentication protocols: Some misconceptions and a new approach. *Proceedings of IEEE Computer Security Foundations Workshop VII*. Los Alamotis, CA: IEEE Computer Society Press, 1994: 178–186.

[Meyer 1997] Meyer, B. The next software breakthrough. *Computer*, 30(7), July 1997: 113–114.

[Nikander 1997] Nikander, P. Modelling of cryptographic protocols. Licentiate's thesis, Helsinki University of Technology, Helsinki, Finland, December 1997.

[O'Malley 1992] O'Malley, S.W., and L.L. Peterson. A dynamic network architecture. *ACM Transactions on Computer Systems*, 10(2), May 1992: 110–143.

[Orman 1994] Orman, H., S. O'Malley, R. Schroeppel, and D. Schwartz. Paving the road to network security, or the value of small cobblestones. *Proceedings of the 1994 Internet Society Symposium on Network and Distributed System Security*, February 1994.

[Sahlin 1997] Sahlin, B. A Conduits+ and Java implementation of Internet protocol security and Internet protocol, version 6. Master's thesis, Helsinki University of Technology, Helsinki, Finland, 1997.

[Schmidt 1995] Schmidt, D.C. Using design patterns to develop reusable object-oriented communication software. *Communications of the ACM*, Theme Issue on Object-Oriented Experiences, M.E. Fayad and W.T. Tsai, editors, 38(10), October 1995: 65–74.

[Simmons 1994] Simmons, G.J. Cryptanalysis and protocol failures. *Communications of the ACM*, 37(11), November 1994: 56–65.

[Thayer 1997] Thayer, R., N. Doraswamy, and R. Glenn. *IP Security Document Roadmap*, Internet Draft draft-ietf-ipsec-doc-roadmap-01.txt (work in progress). Internet Engineering Task Force, July 1997.

[Timo 1996] Timo, P.A., and P. Nikander. A modular, STREAMS based IPSEC for Solaris 2.x systems. *Proceedings of the Nordic Workshop on Secure Computer Systems*, Gothenburg, Sweden, November 1996.

[van Renesse 1996] van Renesse, R., K.P. Birman, and S. Maffeis, Horus, a flexible group communication system. *Communications of the ACM*, 39(4), April 1996.

[Wu 1997] Wu, J., ed. *Component-Based Software with Java Beans and ActiveX*. White paper. Sun Microsystems, www.sun.com/java-station/whitepapers/javabeans/ javabean_ch1.html, August 1997.

[Zremski 1997] Zremski, A.M., and J.M. Wing. Specification matching of software components. *ACM Transactions on Software Engineering and Methodology*, 6(4), October 1997.

[Zweig-Johnson 1990] Zweig, J.M., and R.E. Johnson. The Conduit: A communication abstraction in C++. *Usenix C++ Conference Proceedings*, pp. 191–204, San Francisco, CA, April 9–11, 1990. The Usenix Association, 1990.

CHAPTER 24

Dynamic Database
Instance Framework

It is common to integrate object and relational designs. For example, object and relational entities must interact whenever object technology replaces legacy relational systems or when object-oriented (OO) client applications access and control data stored in a relational or hierarchical format. They also interact when an object layer bridges two or more relational databases and translates and migrates data between them. An object-oriented bridge can be faster and more powerful than a relational design developed using structured query language (SQL) or a procedural programming language. A third form of object-relational interaction occurs in low-level database engines that support hybrid object and relational interfaces. In spite of the many advantages of object technology, the interface between object and relational architectures often causes problems.

One danger is that the object-oriented design will become contaminated with undesirable features from the relational or hierarchical model. For example, the design might violate encapsulation, rely on vendor-specific database implementations, and suffer the performance penalties associated with cross-network queries and joins. A less obvious but perhaps more insidious risk occurs from the architectural mismatch between the relational and object paradigms. Sometimes the mapping between the object and relational domains becomes increasingly intricate as the project unfolds and emerges as a "black hole" consuming hundreds of hours of developer time while contributing little or no value to the final system. This risk is particularly acute in data warehousing applications that contain complex relational schemas or a very large number of tables.

To mitigate these risks, Grady Booch recommends interposing an object layer between OO and relational systems: For most cases, it is reasonable to approach the design of a data-centric system by devising a thin object-oriented layer on top of a relational database management system (RDBMS) [Booch 1996]. If the performance of navigating around the domain model is the central concern, consider providing persistence through an object-oriented database management system (OODBMS).

In practice, this object layer is often implemented using specialized libraries or commercial application frameworks that allow objects to read, insert, update, and delete elements stored in a relational database. One particularly elegant implementation of Booch's concept is a data repository object that encapsulates the contents of a single database row and the obligatory database access methods previously listed. Several commercial software vendors offer products that incorporate this design [Booch 1996]. It offers many benefits to developers, including insulation from compiler variances, ability to transparently connect between incompatible relational databases, and the higher automation and control offered by an object-oriented programming language.

A simple employee identification system might be implemented in a relational table as follows:

RELATIONAL DATABASE SCHEMA

Table__   EMPLOYEE

NAME_____STRING

SOCIAL_SECURITY_NUMBER   STRING

A static repository object representation of this relational structure contains data attributes of the relational model and also provides methods for accessing the underlying database.

```
Repository Class Interface:

class Employee
{
    public:
            Employee();
            Employee( DatabaseHandle& aDB );
            read();
            insert();
            delete();

    protected:
            DatabaseHandle        _aDB;
            String                _name;
            String                _ssn;
};
```

Although the approach suggested by Booch is an effective solution for small to medium-size projects, the design breaks down as the project increases in scale, especially when databases contain more than 100 to 200 tables, complex schema relationships, and many gigabytes of physical data [Booch 1996]. In these cases, the number of classes and lines of code become prohibitively large and cease to be cost-effective in terms of systems development and maintenance. This problem is magnified when more than one relational format is translated. For example, a company acquires another firm and then translates the new firm's data so that it conforms to existing data definitions and standards. In this scenario, a minimum of two repository objects are required per table (one for the internal data format, one for the external format). If the data in the external database tables does not map exactly into the internal table definitions, there may be a many-to-one or a one-to-many relationship between external and internal table formats. This increases the number of classes and line-of-code problem by factor n, where n represents the number of mappings required when translating the data to conform to internal standards and controls. Another negative feature is that developers must modify and recompile the repository objects whenever external or internal database tables are changed.

The Dynamic Database Instance framework addresses these concerns by replacing statically defined classes with instances of objects that are configured dynamically at runtime. The framework typically generates a large number of runtime objects from a very small number of classes. This reduces program maintenance and increases automation because runtime objects do not need their class definitions redefined whenever a relational database schema is changed.

24.1 Dynamic Database Instance Overview

The Dynamic Database Instance framework avoids directly mapping classes to tables by inspecting database schemas at runtime and dynamically configuring in-memory database objects. It replaces compile-time constructs with runtime constructs.

The framework is built using three design patterns: Instance, Mediator, and Abstract Factory. The Instance Pattern is a newer and less well known design pattern than Mediator and Abstract Factory. It is described by Gamma, Helm, and Vlissides in their tutorial, *Design Patterns Applied*. The Instance pattern is used twice: once to create the Row Instance mapping and a second time to create a Database Instance mapping. The Factory and Mediator patterns correspond to the patterns defined by Gamma et al. in the text, *Design Patterns* [Gamma 1995, 1996]. Figure 24.1 shows the Instance Design pattern.

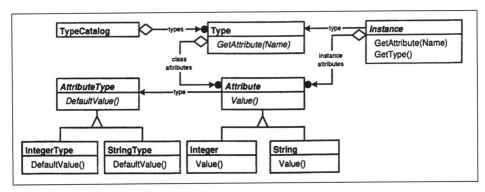

Figure 24.1   Instance Design pattern.

The Dynamic Database Instance framework contains low-level objects that present abstractions of the low-level behavior of tabular databases and hierarchical file structures. The behavior of these objects is structured by the Instance, Mediator, and Abstract Factory patterns.

Because it is a framework, Dynamic Database Instance contains *priority-inversion* (default behavior that is defined by the framework and not the developer), as shown in Figure 24.2. Default behavior is configurable into three modes: Object-Relational, Migration, and Translation. Object-relational mode maps a single layer of runtime objects to an underlying database. Migration mode creates an object bridge between two or more relational databases, and Translation mode creates a translation layer between two or more relational databases.

The framework may be scaled upward by integration with enterprise-wide object technologies such as Common Object Request Broker Architecture (CORBA) or by constructing distributed Internet applications or agents. Our attention is now directed to the specific classes and objects of the framework, their properties, and collaborations.

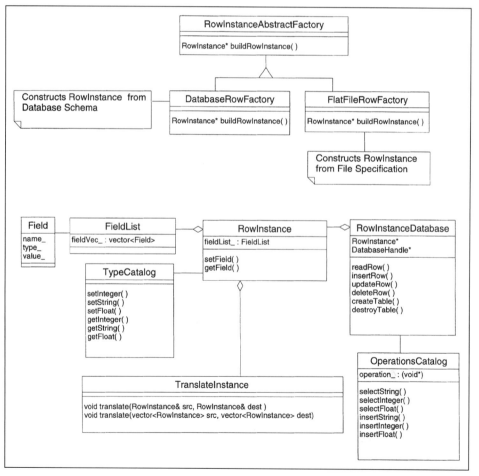

Figure 24.2   Dynamic Database Instance framework classes.

24.2 Dynamic Object Configuration

The Dynamic Database Instance life cycle contains five stages:

1. Inspect schema information.

2. Construct a generic Row Instance from schema information.

3. Bind Row Instance with a specific Database Instance.

4. Perform application-specific tasks with the Database Instance and possibly other Database Instance objects.

5. Deallocate resources (database connections, network resources, and memory).

At startup a subclass of the Abstract Factory pattern inspects the database schema and creates one or more Row Instance objects. The Abstract Factory pattern insulates the system from needing to understand the schema definitions of each database. Database vendors often define table schemas in a complex and/or proprietary format, so it is desirable to isolate this behavior from the rest of the system.

The Row Instance object is vendor-neutral by design. For example, a Row Instance object created from an Oracle database is interchangeable with a Row Instance object created from a Sybase database, a DB2 database, or from a flat file. It serves as the bridge between otherwise incompatible relational, object, and hierarchical structures. Each Row Instance object contains a collection of the attribute types and values of elements in a database table. In strongly typed languages such as Java or C++, a Type Catalog object maintains a collection of mappings between types and values to allow runtime type casting of values as they are passed to and from the Row Instance. An alternate implementation of the framework might use generic programming techniques (templates and runtime type information) to dispense with the Type Catalog component. Weakly typed languages such as Smalltalk offer a third alternative to Type Catalogs and generic programming techniques. When programming the Instance Pattern, dynamic elements such as the Type Catalog must be designed with care. If unnecessary overhead exists, it may lead to a performance bottleneck.

To be truly useful, a Row Instance object needs capabilities such as methods to read, insert, and delete data from a database. Implementing this behavior requires vendor-specific information. The Dynamic Database Instance framework isolates proprietary routines in specific subclasses, each of which understands the syntax and characteristics of the target relational database. Vendor-neutral Row Instance objects bind to vendor-specific database instances by aggregation. For example, clients may construct a Row Instance from a specific database (Sybase) and then bind the Row Instance object with a set of DB2 database operations. This technique is useful when porting or migrating databases from one environment to another. Or clients may create two or more Row Instance objects from separate databases or hierarchical files and then simultaneously bind them with two or more Database Instance objects at runtime. This configuration allows runtime communication and data exchange between incompatible databases.

Implementing the Database Instance class is challenging because relational databases often associate each operation to a specific type. For example, a database might provide a separate read, update, insert, and delete method for each type stored in the database. The Operations Catalog object manages the myriad combinations of database operations and types. It binds the types passing in and out of the Database Instance with their corresponding operations and selects and executes the appropriate low-level relational database operation. The Operations Catalog also translates proprietary, nonstandard data types and reconciles subtle differences between various vendor interpretations of the ANSI and Xopen standards. Like the Type Catalog, it must be very carefully designed to ensure maximum performance.

24.3 Translation and Migration Services

Migrating data between two or more relational databases often involves more than just copying data records. It may also require reconciling incompatible table and field definitions, overcoming proprietary database limitations, and translating between differing data formats and data types. More than one Row Instance object may be required to address these problems. For example, a Row Instance Object might receive input from a legacy relational database, modify the results, and store the modified data in a second Row Instance object associated with an object database.

This scenario is effective only if all field names and types are identical. This rarely occurs in practice. A more typical scenario involves translating one collection of types and values into a dissimilar type-value collection. To accomplish this, a separate Translation Object automates translation services between source and destination rows. This design corresponds to the Mediator pattern identified in [Gamma 1995].

The definitions that map the incoming and outgoing rows are stored in a Translation Catalog object. The Translation Catalog is accessed at runtime and provides information concerning the translation that operations provide. Typical items in this catalog include Rename, Convert Date, ASCII-EBCIDC, and other useful translation parameters. If highly specialized and elaborate translations are necessary, developers may subclass or extend the Translation Catalog in the same manner as the Operations Catalog described earlier.

A more sophisticated version of the Translate Object combines an ordered collection of Row-Translate-Row structures (see Figure 24.3). This enables many-to-one, one-to-many, and many-to-many translation operations to be performed on collections of database row objects.

Developers customize object-oriented frameworks to solve specific application problems. In the Dynamic Database Instance framework, the bulk of framework customization usually occurs in the translation layer. In favorable circumstances, it may be possible to replace the customization step with a standardized component that is reused across multiple applications. The following C++ interface illustrates one possible configuration providing translation capabilities. This configuration provides for one-to-many, many-to-one, and many-to-many mappings between source and destination relational or object database:

```
class Translate{    Translate();    virtual ~Translate();
    void translate( Row Instance& src, Row Instance& dest );
    void translate( vector<RowInstance>& src, vector<RowInstance>& dest)
};
```

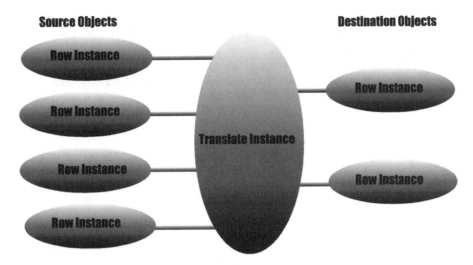

Figure 24.3 Translation Object configuration.

Developers have great latitude in implementing the translation functions. A loose translation algorithm might copy all fields from database 1 that have the same field name as fields in database 2. A stricter translation algorithm might apply global type translations to a given field name. The Translation Catalog object is useful for automating these global translations. The Global translation mode is particularly useful if a target database uses a different set of primary key-types than the source database, but all other aspects of the schema are identical. Translations may also be detailed down to the field-by-field level. These highly specific translations are not as automated as the looser translation algorithms described.

If properly implemented, Translation Objects are capable of extremely high performance. Tests conducted by the authors on databases ranging from 1 to 30 gigabytes revealed less than 1 percent performance degradation when compared with data loads and extracts where no translation took place. Of course, the complexity of translation algorithms will play a large role in determining the ultimate performance achieved.

24.4 Using Dynamic Database Instance

Clients interact with the Dynamic Database Instance framework by instantiating a Row Instance Database object and various translation objects. The Row Instance object may be created from a flat file, database, or other instantiation mechanism. Once the Row Instance object is constructed, it is typically bound to a specific database instance at constructor time:

```
Databasehandle aHandle(userid, login, password, database);
    DatabaseInstance aDBInstance(RowInstance& aRow, aHandle);
    aDBInstance->readRow();  // read a row
    aDB->field("price", 103.96); // reset a specific field
```

The ability of a Row Instance object to adapt to databases of arbitrary complexity without recompilation presents significant potential for automation when compared to statically compiled object designs. The greater flexibility of the design also improves time to delivery in many instances. In rough benchmarks obtained by comparing projects of similar size using static objects versus dynamic objects, we have observed productivity increases of 300 to 400 percent in time to delivery for small- to medium-scale projects (static objects do not scale well to very large projects, so a comparison is impractical). The productivity improvement is even when dynamic object-oriented methods are compared with relational methods such as SQL. In their role as consultants at several major U.S. corporations, the authors have observed productivity increases larger than 1800 percent in large data warehousing projects.

24.5 Consequences

It is hard to implement a Dynamic Database Instance framework. A single project can afford to build this framework only if it is very large. Once it is finished, however, it can be used in even small-scale projects. An object-relational system that uses it will take less time to develop and be smaller and more flexible than procedural methods such as SQL.

Implementations of the Dynamic Database Instance framework should use a commercial library to handle low-level relational database access methods. Commercial object class libraries make the framework more portable by insulating developers from differences in relational database data storage conventions and SQL standards, and by shielding developers from differences between various compiler implementations.

24.6 Scaling to Higher Levels of Organization: CORBA and the Internet

The performance overhead of cross-network queries and joins is one of the chief drawbacks of the relational model in distributed computing environments. Dynamic Database Instance objects are ideal for distributed database applications because they are configured at runtime, and the same object may access databases distributed across a network independent of the host operating system, client operating system, or proprietary RDBMS. Network overhead may also be reduced by passing Dynamic Database Instance objects to relational databases, performing local queries and joins, and returning result sets. This technique greatly improves network efficiency when accessing distributed relational systems.

Dynamic Database Instance objects may be embedded in Object Request Brokers and deployed in distributed systems at the enterprise level of organization via CORBA. As CORBA and other request brokers become ubiquitous on the Internet, the Dynamic Database Instance objects may be used for client-to-server, server-to-client, and server-to-server communications. The advantages of runtime configuration become even more valuable in distributed environments where applications must routinely access previously unknown databases and database formats.

24.7 Summary and Emerging Trends

Dynamic Database Instance reflects several emerging trends in object technology:

- Runtime configuration to unknown interfaces and data structures (CORBA DII, Web-based object browsers, CORBA-DSI gateways)
- Abstract configuration of business objects

All of these initiatives use multiple layers of abstraction that are configured at runtime. This approach trades efficiency for flexibility and rapid development. We predict that dynamic runtime configuration techniques will become even more important as systems development moves from the enterprise scale to truly global levels of organization made possible by the Internet.

24.8 References

[Booch 1996] Booch, G. *Object Solutions: Managing the Object-Oriented Project.* Reading, MA: Addison-Wesley, 1996.

[Gamma 1995] Gamma, E., R. Helm, R. Johnson, and J. Vlissides. *Design Patterns: Elements of Reusable Object-Oriented Software.* Reading, MA: Addison-Wesley, 1995.

[Gamma 1996] Gamma, E., R. Helm, and J. Vlissides. *Design Patterns Applied: OOPSLA 1996 Tutorial Notes,* San Jose, California, October 6–10, 1996.

CHAPTER

25

Compound User Interfaces Framework

Most interest in object-oriented programming so far focuses on implementation aspects such as the question of how a large software system should be structured into objects. From a user's point of view, it is not visible, whether the software system is built using object technology or some other implementation means. It is not relevant either. This is where component software takes a step beyond orthodox object-oriented programming. Components are meant to be visible to the end user of software, or at least to its systems integrator. In general, it must be possible to treat a component as a shrink-wrapped, marketable piece of software, which can be integrated with other components that have been developed and deployed by other parties (such as other companies). A customer may buy and compose components of vendors that are completely unaware of each other.

A component is a unit of composition with a contractually specified interface and explicit context dependencies only. Components can be deployed independently of each other and are subject to composition by third parties. A more complete definition of the term *software component* was developed at the 1996 Workshop on Component-Oriented Programming [Szyperski 1997]. According to this definition, a component is a blackbox where all interactions go through its specified interface. Independent deployment means that version problems and binary packaging and distribution issues must be addressed. Where object technology is used to implement a component, the component is typically a package that contains a number of cooperating classes

This chapter is in part based on the book, *Component Software: Beyond Object-Oriented Programming* [Szyperski 1998)].

and possibly a few objects that serve for configuration or parameterization purposes (resources).

When discussing software components, most current emphasis is on the construction of individual components and on the basic wiring support for components. Solving these problems is necessary, but not sufficient. The goal of components is to enable useful integration of independently developed components (for example, see [Szyperski 1998]). But how can such components work together in a meaningful way, if they solve problems from completely different application domains? They cannot. There must be a common ground, a common context that allows the components to communicate in the same language. A wiring standard, as provided by an object model, is not enough: For example, there exists no useful interaction between a device driver implemented as a Component Object Model (COM) component and a spreadsheet that is also implemented as a COM component. They have no common ground.

A *component framework* creates such a common ground. A component framework is a software entity that sets a standard for components in a certain problem domain and allows instances of these components to be plugged into the component framework. The component framework establishes environmental conditions for the component instances and regulates the interaction between component instances. Component frameworks can come alone and create an island for certain components, or they can themselves cooperate with other components or component frameworks. It is thus natural to model component frameworks themselves as components.

What precisely is it that a component framework contributes to a system's architecture? If its purpose were to collect useful facilities, then it would be no more than a traditional toolbox-style library. Since, by construction, a component framework accepts dynamic insertion of component instances at runtime, it also has little in common with orthodox application frameworks—the primary focus of this book. In fact, implementation inheritance is not normally used between a component framework and the components that it supports, because inheritance poses special problems in the context of component software [Szyperski 1998].

The key contribution of a component framework is partial enforcement of architectural principles. By forcing component instances to perform certain tasks through mechanisms under control of the component framework, the component framework can enforce policies. To use a concrete example, a component framework might enforce some ordering on event multicasts and thus exclude entire classes of subtle errors caused by glitches or races that could otherwise occur.

25.1 BlackBox Component Framework

The BlackBox Component Framework (formerly called Oberon/F) is part of the BlackBox Component Builder, a component-oriented rapid development tool and component-oriented programming environment [Oberon 1997]. The BlackBox Component Framework (BCF) is one of the few available component frameworks and focuses on components for compound-document-based client applications with rich graphical user interfaces, in combination also called *compound user interfaces*. For a comparison with some other component frameworks, see *Section 25.3*.

As the name suggests, BCF builds on the principles of blackboxes (abstraction) and reuse through object composition. Figure 25.1 presents an overview of the BlackBox architecture. The framework consists of a core set of layered modules and an open set of *subsystems*. Each subsystem (boxes with bold frames in Figure 25.1) is itself a set of layered modules. The component builder *is* the component framework extended by a development subsystem, providing compilation, debugging, browsing facilities, and repository services, as well as documentation and source wizards. In Figure 25.1 this Dev subsystem is shown to the right, but above the Text and Form subsystems: It builds on these two other subsystems.

All parts of BlackBox, except for those shaded in Figure 25.1, are platform-independent. The lightly shaded modules still have portable interfaces. Even the look-and-feel of the platform's native compound document architecture is abstracted from; currently, mappings for Object Linking and Embedding (OLE) and OpenDoc exist. (OpenDoc is now defunct, but see *Section 25.3.*) Wrapping of platform-specific controls similar to Java's peer classes is used to maintain platform look-and-feel precisely. Platform-specific features can be accessed, but components that refrain from doing so are themselves fully platform-independent. The modules and subsystems on the left side of Figure 25.1 provide standard programming interfaces. Those on the right side are either optional (such as structured query language, SQL, or the Dev development subsystem), are not normally imported by components (such as module Windows), or are platform-specific (such as Host subsystem).

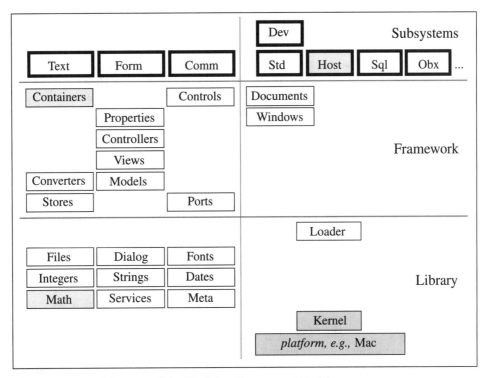

Figure 25.1   Architecture of the BlackBox Component Builder.

The BlackBox Component Framework focuses on visual components (or, more exactly, components that implement visual objects)—a flexible concept as proved by VisualBasic, OLE, and now ActiveX controls and JavaBeans. The cornerstone of visual component objects is their visual appearance and interaction with their containing and contained component objects. The central abstraction in BlackBox is thus a *view*. BlackBox views can be fully self-contained; that is, they are implemented as one single type. For more complex views, and container views in particular, a proper split into models, views, and controllers is used to enhance configurability and master complexity.

The BlackBox architecture is based on a number of design principles and patterns. Some of them are particularly characteristic of BlackBox: the Carrier-Rider-Mapper separation, the Directory objects, the Hierarchical Model-View separation, the Container Modes, and the Cascaded Message Multicasting services. Each of these patterns and approaches is explained further in the following subsections.

25.1.1 Carrier-Rider-Mapper Design Pattern

This design pattern is ubiquitous in the BlackBox framework and its uniform application greatly contributes to the understandability of the framework. The key idea is to separate data-carrying objects (carriers), access paths to data in these objects (riders), and data-formatting filters (mappers). This pattern originated in the Ethos system [Szyperski 1992], then still under the name Carrier-Link-Rider Separation.

A carrier maintains data that is logically accessible by position (coordinate). The abstract carrier interface opens a dimension of extensibility: Many concrete implementations can implement a given carrier interface. A rider encapsulates an access path to a carrier's data at a certain position. Riders are created by their carriers and usually have privileged access to the carrier's implementation. Therefore, a rider can efficiently maintain client-specific access state to a carrier. (The separation into carriers and riders is related to the Iterator pattern [Gamma 1995].) Clients use the combination of a carrier's direct interface and the provided rider interfaces to access a carrier.

Together the carrier and rider interfaces form a bottleneck interface that decouples clients from the potentially many carrier implementations. Mappers are used to provide interfaces more suitable for specific clients than the raw carrier and rider interfaces, but as such are a convenience feature that is optional. Decoupled by the bottleneck interface, mappers form a dimension of extensibility that is orthogonal to that of carriers. (The separation into riders and mappers is related to the Bridge pattern [Gamma 1995].) Figure 25.2 illustrates the relations between clients, mappers, riders, and carriers.

Table 25.1 illustrates the rich use of this design pattern in the BlackBox framework.

Using the file system abstraction as an example, the following program fragment illustrates how a specific file object and a specific mapper are combined. Code examples are given in the preferred language of BlackBox: Component Pascal, a component-oriented programming language and a descendent in the Pascal/Modula/Oberon line

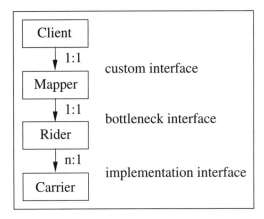

Figure 25.2   Carrier-Rider-Mapper separation.

of languages. Detailed knowledge of Component Pascal is not required to follow this chapter. Where unusual features appear for the first time, they are briefly explained. For more information see the Oberon microsystems Web site at www.oberon.ch.

A file is a typical carrier of data (bytes) with a one-dimensional organization (position of byte in file). A BlackBox file object is implemented by some file system; there could even be several such implementations coexisting, dynamically selected as needed. A file rider is an object a file object returns upon request and that refers to a specific position in the file object. Riders can be used to read from or write to file objects. Unlike integers used to represent positions in files, a rider is an abstraction controlled by its carrier. For example, a file rider can never point to positions outside of the file and can internally hold direct references to file buffers or other position-specific information.

In this example file riders do not directly surface. Instead, a mapper is used to create a higher-level access mechanism than reading and writing of bytes. The mapper used is the standard object writer controlling externalization:

```
VAR f: Files.File; w: Stores.Writer; pos: INTEGER;
...
f := ...;
w.ConnectTo(f); w.SetPos(pos); w.WriteStore(someObject)
```

The writer's ConnectTo method requests a new rider from the file and attaches it to the writer. In the example, the mapper is then asked to position itself at position pos. The mapper itself then advances the rider to pos. The writer is now able to handle requests to externalize objects by writing a linear sequence of bytes to the file, using the rider as a bottleneck interface.

The generalization of the Carrier-Rider-Mapper pattern to the other areas of application in BlackBox previously mentioned is quite straightforward. The form system is an example where no standard mappers are defined: The simple access to individual elements (views) in a form via form riders serves all standard needs. However, for more involved access patterns, form mappers could be introduced.

Table 25.1   The Usage of Carrier-Rider-Mapper Design Pattern in the BlackBox Framework

FILE SYSTEM ABSTRACTION LAYER		
■ mapper	Stores.Reader, Stores.Writer	*internalize/externalize objects*
■ rider	Files.Rider	*random access byte read/write*
■ carrier	Files.File	*file abstraction (positional streams)*

DISPLAY SYSTEM ABSTRACTION LAYER		
■ mapper	Ports.Frame	*coordinate transformation*
■ rider	Ports.Rider	*clipping area*
■ carrier	Ports.Port	*pixel-map abstraction*

TEXT SUBSYSTEM		
■ *mapper*	TextMappers.Scanner, TextMappers.Formatter	*formatted scanning/printing*
■ *rider*	TextModels.Reader, TextModels.Writer	*positional reading/writing of text elements*
■ *carrier*	TextModels.Model	*attributed sequence of elements (characters and embedded views)*

FORM SUBSYSTEM		
■ mapper	(no standard form mappers)	
■ rider	FormModels.Reader, FormModels.Writer	*2D positional reading/writing of form elements*
■ carrier	FormModels.Model	*attributed z-ordered list of 2D-positioned elements*

25.1.2 Directory Objects

Blackbox abstraction in BlackBox is taken to the extreme, in that not even the names of implementations of abstract interfaces are made public. As a consequence, the use of language-level NEW statements (Java: new functions) is ruled out as these would require the class name. Instead, new objects are created using factory objects or factory methods. Factory objects—for historical reasons they are called *directory objects* in BlackBox—are used where a new object is needed and no similar object is available. Such directory objects point to the currently selected default implementation in a certain context. (Directory objects are a specialization of the standard *Abstract Factory* [Gamma 1995].)

Each module introducing a new abstraction also provides a configurable directory object: the system-wide default for all cases where no more specific directory object is available. For example, consider the following (slightly simplified) excerpt of the file system abstraction:

```
DEFINITION Files;
TYPE
    File = ...;
    Directory = POINTER TO ABSTRACT RECORD    (* an abstract class *)
        (d: Directory) New (path: ARRAY OF CHAR): File, NEW, ABSTRACT;
        (d: Directory) Old (path, name: ARRAY OF CHAR): File,
NEW, ABSTRACT;
        ...
    END;
  VAR dir-: Directory;    (* dash mark indicates read-only variable *)
END Files.
```

A file directory object can be asked to open an existing old file by name or to create a new one that initially has no name. (This application in the file system gave directory objects their name.) The standard file system is accessed through configuration variable Files.dir:

```
VAR f: Files.File;
...
f := Files.dir.Old("/dev", "null" )
```

In many situations an object of similar qualities to the one at hand is required. For example, when transforming an attributed data model, a buffer for temporary copies may be required. To avoid loss of specific attributions, the buffer and the data model should be instances of the same implementation. For such cases, BlackBox supports cloning of most objects, where a clone is an empty copy of its original (the template of the Template Method pattern [Gamma 1995]). Note that this is different from (deep or shallow) copying since the source object's specific state is dropped and a freshly initialized object is returned instead.

```
VAR t, t1: TextModels.Model;
...
t := ...;
t1 := TextModels.CloneOf(t);
t1.InsertCopy(t, 0, 42);    (* avoid loss of attributions *)
...    (* change t1 - e.g., capitalize all lowercase characters *)
t.Replace(0, 42, t1, 0, t1.Length())    (* atomically update *)
```

Consider a case where the implementation of text t adds new attributes to those defined in the standard text interface. For example, t1 might maintain an outline-level attribute. If t1 was created independently of t, support of this special attribute would not be guaranteed and the InsertCopy operation would potentially have to drop this attribution. By using a clone, this loss is avoided since t and t1 are instances of the same text model implementation.

25.1.3 Hierarchical Model-View Separation

The original Model/View/Controller (MVC) framework [Krasner-Pope 1998] is flat and thus unable to support compound documents. Most more recent MVC-based frameworks do allow for the nesting of views inside views, where each view then has its model. The BlackBox approach to the recursive embedding of models and views is different and, in its being different, directly responsible for some of the more interesting capabilities of BlackBox. Nevertheless, BlackBox defines a compound document model that is easily mapped to standard platforms, such as OLE or OpenDoc.

To the programmer, BlackBox presents a hierarchical version of the original MVC framework (HMVC). The HMVC framework is designed to accommodate very lightweight visual components as well as full-fledged heavyweight container components. For example, a view that merely displays something need only implement a single method (Restore) and is immediately usable as a first-class citizen. This is in contrast to approaches that either only support noncontainer objects, such as today's Java, or complicate the implementation of even simple objects, such as OpenDoc or OLE/ActiveX. (ActiveX is interesting in that it does allow for extremely lightweight objects that do not implement any of the OLE interfaces; however, such objects then also do not have a visual presence.)

Views in BlackBox provide visual presentation of data and can be context-sensitive, active, and interactive. A view is a rectangular display object, may be transparent, and can overlap other views. Views may be embedded recursively where some views also function as containers. A BlackBox compound document itself is an outer-level view. Besides directly presenting visual information, a view can also function as an anchor for arbitrary objects "under the hood." For example, a view can be just an icon but refer to the results of a database search. Views are mapped by BlackBox to platform-specific abstractions—for example, to both OLE containers and servers. The framework shields view programmers from platform-specific issues, including look and feel.

A view may have a separate model, enabling multiple views to display the same model in different ways or from different perspectives (Observer pattern [Gamma 1995]). Models represent and manage data presented by views. A view can also have a separate controller, enabling the configuration of a view with a controller of the user's choice. Controllers interact with users and interpret user input.

Views—but also, where present, models and controllers—are all modeled as persistent objects in BlackBox. Their state is stored as part of the containing document. For models, persistence is an expected property. For views and controllers, an explanation is in order. First, the actual choices of view and controller implementations matter and should be preserved. For example, where one view component may display a model containing a table of numbers graphically, another view component may display the same model as a textual table. Likewise, different controllers may support different styles of editing such a view. Second, a view may be set to display a specific section of a model (scrolling, panning, zooming, and so forth) and may have various adjustable display properties (such as showing or hiding marks). These settings should be preserved as well. Finally, controllers may save the mode of a container view to which they belong (see *Section 25.1.4* on container modes).

In the HMVC approach, a *model* can contain nested views. This is important, since the choice of view settings of a nested view needs to be consistent across the possibly many views onto the outer model. Notice that HMVC is very different from other recursive MVC extensions that normally promote embedding of views in views (or models in models), but *not* of views in models. By tightly interweaving the embedding of models and views, HMVC can capture complex scenarios in a natural way. For example, the view that displays a particular model can be chosen externally without requiring the model to know anything about the set of views that could be used. It is the role of the next outer model (and eventually the enclosing document) to abstractly hold the chosen view and thereby to make the choice persistent.

Figure 25.3 shows a scenario where a document is visible in two windows, one showing the document itself and the other showing separately an embedded view. The document, as shown, consists of an outer text that contains several embedded game views. (By coincidence, the game is called BlackBox as well. The English mathematician, Eric W. Solomon, whose games are distinguished by being easy and simple, but very interesting, has invented it.) One of the embedded graphical game views is displayed a second time and this time enlarged in a separate window. Figure 25.4 shows how this scenario is supported by a hierarchy of an outer text view displaying a text model, which itself contains an embedded game view displaying a game model.

Documents in BlackBox are simply the root views of a model-view hierarchy. A root window uniquely displays a document, but an arbitrary number of child windows

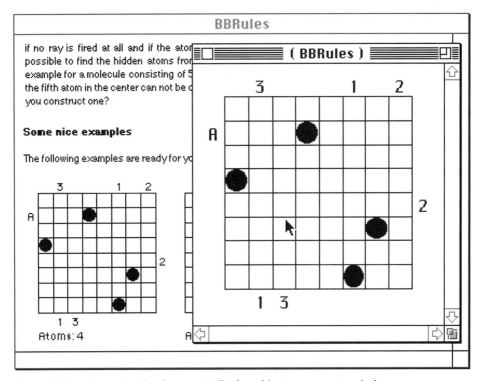

Figure 25.3 Scenario of a document displayed in two separate windows.

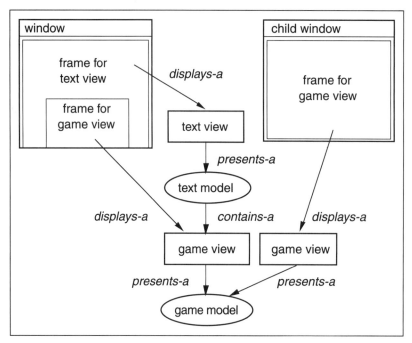

Figure 25.4   Models, views, and frames (corresponds to the scenario in Figure 25.3).

may display other sections of the same document or views embedded into that document. Child windows can be opened and closed freely—they represent no persistent state. Opening and closing root windows opens and closes documents. Closing a root window also closes all child windows onto the same document.

The root view of each window is a unique view to allow for separate scrolling, panning, and so on. The root views' models, as well as any views embedded in them, are shared with other windows displaying the same document. The framework's message propagation mechanisms built on this sharing to automatically establish consistent and simultaneous update of all windows onto a document.

A view may thus be embedded in a model that is displayed by several views, possibly in several windows, and even on different display devices. A *frame* object represents each individual visual appearance of a view in a window. Frames are mappers onto abstract display devices called *ports*. While views in a document form a directed acyclic graph, frames form a tree per window. Figure 25.5 shows how models, views, and frames are arranged when using a child window to display the original document rather than an embedded view.

25.1.4 Container Modes

Traditional visual component systems distinguish the use of pre-assembled component instances from assembling component instances. An example for the former is filling in a predesigned form; an example for the latter is designing a new form. For

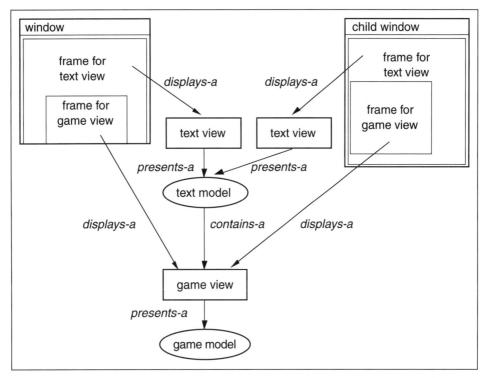

Figure 25.5 Models, views, and frames in the case of two windows onto the same document.

example, a VisualBasic form is either under construction and its controls are inactive, or it is frozen and its controls are active. The same split is advocated for JavaBeans, where a bean is either in assembly or in use mode, differentiating between build and use time. For many applications, this split is justified: Different people create and use forms.

However, compound document systems naturally unify construction and use of assemblies of visual component instances. For example, some outer levels of a compound document may be frozen—that is, turned into a fixed form—while at inner levels it is still possible to arrange new component instances. There is nothing wrong with filling component instances into the fields of a form, if the form designer permitted this. A form's field could, besides text or numbers, easily accept pictures and other media encapsulated by instances of visual components.

Strictly separating build and use time is quite restrictive and rules out many advanced applications. At the same time, the strict separation also has its advantages: The user of a prefabricated form, for instance, cannot accidentally damage the form while trying to fill it in. The BlackBox container framework has a unique concept to take advantage of the unification without losing control: *container modes*. Despite its simplicity, this concept is perhaps one of the most powerful found in BlackBox.

Using a special editor, containers on any level of a document can be set into one of several modes. The four standard modes are listed as follows.

Edit mode. The contents of the container can be selected, edited, and focused; this is the default used by a document editor where nested contents can be both edited and used, for example, in a text editor.

Layout mode. The contents of the container can be selected and edited, but not focused. This is the default used by a visual designer or component builder. Note that a BlackBox view can be *active* even if it is not focused—like ActiveX and OpenDoc objects, but unlike traditional OLE objects.

Browser mode. The contents of the container can be selected and activated, but not edited. This is similar to standard Web pages where HTML-defined text can be selected and embedded controls can be focused; a typical use is for online documentation and machine-generated reports.

Mask mode. The contents of the container can be activated, but neither selected nor edited; this is the default used by a predesigned form.

The other four combinations of selectable, editable, and focusable settings are also possible. For example, a container can be fully frozen by allowing none of these operations, or it can form a palette by permitting selections, but neither editing nor focusing. (Permitting editing but not selecting seems less useful.)

no edit, no select, no focus—*frozen*

no edit, no select, focus—*mask*

no edit, select, no focus—*palette*

no edit, select, focus—*browser*

edit, no select, no focus

edit, no select, focus

edit, select, no focus—*layout*

edit, select, focus—*edit*

The modes can be individually set for each container in a document, including the outermost one. Hence, a human designer or a programmed document generator can fully determine the degree of flexibility left to the user of a document. Documents can thus range from fully static and immutable to freely editable templates. The mode-switching commands can be made unavailable to some users to avoid confusion or to prevent intentional misconduct. It is the spectrum of possibilities that is uniformly covered by modal containers that allows BlackBox to serve so many aspects of compound documents and compound user interfaces with a relatively small number of concepts.

25.1.5 Cascaded Message Multicasting Services

BlackBox uses first-class *message objects* to decouple the sources of events from models, views, and display frames. Unlike ActiveX or JavaBeans, most BlackBox component instances do not need to be connected explicitly to cooperate—implicit connections are made and maintained by the framework. Essentially, change propagation is based on multicasts instead of registration of observers with observables. (A discussion of some performance-related issues follows later in this subsection.) The result is a lightweight and intuitive programming model, but also a potential minefield for subtle errors. Message or event multicasting raises some important problems. In particular, the relative ordering of incoming messages needs to be looked at carefully.

For example, consider a model displayed by two views. A change to the model's contents causes a notification message to be multicast to all views displaying that model. If the first view decides, as a result of receiving the notification, to change the model's contents again, then a second notification message is multicast. There are two possibilities: The second view receives the two notifications either in the order sent or in the reverse order. Often, a reverse order could be devastating, since the second view would receive incremental change notifications in noncausal order. If this view used these notifications to update its display incrementally—for example, to avoid screen flicker—then an inconsistent display could result. Note that this problem is *not* related to the BlackBox mechanisms to distribute messages. For example, event multicasting in JavaBeans to registered listeners or in COM to connected objects suffers from the same problem.

A general but very heavyweight solution to the ordering problem is to buffer all messages in queues and equip all recipients with their own threads. The messages are then delivered in causal order, where the separate threads allow for independent processing of messages. This approach is practicable in a truly distributed system with its physically separate processors and is the cornerstone of message queuing systems. In a compound document setting this approach would lead to a separate thread for every instance of every visual component used in any of the open documents. In addition, it would force all messages to be heap-allocated. (Interestingly, both JavaBeans and COM use heap-allocated event objects, although in many cases this is not strictly required.)

The BlackBox component framework follows a different and more lightweight approach. Messages are normally allocated on the sender's stack frame and are delivered in natural recursive call order (depth first), but the framework prohibits recursive sending of messages with overlapping semantics. When the first view in the preceding example tried to change the model's contents while a change notification was still in progress, the system would raise an exception. If the view still wanted to cause that change it would have to delay the change by registering a *deferred action* with the Black-Box framework. This action would be executed after the currently ongoing change notification terminated, causing nested change requests to be serialized.

Note that direct registration of observers with subjects (observables) would render it impossible for the framework to detect and intercept errors that would cause noncausal message propagation. Routing all messages through the BlackBox component framework allows it to enforce certain protocols of interaction or at least stop interactions that are about to violate important protocols. The gained robustness of the overall system, despite its high degree of dynamic configurability, is remarkable.

If all BlackBox messages went through the same multicasting channel, the framework could not reasonably block nested message sends. To see why, consider the following typical message chain. The user presses a key and, in reaction, the framework sends a message to the current focus view. The focus view delegates the message to its controller, which interprets it and requests a change to the contents of its model. The model performs the change and sends a notification message to its views. Each view computes the required changes to its displayed contents and sends a message to each of the frames displaying (part of) the view on one of the display devices. Figure 25.6 illustrates how BlackBox propagates messages in a three-stage cascade.

Obviously, it would be painful to force serialization of these logically noninterfering messages. To solve this problem, the BlackBox framework provides *cascaded message multicasting*. For each of the three messaging levels indicated here and numbered 1 to 3 in Figure 25.6, a separate multicasting mechanism with a separate recursion barrier is provided. First, a *controller message* is sent along the focus path—this is a forwarded unicast, as any container on the way to the focused view can intercept and possibly modify the message (the focus path is a *Chain of Responsibility* [Gamma 1995]). The view consuming this message, usually the focus view, can now request a model change. This change causes a *model message* to be multicast to all views displaying the model. Each of these views can then multicast a *view message* to all frames mapping the sending view onto one of the display devices.

The rules enforced by the framework are quite simple but catch most misbehaving components right when the error occurs rather than leaving behind visual trash or even inconsistent document states. The first rule is that a model cannot send a model message while another message sent by the same model is still on its way. The second rule is that a view cannot send a view message while another message sent by the same view is still on its way.

How does BlackBox efficiently distribute a message to its destinations without forcing interested recipients to explicitly register with the message's source? By using *source-addressed messages* the system limits distribution of messages to genuinely interested recipients *without* maintaining explicit dependency lists. The idea is that every message is tagged with the source object that sent the message. Potential message recipients indicate whether they are interested in a particular source when asked by the framework (instead of registering ahead of time).

In some exceptional cases the source of a message needs to send a message to sinks that are not even aware of the source's identity; source addressing fails to handle such

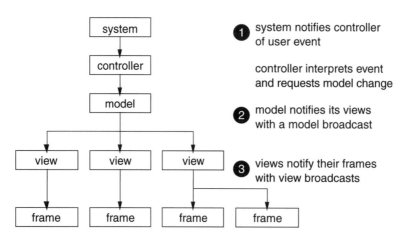

Figure 25.6   Three-stage cascaded message propagation in BlackBox.

cases. Note that in such cases explicit dependency lists (registered listeners) would not help either: The sink would not know which source to register with. For these occasions, BlackBox also supports *domaincasting* of model and view messages: Such messages are sent to all views and frames, respectively, that belong to a given document. Finally, *omnicasting* of view messages can be used to broadcast to all currently open documents.

The absence of a source address forces the framework to impose very strict recursion barriers on domain- or omnicast messages. As a result, domaincasts can be nested only if addressing different documents, and omnicasts cannot be nested at all. Besides these restrictions, omnicasts are also less efficient than domaincasts, which are less efficient than multicasts. Since all these message distribution mechanisms are restricted to *visible* destinations, they all still perform very well. To make up for the possible miss of relevant messages while being invisible, views need to check their consistency and lazily update themselves when inconsistencies are discovered once they become visible. (Similar lazy updates may be required in other forms of processing that reveal views, such as printing.)

25.2 Advanced Applications Based on Compound Documents

The BlackBox compound document model is powerful and flexible enough to support radically different application models. In particular, the provided standard text containers allow for interesting user-interface variations when compared to the more traditional form containers. Essentially, interfaces based on text containers are more like Web pages than like dialog boxes or forms, as known from VisualBasic style applications. However, both recursive container embedding and container modes allow for interfaces that go well beyond either Web-style interfaces or traditional forms. Also, since all BlackBox components have genuine programming interfaces, there is no need for separate automation or scripting interfaces. Using these programming interfaces, it is simple to synthesize on-the-fly user interfaces that exactly meet their requirements. This is similar to Web pages synthesized by Common Gateway Interface (CGI) scripts—for example, to report on the results of a search.

A first example of such novel interfaces is the BlackBox Component Builders debugging support. For instance, it is possible to select a view in an open document and inspect its current state. The inspection command uses the BlackBox reflection mechanism to inspect the state of the selected view. It then generates a text displaying all fields of the view object together with the values that each field had at the time of inspection. The generated text contains controls (embedded views) to continue inspection. Link controls allow the chasing of pointers (object references) and inspecting of the objects they point to. Folding controls allow the expanding or collapsing of parts of the inspected object to reveal or hide the state of subobjects. Figure 25.7 shows a typical screen, where a text view has been selected and state inspection requested. The user then asked for the state of the view's model. Since all displayed information is just regular text, the displayed material can be dragged and dropped, for example, to create an e-mail message to a help desk or to write a report.

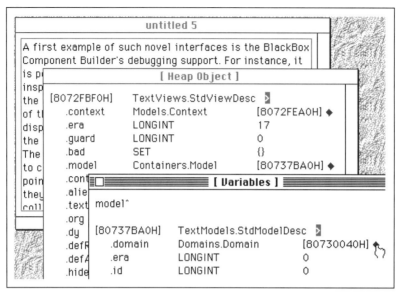

Figure 25.7 Interface generated by the BlackBox Component Developer debugger.

A second example of the unusual interfaces that become possible when generating compound user interfaces is the Debora discrete circuit simulator implemented using BlackBox [Heeb 1993]. Figure 25.8 shows a typical user interface, as synthesized by Debora. Again, the outer container is a text. This time, the actual simulation results are displayed by embedded trace views. A trace view is *text-context-aware:* If it finds that its container is a text, then it extracts the name of the signal that it should display from the surrounding text. In Figure 25.8, signal names are "Clock," "Enable," and so on. They correspond to names of signals in the simulated circuit—in this example, a cyclic 13-state counter.

25.3 BlackBox and Some Other Component Frameworks

As mentioned in the introduction to this chapter, there are very few true component frameworks available today. For example, it might seem that JavaBeans is a component framework for Java, while it really just defines a wiring standard for Java components. Enterprise JavaBeans is a component framework and so are some of the more recent additions to JavaBeans, collectively known as the *Glasgow extensions*. However, neither of these recent contributions addresses issues of compound user interfaces.

In the Microsoft component world, ActiveX probably gets closest, but does not directly address the issues of compound user interfaces. Clearly, compound user interfaces can be built using the OLE conventions for compound documents and ActiveX controls. However, instead of providing a component framework, a set of conventions is published that, if followed, promises interoperability. In fact, every ActiveX container re-implements a good part of the complexity of the OLE/ActiveX model from

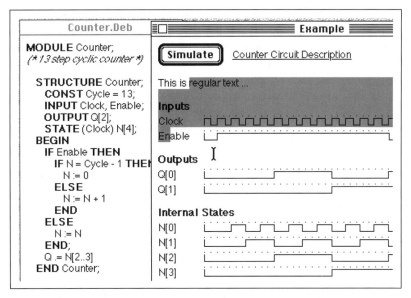

Figure 25.8 Interface generated by the Debora discrete circuit simulator.

scratch, allowing for a very real problem of incompatibilities between ActiveX containers.

While OpenDoc as such is now long gone, it remains one of the very few approaches fundamentally based on compound user interfaces. In many ways, BlackBox is similar to OpenDoc. Both are component frameworks for mostly visual components. Both have the notions of general containers and recursive embedding. Both use compound documents for everything, including their entire user interface. This similarity is not surprising, since the BlackBox component framework is designed to allow for natural mapping to both OpenDoc and OLE. Even on the level of compound document modeling, OpenDoc and BlackBox are at least superficially similar. Where OpenDoc uses parts, frames, facets, shapes, and canvases, BlackBox uses views, contexts, frames, port riders, and ports, respectively.

BlackBox is less complex—and less powerful—than OpenDoc in that it supports a more restrictive document model. For example, there is no generic support for document versioning. Also, BlackBox currently does not support general object linking, although it does support Web-like hyperlinking.

BlackBox goes beyond OpenDoc in that it also has a fully integrated development environment. Component Pascal is used as the one language for all purposes, from performance-critical low-level programming, to interfacing to external, platform-specific dynamic link libraries, to implementation of new components, to scripting. This very broad use of a single language is unparalleled in the industry. Java, for example, is not advocated for scripting; JavaScript is used instead. Also, Java is not at all apt for systems programming.

A proof of concept: All of BlackBox—including its garbage collector, compiler, top-level interpreter, reflection service, platform-specific interfacing, command and script packages, and all standard components—is solely implemented in Component Pascal. This impressive bandwidth is possible because Component Pascal is a small, simple, efficient, and effective language that can be used in layers. Script authors, for example, need not be aware of the majority of the language features. Implementers of simple components can still ignore substantial parts of the language. To the other extreme, no one but systems programmers needs to be aware of the low-level features of the language. Language-established safety properties strictly hold for all but the low-level features, which therefore can be statically excluded at compile-time, if desired.

Still, BlackBox avoids the single-language-island syndrome by supporting the standard object model of the underlying platform—most prominently, COM on Windows platforms. A direct-to-COM binding of an extended Component Pascal compiler allows for native programming of COM components. Components programmed using any other language or environment can be used by BlackBox components, and vice versa. On COM platforms, BlackBox is fully OLE-enabled; BlackBox is both an OLE server and an OLE container. OLE automation is fully available to the Component Pascal programmer or script author. Figure 25.9 shows an example of a simple module that uses the Microsoft Excel spelling checker to check the spelling of the current focus text; following a typical scripting approach, the checking command is implemented using a single procedure.

This simple script module acquires a reference to an Excel application component object and stores it in a global variable. The result is efficient checking once Excel starts up. However, the Excel server is also locked in memory for the lifetime of module Test-Spellcheck. A sophisticated implementation would release the Excel object, for example, after the spelling checker had not been used for a while. (It is, of course, also possible to provide a library abstraction that caches such objects and internally implements the timeout release, such that the burden on script authors is reduced.)

The BlackBox Component Builder, incorporating the BlackBox Component Framework, is a commercial product. As an extension of BlackBox, a cross-development system extension called *JBed IDE* is available. JBed IDE allows the development of Component Pascal components for embedded real-time applications for the real-time operating system *JBed*. JBed is a component-oriented operating system for hard real-time applications, featuring a unique deadline-driven scheduler and real-time garbage collector supporting components in Java class file format (bytecode). BlackBox and JBed allow the development of embedded industrial automation applications and Windows NT–based visualization software using the same programming language, the same integrated development environment (all user interface controls can also be linked to remote sites, such as a JBed application), and some of the same library components. In this combination, the unique potential of compound user interfaces is brought to the front ends of industrial real-time systems.

A fully functional education version of BlackBox for Windows 3.1/95/98/NT and Mac OS 7/8 is available free of charge from Oberon Microsystems' Web site (www.oberon.ch/).

25.4 Summary

Compound user interfaces, the most recent development on the user interface front, can be seen as a merger of more traditional graphical user interfaces and compound documents. The key idea is that all user interface elements are modeled as elements of compound documents: A dialog box is seen as a document displayed in a specific

```
MODULE TestSpellcheck;
  IMPORT CtlExcel, CtlT, TextControllers, TextMappers, TextViews;
  VAR app: CtlExcel.Application;

PROCEDURE Next*;
  VAR c: TextControllers.Controller; s: TextMappers.Scanner;
    res, beg, pos: INTEGER; ch: CHAR;
BEGIN
  c := TextControllers.Focus();
  IF c # NIL THEN    (*focus controller exists and is text controller *)
    IF c.HasSelection() THEN    (*selection exists; start at its end *)
      c.GetSelection(beg, pos)
    ELSIF c.HasCaret() THEN    (*caret exists; start at its position *)
      pos := c.CaretPos()
    ELSE    (* else start checking from the beginning of the text *)
      pos := 0
    END;
    s.ConnectTo(c.text); s.SetPos(pos); s.Scan();
    WHILE ~s.rider.eot  &  ( (s.type # TextMappers.string)
        OR app.CheckSpelling(CtlT.Str(s.string), NIL, NIL).Boolean() )
    DO
      (* while there is more text and the current token either is not
         a word or is found in the dictionary, skip white space and
scan
         in the next token *)
      s.Skip(ch); pos := s.Pos() - 1; s.Scan()
    END;
    IF ~s.rider.eot THEN
      (* found a word not in Excel's dictionary - select and show it *)
      TextViews.ShowRange(c.text, pos, s.Pos() - 1,
TextViews.focusOnly);
      c.SetSelection(pos, s.Pos() - 1)
    ELSE    (* checked entire text *)
      c.SetCaret(c.text.Length())    (*remove selection *)
    END
  END
END Next;

BEGIN
  app :=
CtlExcel.ThisApplication(CtlExcel.NewWorksheet().Application())
END TestSpellcheck.
```

Figure 25.9 Example script to spell-check arbitrary text.

mode and containing various controls. This unification holds great promise, as it finally reunites the intuitively close concepts of documents and forms, as known from the paper-based office.

Implementing graphical user interfaces without guidance is hard; application frameworks come to the aid, as illustrated in several other chapters of this volume.

Implementing software components for compound documents is even harder, as it is generally harder to build component software than it is to build monoliths. Traditional application frameworks—with their largely whitebox-reuse-oriented approach—do not significantly help to tackle the chore of building software components that, in their instances, live and manifest themselves in compound user interfaces and in compound documents as a special case. We introduced the BlackBox Component Framework, a framework that emphasizes components and blackbox reuse and that specifically targets compound documents. Some selected aspects are studies in detail, including the message propagation mechanism provided to flexibly couple component instances and allow them to interact. Beyond the scope of BlackBox itself, the presented solutions can serve as a general repository of ideas and approaches in the domain of compound user interfaces.

25.5 References

[Gamma 1995] Gamma E., R. Helm, R. Johnson, and J. Vlissides. *Design Patterns: Elements of Reusable Object-Oriented Software*. Reading, MA: Addison-Wesley, 1995.

[Heeb 1993] Heeb, B.U. *Debora: A System for the Development of Field Programmable Hardware and Its Application to a Reconfigurable Computer*, Series Informatik Dissertationen der ETH Zürich 45. Verlag der Fachvereine Zürich, 1993.

[Krasner-Pope 1998] Krasner, G.E., and S.T. Pope. A cookbook for using the Model-View-Controller user interface paradigm in Smalltalk-80. *Journal of Object-Oriented Programming* 1(3): 26–49.

[Oberon 1997] Oberon Microsystems., *BlackBox Developer and BlackBox Component Framework*. Oberon Microsystems, www.oberon.ch, 1997.

[Szyperski 1992] Szyperski, C. Insight Ethos: On Object-Orientation in Operating Systems. Ph.D. thesis, ETH no. 9884, Informatik Dissertationen der ETH Zürich 40. Verlag der Fachvereine Zürich, 1992.

[Szyperski 1997] Szyperski, C., and C. Pfister. Workshop on component-oriented programming—WCOP 1996, Summary. In *Special Issues in Object-Oriented Programming—ECOOP 1996 Workshop Reader*, pp. 127–130, M. Mühlhäuser, editor. Heidelberg: dpunkt Verlag, 1997.

[Szyperski 1998] Szyperski, C. *Component Software—Beyond Object-Oriented Programming*. Harlow, England: Addison-Wesley, 1998.

PART

Six

Experiences in
Application Frameworks

Part Six discusses experiences and lessons learned in the application framework arena. Part Six has three Chapters, 26 through 28.

Chapter 26, "Framework Development Using Patterns," shows how framework development can be aided by using common design patterns. A good example is hard to find, though, because most frameworks are too complex, their domains are rather specific, and their implementations are often proprietary. However, this chapter discusses a file reader framework, and it is small enough to be a good example. This is a real framework that is in use in both Smalltalk and Java, but it is simple enough to describe here.

Chapter 27, "Experiences with the Semantic Graphics Framework," presents some experiences gained in evolving a framework architecture through its application in a number of projects over a period of years. The evolution of the framework is considered from various perspectives, such as architecture, influence of programming language, and framework and organizational issues. For each perspective, the initial situation, the objectives that were aimed for, the evolution observed, and major findings are discussed.

Chapter 28, "Enterprise Model-Based Framework," describes a scalable strategy for model-based development as implemented at a major financial services institution. The architecture uses a layering of frameworks that abstract and insulate custom code from the details of a variety of enterprise required services. Model/View/Controller and Abstract Factory design patterns, among others, allow loose coupling and abstraction at a business entity level. The architecture leverages a number of NeXT Software's frameworks and the runtime adaptability afforded by Objective-C to implement generic objects and a generic application programmer interface (API). This minimizes the requirement for custom code. The frameworks implementing the architecture are capable of reading business model information at runtime and generating the entities necessary for the application. This approach serves as an alternative to code generation since it dispenses with the configuration and versioning overhead associated with strategies requiring generated classes specific to the application.

CHAPTER 26

Framework Development Using Patterns

This chapter shows how framework development can be aided by using common design patterns. I've written several frameworks and want to illustrate the typical process for designing one and how patterns are helpful. A good example is hard to find, though, because most frameworks are too complex, their domains are rather specific, and their implementations are often proprietary. However, one subsystem I've built is a file reader, and it turned into a typical framework, but one small enough to be a good example. This is a real framework that is in use in both Smalltalk and Java, but it is simple enough to describe here.

26.1 The File Reader

The File Reader is a subsystem developed as a framework for reading record-oriented flat files into domain objects. For example, the File Reader can convert the record data shown in Figure 26.1 into the object structure shown in Figure 26.2.

The File Reader does not automatically know how to convert the data into objects. Rather, a client has to initialize the File Reader with the record format, the domain

```
John Smith  |  123 Main St.  |  Lalaland  |  CA  |  12345  |  408-555-1212
```

Figure 26.1   Contents of a typical data record.

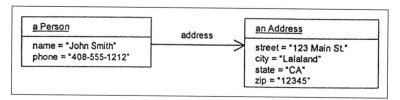

Figure 26.2 Object structure of a typical data record.

model, and the mapping between them. With that information, the File Reader can then read a record of the specified format into objects from the specified domain.

Although the File Reader's task is fairly simple, the task requires a great deal of flexibility. The File Reader must be able to support the limitless number of possible record format combinations. It needs a fairly simple interface that enables the client to describe the data mappings and direct the file reading. It also needs to be extensible, so programmers can add new format types.

26.2 Initial Design

The initial design for the File Reader is fairly simple. It needs to be able to read one record at a time, and a record is a set of fields. Figure 26.3 shows the initial class structure of the file reader.

To read the next object, the File Reader reads the next record, which reads the fields.

26.3 Composite Fields

One shortcoming of this design is that it cannot handle nested objects. A nested object appears in a record as a series of fields that go together to create a subrecord within the record. An example is the four fields inside a person record that describe its address: street, city, state, and zip. They are neither the entire record nor a single field, but are a set of fields that go together to form an address subrecord of the person record.

To handle nested objects, the design needs a collection field class that can contain an unlimited number of fields, but acts as a field itself. However, a nested object can itself contain nested objects, so a collection field needs to be able to contain other nested fields.

This is an example of the Composite pattern [Gamma 1995]. Composite makes an object and a group of objects act the same, so that a system can build object trees where branch nodes behave the same as leaf nodes. The File Reader's collection field should be a composite field that behaves the same as a leaf field, as shown in Figure 26.4.

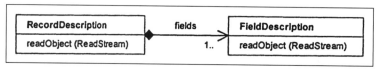

Figure 26.3 Initial class structure of the File Reader.

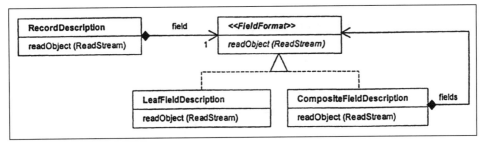

Figure 26.4   The Composite pattern in the File Reader.

This way, any field can now be a composite field that contains other fields. Notice that a record now needs to contain only a single field; whereas before, it might have contained multiple fields, now it can contain just a single composite field.

26.4 Decorator Fields

The difference between a record and a field was rather clear, but composite field now blurs the distinction. A composite field is a series of fields that act as one, whereas a record is a field or group of fields delimited by an end-of-record mark. An object's data does not necessarily have to be stored in a record; any series of fields will do as long as the File Reader knows when it has reached the last field for the object. Thus, the record structure is optional.

This is an example of the Decorator pattern [Gamma 1995]. A decorator is a wrapper object that adds behavior to the subject it decorates without changing the subject's interface. Decorators can be nested to add multiple behaviors. The main difference between a composite and a decorator is that a composite can contain multiple children, whereas a decorator contains exactly one child. Decorator is a flexible alternative to subclassing because a decorator can be added to any object from a hierarchy, whereas a subclass can only extend a single class in a hierarchy. (To simplify the diagram, the composite class is not shown here.) Figure 26.5 shows the use of the Decorator pattern in the File Reader.

This way, a record can be used to decorate a leaf field or a composite field, or it might not be used at all. A record field can even be used to decorate another record field. This way, if the record for an object can itself contain records (with their own delimiters), the File Reader can read it.

26.5 Adapter Fields

Once a field's data is read, the data must then be stored in the result object. By default, a result object is an array, since that's the simplest way to return an object's data. However, a result object will typically be a domain object, since that's the easiest way for an object system to store and use the data.

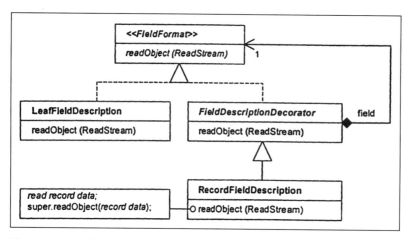

Figure 26.5 The Decorator pattern in the File Reader.

This leads to two issues: What object should be responsible for taking a field's data and storing it into a result object? And how will this object know whether the result object is an array or a domain object? This new storing object is like a decorator, in that it could need to be wrapped around any field description. However, the storing objects don't need to be nested like the decorators; the composite field that represents the result object needs exactly one storing object for each field. This means that a composite field won't actually contain leaf fields directly. Instead, a composite field will contain storing fields, each of which contains a leaf field (which might in fact be a decorator and/or another composite field).

This is an example of the Adapter pattern [Gamma 1995]. An adapter is a wrapper object that converts one object's interface to another. The adapter may also add behavior to its subject, like a decorator can, but its main purpose is to convert an object's interface. Thus, a decorator preserves the interface of its subject, whereas an adapter converts the interface. (To simplify the diagram, the decorator and leaf classes are not shown here.) Figure 26.6 shows the Adapter pattern in the File Reader.

This way, when a composite initializes its result object, it also makes sure to populate itself with the right type of field adapters. Each field adapter uses its field description to read the data, then stores the data into the result object using the appropriate protocol.

26.6 Null Fields

Another requirement is that sometimes a record contains fields that the corresponding object doesn't need. When reading from sequential data files, there's no easy way to skip over small amounts of data that are not needed, so the File Reader needs a way to read this data but then ignore it. Having read the data for a field, rather than storing the data into an array or result object, the File Reader should just ignore the data.

This is an example of the Null Object pattern [Woolf 1998]. A null object is one with

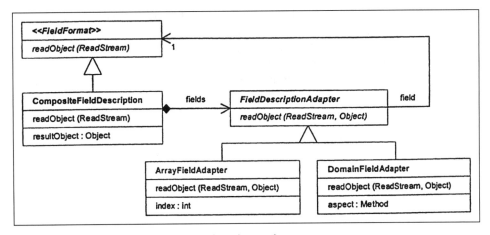

Figure 26.6   The Adapter pattern in the File Reader.

the same interface as its corresponding real object, but which implements that interface to do nothing. A null is preferable to using a null (Java and C++) or nil (Smalltalk) constant because it doesn't have to be tested for specifically and encapsulates the "do nothing" behavior to hide it from the client.

The File Reader implements this null object as another subclass of FieldDescription-Adapter, an adapter that stores its value into the result object by doing nothing.

26.7 Format Tree Builder

The File Reader uses the field description classes to build format trees. A format tree, an object tree of field descriptions that describes the mappings from a record's format to its corresponding domain object's model, determines how the File Reader reads records and creates domain objects. The more complex the mappings, the more extensive the format tree structure. Thus, the major task for a client using the File Reader is to build the appropriate format tree. Because of the potential complexities of these trees, building them can be difficult. Furthermore, the data mappings the trees represent often change because of evolving requirements, so the code to build the trees has to be as straightforward and easy to maintain as possible.

The File Reader needs a layer of Application Programmer Interface (API) code to assist the client in building these trees. This allows the client to tell the API what tree structure it needs, while leaving the details of building the tree to the API, encapsulating the details, and hiding them from the client. This API can easily be encapsulated in a single class responsible for building format trees.

This is an example of the Builder pattern [Gamma 1995]. A builder separates the process of building a complex structure from the description of that structure. This keeps the description as simple as possible and hides the building details. This is especially useful when the same set of instructions can be interpreted differently to build different but equivalent structures.

The FormatTreeBuilder class is the File Reader's public interface that hides the rest of the framework's classes. A client tells a builder what the tree should do and the builder takes care of building the tree. For example, the code to build a format tree for reading the person/address data described earlier is shown as follows. First, here's the Smalltalk version of the code (the code is indented to show the nesting in the format tree):

```
| builder |
builder := FormatTreeBuilder fieldDelimiter: $|.
^builder
  startCompositeResultPrototype: Person basicNew;
    addStringFieldWithAspect: #name;
    startCompositeResultPrototype: Address basicNew;
      addStringFieldWithAspect: #street;
      addStringFieldWithAspect: #city;
      addStringFieldWithAspect: #state;
      addStringFieldWithAspect: #zip;
    endCompositeField;
    addFieldWithAspect: #address;
    addStringFieldWithAspect: #phone;
  endCompositeField;
  recordField;
  characterStreamFormat
```

Second, here's the Java version of the same code (again, indented to show the format tree):

```
FormatTreeBuilder builder = new FormatTreeBuilder();
builder.setFieldDelimiter('|');
builder.startResultField(new Person());
  builder.addStringField(this.setNameSpec());
  builder.startResultField(new Address());
    builder.addStringField(this.setStreetSpec());
    builder.addStringField(this.setCitySpec());
    builder.addStringField(this.setStateSpec());
    builder.addStringField(this.setZipSpec());
  builder.endCompositeField();
  builder.addField(this.setAddressSpec());
  builder.addStringField(this.setPhoneSpec());
builder.endCompositeField();
builder.recordField();
return builder.streamFormat();
```

(Each of the preceding set*Something*Spec( ) methods returns a MethodSpec, an object the File Reader uses for creating instances of java.lang.reflect.Method. For example, setNameSpec( ) returns a MethodSpec that creates a Method to invoke Person.set-Name(String).)

This mapping is the only code the client must implement to use the File Reader. By using the builder interface, the client contains a straightforward description of the record format and its mappings to the domain model. This description is easy to break into reusable parts (to separate the address mappings from the person mappings, for example) and to maintain as the mappings change. It hides the field description classes from the client so that the client is not bound to any particular implementation of the framework.

26.8 Subsystem or Framework?

Is the File Reader a framework or just a subsystem? It's a subsystem in that it consists of multiple classes—FieldFormats, FieldDescriptionAdapters, FormatTreeBuilder, and so on—and multiple instances of those classes to accomplish one overall task: reading a file. What makes it a framework is that its class structure is extensible, yet the rest of the subsystem will work—unchanged—with the new parts as they're introduced.

For example, when the File Reader needed to be able to read a new kind of record format, such as a set of repeating fields, I added new kinds of FieldFormats to handle the task. Similarly, in the port to Java, I added a new field adapter class to the Field-DescriptionAdapter hierarchy that can get and set the values of an object's public fields. Thus, the File Reader is typically used as a blackbox subsystem; but when that's inadequate, it can be opened up and extended as a whitebox framework.

26.9 Summary and Lessons Learned

The process for developing the File Reader illustrates a number of important points for framework development.

Requirements should be general. The purpose of the File Reader is to read data records into domain objects. It must support a limitless variety of possible record formats and domain models, but the types of structures are limited and predictable. These are rather broad requirements that specify the behavior of the system, not its implementation. The more specific a framework's requirements are, the less reusable the framework will be.

Functionality grows iteratively. The File Reader did not initially implement all of the functionality it eventually needed. At first, it could handle only very simple record structures, but then it grew to handle additional cases. Each new user of the File Reader seems to discover a new type of record structure that the framework should handle, so the framework's growth is never complete.

Polymorphic hierarchies aid extensibility. The File Reader framework is primarily one hierarchy: a set of interchangeable field description classes. The framework supports a variety of different field descriptions, but collaborates with all of them through the generic FieldFormat interface. This allows new classes to be added to the hierarchy without changing the rest of the system, and for the system to eventually use classes that haven't even been created yet.

Patterns aid framework development. A pattern is not a framework, but a good framework contains good patterns. Patterns often solve problems in a framework's design. Developing the File Reader demonstrates that when a new feature must be added, the right pattern can show exactly how to add the feature.

The development of the File Reader illustrates all of these lessons, and they're all applicable to the development of any framework.

26.10 References

[Gamma 1995] Gamma, Erich, Richard Helm, Ralph Johnson, and John Vlissides. *Design Patterns: Elements of Reusable Object-Oriented Software*. Reading, MA: Addison-Wesley, 1995.

[Woolf 1998] Woolf, Bobby. Null object. In *Pattern Languages of Program Design 3*, Robert Martin, Dirk Riehle, and Frank Buschmann, editors. Reading, MA: Addison-Wesley, 1998.

27

Experiences with the
Semantic Graphics Framework

Like many companies, ABB embraced the object-oriented paradigm with goals such as building systems that are of better quality, are more flexible, are easier to maintain, and so forth. A cornerstone to reaching these goals was the trust that a proper application of object-oriented principles will lead to a significant amount of reuse and a solution to the nagging feeling that significant efforts expended in building software systems belonged in the category of reinventing the wheel. The result of adopting and systematically applying the object-oriented approach led to the creation of an objected-oriented framework for the domain of graphical engineering. In this chapter we present some experiences gained in evolving a framework architecture through its application in various projects over a period of years. The chapter is organized as follows. The evolution of the framework is considered from various perspectives, presented in sections. For each perspective we consider the initial situation, the objectives that were aimed for, the evolution we observed, and major findings. *Section 27.1* outlines the history of the ABB Semantic Graphics Framework (SGF). *Section 27.2* is concerned with the architecture and trade-offs made in its evolution. In *Section 27.3* we consider how programming languages and significant know-how sources influenced the SGF. *Section 27.4* summarizes a set of framework metrics that have been defined and how they trace significant changes in the evolution of the framework. In *Section 27.5*, we briefly look at organizational issues. *Section 27.6* and *Section 27.7* summarize our conclusions.

27.1 Semantic Graphics at ABB

We consider the need in the application domain addressed by the framework and how the applications affected the evolution of the framework.

27.1.1 Initial Situation

The SGF is based on a portable commercial class library (providing graphical user interface basics and so on) and supports the development of Graphical Engineering applications. The major components of the SGF are a configurable graphical editor and a set of classes designed to be refined with specific application know-how. The need for a framework in this domain arose from the painful realization that standard offerings of graphical tools did not (in 1992—and maybe not in 1998) cover all the requirements for specialized engineering. Two apparent options were adapting standard tools or developing one-off solutions. There had been negative experiences with both. Adaptation often took longer than expected and was not able to meet important initial and, especially, later emerging requirements. One-off solutions took a long time to develop, were of high risk, and had a high price.

27.1.2 Objectives

The objective from the perspective of an engineering department was to get specialized in-house engineering tools for an acceptable cost. From a tool developers/ software provider perspective set to satisfy several such demands, the objective was to identify and capture the common part of such tool requirements, thus building a platform allowing for customizable solutions. From the Corporate Research perspective, building the SGF had two goals: first, a way of gaining experience in design and implementation of reusable classes and application frameworks and, second, a practical way for achieving the transfer of object-oriented know-how into the business units.

27.1.3 Evolution

The SGF emerged as the common core of two engineering tools completed at the ABB Corporate Research Center at Heidelberg, Germany, in 1993, using C++ and a commercial base library.

First Applications

The first SGF applications were engineering tools providing graphical shells around existing FORTRAN programs. One requires a complex input data file that contains the topology, as well as engineering data of components modeling the airflow through a gas turbine; the other is used for calculating steam cycle processes. In each case a specific graphical editor provides domain symbols, associated data dialogs, and system consistency checks. The input file is generated and, in addition, the output file of the calculation program is scanned and results are inserted into the drawing or are made accessible through the respective components (using object-specific behavior). Efforts for developing each of these applications required about six person-months.

Catalyst for Further Projects

The fact that sample applications were available generated interest, while the underlying framework enabled solutions to be provided more rapidly than in the past. In the following two years several graphical shell–type projects were built using the SGF for calculation programs modeling systems with thermodynamic, electrical, and mechanical components, as shown in Figure 27.1. The projects were typically two-person efforts and, depending on the complexity of the applications, took around 6 to 12 months to complete. The framework was found to be well suited for applications of this type. The effect for the framework was more a ripening process than addition of concepts. For example, a help feature was added and internal structures were cleaned up. With additional developers working with the framework, the need for documentation and training emerged.

More Ambitious Framework Applications

A further application of the SGF is a set of CASE tools developed to support a specific software development and configuration process for production control systems. The Modeler, the Configurator, and a high-end prototype were not only based on the SGF, but also share an additional layer of common components. One example is the extension of the connection concept by a conduit. A conduit connection between two elements allows specific connections between internal parts of these elements. These common components were recognized as candidates for inclusion in the framework itself, but this never eventuated (refer to *Section 27.5*).

There are a number of ways to represent the structure of a system in graphical editors. We will consider a few.

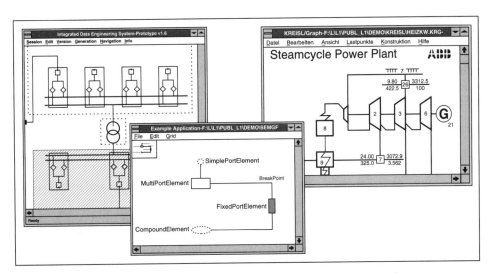

Figure 27.1   An SGF demonstrator (bottom) and two application examples.

Flat/flat. This is the trivial case, where all components of a system are at the same level (flat) and all are accessible in one graphical editor.

Deep/deep. In this case, the application is hierarchical (deep) and matched by a hierarchical set of editors. Internals of components are edited in a separate editor with its own window.

Deep/flat. Here the hierarchical structure of the system is manipulated in a single graphical editor, but details are hidden or revealed depending, for example, on the zoom level.

The first applications of the SGF mapped into the flat/flat case, but, later, different solutions were used to represent hierarchical system structures. On the positive side we note that the framework provided all necessary base elements and was flexible enough to allow several solutions. On the negative side we note the lack of support and guidance for using either solution within the SGF. As a result, different applications contain different solutions and the generic aspect of neither has been captured in the framework.

The production use of SGF applications revealed shortcomings in the ability to deal with bulk data. The mysterious crashes of one application were traced back to an index overflow when the object model was serialized for persistent storage. The fault was due to a simplistic assumption within the commercial base library that an index within the 64K limitations of a Windows data segment would suffice. From an applications developer's view the SGF was at fault since it had never been tested with bulk data of that order. Here the framework had to be modified to ensure that faults in the libraries used did not affect the framework user.

Large Applications

The largest application built on the SGF is an integrated data engineering system for configuring complex power distribution networks with transmission lines, stations, substations, and their internals. Such systems contain, for example, up to 100,000 switches, 20,000 lines, and, for each element, a set of associated (and interdependent) configuration information. While the network is entered with the graphical editor, the topology information is derived and verified and, together with data from configuration dialogs, entered into an ORACLE database used by the network control system. The major benefits of this approach are saving of engineering effort and consistency between database and graphical representation. There were several internal versions and the first official release was made after an effort of around 10 person-years.

This application is on a scale that went beyond the limits of the framework. First, the underlying commercial library itself is not handling such large amounts of elements efficiently. Second, the graphical editor framework had not been designed for huge numbers of elements. Performance became a major issue, as thousands of elements are considered for manipulation in a graphical editor. Even seemingly trivial operations like selecting an element or copying it with its associated aspects could take an unacceptable amount of time. The effect on the framework was very significant. It was decided that access to the source of the commercial library would be used to tune critical aspects for performance and to move to a different base library for future framework development.

27.1.4 Findings

While some hard lessons had to be learned, the overall finding is that the framework approach produces a positive impact. This has been recognized within ABB and outside. This section lists key findings.

- Guided by two concrete application needs with overlapping requirements, a framework could be developed in conjunction with the first projects. The domain of graphical engineering was in demand and the SGF could successfully be used as the basis for additional projects. A range of 10 applications has been built in cooperation with various organizational units within ABB.

- As more complex application areas were tackled, a number of problematic issues emerged. Performance for large projects became the most significant problem. This is a result of the framework initially being developed in conjunction with (relatively) small applications.

- With several framework projects taking place in parallel, the tendency for separate development paths increased.

- Performance tests with bulk data—even above initially anticipated amounts—are important for a framework that claims to be applicable to a variety of application domains.

- Framework designers need the courage to consider significant changes, including change to a different base library or a new development.

The impact of applications, which could be delivered faster and with more advanced features, provided tangible benefits. One SGF application alone led to a saving of 1200 engineering hours per year through increased productivity of designers. For another application, the benefit was the ability to produce an advanced, customizable product, which, according to customer surveys and prerelease versions, is set to increase market share. Reuse benefits internal to ABB had accumulated to 9.5 person-years by the end of 1996. At that time the SGF application won the Object Management Group–sponsored Object Application Award.

27.2 Major Concepts and Architecture

The SGF emerged as a successful framework for multiple projects because it provides some powerful general concepts, which give the needed flexibility for variants in applications of graphical engineering. Here we look at how such flexibility became part of the SGF architecture.

27.2.1 Initial Situation

When the SGF was designed, many of the applications that were later built using this framework could not be envisaged. The fact that two different applications provided guidance in the development was most helpful. There was no widespread analysis phase or an attempt to collect needs of other potential users. The crux was to focus on a clear core functionality to be provided by the framework. The first architecture was very much a no-frills version with less than 100 core classes.

27.2.2 Objectives

Architectural choices were considered in terms of how they help to implement increased reuse (or the avoidance of duplication) and whether they satisfy basic needs for graphical engineering. That is, the architecture would suffice to cover the essential needs of the applications being built at this time. For flexibility the approach was to provide hooks for customization, as they were foreseeable. Extensions due to possibly emerging future requirements were not built in. Rather the approach was to trust that essential objects and services, containing as few specifics as possible, would be useful (and customizable) for other applications in the same domain.

The general approach taken was to build a lightweight framework that is customizable in a layered fashion. Figure 27.2 illustrates how the SGF is focusing on its domain. If additional framework benefits are to be gained—for example, in the domain of network control (electrical, water, oil, gas, and sewerage networks)—then these are to be implemented in an additional layer, addressing the more specific domain.

27.2.3 Evolution

First we provide an overview of major class clusters in the SGF architecture. Then we illustrate, by looking at several examples, how the architecture of the SGF evolved.

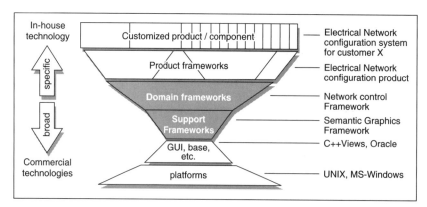

Figure 27.2   Layered architecture of the SGF.

Major Class Clusters of the SGF

This summary is intended to provide an impression of the major groups of classes and their interworking.

VObject is the root of the class hierarchy comprising all classes of C++/Views and SGF.

SKernel and its subclasses form the model of an application. They define how a system (SCoordinator) like a power plant is composed of components (SComponent) or subsystems (SSystem) like machines, pipes, or electric devices, and how these behave. In the following, such components or subsystems are called *application objects.*

Graphical aspects (SDisplayList, SDisplayElement) define how application objects are viewed and edited on the screen. Similar to the nodes and edges of a graph, the graphical aspects are partitioned in objects having a position (SPositionElement) and in connections between such objects (SConnection).

Views Applications start by displaying an SMainWindow on the screen.

The generic graphical editor SGraphicEditor is the major user interface to view and/or edit application objects via their graphical aspects.

STextView and SDataViewDialog are used to edit texts and data sets.

The Clipboard functionality is implemented by SClipContents and SClipContentsType.

General Concepts

One of the general concepts is support for graphical hierarchies. For example, detail levels may be represented as subdrawings in separate editors. Connectivity between components of higher and lower levels of the graphical hierarchy is kept consistent. Another general concept is the Coordinator-Aspect-View triple. The concept of coordinated aspects (a variation of the Model/View/Controller paradigm (see also Figure 27.3 in the sidebar titled *Major Classes of the SGF*)) supports systematically partitioning application complexity. Each application object can be represented in the framework by a coordinator, which is responsible for consistency between the graphical representation (graphic aspect), the engineering data (data aspect), textual information, and other aspects, such as interface representations. This is illustrated in Figure 27.4.

A (customizable) mechanism for updating and change propagation is also provided. These general concepts are a core part of the SGF and have been stable over the years. The Coordinator-Aspect concept was found to be useful for several later emerging needs. For example, the representation of an engineering object in a relational database can be realized as one additional aspect.

Graphical Editor

In addition to typical functionality (rubber-banding, zooming, standard and reduced printing), the SGF graphical editor uses the Coordinator-Aspect concept to provide semantic copy and paste; in other words, not only graphics but also their semantics (such as associated data) are copied. This is vital for engineering applications where hierarchies of components with various associated information aspects need to be

Major classes of the SGF are shown in an inheritance hierarchy in Figure 27.3. The groupings of classes are illustrated by colors (refer to the legend). It is intended to provide more detailed information about the evolution of an object-oriented framework in an industrial setting.

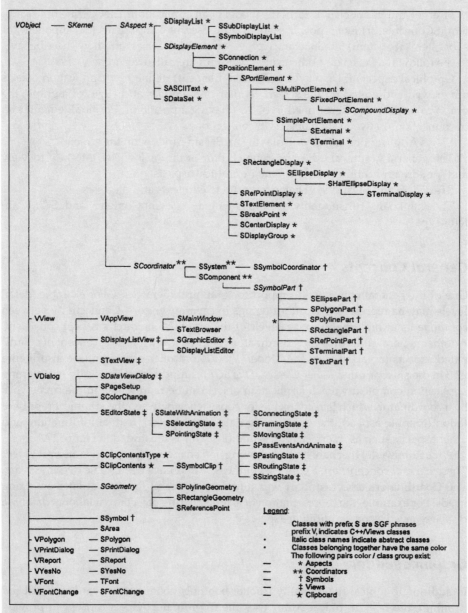

Figure 27.3 Major classes of the SGF in an inheritance hierarchy.

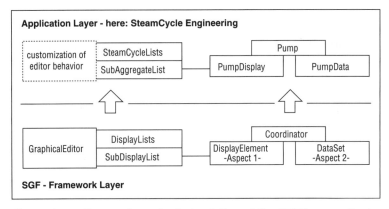

Figure 27.4   Excerpt from the instantiation of the SGF for a particular application.

manipulated. The graphical editor also allows for customizing object behavior. For example, the type of connections accepted, consistency checks, restrictions on selection and moving can be defined for individual and groups of components. The graphical editor is also an essential concept of the SGF. For each application, one or more graphical editors are customized. Here it was found that the original implementation of the editor was not sufficiently flexible. In a redesign of the editor, states were represented as classes, which can be subclasses for customization (see also Figure 27.5).

Symbol Editor

Symbols used to represent components in a drawing can be defined using a symbol editor. The shape of the symbol, terminals (in other words, where the symbol can carry connections), and reference points (where additional, computed information, such as labels, should be placed) can be specified.

   The symbol editor can also be used as part of an application, to enable the end user to define new symbols. Symbols are stored in a platform-independent format. The symbol editor was a later addition to the SGF, in response to the recurring demand for changes to symbols by end users.

Synchronized Graphical Views

Several graphical views (editors or read-only views) can be open at the same time (typically with different zoom factors or scrolling offsets). All views are kept up to date. One instantiation of this concept, which became popular in applications of the SGF, is a small subview showing an overview of the complete world picture of the respective editor. Again, this is an addition that emerged only as more complex applications were developed.

Object Persistence

Entire systems (that is, graphics and their semantics) can be written to disk. This mechanism takes a version number to facilitate coping with changes of object definitions over time. The need for a version number was soon realized. This allows application builders (and SGF maintainers) to read in objects stored by a previous version of the application (using getFrom) and check (if version is lower than currentVersion) whether update activities need to be initiated.

This serialization mechanism was appropriate for small to medium applications. Complex applications typically require a persistence mechanism in conjunction with a database. This was realized in applications for the databases ORACLE and Microsoft ACCESS but was never fully integrated into the framework.

Customizability–Tailoring to Configuration

We use the terms *configuration* and *tailoring* to distinguish between activities of blackbox customization and whitebox customization. The differences in effort and competence requirements are illustrated in Figure 27.5.

The customizability of the SGF is based on the mechanisms of object technology (subclassing, refinement, redefinition, polymorphism, clustering). Specific extensions are designed for—for example, by providing custom classes, clusters, and redefinable states for a finite state machine. These are whitebox customization mechanisms in the framework. Such tailoring can only be done by people with a good understanding of the internals of the framework. Initially, tailoring was the only way to customize the SGF. A very pragmatic philosophy was adopted for adding tailoring support. Only if it can be shown that more than one application will benefit is a change in the SGF considered.

The symbol editor is an example of blackbox customization (for example, the user does not have to know about the internals to be able to define customized behavior). It also exemplifies the balance between efforts at the framework layer versus effort at the application layer (see Figure 27.5). For the symbol editor, another 100 classes were added to the SGF to address only *one* aspect of customization.

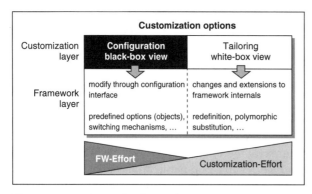

Figure 27.5 Customization options.

27.2.4 Findings

This section lists major lessons learned and findings about the preceding approach.

- The preceding approach is of the type bottom-up and is quite different from what we may call a top-down framework approach. Top-down framework development endeavors to cover a large number of applications straight off. It necessitates a significant amount of requirements modeling across various user groups to ensure that all aspects are covered in the framework.

- The goal to keep the SGF extensively customizable and the iterative bottom-up approach led to a framework in which customization is more whitebox than blackbox.

- The key concepts, which are general and simple enough to survive many years of framework usage, emerge as the core strength.

27.3 Influence of Programming Languages

The SGF has been influenced by a number of object-oriented programming languages and some other significant know-how sources.

27.3.1 Initial Situation

The initial prototype of the SGF was written in Smalltalk. The language was chosen for being object oriented and for being embedded in an environment supporting rapid prototyping and graphics. Although Smalltalk was chosen for the prototype, it was apparent from the start that it would not be a widely accepted choice for implementing solutions for ABB business units where such solutions would be embedded in existing software systems most likely written in FORTRAN, C, and C++.

27.3.2 Objectives

The focus in developing a graphical application was on OO principles (rather than language gimmicks). There was a conscious effort to apply OO principles explicitly, thus building up exemplary experiences for demonstrating and transferring object-oriented know-how via Corporate Research into the business units. Programming languages were seen as a medium for reaping the benefits promised by the object-oriented approach.

27.3.3 Evolution

In this section, we consider the various sources of influence.

Influence of Smalltalk

The language of the prototype has influenced the SGF in several ways. Smalltalk helped to install a culture of rapid development cycles for the SGF. This environment very much encourages the "code a little, test a little" approach. Today this has been formalized for bigger SGF projects in the form of baseline-oriented development. In a project with seven people, there are, for example, baselines defined in approximately six-week intervals. There are shorter cycles within this time frame, but the baselines provide the visible progress measures. Other influences of Smalltalk include some naming conventions—for example, getTerminalOppositeTo (this); the single rooted hierarchy; and maybe some messy aspects in the inheritance relations. These influences were further reenforced when the production version of the SGF was built on a commercial library, which itself was strongly influenced by Smalltalk [Jacobson 1992].

Influence of Class Library: C++Views

This set of classes provided the basis on which SGF classes were built (refer to Figure 27.2).

> **NOTE** C++Views was selected at the time because it provided the essential functionality required, it offered portability across Unix and Windows platforms, it was implemented in a widespread language (C++), it came with source code, and there was no fee for runtime licenses.

The class library enforced conformity in certain ways (for example, the use of the persistence mechanism via the methods getFrom and putTo) and it encouraged adopting its style by simply providing the sources from which many SGF classes were derived. At the time the library was adopted there were additional limitations to C++: Neither templates nor runtime type information were available and there were inconsistencies with deallocation. The solution for the first in C++Views is to sacrifice type information; for example, any elements in container classes such as VSet and VDictionary are of the most general class VObject. Proper solutions for the last two shortcomings mentioned were provided by C++Views and used in the SGF. As C++ matured, some shortcomings were removed in the language, yet the interim solutions still remain.

Influence of C++

There are obvious influences from the underlying programming language, yet it is apparent that in the SGF there has been a conscious limitation to using the object-oriented features of the language. For example, friend classes are a very rare exception and attributes are safely accessed via method calls. Yet shortcomings of C++ are apparent in the framework and in the applications built on it. The fact that there is no support for covariant redefinition (as there is in Eiffel [Meyer 1988]) makes typecasting in refined methods a common occurrence. Just for one application built on the SGF, a grep listing of the lines containing a typecast showed more than 400 entries. As an SGF developer overstated it, "Every third line is a typecast." There are crutches to avoid the worst effects of such casting and they have been used—for example, checking with an assert statement the validity of the typecast and, even better, supporting this systematically with an appropriate macro. In any case, the influence of C++ remains apparent.

Influence of Eiffel

Why mention Eiffel? Eiffel is regarded as the programming language that has most consciously been designed to meet software engineering principles and to map cleanly object-oriented principles into programming features [Meyer 1988, 1992]. Through exposure to publications of Eiffel and previous experience with programming in Eiffel, the developers at ABB Corporate Research were inspired to adopt ideas from the Eiffel style. Here are some examples. All methods are by default declared as virtual to allow for future redefinition. The principle of *design by contract* has manifested itself in use of pre- and postconditions, which are checked via macros named *require* and *ensure*. Also, a redesign of an early monolithic version of the state machine in the SGraphicEditor implements the design described in [Mora 1992], where each state is encapsulated in a separate class. Recently a master's thesis looked at how the SGF could benefit from adopting additional lessons from Eiffel programming [Weinand 1988].

Influence of Frameworks and Design Patterns

The description of the ET++ framework provided some inspiration [Gamma 1995]. The benefit of design patterns was realized most dramatically when standard patterns as described in [Gamma 1995] were utilized for better documentation of the SGF. First, it emerged that core functionality of the SGF was making use of design patterns (for example, the Factory pattern for limiting refinement of special domain objects to one class or the Coordinator-Aspect-View pattern as a new variant). Second, it became clear that exposing such patterns explicitly provided for clarity in design, choice of options, and improved communication between SGF and application designers.

27.3.4 Findings

This section introduces five more findings.

- Pragmatics often dictate the use of a compromise language such as C++; this also happened for the SGF. The language choice had to be accepted, but at the same time it was found most valuable to put object-oriented principles first.

- Smalltalk, Eiffel, and design patterns were valuable sources of influences.

- Some relatively simple measures were found to provide fast payback (see subsequent text).

- Thinking in terms of design by contract and enforcing it with systematic use of pre- and postconditions reduced time spent chasing elusive errors.

- Adopting design patterns for making and documenting design choices greatly improved the understandability of such choices and helped to lift the communication between team members to a higher and more concise level.

27.4 Metrics on Framework Evolution

The SGF was used as a test case for a new method of using object-oriented metrics to guide framework evolution. A group of metrics was applied. The interpretation of the measurements gave hints on places in the framework that needed to be restructured. The hints were discussed with the chief designer and feedback was received in the following categories:

FEEDBACK RECEIVED	PERCENTAGE OF HINTS
Agree	67
Disagree	22
Indifferent	11

All hints aimed at improving the internal structure of the framework to provide for better maintainability and reusability.

27.4.1 Initial Situation

The development process of object-oriented frameworks is highly iterative. Continuous monitoring and improvement of their design is essential because of their long-term use.

The primary goal of frameworks is to be reused in as many applications as possible with as few changes as possible [Rösel 1996]. The application of object-oriented design-principles such as modularity, abstraction, and decoupling (good design) leads to better maintainability and reusability. However, the object-oriented paradigm alone does not guarantee good design. Developers have to understand design-principles and to check whether these have been obeyed. Therefore, framework development needs experienced software engineers. Frameworks never achieve a perfect form in their initial design or after only a few iterations. Development proceeds iteratively and incrementally. A continuously enhanced program gets more and more complex, its inner structure more and more disorderly, unless countermeasures are taken to consolidate its design. Therefore, every phase of functional extension is followed by a consolidation phase, where design and implementation are inspected and restructured. One of the goals of framework development is to get a stable framework after a few iterations. Thus, the probability of having to change large parts of a framework's instantiation is diminished. Currently, the consolidation phase means a lot of manual work. Code reviews are made to reveal parts of the framework that have to be reorganized in order to comply with a good design style. The initial situation for the SGF can be described as follows:

- Consolidation needed a lot of experience on the side of the developers.

- The criteria for when to restructure were chosen individually by every developer depending on the individual level of experience.

- The process of how to find out when and where to restructure was ad hoc and not formalized.

- Different software engineers could produce different results for the consolidation of the same piece of software.

By using design metrics as described in the following paragraphs, the consolidation phase is made more efficient and effective. Developers are provided with hints about where and how to restructure and consolidate their framework.

27.4.2 Objectives

As the test case for a Ph.D. study [Erni 1996], design metrics were applied to the SGF. For this thesis, the objective was to verify the meaningfulness of the metrics and associated methods for interpretation. For the developers, the goal was to improve quality—that is, modify structural aspects to achieve better reusability. For the use of metrics, one objective was to spot classes or groups of classes that should be subject to reorganization in the next consolidation phase.

In order to define and quantify software quality, quality models are used that split quality into factors and criteria and assign metrics to the criteria [Meyer 1992]. For the SGF, the focus was on a subset of the quality factors that is connected to reusability, as reusability is the most important quality goal for object-oriented frameworks, and with it come flexibility and understandability.

Quality assurance in design is achieved by exploiting design heuristics. For different design methods, guidelines for good design and programming style have evolved over time (heretofore, we called these guidelines *design rules*). The majority of object-oriented design rules are concerned with three *design principles*.

Modularity. A system is modular if it fulfills five criteria. These are modular decomposability, modular composability, modular understandability, modular continuity, and modular protection [Mora 1992].

Abstraction. The quality of an abstraction is determined by the criteria of low coupling, good cohesion, simplicity (see subsequent text), sufficiency, and completeness [Booch 1996].

Simplicity. The less complex the design, the easier it is to understand, extend, and reuse. The complexity of a software system has two facets: its size (for example, the number of components) and the degree of interdependency/connection (that is, the information flow and coupling among the components).

Figure 27.6 shows the combination of design principles, design rules, and design metrics of different authors into a quality model.

From the variety of object-oriented metrics, 16 were chosen to analyze the SGF. The selected metrics were grouped using a quality model like the one in Figure 27.6 into three groups called *multi-metrics:*

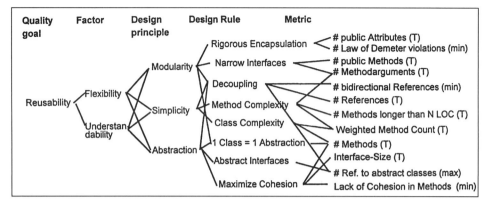

Figure 27.6 Extended quality model for framework design. (Min: A zero-value is optimal. Max: the larger the value the better. T: the value is limited by a threshold.)

Metrics for class and method complexity. If a class or method is too complex, it probably implements more than one abstraction and is a candidate for partitioning. Furthermore, it will be harder to understand and debug. If the complexity is too low, then the class or method might not constitute a meaningful abstraction.

Metrics for coupling. Classes or groups of classes that are tightly coupled will increase the effort required for debugging (more classes have to be looked into) and will increase the likelihood of introducing consecutive errors during debugging (changes affect more classes).

Metrics for cohesion. If a class shows bad values for the cohesion metrics, it is likely to embody more than one abstraction and is a candidate for partitioning.

27.4.3 Application of Metrics

Having selected the metrics, the next question is how to interpret the measurement results. Interpretation of measurement results is covered in the following section.

Interpretation of Measurement Values

When using design-metrics, one must know when a measured value indicates the need for an adjustment. We are looking for a function that divides the set of measurement values into *critical* values and *normal* values. There are different approaches in order to define such a function. The first is to use thresholds; the second is to monitor changes in measurement values when applying metrics to different versions of a component over time.

With the information from the design rules, the quality, and the measurement values, explanations can be generated that help developers to understand the measurement values.

There are no ubiquitous, predefined thresholds for metrics. Usually, average values calculated from previously derived measurement databases [Beck-Johnson 1994; Meyer 1988] or project- or department-specific guidelines are used. We propose two alternative sources for the value of a threshold:

1. DeMarco states: "The best way to judge a metric value is by comparison to similar projects, . . . produced by the same company, in the same language and which have the same processing bias" [DeMarco 1982]. Trivially, a software system is similar to itself. Thus, one alternative is a threshold calculated from the average and standard deviation of the metric values for the software under investigation.

2. The other alternative is deriving thresholds from statements in design-rules.

Alternative 1 uses well-known statistical methods. It represents the thesis that components of a software system that was developed at one location by a team of people show certain similarities in the style of their design and implementation that should be reflected in a set of similar metric values. Values that are outside an interval of average plus/minus standard deviation (above if the design rule implies a minimized value, below if it implies a maximized value) are considered to be outliers.

DeMarco proposed comparing one program with another similar program. Viewing this statement from a different perspective, we can state that different versions of the same software are very similar software packages and can be compared. However, the goal is not to get thresholds from the metric values of earlier versions, but to compare versions and interpret the changes of the metric values over time. Clapp states: "Data trends over time are often better indicators of potential problems than the actual values, because they can show when deviations . . . are temporary, fluctuating, growing, or diminishing" ([Chidamber 1994, p.108]).

In the iterative development process of object-oriented frameworks, the software reaches a kind of stable state after each consolidation phase, given that no new functionality is added. Whenever a new iteration brings additional functionality into the framework, the inner structure of the software gets more complex. In this process, problem spots may be created that decrease maintainability and make further development more difficult. By monitoring the trends of certain types of metrics throughout all subsequent versions of a software system—for example, before and after a phase of functional extensions—developers are able to spot problematic components and resolve problems in the consolidation phase.

The trend of the metric values, whether growing, diminishing, or unchanged, is compared to the limitations that interpretation models or design rules put on a metric value. If the model or design-rule proposes an upper limit to the metric value and the numbers of a trend are growing, then we mark the trend as critical, and vice versa for lower limits and diminishing trends.

Case Study: Using Metrics for Identifying Critical Spots

A set of tests is aimed at improving the current version of SGF by identifying problem spots in the software and giving hints about where and how to restructure the framework for consolidation purposes. For this, the consecutive versions 2.1 and 2.2 of the SGF were measured using the three groups of metrics previously described (complexity, cohesion, coupling), providing more than 900 measurement values (2 times 31 classes, 16 metrics each). From these values, outliers and trends in values were calculated and 45 statements about problem spots were identified, which means a drastic reduction in the amount of measurement information. The results were enriched with some additional information, as shown in the Table 27.1.

Table 27.1 presents classes with critical spots, tables of values for the multimetrics (with critical values indicated), the interpretation, and an explanation for the metric value. At the same time, the developer made use of a class browser to look up the origin of metric values in his source code, guided by the explanations. With these prerequisites fulfilled, a design review was conducted together with the developer. The developer had to understand the meaning and interpretation of the measurement values and give feedback in three different categories:

Agreement. The analysis results conveyed helpful or very important information for the next consolidation phase.

Disagreement. The analysis results are proposing refactorings that do not make sense either because of the role of the class or because the abstraction embodied in the class cannot be split for reasons of efficiency.

Indifference. The analysis results do not convey useful information.

27.4.4 Findings

Metrics can be used as an integral part of the design process to assist software developers in improving their product quality. Major questions are which criteria make it possible to measure positive and negative elements of systems design and how such measurement results can be used to improve the design process [Evagelist 1983]. The application of simple product metrics to entire programs, like measuring the average module interface size of a system, can only indicate certain problems but does not relate measurement results back to design principles. It can be very difficult for the developer to decide on the right action to take upon receipt of a particular metrics value.

Design metrics improve this situation by relating knowledge about good design (*design rules* or design heuristics) to characteristic structural system properties [Erni 1996] and [Berry-Meekings 1985]. Most object-oriented metrics deal with structural properties such as the depth of inheritance trees. Therefore, we find metrics mostly on the design level. Examples are Chidamber and Kemerer's *metric suite* [Chidamber 1994] and Abbott, Korson et al.'s *design complexity metric* [Abbott 1994]. The use of such design metrics as part of the development process has two problems.

First, complex metrics are often used—that is, metrics that combine several simple metrics into one formula. The measurements produced by a complex metric are very difficult to relate back to particular properties of the system under consideration. Often it is hard to trace backwards to the constituent of the formula that is responsible for the produced value and know how to improve it. An example of such complex metrics is *interaction-level* metrics proposed in [Abbott 1994].

Second, for most design metrics no criteria or thresholds are given to judge whether a value indicates a critical situation that needs improvement. This makes the interpretation of measurement results rather difficult.

The approach presented in [Erni 1996] avoids the first problem by using only simple metrics together with appropriate strategies for getting a similar level of abstraction as

Table 27.1 Example of Metric Use in Framework Evolution

CLASS	GROUP OF METRICS	V2.2 OUTLIER	TREND 2.1-2.2	INTERPRETATION	FEEDBACK	BACKGROUND
Text Element	Complexity	NO	Increase	Simplify methods; class is more complex.	Disagree	Increased portability and size through IFDEF-statements. No design flaw, no reorganization.
Main Window	Cohesion	LOW	Decrease	Bad cohesion; values must not be descending!	Agree	Class not well designed, single-instance class with multiple tasks.
Kernel	Complexity	LOW	None	Class does not constitute meaningful abstraction.	Agree, important hint	Class experienced several reorganizations and was simply forgotten.

achieved by complex metrics. Furthermore, it proposes a systematic approach for defining application-specific thresholds and interpreting measurement values using trend analysis.

This opens the door for a tight coupling of the software development steps and the usage of a metrics tool; the design rules reflecting particular quality goals of the developer are an integral part of the metrics tool. The tool is used to assess the software. It interprets metric values and transforms them into statements at about the level of abstraction expressed in design-rules. In addition, it supports the designer in localizing problem spots by providing explanations of each value. Thus, the software engineer gets direct assistance in applying particular design rules that improve the structure of his or her software.

The metrics approach that was tried out for the SGF especially supports evolutionary development. It was found to be valuable during the consolidation phase, as in each iteration, where design is cleaned up; it also provides an objective, repeatable mechanism to support review and to give advice on how the framework should further evolve.

27.5 Organizational Issues

Developing the SGF and developing applications with this framework have brought up several organizational issues. In [Holland 1992] several organizational models for supporting development in the context of object technology are described, including an Ad Hoc Model, an Expert Services Model, and a Product Center Model. We look at some of these issues and also consider how they have been dealt with in other framework projects within the organization.

27.5.1 Initial Situation

Since the SGF was the first framework developed in the organization, there was no previous experience or culture for this type of approach. The group that developed the framework is situated in a research organization, which had been charged to explore technology and develop prototypes—where should a product be supported?

27.5.2 Objectives

The objective was to take full advantage of the opportunities arising from a framework-based approach. Therefore, current organizational settings were not taken for granted.

27.5.3 Questions That Arose during the Evolution of the Framework

The organization of the SGF was started in an Ad Hoc Model for Reuse and has evolved into an Expert Services Model. The success of SGF implementations and the spread of their use are possible only in conjunction with the services of some key people. We have recognized that the SGF should be treated more like a product, but several questions have to be addressed before the organizational setting reaches the level of a Product Center Model as described in [Holland 1992].

Ownership Issues

Who owns a framework used across domains? How should maintenance and warrantees be handled? How are financial investments shared and benefits distributed?

The SGF can be applied in the broad domain of Graphical Engineering and is therefore of interest to a number of business units within ABB. None of these businesses has a primary focus on building or maintaining software of this generic nature. The internal informatics unit did not have appropriate resources and the transfer to a (small) external software house was regarded as too risky. Thus, the responsibility stayed with Corporate Research. In January 1998 an Advanced Software Center was established in ABB Informatik, Germany, to bridge the gap between research and application.

For a business area–specific framework built on top of the SGF (for example, in the domain of network control), the ownership issue is clear. Here a business unit takes responsibility for further developments, maintenance, and profits associated with this product.

People Issues

How should appropriate expertise be built up—by using external experts, by acquisition, by retraining, or by using a combination of these methods? How should you handle staff who cannot make the change?

If good designers are a precious commodity, then good framework designers are even more so. That a number of good people were available to evolve the SGF was more the result of chance than organization. Only four core people were involved in developing the SGF and applications in the originating location. The transfer to others was done within the context of projects in small teams. This way, pockets of SGF know-how developed (three smaller ones and one larger), making a total of nine people. At the originating site, only two people remain involved with the SGF and the know-how must be classified as vulnerable.

From the SGF and other framework projects emerging in the organization, it became apparent that the quality of the people involved is particularly critical, since the effects of design decisions are multiplied to all projects building on the framework. Therefore, training is regarded as important, but the question is, how to go about it? The experience with general introductory courses has been mixed. In any case, the framework-specific training must be done by key people with a sound understanding of the framework internals and experience in instantiating the framework.

Process Responsibilities

How can framework upgrades be synchronized with application development? How are the additions of application developers that have generic value to be recognized and included?

The two distinct processes associated with frameworks are illustrated in Figure 27.7. The framework development process is executed at first very much in iteration with application development. For the SGF this was a period of about two years (including a six-month prototyping phase). Then stabilization should occur, allowing the framework process to work in longer time frames, while more applications are being developed in parallel. Organizational responsibilities and interactions have to be assigned for the two types of processes to work effectively. One key for succeeding in this is identified by the box labeled "usage" in Figure 27.7. The organization must be ready to use the frequent baselines of the development and provide early feedback.

One important aspect is the decision about which additional features are to be included in the framework. For the SGF, the pragmatic approach was to leave as much responsibility as possible with the application developer and provide advice from the framework developer side. If application needs seemed to expose a shortcoming in the SGF, the application developer had to come up with one or more proposals for a solution—one of these should be under the application developer's control (it should not involve a new release of the SGF). This arrangement worked well to keep the framework stable; on the other hand, there are several cases where we found that good generic solutions were implemented within applications that did not flow back into the SGF.

Example: A Large Organizational Change

For a domain other than Graphical Engineering, a technology study was made within a business area of the company. A framework-based development approach promised new opportunities. Therefore, a business study was commissioned, resulting in a proposal for an alignment of several organizational entities to take advantage of the business opportunities. A new business unit was established, responsible for developing and marketing a framework-based platform. Some 11 application development centers are designated users.

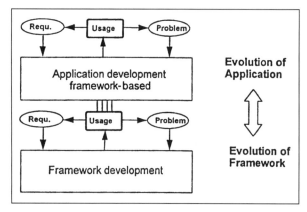

Figure 27.7 Dependencies between framework processes. (Note: The usage of the framework *is* the application development.)

Whether this endeavor will become a business success, it is too early to say. But we know already that without the conscious reorganization and the addressing of the associated financial issues no common (framework) development could have taken place.

27.5.4 Findings

Leveraging the potential of a framework approach requires organizational changes. Such changes cover a broad range:

- Recognizing and fostering designer ability and potential
- Training and mentoring team members over several months
- Reorganizing the developers into a framework team and a team of application developers
- Committing to substantial framework development efforts and times before application instances are built on top
- Defining processes for synchronizing framework and application development (here baseline-focused development is found useful)
- Considering new organizational entities to carry the framework through to a product level

Some of these changes were realized during the evolution of the SGF; others are still pending; and for some issues we are hoping that we will do better next time.

27.6 Framework Lessons Learned: Some Theses

In this chapter we summarize our experience in terms of several propositions. They express findings that are also likely to be applicable to other organizations evolving frameworks.

27.6.1 Thesis 1: No Framework Success without Application Success

What distinguishes a *successful* object-oriented framework from others? In our experience the primary point of distinction is the number of applications that have been successfully realized using the framework. Therefore, the driving force must be the applications. The first two or three applications provide the essential requirements. As a check, ask the following question: Are we able to succinctly state the domain the framework is addressing (see Chapter 1)? While the framework architect will keep openness and extendibility for future applications in mind, we found it vital to accept the reality that there will be no future applications unless these first few are out there within the window of opportunity. Some chances for better design decisions, better documentation, and so on, have been sacrificed to this pragmatic view. This has hurt. Looking back, we find that without some wounds of this kind we may have a framework that is better but unsuccessful.

27.6.2 Thesis 2: No Framework without Customizable Architecture

Customizable architecture is the key to fulfilling the demands of the variants required by applications in the framework domain. Designer know-how and modeling techniques are vital, but in our experience they must be consciously focused on identifying key concepts that are general and simple enough to survive many years of framework usage (see Chapter 2). Design patterns can help to address the variable hot spots with flexible designs that are maintainable. Effort spent for customization should be consciously evaluated to determine if it is best spent in configuration or tailoring, at the framework layer or at the application layer.

27.6.3 Thesis 3: OO Principles Are More Important than Language Choices

Whether the framework is implemented in Java, Smalltalk, C++, or some other language, without a sound foundation on object-oriented principles it will not deserve to be called a framework. Design by contract and use of design patterns were two adoptions that provided a good payback (see Chapter 3).

27.6.4 Thesis 4: The Law of Increasing Entropy Applies to Framework Evolution

This law of the universe tells us that a framework will deteriorate as it is developed and maintained unless conscious efforts are expended to counteract this. The metrics support for the framework designer previously presented (see Chapter 4) is a way to provide objective checks where such efforts are most needed.

27.6.5 Thesis 5: No Framework without Organizational Changes

It is our experience that successfully developing and utilizing an object-oriented framework requires organizational changes (see Chapter 5). While here, too, an iterative approach with small changes may be useful, it is our recommendation to not leave such developments to chance. Defining the organizational responsibilities and interaction processes is a prerequisite for creating a win-win situation for framework suppliers and framework users. The goal should be to implement a Product Center Model for utilizing the potential of good framework developments.

27.6.6 Thesis 6: No Framework Benefit without Commitment and Investment

We found that a framework:

- Takes longer to build than traditional libraries, as it contains additional design information

- Takes longer to learn than traditional libraries, as more complex interfaces must be understood

- Requires more careful design than individual programs

- Requires better documentation and support than individual programs

- Changes the software life cycle, as efforts are shifted, for example, from designing individual systems to deriving systems from or integrating systems with the framework design

- May require rework in existing derivations when changes are made to it

In our experience the cost of a framework may be 50 percent of the total cost of the first three applications. Once three or more applications are implemented and being used the framework will most likely have paid for itself. To reach this pay-off level significant commitment and investment are required.

27.7 Summary

The Semantic Graphics Framework evolved over a period of years from a prototype to a framework used in several industrial applications. The approach resulted in tangible benefits and is therefore regarded as a success. The lessons learned in the process are to a large extent old lessons in a new form.

It is common knowledge that aspects such as architecture, documentation, metrics, process, and organization are important for producing successful software. One challenge is to apply the principles of these areas to the framework approach and refine appropriate actions in accordance with the emerging needs. On the one hand, frameworks are the same (a complex software system, a product, and so on); on the other hand, they are different. New ways of abstracting complexity are available, new skills are required, faster development cycles are possible, and new types of metrics are necessary.

The experiences gathered during evolution of the SGF were particularly valuable to us through the mix of activities possible through our role of being responsible for technology transfer rather than pure product development. This helped us to stick with a more systematic approach not dominated by deadlines alone, yet directly driven by practical applications in various industrial domains. Of course, many aspects of the development could be improved in hindsight and reporting the experiences helps to pinpoint places for improvements.

We hope that the reader will benefit from our reflection on some experiences, as we too have greatly benefited from experiences reported by other framework developers.

SAMPLE EXCERPT OF SGF CONCEPT BOOK

The purpose of this sidebar is, first, to show how systematic documentation techniques for a framework were applied in the SGF and, second, to provide some glimpses into more details—for example, updating via the Coordinator-Aspect-View triple. The symbol {...} indicates where very specific information has been skipped.

Intent

When changing the state of objects in a system, dependent objects must be informed about these changes, thus allowing these objects to update their state appropriately.

In SGF, the updating of dependent objects is done mainly to ensure consistency between data structures and to update views after data changes.

To get a better understanding of the problems involved in change propagation, read the first three paragraphs of the Motivation section in the design pattern description of Observer in [Gamma 1995]. In this description, "Subject and its observers" corresponds to "an aspect and its dependent objects as coordinators, other aspects and views."

Interface

See the Related Classes and Methods section later in this sidebar, as there is no one single interface.

Design

Change propagation in SGF is implemented by sending messages along the data structures to the dependent objects. Objects being changed (usually aspects) inform their dependent objects—their coordinators, other aspects, and views—about the changes. These objects may react appropriately, for example, by passing the request to other objects or by updating their presentation.

In the following, the default behavior provided by SGF is presented. The general message flow presented in Figure 27.8 comprises three main parts, which are explained in more detail in the following sections.

General Message Flow of Change Propagation in SGF

The general message flow being provided as default behavior by SGF is depicted in Figure 27.8. The steps are as follows:

0. The user changes an aspect.

1. The aspect being changed notifies its views to update their presentation.

2. The aspect being changed notifies its coordinator to update itself (by aspectChanged( )).

    First, the coordinator passes this request to its other aspects, which pass the request to their views; that is, all other aspects and the corresponding views are updated.

3. Afterward, the coordinator {...}

Avoiding Multiple Updates

If an object is manipulated, an update message is propagated to its dependent objects. The update message may cause several objects to update themselves, which may lead to additional update messages to *their* dependent objects, and so on (recursive). Thus, *one* object manipulation can lead to many update messages and a graphical view, which is dependent on its presented objects, may get *several* update messages due to only *one* object manipulation. {...}

If each update message would cause an immediate update on the corresponding view, this would result in multiple updates of the view, although only one object was manipulated. {...} Therefore, SGF provides the possibility of avoiding this inefficiency by allowing display elements to delay the updating of corresponding views until all dependent objects have updated themselves. {...} The starting/stopping of collecting updates may be nested.

```
MethodChangeSomething()        // method of display element
{
    myDisplayList -> collectUpdates();      // start collecting
    "do something that may cause updates";
    myDisplayList -> stopCollectingUpdates();   // stop collecting
}
```

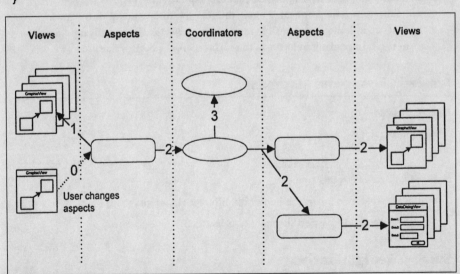

Figure 27.8 General message flow for change propagation.

Continues

SAMPLE EXCERPT OF SGF CONCEPT BOOK *(Continued)*

Further Remarks

Propagate changes only horizontally (default behavior).

   The default behavior provided for SGF propagates changes only horizontally, not vertically along the coordinator hierarchy. In the vertical (upward) direction, only some flags are set, indicating that some update requests should be performed to this (sub)system at a later stage.

Related Patterns and Concepts

This section contains references to related patterns and concepts to this SGF concept.

   Design pattern Mediator (273)

   Design pattern Observer (293)

   Design pattern Chain of Responsibility (223)

- Coordinator with Mediator and Observer responsibilities
  The role of coordinators for change propagation is somewhere between Mediator and Observer. The section, Related Patterns of Observer, in the design pattern book states: "Mediator: By encapsulating complex update semantics, the ChangeManager acts as mediator between subjects and observers."
     Coordinators do just this. They coordinate and manage most of the updating.{...}

- Coordinator hierarchy similar to ChainOfResponsibility
  Requests may be propagated along the coordinator hierarchy, thus allowing other coordinators, responsible for updating objects after specific modifications, to react. The default behavior is to set the change indicator flag.

Related Classes and Methods

Related classes:

- SCoordinator
- SAspect {...}

Methods implementing this concept:

- [update]-methods (many methods with different signatures exist)
- void [SCoordinator::aspectChanged] (SAspect) {...}

Sundry: Reorganization

- The implementation of an updateDeep( ) functionality could be supported by SGF (at the moment, it is only supported in another application named K2). {...}

27.8 References

[Abbott 1994] Abbott, D.H., et al., A proposed design complexity metric for OO development. Clemson, SC: Clemson University, 1994.

[Beck-Johnson 1994] Beck, K., and R. Johnson. Patterns generate architectures. *Proceedings ECOOP* 1994, Bologna, Italy, July 1994. LNCS 821, pp. 139–149, M. Tokoro and R. Pareschi, editors. Springer-Verlag.

[Berry-Meekings 1985] Berry, R.E., and B.A.E. Meekings. A style analysis of C programs. *Communications of the ACM* 28(1), January 1985.

[Booch 1996] Booch, G. *Object Solutions: Managing the Object-Oriented Project.* Reading, MA: Addison-Wesley,1996.

[Chidamber 1994] Chidamber, S.R., and C.F. Kemerer. A metrics suite for object-oriented design. *IEEE Transactions on Software Engineering* 20(6), June 1994.

[DeMarco 1982] DeMarco, T. *Controlling Software Projects.* Englewood Cliffs, New Jersey: Yourdon Press, 1982

[Erni 1996] Erni, K. *Anwendung multipler Metriken bei der Entwicklung von objektorientierten Frameworks.* Münster, Germany: Krehl-Verlag, 1996.

[Evagelist 1983] Evangelist, W.M. Software complexity: Metric sensitivity to program structuring rules. *Journal of Systems and Software* 3(3), September, 1983.

[Gamma 1995] Gamma, E., R. Helm, R. Johnson, and J. Vlissides. *Design Patterns: Elements of Reusable Object-Oriented Software.* Reading, MA: Addison-Wesley, 1995.

[Holland 1992] Holland, I.M. Specifying reusable components using contracts. *Proceedings ECOOP 1992*, Utrecht, The Netherlands, June 1992. LNCS 615, pp. 287–308, O. Lehrmann Madsen, editor. Springer-Verlag.

[Jacobson 1992] Jacobson, I. *Object-Oriented Software Engineering.* Reading, MA: Addison-Wesley, 1992.

[Meyer 1988] Meyer, B. *Object-Oriented Software Construction.* Prentice Hall International (UK), 1988.

[Meyer 1992] Meyer, B. *Eiffel—The Language.* Englewood Cliffs, NJ: Prentice Hall, 1992.

[Mora 1992] Mora, A., and A. Cosculluela. A metrics approach to the software reuse problem. *Proceedings of the 3rd European Conference on SW Quality,* Madrid, Spain, 1992.

[Rösel 1996] Rösel, A. Succeeding with frameworks (Erfolge mit object-orientierten frameworks). *Proceedings—Object World Conference,* Frankfurt, Germany, October 1996.

[Weinand 1988] Weinand, A., E. Gamma, and R. Marty. ET++—An object-oriented application framework in C++. *Proceedings OOPSLA 1988, ACM SIGPLAN Notices* 23(11), November 1988.

CHAPTER 28

Enterprise Model-Based Framework

Experience has indicated that large-scale enterprise development poses a variety of challenges to both developers and managers. In addition to constraints of distribution and scalability in a potentially heterogeneous hardware infrastructure, the implementation of business logic for a particular vertical market can be quite demanding. These requirements have led to proposals for standardization and generalization as suggested by the Object Management Group (OMG). While the particulars of a vertical market are myriad, there are similarities in the implementation of business software that can be abstracted and encapsulated. Further, it should be possible to separate the roles assumed by objects from the objects themselves, thereby giving rise to generic objects that can assume a variety of roles as needed. This chapter describes a particular instance of this approach as implemented at a major financial institution.

The discussion assumes the reader has knowledge of design patterns on the level of Gamma et al. [Gamma 1995], distributed computing on the level of Orfali et al. [Orfali 1996], and a familiarity with basic object-oriented technology and tactics such as dynamic typing and dynamic binding as applied to the enterprise development environment.

28.1 Background

The strategy discussed grew out of a requirement by the client institution for mission-critical applications that needed to adapt quickly and efficiently to business dynamics.

The resulting infrastructure was commissioned by a strategic initiative. The initiative was a response to market forces and advancing technology, which required the organization to:

- Respond faster to changing business conditions
- Give customers computational access to business services
- Improve the return on investment in computing resources

Since most of the organization's business is conducted electronically, using software developed in house, these requirements could not be met without:

- Making the software development process more efficient and predictable
- Making the software products more reliable
- Obtaining greater leverage from existing software products
- Efficiently incorporating new technologies

In order to satisfy these requirements, it was decided that the infrastructure had to fulfill several key cultural and developmental objectives that included freeing the enterprise developer from common development tasks, favoring long-term versus short-term thinking, as well as using as much proven commercial-off-the-shelf (COTS) technology as possible in order to reduce the maintenance load.

In addition to the needs set forth by the initiative, the architecture and its implementation had to provide an environment for good business software development—for example, discourage ad hoc data and process redundancy, abstract business rules, and work flow from both storage technologies and presentation interfaces as well as provide interoperability with other systems including legacy applications.

28.2 Management Decisions

The rather ambitious design requirements were accompanied by requirements from the managerial team prior to the development of the infrastructure. Among these were the use of NeXT products and technologies for the enterprise and the need for applications to build on the requirements and functionality of their predecessors. The NeXT technologies, in particular, included the OpenStep development and deployment environment, the Enterprise Objects Framework (EOF), and the WebObjects Framework (WOF). The glossary provides a short description of each of these technologies.

28.3 Development Team Decisions

A key decision made by the development team was the use of models to reduce the amount of custom code required to implement complex functionality. This section describes the use of metadata-based programming.

28.3.1 Model-Based Development

Models are a form of metadata. Metadata is data that describes the structure of something like an application, a process, or a group of related business objects. For example, an object model might define object types, such as Loan, Vendor, and Property. In addition to their names, it might also identify their attributes (PhoneNumber, Loan-Amount, and so on), the types of those attributes (String, Number, Date, Money, and so on), and the relationships allowed between the objects (for example, a Property contains zero or more Loans by reference).

These descriptions are stored in concise formats, which can be consumed by frameworks that know how to interpret the information. Using the information, the frameworks can make a large number of decisions without the help of custom code supplied by a developer. For example, using metadata, a framework that provides object persistence could extract the attribute values from the Loan, Vendor, and Property objects previously described and store them in a database without requiring any help from custom code. Later, using the same metadata, the framework could load the data from the database and reconstruct the objects in memory, again without custom code. The metadata used by this framework would describe the objects to be stored and retrieved, the database schema, and the mapping between the objects and the schema.

Of course, some custom code is required in many cases, since models cannot describe every conceivable aspect of a complex application. In practice, however, the amount of custom code required to implement a piece of custom functionality is radically smaller than would have been necessary without a model. The code is tightly constrained by the framework to specific tasks, since its role is to modify standard functionality, not to create new functionality from first principles. It therefore tends to be simple, easy to test, and easy to maintain.

Replacing custom code with metadata is a general design pattern used throughout the infrastructure. This pattern is used repeatedly, to the point that developers using the infrastructure focus more on model building than on coding. This shift in focus is significant because it lowers the level of expertise needed to develop business applications. It also promotes reuse, because models are less idiosyncratic than code and less dependent on the computing environment, or on a particular coding style or technology. In fact, most of the business logic developed with this technique will survive implementation technology changes without breakage, because it is not dependent on any particular programming language or tool.

To the reader familiar with 4GLs, the shift in focus described here is reminiscent of a 4GL's effect on the development process. Indeed, the infrastructure gives the application developer an experience very much like the experience of working with a 4GL. Since programs are better than people at writing formatted files, the infrastructure provides graphical tools to generate the metadata. These tools support the abstractions defined by the models, using terminology and visual cues to focus the developer's attention on high-level tasks, instead of on the syntax of the metadata being produced. The developer uses the tools to build the structure, then writes a small amount of highly focused code to implement the business logic.

Because of the similarity to 4GLs, it is reasonable to ask if the infrastructure yields productivity gains similar to those realized with 4GLs. In practice, this has proven true, as clients of the infrastructure report a dramatic reduction in the number of lines of code required, and a related reduction in testing and maintenance costs. The last section of this chapter describes the experiences of several early adopters and enumerates the windfalls and the difficulties they encountered in using the infrastructure.

Despite these similarities, the infrastructure differs from most 4GLs in terms of extensibility. Instead of confining the developer within a restrictive language box, the infrastructure uses a native language for application development and exposes the underlying machinery as an extensible public application programmer interface (API) in the same language. This allows experienced developers to extend or even replace the supplied functionality, something that usually cannot be done with a 4GL. Thus, the infrastructure will never stand in the way of implementing something required by an application. This difference is important to the client organization, where a variety of technologies coexist, and where new technologies are constantly being added to the computing environment. These factors place a premium on the ability to modify the infrastructure to meet changing requirements or to incorporate components supplied by other parts of the organization.

The infrastructure's emphasis on metadata dovetails nicely with the formalization of the development process required by object technology. In fact, the infrastructure and the development process defined by the initiative were designed to work together. At each step of the process, the activities that capture and elaborate the content of the application are used directly to create the models used by the frameworks at runtime. This direct integration enforces the process, improves the fidelity of the translation from requirements to analysis to design to implementation, and automates a significant amount of work that previously had to be done manually.

In particular, the object model plays a central role in this approach. In this case, the Object Modeling Technique (OMT) methodology was used [Rumbaugh 1991] to describe the object model. However, it should be apparent that the choice of methodology affects the implementation only to the extent that the formalism allows accurate, concise description of the business system. Unified Modeling Language (UML), Booch, or some other methodology could just as easily have been implemented [Booch 1996].

Architectural Layering

Another key decision by the development team was the use of a layered architecture. As a general design pattern, layering is a technique for managing complexity. Most large software systems are broken into layers, each layer defining abstractions to be used by the layers above. Compile and runtime dependencies between layers can be described with dependency graphs.

One of the most widely known application layering strategies is client-server. The separation of duties between client and server was instrumental in establishing distribution as a viable design strategy, supporting innovations like heterogeneous platform integration and the graphical user interface. This approach fails, however, to provide adequate separation between business logic and the user interface, and embeds the business logic in the user interface or application control code. This prevents effective sharing of the business logic among multiple processes.

The shortcomings of client-server gave rise to what is commonly known as *three-tier* architecture. With the three-tier approach, the application control and business logic are broken out into a middle tier and can be shared by different front ends. This is a significant improvement over client-server, but does not go far enough in making the business logic reusable across multiple applications.

The shortcomings of three-tier gave rise to what is commonly known as *application integration,* sometimes referred to as *service-based architecture.* This approach breaks coarse application functions into discrete reusable components called *services,* each encapsulating a well-defined piece of a business process. These components can be combined to build distributed programs and can be reused in many different applications.

The infrastructure defines and implements a service-based architecture. The architecture, illustrated in Figure 28.1, has five layers:

Presentation layer. Interacts with a user above and with the application layer below. It is responsible for presenting views on the application's state and actions to an end user, and for conveying end-user actions to the application.

Application layer. Interacts with the presentation layer above and with anything below. It is responsible for implementing the business process represented by the application, managing the dialog with the presentation layer and coordinating the activities of the services and business objects used by the application.

Service layer. Interacts with anything above or below. It is responsible for implementing discrete functions used by larger business processes.

Persistence layer. Interacts with anything above and with the data layer below. It is responsible for managing the storage and retrieval of the business objects used by the layers above.

Data layer. Interacts with anything above and with the physical storage below. It is responsible for managing the physical backing stores used by the persistence layer.

Standard APIs are defined for all of the layers except the service layer. Because the service layer can be recursively composed (in other words, allowing services to use other services), this could be called an *n*-tier architecture.

It is important to note that the layers are logical, not physical, and that physical partitioning is possible but not required. The APIs and interaction semantics between the layers are unaffected by partitioning. In the current implementation of the infrastructure, the top four layers reside in a single address space. Robust physical partitioning of these layers would require mediation by reliable and/or transacted messaging services, as illustrated in Figure 28.2. The incorporation of message-oriented middleware is planned, but has not yet been implemented.

Between the persistence and data layers, an X/Open DTP monitor may be introduced to support distributed transactions and data replication, as illustrated in Figure 28.3. The incorporation of a transaction monitor is planned, but has not yet been implemented.

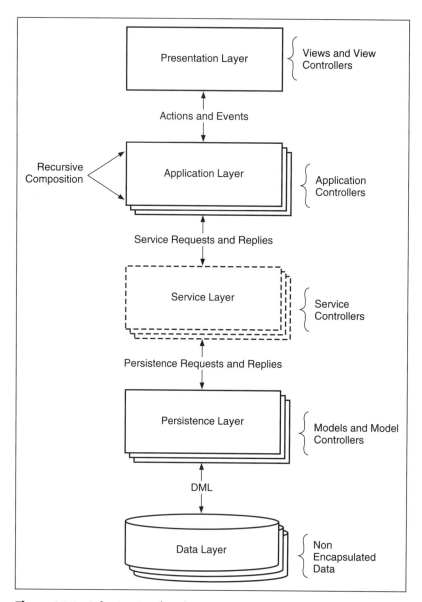

Figure 28.1   Infrastructure layering.

The presence of different transaction forms at different levels of the architecture is intentional and necessary. The transactions between the persistence and data layers are used for database federation and are not suitable for the interactions that occur higher in the architecture. Similarly, the message-oriented transactions that occur higher in the architecture may involve queuing, broadcasting, asynchronous delivery, and other quality-of-service characteristics that are unsuitable for database federation.

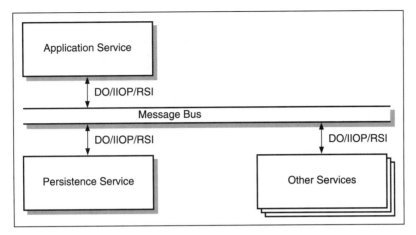

Figure 28.2 Physical partitioning above the data layer using message-oriented middleware.

28.4 Structure

The infrastructure can be divided along functional lines into frameworks, as illustrated in Figure 28.4. A description of each framework follows. The frameworks themselves were implemented using OpenStep Bundles and Frameworks. A description of Bundles is provided in Appendix A, "Glossary."

28.4.1 Model Object

The Model Object Framework provides object brokerage and other core abstractions. It implements a subset of the Common Object Request Broker Architecture (CORBA) specification. This framework captures information about domain objects from the

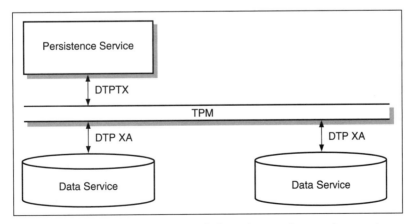

Figure 28.3 Physical partitioning below the persistence layer using a transaction monitor.

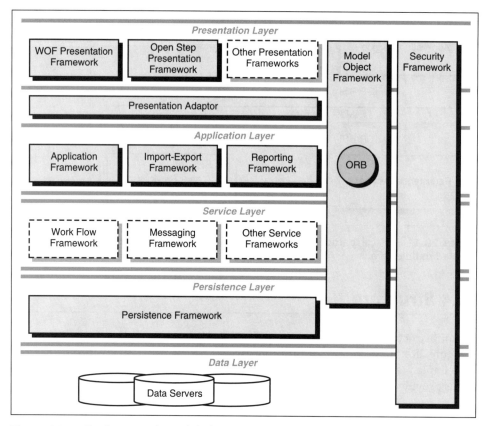

Figure 28.4 The frameworks and their positions in the layered architecture.

object analysis and design activities performed by the developers. This information is then used at runtime to automate standard functions. The Model Object Framework also provides logging and exception handling, routes objects to and from object storage services, defines the resource name space, assigns object identifiers, manages runtime configuration, performs domain object validation, manages query editing and processing, and supplies commonly used utility functions. The Model Object Framework is used throughout the top four layers of the architecture.

28.4.2 Persistence

The Persistence Framework manages the storage of domain objects in relational databases through an easy-to-use access layer based on NeXT's EOF 2.0 [Apple 1996, 1997a, 1997b]. It allows decoupling of the application code from database semantics. While EOF and relational databases were used for most applications created with the infrastructure, alternative forms of storage, including flat files, are also supported. The persistence framework resides in the persistence layer.

28.4.3 Import-Export

The Import-Export Framework provides a standard architecture for bulk data processing and includes a job scheduler, a batch controller, a configurable data file parser, and a data validation and formatting facility. Using this framework, developers build batch utilities with a graphical tool. They do not have to write any custom code in most cases. The Import-Export Framework resides at the service layer of the architecture.

28.4.4 Application

This framework manages control flow, querying, error handling, change buffering, configuration, and many other functions. With this framework, no custom code is required for most common application functionality. In this case study, the application framework was designed to implement most form-based applications typical of information technology (IT) environments. While less well suited for analytical applications, the framework could be augmented to allow for other application requirements. The Application Framework can be used at the application and service layers.

28.4.5 Presentation Adapter

The Presentation Adapter maps user interface actions and events to application actions and events, and vice versa. This mapping decouples the application from the user interface and discourages placement of business logic in the user interface. This adapter represents a point of integration between technology domains and can be used as a boundary between internal and external systems. The Presentation Adapter implements the thin client interface and can be implemented on a variety of platforms. It insulates the rest of the application from the OpenStep and Web Objects Framework (WOF) presentation technologies. The Presentation Adapter resides at the boundary between the presentation and application layers.

28.4.6 OpenStep Presentation

The OpenStep Presentation Framework provides a standard skeleton for constructing user interfaces based on OpenStep. Using a Model/View/Controller (MVC) architecture, this framework allows developers to build graphical user interfaces (GUIs) entirely with graphical tools. They do not write any custom code in most cases. The framework manages the movement of data between domain objects and the user interface, and interacts with the Presentation Adapter to send user actions to the application and to respond to application events. The OpenStep Presentation Framework resides at the presentation layer [NeXT 1996].

28.4.7 WOF Presentation

The WOF Presentation Framework works with NeXT's Web Objects Framework (WOF), a tool for building HTML (World Wide Web) based user interfaces [Apple

1997b]. It wraps the HTML language with object-based APIs, provides a way to bind object data to HTML pages, and uses a scripting language to manage screen transitions. The WOF Presentation Framework resides at the presentation layer [NeXT 1996].

28.4.8 Security

The Security Framework ensures the secure execution of applications based on the infrastructure. The functions performed by this framework include (1) authenticating users and hosts, (2) authorizing operations on protected resources, (3) preventing unauthorized reading or writing of protected data outside trusted processes, and (4) recording operations for auditing and accountability. The Security Framework resides in all five layers of the architecture.

28.4.9 Reporting

This framework is intended to address the reporting requirements typical of most projects at client organization through direct use of the infrastructure, eliminating the need for third-party products that require schema transformation. The Reporting Framework includes a reporting engine, a layout application, and a report viewer. The reporting engine resides at the service layer of the architecture.

28.4.10 Work Flow

The Work Flow Framework has not yet been implemented. It is envisioned as providing control flow and management services to coarse-grained business processes. Using a business process model, it will drive applications, tools and services, tracking status and exceptional conditions, and the application of rule-based logic to adapt to a variety of conditions.

28.4.11 Messaging

The Messaging Framework has not yet been implemented. It is envisioned as providing transacted messaging services to the distributed implementation of the infrastructure. This framework will be implemented using CORBA/COM+ or another well-accepted messaging layer. A number of third-party products could be used in its implementation [Orfali 1996].

28.5 Tools

In order to simplify deployment, the infrastructure incorporates a variety of tools, including model compilers, batch drivers, database configuration tools, and object modeling tools.

28.6 Implementation Strategies

This section discusses two different implementation strategies: primitive semantics and extended semantics.

28.6.1 Primitive Semantics

The NeXT technologies used to implement the infrastructure provided several semantic features that made the implementation simpler and more generic. These features favor runtime adaptation including dynamic typing, dynamic binding, introspection, and *key-value coding*. See the glossary for a description of key-value coding.

28.6.2 Extended Semantics

The most important semantic extension defined by the infrastructure is an object type called a *model object*. Model objects are derived from entity objects and are the primary vehicle for managing business data. They are at the heart of most infrastructure functionality and play a central role in the development and deployment of infrastructure-based software. The model object provides a generic container for data and a generic API to access and mutate the data. The role of the model object is business-specific.

A model object has three essential properties: an interface, an identifier, and a reference handler. The interface defines an abstract type and describes its characteristics. These descriptions are stored in archives called *interface repositories* and support the formal separation of model object interfaces from their implementations. Identifiers are used to assert uniqueness across address spaces and object stores. Reference handlers make a model object's persistent storage location independent of its type.

Additional semantic extensions include a collection protocol, dynamic state and behavior binding, change and death notification, shared instances, and type coercion and formatting.

28.7 Minimizing Dependencies

Among the design goals for the infrastructure were maximizing interoperability and minimizing coupling between infrastructure elements. In order to achieve these goals, a number of design patterns were employed. Among them were name spaces, abstract factories, and notification.

One of the most unusual decoupling strategies employed was the use of abstract qualifiers to eliminate database dependencies. Abstract qualifiers are first-order predicates that can be evaluated against objects using key-value coding. This allowed clients to treat local and remote collections uniformly, despite their radically different underlying implementations, without sacrificing performance.

28.8 Deployment and Learning Curve

The infrastructure thus far has been used in more than 10 production systems. The first 2 of these served as important sources of feedback to the infrastructure development team. Opinions differed significantly between them regarding the difficulty of learning to use the infrastructure.

The earlier of the two projects used prerelease versions of the infrastructure. Team members found the learning curve steep, claiming that it was almost a year before they were fully productive. They attributed this to using unstable code, with no examples and minimal documentation. Many of the problems were due to the bugs in early releases of EOF. The project had a large object model, with several levels of inheritance and every possible permutation of relationship semantics. It therefore exercised many portions of the infrastructure and exposed corner cases that had not been adequately tested.

The second project, which started with a later prerelease version, characterized the learning curve as minimal. Developers with little or no previous exposure to EOF or OpenStep became productive relatively quickly. They attributed this to the infrastructure's hiding of the lower-level EOF interfaces, and particularly the persistent collection metaphor. The concept that challenged them the most was model-based application flow, but all of the team members were able to become productive through study and experimentation. The user interface and batches were developed quickly and required minimal code.

Both teams considered the infrastructure effective in promoting reuse across the entire architecture and concluded that the benefits of using the infrastructure outweighed the effort involved in learning to use it well.

28.9 Infrastructure Effects on the Development Process

The project teams found that using the infrastructure allowed developers to focus on analysis and design and to spend less time in implementation. The developers wrote primarily business-specific code and attributed this fact to the amount of standard functionality supplied by the infrastructure. They also found the infrastructure easy to extend and developed many components that they considered candidates for reuse on other projects, particularly application model controllers.

The project teams considered the integration with Rational Rose and the automatic generation of the entire persistence model to be major accomplishments, and they claimed that it improved the quality of their analysis and design work. They attributed this to both the time savings that resulted from the persistence model generation and the direct use of object models at runtime. In particular, they observed that the direct use of object models at runtime forced the team to keep the models current, improving the quality of the documentation.

The project teams observed that the infrastructure's use of models fit naturally with development activities and deliverables. For example, they noted that adornments added to the Rose models for the sake of the model compiler captured important design decisions. Similarly, they found that use cases and GUI flow diagrams generated during requirements capture were easy to render as application flow models, and that process cases were easy to render as batch specifications.

Finally, the project teams claimed that the layering of the architecture effectively separated presentation, application flow, and business logic, leading to clean designs and implementations.

28.9.1 Metrics

The metrics shown in Tables 28.1 through 28.5 were gathered by the first project team.

28.10 Summary

This chapter describes an infrastructure for model-based programming implemented at a major financial institution. The key merits of this approach are rooted in the use of abstractions that support the specification of business entities. The developer is consequently freed from considering the details of common programming tasks and can focus on business logic. While superficially similar to 4GLs in the user experience, the infrastructure differs from 4GLs in that it does not prevent developers from changing or extending the infrastructure. The details of the implementation were too numerous to describe here and were consequently mentioned only in passing. Significant to the implementation, however, were the use of runtime adaptation and storage abstraction as provided by NeXT technology and the Objective-C language. Qualitative and quantitative surveys of the learning curve and the effect of the infrastructure on the development process indicate a reasonable learning curve, a positive user experience, and a net increase in developer productivity.

Table 28.1 WOF Presentation Metrics

Learning Curve	Low
Utility	High
Web Objects Script Methods	646
Web Objects Script Statements	2238
Lines of Web Objects Script	3221
Web Objects Script Instance Variables	271
Lines of Web Objects Configuration	3095

Table 28.2 Application Metrics

Learning Curve	High
Utility	High
Model Files	53
Model File Lines	7989
Query Specifications	15

Table 28.3 Model Object Metrics

Learning Curve	High
Utility	Moderate
Lines of Code	13608
Model Elements	1343
Enumerations	54
Attributes	693
Relationships	114
By Reference Relationships	60
By Value Relationships	48
Uses Relationships	6
Methods	102

Table 28.4 Persistence Metrics

Learning Curve	High
Utility	High
Persistent Classes	96
Methods	483
Validation Methods	29
Predicate Methods	14
Statements	3004
Lines of Code	5896

Table 28.5 Import-Export Model Metrics

Learning Curve	Low
Utility	High
Batch Specifications	11
Batch Specification Lines	1365
Query Specifications	23
Custom Classes	9
Methods	23
Statements	270
Lines of Code	437

28.11 References

[Apple 1996] *Enterprise Objects Framework Developer's Guide.* Apple Computers, 1996.

[Apple 1997a] *Using Enterprise Objects Framework with OpenStep.* Apple Computers, 1997.

[Apple 1997b] *WebObjects Developer's Guide.* Apple Computers, 1997.

[Booch 1996] Booch, G., I. Jacobson, and J. Rumbaugh. *The Unified Modeling Language for Object-Oriented Development.* Rational Software Corporation, www.rational.com/uml, 1996.

[Gamma 1995] Gamma, Erich, Richard Helm, Ralph Johnson, and John Vlissides. *Design Patterns: Elements of Object-Oriented Software.* Reading, MA: Addison-Wesley Longman, 1995.

[NeXT 1996] *Discovering OpenStep: A Developer Tutorial.* NeXT Software, 1996.

[Orfali 1996] Orfali, Robert, Dan Harkey, and Jeri Edwards. *The Essential Distributed Objects Survival Guide.* New York: John Wiley & Sons, 1996.

[Rumbaugh 1991] Rumbaugh, James, Michael Blaha, William Premerlani, Frederick Eddy, and William Lorenson. *Object Oriented Modeling and Design.* Englewood Cliffs, NJ: Prentice Hall, 1991.

The definitions in this glossary are arranged in alphabetical order and were contributed by the authors of this book. A definition may be a single word, such as *component*; a phrase, such as *design patterns*; or an acronym, such as *UML.* Multiple definitions are also included, using enumeration.

The following cross-references are used to show the relationships between definitions and to indicate their respective chapters:

See refers to a different entry for the definition of a synonym.

See also refers to similar and related definitions.

(#) indicates the chapter in which the term is discussed.

Note: **Boldface** marks terms that appear elsewhere in the glossary.

Absent object/cluster. An absent object/cluster is one that is not loaded in the current address space *(20)*.

Abstract object. Object serving as a common reference model for both controller (in other words, the application) and views (in other words, the user interface) *(15)*.

Action. A CSP++ class that corresponds to a CSP **event.** Actions can be used for synchronizing with other **agents** or interfacing with user-coded external routines. Subclasses are *atomic* actions, which do not pass data, and *channel* actions, which do *(9)*. *See also* **Channel.**

Action rules. Rules triggered by events that conditionally perform some action. Action rules are used to add extra semantics (business rules) or to add extra functionality *(3)*.

Active object-oriented database system. A database system based on an active object-oriented data model. It extends passive object-oriented database systems with the possibility to define reactive behavior in terms of Event/Condition/Action rules *(Sidebar 2)*.

Activity. An activity is a thread that is capable of executing in several address spaces, at the same or different nodes, at different times (but in, at most, one address space at a time) *(20)*.

Agent. (1) A CSP++ class that implements a CSP **process.** In software it would constitute a schedulable thread of control *(9)*. (2) A software module that is autonomous, proactive, reactive, and social. A strong agent is also knowledge based or intelligent *(6)*.

Agent advertisement. The commitment of an agent to taking on a well-defined class of future service request. It is a declaration that contains a specification of the agent's capability with respect to the type of request it can accept *(7)*.

Agent capability. In a multiagent system this is the knowledge about what types of services can be requested from a provider agent *(7)*.

Agent languages. Agents communicate with each other in order to collaboratively provide a solution to a particular problem. In order to communicate, they message each other in a language in which they can best represent the information *(6)*.

Agent name server (ANS). Specialized software agent that in a multiagent system is responsible for the resolution of logic agent names to transport addresses *(7)*.

Agent preference. In a multiagent system this is the knowledge about what types of information have utility for a requester agent *(7)*.

Agent society. A group of agents coexisting in the same environment and functioning together *(6)*.

Allocation. The temporal interval when an operation is assigned to a certain resource *(21)*.

Application code. The code that implements the methods required by an object's type *(20)*.

Application-directed clustering. In application-directed clustering, clusters are explicitly made visible to applications, which are then made responsible for the assignment of individual objects to clusters based on application-specific knowledge *(20)*.

Application domain. Specific application areas where IBM SanFrancisco is providing default implementation. The application domains that are being addressed by the initial releases of SanFrancisco include the business financials (accounts payable, accounts receivable, and general ledger), order management (processing sales orders and purchase orders), and warehouse management (functions for internal stocking/tracking as well as shipping) *(Sidebar 3)*.

Atomic object. Noncompound terminal object that might still feature a rich infrastructure (for example, a graphics editor) but without the capability to include and manage generic objects *(15)*. *See also* **Compound object.**

Attribute. Named basic property of an **object,** typically represented by some elementary data type like Boolean, Char, Integer, or Real *(15)*.

Authorization rules. Access control relies on a rule-base of authorization rules *(3)*.

Base Object Model classes. These classes provide the basic building blocks that are used to create SanFrancisco applications. Application objects are built by inheriting from the appropriate base class to provide access to the necessary infrastructure services *(Sidebar 3)*.

Bottleneck interface. The bridging interface between two independently extensible abstractions. The bottleneck interface itself cannot be extended without risking the loss of some of the extended abstractions on either side of the interface. An example is the carrier/rider interface provided by the **Carrier-Rider-Mapper Separation pattern** *(25)*.

Broadcast. Strategy of message spreading by a **compound object** to its components. Typically used to notify components about state changes of a model object *(15)*. *See also* **Model**.

Broker agent. A specific type of **middle agent** *(7)*.

Bundle. A directory containing application resources (for example, images, configuration information, shared libraries. In OpenStep, a framework is a bundle that contains a sharable library *(28)*.

Business policy. Context-dependent and time-dependent organizational knowledge, which captures the core information making up the competitive factor of an enterprise *(Sidebar 1)*.

Business process. A procedure whereby documents, information, or tasks are passed between participants according to a defined set of rules to achieve, or contribute to, an overall business goal *(Sidebar 2)*.

Cache-based dispatch technique. A technique that first looks in a cache to see if a method for a given class/selector pair has already been computed. If not, some cache-miss algorithm is used for dispatch and the resulting information is cached for later use. Caches may be global (LC) or call-site-specific (IC and PIC) *(16)*.

Call by cloning. Reuse of an object (generic or prefabricated) as a template, that is, by producing a fresh and independent clone *(15)*.

Call by reference. Reuse of a prefabricated object by reference. Typically used to include some public object in a document via a camera view *(15)*.

Camera view. View of some visual object, acting as a **model**. Typically used to display multiple excerpts of a complex **document** *(15)*.

Capacitive reasoning. The process of reasoning about the limited capacity of sharable resources *(21)*.

Carrier-Rider-Mapper Separation pattern. A pattern that combines a number of known simpler design patterns in a way that proved generally useful. Carriers are responsible for the maintenance of data arranged according to some coordinate system. Riders are created by carriers to abstractly represent positional access by clients. Mappers are optional objects that lift the raw abstraction provided by riders to something closer to certain classes of clients *(25)*.

Cascaded message multicasting. A mechanism to propagate messages according to architectural stages of change propagation. At each stage, the cascading multicast mechanism imposes certain restrictions to ensure that efficient delivery is possible, while at the same time ruling out incorrect delivery orders that would lead to inconsistencies *(25)*.

Channel (CSP). A named unidirectional, nonbuffered interprocess communication port. When two **processes** engage in an **event** whose name is a channel, data is passed from the process using the output symbol (!) to the process using the input symbol (?) *(9)*.

Class. A class is a set of objects that share a common structure and a common behavior. Also used to refer to the code to be bound to an object *(20)*.

Cloning. Producing an exact but independent copy of an object, including its behavior *(15)*.

Cluster. A cluster is a set of objects that form a unit of loading and unloading into and out of address spaces *(20)*.

Codesign, hardware/software. An approach to automating the design of embedded systems that moves from high-level specifications, through partitioning into hardware and software portions, into hardware and software synthesis, including generation of the hardware/software interface. Cosimulation of interacting hardware and software is used to verify the resulting system. An important purpose of codesign is to facilitate the exploration of design alternatives. This involves moving functionality between software and hardware in order to satisfy constraints *(9)*.

Collaboration language. Agents collaborate with each other via conversational protocols *(6)*.

Columbus Inspector. Tool to interactively query and alter attributes and links (properties) of objects *(15)*.

Common business objects. Objects that are used in more than one application domain *(Sidebar 3)*.

Communicating sequential processes (CSP). A design formalism that uses algebraic statements to model a system in terms of concurrent processes *(9)*.

Compiled object module. A file containing object code (native processor instructions) and sufficient information for a tool to compose it with other such files and execute it on an operating system. An object module is usually generated by a compiler from a fragment of source code (for example, in the C language) *(10)*.

Complete behavior. The set of all methods understood by a particular class *(16)*.

Component framework. A collection of rules and interfaces (contracts) that govern the interaction of components plugged into the framework. A component framework typically enforces some of the more vital rules of interaction by encapsulating the required interaction mechanisms *(25)*.

Composition, parallel versus interleaved (CSP). Designating that a set of processes is to execute concurrently. Parallel composition allows for communication and synchronization of the composed processes; interleaved composition does not *(9)*.

Compositional modularity. A programming model in which modules are adapted and composed using a suite of operators, each of which supports an individual effect of object-oriented (OO) programming such as combination, encapsulation, rebinding, or hierarchical nesting *(10)*.

Compound document. Hierarchically composed document, where each part of the document is supported by specific software components. Dynamic loading on demand of such components is required to handle arbitrary incoming documents *(25)*.

Compound object. Object with encapsulated contents called **components**. Components are generic **objects** whose exact type need not be known by the compound object. Compound objects act as parents of their contents and must implement the **parental control** message propagation rule. Typical forms are **containers** *(15)*.

Compound user interfaces. Generalizing the concept of **compound documents** to user interfaces. A compound user interface models every aspect of a user interface as a form of document and, in its purest form, eliminates the concept of applications. Instead, application-specific functionality is acquired as needed by composing parts into documents or user interfaces that cause new software components to be loaded into the system *(25)*.

Constraint. (1) A relation that links a set of variables, each associated with a set of domain values, by means of arithmetic, logic, and functional operators *(13)*. (2) A relation between two or more scheduling objects that differentiate feasible from infeasible solutions. Constraints may exist that rule out certain allocations. Furthermore, objective functions may exist that differentiate good from not so good solutions. There are two subproblems: the finding of good sequences of operations on a resource and the finding of the temporal allocation *(21)*.

Constraint programming. Programming paradigm that distinguishes itself in that it allows the developer to state a computational problem in a declarative way as a **constraint satisfaction problem** *(13)*.

Constraint satisfaction (CS) problem. This consists of a set of logical variables that represent the characteristic parameters of a system for a given computational problem and a set of constraints between those variables that represent the invariant properties of the system *(13)*.

Container. A container is a (1) (logically or physically) contiguous area of (secondary) storage *(20)*; (2) **compound object** of container type. Typically a panel or a desktop *(15)*.

Content analysis. An accepted research technique in the social sciences concerned with the analysis of the content of communications. A central idea in content analysis is that the many words of a text can be classified into fewer content categories that are presumed to have similar meaning. On the basis of this categorization, the researcher tries to draw valid inferences from the text *(2)*.

Context-sensitive processing. Context-dependent message handling by a component or **model**. Typically used by components to distinguish between unlocked and locked containers and by visual model objects to distinguish between user environments and developer environments *(15)*. *See also* **User view; Developer view**.

Copy swizzling. Copy swizzling is a form of **eager swizzling** in which the object being swizzled is copied to a different memory region during swizzling *(20)*.

Core business process. The basic object-oriented structure and behavior that all applications in the given domain would require. They are a starter set for an application and are designed to be extended and modified into complete applications *(Sidebar 3)*.

Datafeed handler. A class of applications in which the primary function is to deliver data to a number of subscribers *(12)*.

Deductive learning. Models are derived from facts and examples observed in the real world *(5)*.

Deep copy. Copy of a **compound object** containing copies of the original contents *(15)*.

Defining class. The class in a **method node** that contains the native method definition for a selector *(16)*.

Dependent classes. The set of classes that inherit a particular native definition from a **defining class,** together with the defining class itself *(16)*.

Descriptive construction. Using a functional description to specify some custom object composition *(15)*.

Descriptor. A descriptor is a representative for an **absent object** *(20)*.

Design pattern. An object-oriented design that solves a problem that is found in multiple applications and application domains *(Sidebar 3)*.

Design space exploration. The ability of a modeling tool or environment to automatically or semi-automatically search the design space for feasible design alternatives by considering different architectures and components *(18)*.

Design Specification Language (DSL). An object-oriented, executable modeling language with synthesis and design space exploration capabilities for the rapid prototyping of real-time distributed systems *(18)*.

Developer view. Camera view representing a graphical developer environment. Allows the construction, editing, and altering of graphical user interface (GUI) elements *(15)*.

Dictation. Use of speech input for text entry or document creation *(4)*.

Directory object pattern. Specialization of the Abstract Factory pattern. A directory object represents a particular configuration choice by evaluating context and parameters to create and return an object upon request. For example, a directory object representing the currently configured abstract file system may return file objects by name *(25)*.

Dispatch. The runtime process of determining the address of the function code to execute for a given function name and receiver type *(16)*.

Display space. Hierarchic structure of all currently visible objects. Logically a DAG (direct acyclic graph) with edges joining at model objects (visual or abstract). The display space is a compound object itself *(15)*. *See also* **Model**.

Distributed object. A synonym for **global object** *(20)*.

Document. Special kind of **object** that is identifiable by the file system, is self-contained, and features an adaptive visual representation *(15)*.

Domain analysis. The process of identifying, collecting, organizing, and representing the relevant information in a domain to support reuse of software artifacts for systems to be built in this domain *(21)*.

Domain knowledge. The overall knowledge (heuristic and formal) about a specific domain; for example, about a medical diagnosis or an engineering problem *(5)*.

Dynamic type. The actual type (class) of an object at runtime. This may differ from the static type of a variable that is bound to the object *(16)*.

Dynamism. Techniques that allow the software to adapt to runtime changes. This includes the use of dynamic typing, dynamic binding, delegation, and metaobject protocols *(28)*.

Eager swizzling. A form of swizzling in which all the references contained within an object are swizzled as soon as the object is loaded into an address space *(20)*.

Eeyore. Eeyore is the storage subframework of the Tigger framework, that is, a set of classes supporting containers and storage objects *(20)*.

Electronic commerce. Marketplaces that operate over the Internet *(6)*.

Endpoint. An endpoint represents a network address *(20)*.

End-user objects. End-user objects represent the specific business model *(3)*.

Enterprise integration. Information technology to bring together diverse aspects of a company or enterprise *(6)*.

Enterprise Objective Framework (EOF). This NeXT framework provides mappings from database schemas to object models, thereby insulating client code from database-specific semantics *(28)*.

Event (CSP). An abstract named activity that a process engages in. Events are often defined to represent real-world occurrences originating in the system or its environment *(9)*.

Event/condition/action rule. Monitors the situation represented by the event and the condition, and executes the corresponding action when the event occurs and the condition holds true *(Sidebar 1)*.

Executable specification. A high-level description of a system that, in addition to its descriptive use, also functions as source code for simulation, logical verification, and/or synthesis. **VHDL** is an executable specification language *(9)*.

Expert rules. Knowledge extracted from domain experts, represented in the form of if-then rules *(5)*.

Extended Style Notation (ESN). A front-end language to support reuse of structure, both at the topological level and at the architectural level, in the development of component-based systems *(18)*.

Extensional reuse. Refers to the type of structural reuse in which a reusable artifact is used at a given abstraction level to produce another reusable artifact of the same abstraction level *(18)*.

Extent. An extent is a group of objects belonging to a common owner *(20)*.

Externalizing. Translating the internal data structure of an object (and its components) into a persistent linear form *(15)*. *See also* **Persistent representation.**

FDR. A powerful simulation and model-checking tool for specifications written in CSP (see Roscoe 1994) *(9)*.

First-class modules. A module that can be manipulated in a manner similar to other data types within a running program *(10)*.

Forward-chaining rules. A forward-chaining rule consists of two parts: a left-hand side, or condition, and a right-hand side, or action. The condition is roughly a first-order formula, and the action is a sequence of primitive changes to a set of objects. The intended meaning of the rule is that the condition is matched against a collection of objects, possibly binding some variables in the rule to some of these objects, and then the action of the rule is run, using the bindings generated in the condition match *(14)*.

Foundation. The distributed object-oriented infrastructure that is used to build the common business objects and core business processes. It contains the **Base Object Model classes** and **Utilities** *(Sidebar 3)*.

Framework development method. A development method aimed at developing reusable software frameworks. Such a method differs from traditional development methods, in that no specific application is built. Traditional analysis techniques such as use cases and prototyping cannot be employed *(2)*.

Functional view. Camera view associated with some semantics *(15)*. *See also* **User view; Developer view.**

Fuzzy AND. Fuzzy logic operation whereby the minimum value is selected among a set of values. In the CNM neural network model, it refers to the operation done by the neurons in which the minimum input value is selected *(5)*.

Fuzzy OR. Fuzzy logic operation whereby the maximum value is selected among a set of values. In the CNM neural network model, it refers to the operation done by the neurons in which the maximum input value is selected *(5)*.

Gadgets toolkit. Toolkit supporting the construction of objects. Includes interactive composer tools and a functional programming interface for descriptive constructions. Also includes a framework (set of classes) representing prefabricated standard components such as text fields, buttons, and sliders *(15)*.

Generalized block structure. The possibility to nest any kind of block construct within any other kind of block construct to an arbitrary nesting depth. Generalized block structure implies that each instance of a block (activation record or object) will exist in the context of an instance of its enclosing block and will have access to all attributes (variables, methods, and classes) of that enclosing instance. This was pioneered in Algol, whose block constructs are the procedure and statement block, which could be nested arbitrarily and to any depth *(19)*.

Generalized inheritance. Generalized inheritance is supported if the notion of inheritance can be applied to any abstraction mechanism in the language, such as classes, methods, processes, and exceptions *(19)*.

Generalized text. Stream of objects represented by (library, object) pairs, of what ordinary characters (font, ASCII-code) are just special cases, if font is regarded as an object library consisting of mere character glyphs *(15)*. *See also* **Object library**.

Generalized virtuality. Generalized virtuality is supported if virtuality can be applied to all kinds of abstraction mechanisms in the language, such as classes, methods, processes, and exceptions *(19)*.

Generic object interface. Message interface accepting an open hierarchy of message types. Message handler is of the form Handle (me: Object; VAR M: Message), where me is the receiver object and M is the base message type *(15)*.

Generic runtime library. A library that provides common runtime support for a set of languages supporting distributed or persistent programming, which have similar requirements *(20)*.

Global object. A global object is one that is simultaneously accessible from multiple address spaces *(20)*.

Global (object) reference. In a language for distributed programming, global (object) references are those references that are transmitted between nodes *(20)*.

Graphics recognition. A process that groups the raw wires resulting from the vectorization stage according to certain syntax rules, recognizes these groups as types (for example, lines) of graphic objects, and determines their attribute values. Usually both vectorization and graphics recognition may be referred to the same entire process that converts raster pixels to vector form graphic objects *(22)*.

GRT object. A container for one or more **language objects** that can be uniquely identified and to which code implementing the interface to the contained object(s) can be bound dynamically by the appropriate LSRT *(20)*.

Hardware. As the term is used here, it primarily refers to digital logic, typically built in the form of integrated circuits or by configuring field-programmable devices *(9)*.

Hierarchical Model/View/Controller (HMVC). A specific extension of the classic Model/View/Controller separation to support compound documents. HMVC allows embedding of views into models *(25)*.

Hierarchical nesting. A mechanism by which modules may be associated with names within other modules *(10)*.

Hybrid intelligent system. Combines several different artificial intelligence approaches, such as expert systems, neural networks, fuzzy logic, and genetic algorithms, in a single architecture *(5)*.

Immature object. A **GRT object** to which no **object identifier** has been allocated *(20)*.

Incremental processing. Gradual processing of a message by intermediate stations (that is, containers) of the target object. Used, for example, to compute absolute screen coordinates and overlap masks of visual objects in the display space *(15)*.

Indexcards. Forms *(3)*.

Inductive learning. A bottom-up learning approach, whereby the concept formulations are derived from the observations of particular occurrences of a phenomenon *(5)*.

Information agent. A specific type of **software agent** that is tightly coupled to information sources so as to find information in response to queries and actively monitor them for specified conditions *(7)*.

Inheritance conflict. If a class inherits two different methods for the same selector from two different parent classes, an inheritance conflict occurs. This is only possible if a language supports multiple inheritance *(16)*.

Inheritance management. The propagation of method definitions to subclasses that do not contain native definitions for those methods and the detection of **inheritance conflicts** that arise *(16)*.

Inline caching (IC). A cache-based dispatch technique in which a single method address is stored at a call site and guarded by a check for the correct dynamic type of the receiver. If the check fails, a cache-miss technique is used to obtain the correct method address and it is inserted at the call site *(16)*.

INNER statement. When inheritance is allowed for methods, a need arises for specifying how to combine the code of the super- and submethods. The Simula and BETA languages solve this problem by allowing INNER statements to be inserted in the code of the supermethod. The code of a submethod will thus be executed at the places of the INNER statements. This gives the framework control over method combination. This is related to the notion of SUPER in languages like Smalltalk, which, however, works in the reverse direction and only for virtual methods *(19)*.

In/out baskets. Baskets that maintain lists of incoming and outgoing work *(3)*.

In-place swizzling. A form of eager swizzling in which the object being swizzled is not copied to a different memory region during swizzling *(20)*.

Intentional reuse. Refers to the type of structural reuse in which an artifact is reused at a given abstraction level to produce a final artifact of the same abstraction level or another artifact of a lower abstraction level *(18)*.

Interactive construction. Using interactive tools (built-in editors, **Gadgets toolkit,** Columbus inspector) to construct, customize, and compose an object *(15)*.

Interactive scheduling. A form of scheduling whereby a human scheduler, together with a scheduling program, builds a **schedule** *(21)*.

Interface agent. A specific type of software agent that manages a graphical interface in order to interact with the user receiving user specifications and delivering results *(7)*.

Internalizing. Translating the persistent linear form of an object into an internal data structure *(15)*. *See also* **Persistent representation.**

Iterative improvement method. A search method that applies local changes to find improved solutions. These improvements are iteratively searched for until some stopping criterion is reached. Examples are **tabu search, simulated annealing,** and genetic algorithms *(21)*.

Job. A concept to collect all operations required for one order *(21)*.

Joint application development. A method of developing software systems wherein technical members and users jointly develop the software systems *(12)*.

Kanga. The communications subframework of the Tigger framework, that is, a set of classes supporting endpoints *(20)*.

Key-value coding. The representation of the states of a business entity as a set of named values. This allows the client code and infrastructure to interact with the entity without knowledge of the entity's class. The entity's states may be queried and set by accessing these values by name *(28)*.

Knowledge independence. In analogy to data independence, this notion of independence is achieved by factoring shared knowledge out of applications and expressing it in the database schema, preferably within objects and rules *(Sidebar 1)*.

Language object. A synonym for **object** *(20)*.

Language reference. Those object references supported by the runtime of some particular object-oriented programming language *(20)*.

Language-specific runtime library. A library that provides the runtime support for a particular programming language *(20)*.

Layered agent architecture. Categorizing an agent's functionality into layers, where each layer is dependent on its neighbors *(6)*.

Lazy swizzling. A form of swizzling in which the individual references contained within an object are not swizzled until the first time that an attempt to dereference them is made *(20)*.

Lazy transaction semantics. A representation whereby a transaction is not opened until the transaction is ready to be committed *(12)*.

Learning mechanism. The procedure used to perform the learning process, the function of which is to modify the synaptic weights of the network in an orderly fashion so as to attain a desired design objective *(5)*.

Line. The generic name of an abstract class of graphic objects in line drawings, each of which is the trace of a nonzero-width pen that moves from a start point to an end point, follows a certain trajectory, which is possibly constrained by a geometric (for example, circular) function, and optionally leaves invisible segments according to some pattern (for example, dashed or dash-dotted) *(22)*.

Link. Named reference from one **object** to another, for example, representing some **view model** relationship *(15)*.

Load (an object/cluster). Loading an object/cluster makes it accessible in some address space *(20)*.

Logical data unit. Smallest unit of information that can be exchanged between two systems *(12)*.

Machine Drawings Understanding System (MDUS). An experimental system developed by Liu and Dori (1996) for vectorization and graphics recognition *(22)*.

MatchMaker agent. A specific type of middle agent *(7)*.

Mature object. A GRT object to which an **object identifier** has been allocated *(20)*.

Mental model. A hypothesized inner representation of objects and events in human memory *(2)*.

Message protocol. Set of message types and rules governing the handling and propagation (for example, forwarding, delegating, absorbing) of messages within objects in general and **compound objects**, including the **display space** in particular *(15)*.

Message time-stamp. Unique identification stamp allowing a receiver object to detect multiple arrivals of a message *(15)*.

Meta-CASE environment. A CASE (Computer Aided Software Engineering) tool that allows the user to create and customize the methods that the tool supports *(2)*.

Metamodel. Describes structure and constraints of an object model *(3)*.

Method dispatch. The runtime determination of a correct method address for a given selector and receiver object, based on the dynamic type (not static type) of that receiver *(16)*.

Method node. A data structure that represents a set of classes, all of which use the same native method definition. The method node does not store this set of classes, but can compute the set from its defining class, selector, and the extended dispatch table that contains the method node. The method nodes for each selector form an induced subgraph of the inheritance graph in which the nodes are the **defining classes** for that selector *(16)*.

Middle agent. In a multiagent system, a specific software agent that can provide information about other agents. In particular, it can provide the names of the agents that offer a specific service *(7)*.

Mixed-initiative scheduling. An interactive scheduling form where human scheduler and scheduling program try to improve a schedule alternating *(21)*.

Mobile objects. These are **Self-contained objects** featuring a portable description of their program code *(15)*. *See also* **Slim binary**.

Mobility. The ability to migrate to another location *(6)*.

Model. Notion referring to the Model/View/Controller (MVC) design pattern *(15)*.

Model-based programming. The implementation of business metadata in terms of generic objects and factories, which consume model information and create the necessary business entities as needed *(28)*.

Module. A naming scope consisting of a collection of names, some of which are associated with values. Values are domain-specific; for example, they may be programming language data types, methods, fragments of compiled code, or fragments of text. Values may contain self-references *(10)*.

Multiagent system. [1] An organization of collaborating software agents *(7)*. [2] A software system in which **agents** are the primary components *(6)*.

Multicriteria objective function. An objective function that considers different criteria such as minimizing due date violations, minimizing flow time of jobs, and minimizing the total makespan *(21)*.

Multilayer feedforward neural network. Neural network topology formed by several layers (one or more hidden layers) in which the processing signal flows from the bottom layer to the top layer without feedback *(5)*.

Navigation. Use of speech input for data entry, transaction processing, or command and control *(4)*.

Near instantaneous. A quality of service (QoS) attribute to denote that service is provided instantaneously within the context of the operating conditions *(12)*.

Nested hooks. A hook is a location in the framework that can be specialized by the application programmer. Nested hooks utilize the general block structure by allowing a hook (class or method) to contain any number of local hooks (other classes or methods), each of which may contain any number of local hooks, and so on to any suitable depth. Most object-oriented programming languages support only a special case: the two-level nested hook consisting of a class containing local method hooks. With general support for nested hooks, other forms are possible: for example, nested class hooks (class hooks nested inside class hooks), and nested method hooks (method hooks nested inside method hooks) *(19)*.

Neuron. Signal processing element of a neural network model *(5)*.

Neuron activation. Defines the output of a neuron in terms of the activity level at its input *(5)*.

Neuron layer. A level formed by neurons in a neural network topology. In general, a neural network model has at least two layers: the input layer consisting of input neurons and the output layer consisting of output neurons. Normally, a neural network model has three layers including a middle layer, or hidden layer, consisting of hidden neurons, as in the backpropagation neural network model *(5)*.

Nonreflexive language. A language that is not reflexive *(16)*. *See also* **Reflexive language.**

Nonsharable resource. A resource that can be used by only one operation at a time *(21)*.

Nonstatically typed language. A language that does not require variables and method returns to be statically typed *(16)*.

Oberon's type extension facility. Generic interfaces are ready to accept messages of any variant type Message1, Message2, and so on, of Message. New message variants can be introduced at any time without invalidating the interface *(15)*.

Object. [1] A software entity with identity, state, and behavior *(20)*. [2] An entity with encapsulated state and behavior. Behavior is expressed as the handling of messages according to a well-defined protocol. Object kinds are either abstract or visual. Object granularity ranges from character glyph to document and full desktop *(15)*. *See also* **Message protocol; Model; View; Generalized text.**

Object fault. Occurs when an attempt to access an **absent object** is made *(20)*.

Object fault avoidance. Ensures that no object faults occur by ensuring that objects are always loaded in the current address space before any access to them is attempted *(20)*.

Object fault detection. Traps attempts to access absent objects, causing the object to be loaded before the access proceeds *(20)*.

Object identifier. Unambiguously identifies an object *(20)*.

Object library. Indexed collection of **objects**. Contains **persistent representations** of objects together with their **components**. Kinds are either public or private. Object libraries also serve as generalized fonts for generalized texts *(15)*. *See also* **Generalized text; Private object library; Public object library.**

Object model. Describes **objects,** associations, and **constraints** *(3)*.

Object reference. An object reference allows the object to which it refers to be located and accessed *(20)*.

Object store. The persistency component *(3)*.

On-the-fly code generation. Translation of a unit of program code to machine code at loading time *(15)*.

Ontology. [1] Collection of logical descriptions of special-purpose concepts common to a specific knowledge domain *(7)*. [2] Concepts and terminology that are pertinent to a particular discipline or specialty *(6)*.

OpenStep. NeXT's Objective-C–based software development and deployment environment *(28)*.

Operation. An activity to be performed in a workshop to produce some ordered product *(21)*.

OPS5. The standard rule-based programming system of the 1980s. It provides the basic implementation of rule-based programming systems and forward-chaining rules *(14)*.

Order. The specification of what product will be produced and with that what operations it will be scheduled *(21)*.

Owl. The GRT subframework of the Tigger framework, that is, a set of classes supporting **global** and **persistent objects** and, optionally, **clusters** *(20)*.

Parental control. Main rule of the **message protocol** used in our framework. Says that messages must not be sent (directly) to a **component** from any instance but its **container** *(15)*.

Partitioning. Decomposing system into functionally independent vertical components or subsystems *(12)*.

Performative. Communication primitive that corresponds to a specific linguistic action (for example, query, answer) *(7)*.

Perplexity. A measurement of the number of equally likely word choices, given a sequence of words *(4)*.

Persistent object. An object that may outlive the execution of the program that created it *(20)*.

Persistent representation. Linearized representation of an object (including its components) without dependence on or reference to any random access memory *(15)*.

Plan. A set of activities to be performed by an agent *(Sidebar 4)*.

Polymorphic inline caching (PIC). A **cache-based dispatch technique** in which each call site invokes a special stub routine that contains the method addresses of all previously invoked methods. If the correct method is not already cached, then a cache-miss technique is used to obtain the correct method address and the stub dynamically grows *(16)*.

Prefabricated component. Prefabricated member of a **public object library**. Ready to be reused in compound objects by cloning or by reference. Identified by a qualified name of the form Library.Object *(15)*.

Prepare an object. Preparing an object makes it ready to be accessed by other objects *(20)*.

Private object library. Anonymous object library that typically collects the components and private objects of a compound object or a document *(15)*.

Process (CSP). An abstraction for a locus of control that engages in a sequence of **events,** some of which may synchronize it with other concurrent processes. A process may be defined in terms of other processes *(9)*.

Process plan. A temporal plan that prescribes how a product may be produced in a given workshop *(21)*.

Product manager. An important marketing decision maker who is responsible for development, pricing, distribution, advertising, and sales promotion of one or more products *(2)*.

Promote an object. An object is promoted when first allocated an object identifier *(20)*.

Pronunciation. A phonetic representation of a word *(4)*.

Properties. Describe attributes and associations (references to other objects) of an object *(3)*.

Property expressions. Describe chains of properties, by following associations *(3)*.

Proxy. A representative for an absent object to which code implementing the interface to the object is bound and that can therefore be invoked as if it were the object that it represents *(20)*.

Public object library. Named object library. Members can be identified by qualified names of the form Library Object, where Object is the index or the name of the desired object *(15)*.

Publisher. Source of data in a data feed handler system *(12)*.

Punishment algorithm. An algorithm specific for CNM, which decreases the synapse weights that lead to a wrong hypothesis (applied during the training process) *(5)*.

Query expressions. Represent in an abstract way queries to be executed. A query (expression) can be stored and reused *(3)*.

R++. An implementation of a **forward-chaining rule** extension to C++. This extension provides rules that are tightly integrated into C++, to the point that R++ rules look and act very much like C++ methods, except, of course, that they are executed in response to changes to C++ objects, instead of via explicit calls *(14)*.

Refactoring. The process of redesigning, for example, a class library, without changing the overall behavior, for instance, to remove redundant code *(3)*.

Reflexive language. A language in which methods or new classes can be defined at runtime. For example, Smalltalk is fully reflexive, Java is partially reflexive, and C++ is not reflexive *(16)*.

Reify. To make concrete—the opposite of the verb *to abstract (10)*.

Reinversion of control. A new approach to software integration that distinguishes itself from the more common approach of object-oriented application frameworks in that it allows the developer to create relationships between software components and to determine the information and control flow between them by customizing the variable aspects of each single component *(7)*.

Remote object invocation. An invocation on an object located in a node or address space other than that of the invoking object *(20)*.

Requirements gathering. A phase of software engineering in which users needs are formalized *(12)*.

Resource. May be a machine, a tool, space, energy, or something else required to perform an operation *(21)*.

Resource query. Query asking **objects** about the resources (typically program modules and object libraries) they depend on *(15)*.

Reward algorithm. An algorithm specific for CNM that increases the synapse weights that lead to a correct hypothesis (applied during the training process) *(5)*.

Robin. The protection subframework of the Tigger framework, that is, a set of classes supporting extents and related abstractions *(20)*.

Role. A position to be fulfilled by an agent in a team *(Sidebar 4)*.

Roo. The threads subframework of the Tigger framework, that is, a set of classes supporting threads and related synchronization mechanisms *(20)*.

Rule-based programming systems. A class of programming systems that are based around **forward-chaining rules**. They consist of a working memory of objects and a collection of rules that run over these objects. The system proceeds by matching all the rules against all the objects. The successful matches are graded and the best rule is run. The match-grade-run loop is continued until there are no matching rules to run *(14)*.

Rule pattern. In analogy to design patterns, rule patterns capture basic business knowledge recurring in various application environments. They both categorize rules according to different types of business policies, and at the same time provide an abstraction mechanism for specifying rules in an application-independent manner *(Sidebar 1)*.

Sales promotions. Marketing events aimed at having a direct impact on the buying behavior of consumers. Examples of sales promotions are price-offs, premiums, cash refunds, samplings, and coupons *(2)*.

Satisfaction degree. A degree of satisfaction of a constraint *(21)*.

Scenario. Operating procedures to be followed by frameworks and their teams of agents during services realization *(Sidebar 4)*.

Schedule. The solution of the scheduling process; an allocation of resources with jobs and operations *(21)*.

Schedule evaluation. An evaluation of the objective functions *(21)*.

Scheduling. The activity of planning and allocating operations to resources. The result of this activity is a **schedule** *(21)*.

Scheduling task. A basic action a human user or a computer program can perform to change the schedule. Examples are the allocation of a new operation, or the swap of two operations on a resource *(21)*.

Selector. The signature of a method *(16)*.

Self-contained object. An **object** linked together with its resources (typically program modules and **object libraries**) *(15)*.

Self-reference. A reference to a name defined in a module from within the module itself. For example, a method associated with a name in a module can refer to the value associated with another name in the module *(10)*.

Self-referential name space. Also known as **module** *(10)*.

Semantic graphics. Graphical representations that have a synchronized link to the information of associated semantic information. An example is the graphical representation of an electric motor showing contact points for electrical connections and mechanical connections. This representation has associated engineering data, including information about voltage rating and maximum mechanical load. Connecting graphical elements in a semantic graphics context allows the validity to be checked based on the associated semantic information *(27)*.

Service. Needs to be satisfied by frameworks and their teams of agents *(Sidebar 4)*.

SGF. Semantic Graphics Framework *(27)*.

Shallow copy. Copy of a compound object containing references (for example, by **camera views**) to the original contents *(15)*.

Sharable resource. A resource that may be used by several operations at the same time. A maximal capacity may constrain the maximal number of operations *(21)*.

Simulated annealing. An optimization method based on ideas from statistical physics whereby the annealing of a solid to its ground state (the state with minimum energy) is simulated *(21)*.

Singular objects. An object that is declared with an anonymous class (or anonymous subclass). This is usually done by allowing class specialization and object instantiation to be done in the same declaration *(19)*.

Slim binary. Preprocessed, highly compact, and processor-independent form of a unit of program code. Serves as input to an on-the-fly code generator *(15)*. *See also* **On-the-fly code generation.**

Softbot. The name given to a system handled as only one agent and embedded into a larger system *(8)*.

Soft constraints. Constraints that may be violated. The resulting schedule is still feasible, but its evaluation my be worse *(21)*.

Software agent. (1) An autonomous entity that can execute plans *(Sidebar 4).* (2) Integrated system that incorporates major capabilities drawn from several research areas: artificial intelligence (AI), databases, programming languages, and theory of computing. In distributed AI, agents are software units of design that can be customized and composed with other similar units to build complex systems *(7).*

Software bus. Metaphor used for a universal and well-defined message protocol to symbolize the analogy to the concept of a hardware bus that allows complying units to plug in and participate *(15).*

Source-addressed messaging. In contrast to orthodox destination addressing, source addressing labels a message with its source and then offers potential destinations a choice of whether they want to receive the message or not. Source addressing needs to be combined with other approaches to allow for efficient messaging *(25).*

Static type. The type of a variable or return type as specified by a declaration in the language *(16).*

Storage object. A unit of secondary storage *(20).*

Structural reuse. Type of reuse based on the identification and abstraction of recurring structural patterns in system development; similar to design reuse, but it addresses only the organizational structure of a system or subsystem *(18).*

Style (architectural style). The term frequently used in software architecture literature to refer to reusable organizational patterns or reusable architectures; also refers to the generic architecture of a class of systems, or some type of generic, high-level structural abstraction of a class of systems *(18).*

Subscriber. Recipient of data in a data feed handler system *(12).*

Swizzling. The conversion of references in loaded objects from a form used to refer to stored objects to an alternative form optimized to refer to loaded objects *(20).*

Synapse. The connection between two neurons *(5).*

Synthesis, hardware and software. The automated processing of a specification into a hardware or software end product. In the case of software, the end product is binary machine code, or source code that can be readily compiled into it. In the case of hardware, it means a manufacturable circuit description (for example, netlist) or source code (such as **VHDL**) from which the circuit description can be automatically created *(9).*

System objects. Represent objects in the repository required for proper functioning of the framework tools *(3).*

Table-based dispatch technique. A technique that precomputes the appropriate method address for each class/selector pair and stores them in a table so that at dispatch-time only a single table lookup is necessary to obtain the correct address *(16).*

Tabu search. An iterative improvement method that uses a dynamic memory (the tabu list) that stores attributes of past solutions of the search process. In a short time, memory characteristics of recent solutions are stored to avoid reversals or cycles in search. A long-term memory is used to define phases of intensified and diversified search *(21).*

Target-oriented dispatching. Dispatching of a message within a **compound object** toward some target component according to the principle of **parental control**. By rule, the message must traverse all paths leading toward the target object *(15).*

Task agent. A specific type of software agent that supports decision making by formulating problem-solving plans *(7).*

Team of agents. A set of agents that cooperate in order to achieve a common goal *(Sidebar 4)*.

Template (architectural template). An abstract representation of the structure of a component-based system in terms of a set of components with multipoint interfaces and point-to-point interface connections between these components *(18)*.

Temporal reasoning. A basic inference technique for achieving temporal consistency of schedules *(21)*.

Temporal relation. A relation between time points or time intervals *(21)*.

Thesaurus. Indexing vocabulary having its own semantically meaningful structure, such as a generic/specific taxonomy of descriptors (indexing keywords) and synonyms (providing additional access paths during searches) *(3)*.

Think-aloud protocols. A written report of a verbalized think process *(2)*.

Time intervals. Composed from two time points and used to specify the temporal information of operations, jobs, and schedules. The distance between both time points is the duration of the interval *(21)*.

Time points. The basic objects on which temporal reasoning is applied *(21)*.

Topology. A high-level abstraction of the underlying structure of a system as a graph with typed nodes and singular, featureless edges, where the nodes represent abstract components and the edges represent the relatedness of the components *(18)*.

Transparent clustering. A form of clustering in which **clusters** are not (necessarily) made visible to applications, and objects are assigned to clusters by the runtime system itself *(20)*.

Typical input. These **Slim binaries** may be iterated to produce optimized code *(15)*.

Unload (an object/cluster). Unloading an object/cluster makes it inaccessible in the address space from which it is being unloaded *(20)*.

Upcall code. Code that implements the upcall methods to be bound to GRT objects containing language objects of a particular type *(20)*.

User view. Camera view representing a graphical user environment. Allows the use but no editing or altering of displayed GUI elements *(15)*.

Utilities. Provide services that will be needed by most applications built using SanFrancisco components. The utilities provide completed function and are designed to be used as is, rather than being extended or modified *(Sidebar 3)*.

Vectorization. Also known as raster to vector conversion, is a process that finds the vectors (straight line segments in the basic stage and other graphic objects in the graphics recognition stage) from the raster images. Vectorization is referred to as the basic stage *(22)*.

VHDL. Literally, "VHSIC Hardware Description Language," where VHSIC in turn stands for "Very High Speed Integrated Circuit." Originally created as a means of describing circuits, VHDL came to be used to input circuit descriptions for simulation. Now it is also used as an input to hardware **synthesis** tools. It can be viewed as a programming language for hardware engineers, which has gained popularity over earlier methods relying on drawing circuit schematics *(9)*.

View. Notion referring to the Model/View/Controller (MVC) design pattern. Visual representation of some abstract or visual **model** *(15)*.

Vocabulary. Set of words or phrases that can be translated by a speech recognition system *(4)*.

WOF. NeXT's WebObjects Framework. This framework provides utilities for the creation of HTML and Java-based dynamic Web sites *(28)*.

Word-usage model. Statistical information on word sequences that assist a speech recognition system by biasing the output toward high-probability word sequences *(4)*.

Work flow management system. Used to design and streamline business processes and, thus, is a set of tools used to specify business processes, their required and modified data, and their interfaces to users and applications (commonly referred to as **agents**) involved in the business process. Besides this modeling perspective, work flow management systems also support the execution (enactment) of business processes *(Sidebar 2)*.

Index of Authors

This author index is arranged in alphabetical order by last name and includes the following information for each author: last name, first name, affiliation, country, primary e-mail, URL, chapters contributed, and a brief biography.

Ahmed, Amal. AT&T Network and Computing Services, USA, Chapter 14, pp. 309–321.

Banavar, Guruduth, Ph.D. IBM T.J. Watson Research Center, Middletown, NJ, USA, e-mail: banavar@watson.ibm.com, URL: www.research.ibm.com/people/ b/banavar, Chapter 10, pp. 225–239.

Guruduth Banavar received a Ph.D. from the University of Utah in 1995 after a B.E. from Bangalore University and an M.S. from Arizona State University. He has since been working as a research staff member at IBM's T.J. Watson Research Center in New York. At IBM Research, he has developed frameworks for building distributed applications with programming models based on both data sharing and message passing. His publication record includes best paper distinctions at the Institute of Electrical and Electronics Engineers (IEEE) International Workshop on OO Operating Systems 1996 and the IEEE International Conference on Distributed Computing Systems 1997. He has served on the program committees of the IEEE International Conference on Distributed Computing System (ICDCS) and International Performance, Computing, and Communications Conference (IPCCC) conferences and is on the doctoral thesis committees of students at the University of Utah and the University of Michigan.

Beckenkamp, Fábio Ghignatti. University of Constance, Constance, Germany, e-mail: beckenkamp@acm.org, URL: www.altissimo.com, Chapter 5, pp. 95–112.

Fábio Ghignatti Beckenkamp is a research assistant in the Software & Web Engineering Group at the University of Constance. He applied artificial intelligence techniques to various real-world decision support systems, mainly based on neural networks. Fábio received his bachelor's degree in computer science from the Pontifical Catholic University of Rio Grande do Sul, Porto Alegre, Brazil, and his master's degree in computer science from the Federal University of Rio Grande do Sul in Porto Alegre.

Brugali, Davide, Ph.D. Department of Automatica e Informatica, Politecnico di Torino, Italy, e-mail: brugali@polito.it, URL: www.polito.it/~brugali, Chapter 7, pp. 155–171, and Chapter 13, pp. 279–307.

Davide Brugali is a postdoctoral research fellow at the Department of Automatica e Informatica of the Politecnico di Torino, Turin, Italy, where he has received a Ph.D. in computer science. He received a master's degree in electronics engineering at the Polytechnic of Milan, Italy, in 1994. His main research activity concerns the techniques to build and reuse software, such as design patterns, application frameworks, component development, and software agents. He is also doing research in the field of mobile robotics, multiagent systems, distributed systems, and constraint programming. He has been coorganizer of the OOPSLA 1997, 1998, and 1999 Mid-year Workshops on Applied Object Technology for Manufacturing. In 1997, he spent one year at the Robotics Institute of Carnegie Mellon University doing research in the group of Dr. Katia Sycara.

Cahill, Vinny, Ph.D. Department of Computer Science, Trinity College, Dublin, Ireland, e-mail: vinny.cahill@cs.tcd.ie, URL: www.dsg.cs.tcd.ie/, Chapter 20, pp. 485–519.

Vinny Cahill currently leads the Distributed Systems Research Group in the Computer Science Department at Trinity College, Dublin, where he is also course director for the master's program in networks and distributed systems. He has been doing research in the area of distributed object systems for a number of years and holds a Ph.D. from Trinity College. His current research is particularly concerned with the use of object-oriented techniques such as frameworks, design patterns, and reflection to build dynamically adaptable system software.

Campo, Marcelo R., Ph.D. Department of Computer Science, UNICEN University, Argentina, e-mail: mcampo@exa.unicen.edu.ar, URL: www.exa.unicen.edu.ar/~mcampo, Chapter 11, pp. 241–270.

Marcelo Campo is an associate professor at the Computer Sciences Department of UNICEN University, Argentina, teaching software architecture and object-oriented programming courses at undergraduate and graduate levels. He received a systems engineer degree from UNICEN University at Tandil, Argentina, in 1988 and a Ph.D. in computer science from the UFRGS at Porto Alegre, Brazil, in 1997. In 1997 he organized the First Argentine Symposium on Object-Orientation. His current research interests are object-oriented application frameworks for dynamic simulation, intelligent support for framework design and instantiation, architecture-driven design methods, and information visualization systems.

Chande, Suresh B. Software Technology Laboratory, Nokia Research Centre, Helsinki, Finland, e-mail: chande.suresh@research.nokia.com, Chapter 6, pp. 113–153.

Suresh B. Chande is from Bangalore, India, and received his bachelor's degree in computer science from B.M.S.C.E, Bangalore, India. He worked in India as a software consultant for SPA and Jakson Engineers for a short period of time. He received his master's degree in information technology at R.M.I.T, Melbourne, Australia on Software Agents. Currently, he is working for Nokia Research Centre, Helsinki, Finland, as a software engineer in the software technology laboratory.

Chatterjee, Arunava, Ph.D. Inline Software Corporation, Sterling, VA, USA, e-mail: bob@inline-software.com, URL: www.inline-software.com, Chapter 28, pp. 659–673.

Originally a research physicist, Arunava Chatterjee has most recently been a consulting engineer for Apple Computers. During his physics research he designed and implemented frameworks for simulation and image processing. As a consultant he has been a principal developer on On-Line Analytical Processing (OLAP) and On-Line Transaction Program (OLTP) systems for the Department of Defense, telecommunications, airlines, and state government. In addition to participating as a lead developer in systems with distributed technologies, he has also served as a business analyst and database architect.

Courdier, Rémy. IREMIA, University of La Réunion, France, e-mail: courdier@univ-reunion.fr, URL: www.univ-reunion.fr/~mas2, Chapter 8, pp. 173–191.

Rémy Courdier is senior lecturer at the University of La Réunion, Indian Ocean, France. His interests focus on the methodology of development of multi-agent systems. With that aim, he investigates the intrinsic properties and differences between the object and agent paradigms. This promising work continues previous engineering experiences undertaken in the industrial context of Schneider R&D in Sophia-Antipolis, France, where he worked as project leader for seven years.

Dalebout, Arco. Rotterdam School of Management, Erasmus University Rotterdam, The Netherlands, e-mail: adalebout@fac.fbk.eur.nl, URL: www.fbk.eur.nl/FBK/VG3/, Chapter 2, pp. 7–25.

Arco Dalebout was a Ph.D. student in the Marketing Department of Erasmus University, Rotterdam, The Netherlands, where he studied the design and use of marketing software. Some of his projects involved applying object modeling to the marketing domain and using case-based reasoning for supporting sales promotion decision making. *Arco unfortunately died much too young on April 8th, 1999, while this book was still in production. His great enthusiasm and ideas will continue to influence his colleagues, friends and family.*

Devos, Martine. Requirements Architect, Brussels, Belgium, e-mail: mdevos@argo.be, URL: www.argo.be/persoonlijk/mdevos/marteng, Chapter 3, pp. 29–64.

Martine Devos graduated summa cum laude in business informatica at the Brussels Free University, and as economist at the State University of Ghent. She recently joined EDS as a requirements architect. She has been director of the Information Systems Department at Argo since 1992 and previously worked as a teacher, a technical consultant, and a project leader for the Belgian Minister of Education and the Civil Service. She is cochair of EuroPlop 1999.

Dori, Dov, Ph.D. Industrial Engineering and Management, Technion Institute of Technology, Israel, e-mail: dori@ie.technion.ac.il, Chapter 22, pp. 541–553.

Dov Dori has been a faculty member at the William Davidson Faculty of Industrial Engineering and Management, Technion, Israel Institute of Technology, since 1991. He received his B.Sc. in industrial engineering and management from Technion in 1975, his M.Sc. from Tel Aviv University in 1981, and his Ph.D. in computer science from Weizmann Institute of Science, Rehovot, Israel, in 1988. Between 1987 and 1990 he was assistant professor in the Department of Computer Science, University of Kansas. Between 1996 and 1998 he was head of the Area of Information Systems Engineering. In 1995 his team won first place in the Dashed Line Recognition Contest held during the First International Association for Pattern Recognition (IAPR) Workshop on Graphics Recognition at Pennsylvania State University. Dov Dori is associate editor of the Institute of Electrical and Electronics Engineers (IEEE) *Pattern Analysis and Machine Intelligence—T-PAMI* and the *International Journal of Document Analysis and Recognition* and is on the editorial board of the *International Journal of Pattern Recognition and Artificial Intelligence.* He is a senior member of the IEEE, a member of the IEEE Computer Society, the Association for Computing Machinery (ACM), and International Association for Pattern Recognition (IAPR).

Dorn, Jürgen, Ph.D. Institut für Informationssysteme, Technische Universität Wien, Vienna, Austria, e-mail: dorn@dbai.tuwien.ac.at, URL: www.dbai.tuwien.ac.at/staff/dorn/, Chapter 21, pp. 521–539.

Jürgen Dorn received his M.S. and Ph.D. degrees in computer science from Technische Universität Berlin, Germany. From 1989 to 1996 he has headed the Knowledge-based Scheduling group of the Christian Doppler Laboratory for Expert Systems in Vienna. Currently he works as a professor at Technische Universität Wien, Austria. His research interests include real-time planning, knowledge-based systems, case-based reasoning, and software engineering.

Erdogmus, Hakan. National Research Council of Canada, Institute for Information Technology, Ottawa, Ontario, Canada, e-mail: Hakan.Erdogmus@nrc.ca, URL: wwwsel.iit.nrc.ca, Chapter 18, pp. 403–450.

Hakan Erdogmus is a research officer with the Institute for Information Technology, National Research Council of Canada, Ottawa. He joined the Software Engineering Group of IIT in 1995. His research activities are centered around formal methods, reuse, software architecture, and design patterns. He holds a doctoral degree in telecommunications from Institut national de la recherche scientifique of Université du Québec and a master's in computer science from McGill University, Montreal.

Erni, Karin, Ph.D. ABB Calor Emag Schaltanlagen AG, Mannheim, Germany, e-mail: karin.erni@deace.mail.abb.de, URL: www.abb.de/deace/, Chapter 27, pp. 629–657.

Karin Erni is responsible for control system development within ABB Utility

Automation, Germany. After earning a degree in computer science from Technical University of Karlsruhe with emphasis on knowledge-based systems and object-oriented software development, she worked for several years as a software engineer and project leader at ABB Corporate Research, Germany. She earned her Ph.D. in computer science in the field of object-oriented design metrics at Technical University Karlsruhe in 1996. For her Ph.D. studies, she monitored the development of the Semlib with design metrics that gave hints on needed restructuring.

Fayad, Mohamed E., Ph.D. Department of Computer Science and Engineering, University of Nebraska, Lincoln, USA, e-mail: fayadm@acm.org, m.fayad@computer .org, URL: www.cse.unl.edu/~fayad, lead editor of this book, front matter, back matter, book parts, and Chapter 1 (pp. 1–6), and the book Web site materials.

Mohamed Fayad is an associate professor of computer science at the University of Nebraska, Lincoln. He was an associate professor of computer science at the University of Nevada from 1995 to 1999. He has more than 15 years of industrial experience. He has been actively involved in more than 60 object-oriented projects for several companies. He has been the guest editor of six theme issues: *CACM's OO Experiences* (October 1995), *IEEE Computer's Managing OO Software Development Projects* (September 1996), *CACM's Software Patterns* (October 1996), *CACM's OO Application Frameworks* (October 1997), *ACM Computing Surveys—Application Frameworks* (September 1999), and *IEEE Software's Software Engineering in-the-Small* (May/June 2000). He has published articles in *IEEE Software, IEEE Computer, Journal of Object-Oriented Programming (JOOP), ACM Computing Surveys*, and *CACM*. He is a distinguished speaker and has given lectures, tutorials, and seminars at national and international conferences, universities, and companies. He is a senior member of the Institute of Electrical and Electronics Engineers (IEEE), a senior member of the IEEE Computer Society, a member of the Association for Computing Machniery (ACM), and he serves on several conference program committees, such as TOOLS USA '96 and Hong Kong QSD '96. In addition, he is an *IEEE* Distinguished Speaker; an associate editor, editorial advisor, and a columnist for *Communications of the ACM IEEE Software,* Al-Ahram (the Egyptian Newspaper); editor-in-chief of *IEEE Computer Society Press—Computer Science and Engineering Practice Press (1995–1997);* and an international advisor for several universities. He received an M.S. and a Ph.D. in computer science from the University of Minnesota at Minneapolis. His research topic was entitled, "Object-Oriented Software Engineering: Problems and Perspectives." He is the lead author of *Transition to OO Software Development* (John Wiley & Sons, 1998) and lead editor of this three-volume work on object-oriented application frameworks (John Wiley & Sons, 1999).

Franz, Michael, Ph.D. University of California, Irvine, USA, e-mail: franz@uci.edu, URL: www.ics.uci.edu/~franz, Chapter 15, pp. 323–338.

Michael Franz is an assistant professor in the Department of Information and Computer Science at the University of California, Irvine. His research interests are programming languages and their implementation, extensible component-based software systems, machine-independent program representations, and dynamic code generation and optimization. He received a Dr. Sc. Techn. degree in computer science and a Dipl. Informatik-Ing. degree, both from ETH Zurich. Further information about Franz and his work can be found at www.ics.uci.edu/~franz.

Gardner, William B. Computer Science Department, Trinity Western University, Canada, e-mail: wgardner@twu.ca, URL: faith.csc.twu.ca/~wgardner, Chapter 9, pp. 197–223.

Bill Gardner graduated from M.I.T. in computer science (B.S.E.E., 1974). After studying teaching at the University of Toronto (B.Ed., 1975), he worked at Litton Systems Canada as a software engineer, with an emphasis on embedded systems and operating systems. He is an assistant professor of computer science at Trinity Western University, meanwhile finishing his Ph.D. in the VLSI Design and Test Group of University of Victoria's Department of Computer Science. His research interests are hardware/software codesign, object-oriented microprocessor simulation, reconfigurable computing, and object-oriented application frameworks.

Greenfield, Jack. Inline Software Corporation, Sterling, VA, USA, e-mail: jack@inline-software.com, URL: www.inline-software.com, Chapter 28, pp. 659–673.

A leader and innovator in component software technology for more than 16 years, Jack Greenfield has led development of several generations of component-based tools for building mission-critical custom applications in the enterprise, including NeXT Software's Enterprise Objects Framework and the business infrastructure of a Fortune 50 financial institution.

Gutknecht, Juerg, Ph.D. ETH Zürich, e-mail: gutknecht@inf.ethz.ch, URL: www.cs.inf.ethz.ch/group/gutknecht, Chapter 15, pp. 323–338.

Juerg Gutknecht is a professor of computer science at ETH Zürich. His main fields of interest comprise programming paradigms, environments, and languages. After receiving his Dr. Sc. in mathematics in 1977, he was involved in the document processing part in the Lilith/Modula project and, from 1986, in close collaboration with Niklaus Wirth, he developed the Oberon language and system. Since 1992, he has been working on different evolutions of Oberon, aiming at reusable components and active objects.

Hedin, Görel, Ph.D. Department of Computer Science, Lund University, Lund, Sweden, e-mail: Görel.Hedin@dna.lth.se, URL: www.dna.lth.se/~gorel, Chapter 19, pp. 451–479.

Görel Hedin received her Ph.D. in computer science from Lund University in 1992. Since 1998 she has been an associate professor in the Department of Computer Science, Lund University. Her research interests are focused on object-oriented languages and implementation techniques and she has been active in this area since around 1985. She has developed extensions to attribute grammars to support object-oriented languages and tool support for development of domain-specific languages.

Holst, Wade. University of Alberta, Canada, e-mail: wade@cs.ualberta.ca, URL: www.cs.ualberta.ca/~wade, Chapter 16, pp. 339–367.

Wade Holst is completing a Ph.D. in computing science from the University of Alberta and plans to continue in an academic career. His research areas involve object-oriented programming languages, programming environments, and web-based programming paradigms. He also has interests in compiler technology, distributed computing, complexity theory, and mathematics.

Janello, David A. Chapter 24, pp. 589–597.

Johnson, Ralph E., Ph.D. Department of Computer Science, University of Illinois at Urbana-Champaign, USA, e-mail: johnson@cs.uiuc.edu, coeditor of this book.

Ralph E. Johnson is on the faculty of the Department of Computer Science at the University of Illinois. He is the leader of the UIUC patterns/Smalltalk group and the coordinator of the senior projects program for the department. Ralph's professional interests cover nearly all things object-oriented, especially frameworks, patterns, business objects, Smalltalk, Common Object Model (COM), and refactoring. He has been to every Object-Oriented Programming, Systems, Languages, and Applications (OOPSLA). He received his Ph.D. and M.S. from Cornell and his B.A. from Knox College. He is a member of the Association for Computing Machinery (ACM) and the Institute of Electrical and Electronics Engineers (IEEE) Computer Society. He is a coauthor of *Design Patterns: Elements of Object-Oriented Software* (Addison-Wesley, 1996). He is also a coeditor of this three-volume work on object-oriented application frameworks (John Wiley & Sons, 1999).

Johnson, Verlyn, Ph.D. International Business Machines, Rochester, Minnesota, USA, e-mail: verlyn@us.ibm.com, Sidebar 3, pp. 68–72.

Verlyn M. Johnson is a member of the San Francisco team in Rochester, Minnesota. His background is in the areas of database administration and support of application development programmers. Currently he is working to understand developer requirements for San Francisco and to promote San Francisco in standards organizations.

Kannan, Raman, Ph.D. GovPX, Inc., New York, NY, USA, e-mail: rkannan@govpx .com & asset@acm.org, Chapter 12, pp. 271–291.

Raman Kannan is a practitioner with interest and experience in distributed artificial intelligence environments, distributed computing environments, object orientation, software process and technology, and change management. He has often published the results of applying these technologies in various disciplines including concurrent engineering and financial markets. He is currently employed by GovPX, Inc. He has a Ph.D. in physics and an M.S. in computer science, both from West Virginia University.

Kappel, Gerti, Ph.D. Department of Information Systems, University of Linz, Austria, e-mail: gerti@ifs.uni-linz.ac.at, URL: www.ifs.uni-linz.ac.at/ifs/staff/staff .html, Sidebar 1, pp. 26–27, and Sidebar 2, pp. 65–67.

Gerti Kappel received her Dipl.-Ing. degree and her doctorate in computer science from Vienna University of Technology, Vienna, Austria, in 1984 and 1987, respectively. From 1987 to 1989 she was a visiting researcher at Centre Universitaire d'Informatique, Geneva, Switzerland. Presently, she is a professor of computer science at the Johannes Kepler University of Linz, Austria, where she directs the Information Systems subdivision. Her current research interests include active object-oriented database systems, object-oriented software engineering, and applying database technology to workflow management and the

WWW. She is a member of the Association for Computing Machinery (ACM), the Institute of Electrical and Electronics Engineers (IEEE), German Informatics Society (GI), and Austrian Computer Society (in English) or Österreichische Computer Gesellschaft (in German) (OCG).

Kendall, Elizabeth A., Ph.D. Departments of Computer Systems Engineering and Computer Science, Royal Melbourne Institute of Technology, Australia, e-mail: kendall@rmit.edu.au, Chapter 6, pp. 113–153.

Elizabeth A. Kendall has a BSME from the Massachusetts Institute of Technology and a master's degree and a Ph.D. from the California Institute of Technology. She worked for many years in the U.S. aerospace and defense industries in research and development at Xerox, Lockheed, Boeing, and other companies. Throughout the 1990's, she has been an academic in Australia and New Zealand. Her research interests now center on the application and extension of object-oriented techniques to agent-based systems. This has included patterns, frameworks, and analysis techniques. She is also directing research in agent applications, including enterprise integration, computer-based learning, and network management.

Knudsen, Jørgen Lindskov, Ph.D. Department of Computer Science, University of Aarhus, Denmark, e-mail: jlknudsen@daimi.au.dk, URL: www.daimi.au.dk/~jlk, Chapter 19, pp. 451–479.

Jørgen Lindskov Knudsen received his Ph.D. in computer science from Aarhus University in 1986 and since 1988 has been an associate professor in the Department of Computer Science, Aarhus University. Since 1982 he has been involved in research within object-oriented technology, especially languages and environments. Within object-oriented languages, he has primarily worked with the BETA programming language, and within environments primarily with the Mjølner System. He is the managing director of Mjølner Informatics, an Aarhus-based software and consultancy company, which is the supplier of the BETA language and the Mjølner System.

Krishna, P.V. Murali. Software Technology Laboratory, Nokia Research Center, Finland, e-mail: murali.krishna@research.nokia.com, Chapter 6, pp. 113–153.

Murali Krishna is currently working at Nokia Research Center, Helsinki, Finland, as a software engineer. He received a baccalaureate in electronics and communications engineering from J.N.T. University, Anantapur, India, and an M.S. in computer systems engineering from RMIT University, Australia.

Lederer, William G. Chapter 24, pp. 589–597.

Lindstrom, Gary, Ph.D. Department of Computer Science, University of Utah, Salt Lake City, UT, USA, e-mail: gary@cs.utah.edu, URL: www.cs.utah.edu/~gary, Chapter 10, pp. 225–239.

Gary Lindstrom is a graduate of Carnegie-Mellon University, where he earned B.S. and M.S. degrees in mathematics and a Ph.D. in computer science. He is a professor of computer science at the University of Utah, having taught previously at the University of Pittsburgh. He has served as an Institute of Electrical and Electronics Engineers (IEEE) Computer Society Distinguished Visitor and has been awarded the University of Utah College of Engineering Outstanding Teaching Award. He was the founding editor-in-chief of the *International Journal of Parallel Programming* and coedited the book, *Logic Programming: Functions, Relations and Equations*. His research has been supported by the National Science Foundation (NSF), Advanced Research Projects Agency (ARPA), DoD/Office of Naval Research (ONR), and industrial sponsors MCC, IBM, Xerox, NCR, and L.M. Ericsson. He served on the NSF Computer and Computation Research Advisory Committee from 1988 to 1992 and as a consultant to the United Nations.

Liret, Anne. LIP6 Laboratory, University of Paris, France, email: Anne.Liret@lip6.fr, URL: www-poleia.lip6.fr/~liret, Chapter 17, pp. 369–401.

Anne Liret is pursuing a Ph.D. at the LIP6 laboratory (University of Paris 6), where she studies the combination of formal reasoning techniques and constraint satisfaction. She has extended the BackTalk framework with a collaboration mechanism and formal techniques such as constraint rewriting and deduction of redundant constraints.

Litman, Diane J., Ph.D. AT&T Labs—Research, Florham Park, NJ, USA, Chapter 14, pp. 309–321.

Diane J. Litman is a principal technical staff member at AT&T Labs—Research. She received her Ph.D. in computer science from the University of Rochester in 1986. She joined the Artificial Intelligence Principles Research Department at AT&T Bell Laboratories in 1985 and went to AT&T Labs—Research when AT&T split up. From 1990 to 1992 Diane was an assistant professor of computer science at Columbia University. Diane's research is in the area of artificial intelligence and includes contributions in computational linguistics, knowledge representation and reasoning, plan recognition, applications of machine learning, and user modeling.

Maamar, Zakaria, Ph.D. Defence Research Establishment Valcartier, Canada, e-mail: zakaria.maamar@drev.dnd.ca, Sidebar 4, pp. 192–194.

Zakaria Maamar is currently a scientist at the Defence Research Establishment Valcartier (DREV), Quebec. He has led research on software agents and object-oriented frameworks for interoperability issues. His current research interests are business objects and work flows. Zakaria received his M.Sc. and Ph.D. in computer sciences from Laval University, Quebec.

Marcenac, Pierre, Ph.D. IREMIA, University of La Réunion, France, e-mail: marcenac@univ-reunion.fr, URL: www.univ-reunion.fr/~mas2, Chapter 8, pp. 173–191.

Pierre Marcenac is a professor at the University of La Réunion, Indian Ocean, France. He is head of the MultiAgent Systems research team at IREMIA (Institut de Recherche en Mathématiques et Informatique Appliquées). His work is now oriented toward the definition of software platforms and agent-based environments. He is the author of more than 40 scientific records in the area of software engineering and application development. He defended an "Habilitation à Diriger les Recherches" in 1997.

Mishra, Anil. AT&T Network and Computing Services, Middletwon, NJ, USA, Chapter 14, pp. 309–321.

Anil Mishra is a principal technical staff member at AT&T Labs. He received his M.S. in computer science from New Jersey Institute of Technology, Newark, in 1987. He was a consultant in the area of object-oriented applications development prior to joining AT&T Bell Laboratories in 1990. He is one of the original members of the R++ team and participated in the design of R++ and implemented R++ 1.0 translator. His interests include object-oriented programming, rule-based programming, and distributed object computing.

Nikander, Pekka, Ph.D. Ericsson Research Nomadiclab, Jorvas, Finland, e-mail: pekka.nikander@ericsson.com, Chapter 23, pp. 555–587.

Pekka Nikander is a research manager at Ericsson Research at Jorvas, Finland. Before joining Ericsson in 1998 he spent nine years leading a Finnish pioneer Internet company, Nixu. He is the main author of the first Finnish Internet Security book, published in 1996. Nikander has a Ph.D. in computer science and engineering from Helsinki University of Technology.

Pachet, François, Ph.D. Sony Computer Science Laboratory, Paris, France, E-mail: pachet@csl.sony.fr, URL:www-poleia.lip6.fr/~fdp, Chapter 17, pp. 369–401.

François Pachet, a civil engineer, got his Ph.D. in computer science/artificial intelligence from University of Paris VI, where he has been an assistant professor for 5 years. His research focuses on embedding inference techniques in object-oriented programming languages. He is the author of the NéOpus system, which integrates first order production rules in Smalltalk. He now heads the music research team at Sony Computer Science Laboratory in Paris, where he applies various object-oriented techniques, including constraint satisfaction programming, for designing and building interactive multimedia systems.

Pärssinen, Juha. Technical Research Centre of Finland, VTT Finland, e-mail: juha.parssinen@vtt.fi, Chapter 23, pp. 555–587.

Juha Pärssinen is a research scientist at the Technical Research Centre of Finland. He worked for three years at Nokia Telecommunications as a software designer. He has an M.Sc in computer science and engineering from Helsinki University of Technology, and he is currently writing his doctoral thesis on object-oriented protocol engineering.

Patel-Schneider, Peter F., Ph.D. Bell Labs Research, Murray Hill, NJ, USA, Chapter 14, pp. 309–321.

Peter F. Patel-Schneider is a member of the technical staff at Bell Labs Research. He received his Ph.D. from the University of Toronto in 1987. In August 1997 he rejoined Bell Labs. From 1983 to 1988 he worked in the artificial intelligence (AI) research group at Fairchild and Schlumberger. Peter's research interests center on the properties and use of description logics. He has designed and implemented large sections of CLASSIC, a description logic–based knowledge representation system.

Pathak, Chirag V. Nokia Telecommunications, Helsinki, Finland, Chapter 6, pp. 113–153.

He earned a bachelor of engineering degree in the electronics and telecommunication field in India and an M.S. in information technology from Royal Melbourne Institute of Technology, Australia.

Pfister, Cuno, Ph.D. Oberon microsystems, Inc., Zürich, Switzerland, e-mail: pfister@oberon.ch, URL: www.oberon.ch/, Chapter 25, pp. 599–618.

Cuno Pfister is cofounder and managing director of Oberon microsystems, Inc., Zürich, Switzerland. He received his Ph.D. in computer science in 1993 from the Swiss Federal Institute of Technology (ETH), Zürich, Switzerland, under the supervision of Professor Niklaus Wirth. He is coarchitect of BlackBox Component Builder and codesigner of Component Pascal.

Pree, Wolfgang, Ph.D. University of Constance , Germany, e-mail: pree@acm.org, URL: www.altissimo.com, Chapter 5, pp. 95–112.

Wolfgang Pree is a professor of computer science at the University of Constance and head of the Software & Web Engineering Group. His research interest is software engineering, in particular, object and component technology, software architectures, and human-computer interaction. He is the author of *Design Patterns for Object-Oriented Software Development* (Addison-Wesley, 1995). He was a visiting assistant professor at Washington University in St. Louis (1992–1993) and a guest scientist at Siemens AG Munich (1994–1996).

Price, Roberto Tom, Ph.D. UFRGS-Instituto de Informatica, Brasil, e-mail: tomprice@inf.ufrgs.br, URL: www.inf.ufrgs.br/~tomprice, Chapter 11, pp. 241–270.

Roberto Tom Price has a degree in engineering, a diploma in computing, a master's degree in management, and a doctoral degree in applied sciences. He is the director of a computing unit and the dean of a computer science institute; he has taken part in a number of program committees for workshops, symposiums, and conferences and has sat on advisory committees for research supporting agencies.

Rausch-Schott, Stefan, Ph.D. Department of Information Systems, University of Linz, Austria, e-mail: stefan@ifs.uni-linz.ac.at, URL: www.ifs.uni-linz.ac.at/ifs/staff/staff.html, Sidebar 1, pp. 26–27, and Sidebar 2, pp. 65–67.

Stefan Rausch-Schott received his master's degree and his Ph.D. in computer science from the Johannes Kepler University, Linz, Austria, in 1991 and 1997, respectively. From 1991 to 1993 he was a member of the Research Institute for Applied Knowledge Processing (FAW), Hagenberg, Austria. Since 1993, he has been affiliated with the Department of Information Systems at the Johannes Kepler University of Linz.

Retschitzegger, Werner, Ph.D. Department of Information Systems, University of Linz, Austria, e-mail: werner@ifs.uni-linz.ac.at, R\URL: www.ifs.uni-linz.ac.at/ifs/staff/staff.html, Sidebar 1, pp. 26–27, and Sidebar 2, pp. 65–67.

Werner Retschitzegger studied business informatics at the Johannes Kepler University of Linz. From 1990 to 1993, he worked for the Research Institute for Applied Knowledge Processing (FAW), where he was involved in various industrial and research projects concerning the application of relational and object-oriented database systems in the areas of Computer Integrated Manufacturing (CIM) and configuration management. Since 1993, he has been affiliated with the Department of Information Systems at the Johannes Kepler University of Linz. He received his Ph.D. in 1996.

Ros, Johannes P. AT&T Network and Computing Services, Middletown, NJ, USA, Chapter 14, pp. 309–321.

Rösel, Andreas. ABB Informatik GmbH, Mannheim, Germany, e-mail: andreas.roesel@deinf.mail.abb.de, URL: www.abb.de/deinf/, Chapter 27, pp. 629–657.

Andreas Rösel is manager of the Advanced Software Center (ASC) at ABB Informatik, Germany. He has some 16 years' experience in software engineering, consulting, and lecturing. In 1982 he gained his degree in communications engineering in Germany, then continued studies of computer science in Australia, which he completed with a master's degree in software engineering. He worked for several years as a software engineer for Westinghouse, then lectured at the University of Queensland (Brisbane) in software engineering and object-oriented (OO) technologies. In 1993 he returned to Germany to take up a consulting position at the ABB Corporate Research Center in Heidelberg.

Roy, Pierre, Ph.D. CREATE Laboratory, University of California, Santa Barbara, USA, e-mail: pierre@create.ucsb.edu, URL: www-poleia.lip6.fr/~roy, Chapter 17, pp. 369–401.

Pierre Roy got a Ph.D. from the University of Paris VI (LIP6 laboratory).

He is developer the BackTalk framework. He has published several papers dealing with the integration of constraint satisfaction techniques with objects and has presented tutorials on these matters at various international conferences, including IJCAI'97 in Nagoya, Japan. He has been an associated researcher at the SONY-CSL laboratory in Paris and is now working as a computer music researcher at the CREATE laboratory (UC, Santa Barbara).

Schmidt, Douglas C., Ph.D. Department of Computer Science, Washington University, St. Louis, Missouri, USA, e-mail: schmidt@cs.wustl.edu, URL: www.cs.wustl.edu/~schmidt, coeditor of this book.

Douglas C. Schmidt is an associate professor in the Department of Computer Science and in the Department of Radiology at Washington University in St. Louis, Missouri. His research focuses on design patterns, implementation, and experimental analysis of object-oriented techniques that facilitate the development of high-performance, real-time distributed object computing systems on parallel processing platforms running over high-speed ATM networks. He received B.S. and M.A. degrees in sociology from the College of William and Mary in Williamsburg, Virginia, and an M.S. and a Ph.D. in computer science from the University of California, Irvine (UCI) in 1984, 1986, 1990, and 1994, respectively. He is a member of the USENIX, the Institute of Electrical and Electronics Engineers (IEEE), and the Association for Computing Machinery (ACM). He is also a coeditor of two volumes of this three-volume work on object-oriented application frameworks (John Wiley & Sons, 1999).

Schnettler, N. Peter. Chapter 24, pp. 589–597.

Serra, Micaela, Ph.D. Computer Science Department, University of Victoria, Victoria, British Columbia, Canada, e-mail: mserra@csr.uvic.ca, Chapter 9, pp. 197–223.

Micaela Serra received her B.Sc. degree in computer science (gold medal) from the University of Manitoba, Winnipeg, Manitoba, Canada, in 1983 and her M.Sc.

and Ph.D. degrees in computer science from the University of Victoria, Victoria, British Columbia, Canada, in 1984 and 1987, respectively. Currently, she is a professor in the Department of Computer Science, Faculty of Engineering, University of Victoria. Her research interests are testing algorithms for digital circuits, computer-aided design (CAD), finite fields, and hardware/software codesign. She was the recipient of a 67 Science and Engineering Postgraduate Scholarship from the Natural Sciences and Engineering Research Council.

Srinivasan, Savitha. IBM Corporation/Research Division, San Jose, California, USA, e-mail: savitha@almaden.ibm.com, Chapter 4, pp. 77–93.

Savitha Srinivasan is a software engineer at the IBM Almaden Research Center in San Jose, California. She received a B.S. in electrical engineering in India, and an M.S. in computer science from Pace University.

Sycara, Katia, Ph.D. School of Computer Science, Carnegie-Mellon University, Pittsburgh, Pennsylvania, USA, e-mail: katia@cs.cmu.edu, URL: www.cs.cmu.edu/afs/cs.cmu.edu/user/katia/www/katia-home.html, Chapter 7, pp. 155–171.

Katia Sycara is a senior research scientist (associate research professor) in the School of Computer Science at Carnegie-Mellon University. She holds a B.S. in applied mathematics from Brown University, an M.S. in electrical engineering from the University of Wisconsin, and a Ph.D. in computer science from the Georgia Institute of Technology. She is author of a book on manufacturing. She is the general chair of the Second International Conference on Autonomous Agents (Agents '98), and has chaired the DARPA Conference on Planning, Scheduling and Control in 1990. She is a founding editor-in-chief of the new journal, *Autonomous Agents and Multi Agent Systems*; the area editor for artificial intelligence (AI) and management science for the journal, *Group Decision and Negotiation;* and sits on the editorial board of *IEEE Expert, AI in Engineering,* and *Concurrent Engineering.* She has served as special editor of the *IEEE Transactions on System, Man and Cybernetics for Planning, Scheduling and Control,* and as a guest editor for the Spring 1998 *AI Magazine* issue on "The Many Faces of Agents."

Szafron, Duane, Ph.D. University of Alberta, Canada, Chapter 16, pp. 339–367.

Duane Szafron received a Ph.D. in applied mathematics from the University of Waterloo in 1978. He is currently a professor of computing science at the University of Alberta. He has been doing research in object-oriented computing since 1980, including language design, language implementation, programming environments, and object bases. He is also the president of Sunrise Software, which has developed the CHILDS library system for school libraries, and he is one of the founders of BioTools, a supplier of next-generation bioinformatics software.

Szyperski, Clemens, Ph.D. School of Computing Science, Queensland University of Technology, Australia, e-mail: c.szyperski@qut.edu.au, URL: www.fit.qut.edu .au/~szypersk/, Chapter 25, pp. 599–618.

Clemens Szyperski is associate professor in the Faculty of Information Technology at Queensland University of Technology (QUT), Brisbane, Australia. From 1992 to 1993 he held a postdoctoral fellowship from the International Computer Science Institute (ICSI) at the University of California at Berkeley. In 1992, he received his Ph.D. in computer science from the Swiss Federal Institute of Technology (ETH), Zürich, Switzerland, where he designed and implemented the extensible operating system Ethos under the supervision of Professor Niklaus Wirth and Professor Hanspeter Mössenböck. In 1987, he received a degree in electrical engineering/computer engineering from the Aachen University of Technology (RWTH), Germany. In 1993, he cofounded Oberon microsystems, Inc., where he has since served as director of research. In 1997 Oberon microsystems released the new component-oriented programming language, Component Pascal. He was a key contributor to both BlackBox and Component Pascal. In 1998 he published *Component Software—Beyond Object-Oriented Programming* (Addison-Wesley), now frequently cited as the definitive text on component software.

Tanir, Oryal, Ph.D. Bell Canada, Montreal, Canada, e-mail: Oryal.Tanir@bell.ca, Chapter 18, pp. 403–450.

Oryal Tanir is a senior consultant and director of research within the Quality Engineering and Research organization of Bell Canada in Montreal. He has been an employee of Bell Canada since 1986. He holds a Ph.D. and a master's degree in electrical engineering from McGill University in Montreal. He is an active researcher within the discrete event simulation milieu and has published a book and many papers on the subject. He is chairman of the Institute of Electrical and Electronics Engineers (IEEE) P1173 working group on simulation as well as a member of the Association for Computing Machinery (ACM) and the IEEE computer and IEEE communications societies.

Tilman, Michel. System Architect Unisys, Brussel, Belgium, e-mail: mtilman@argo .be, Chapter 3, pp. 29–64.

Michel Tilman graduated summa cum laude in mathematics from the Brussels Free University in 1981, specializing in functional analysis, locally convex spaces, and stochastic process theory. He started his professional career in the Mathematics Department of the Faculty of Applied Sciences as assistant-researcher, where he was involved in research on non-Archimedean analysis. In 1989, he went to SoftCore, a spin-off company of the Brussels Free University, developing electronic document and work flow management applications. In 1994, he joined Unisys Belgium as senior system architect for the Argo framework.

van Hillegersberg, Jos, Ph.D. Rotterdam School of Management, Erasmus University, Rotterdam, The Netherlands, e-mail: jhillegersberg@fac.fbk.eur.nl, URL: www.fbk.eur.nl/FBK/VG1/JVH/, Chapter 2, pp. 7–25.

Jos van Hillegerberg is an assistant professor of information systems at Erasmus University, Faculteit Bedrijfskunde. He completed his Ph.D. on metamodeling-based integration of object-oriented systems development. His current research interests include adoption of OO technology and component-based development.

Vergo, John. IBM Corporation/Research Division, Hawthorne, New York, USA, e-mail: jvergo@watson.ibm.com, Chapter 4, pp. 77–93.

John Vergo is a research staff manager at the IBM T.J. Watson Research Center in Hawthorne, New York. He received a B.S. in mathematics and psychology from the University of Albany, and an M.S. in computer science from Polytechnic University.

Wenyin, Liu, Ph.D. Microsoft Research, Beijing, PR China, e-mail: wyliu@microsoft .com, Chapter 22, pp. 541–553.

Liu Wenyin is a researcher at Microsoft Research, China. He received his B.Eng. and M.Eng. in computer science from the Tsinghua University in 1988 and 1992, respectively, and his D.Sc. in information management engineering from Technion—Israel Institute of Technology in 1998. His research interests include automated engineering drawing interpretation, pattern recognition, software engineering, object-oriented programming, object-process methodology, artificial intelligence, and computer graphics. He also won a third prize in the First International Java Programming Contest (ACM Quest for Java '97), sponsored by the Association for Computing Machinery (ACM) and IBM, in 1997. He is a member of the Institute of Electrical and Electronics Engineers (IEEE), the IEEE Computer Society, and the ACM.

Wierenga, Berend, Ph.D. Rotterdam School of Management, Erasmus University, Rotterdam, The Netherlands, e-mail: bwierenga@fac.fbk.eur.nl, URL: www.fbk .eur.nl/FBK/VG3/, Chapter 2, pp. 7–25.

Berend Wierenga holds a Ph.D. in marketing from Wageningen Agricultural University in The Netherlands. He is a professor of marketing at the Erasmus University in Rotterdam and has held visiting positions at Stanford University, the Wharton School of the University of Pennsylvania, and the European Institute of Business Administration (INSEAD), Fontainebleau, France.

Woolf, Bobby. Independent consultant, Cary, North Carolina, USA, e-mail: woolf@acm.org, Chapter 26, pp. 621–628.

Bobby Woolf is an independent consultant in Cary, North Carolina, specializing in frameworks and components design and development in Java and Smalltalk. He previously worked at Ascent Logic Corp. in San Jose, California, on one of the world's largest Smalltalk applications; at Knowledge Systems Corporation in Cary, North Carolina, and at SilverMark in Raleigh, North Carolina. He was the program chair of PLoP (Pattern Languages of Programming) '99. He is a coauthor of *The Design Patterns Smalltalk Companion* (Addison-Wesley, 1998).

About the CD-ROM

The CD-ROM contains close to 700 MB of materials related to thirteen chapters, a sidebar, and an invited framework called EFLIB. The CD-ROM includes:

- Design pattern implementations
- Case studies
- Sample models
- Framework code
- Demos
- Manuals and documentation

Each of the chapters that are included on the CD-ROM have a readme file that describes the contents specific to its chapter, how to navigate through the CD contents, how to use the software contained on the CD-ROM, and how to get technical support.

Additional information regarding individual framework projects can be found at the contributors' URLs included in the readme file for each chapter. Updates, if any, to the CD materials will be available on the companion Web site at www.wiley.com/compbooks/frameworks.

CD-ROM Table of Contents

EFLIB: An Invited Framework

Johan Larsson

The Extended Function Library (EFLIB) has evolved from a Pascal function library into a framework-like Object-Pascal library (prototype 5) and a complete object-oriented framework (prototype 7). EFLIB is subject to research at Uppsala University. It is a large-scale experiment with the aim to try to provide generic components unified under a common architecture. The goal is to make EFLIB a system that promotes and enforces reuse thinking within a large enterprise, without exposing programmers to complexity dilemmas or learning curve problems. EFLIB is currently financed by NUTEK, the Swedish National Board for Industrial and Technical Development. Published research results are included on the CD-ROM, as are abstracts, source code for prototype 5, documentation, and tools.

Index

A

ABB Semantic Graphics
Framework. *See*
Semantic Graphics
Framework

Abstract Factory Method
pattern

agent systems frame-
work, 122, 123–124

Déjà Vu scheduling class
library, 524

Dynamic Database
Instance framework,
591, 592, 593

Etyma, 231

abstraction, 339, 643
design levels, 408–410

abstraction scales, 245

abstractor objects, 244

access-limited rules, 315

access paths, 315

ACME, 444, 445

Action class, CSP++, 207,
209

action rules, Argo
repository-based
framework, 40–41,
58–61

ActionsAPI class, 141–142

active actions, 163

Active Object pattern

agent systems frame-
work, 122, 126–127,
135, 136, 149

speech recognition
framework, 82

Active Object with Future
pattern, agent sys-
tems framework, 128,
131–134

ActiveVariable class,
300–304

active vocabulary, 78

Active-X, 325

BlackBox contrasted,
614–615

actors, 156

Adapter pattern

agent systems frame-
work, 120

File Reader, 623–624

Java Conduits, 564

speech recognition
framework, 82, 84–86,
91

AddClassLink algorithm,
350, 351

invocation cost, 360

AddMethodNodeChild
algorithm, 353

AddSelector algorithm,
350–351

invocation cost, 360

Aesop, 444

affective relations, interdependent changing
objects, 309–315

agent-based systems,
115–116

Agent Builder pattern,
agent systems frame-
work, 138–139

Agent class, CSP++, 207,
208–209

Agent-oriented frame-
works, 73–75, 192

agent-oriented Java
framework

agent model, 183–185

agricultural biomass
application, 189–190

application generation,
186–188

GEAMAS layer, 176,
178–179

Java implementation,
186–188

Publishers Since 1807